Studies in Legal History

Published by The University of North Carolina Press
in association with the American Society for Legal History

SAMUEL E. THORNE
Photograph by John Chapin

On the Laws and Customs of England

Essays in Honor of Samuel E. Thorne

Edited by Morris S. Arnold, Thomas A. Green, Sally A. Scully, and Stephen D. White

The University of North Carolina Press
Chapel Hill

The editors wish to thank Elizabeth B. Clark, Victoria D. List, and Sheldon J. Tepler for their editorial assistance in the preparation of this volume, and the William W. Cook Endowment Fund for The University of Michigan Law School for its generous financial support.

Manufactured in the United States of America
Library of Congress Cataloging in Publication Data
Main entry under title:

On the laws and customs of England.

(Studies in legal history)
Bibliography: p.
Includes index.
CONTENTS: Simpson, A. W. B. The laws of Ethelbert.—Tabuteau, E. Z. Definitions of feudal military obligations in eleventh-century Normandy.—Milsom, S. F. C. Inheritance by women in the twelfth and early thirteenth centuries.—[etc.]
1. Law—Great Britain—History and criticism—Addresses, essays, lectures. 2. Customary law—Great Britain—Addresses, essays, lectures. 3. Thorne, Samuel Edmund, 1907– —Addresses, essays, lectures.
I. Thorne, Samuel Edmund, 1907– II. Arnold, Morris S.
III. Series.
KD606.06 349.41 80-11909
ISBN 0-8078-1434-2

For Samuel E. Thorne

Contents

Introduction

The essays that follow are published in honor of Professor Samuel E. Thorne. They are intended as a tribute to him and to his lifelong study of English legal history from the eleventh to the seventeenth century. Working back in time from the age of Coke to the age of Bracton and beyond, Professor Thorne has made many important contributions to the study of the common law and to the history of English society; and in his capacity as author, teacher, and colleague, he has given encouragement and inspiration to many scholars in his field.

Most of Professor Thorne's early work dealt with the Tudor and early Stuart periods. In his studies on statutes and statutory interpretation, on early Tudor "fiscal feudalism," and on Sir Edward Coke, he traced important changes in early modern ideas about law and law making and related these shifts in legal ideas to the development of the early modern state. In some of these works, and more particularly in his remarkable essay "Tudor Social Transformation and Legal Change," he also showed how changes in legal doctrine could be connected with broader social and economic developments. Although Thorne's work on Tudor-Stuart law often focused on the ways in which lawyers manipulated medieval precedents in order to maintain the illusion of legal continuity in a period of rapid social change, it also took account of the very real continuity between medieval and early modern English law. It is not surprising, therefore, that ultimately he should have turned his full attention to the formative period of the common law, the twelfth and early thirteenth centuries. He has demonstrated that this era, like the Tudor-Stuart period, witnessed greater changes in legal ideas and practice than earlier historians realized. In his influential article on early English feudalism, he identified major changes that occurred in the law of real property during the twelfth century and suggested that they were integrally related to important modifications in the structure of English feudal society. Moreover, in the study of Bracton's *De Legibus* that has occupied him for the past quarter century, he has demonstrated that the complex textual history of this work provides a guide to the development of legal rules and legal thought under the Angevins and Henry III. His monumental edition and annotated translation of the *De Legibus* has made it possible for future scholars to write the intellectual and social history of the common law during this crucial period and to attain the objectives that he outlined for legal history in his early essay on social and legal change.

Although Professor Thorne has studied an unusually wide range of legal topics over many different periods of English history, he has developed a unified and coherent approach to his subject. Two types of legal scholarship are repeatedly represented in his writings: the reconstruction of legal doctrine and legal ideas through the editing and analysis of major texts; and the study of the relationship between legal change and other historical developments. As practiced by Professor Thorne, these two types of scholarship are complementary and often interdependent. His work reflects his view that sociological studies of the law must be based upon the meticulous, technical analysis of texts, and that the study of such texts should ultimately lead to broad conclusions about the history of English society.

The essays published here are animated by similar ideas about the methods and objectives of English legal history. Although they deal with various topics and historical periods and exemplify diverse methods of studying legal history, they generally proceed from the study of legal texts to the reconstruction of legal doctrine and ideas; and they then address broader problems concerning the relationship of legal theory to legal practice, the functioning of legal doctrines and ideas in a social context, and the complex interconnections between legal change and social development. Thus, although each of these essays has its own distinctive subject matter and historiographical setting, yet the entire collection reflects trends in English legal history that Professor Thorne has been instrumental in initiating.

In the opening essay, Professor Simpson discusses the earliest document in English legal history, the laws of Ethelbert. Through an examination of the possible reasons for its promulgation in the very early seventh century, he considers several important problems in the study of both Anglo-Saxon and later English law. The codes or dooms that English kings issued periodically from the seventh to the earlier eleventh century may tell us much about Old English legal ideas and practice. But historians who use them must first determine what they were, why they were issued, and how they were related to English legal practice. Were they relatively accurate redactions of existing legal customs, royal mandates for legal change, or edicts that included provisions of both types? If they merely codified existing practice, why were they adopted? And if they were designed in whole or in part to change the law, how successful were they in doing so? By raising these questions with reference to Ethelbert's code, Simpson touches on important questions about the relationship between written law and legal practice and about the extent to which English kings modified customary norms that embodied the well-established values of their subjects. In addition, when he shows that Ethelbert's code may provide evidence of a conflict between customary ideas about redress for violent wrongs and the ideas of a newly converted king on this subject, he demonstrates that the study of this kind of text can help us to understand the moral concerns of early medieval communities.

By treating a seventh-century Anglo-Saxon lawbook as our earliest common-law text, Simpson joins with several other contributors to this volume in stressing the continuity between Anglo-Saxon and later English law. The essays by Dr. Hyams and Professor Beckerman, especially, support the view that much of the Old English legal culture survived the conquest and continued to be a vital element in English law long after 1066. Not only did the Anglo-Saxons create administrative mechanisms, like the shire, the tithing, and the writ, that later became part of the institutional framework for the "classical" common law; they evolved legal procedures that the conquest did not destroy and may not even have profoundly altered. Anglo-Saxon law also gave formal expression to certain fundamental, if conflicting, ideas about "wrongs" and compensation for wrongs; these ideas, too, survived the conquest. Finally, Anglo-Saxon law apparently developed in a society whose members did not clearly distinguish legal rules from other sorts of norms, and a similarly undifferentiated legal system continued to exist in twelfth-century England.

Whereas Hyams and Beckerman emphasize the continuity of English legal history by showing how aspects of Anglo-Saxon legal culture survived the conquest, Professor Tabuteau makes a similar point by questioning the view that the Norman invasion revolutionized English landholding practices. By demonstrating that a well-defined system of military service for feudal tenancies did not exist in Normandy in 1066 or even in 1106, she shows that eleventh-century Norman law could not have served as a model for the royal establishment of a well-defined system of feudal tenure in postconquest England. Her work therefore suggests that Anglo-Norman feudalism was not a uniform order which kings or dukes imposed and which simply became more systematic and more subject to royal control during the twelfth century. Instead she encourages us to see it as a set of unsystematized practices, varying considerably from lordship to lordship, largely shaped by local rather than royal, political pressures, and developing under the possible influence of Anglo-Saxon legal principles.

Nevertheless, Tabuteau's suggestion that Henry I's government may have done much to create the more systematic feudal tenure of England and Normandy after 1130 acknowledges that royal government eventually came to play an important part in organizing and regulating feudal legal practices. Her work, therefore, lends some support to the generally held view that we can reconstruct the development of common-law institutions by studying the various administrative mechanisms that English kings intermittently used to regulate feudal practice. This evolutionary process may be observed in the development of royal administrative machinery, both central and local, for dispensing justice and overseeing the actions of feudal and communal courts; the creation of a system of common-law remedies that litigants could use in an increasing number of civil cases; the elaboration of a system of royal criminal justice; and the growth of distinctive common-law procedural devices, notably the jury. These institutional developments are now well known, and although questions remain about the pace at which development occurred, about the intentions of the kings and royal advisors who promoted them, and about the kind of institutions that may have served as models for them, it is generally agreed that these changes both reflect and help to explain the birth of the common law.

Professor Milsom, however, has recently noted several limitations of this approach to the early history of the common law. His principal contention is that previous historians have greatly oversimplified the legal developments that occurred in England roughly between 1150 and 1250. According to Milsom, the common law of Glanvill's day grew up in "a seignorial world" that had much in common with the one discussed by Tabuteau. In addition, he maintains that royal judicial officers who provided the early remedies to litigants neither changed nor wished to change the principles according to which that world worked, but simply wished to control it and make it work in accordance with its own disparate, but established legal principles. Although common-law judges developed common-law principles of property that came to be applied in royal courts, those principles did not appear, so the argument runs, until well after the advent of early common-law remedies. According to this view their appearance resulted not from a rational, governmentally inspired plan, but from the accident of litigation.

In his contribution to this collection, Milsom shows how inheritance rights of women developed in the late twelfth century. He maintains that the forces that produced these abstract rights had two main aspects: the primary one feudal and "contractual"; the other internal to the family. Formal legislation played no part in this process in which the king participated by example and command rather than by rule making. Initially, the purpose of inheritance customs was simply to identify a suitable male substitute for deceased tenants; a woman's "rights" in these circumstances were therefore ancillary to this aim. It was the pressure of the need for family settlements on an essentially contractual feudal world where only men counted that eventually produced the property rights of women.

Dr. Hyams adopts a similar approach to the early history of the common law in his essay on the ordeals. Like Milsom, Hyams pictures medieval legal change as a gradual and complex process that cannot be divided into self-contained periods or explained solely—or even mainly—by reference to royal policies or judicial fiat. Unlike Milsom and Tabuteau, however, he illuminates the history of the common law by studying procedural practices that did not survive to become parts of this legal system. In his view, historians cannot understand how and why the new proofs were developed without determining how the older ones worked and why they died out; and he maintains that conventional answers to these questions are unsatisfactory. He denies that the ordeal was a crude, barbaric practice that had a static history until it was suddenly abolished by enlightened churchmen and rational-minded judges and rulers. Instead, he argues that in a particular sort of society, the ordeal performed "a sensible function in a useful way" and that the process of abandoning it had been under way long before the time at which it was completely superseded by other modes of proof. He also treats the ultimate demise of the ordeal as "the cumulative effect of individual acts that arose from actual cases." He argues that this procedural development was due to changes in English social structure and social attitudes, rather than to governmental dictate or to intellectualized propaganda. By rewriting the history of the ordeal from an anthropological perspective, Hyams performs several distinct tasks. Not only does he develop a complex model of medieval legal change and use it to help explain the common law's eventual adoption of other modes of proof, he also identifies important links between pre- and postconquest legal practice and shows how the study of one seemingly exotic legal practice can contribute to our understanding of medieval thought and social structure.

In the essay that follows Hyams's study of the ordeal, Professor Donahue adopts a similarly indirect approach to the study of English legal culture. By studying the use of witnesses in English church courts during the thirteenth and fourteenth centuries, he is able to detect the influence of emerging common-law institutions and legal ideas on the Romano-canonic system. Donahue demonstrates that such influence could operate even where the canon law was allegedly more highly developed than the common law. At an early date, the canon law had been embodied in a formal academic system and had created a theory of judicial proof that was formal precisely where the common law was not. Inquisition of witnesses by highly trained judges, rather than the taking of verdicts from a group of laymen, was the accepted canonical fact-finding process. Yet, as Donahue shows, the judges who presided over English church courts did not always apply the letter of the academic law. Instead, they created a law of proof that was actually an amalgam of textual prescription and judge-made law. It appears that this living law of proof was shaped in part by the attitudes of litigants, who entered church courts with expectations created in a world where jury verdicts were the most common form of proof.

Whereas Donahue shows how and why a particular procedure used in one court system was at least partially adopted in another, Professor Beckerman examines an instance in which one group of English courts failed to embrace a doctrine that was accepted in others. Beckerman seeks to document and explain the failure of common-law courts to follow local courts in providing remedies and compensation for loss of honor. His approach to this problem in the history of substantive common-law doctrine is a novel one. Beckerman turns away from the traditional practice of tracing the gradual emergence and elaboration of legal principles in the judicial decisions of royal judges. He instead gives considerable attention to local courts and to customary norms that were not necessarily embodied in common-law formal legal rules, and he attempts to explain why common-law rules sometimes failed to conform to accepted social norms or to follow the linear developmental patterns that historians have often searched for in medieval legal history. After showing that litigants were compensated for loss of honor in the Anglo-Saxon and Anglo-Norman periods and that they later received such compensation in local courts, Beckerman asks why they were given no such remedies in the developed common-law courts of the thirteenth century. He finds an answer to this question through the examination of common-law procedures.

The substantive and methodological implications of Beckerman's article are complex and establish his intellectual kinship with several of the other contributors to this volume. In the first place, his study also supports the view that important Anglo-Saxon legal ideas survived the conquest, and that even when they failed to be incorporated into the common law, they are essential to an understanding of it: the very reasons for nonincorporation tell us much about the nature of the enterprise on which the creators of the common law believed themselves engaged. Secondly, his work testifies to the importance of English local courts throughout the medieval period. He argues that these courts should not be seen as intellectually passive bodies that were capable only of absorbing royal doctrine. Finally, he does not assume that common-law rules invariably reflect some particular community sentiment, class interest, or even judicial policy. Instead, he focuses his attention on the complicated workings of common-law procedure. Although the procedures that he discusses were ultimately animated by the politically based concept of the king's peace, he shows that this concept was sometimes so rigidly construed that it could not serve as the basis for a wide range of tort remedies.

Beckerman's essay and the two that precede it serve to remind us both of the conceptual limitations of academic legal rules and of the potential richness of those rules as they are applied in practice. They go beyond the traditional enterprise of tracing doctrine and even beyond the demonstration of disparity between legal and social norms: they investigate the tension that the disparity produced and seek to illustrate the ways in which formal institutions for conflict resolution dealt or failed to deal with that tension. This concern with the dynamics of institutions that fuse official and formal with lay and open-ended processes is relevant to the increasing body of social history now being written on the basis of the medieval trial records. By clarifying the nature of the processes that affect prosecutions, verdicts, and judgments, the work of contemporary legal historians promises to complement and strengthen the important work of quantitative analysts of social behavior.

Professor Sutherland reminds us both of the importance of the most formal aspects of common-law reasoning and of the dangers of assuming that legal texts contain facts about social reality. Within the tightly bounded world of medieval common-law actions trial process went forward in rigid, formal pleadings. For every action there was a prescribed defense, and limitations imposed on the types of accepted defenses produced relatively formulaic responses that often hid the facts. Although historians once failed to recognize that formulaic entries in the rolls rarely tell us what happened in a case, they now see that common-law pleadings were sometimes fictional. But they have not analyzed closely the significance of this peculiar, artificial form of legal argumentation. The intellectual structure of pleading has largely been ignored by legal historians, who have focused instead on procedure and doctrine, and by social and intellectual historians as well. In his essay on "color," Sutherland thus embarks on the study of a relatively unknown subject. In it, he attempts to show how pleadings became highly artificial and divorced from the actual facts of cases, and to explain why this stylized form of discourse came to be tolerated. He also considers the question of what the acceptance of this system of pleading may suggest about later medieval ideas concerning law and legal rules. He demonstrates that even the most artificial and abstruse forms of common-law discourse can be seen as the outgrowth of a particular type of legal ideology, and that by examining it we can gain an insight into the attitudes of lawyers who, though they constituted only a tiny minority of English society, nevertheless exercised a profound influence on it.

Although later medieval common lawyers were comfortable with the most formal aspects of private-law reasoning and pleading discussed by Sutherland, Professor Gray argues that their concept of the nature of law was perhaps not confined to the ideas of this private-law world. It has been claimed that fifteenth-century lawyers lacked both the language and the conceptual framework to analyze conflicts among royal authority, parliamentary power, and personal rights and that lawyers acquired this capacity only in the aftermath of the Reformation Parliament. According to Gray, however, medieval lawyers did not favor private-law arguments and metaphors because of an inability to understand what would later be called "public law." Gray draws novel and challenging conclusions from his analysis of Lancastrian legal language. In some cases, he maintains, common lawyers used the language of private law when discussing cases involving the king or Parliament simply because those cases really raised nothing more than private-law issues. In other instances they used such language because it provided helpful analogies, tactically useful arguments, or straightforward descriptions for discussing what were actually perceived as public, as opposed to private, issues. His essay cautions us against being so overawed by the technicality of common-law argumentation that we fail to perceive its nuances. It also reminds us that medieval lawyers were not mere captives of common-law reasoning but could often manipulate it artfully when they found it convenient to do so.

The studies of Gray and Sutherland on the developed common-law system of the later Middle Ages provide a useful background to the problems raised in the final six essays on law and legal change in the Tudor-Stuart period. Sutherland's essay gives some indication of why Tudor monarchs, statesmen, lawyers, litigants, and members of Parliament should have wished to make major alterations in a technical and artificial legal order that seems, at least in retrospect, to have been singularly ill adapted to the needs of a postfeudal society. Gray's article, on the other hand, helps us to understand why many postmedieval proponents of legal change chose to preserve elements of the medieval common law.

He suggests that medieval lawyers had developed principles and modes of argument that were sophisticated and supple enough to be used during the sixteenth and seventeenth centuries to legitimate expansions in royal power, defenses of private rights against royal encroachment, innovative judicial decisions, and the promotion of new economic and political interests.

Like most writers on Tudor-Stuart legal history, Garrett-Goodyear, Ives, Barton, Baker, Barnes, and Yale are concerned with the problems of tracing, explaining, and characterizing legal change. For they are studying a period in which important legal developments occurred with unprecedented rapidity and in which increasing numbers of people engaged in public and highly politicized debates about what the law was or should be. During the early Tudor period, monarchs, royal servants, and members of Parliament often thought it necessary to create new courts and strengthen old ones and to override established private rights. They also wished to modify criminal law and procedure, to establish new sorts of economic regulations, to make significant statutory changes in English private-law doctrine, and to effect revolutionary changes in the English church. Many of these attempts to transform medieval law were successful, but few of them went completely unopposed. Similarly, the efforts of Tudor and early Stuart judges, reporters, and treatise writers to modify existing common-law rules, to develop the law administered in non-common-law courts, and to clarify the relationship between different jurisdictions did not silence contemporary critics of English law. During the later Elizabethan and early Stuart periods, legal controversies arose in the courts, in Parliament, and elsewhere about the nature and scope of royal authority, about the privileges and powers of Parliament, and about the liberties of English subjects. Under Charles I, these controversies gradually led to the creation of competing legal ideologies, one of which supported more extreme royalist claims to power and the other of which was designed to protect private rights against what was perceived as a royalist attack. By the time of the English Revolution, these diverse movements for change had led to important alterations in English legal doctrine, judicial institutions, and constitutional theory. But these changes were usually portrayed as attempts to restore or preserve the ancient law of England.

Professor Garrett-Goodyear and Dr. Ives examine two legal developments associated with the policies of early Tudor royal government: the revival of quo warranto proceedings against franchise holders; and the royal attacks on the privilege of sanctuary. These two developments have generally been portrayed as parts of an organized royalist program to increase the power of the Tudor state and to develop an ideology that would legitimate this political process. Although Garrett-Goodyear and Ives do not directly attack this traditional position, their studies suggest that it should be elaborated if not modified. Previous historians have maintained that early Tudor lawyers revived the long-dormant procedure of quo warranto in order to repress private jurisdictions and centralize judicial power in a sovereign state. Garrett-Goodyear, however, raises certain doubts about the validity of this interpretation. He concedes that early Tudor lawyers enhanced the power of Tudor monarchs by developing theories that justified attacks on private jurisdiction. But he goes on to argue that this attack was relatively unsystematic and sometimes served only the short-term interests of particular politicians and not the state. He also shows that legal doctrines and procedures originally developed to promote royal interests could, in fact, be used with advantage by the very local magnates whom the crown wished to bring under control. Moreover, by establishing that the early Tudor attack on franchises was largely unsuccessful, he demonstrates the enduring character of the medieval view that private jurisdiction was a property right and therefore entitled to legal protection. He shows also that local political interest groups were often able to frustrate royalist attempts to centralize justice.

Although Dr. Ives's essay on the law of sanctuary demonstrates that early Tudor monarchs sometimes succeeded in expanding their powers by overriding ancient rights and privileges, his work, like Garrett-Goodyear's, suggests that historians can better understand this process if they study not only royalist legal doctrines and procedures but also the ways in which these doctrines and procedures were applied in particular cases. Ives describes in detail Henry VIII's attempts to destroy the privilege of sanctuary in an effort to undermine the power of one of his political foes. Although his work suggests that the early Tudor attack on sanctuary did not proceed much more systematically than the attack on private jurisdiction, Ives also makes it clear that it was considerably more successful. His work and Garrett-Goodyear's therefore force us to ask why some royalist efforts to centralize justice and destroy old privileges worked, whereas others did not. Garrett-Goodyear's study suggests that such royalist initiatives could fail when they led to the creation of legal procedures that could be employed by local authorities and when they involved attacks on well-established, well-defended rights. Ives's study indicates that early Tudor monarchs could expand their powers when they attacked private rights in ways that mere subjects could not easily emulate, when the rights they attacked were already unpopular, and when they picked opportune moments for moving against their political opponents. The question remains as to which of these two lessons was the more important one for post-Reformation royalism.

Drs. Barton and Baker take us back to the world of common-law doctrine and show us how significant changes occurred in two branches of the law: real property and contract. Taken as a whole, developments in English private law during the Tudor-Stuart period can often be portrayed as judicial responses to the changing needs of different economic and social interest groups. But because these changes were actually made on a case-by-case basis by judges who rarely gave explicit consideration to the social, political, or economic implications of their decisions and who felt bound to harmonize their decisions with precedent, historians cannot fully explain them simply by showing that they promoted some general social or economic interest. Instead, scholars must also try to show how changing attitudes of judges responding to problems raised by new cases gradually led to the creation of new legal rules and principles. Barton and Baker therefore attempt to trace and explain changes in legal doctrine by analyzing the tortured analytical processes by which such changes ultimately took shape.

Though he concentrates on developments during the last decades of the sixteenth century, Dr. Barton's essay is a contribution to the study of the transformations of property law that were initiated by the Statute of Uses (1536). This act can be considered as part of the royalist program dealt with by Garrett-Goodyear and Ives, because one of its principal purposes was to prevent landowners from evading feudal incidents due to the crown. Like most legislation, however, the Statute of Uses had unforeseen effects, and its social impact ultimately depended upon the way in which it was later interpreted by the judges, whose principal devotion was as much to common-law principles and rights as to the safeguarding of royal revenues. Barton shows that the latter part of Elizabeth's reign saw a judicial controversy on the question whether one could confer an interest on someone not yet born. This question was of serious importance to landholders who sought to secure the long-term social and economic position of their families; it was also of concern to the crown, which stood to lose substantial revenues if such future interests were held to be valid. The debate, only one of many controversies engendered by the application of the Statute of Uses, ended in a sort of compromise. The rules that emerged from this compromise remained in force long after the demise of the feudal incidents and thus left their mark on the development of modern property law.

Dr. Baker turns to a subject that has attracted great interest in recent times: the process by which modern contract law emerged out of the law of tort through the development of the writ of *assumpsit*. Perhaps the last feature of this process that remains mysterious concerns the adoption in England of the rule of consideration. This problem has been studied by economic as well as legal historians, who have seen the rise of contract as an important index of the way in which the Tudor state promoted mercantile interests. Baker has turned his gaze inward to the development of common-law principles, finding the source of contract law in the evolution of doctrine rather than in social pressures, class interests, or Renaissance jurisprudence. He reminds us how important the internal history of common law remained even at the moment of the greatest apparent conjunction between legal and mercantile elites.

Tudor and early Stuart legal change, even at the purely doctrinal level, was by no means the sole preserve of the common-law courts. Mercantile law, for example, an important aspect of which Baker examines, developed also in the Court of Admiralty. Moreover, theories of common-law jurisdiction emerged out of the competition and conflict between common law and so-called prerogative courts. The principles of this new law of jurisdiction were articulated by courts on either side of their common border.

Because they consumed the attention of contemporary writers and men of politics, the tensions between common-law courts and the courts of Star Chamber, High Commission, Equity, Requests, and Admiralty have been analyzed in great detail. Historians are only now coming to appreciate the degree to which these parallel systems were complementary rather than in conflict. Even where there was conflict there was also similarity in approach to legal reasoning. Professor Barnes's study of an important mid-Jacobean Star Chamber case suggests that Star Chamber judges shared the concern with precedent that has long been taken as the hallmark of the common-law courts. Moreover, in Star Chamber, as in the common-law courts, precedent could be manipulated and made to serve the purposes of judges whose real concern was with the demands of policy. Far more than the common-law courts, however, to the extent that Star Chamber bound itself by precedent it was denying its extraordinary and creative judicial powers. As Barnes's essay suggests, ultimately the "dignity" of Star Chamber could be diminished by reliance on precedent and Coke's "reason of the law." Royalist attitudes shared many of the tendencies of, but were not entirely consonant with, the drift of the developing contemporary legal mentality.

The essays by Barton, Baker, and Barnes illuminate some of the main intellectual traits of Elizabethan and early Stuart lawyers. Although lawyers were prepared to make changes in the law on a short-term basis, they nevertheless felt impelled both to show that such changes were consistent with preexisting legal doctrines and institutions and to formulate broad legal principles from which new rules could be deduced. It is this academic, rationalizing spirit that enhanced sixteenth- and early seventeenth-century fascination with medieval precedent, drawn largely from the abridgments and the early printed Year Books, and it is this spirit that Coke's *Reports* reflect. In the early seventeenth century, this same academic interest was expressed in more polemical and political terms when jurists like Coke came to view early Jacobean use of some prerogative courts as an attack on the common law, and when many Caroline M.P.'s attacked the royal courts for undermining the liberties of English subjects. This emerging opposition to the crown turned to history, mainly to constitutional and legal history, not only because it provided them with a wealth of useful common-law precedents, but also because they saw it as a source of basic legal and moral principles underlying government and personal liberties generally. They turned to history, in short, for their understanding of fundamental law.

Contemporaries turned their partly antiquarian, partly polemical attentions not only to the Year Books and to Magna Carta but also to the rolls of Parliament and to the Anglo-Saxon dooms, frequently reading postconquest developments into preconquest England. In the concluding essay, Dr. Yale demonstrates that writers from Coke on made similar use of Bracton's *De Legibus* and thereby accorded it a kind of authority it had not had for several centuries. Like the revival of Magna Carta, however, the revival of Bracton outlived the early seventeenth-century crisis that occasioned it. For Bracton's *De Legibus*, revived by late Tudor jurists as an ornament to their treatises, and made prominent by all sides in early Stuart political debate, became in the hands of Selden a source for a more dispassionate form of historical analysis. Bracton and the birth of modern English historical scholarship are inseparable. From Selden's day to ours, the text known as "Bracton" has remained central to an understanding of the laws and customs of early English society.

Morris S. Arnold
Thomas A. Green
Sally A. Scully
Stephen D. White

On the Laws and Customs of England

1 The Laws of Ethelbert

A. W. B. Simpson

Professor S. E. Thorne from time to time used the opportunity provided by a public lecture to try out a new way of looking at a historical problem—one of these lectures, for example, delivered at Gray's Inn in 1959, and still unhappily difficult to obtain, revitalized the study of the early history of the Inns of Court.[1] I was myself privileged to hear one such lecture many years ago in Oxford. In this essay, which began as a lecture, I should like to follow his example by floating the idea that the laws of Ethelbert need to be looked at in a curious way to be understood, but I must disclaim at once anything more than the modest hope that I can raise problems which wiser heads may settle.

The earliest known event in Anglo-American legal history is naturally of some special interest to a law teacher at my university, for it was the promulgation of the laws of King Ethelbert of Kent and, if it is realistic to give the event a location, it may well have happened in Canterbury itself. It is there that lie the mortal remains of the king and of Bertha his queen, buried in the mausoleum of St. Peter and St. Paul, now familiar to tourists as St. Augustine's Abbey, which he started to build before his death to house the bodies of the kings of Kent and the archbishops of Canterbury. There was an element of compromise about the site, adjacent as it was to a pagan shrine; indeed, two cult objects from the shrine have survived, and were found in modern excavations beneath the Abbey church.[2] Ethelbert died on the twenty-fourth day of February in A.D. 616, almost exactly thirteen and a half centuries ago. He had ruled approximately fifty-six years, since about A.D. 560, and he belonged to only the third generation after the invasion. His reign is about as close to us as it is to the traditional date of the founding of Rome—753 B.C.; inevitably, King Ethelbert is a shadowy figure. What little we know of him has come down to us principally because he was the king to whom Pope Gregory sent Augustine's mission, a mission that was to some degree at least successful. As the Venerable Bede put it, Ethelbert was the first king of the English to enter the Kingdom of Heaven and, because Augustine brought salvation, that represented success.[3] If Bede is correct on his entry (and it is hardly

1. Samuel E. Thorne, "The Early History of the Inns of Court with Special Reference to Gray's Inn," *Graya*, no. 50 (1959), pp. 79–96.

2. Pope Gregory advised in favor of the use of pagan temples for Christian purposes, so long as they were well built and purified. See Bede, *Historia Ecclesiastica Gentis Anglorum*, I.30 (Letter to Mellitus, A.D. 601), ed. Bertram Colgrave and R. A. B. Mynors (Oxford, 1969), II.4 (p. 149).

3. Bede, *Historia*, II.5 (p. 149).

a historical question), it must, I think, have caused something of a stir, for Ethelbert, according to the genealogies, was a great-grandson of Hengist (who, with his brother Horsa, according to one view, was some sort of horse), and a direct descendant through only seven generations of the god Woden; descent from the god was standard in the genealogies of the Saxon monarchs. For Ethelbert was a king in a very different sense from the essentially secular sense understood today. He was a divine figure, part priest, part god, part ruler, part general; and he ruled a people, not a territory. Only because of their contemporary location did his dominion extend as far north as the Humber, and as far west as around Worcester. Furthermore, he was but one king amongst a number of Saxon kings; there may indeed have been more than one king in Kent. He was, however, a superior king, the third such to enjoy *imperium* over all the southern kingdoms. The *Anglo-Saxon Chronicle* calls such superior kings *bretwaldan*, though it is not at all clear in what their overlordship consisted. But in modern terminology, Ethelbert, our first lawgiver, is best, I think, described as a tribal chief, and a paramount chief as well.

King Ethelbert's place in history principally depends upon Bede's account of his conversion to Christianity, and his association with the establishment of the see of Canterbury. To legal historians, however, his fame has another basis; at some point after his conversion, traditionally in 597, but before the death of Augustine in ca. 605 (both dates, I fear, being irredeemably uncertain), he was responsible for the promulgation, perhaps in 602 or 603, of a set of laws that have, by the skin of their teeth, survived.[4] Although it is possible to raise doubts about the precise state of our text, in the main in this essay I shall avoid discussion of the textual difficulties, and proceed generally on the assumption that they have survived in something closely resembling the original form. These laws have two special claims upon our attention. The first is that they are the earliest set of written laws of any Germanic people in Europe. The second is that they constitute the earliest text, so far as we know, ever written in the English language. Bede, in the history he wrote a century and a quarter later, extols the virtues of Ethelbert, and tells us that "Among other benefits which he conferred upon the race under his care he established with the advice of his counsellors a code of laws after the Roman manner. These are written in English and are still kept and observed by the people."[5] The laws have survived in a single manuscript, the *Textus Roffensis*, in the cathedral library at Rochester; at one point it was even dropped in the sea, and no doubt over the centuries it has had other near escapes. The manuscript dates from around 1120, and was probably copied from a Canterbury manuscript that has long been lost. The *Textus Roffensis* also contains the only text of the later Kentish laws

4. The basic edition is in F. Liebermann, *Die Gesetze der Angelsachsen*, 3 vols. (Halle, 1903–16), at 1:3–18. A convenient text with translation is in F. L. Attenborough, *The Laws of the Earliest English Kings* (Cambridge, 1922), at pp. 4–17.

5. Bede, *Historia*, II.5 (p. 151).

of Hlothere and Eadric (ca. 670) and of Wihtred (ca. 695). Other collections of preconquest laws survive, such as the laws of Ine of Wessex (ca. 690); some laws, which we know once existed, such as the laws of Offa of Mercia, have been lost. But in English history the laws of Ethelbert have no rival in antiquity, and they possess the particular interest that must attach to the very first collection of all. There is indeed no reason to believe that there ever were any earlier English or Germanic laws.[6] They provide us, then, with the first information we have on English law, which was to become one of the two great systems of legal thought produced in western Europe, the common-law system. It is a curious reflection that some seventy years earlier, at the other end of Europe, the Emperor Justinian in Byzantium had been responsible for producing the great codification of Roman law, the *Corpus Iuris Civilis*, which was to become the basis for the other great system—Roman or civil law. But as the common law was, as it were, just beginning in A.D. 600, Roman law already possessed an intellectual history stretching back to the early Roman code, the Twelve Tables, promulgated, so tradition has it, in 451 B.C.; the common-law system arrived late on the scene.

The text of the laws begins with a preamble, no doubt a later addition to the original text, which states that "These are the dooms which Aethelbert established in the lifetime of Augustine." The word *domas*, commonly rendered as "dooms," is almost untranslatable, and the same may be said for Bede's description or title—*decreta iudiciorum*. The nearest equivalent is "judgments," and the difficulty we have in finding an equivalent for the contemporary description is not without its significance. Today, of course, we draw a distinction between legislation on the one hand and adjudication on the other; the nature of the two activities and the distinction between them provides endless amusement for legal philosophers. Essentially, however, legislation involves the idea of laying down abstract general rules to deal with situations that, it is thought, will arise in the future: adjudication on the other hand involves giving decisions in particular cases after they have arisen. But this distinction was not part of the intellectual stock of ideas of the seventh century. So what we think of as the *laws*, the legislative code, that is, of King Ethelbert, consisted in the eyes of contemporaries as a set of judgments pronounced by a king (and his council of elders)[7] who did not think there was any critical difference between pronouncing abstract decisions of a general character for the future and giving particular decisions in concrete cases. The king and his counselors proceed to give judgments without waiting for any actual disputes to come before them. *If* this or that happens, this is the judgment. Ethelbert then in a sense legislated without knowing that this was what he was doing, without realizing that he was employing a new and immensely important social technique. For, since Ethelbert's time, legislation has become a major instrument of social control, though

6. There are earlier Welsh laws.

7. Bede, *Historia*, II.5 (p. 150), says "cum consilio sapientium" ("with the advice of wise men").

it took a very long time for its potentiality to be realized. For example, in one recent year, Acts of the British Parliament and statutory instruments covered nine thousand pages of print in the standard edition. The predominant function of modern government has come to be legislating. King Ethelbert, I fear, started it all.

His laws modestly comprise a mere ninety distinct clauses.[8] Now the first problem that confronts anyone who compiles a collection of this kind is determining a suitable arrangement and, when the collection is the first ever, the problem is particularly acute. Though some have seen in the laws nothing more than a loose association of ideas, it seems to me that the arrangement is in the main quite systematic. The laws are largely concerned with prescribing money payments, as "compensation"[9] (if that is the right concept, and it probably is not) for wrongs. We start with sixteen clauses dealing with situations where the compensation payable depends upon the status in society of the victim, and we start from the most important end—the church and churchmen.[10] We then proceed down the social scale through the king[11] to noblemen[12] and finally to commoners.[13] We then have four clauses (17–20), rather oddly inserted at this point, dealing with secondary participation in wrongdoing—the sort of thing we call aiding and abetting—and these fix appropriate levels of compensation. For example, clause 20 deals with liability for lending weapons that are used in homicide, a matter that still gives rise to legal problems in our time. I guess the compiler could not think where these clauses should come, but put them in early because they involved an element of general principle. The next six clauses (clauses 21–26) deal with killings, and the payment of the wergild, literally the "man-price" or "man-value," which was payable to the kin of the dead person. The text, and we must remember that our manuscript was written five hundred years after Ethelbert's time, is somewhat disorderly between clauses 24 and 33. Thus, clause 24 seems out of place in the middle of the section on homicide because it deals with compensation for putting bonds on a freeman. But the text is defective at this point, and I suspect in any event that both clauses 24 and 25 may be corrupt. We move on in clauses 27–29 to deal with breaking and entering, and then again we have three clauses that seem to be in the wrong place. Clause 30 deals with the payment of wergild, and should come earlier with the other clauses on homicide. Clause 31 is in like case, though perhaps it would fit in later in the section on the family. Clause 32 is a mystery, for it deals with damage to a *hamscyld*, and nobody knows what this was with any degree of certainty, more particularly because the word occurs only here: "the enclosure of a dwelling," Attenborough's translation, is a plausible conjecture.

8. The division into *numbered* clauses is not a feature of the original MS.
9. In the original, *bot*, a word etymologically connected with "better."
10. Cl. 1.
11. Cl. 2–12 incl.
12. Cl. 13–14.
13. Cl. 15–16.

We then proceed to deal with assault, battery, and grievous bodily harm, and this in minute detail. For clauses 33 to 72 contain an alarming list of possible acts of violence, and for each a precise sum by way of compensation is provided. The arrangement within this section is basically anatomical. We begin at the top, with pulling of hair in clause 33. The next clause is for harder pulls, involving an element of scalping. With odd lapses we then move down the Anglo-Saxon human anatomy, reaching the fingernails by clause 55 and eventually the toenails by clause 72. One cannot but admire the dogged determination with which the laws attempt (but of course fail) to cover every possible form of mayhem, and to fix with precision the appropriate sum of money. Only in one place, clause 65, is there any sign of flagging; here the legislation gave up, and left the assessment for laming to friends. "If a thigh is broken," the clause says, "12 shillings shall be paid as compensation. If he becomes lame, the settlement of the matter may be left to friends." After we have completed this gory catalogue we move on in clauses 73–84 to deal with aspects of what we now call family law, and finally, by a natural sequence of thought, we conclude with six clauses concerned with law relating to the family retainers, that is to say, servants and slaves. The dooms are, in the main, tidily arranged in a systematic way.

The money payments (to use a neutral term) referred to in the laws are presented in terms of three concepts—*bot*, *geld*, and *wite*. It is quite radically mistaken to think of the laws as dealing with crimes, a modern and wholly irrelevant conception. *Bot* is usually translated as *compensation*, and appears in the laws when damage has been caused or rights violated. *Geld*, which means value, is the concept involved whether there is something in the nature of total loss—death, a foot struck off, genitals destroyed—or where, as in the case of theft from the church, the sum payable is a multiple of the thing's value. *Wite* appears in only one clause, clause 9: "If a freeman robs a freeman, he shall pay threefold compensation [*bot*] and the king shall take the fine [*wite*][14] or [? and] all the man's goods." In two other clauses (clauses 2, 84), payment is to be made to the king as well as to the immediately wronged person, but these clauses do not indicate under what description the money is payable. Clause 6 provides for a payment of fifty shillings to the king when a freeman is killed for infringement of his rights as lord (to *drihtingbeage*); this probably corresponds to the concept of *manbot* found in later laws (e.g., Ine, clauses 70, 76), a payment for the infringement of the lord's rights as lord; it is therefore a form of *bot*.

Now the laws of Ethelbert and of other Anglo-Saxon kings are often called "codes," but if we mean by a code a comprehensive statement of the law in general, or even the law on one particular subject, it is quite obvious that Ethelbert's laws do not constitute a code in that sense at all; the dooms deal with only a limited selection of matters. Before they were

14. *Wite* means "punishment," "fine," "torture," "misery," "penance." Here it seems reasonable to translate it as "fine."

promulgated, all the law was customary law, depending upon traditions accepted by the older and more important members of the community, and in particular by the paramount chief or king and his advisers and counselors. Most law at most stages in human history has been customary law of this kind, and much contemporary law even today is of this character. After the promulgation of Ethelbert's laws, most Kentish law continued to be customary law, and the first question that this observation suggests is why they were promulgated at all. Why was the king not content to leave matters to be regulated in the traditional way by orally transmitted custom? What was the problem or the event that prompted King Ethelbert and his wise men to have recourse to what T. F. T. Plucknett once called the "desperate expedient" of written legislation, something that had never been used before in England? No doubt, sooner or later, *someone* would have taken the plunge, but the earliest laws of Wessex are nearly a century later (ca. 695) and the lost laws of Offa of Mercia (757–96) nearly two; later legislators were indeed inspired to some degree by the example of King Ethelbert. So it is reasonable to ask why it was first done when it was first done.

One explanation was suggested a very long time ago by the very first historian to consider the matter—the Venerable Bede himself—and it has been adopted by virtually all subsequent historians in one form or another. Bede presents the legislation as a consequence of the success of St. Augustine's mission.[15] For the story of this mission we are mainly dependent upon Bede's *Ecclesiastical History of the English People*, which he completed in A.D. 731. Gregory the Great, later St. Gregory, was elected pope in the year 590. The story is that one day before he became pope he was in the slave market in Rome, and spotted a group of particularly handsome boys up for sale. On inquiry he was told that they were from Britain and were pagans. He remarked, rather rudely, with a sigh: "Alas that the author of darkness should have men so bright of face in his grip, and that minds devoid of inward grace should bear so graceful an outward form."[16] Conversation proceeded, and he was told that the boys were *Angli*, and came from the kingdom of Deira, whose king was Aelle. Having cracked three perfectly appalling puns, only one of which is, mercifully, generally known,[17] he unsuccessfully asked the pope to send a mission to England. One may well wonder what the good Gregory was doing in the slave market anyway, and the answer may be that he was considering buying some English slaves. We know from a letter of his in 595 or thereabouts that he had a plan to buy some English slaves and train them as missionaries to the English.[18] His missionary ideas were put

15. Bede, *Historia*, II.5 (p. 151).

16. Ibid., II.1 (p. 135).

17. Pun number two indicates that the English shall be saved from the wrath of God (*de ira*); pun three suggests that Aelle's land ought to resound to cries of "Alleluia."

18. The letter is printed in Arthur James Mason, *The Mission of St. Augustine to England according to the Original Documents, Being a Handbook for the Thirteenth Centenary* (Cambridge, 1897), p. 17.

into effect only when he become pope himself, and in 596 St. Augustine, prior of the monastery of St. Andrew in Rome, was put in charge of the mission, which set out for England; Augustine was to be consecrated bishop if his mission was successful. En route, the nerve of the whole party cracked at the prospect of going to a "barbarous, fierce, and unbelieving nation whose language they did not even understand," but Pope Gregory succeeded in restoring morale, and as part of the process promoted Augustine to be abbot. About forty strong, the party reached the Isle of Thanet, probably in the spring of 597, and, after some initial nervousness, King Ethelbert came over to Thanet across the Wantsum Channel and met them. He allowed them to conduct their mission, and to move to Canterbury, where they operated from the Church of St. Martin's, just outside the city, which still exists as the oldest continuously used Christian building in the country. Ethelbert was soon converted and baptized, traditionally on Whit Sunday, 2 June 597, and, by Christmas that year, mass baptisms were under way—ten thousand at a time. In 601, Pope Gregory sent Augustine the *pallium*, together with reinforcements, Mellitus, Justus, Paulinus, and Rugianus. By 601, Augustine was performing so many miracles that Gregory was impelled to write him a cautionary letter on the subject. Work began on the building of new churches and the restoration of old ones and on the monastic mausoleum of St. Peter and St. Paul, now known as St. Augustine's, where Augustine and King Ethelbert were to be buried, with their successors. In 604, Mellitus was consecrated bishop and set to work on the East Saxons, whose king was Ethelbert's nephew Saeberht; and on his success, Ethelbert built the Church of St. Paul's in the city of London, which was his see. Justus was consecrated the first bishop of Rochester, where Ethelbert built St. Andrew's. Probably in 605, Augustine died and was succeeded by Laurentius, and in 616 by Ethelbert; our laws were promulgated sometime before Augustine's death in 605 and probably after 601.

The whole story of St. Augustine's mission is presented by Bede as a success story. Ultimately, a historian cannot judge the matter, for what St. Augustine was bringing to the English was salvation, and historical evidences do not throw any light on his success in that. Insofar as the mission was outwardly successful, some credit must presumably go to Ethelbert's Frankish queen, Bertha, who was a Christian when they married, and to her bishop, the shadowy figure Liudhard, and also to the Christian community that must have existed in Kent before Augustine arrived. Bede does himself bear witness to some setbacks; thus he recounts the disastrous attempt by Augustine to establish relations with the Celtic church.[19] He also recounts how, after Ethelbert's death, official support for Christianity collapsed—Eadbald, Ethelbert's son, promptly reverted to pagan ways and married his stepmother.[20] On the death of the converted King Saeberht, his three sons expelled the missionaries

19. Bede, *Historia*, II.2 (p. 139).
20. Ibid., II.5 (p. 151).

from amongst the East Saxons. Bishops Mellitus and Justus fled to Gaul, and Laurentius nearly followed but, as he lay asleep in St. Augustine's, St. Peter flogged him and told him to pull himself together. The marks so impressed King Eadbald that he became a Christian, and matters began to look up again.[21]

Now, part of the evidence for the success or failure of the mission must be sought in the laws, and Bede himself explained the laws partly by reference to the success of Augustine's mission. In speaking of the laws he says: "Among these he [i.e., Ethelbert] set down first of all what restitution must be made by anyone who steals anything belonging to the church or bishops or any other clergy; these laws were designed to give protection to those whose coming and whose teaching he had welcomed."[22] The obvious reference is to the first clause of the laws, which states that "God's property and the church's shall be compensated twelvefold. A bishop's elevenfold. A priest's property ninefold; a deacon's property sixfold; a clerk's property threefold. Breach of the peace shall be compensated doubly when it affects a church or a meeting place." The idea, in the form now generally accepted by historians, is that Augustine and his followers constituted a new class or category in society, whose place in the scheme of things was simply not defined by customary law. Existing law, it is supposed, would have defined how compensation was to be made for theft from, for example, a commoner or nobleman, but some decision had to be taken on the going rate for various grades of churchmen. This need, the argument runs, generated the laws of Ethelbert. I find this explanation most unsatisfactory, and I wish both to question it and to suggest alternatives.

Bede's explanation relies exclusively on clause 1, which it certainly explains, but it does not seem to explain the rest of the laws—the other eighty-nine clauses, which do not mention the church at all. Indeed, to be fair to Bede, he does not as it were press his explanation. And in the case of clause 1 there are difficulties.[23]

The first is the scale of compensation laid down, which contrasts oddly with that provided by clause 4, which states that "If a freeman robs the King, he shall pay back a ninefold amount." It seems hardly conceivable that a priest's property and that of the king ranked at the same level. Furthermore, insofar as the later laws deal with the matter at all, they indicate no tradition of such extraordinary treatment for the church. Thus the Kentish laws of Wihtred (695) equate the position of the church with that of the king, providing that the *munbyrd* (protection) of the

21. The view that Bede overstated the success of St. Augustine's mission may well be correct; but to be fair he does record the setbacks.

22. Bede, *Historia*, II.5 (p. 151).

23. H. G. Richardson and G. O. Sayles, *Law and Legislation from Aethelberht to Magna Carta* (Edinburgh, 1966), pp. 2 ff., argue that cl. 1 is an interpolation, an argument related to their general skepticism over Ethelbert's conversion. But they do not face up to the problem of explaining the interpolation—there was *some* version of cl. 1 in Bede's time. Nor do they provide any positive explanation of Ethelbert's venture into legislation.

church should be fifty shillings—the same as that provided in Ethelbert's laws for the king (clause 8).[24]

The second difficulty is that, apart from clause 1, the laws do not deal with the special position of the church and churchmen at all; for example, there is no special ruling on the *munbyrd* of the church, though there is on that of the king and of commoners, nor on slaying of or injuries to priests or churchmen, or injury to church property. The Kentish laws of Hlothere and Eadric (ca. 673–86) again contain no reference to the church. Wihtred's laws, nearly a century later, are the earliest laws to concentrate upon fitting the new institution into society, for they contain no less than fifteen clauses, out of twenty-eight, which explicitly deal with the church and its position in society or presuppose its existence,[25] and seven more of obvious Christian significance;[26] the contrast with the laws of Ethelbert is very striking.

The third is that there is independent evidence in Bede's *History* that St. Augustine was particularly interested in the problem with which the first clause deals, and the passage in the laws seems to be quite out of line with the church's view on theft from the church. In 600 or 601, Augustine sent to Pope Gregory a series of nine questions that, Bede tells us, seemed urgent, and Pope Gregory promptly replied to them.[27] The third question Augustine asked Gregory was "how one who steals from the church should be punished." Pope Gregory's reply was in some ways not very helpful, for he stated: "My brother, you must judge from the thief's circumstances what punishment he ought to have. For there are some who commit theft though they have resources, while others transgress in this matter through poverty. So some must be punished by fines, and some by a flogging, some severely and some more leniently." He added that "love must dictate the method of correction, so that we do not decide on anything unreasonable." Turning then from the question of *punishment* to that of *compensation*, he said: "You should also add that they ought to restore whatever they have stolen from a church. But God forbid that the church should make a profit out of the earthly things it seems to lose and so seek to gain from such vanities." From this passage it seems likely that Gregory knew that legislation was intended (hence the phrase "you should add"),[28] and he gave advice as to the form it should take. What is very surprising is that there seems little connection between Gregory's advice and the solution adopted by the laws.

Any explanation of Ethelbert's legislation that depends exclusively on

24. Wihtred, cl. 2. For the text of Wihtred's laws, see Liebermann, *Gesetze*, 1:12–14; and Attenborough, *Laws*, pp. 24–31. The evidence of the *Penitential of Theodore*, attributed to Theodore of Tarsus, archbishop of Canterbury, A.D. 668–90, also does not suggest so privileged a position for the church; the compensation for theft from churches is fourfold only. See J. T. McNeill and H. M. Gamer, *Medieval Handbooks of Penance* (New York, 1965), at p. 186.

25. Wihtred, cl. 1–4, 6–8, 16–22, 24.

26. Wihtred, cl. 5, 9–15.

27. Bede, *Historia*, I.27 (p. 79).

28. *Addes etiam* is the Latin.

clause 1 is, therefore, built upon an unsure foundation. There are certainly grounds for suspecting the authenticity of the clause in the form we now have it and, even assuming it to be genuine, we still have to explain the rest of the legislation and the disparity between Gregory's advice and the laws. So far as this is concerned, there are again a number of explanations that are possible. The most radical is that the correspondence between Augustine and Gregory is spurious and never happened. But assuming that it did, it seems to me that we can still accept Bede's explanation, but explain the disparity in two ways. The first is that Augustine's hold over Ethelbert was not very great, and Ethelbert's conversion somewhat skin deep, a view for which there is other evidence. The second is that Gregory was dealing in a set of conceptions largely alien to Ethelbert and his counselors, with ideas they did not understand. Gregory is recommending *punishment*, graded according to guilt, on the one hand, and simple *compensation* on the other; he distinguishes what is to be done to the thief, and what is to be done to put things right for the victim, between criminal and civil law. The laws of Ethelbert have, in fact, only the slightest reference to punishment in one clause; the predominant notion with which they are concerned is *bot*—we translate this "compensation"—as an alternative to simple retaliation, rather than as economic restitution, and in the case of a thief, retaliation would normally involve killing.[29] To provide an alternative to retaliation one needs a substantial payment, and this is what the laws offer; we cannot regard it as either a civil or a criminal remedy.

It is natural enough to expect to find elsewhere in the laws, if not an explicit reference to the church, at least a reflection of Christian influence. But there is one other clause that surprisingly reveals a curious lack of this influence, and this again seems to support the view that Ethelbert was not very strongly influenced by Augustine. One of the other questions that Augustine posed to Pope Gregory relates to marriage. His fifth question was, "Within what degree may the faithful marry their kindred; and is it lawful to marry a stepmother or a sister-in-law?" Gregory replied that in no circumstances must there be marriages between those twice removed, and that marriage to a sister-in-law or stepmother is gravely sinful. The English who have contracted such marriages in ignorance are to be received into the church, but must in future abstain from sexual relations; for the future they are to be excommunicated. If we turn to the laws of Ethelbert, we might expect appropriate provisions in the clauses dealing with marriage and the family, but if Augustine tried (one suspects that Queen Bertha would try, too) to convince King Ethelbert and his counselors, he dramatically failed. Discussion of the subject may, however, have prompted clauses 75 and 76, which provide compensation

29. Thus, Wihtred's laws (A.D. 695), cl. 25 and 26, provide that if a man is killed while thieving no wergild is payable; if he is caught, i.e., detained, the king is to decide whether he be killed, sold beyond the sea, or ransomed for his wergild. Ine's laws (ca. A.D. 690) are similar. For the text of this latter code, see Liebermann, *Gesetze*, 1:88–123; and Attenborough, *Laws*, pp. 36–61.

(presumably to a guardian) when a widow is married by someone who is not entitled to marry her. The clause, however, clearly recognizes that in some situations someone had a right to marry a widow, and we can guess that the right resided either in a brother-in-law or in a stepson. Ironically enough, King Ethelbert's own widow was married by his son Eadbald—apparently the widow was not Bertha but some subsequent wife. The *Anglo-Saxon Chronicle* records that in marrying the widow he followed heathen custom. Bede recounts, however, with some satisfaction, that no good came of this, for Eadbald was "afflicted by frequent fits of madness and possessed by an unclean spirit." Bede obviously thought it served him right.

Bede's explanation for the promulgation of the laws is therefore problematical and, even if it does explain clause 1, fails to explain the main body of the legislation. All Bede offers as a makeweight is the statement that Ethelbert's legislation was imitative of Roman legislation—the laws, he says, were promulgated *iuxta exempla Romanorum*. One may look in vain in the laws for any Roman influence on their *substance*; there is no question of any borrowing of Roman law conceptions or rules; nor were the laws written, as one might have expected, in Latin. It is perhaps conceivable that some account of the codification of the Emperor Justinian had filtered through from the East, as perhaps had knowledge of the code of Theodosius. But mere imitation of Roman written codes provides a very unsatisfactory explanation of the major part of Ethelbert's laws. I think there are other ways in which the laws can be explained in terms of Christian influence and the Augustinian mission, without having recourse to the wilder speculations of those who suppose that there may have been earlier models.[30]

If one looks at the laws, they are mainly concerned to provide scales of money payments for various kinds of wrongs, in the form of either *bot* or *geld*, as I have explained. Whether what is involved is homicide, or theft, or scalping, the laws provide for an appropriate payment, and they give the impression of a society in which anything from murder down to a punch-up could be sorted out by, as it were, writing a check. But it is about as certain as can be that seventh-century Kent was not like that at all. Whether it was a more or less violent society than we have today it is quite impossible to tell—one may guess that it was a society in which the boundary between peacetime and wartime was not as clear as today, but it is quite possible that, in peacetime, it was fairly peaceful. It was, however, a society in which the institution of the blood feud existed, and one in which the likely and acceptable reaction to wrongdoing was not payment of money but retaliation, by either the victim or his kin. This we know not simply from comparative evidence, but from the later Saxon

30. Richardson and Sayles attempt to explain the laws without reference to Christian influence because they reject the authenticity of cl. 1, reject the evidence for Ethelbert's conversion, and reject the connection between literacy and the church; they end up vaguely premising ghostly earlier models. In the process, Bede's argument has to be rejected on weak grounds. See *Law and Legislation*, pp. 1–13, 157–69.

laws, which expressly recognize the legitimacy of retaliation and the feud. Thus, for example, the earliest laws of Wessex, those of Ine (ca. 690), have this provision on theft: "If a thief is taken he shall die the death, or his life shall be redeemed by the payment of his wergeld." And later on we have, for example, this: "He who kills a thief shall be allowed to declare with an oath that he whom he killed was a thief trying to escape, and the kinsman of the dead then shall swear an oath to carry on no feud against him. If however he keeps it secret, and it afterwards comes to light, then he shall pay for it." And some four centuries after the laws of Ethelbert, King Edmund, recognizing the prevalence of the blood feud as a reaction to violence, produced a special code regulating an institution that he was powerless to stop.[31] Indeed, much Anglo-Saxon legislation is concerned with the provision of alternatives to retaliation and the blood feud, and forms part of the long process whereby eventually the law comes to recognize no right of retaliation at all, but only a right of self-defense, provocation alone counting at most as a mitigating factor. It is quite inconceivable that this process had proceeded far in King Ethelbert's time.

The position some sixty or so years later is made abundantly clear by a work compiled from the opinions of Theodore, the then archbishop of Canterbury. In this, the *Penitential of Theodore*, opinions are given as to the appropriate scale of penance for killing:

> 1. If one slays a man in revenge for a relative, he shall do penance as a murderer for seven or ten years. However, if he will render to the relatives the legal price, the penance shall be lighter, that is [it shall be shortened] by half the time.
> 2. If one slays a man in revenge for a brother, he shall do penance for three years. In another place it is said that he should do penance for ten years.
> 3. But a murderer, ten or seven years.[32]

There is here explicit recognition of the feud, combined however with condemnation of it. The church dealt in ideals but accepted realities.

What Ethelbert's laws were plainly concerned with was to provide, in the form of fixed money payments, an alternative to retaliation and the feud. It is clear from the laws that a system already existed whereby this could be agreed upon by the injured party or his kinsmen, and clause 65 indeed retains this in the case of laming. But haggling and bargaining between the quarreling families is a difficult and indeed dangerous operation, and one can see the enormous advantage of having a fixed tariff providing definite alternatives to counter-violence. This the laws provided, and I suspect that Christian influence lay behind this. There is indeed some direct evidence for this view in a passage written by King

31. For Edmund's code, see Liebermann, *Gesetze*, 1:186–91; and A. J. Robertson, *The Laws of the Kings of England from Edmund to Henry I* (Cambridge, 1925), pp. 8–11.
32. See McNeill and Gamer, *Medieval Handbooks of Penance*, p. 187.

Alfred. Somewhere about 892, Alfred compiled a set of laws and wrote a long introduction to them. In it he explains that his laws incorporate much earlier legislation going back to Ethelbert's laws. He tells us: "After it came about that many people had received the faith of Christ, many synods were assembled throughout all the earth, and likewise throughout England, after they had received the faith . . . they then established, for that mercy which Christ taught, that secular lords might with his permission receive without sin compensation in money for almost every misdeed at the first offence, which compensation they then fixed."[33]

What was involved, according to this passage, was the establishment of the idea *that it was not sinful to accept compensation*, and the point of this is that in societies where the feud exists it is regarded as the *duty* of the injured person or his kin to retaliate—they behave dishonorably if they do not do so. Recidivists could of course expect no mercy at all; only first offenders could enjoy the new system. What the laws of Ethelbert were concerned to introduce into society was a new idea—that it was not wrong to take money instead of blood. This represents a dramatic change, and we can see in the laws the attempt inspired by the church to introduce a new and merciful alternative to the tradition of retaliation. It seems to me, however, that it is not conceivable that this alternative was originally compulsory, and if this is right the laws involve legislation in a restricted sense—they are permissive laws only; their unreality reflects their idealistic quality, which resembles the penitentials, and is the best evidence of their Christian genesis. They provide as it were a recommended alternative that *may* be used, and the alternative system is made more likely to be used by being as precise as possible. It may well be that the money payments were fixed at a higher level than was realistic, and the outcome of a settlement in reality would be either the surrender of the wrongdoer into debt slavery, or the payment of some lesser sum; this is suggested by modern studies of the feud, but there is no way of telling what actually happened in Ethelbert's time. A realization of this, and of the fact that laws can represent aspirations only, is the key to understanding Anglo-Saxon legislation.

There are, I think, two other ways in which promulgation of the laws of Ethelbert is related to the influx of Christianity. The first arises in the following way. We naturally think of Augustine as bringing a religion to Canterbury, or at least furthering the spread of one that already was practiced there. The Christian church, however, also brought with it another enormously important possession and this was technological—churchmen knew how to read and write. This made possible the laws of Ethelbert. Given the illiteracy of society, one may well wonder what the point of having written laws was at all—there would be little point in distributing copies amongst a population unable to read or write. The written text probably served as an *aide memoire*, from which the laws could be read out by clerics to leading and important citizens. We have

33. Liebermann, *Gesetze*, 1:15.

indeed an early illuminated manuscript from the ninth century that illustrates this—it shows Moses reading out the tables of the law, and the Anglo-Saxon scribe was no doubt depicting a scene with which he was familiar.[34] The audience may indeed have come to learn the laws by heart—some later laws are in alliterative prose. The use of the local language—Old English—and not Latin, the natural language of Augustine and his followers, connects with the function of the text, for there would be no point in reading out Latin laws to Anglo-Saxon elders.[35] Later, when law becomes the preserve of lawyers, the use of the vernacular ceases to be important, and English law came to be expressed in languages not known by the populace—Latin and Norman French. What is a little mysterious, however, is the alphabet used.[36] The Latin alphabet could not cope happily with Old English, and the text of the laws is written in a combination of the Latin alphabet and certain runic characters taken from the Germanic runic alphabet—which was used only for magical purposes or for inscriptions. The idea of combining the two was developed in the Celtic church, and so there lies behind the text of the laws Irish or Celtic influence. We can only guess at how this came about: there were contacts between the Celtic church and the Franks, and Augustine himself attended two disastrous synods with the British church. The use of the mixed alphabet suggests, however, that Christianity in seventh-century Kent had closer links with Celtic Christianity than Bede's own account records; Bede of course had little use for Celtic Christianity.

A further aspect of Christian influence on the laws is suggested by their similarity to a peculiar and at times entertaining form of early Christian literature—the penitentials.[37] The Christian notion of penance for sin gave rise to an obvious problem: what was the right form and quantity of penance for each particular sin? In the Celtic Christian communities of the fifth century there evolved a special form of literature directed to working out a comprehensive set of answers to all possible problems. One of the earliest surviving penitentials is that attributed to Finnian of Clonard, an Irish monk who died in about A.D. 550. The following extracts are typical:

> But if he is a cleric and strikes his brother or his neighbor or sheds blood, it is the same as if he had killed him, but the penance is not the same. He shall do penance with bread and water and be deprived of his clerical office for an entire year, and he must pray for

34. British Library Additional MS 10546, reproduced in R. H. Hodgkin, *A History of the Anglo-Saxons*, 3d ed., 2 vols. (London, 1952), 2:pl. 76, facing p. 611.

35. Richardson and Sayles (see *Law and Legislation*, p. 9) seem to assume that written laws could have no function unless literacy was widespread. This is a mistake; indeed, in modern times in colonial territories, written laws have commonly operated in illiterate societies. Reading is only one means of access to a written text.

36. For discussion, see Richardson and Sayles, *Law and Legislation*, pp. 159 ff., where it is argued that long before Augustine's time, English was being written in Kent, the local inhabitants having themselves combined the use of the Roman and the runic alphabets.

37. See McNeill and Gamer, *Medieval Handbooks*; and Thomas Pollock Oakley, *English Penitential Discipline and Anglo-Saxon Law in Their Joint Influence* (New York, 1923).

> himself with weeping and tears, that he may obtain mercy of God, since the Scripture says: "Whosoever hateth his brother is a murderer," how much more he who strikes him.
>
> But if he is a layman, he shall do penance forty days and give some money to him whom he struck, according as some priest or judge determines. A cleric, however, ought not to give money, either to the one or to the other.
>
> If a cleric commits theft once or twice, that is, steals his neighbor's sheep or hog or any animal, he shall do penance an entire year on an allowance of bread and water and shall restore fourfold to his neighbor.
>
> If however he does it not once or twice but of long habit, he shall do penance for three years.[38]

Another example, though later than Ethelbert's time, is the penitential of Theodore of Tarsus, archbishop of Canterbury from 668 to 690, which, curiously enough, takes a milder view of theft than does Ethelbert's clause 1. A typical passage states that "Money stolen or robbed from churches is to be restored fourfold; from secular persons, twofold."[39] There is an obvious similarity between the penitentials that set out to assign to each sin the exactly appropriate penance, and the early laws that attempted to set out for each wrong the precisely appropriate compensation, and it may well be that the penitentials are the source of the technique attempted by the apparently secular laws of Ethelbert: this again would suggest a Celtic influence at work in seventh-century Kent. If, however, we are to understand the earliest known English legislation, we must concentrate attention not so much upon their detailed content as upon providing a general explanation of their genesis and their function; and to do this requires us to think ourselves back into a world in which legislation could perform a rather different function from anything we encounter today. The laws are an expression of aspirations, not a compulsory and enforceable set of regulations.

38. McNeill and Gamer, *Medieval Handbooks*, p. 88.
39. Ibid., p. 187.

2 Definitions of Feudal Military Obligations in Eleventh-Century Normandy

Emily Zack Tabuteau

There are two current schools of thought on Norman feudal practices in the eleventh century. Charles Homer Haskins and Henri Navel, writing in the first half of this century, argued that Normandy in the eleventh century was one of the most thoroughly and systematically feudalized areas of Europe and that it had become so at a remarkably early date, probably by 1035 and certainly by 1050.[1] Perhaps because it fit so well with John Horace Round's thesis concerning the introduction of knight service into England by William the Conqueror in the years immediately after 1066, this view achieved virtually complete acceptance. Recently, however, a few scholars have suggested that Norman feudal obligations at the time of the conquest of England were less clearly defined than has generally been supposed;[2] and one scholar, D. J. A. Matthew, has largely denied the importance of feudal institutions in Normandy at that date.[3] Neither extreme view—that of Haskins and Navel or that of Matthew—is entirely correct, and their protagonists may have somewhat misconceived the problem. Many aspects of "fully developed feudalism" are indeed notably lacking in eleventh-century Normandy. Their absence, however, is rarely total; and references to lords and men, to benefices, fiefs, and honors, to homage and fealty and service occur quite frequently in the contemporary documents, albeit usually without the elaboration of detail that scholars would like. The problem in interpreting the Nor-

1. Charles Homer Haskins, *Norman Institutions* (1918; reprint ed., New York, 1960), pp. 5–24; Henri Navel, "Recherches sur les institutions féodales en Normandie (région de Caen)," *Bulletin de la Société des antiquaires de Normandie* 51 (1948–51): 5–176, and his earlier articles cited there. It would be impractical to cite all the scholars who have accepted their conclusions.

2. David C. Douglas, "The Rise of Normandy," *Proceedings of the British Academy* 33 (1947):101–30, at 117–19; David C. Douglas, *William the Conqueror: The Norman Impact upon England* (Berkeley and Los Angeles, 1964), pp. 96–103; L. Musset, in *Revue historique de droit français et étranger*, 4th ser. 29 (1951): 150, and in Michel de Boüard, ed., *Histoire de la Normandie* (Toulouse, 1970), p. 124; Joseph R. Strayer, review of the *Recueil des actes des ducs de Normandie (911–1066)*, ed. Marie Fauroux, in *Speculum* 37 (1962): 607–10, at 609; C. Warren Hollister, "1066: The 'Feudal Revolution,'" *American Historical Review* 73 (1968): 708–23, at 721–22; Jean Yver, "Les premières institutions du duché de Normandie," *I Normanni e la loro espansione in Europa nell'alto medioevo*, Settimane di studio del Centro italiano di studi sull'alto medioevo, vol. 16 (Spoleto, 1969), pp. 299–366, at 334–35, 594; the remarks of Antonio Marongiu, in *I Normanni*, pp. 590–91.

3. D. J. A. Matthew, *The Norman Conquest* (New York, 1966), pp. 57–68, 145–46.

man evidence may result from an unwarranted assumption that all the features normally associated with feudal relationships were coeval with the establishment of the relationships themselves. Instead, the most sensible conclusion about the development of Norman feudal tenure may be that by 1066 a set of developing but unsystematized feudal practices existed in Normandy, which were introduced into England by its Norman conquerors; and that, thereafter, these practices gradually developed in both countries in the direction of greater precision and limitation, perhaps attaining earlier in England, because of the situation of the conquerors, a degree of systematic elaboration unknown in Normandy until the same men tried to remake Norman conditions in the image of their newly acquired territory. Suggestions to this effect have been made by several of the scholars who express doubts about the views of Haskins and Navel, but they concentrate on the period from 1066 to 1087 as the crucial one for Normandy as well as for England.[4] On the basis of the evidence to be presented here, it seems to me that for Normandy at least the widespread existence of definitions of feudal obligations cannot be demonstrated at any time before 1100. Such definitions may well not have become common until the early twelfth century.

Such a conclusion must derive from evidence from the eleventh century. Haskins and Navel based their views principally upon a study of twelfth-century documents that they thought could be made to cast light on eleventh-century conditions, concentrating on the inquest concerning the bishopric of Bayeux made in 1133 and the inquest concerning all of Normandy made in 1172. The temptation to use these two systematic surveys as sources about earlier times is great, because references to enfeoffments, feudal tenure, and feudal obligations are meager and obscure in eleventh-century sources. Nevertheless, it is better to tolerate gaps in our knowledge than to read back into the eleventh-century conditions that did not exist until the twelfth. Feudal tenure in Normandy in the eleventh century, as it emerges from the eleventh-century sources alone, seems less precocious and less well organized than has usually been thought.

This is not to deny that tenure was widespread within the Norman upper class in the eleventh century; on the contrary, it would appear that tenurial relations were spreading ever wider among the laity.[5] Tenure, however, need not imply that any particular type of service is due from the tenement. A good many Norman tenements of the eleventh century were held, for example, for rent.[6] It must not be assumed that all the

4. Strayer, review of Fauroux's *Recueil*, pp. 609–10; Douglas, *William*, pp. 98, 101–2, 103, and esp. 283; Hollister, "1066," p. 722; Yver, "Premières institutions," pp. 335, 594.

5. Emily Zack Tabuteau, "Ownership and Tenure in Eleventh-Century Normandy," *American Journal of Legal History* 21 (1977): 97–124.

6. See Emily Zack Tabuteau, "Transfers of Property in Eleventh-Century Norman Law" (Ph.D. diss., Harvard University, 1975), pp. 183–98, 200–202; and W. E. Wightman, *The Lacy Family in England and Normandy, 1066–1194* (Oxford, 1966), pp. 215, 220–21. There has been little study of nonfeudal services in Normandy, doubtless because of the

tenements that demonstrably existed in eleventh-century Normandy were held for specifically defined services of a feudal nature—or even that a tenement called *beneficium* or *feodum*, and said to be held for one or more distinctively feudal services, was held for all the types of service ordinarily thought to have issued from a fief or for only those types of service.

In the generally accepted model of a fully developed feudal system, a vassal's obligations to his lord include such varied duties as host service, castle-guard, suit of court, escort and messenger service, aids, and feudal incidents such as relief, wardship, marriage, and escheat, all of them governed by conventional limitations as to type, occasion, amount, and so on. All these obligations are mentioned at least occasionally in eleventh-century Norman sources, which is doubtless why it has sometimes been asserted that the full model was in existence in Normandy at that time.[7] In fact, however, an analysis would show that, in most if not all cases, Norman habits in the eleventh century were markedly anomalous in terms of the model. Such an analysis would be quite lengthy.[8] Because host service is usually treated as the most central of a vassal's obligations to his lord, and because the signal characteristic of the Norman feudal "system" as it has been elucidated by Haskins and Navel and their followers is the precise definition of the military service owed to the duke by his vassals and, consequently, to the ducal vassals by their own men, I shall concentrate on this aspect of the problem. In order to substantiate the conclusion that feudal military obligations in the eleventh century were much less precisely defined than Haskins and Navel believed, it will be necessary to demonstrate why the twelfth-century evidence upon which they relied cannot be used to argue about eleventh-century condi-

---

general assumption that all honorable tenure was feudal. On the blindness sometimes induced by the concept of feudalism, see the valuable remarks of Elizabeth A. R. Brown, "The Tyranny of a Construct: Feudalism and Historians of Medieval Europe," *American Historical Review* 79 (1974): 1063–88.

7. E.g., William J. Corbett, "The Development of the Duchy of Normandy and the Norman Conquest of England," in *Cambridge Medieval History*, vol. 5 (Cambridge, 1929), pp. 481–520, at 484, 511–12, and passim. Some scholars have suggested that developed feudal organization was or may have been imposed on Normandy at the time of the Viking conquest; see Jacques Boussard, "Services féodaux, milices, mercenaires dans les armées, en France. aux Xe et XIe siècles," *Ordinamenti militari in Occidente nell'alto medioevo*, Settimane di studio del Centro italiano di studi sull'alto medioevo, vol. 15 (Spoleto, 1968), pp. 131–68; at 157–58; Maurice Rabasse, *Du régime des fiefs en Normandie au moyen-âge* (Paris, 1905), par. 4; Henri Prentout, *Etude critique sur Dudon de Saint-Quentin et son histoire des premiers ducs normands* (Paris, 1916), pp. 263–64 and n. 1, 298–300, and the references there; Henry R. du Motey, *Origines de la Normandie et du duché d'Alençon* (Paris, 1920), passim; Robert Génestal, "L'histoire du droit public normand," *Bulletin de la Société des antiquaires de Normandie* 37 (1926–27): 75–151, at 80–81, 98; Robert Besnier, *La coutume de Normandie: Histoire externe* (Paris, 1935), p. 23; and Paul Chesnel, "Comment fut effectué par Rollon le partage des terres néo-normandes," *Revue de l'Avranchin* 29 (1936): 66–73, at 68.

8. It is done in Tabuteau, "Transfers of Property," pp. 346–484.

tions before considering the picture presented by the eleventh-century evidence when that evidence is considered on its own.

The most structured argument for the existence of precisely defined feudal obligations in Normandy by the middle of the eleventh century is that given by Haskins. He argues that the quotas of knight service which the Inquest of 1172 records as due to the duke from the abbeys of Normandy were established before the death of Duke Robert the Magnificent in 1035.[9] He asserts that the Bayeux Inquest records the conditions on the estates of the bishopric in the late eleventh century and that parts of it record obligations which were in existence before 1047.[10] He uses a charter allegedly issued by Henry I in 1128 as evidence of precise obligations owed to and by the abbey of Saint-Evroul by 1056 at the latest[11] and combines the Inquest of 1172 with a charter of 1066 to demonstrate the existence by 1066 of an honor of exactly ten knight's fees.[12] On the basis of this and similar evidence, Navel reaches the same conclusion as Haskins: that the establishment of precise quotas of service owed to the duke had occurred by the end of the reign of Robert the Magnificent.[13] Each of these pieces of evidence must be considered in turn, for they are by and large independent of one another.

There is no doubt that the Bayeux Inquest expresses defined obliga-

9. Haskins, *Norman Institutions*, pp. 8–10, partially quoted below, at text accompanying n. 51. See also Navel, "Recherches," pp. 164, 173–74. This conclusion is widely accepted.

10. Haskins, *Norman Institutions*, pp. 14–18, 201–2. See also Henri Navel, "L'enquête de 1133 sur les fiefs de l'évêché de Bayeux," *Bulletin de la Société des antiquaires de Normandie* 42 (1934):5–80; and John Horace Round, "The Bayeux Inquest of 1133," in *Family Origins and Other Studies*, ed. William Page (London, 1930), pp. 201–16, at 202–5. Commenting on Navel's research on the area around Caen, R. Allen Brown, *The Normans and the Norman Conquest* (New York, 1968), p. 41, suggests "that, if anything, the Caen region is likely to have been more backward in these matters than Upper Normandy."

That the Bayeux Inquest reflects eleventh-century conditions is almost universally accepted; even Matthew, *Norman Conquest*, p. 59, agrees that the Inquest "incorporates some older material." To my knowledge, David R. Bates, "Notes sur l'aristocratie normande: 1. Hugues, évêque de Bayeux et sa famille," *Annales de Normandie* 23 (1973): 7–38, at 17, is the only recent scholar who rejects this conclusion; he does not explain his reasons for doing so.

11. Haskins, *Norman Institutions*, pp. 11–14, partially quoted below, at text accompanying n. 72. Navel, "Recherches," p. 88, also accepts this document as an accurate account of eleventh-century affairs but does not emphasize it.

12. Haskins, *Norman Institutions*, pp. 18–19. This, in turn, leads him to conclude, p. 19, that "the assignment of the service of five knights for the original holdings of the bishopric in the Avranchin," which is also recorded in the Inquest of 1172, must be earlier than 1066. I do not see that this follows.

13. Navel, "Recherches," passim, esp. pp. 60, 164, 173. Navel's additional evidence concerns vavassors, lesser military tenants who, under this name, are peculiar to Normandy. Their obligations, too, according to Navel, were fixed by the mid-eleventh century and probably much earlier (ibid., pp. 106–7, 113–15, 146–50; Henri Navel, "Les vavassories du Mont-Saint-Michel à Bretteville-sur-Odon et à Verson [Calvados]," *Bulletin de la Société des antiquaires de Normandie* 45 [1937]: 137–65, at 141–51, 164).

tions of the bishop to the duke and of the bishop's vassals to their lord. The longer of the extant versions of the Inquest says that the jurors "said that the bishop of Bayeux owed the lord of Normandy ten knights for the service of the king of the French, and that ten knights of the bishopric did this service through one knight for forty days. And they also said that the same bishop owed the service of twenty knights on the marches of Normandy for forty days, wherever the king [i.e., the duke] should wish, and five knights did this service through one."[14] The bishop, therefore, is owed the service of 100 knights and owes 20 and 10, respectively, to the duke and to the king of France through the duke. The Inquest then lists the bishop's tenants and how many knight's fees each holds or how much service he owes;[15] when added up, however, these figures amount to just under 120 knights, not an even 100.[16] The discrepancy is variously explained: Haskins refers briefly to the figure of 120 as "a long hundred";[17] Navel rejects this and suggests that the quotas owed to the duke and the king were "une sorte de forfait consenti autrefois par le duc à une époque où les fiefs de l'évêque de Bayeux dépassaient d'assez peu la centaine."[18]

14. Navel, "Enquête," p. 14: "Isti jurati dixerunt quod episcopus Baiocensis debebat domino Normanniae decem milites ad servicium regis Francorum, et quod decem milites episcopatus faciebant hoc servicium per unum militem per quadraginta dies. Dixerunt etiam quod idem episcopus debebat servicium viginti militum in marchis Normanniae per quadraginta dies, ubicumque rex vellet, et istud servicium faciebant quinque milites per unum." Cf. ibid., p. 17: "unumquodque feodum quinque militum facit servicium unius militis in marchis Normanniae, et duo eorum servicium regi Franciae." In ibid., p. 15, Robert earl of Gloucester testifies that for his fee of ten knights "debeo servicium unius militis ad servicium regis Franciae; ad servicium domini Normanniae debeo servicium duorum militum in marchis per quadraginta dies . . . ," and that for fees of eight and seven knights together "debeo ad servicium regis Franciae militem unum et dimidium, et ad servicium in marchis Normanniae servicium trium militum per quadraginta dies." This is the only passage in the Inquest that is in the first person. This text of the Inquest can also be found in J. N. de Wailly, L. V. Delisle, and G. M. G. Jourdan, eds., *Recueil des Historiens des Gaules et de la France*, vol. 23 (Paris, 1876) (hereafter cited as *HF*), pp. 699–702.

A much shorter version of the Inquest is preserved in *Red Book of the Exchequer*, ed. Hubert Hall, 3 vols., Rolls Series (London, 1896), 2:645–47. It summarizes the material on military service thus (pp. 646–47): "Episcopus Baiocensis debet invenire x optimos milites ad servicium Regis Francorum per xl dies; et ad eos procurandos, debet capere in unoquoque feodo militis xx*s*. Rothomagensis monetae. Cum autem inveniet Duci Normanniae xl [*sic*] milites per xl dies, debet capere in unoquoque feodo militis xl*s*. praedictae monetae. . . . " This text is also published in *HF*, 23:698–99.

15. Navel, "Enquête," pp. 14–23.

16. I calculate 119¾ knights on the basis of the figures in Navel's edition of the Inquest; but it should be noted that Navel restores, on the basis of the version of the Inquest in the Red Book of the Exchequer, an entry for two knights that is not in the text printed in *HF*, vol. 23. Some earlier scholars therefore give the total for the French version as 117¾. The figure derived from the French version should be increased by 2 if the higher assessment for Viscount Rannulf's lands (see below, at nn. 28–32 and accompanying text) is used. *Red Book*, 2:646, correctly adds up its total as 119½. It appears to have conflated the last two entries in the French text, resulting in the loss of ¼ of a knight.

17. Haskins, *Norman Institutions*, pp. 15–16.

18. Navel, "Enquête," p. 45; this explanation is further developed by Sarell Everett Gleason, *An Ecclesiastical Barony of the Middle Ages: The Bishopric of Bayeux, 1066–1204* (Cambridge, Mass., 1936), p. 72.

It is difficult to establish the date of the conditions described in the Bayeux Inquest. The Inquest survives in two versions, one in the Red Book of the Exchequer, the other in an early thirteenth-century French register.[19] Neither is the original text,[20] and the only direct authority for believing that the Inquest concerns conditions in Bishop Odo's day, before 1097, comes from documents of 1144 and later.[21] The longer text of the Inquest says merely that "Henry king of England made inquiry concerning the fees of the barons, knights, and vavassors holding of the church of St. Mary of Bayeux and concerning their services, that is, what services they had to do to the same king by the bishop's hand and what [services] they rightfully had to do to the same bishop."[22] Although this passage is admittedly in the past tense, the reason seems to be simply that it reports a past action of the king; and the use of the phrase "the same king" for the person to whom service was owed through the bishop suggests that the scribe thought that Henry was inquiring about conditions in his own day. The use of the past tense in one of the principal passages about service may also be explicable on the basis that the scribe reports what the jurors "said," not what they "say," and the other passages about service are in the present tense. Any argument based on the tenses of the verbs in the extant versions of the Inquest assumes that these passages are verbatim quotations from the lost original, an assumption that by its nature cannot be validated. The French version, however, preserves the statement of Robert earl of Gloucester as a direct quotation in the first person. This passage, more than any other in either version of the Inquest, seems likely to be a verbatim transcription of the original text, and in it Earl Robert testifies in the present tense to his current obligations.[23]

Bishop Odo is mentioned only twice in the Inquest, in both cases in order to identify seven prebends that he created out of land given to the bishopric in 1074.[24] All the individuals in the French version of the Inquest who can be identified were alive in 1133; only when an entry

19. See above, at n. 14.

20. Because each version preserves material not in the other, it is likely that the two are independent summaries of an originally longer document; see Navel, "Enquête," p. 56; Round, "Bayeux Inquest," pp. 206–12; and Gleason, *Ecclesiastical Barony*, pp. 44, 70.

21. Haskins, *Norman Institutions*, pp. 15, 202; Round, "Bayeux Inquest," pp. 203–5.

22. Navel, "Enquête," pp. 13–14: "Henricus, rex Angliae, fecit inquiri de feodis baronum, militum et vavassorum tenentium de ecclesiae Beatae Mariae Baiocensis et de serviciis eorum, videlicet quae servicia facere debebant ipsi regi per manum episcopi, et quae de jure facere debebant ipsi episcopo." The version in the Red Book of the Exchequer has no such introduction.

23. All the passages on service are quoted above, at n. 14. In *Red Book*, 2:645, the quotas of Robert's three ancestors are separately reported, and one of them is said to "have held" (*tenebat*). The only other verb in the Red Book text that concerns a quota is also in the past tense. All the verbs in the French version that refer to quotas of individual men are in the present tense.

24. Navel, "Enquête," pp. 15–16, 21. The transaction of 1074 can be found in V. Bourrienne, *Antiquus cartularius ecclesiae Baiocensis*, 2 vols. (Rouen and Paris, 1902), 1:4–6, no. 3.

takes the form "the fee of so-and-so" is the individual sometimes a man who was a contemporary of Bishop Odo and certainly or probably dead by 1133.[25] The Red Book version sometimes has the names of Odo's contemporaries where the French version has the names of their descendants.[26] Because the two versions are independent, it seems likely that the lost original gave the names of both ancestor and descendant.[27] If this was indeed the case, then the amount of service ascribed to a tenement in the Red Book version need not be the service done by the earlier tenant even when his name is given.

In both versions of the Inquest, Rannulf viscount of Bayeux is said to hold a fief of 7½ knights. Toward the end of the French text, however, there is a description of "the lands that Rannulf . . . held of the fee of the church of Bayeux" which concludes, "These lands the aforesaid Viscount Rannulf held for the service of nine and one-half knights."[28] This passage is part of an addition made to the French version alone at some time between 1162 and 1178, most probably at the time of the Inquest of 1172.[29] Most of the details in the addition were taken from an agreement between a Viscount Rannulf and some bishop of Bayeux, probably Odo, which must date from between 1087 and 1106; but this agreement does not say anything about how much service Rannulf owed.[30] The vis-

25. Namely, the fees of Odo dapifer, Aaloudus the chamberlain, and Corbin d'Agneaux. The fees of William Picoth, Henry de Port, Philip de Briouze, Gilbert de Villers, Hugh Bigot, and Robert Pellevey refer to men who were certainly or probably alive in 1133. The fees of Robert son of Osbert and Odo son of Geneboudus refer to men who are unidentified. See the notes to the text of the Inquest in Navel, "Enquête," pp. 23–35.

26. Robert fitz Hamo, Roger Suard, and Malfillastre for Robert earl of Gloucester; Roger de Courseulles for Walkelin de Courseulles; Henry of Warwick for Robert du Neubourg; Rannulf de Villers for Gilbert de Villers, although it is only a presumption that Rannulf was Gilbert's ancestor. The Red Book version also has Robert de Louvières for "the fee of *Lapier* and Ducy," but this man has not been identified. For "the fee of Guéron," it has Samson of Bayeux, perhaps the cleric of that name who became bishop of Worcester in 1096 and died in 1112. For this Samson's career, see V. H. Galbraith, "Notes on the Career of Samson, Bishop of Worcester," *English Historical Review* 82 (1967): 86–97.

27. Round, "Bayeux Inquest," pp. 207–10; Gleason, *Ecclesiastical Barony*, p. 70. Navel, "Enquête," pp. 41–42, thinks that the Red Book copy represents the original state of the Inquest and that the names of the descendants were substituted in the French version at the time of the Inquest of 1172; this seems less likely than Round's conjecture because, by 1172, several of the men whose names would then have been substituted were certainly already dead.

28. Navel, "Enquête," pp. 21–22: "terrae quae tenuit Ranulfus, vicecomes Baiocassini, de feodo ecclesiae Baiocensis. . . . Has terras tenuit praefatus Ranulfus vicecomes pro servicio novem militum et dimidii." Navel, "Recherches," p. 129, alone notes the discrepancy; he does not attempt to explain it. It is, of course, possible that the *novem* of the addition is a scribal error; but both it and *septem* are written out in the surviving copy, and it is hard to see how "vii" or "vij" could be misread as "ix." The figures cited below, at n. 32, support the reading *novem*.

29. Navel, "Enquête," pp. 39–40; see also ibid., p. 36, n. 140.

30. See below, at nn. 98–100 and accompanying text; see also Navel, "Enquête," p. 37, n. 68. Every viscount of Bayeux was named Rannulf from before 1047 through 1153. Navel, "Enquête," p. 28, n. 26, assumes that the Rannulf of the late eleventh century inherited the earldom of Chester and lived until 1129, but he probably conflates a father

counts of Bayeux inherited the viscounty of Avranches and the earldom of Chester in 1120; but the explanation of the discrepancy in the amount of service due cannot derive from this fact: the Bayeux family inherited after the agreement between Viscount Rannulf and the bishop of Bayeux that was the basis of the enumeration of holdings in the addition to the French version of the text; the discrepancy would seem to have arisen after 1133 rather than before; moreover, the earl of Chester is separately listed in the body of the Inquest as holding a fief of 5 knights.[31] The other extant evidence on the quota of service due from the viscounts of Bayeux suggests that the quota remained 9½ knights.[32] It seems quite possible, therefore, that in the period between 1133 and 1172 the assessment of service due to the bishop from the ancestral lands of the viscounts of Bayeux had been raised from 7½ to 9½ knights. This in turn suggests that the assessments recorded in the Inquest of 1133 were not necessarily at that date fixed for all time and, if so, that there is even less reason to think that they had already been fixed in the eleventh century.[33]

The text of the Inquest as it survives is, therefore, by no means simple and gives little reason to conclude that the purpose of the inquiry was to determine what conditions had been on the fee in the days of Bishop Odo. Moreover, even assuming that its purpose was to describe conditions in Odo's day, there is reason to doubt that the Inquest provides an accurate description of those conditions. The jurors—if they were testifying to the eleventh-century state of affairs—may well, honestly or not, have distorted the facts. The memory of conditions even at the end of Odo's episcopate must have grown hazy in the intervening thirty-six

---

and son of the same name. I prefer the genealogy given by Douglas, *William*, p. 93 and n. 9. For a chart pedigree of the family, beginning with Douglas's Rannulf II, see William Farrer, *Early Yorkshire Charters*, vol. 2 (Edinburgh, 1915), p. 195.

31. Navel, "Enquête," p. 17.

32. The Inquest of 1172 itself, as it records the *servicia debita* only of tenants-in-chief, does not report on the matter. It does, however, ascribe to the earl of Chester a service due of 10 knights "from Saint-Sever and Briquessart," out of over 51½ knights whom the earl had *ad suum servicium* (*HF*, 23:694; *Red Book*, 2:626). Saint-Sever had been the seat of the viscounts of Avranches, who became the first earls of Chester; Briquessart was the seat of the viscounts of Bayeux, who succeeded them as earls. The thirteenth-century records of the services due from Normandy do not list the holding of the viscount of Bayeux as such. *HF*, 23:612, says that the earl of Chester owes 9½ knights plus 1/10 of a knight; in ibid., 23:620–21, a list of the fees held of the earl of Chester adds up to 9½ knights plus 1/16; in ibid., 23:706, the total again is 9½, for which the earl is said to have owed the bishop of Bayeux the service of 2 knights for the king. Ibid., 23:709, however, records the earl as owing 5 knights; but this may be his total obligation to the king from all his possessions. Ibid., 23:637, records him as owing 1½ knights in Pert and Lison; in the Bayeux Inquest, however, this quota was owed by the viscount of Saint-Sauveur, that is, of the Cotentin (Navel, "Enquête," p. 16). Navel, "Recherches," p. 131, says that the holding of the viscounts of Bayeux was one of the fiefs of the bishop of Bayeux which "furent dissociés après la mort des détenteurs de 1133 et partagés entre leurs héritiers. . . ."

33. For different reasons, Matthew, *Norman Conquest*, pp. 65–67, concludes, "The Bayeux evidence . . . suggests that Norman feudal services had not been fixed before the Conquest, but that 'honours' were still in the process of being assembled."

years, especially because the see had been in chaos since Odo's death.[34] Although Round adopted the wording of a writ issued by Geoffrey Plantagenet in 1144 to speak of "the aged jurors of 1133,"[35] there is no reason to think that the jurors of 1133 were particularly aged and some reason to think that some of them were quite young;[36] and Round himself noted that they seem to have "forgotten" that Richard earl of Chester did not become earl until 1101.[37] Moreover, the jurors were the bishop's tenants; and it was certainly more in their interests than in the interests either of the bishop or of the duke that quotas of service should be fixed at a maximum that was only one-fifth to one-tenth (or one-sixth to one-twelfth) of what those quotas might have been.[38] All in all, the Bayeux Inquest of 1133 does not seem a trustworthy source for information about eleventh-century Norman conditions.[39]

34. Gleason, *Ecclesiastical Barony*, pp. 17–25, 41–42.
35. Round, "Bayeux Inquest," pp. 204–5.
36. Navel, "Enquête," pp. 23–25, nn. 3–12.
37. Round, "Bayeux Inquest," p. 210. Richard's name is given only in the Red Book version; the French version has "the earl of Chester." Round, "Bayeux Inquest," pp. 204–5, argues that asking jurors to testify to situations twenty, thirty, even forty years earlier was a "method of obtaining information . . . regularly employed under our Norman kings. . . ." This, of course, is true; but it does not guarantee that the information so obtained was accurate.
38. See Douglas, *William*, p. 101; and Brown, *Normans*, p. 40 and n. 111, on the possible significance of the fixing of quotas.
39. The Inquest contains one additional element that might aid in dating the information in it, namely, the fact that a quota of service is due to the king of France. Perhaps because of the difficulty of finding any time before 1133 when the duke of Normandy would have responded with something like half his available army to a summons for military service from the king, this aspect of the Inquest has occasioned little remark. For a reason that seems to me specious, Matthew, *Norman Conquest*, pp. 62–63, suggests that "the service due to the king of Franks [*sic*] was a mere 'vestigial' service, which survived perhaps two centuries or more," that is, from two centuries earlier than the time of the Inquest. On the basis of an unquestioned acceptance of Haskins's arguments about the Inquest, Boussard, "Services féodaux," pp. 157–58, dates the obligation to "une époque antérieure à la rupture des relations vassaliques entre le duc et le roi de France, rupture qui se situe vers la fin du Xe siècle," rejects the possibility that it dates instead from after amicable relations were formally reestablished in 1119, and suggests that it may date from the concession of Normandy to Rollo in 911.

A survey of the known instances of homage and of military service done by the duke to the king yields little evidence to support any firm date for the creation of the obligation to the king recorded in the Bayeux Inquest. Three modern scholars have attempted to analyze the relationship between the kings of France and the dukes of Normandy in detail. Ferdinand Lot, *Fidèles ou vassaux? Essai sur la nature juridique du lien qui unissait les grands vassaux à la royauté depuis le milieu du IXe siècle jusqu'à la fin du XIIe siècle* (Paris, 1904), chap. 6, portrays the dukes as royal vassals from the establishment of the duchy in 911 until they shifted their allegiance to the dukes of France in 946; this allegiance persisted when the family of the dukes of France ascended the throne as the Capetian kings, and it lasted until 1048, when "l'alliance des Capétiens avec les Normands, ininterrompue depuis plus d'un siècle, cesse bruquement et pour toujours" (p. 198). Ibid., pp. 179–98, chronicles the series of discoverable episodes, between 923 and 1048, when a duke of Normandy did homage or rendered military assistance to a Carolingian or a Capetian; but few details of any occasion are known and none indicates the existence of any conventional number of soldiers to be led or sent by the duke to the royal army. Ibid., p. 200, cites a latest example of mili-

Most scholars who cite the Bayeux Inquest as evidence for eleventh-century conditions insist only that it reflects the situation at the end of the century. Haskins, however, argues that the Inquest as a whole re-

---

tary assistance, from 1071; but the source that Lot cites apparently refers to William fitz Osbern's Flemish adventure of that year, not to a ducal army.

Jean-François Lemarignier, *Recherches sur les hommages en marche et les frontières féodales* (Lille, 1945), distinguishes homage *en marche*, that is, homage done on a frontier in order to signify a peace between equals, from vassalic homage done for a fief. Ibid., chap. 3, esp. pp. 73–100, portrays all the known cases of homage done by the dukes of Normandy to the kings of France between 911 and 1113 as homages of peace, although the distinction between the two types of homage was less clear than it became later in the twelfth century. From the homage that Henry I's son William did to King Louis VI in 1120, following the peace made between Henry and Louis in 1119, the homages were, Lemarignier thinks, vassalic: they were done in return for the grant of Normandy as a fief.

C. Warren Hollister, "Normandy, France and the Anglo-Norman *Regnum*," *Speculum* 51 (1976): 202–42, also discusses homage and military service. According to Hollister, ibid., p. 203, "During the century prior to the Norman Conquest of England there is evidence of only one act of homage of a Norman duke to a French king [in 1060] and even this single instance is a little ambiguous." Nevertheless, on the basis of Haskins's dating of the information in the Bayeux Inquest and Lot's examples of service, he says of the situation in 1120 that "earlier Franco-Norman feudal arrangements . . . clearly carried with them . . . some obligation to render military service to the king of France in return for the ducal fief" (p. 227). At the same time, he thinks that between the battle of Tinchebrai in 1106, whereby Henry I became duke of Normandy, and the agreement of 1119–20, Henry insisted on "absolute Norman independence" (p. 229 and passim) and that after his son's death in late 1120, Henry again attempted "to define the ducal title in such a way as to deemphasize the notion of Norman subordination" (p. 229). Henry did contribute troops to an expedition of Louis VI in 1126, "but since he declined to lead them personally his act could be interpreted as a gesture of amity rather than a vassalic service" (p. 231). Moreover, there were other expeditions to which he did not contribute, and, after 1128, "the necessity of such gestures ceased altogether. During the closing years of the reign, Henry I and Louis VI lived at peace with one another, yet without any pretense of a defined feudal relationship" (p. 231).

Whatever the fine points of disagreement among these three scholars, it seems fairly clear that the obligation on the estates of the bishopric of Bayeux to contribute half their ducal quotas to the royal army must have developed before the diplomatic rupture of 1048 or after the agreement of 1119. The problem remains that, except perhaps in the tenth century, for which the sources largely fail us, Norman contributions to royal French armies seem always to have been rare and not numerically large and to have resembled "gestures of amity" rather than "vassalic service"; yet one would expect a quota to arise as the result of a regularly repeated demand for service.

The contemporary sources for the relations between Norman dukes and French kings are extensively canvassed by the three scholars cited above, and I wish to make only a few remarks. For the Norman attitude to the question, the fundamental text is Dudo of Saint-Quentin's *De moribus et actis primorum Normanniae ducum*, ed. Jules Lair (Caen, 1865), which was written in the early eleventh century about the tenth century dukes. Although Dudo admits Norman promises of military service to King Louis d'Outremer in 943 (p. 226) and to Hugh the Great, duke of France, in 946 (pp. 250–51), he normally insists on the independence of the dukes of Normandy from all superiors; see esp. pp. 169, 247, 250, 263. Dudo's vehement denial of subordination was further developed by several texts that Lot, *Fidèles ou vassaux*, pp. 231–35, and Lemarignier, *Recherches*, pp. 96–100, take as coming from the second half of the twelfth century, but that Hollister, "Anglo-Norman *Regnum*," pp. 229–31, redates to the period between 1120 and 1135, that is, precisely to the period when the question once again became a living issue after more than seven decades in abeyance. The Norman "propaganda line," in other words, was consistent

flects conditions as of mid-century because "it is safe to assume that the amount of the bishop's service to the duke had been determined at least as early as the amount due to the bishop from his vassals."[40] The assumption seems unsafe in general;[41] and the proof that the bishop's vassals' service had been fixed in amount by mid-century concerns only one portion of the estates of the bishopric and is dubious at best. In 1047, because Grimold du Plessis had participated in a revolt against the duke, his lands, which he held from the see of Bayeux, were confiscated. Grimold died in prison, and his lands were given back to the see in 1074. Haskins alleges that what is known of Grimold's honor from the Inquest "indicates that its military obligations had been fixed even before Odo's day,"[42] as Odo became bishop only in 1049 or 1050. The charter whereby Duke William granted Grimold's lands to Bishop Odo in 1074, however, says nothing about their obligations, then or earlier, except to say that—but not how—Grimold had served the bishop from them.[43] The Inquest itself, on the subject of service, says only that the bishop has the service of eight knights from the portion of the honor that remained after Bishop Odo had made seven prebends out of some of it and retained more in his demesne.[44] That these lands had defined obligations in 1133 certainly does not mean that the service was the same in 1047, or even in

---

about Norman independence for over a century. Documents of practice show the same. As Lot, *Fidèles ou vassaux*, p. 192, points out, in a charter dated 968, Duke Richard I refers to Hugh Capet, duke of France, as his *senior* (Marie Fauroux, *Recueil des actes des ducs de Normandie* [911–1066] [Caen, 1961], p. 71, no. 3). No later tenth-century or eleventh-century Norman charter, however, refers to anyone as the duke's lord or reports any superior's consent to a ducal act. Finally, the Bayeux Inquest is the only twelfth-century source that refers to a distinct quota as due to the king of France (after 1204, the distinction ceased to be meaningful because the king of France then succeeded to the position of the duke of Normandy).

If the quota of service due to the king of France according to the Bayeux Inquest represents an old obligation that had not actually been performed for over seventy years (1048–1126), one might wonder why the quota should have been fixed at so high a figure as 10 percent of the bishop's knights, 50 percent of what the bishop owed the duke. Moreover, of all the quotas of service that existed in Normandy in and after 1133, that owed to the king of France was the least likely to be demanded or to be provided if demanded. It is inconceivable that it could have been fixed earlier than and independent of the more actively exercised proffers of military service; but the burden of the other evidence, as I see it, is against the existence of fixed quotas on a wide scale in eleventh-century Normandy. All this tempts me to suggest—as an indisputably unproven conjecture—that the quota of service owed from the estates of the bishopric of Bayeux to the king of France may have been fixed no earlier than the time of the Bayeux Inquest itself and that the matter may then have been raised and settled although recognized by all concerned as largely hypothetical, the question perhaps prompted by the events of 1119–20 and 1126 and the answer perhaps set down more to complete a picture than because anyone concerned expected the quota to come frequently into operation.

40. Haskins, *Norman Institutions*, p. 16.

41. See Brown, *Normans*, p. 40 and n. 112.

42. Haskins, *Norman Institutions*, p. 16.

43. Bourrienne, *Antiquus cartularius*, 1:5, no. 3.

44. Navel, "Enquête," p. 16; also printed by Haskins, *Norman Institutions*, p. 16, and partially quoted in the next note.

1074. One might as well assert the opposite: that the integral amount of service due in 1133 means that the obligation cannot have been imposed before the seven prebends and the demesne lands were separated from the rest of the honor.

The honor of Grimold du Plessis included "the land of Bougy and Danvou, which was half a knight of the aforesaid fee, which land William d'Aubigny held from Grimold as dowry with Grimold's sister."[45] Haskins states that this constitutes "a clear example of early subinfeudation" and continues, "It is entirely possible that the assessment of half a knight's service by which his [i.e., William d'Aubigny's] descendants held these lands was not made until later, but the language of the inquest indicates that they had been held as half a knight's fee in Grimold's time, and the fractional amount of the service would seem to imply the existence of a knight's fee which had been divided before or at the time of the grant to William."[46] It would seem, however, that the language of the Inquest need imply no more than that William was granted land—not, be it noted, as a fief but as his wife's dowry—which at some time was assessed at half a knight's fee. Moreover, the passage that Haskins cites to show that William d'Aubigny's descendants did the service of half a knight for this land[47] comes from the section of the French version of the Inquest that was not added until after 1162. Haskins's first hypothesis, therefore, is preferable to his second one.

Haskins also suggests that "as early as Grimald's time the honor owed the service of ten knights," a statement that he later amends by saying, "The number may not have been ten, but it was pretty certainly a multiple of five."[48] He then goes on to argue that the same was true of other honors recorded in the Inquest, and that this in turn supports Round's view—based otherwise solely on a passage from the later twelfth-century poet Wace—that the Normans of the time of the conquest of England were accustomed to use units of five and ten knight's fees.[49] The argument is quite circular, as it assumes the existence of five- and ten-fee units in the eleventh century in order to prove their existence.[50] There seems, in short, to be no more reason to accept the evidence of the Inquest

45. Navel, "Enquête," p. 16: "De reliquo vero honoris Grimoudi habet episcopus servicium octo militum, cum terra de Bougeyo et de Dampvou, quae fuit de praedicto feodo dimidium militis, quam terram Guillelmus de Albigneyo tenebat de Grimoudo in maritagio cum sorore Grimoudi." Ibid., p. 20, from the addition made after 1162, indicates that this fee was part of the total of eight knights rather than an addition to it. *Red Book*, 2:645, says simply, "Feodum Grimoudi de Plasseiz erat feodum viij militum cum terra de Bugeio et de Daimou [*sic*], quam Grimundus [*sic*] dederat Willelmo de Albinneio cum sorore sua in maritagium."

46. Haskins, *Norman Institutions*, pp. 16–17. Navel, "Enquête," p. 43, draws a similar conclusion.

47. Navel, "Enquête," p. 20.

48. Haskins, *Norman Institutions*, p. 17.

49. Ibid., pp. 17–18. Navel, "Enquête," p. 46, also citing Round, draws a similar conclusion; see also Navel, "Recherches," pp. 61–62. For the passage from Wace, see below, at text accompanying nn. 115–16.

50. The only strictly contemporary evidence that might suggest the existence of such

of 1133 as testimony to the existence in the eleventh century of five- and ten-fee units than to accept its other data as applicable to the eleventh century.

There are similar reasons to doubt the value of other twelfth-century evidence that has been adduced, in the first place that derived from the Inquest of 1172. This was a survey of the service due from the Norman tenants-in-chief to the duke; it frequently also includes the amount of service due to these tenants, but it does not enumerate the subtenants who performed the services that it records. Haskins concluded that the quotas recorded for the abbeys listed in the Inquest were established by the death of Robert the Magnificent, father of William the Conqueror, in 1035, on the following reasoning:

> The list of 1172 is essentially a list of the oldest monasteries of the duchy. If this be the case, it is altogether likely that the erection of these into baronies owing definite quotas of military service took place in the same early period—if not while they were the only monastic establishments, at least while they were the most important ones. Moreover, since the early years of William's reign were hardly a favorable time for so marked a manifestation of ducal authority, this step may well have been taken before the death of Robert the Magnificent, whether entirely in his reign or partly in that of his predecessors we have no means of knowing. Then, for some reason which likewise escapes us, Saint-Evroul was added after its foundation in 1050, thus completing the list as we have it in 1172.[51]

In a note to this passage, he suggests that Saint-Evroul was probably added "because the lands granted to the abbey already rendered knight service to the duke."[52] In fact, however, the evidence is less simple than the conclusions drawn from it imply. Eleven abbeys are listed as owing service in the Inquest. Of these, five are the great old Carolingian abbeys that were refounded in the tenth century—Fécamp, Jumièges, Mont-Saint-Michel, Saint-Ouen, and Saint-Wandrille—which together owe twice as much service as the other six abbeys. These six comprise Saint-Evroul; Saint-Etienne de Caen, not founded until about 1060, "which is evidently assessed not as a barony but for a fief which had come into its possession";[53] the ancient French abbey of Saint-Denis, which owed one

---

units in the eleventh century is the charter of 1066, which Haskins discusses on pp. 18–19. For the significance of this charter, see below, at nn. 80–82 and accompanying text.

51. Haskins, *Norman Institutions*, p. 10. The passage from the Inquest concerning bishoprics and abbeys is printed in ibid., pp. 8–9. The whole Inquest is published in *HF*, 23: 693–99; and *Red Book*, 2:624–45.

52. Haskins, *Norman Institutions*, p. 10, n. 24.

53. Ibid., p. 9. This explanation seems likely; but, as Haskins notes, ibid., n. 20, "The fief of Taillebois [i.e., the fief mentioned in the Inquest as owing service] does not appear in the early charters enumerating the possessions of Saint-Etienne."

knight for Berneval, a domain restored to it in 968;[54] Bernay, founded between 996 and 1017, whose entry occurs twice but does not appear to constitute an assessment;[55] La Trinité du Mont, founded shortly before 1033;[56] and Montivilliers, founded in 1034 or 1035.[57] There is no obvious reason why Saint-Taurin d'Evreux should not appear along with the other abbeys refounded in the tenth century;[58] or why the nunnery of Montivilliers should appear although neither the monastery of Saint-Pierre de Préaux, also founded by 1034 or 1035, nor the monastery of Conches, founded at about the same time, does so.[59] In all, eight Norman

54. This entry is repeated later in the Inquest: *HF*, 23:696; *Red Book*, 2:633. The charter whereby Berneval was restored makes the domain "immunis ab omni hoste aut curte vel districto" (Fauroux, *Recueil*, p. 72, no. 3). Saint-Denis's obligation, therefore, does not date from the time of the restoration of the domain for which it was liable two centuries later.

55. Haskins, *Norman Institutions*, pp. 8–9: "Abbas Bernaii, ad suum servicium ii milites. . . . Abbas de Bernaio habet de feodo suo ii milites." *Red Book*, 2:625–26, has only one entry, in the place of the first entry in the French version, which reads simply: "Abbas de Berniaco, ii milites." The formula *ad suum servicium* is used in the Inquest to denote the number of knights enfeoffed—in contrast to the number owed to the duke—by the abbots of Fécamp, Jumièges, and Saint-Ouen; the abbess of Montivilliers; the bishops of Coutances, Bayeux, and Lisieux; and many of the lay tenants-in-chief. The return of the abbot of Mont-Saint-Michel, the only individual return that survives, says that the tenants-in-chief were asked to report "quot milites unusquisque baronum deberet ad servicium regis, et quot haberet ad suum proprium servicium" (*HF*, 23:703). The *habet* formula of the second entry for Bernay is unparalleled elsewhere in the Inquest, with four exceptions. The first is the entry for Waleran d'Ivry quoted below, at n. 69. The second is this passage from the entry for the bishop of Lisieux: "habet x milites in banleuca Lexoviensi, qui remanent ad custodiendam civitatem donec retrobannus summoneatur, et tunc ibunt cum propriis expensis episcopi. Idem habet ii milites de dono regis Henrici filii Matildis . . . " (Haskins, *Norman Institutions*, p. 8; *Red Book*, 2:625). The third is in *HF*, 23:697, and *Red Book*, 2:638: "Robertus de Auvilers, i militem de ii militibus et quarta parte militis quos habet." The fourth is in *Red Book*, 2:627: in addition to other services, the earl of Leicester "habet [a large number of knights] ad servicium suum de honore de Britolio" (*HF*, 23:694, omits the verb). The last two entries certainly suggest that *habet*, like *ad suum servicium*, meant service due to rather than owed from the tenants-in-chief. In the early thirteenth century, however, the abbot of Bernay owed the king of France the service of 2½ knights (*HF*, 23:636, 710; see also ibid., 23:772).

56. For the date, see J. Laporte, "Les origines du monachisme dans la province de Rouen," *Revue Mabillon* 31 (1941): 49–68, at 55.

57. For the date, see Fauroux, *Recueil*, pp. 228–29, no. 87; and ibid., pp. 233–35, no. 90.

58. The abbey had been reestablished by some date between 962 and 996 (Fauroux, *Recueil*, pp. 75–76, no. 5). Haskins, *Norman Institutions*, p. 10, suggests that the reason for its absence from the list is that it "was subjected to Fécamp by Robert I in exchange for the independence of Montivilliers." This might explain both the absence of Saint-Taurin and the presence of Montivilliers in the list if there were any reason to suspect that an abbey's hierarchical independence had anything to do with its secular obligations; but I see no reason to assume this, and, in the thirteenth century at least, some priories seem to have owed service on their own: see below, at n. 62. In 1272, the abbot of Saint-Taurin was summoned by the king of France but denied that he owed any service (*HF*, 23:747, 751, 765). He does not appear in any of the earlier lists of service in *HF*, vol. 23. Montivilliers was also summoned in 1272.

59. For Saint-Pierre de Préaux, see Fauroux, *Recueil*, pp. 230–31, nos. 88–89. Haskins's

abbeys that had been founded by about 1035 do not appear in the Inquest of 1172.[60] Nor is it easy to see why Saint-Denis should be the only non-Norman abbey on the list although the abbeys of Corbie, Marmoutier, Saint-Bénigne de Dijon, Saint-Père de Chartres, and Saint-Riquier had received possessions in Normandy by 1035.[61] Finally, a good many abbeys both within and without Normandy, founded both before and after 1035, at some time during the eleventh century received donations that included knights, the service of knights, or fiefs—like Saint-Evroul and Saint-Etienne de Caen—or created fiefs themselves but do not appear as owing service in 1172.[62] The list of abbeys in the Inquest of 1172,

---

argument in *Norman Institutions*, p. 10, that this abbey "is barely earlier than Robert's departure for Jerusalem" and therefore "was not sufficiently organized and endowed at the time of William's accession to be assigned definite military obligations" applies equally well to Montivilliers. For Conches, which Haskins does not discuss, see Laporte, "Origines," p. 57.

60. Five that Haskins attempts to explain away in *Norman Institutions*, p. 10, are Préaux; Saint-Taurin d'Evreux; Cerisy (founded by 1032 [Fauroux, *Recueil*, pp. 194–95, no. 64]); Saint-Amand, whose traditional foundation date of 1030 Haskins denies but which had certainly been founded by about 1040 (Laporte, "Origines," p. 56); and Bec (founded at Bonneville in 1034 and moved to Bec in 1039 [ibid.]). Three that Haskins ignores are Conches; La Croix-Saint-Leufroi (in existence in 918 and refounded about 1030 [ibid., pp. 49, 55]); and Lonlay (founded about 1020 [ibid., p. 59]). In 1272 the abbots of Bec and La Croix-Saint-Leufroi were summoned for service by the king of France (*HF*, 23:744, 750). Neither is reported in the records of the results of this summons (ibid., pp. 752–77) to have sent any knights, nor does either appear in any of the earlier lists of service in *HF*, vol. 23.

61. For Corbie, see Fauroux, *Recueil*, p. 21, n. 13. For Marmoutier, see ibid., p. 109, no. 23. For Saint-Bénigne de Dijon, see ibid., pp. 227–28, no. 86; see also ibid., p. 23, n. 26, and p. 26, n. 32. For Saint-Père de Chartres, see below, at n. 89; Fauroux, *Recueil*, pp. 69–70, no. 2; ibid., p. 117, no. 29; ibid., pp. 121–22, no. 32; and ibid., p. 163, no. 50. For Saint-Riquier, see ibid., p. 104, no. 20.

62. Haskins, *Norman Institutions*, p. 10, n. 25, comments on the passage quoted above, at text accompanying n. 51, "The Norman monasteries which appear as arrière vassals in the registers of the French kings in the early thirteenth century are likewise early foundations." As illustrations he cites Lire (founded in 1046), Troarn (founded about 1050), and Cormeilles (founded about 1060). For the entries for these three abbeys, see *HF*, 23:617, 705, 714, 715, 745, 747. In addition, the following Norman abbeys and priories are listed as owing service to the king of France in the thirteenth century: La Trappe (ibid., p. 617), Ivry (ibid., p. 622), Sigy (ibid., pp. 639, 744), Auffay (ibid., pp. 640, 707), Saint-Léger de Préaux (ibid., p. 710, twice), Beaumont-le-Roger (ibid.), Bec (ibid., pp. 744, 750), Bures (ibid., p. 744), Graville (ibid.), Saint-Sauveur d'Evreux (ibid., p. 747; but the abbess denied owing any service [ibid., p. 765]), La Croix-Saint-Leufroi (ibid., p. 750), Jouy (ibid., pp. 750, 751), and Gournay (ibid., p. 751). Those listed on pp. 744 ff. appear to have been considered tenants-in-chief at the time of the listing, in 1272. Jouy-sur-Eure, a Carolingian possession of Jumièges, was restored to that abbey when it was refounded, before 943 (Fauroux, *Recueil*, p. 138, no. 36). The earliest reference to Jouy as a priory that I have been able to find comes from the late twelfth century: J. J. Vernier, *Chartes de l'abbaye de Jumièges (v. 825 à 1204) conservées aux Archives de la Seine-Inférieure*, 2 vols. (Paris and Rouen, 1916), 2:164, no. 202. The abbey of La Croix-Saint-Leufroi was an early foundation: see above, at n. 60. For the abbey of Bec, see the same note. Saint-Ouen's priory of Sigy was founded—initially as an abbey—between 1037 and about 1045 (Fauroux, *Recueil*, pp. 260–62, no. 103); Laporte, "Origines," p. 62, dates the foundation to 1052. The nunnery of Saint-Léger de Préaux was founded before 1047 (Laporte, "Origines," p. 57). The nunnery of Saint-Sauveur d'Evreux was founded between 1055 and 1066

therefore, hardly seems conclusively to establish that quotas of service had been fixed by 1035.

(Fauroux, *Recueil*, pp. 396–98, no. 208). Beaumont-le-Roger was founded as an abbey about 1070 and became a priory of Bec in the twelfth century (Laporte, "Origines," p. 57, n. 3). The abbey of Ivry was founded in 1071 (ibid., p. 63). Gournay-le-Guérin was a priory of Ivry, but I have been unable to determine its precise date of foundation (L. H. Cottineau, *Répertoire topo-bibliographique des abbayes et prieurés*, 3 vols. [Mâcon, 1935–70], 1:col. 1311). Saint-Evroul's priory of Auffay was founded in 1079 (Ordericus Vitalis, *Historia Ecclesiastica*, ed. and trans. Marjorie Chibnall, 6 vols. to date [Oxford, 1969–78], 3:246–50). The abbey of La Trappe was founded in the years after 1122 and was formally endowed only in 1140 (*Gallia Christiana in provincias ecclesiasticas distributa*, vol. 11 [Paris, 1759], col. 747; Cottineau, *Répertoire*, 2:col. 3201). Bures-en-Bray, a small priory dependent on Bec's major priory known as Bonne-Nouvelle or Notre-Dame du Pré, was founded as the result of gifts by Henry I and Geoffrey Plantagenet, the latter in 1149 (Cottineau, *Répertoire*, 1:col. 531; A. A. Porée, *Histoire de l'abbaye du Bec*, 2 vols. [Evreux, 1901], 1:397, 441; ibid., 2:127). The Augustinian priory of Graville-Sainte-Honorine was not founded until 1203 (Cottineau, *Répertoire*, 1:col. 1337). In sum, these monastic vassals hardly seem conspicuously early foundations.

By about 1060, the following Norman abbeys that appear neither as tenants-in-chief nor as rear vassals had been founded: Cerisy, Conches, Fontenay, Lessay, Lonlay, Saint-Amand, Saint-Désir de Lisieux, Saint-Martin de Sées, Saint-Pierre de Préaux, Saint-Pierre-sur-Dive, Le Tréport, and La Trinité de Caen. For the dates of foundation, see Laporte, "Origines," passim. Saint-Sauveur d'Evreux and Saint-Taurin d'Evreux, which were summoned in 1272 but denied owing service, should probably also be included. Several of these abbeys certainly were given knights or fiefs, were owed service by knights, and/or were owed service from fiefs by the end of the eleventh century; see below, at nn. 108 and 120 and accompanying text; Fauroux, *Recueil*, p. 318, no. 140 (Saint-Désir de Lisieux, between 1049 and 1058); ibid., p. 367, no. 183 (Saint-Amand, between about 1042 and 1066); *Gallia Christiana*, vol. 11, *Instrumenta*, col. 129 (Conches, after 1066); Archives départementales de l'Eure (hereafter cited as Arch. Eure), H 262, fol. 220r, a passage not in the version of this charter published in the *Gallia Christiana* (Conches, late eleventh century); Arch. Eure, H 711, fol. 108r–108v, no. 320 (Saint-Pierre de Préaux, between about 1040 and 1072); ibid., fol. 100r, no. 288, where the vassal is called a *balista* (Saint-Pierre de Préaux, before about 1092); Bibliothèque nationale, manuscrit français nouvelle acquisition (hereafter cited as B.N., MS fr. n. a.) 21813, fol. 750 (Saint-Désir de Lisieux, 1068); Archives départementales de l'Orne (hereafter cited as Arch. Orne), *Livre blanc* of Saint-Martin de Sées, fol. 112r (1061); ibid., fol. 47v (1088; partially printed in Haskins, *Norman Institutions*, p. 19, n. 60); ibid., fol. 34r (before 1095); ibid., fol. 10v (1096); and ibid., fol. 43r–43v (1097). In Auguste Le Prévost, *Mémoires et notes pour servir à l'histoire du département de l'Eure*, 3 vols. (Evreux, 1862–69), 1:536–37, two knights are part of the tenement that Roger de Croismare holds from Abbot William of Saint-Pierre de Préaux, who holds from Roger de Beaumont; earlier a knight named Gilbert had held the tenement directly from Roger de Beaumont (between 1078 and 1087). The charter cited below, at n. 90 and accompanying text, records the creation of a fief by the abbess of La Trinité de Caen in 1109. For similar transactions involving churches that were alleged to owe service in the thirteenth century although not in 1172, see below, at n. 64.

The fief for which Saint-Etienne de Caen served in 1172 was the fief of Taillebois. In 1272 it was called the fief of Ros (*HF*, 23:733); for a possible explanation, see ibid., 23:619. In Lucien Musset, *Chartes de Guillaume le Conquérant et de la reine Mathilde pour les abbayes caennaises* (Caen, 1967), p. 108, no. 14, Abbot William created a fief in Caumont-sur-Dive (between 1070 and 1079); in ibid., pp. 75–76, no. 7, a knight and his land at Bapaume are given to the abbey (between 1080 and 1082); in J. H. Wiffen, *Historical Memoirs of the House of Russell*, 2 vols. (London, 1833), 1:522, Hugh de Rosel, who already holds a fief from the abbey, receives another one from Abbot Gilbert, a fief that Musset, *Abbayes caennaises*, pp. 76–77, no. 7, indicates was in Grainville-sur-Odon

It is possible to explain the appearance in the Inquest only of certain abbeys, by and large those founded by the middle of the eleventh century, in a manner which does not mandate that the service of these abbeys had been fixed by the end of the reign of Duke Robert.[63] A change occurred about the middle of the eleventh century in the nature of the possessions given to abbeys: instead of whole estates, new foundations received only scattered possessions and lucrative rights. The change itself may have had nothing to do with feudal considerations: donors may merely have felt less abundantly endowed themselves and, therefore, have made more discriminate donations; and the ecclesiastical reform impulse of the time caused many donations to consist primarily of churches and tithes. Nor does the different structure of the endowments of new abbeys necessarily mean that military service must have been imposed on the large estates of the older abbeys by the time that they were given, at the time of the donation, or—at the latest—in the period when the change in the nature of donations occurred. Instead, it may be that whenever and however fiefs owing military service developed on the lands of Norman abbeys, and whenever and however these fiefs came to owe their military service

(between 1079 and 1096); for two other fiefs held of this abbot, see below, at n. 130 and accompanying text; for another fief acquired by the abbey at some time in the eleventh century, see Léopold V. Delisle and Elie Berger, *Recueil des actes de Henri II, roi d'Angleterre et duc de Normandie*, 3 vols. (Paris, 1909–27), 1:276, no. 154 (recorded in a pancart issued by Henry II).

In Orderic, *Historia Ecclesiastica*, ed. Chibnall, 3:156, and 5:266, Saint-Evroul is given fiefs (in 1073 and 1099 respectively) that were not among those from which it owed service in 1172.

For Norman monasteries founded between 1060 and 1100 that were given knights or fiefs, were owed service by knights and/or were owed service from fiefs, but are not found as rear vassals, see Charles Bréard, *Cartulaires de Saint-Ymer-en-Auge et de Bricquebec* (Rouen and Paris, 1908), p. 1, no. 1 (Saint-Ymer, 1066 or 1067); Bibliothèque nationale, manuscrit latin (hereafter cited as B.N., MS lat.) 17137, fols. 39v–40r (Saint-Sauveur-le-Vicomte, about 1100). For similar transactions involving Norman churches alleged to owe service in the thirteenth century although not in 1172, see below, at n. 64.

For non-Norman abbeys given knights or fiefs, owed service by knights, and/or owed service from fiefs in Normandy, see below, at n. 85, the case from Marmoutier; Benjamin Guérard, *Cartulaire de l'abbaye de Saint-Père de Chartres*, 2 vols. (Paris, 1840), 1:108 (between 1023 and 1027); Fauroux, *Recueil*, p. 341, no. 156C (Saint-Julien de Tours, 1063); ibid., p. 387, no. 199 (Saint-Florent de Saumur, between 1051 and 1066); Le Prévost, *Eure*, 2:506, where the tenant of the fief is called a *vavassor* (Marmoutier, between 1087 and 1106); B.N., MS lat. 12880, fol. 224r (Marmoutier, between 1087 and 1106); and Arch. Orne, H 3351, no. 1 (Marmoutier, late eleventh century). No non-Norman abbey (except Saint-Denis, for its Norman priory of Berneval) is listed as a vassal for land in Normandy in any of the thirteenth-century surveys published in *HF*, vol. 23.

These lists are minimal: they include only men explicitly designated as *milites* or *equites* (except as noted) or lands explicitly designated as *feoda* or *beneficia*. Fiefs whose services were clearly not military have, of course, been excluded, as have all gifts of fiefs where it is not certain that the whole fief was given.

63. Matthew, *Norman Conquest*, pp. 59–65, mounts an elaborate argument against Haskins's use of the Inquest of 1172 and attempts to prove that there is "a direct link" between the abbatial services recorded in 1172 and "the Carolingian military system" (p. 60). Although he makes telling points about the value of some of the evidence, I do not find the argument itself convincing.

to the duke as well as to the immediate lord, only the old abbeys had endowments that were suitable for the creation of such fiefs.[64] Robert Carabie argues that even in 1172 most of the obligation of military

64. This is put forward as a possible explanation of the services from abbeys recorded in 1172 by Jean Yver, "Une boutade de Guillaume le Conquérant: Note sur la genèse de la tenure en aumône," in *Etudes d'histoire du droit canonique dédiées à Gabriel Le Bras*, 2 vols. (Paris, 1965), 1:783–96, at 787, n. 12.

Matthew, *Norman Conquest*, pp. 57–61, and Navel, "Recherches," pp. 164, 173–74, arrive at opposite conclusions on the basis of alleged changes—in opposite directions—in the middle of the eleventh century in donations of knights and/or fiefs to churches. In fact, however, in both halves of the century knights, fiefs, and services that at least may have been military were sometimes granted and sometimes reserved when land was given to churches. For such transfers, in addition to most of the instances cited in n. 62, see below, at nn. 81 and 96 and accompanying text; Fauroux, *Recueil*, p. 220, no. 80 (Saint-Wandrille, between 1029 and 1035); ibid., p. 225, no. 85 (Fécamp, between 1031 and 1035); ibid., p. 246, no. 94 (Fécamp, between 1035 and about 1040); ibid., p. 252, no. 98, twice (Bec, 1041); ibid., p. 261, no. 103 (Sigy, between 1037 and about 1045); ibid., p. 271, no. 110 (Mont-Saint-Michel, between 1037 and 1046); ibid., p. 285, no. 120, the fiefs or services of five different men (Lire, about 1050); ibid., p. 390, no. 202 (La Trinité du Mont, between 1051 and 1066); ibid., p. 394, no. 205 (Saint-Ouen, between 1051 and 1066); ibid., p. 400, no. 210 (Saint-Ouen, between 1055 and 1066); ibid., p. 412, no. 218, and p. 415, no. 218A (Saint-Martin-du-Bosc, priory of Fécamp, between 1059 and 1066); ibid., p. 418, no. 220 (Jumièges, between 1060 and 1066); ibid., pp. 436–37, no. 227 (La Caine, priory of Beaumont-lès-Tours, probably 1066); ibid., pp. 451–53, no. 234, five times (Saint-Wandrille, between 1082 and 1087; in ibid., p. 310, no. 128, one of these gifts is found in a charter datable to between about 1040 and 1053 that does not call the land a fief, as no. 234 does); Bourrienne, *Antiquus cartularius*, 1:29, no. 21 (Bayeux cathedral, between 1035 and 1037); Achille Deville, *Cartulaire de l'abbaye de la Sainte-Trinité du Mont de Rouen* (Paris, 1840), p. 448, no. 50 (between 1037 and 1053); ibid., p. 437, no. 30 (about 1060); P. Laffleur de Kermaingant, *Cartulaire de l'abbaye de Saint-Michel du Tréport* (Paris, 1880), p. 13, no. 3 (1059); Vernier, *Jumièges*, 1:106, no. 32 (about 1080); Musset, *Abbayes caennaises*, p. 61, no. 4, twice (Saint-Etienne de Caen, between 1066 and 1077); ibid., pp. 85–88, four times (La Trinité de Caen, between 1080 and 1082); ibid., p. 121, no. 18 (Saint-Etienne de Caen, between 1079 and 1087); ibid., p. 131, no. 22 (La Trinité de Caen, between about 1080 and 1085?), Arthur du Monstier, *Neustria Pia* (Rouen, 1663), p. 479 (Bec, between 1066 and 1087, concerning a gift made between 1035 and 1066); Delisle and Berger, *Recueil*, 1:271, no. 154 (Saint-Etienne de Caen, late eleventh-century act recorded in the pancart of Henry II); B.N., fonds Moreau, vol. 341, fols. 17r–17v (Fécamp, 1047; one of the references is to a gift that occurred between 1028 and 1035); B.N., fonds Moreau, vol. 21, fols. 26r–26v (Fécamp, between 1028 and 1035); Bibliothèque municipale de Rouen (hereafter cited as Bibl. Rouen), MS 1235 (Y 201), fol. 88r (Cerisy, late eleventh century); Arch. Eure, H 711, fol. 109r, no. 323 (Saint-Pierre de Préaux, late eleventh century); ibid., fol. 122r, no. 377 (Saint-Pierre de Préaux, about 1100); Arch. Eure, H 438, no. 1, par. 11 (Lire, late eleventh or early twelfth century); and probably Fauroux, *Recueil*, p. 303, no. 130 (La Trinité du Mont, 1053). In *Gallia Christiana*, vol. 11, *Instrumenta*, col. 228, the service of two vavassors is given (Lessay, between 1056 and 1084). Gifts simply of vavassors are not included here.

For reservations of knights, fiefs, and services that at least may have been military, see below, at n. 85, the first example; Fauroux, *Recueil*, p. 246, no. 94 (Fécamp, between 1035 and about 1040); ibid., pp. 328 and 330, no. 147 (Saint-Père de Chartres, 1060); ibid., p. 383, no. 197 (Saint-Georges de Boscherville, between about 1050 and 1066); ibid., p. 453, no. 234 (Saint-Wandrille, between 1082 and 1087); Orderic, *Historia Ecclesiastica*, ed. Chibnall, 3:156 (Saint-Evroul, 1073); ibid., 3:174 (Saint-Evroul, 1076); ibid., 3:184 (Saint-Evroul, 1106); Musset, *Abbayes caennaises*, p. 61 (completed by p. 64), no. 4 (Saint-Etienne de Caen, between 1066 and 1077); Paul Marchegay, "Chartes normandes de

service recorded for abbeys in the Inquest was not truly feudal in nature, that is, it was not allocated to specific estates but was instead, for any abbey, "une sorte de forfait qui lui est imposé pour la totalité de sa fortune foncière. . . ."[65] This does not mean that the abbeys themselves did not create fiefs to fulfill their obligations—in fact, Carabie cites one example where he thinks that the military service of an abbey's tenants predates the donation to the abbey of the estate on which they were found[66]—but it implies that the service owed by abbeys in 1172, and the fiefs that they created to perform it, did not necessarily date from the time of the abbeys' acquisition of the estates on which the fiefs were found in 1172.[67] Indeed, Carabie suggests that it was the frequent changes of possession of lay fiefs in the course of the eleventh, twelfth, and thirteenth centuries that permitted gradual definition of the conditions of their tenure;[68] and the Inquest of 1172 itself provides some evidence for this, as not all the quotas in it were fixed beyond all vagueness.[69] The size and

---

l'abbaye de Saint-Florent près Saumur de 710 à 1200 environ," *Mémoires de la Société des antiquaires de Normandie* 30 (1880): 663–711, at 674, no. 9 (about 1082); Paul de Farcy, *Les abbayes de l'évêché de Bayeux*, vol. 4, *Histoire de l'abbaye de Fontenay* (Laval, 1887), pp. 41–42, no. 11 (between 1066 and 1083); B.N., MS lat. 10087, p. 129, no. 374/373 (Montebourg, late eleventh century); B.N., MS lat. 13816, fol. 457/462v, a passage that is not in the version of this charter published in the *Gallia Christiana* (Conches, late eleventh century); and Archives départementales du Calvados (hereafter cited as Arch. Calvados), H 7745, fol. 77v, no. 209 (Troarn, between 1082 and 1109).

A charter printed by Vicomte du Motey, *Le champion de la Normandie: Robert II de Bellême* (Paris, 1923), p. 45, n. 1, which includes a detailed exclusion of both the duke's wars and the immediate lord's wars from an exemption from service, is almost certainly a forgery (Saint-Martin de Sées, ostensibly between 1089 and 1095).

In the following charters, the service mentioned is or appears to be the rear ban and is explicitly or implicitly done by peasants: below, at n. 122 and accompanying text; Orderic, *Historia Ecclesiastica*, ed. Chibnall, 3:246–48 (Saint-Evroul, 1079); ibid., 3:250 (Saint-Evroul, between 1087 and 1106).

These lists are minimal: they include only men explicitly designated as *milites* or *equites* (except as noted) or lands explicitly designated as *feoda* or *beneficia*. Services that were clearly not military have been excluded, even if done for fiefs, as have all gifts of fiefs where it is not certain that the whole fief was given.

65. Robert Carabie, *La propriété foncière dans le très ancien droit normand (XIe–XIIIe siècles)*, vol. 1, *La propriété domaniale* (Caen, 1943), p. 221; see also ibid., p. 222: "Nous croyons donc que les domaines du Mont-Saint-Michel ne sont pas des fiefs." The argument is based on the wording of the entry concerning Mont-Saint-Michel in the Inquest of 1172; but the entries for the other abbeys are less similar in wording than is suggested by ibid., p. 222.

66. Ibid., p. 223. The service was that of the twenty vavassors of Mont-Saint-Michel at Bretteville-sur-Odon and Verson, who together performed the service of one knight. For a detailed analysis of this service and an attempt to demonstrate that the vavassors had a duty to fight even before the domains were given to the abbey, between 1015 and 1024, see Navel, "Vavassories du Mont-Saint-Michel," passim, especially pp. 141–42, 150–51. Navel regards the service of one knight as the feudalization of an originally nonfeudal military obligation.

67. Carabie, *Propriété foncière*, 1:222–23.

68. Ibid., 1:223.

69. William de Roumare had to serve with 3 *or* 4 knights if summoned to serve elsewhere than at Neufmarché (*Red Book*, 2:628; *HF*, 23:694). Waleran d'Ivry, in addition to owing

structure of an abbey's endowment, in short, may have been more important than the date of its foundation—except insofar as the latter conditioned the former—in determining whether the abbey would owe service in 1172.

One final point must be made about the Inquest of 1172. Even if the quotas of service there recorded as due from the abbeys of Normandy could be proved to have been fixed by the mid-eleventh century, this would tell us nothing about the service due from lay fiefs. A quota can be regarded as a limit on the right of the lord to demand more service than the amount fixed. As such, quotas may have been granted to abbeys as ducal boons, motivated by a piety that was irrelevant to the duke's relations with his lay vassals. A decision to require no service at all from a church is an act of even greater piety, which is that much less applicable to the case of lay vassals. Moreover, once a church had been granted a limited liability for service or a total exemption from it, there would be few, if any, occasions on which its liability or exemption might be renegotiated. Lay tenants, on the contrary, died, rebelled, married, challenged each other's rights, committed infractions that put them in their lord's mercy, and so on.[70] Whatever may be the import of the list of abbeys in the Inquest, therefore, it has no implications for the date of the establishment of the assessments due in 1172 from the vast majority of ducal vassals.

The other piece of twelfth-century evidence on which Haskins relies can be disposed of more briefly. This is the alleged confirmation by Henry I of the possessions and rights of the abbey of Saint-Evroul, dated 1128, which includes this description of the creation of the barony of Saint-Evroul between 1050 and 1056:

> I also concede and confirm to them the whole vill of Culley . . . of the gifts of . . . Robert and Hugh de Grandmesnil, which is a *fief d'un haubert*, and another *fief de haubert* of the gift of William Giroie, which is between Touquette and the vill called Villare, which is named Bocquencé, of the fee of Montreuil, from which . . . my father William, with the assent and will of Thierry abbot of the same place . . . and of the aforesaid Robert and Hugh de Grandmesnil and the said William Giroie their uncle, created one barony to do service to him and his heirs in military expeditions and in his other affairs throughout Normandy, so that the knights Richard de Culley

1 knight and having the service of 3½, "habet de Ivreio, viij milites et dimidium, et Regi quod Rex voluerit" (*Red Book*, 2:640; *HF*, 23:697). The tenants of the honors of Conches and Tosny, where there were more than 20 knights, "ad servitium vero Regis nesciunt quot" (*Red Book*, 2:642; *HF*, 23:698). The same is true for the honor of Montfort, where there were over 21 knights (*Red Book*, 2:642–43; *HF*, 23:698). John de Gisors did castle-guard at Neaufle "per iii menses, vel per totum annum, si Regi placuerit" (*Red Book*, 2:643; *HF*, 23:698). The Giffard honor contained over 102 knights, "sed ad servitium regis nescitur quot" (*HF*, 23:696); this phrase is not in *Red Book*, 2:633, which gives the total of knights as slightly over 98¾.

70. Carabie, *Propriété foncière*, 1:222–23; Matthew, *Norman Conquest*, p. 60.

> and Baudry son of Nicholas—to whom the aforementioned Abbot Thierry, with the consent of my father William, gave those two *fiefs de haubert* in inheritance to hold from him—and their heirs will be held to do that service each for his fief with horses and arms and with his expenses, when the abbot of Saint-Evroul will be summoned by me, and they by the abbot, and they will have reasonable tallages granted for the military expeditions and my other affairs in Normandy. If, however, they should default on their service and the abbot is able to prove his summons against them, they will be taken for amercement by me and my successors in their bodies and chattels and the abbot will have the reliefs and the pleas and the other rights that the barons of Normandy have in their *fiefs de haubert*. . . . Again, of the gifts of Arnold Giroie the whole land that is between Touquette and the Charentonne, which is of the fee of Echauffour, which Abbot Thierry gave to Baudry son of Nicholas to hold from him by the service of one vavassor, as much as he will wish to have, with Baudry's wood. . . .[71]

Haskins admits that the charter is suspicious: it does not appear in Orderic Vitalis's account of the history of Saint-Evroul or in any of the cartularies of the abbey; its witness list is copied from an earlier charter and includes a man who perished in 1120; its "form of dating is exceptional and the other final clauses are an obvious imitation of a papal bull." Nevertheless, he attempts to explain these peculiarities and concludes:

> On the whole . . . there does not seem to be sufficient reason for considering the charter a forgery. . . . Even if the initial and final clauses be rejected as spurious, the body of the charter, compared

71. Haskins, *Norman Institutions*, p. 11: "Concedo etiam eis et confirmo totam villam de Cueleio cum ecclesia et omnibus pertinentiis eius de donis sepe dictorum Roberti et Hugonis de Grentemaisnil, que est feodum unius lorice, et aliud feodum lorice de dono Willelmi Geroiani quod est inter Tolchetam et villam que Villaris dicitur, et appellatur Bauchencaium, de feodo de Mosterol, de quibus predictus Willelmus pater meus, cum assensu et voluntate Theoderici abbatis eiusdem loci primi post tempora Sancti Ebrulfi et predictorum Roberti et Hugonis de Grentemaisnil et dicti Willelmi Geroiani avunculi eorum predicte abbatie fundatorum, baroniam unam constituit ad servitium suum et heredum suorum faciendum in exercitibus et aliis negotiis suis per totam Normanniam, ita tamen quod Ric. de Cueleio et Baldricus filius Nicholai milites, quibus memoratus abbas Theodericus illa duo feoda loricarum in hereditatem de se tenenda donavit cum assensu dicti W. patris mei, servitium illud facere tenebuntur quisque pro feodo suo cum equis et armis et cum expensis suis, et heredes eorum, quando abbas S. Ebrulfi a me submonitus fuerit et ipsi ab abbate, et habebunt rationabiles tallias pro exercitibus et aliis negotiis meis in Normannia concessas. Si vero de servitio illo defecerint et abbas submonitionem suam adversus eos probare poterit, in eorum corpora et catalla a me et successoribus meis capietur emenda et abbas relevamenta et placita habebit et alia iura que habent barones Normannie in feodis loricarum suarum. . . . Item de donis Ernaudi Geroiani totam terram que est inter Tolchetam et Carentonam, que est de feodo Escalfoii, quam dedit Theodericus abbas Baldrico filio Nicholai tenendam de se per servitium unum vavassoris, quotiens habere voluerit, cum nemore Baldrici. . . ." The elisions are Haskins's. The full text can be found in *Gallia Christiana*, vol. 11, *Instrumenta*, cols. 204–10, where this passage is in cols. 205–6 and 208. On the basis of the text in the *Gallia Christiana*, I have restored a comma omitted by Haskins, after *Villaris dicitur*.

> with earlier charters for the same house, gives no reason for suspicion. Such comparison shows moreover that even if the charter be declared a fabrication, it contains elements of unquestionable genuineness, while for the passage . . . concerning the knights' fees there is internal evidence that it was reproduced from an older document. The preservation of the names of the original tenants of Cullei and Bocquencé with their obligations expressed in the future tense, as if Duke William were still speaking, constitutes an anachronism which could hardly arise if Henry were making his own statement of the abbey's service, or if a forger were making the statement for him, but would be natural enough if he, or a later compiler, were incorporating into his charter the Conqueror's own formulation of the terms on which these knights' fees were to be held.[72]

The language of the charter does, however, give cause for suspicion, because it includes technical terms that do not otherwise occur in eleventh-century contexts: *baronia*,[73] and *feodum lorice (fief de haubert)*, the Norman term equivalent to the English "knight's fee," which occurs four times in the passage that Haskins quotes. One of the uses of *feodum lorice* appears in the section that Haskins thinks must be quoted from an eleventh-century document, whereas in fact even *feodum militis* does not occur as a technical term in the eleventh century.[74] The language of any part of the charter of 1128 is unlikely to represent eleventh-century conditions. It seems much more closely to resemble "a suspicious charter of the early years of Henry II"[75] concerning a suit between Saint-Evroul and Roger de Bocquencé over knight service due from the *feodum lorice* at Bocquencé.[76] If both these charters were concocted for contentious purposes at a date later than the early reign of Henry II, they can hardly be valid evidence for the situation over a century earlier. Furthermore, the charter of 1128 tells a story of how the abbey acquired Bocquencé that differs from the foundation charter of the abbey;[77] and it twice mistakes the name of one of the eleventh-century tenants, calling him Baudry son of Nicholas instead of Baudry de Bocquencé.[78] Finally, the charter,

72. Haskins, *Norman Institutions*, pp. 12–14.

73. On *baronia*, see Navel, "Enquête," pp. 59–60; and "Recherches," pp. 79, 170.

74. See below, at n. 85 and accompanying text. The clause about amercement in bodies and chattels is also unparalleled, and I have not found the word *catalla* in any other eleventh-century document.

75. Haskins, *Norman Institutions*, p. 12.

76. Delisle and Berger, *Recueil*, 2:72–73, no. 513. For the reasons why this charter is suspect, see ibid., *Introduction* (Paris, 1909), pp. 316–17; and John Horace Round, *Calendar of Documents Preserved in France, Illustrative of the History of Great Britain and Ireland*, vol. 1 (London, 1899), p. 223, n. 3.

77. For the foundation charter, see Fauroux, *Recueil*, p. 290, no. 122; and Orderic, *Historia Ecclesiastica*, ed. Chibnall, 2:34. Haskins notes the difference (*Norman Institutions*, p. 12).

78. Baudry de Bocquencé's father was named Baudry; see the next note. Haskins, *Norman Institutions*, p. 12, n. 30, mentions the problem of the wrong Baudry but does not solve it. Chibnall, in her edition of Orderic, *Historia Ecclesiastica*, 2:82, n. 2, suggests that

even if it reflects eleventh-century events to some extent, may not be significant for Norman developments in that century in general: the de Bocquencé family whose holding is at issue in the charter of 1128 may have had a special military relationship with the dukes, which would mean that, if the family's military arrangements were defined by the middle of the eleventh century, they would nevertheless have no significance for the relationship of anyone else to the duke.[79]

There remains, finally, one indubitably genuine eleventh-century document whose use by Haskins must be challenged: the charter of 1066 for the cathedral church of Avranches, which, he believes, shows the existence by that date of an honor of ten knight's fees and implies the existence of an assessment of five knights on the land of the church at an even earlier date.[80] In fact, however, the charter says merely that five knights who held land in the half of the "land"—not honor—of Saint-Philibert that John bishop of Avranches gave to the cathedral of Avranches were temporarily to commend themselves to John's nephew but were to "hold their land in fee from the bishops of the church of Avranches after the death of Bishop John."[81] Their tenements may well have persisted and developed into the honor composed of five knight's fees that belonged to the church of Avranches in 1172, but there is little reason to believe that they constituted a unit 106 years earlier: the charter speaks only of knights holding land in fee, not of knight's fees or of knight service.[82]

If the twelfth-century evidence is remote and its implications dispu-

---

the charter simply made a mistake. As the name appears twice and the mistake is therefore unlikely to have been purely scribal, this seems to me to be additional evidence that the charter of 1128 is not based on and partially copied from an eleventh-century original.

79. Baudry the German, founder of the family in Normandy, had come from outside the duchy to serve the duke and had been married advantageously at the duke's instance (Orderic, *Historia Ecclesiastica*, ed. Chibnall, 2:82). His son Baudry had held Bocquencé before Saint-Evroul was founded and was the duke's *archearius*, a title, otherwise unknown, which may mean that he was the duke's archer (ibid., 2:34; Fauroux, *Recueil*, p. 290, no. 122).

The other knight of the barony in the mid-eleventh century, according to the charter of 1128, was Richard de Culley. Orderic never mentions such a person, and it is possible that the charter is mistaken here as in the case of Baudry "son of Nicholas." On the other hand, Orderic says that Baudry de Bocquencé had a brother Richard de Neuville (*Historia Ecclesiastica*, ed. Chibnall, 2:82). Because one of the two fiefs making up the alleged barony was Culley, it is possible that the two Richards are one person, and that the scribe of the charter gave Richard the appellation of this fief. Baudry de Bocquencé and another of his brothers were joint tenants of Saint-Evroul for at least some of Baudry's land (see below, at n. 110).

80. See above, at n. 12 and accompanying text.

81. Fauroux, *Recueil*, p. 440, no. 229: "eorum terram post mortem Johannis episcopi de episcopis Abrincatensis ecclesie in fevio tenerent."

82. See also Matthew, *Norman Conquest*, p. 62. Yver, "Premières institutions," p. 335, n. 85, expresses doubt about the relevance of the language of this charter on the grounds that the section under discussion occurs in "une notice rédigée postérieurement à la charte de Guillaume le Conquérant datée de 1066." In fact, however, the notice comes after the signatures to the charter, says that the events narrated occurred before the charter was

table,[83] it is best to concentrate on sources dating from the time about which we should like to know. A systematic review of the contemporary evidence supports the doubts of those scholars who have questioned whether obligations of military service had been defined by 1066 and, indeed, suggests that their doubts may not have gone far enough. It certainly seems unlikely that Normandy was as fully "feudalized" as it is often alleged to have been by the end of the first third of the eleventh century, because five ducal charters of 1025 or thereabouts make clear distinctions between tenure and patrimony and imply that considerable amounts of Norman land were as yet held of no one.[84] Moreover, the eleventh-century sources give little evidence of precise definitions of feudal obligations of any sort, military service included. Technical terminology was wholly lacking: the two apparent references each to knight's fees and to *servicia debita* are mere accidents of phraseology.[85]

Service owed in return for land is mentioned quite often in the eleventh-century documents; but these sources hardly ever specify what service is meant and rarely call the land a fief. When charters or historians mention new enfeoffments, subinfeudations, other creations of a hierarchy of tenure, or transfers of lordship, they rarely state what services the tenants owed; often they do not even say that service was due. Many allusions to unspecified service doubtless refer to agricultural or even to ecclesiastical service. To give but one example of the typical vague reference to service,

---

signed, and itself includes the date (although the construction is such that it is possible that in the original, which is lost, the notice was written in afterwards in a space between the signatures and the date). I do not think that it is necessary to attempt to impugn the contemporaneity of any part of this charter, whose language is simply not as significant as some of its interpreters have felt it to be.

The term *honor* was current in eleventh-century Normandy but appears not to have had a particular technical meaning. It is used most often to refer to a tenement that was vacant or quasi-vacant, such as the honor of Grimold du Plessis of the Bayeux Inquest or the honor of Scollant of William Paynel's agreement with the abbot of Mont-Saint-Michel (see below, at n. 101 and accompanying text).

83. Haskins, *Norman Institutions*, pp. 23–24, also argues that similarities between Norman feudal practices in southern Italy and in Normandy must mean that these practices existed by the time of the departure of the Normans for southern Italy, that is, by the first half of the eleventh century. These alleged similarities, however, are denied by Yver, "Premières institutions," p. 335, n. 86.

84. Tabuteau, "Ownership and Tenure," pp. 100–102.

85. Fauroux, *Recueil*, p. 397, no. 208: "apud Asnerias dedi totum quod in dominio habebam excepto feodo militum, et nemore et aqua" (Saint-Sauveur d'Evreux, between 1055 and 1066). B.N., MS lat. 5441, 1:28: William the Conqueror confirms Humphrey de Bohun's gift of the church of Saint-Georges de Bohun: "id est de beneficio quatuor canonicorum et de feodo unius militis nomine Serlonis quod emerunt fratres predicti monasterii" (Marmoutier, between 1071 and 1082); Haskins, *Norman Institutions*, p. 18, n. 57, regards this as a technical use of the term *feodum militis*. Bibl. Rouen, MS 1193 (Y 44), fols. 30v–31r, no. 17: in return for a life estate given them to settle a dispute, Walter Giffard and William son of Geoffrey "debitum et consuetum servitium Rothomagensi ecclesie et Archiepiscopo inde redderent" (1083). B.N., MS lat. 10086, fol. 102v: Lancelin d'Airan's lord gives part of Lancelin's fief to Troarn for Lancelin to hold from the abbey during his lifetime and, says Lancelin, "illis omne debitum servicium reddam" (about 1100); Lancelin was the priest of Airan.

a particularly tantalizing one, a ducal charter of 1054 or 1055 for Mont-Saint-Michel says, "I concede the land that is called Sainte-Colombe as Neil the cleric, who held it from me as an allod, gave it, whom the monks therefore received among themselves in monastic dress. Moreover, I give the customs and all the services that come from the land, according to the usage of Normandy, to the same saint and monks to possess in perpetuity in the same land."[86] Clearly there was a usage known to apply to all of Normandy that governed some sort of service, but neither the details of the usage nor even the type of service involved is revealed.

Saint Anselm was fond of drawing an analogy between types of knights and types of Christians which provides the best evidence available that the concept of land held for service was widely recognized in Normandy by the late eleventh century: if it had not been, the homily would have made no sense. According to Eadmer, he used to say that "a prince has different kinds of soldiers [*milites*] at his court: he has some who are active in his service in return for the lands which they hold from him . . . [and such men], who serve him for the land which they hold, are already rooted and grounded and have no fear of being torn up so long as they conform themselves to their lord's will."[87] Anselm's description of the services of one of the other types of knights, the mercenaries, leaves no doubt that the service to which he refers is military. A good many charters are quite explicit that knights held land or that particular fiefs were held for service but do not state the services.[88] Several charters refer,

86. Fauroux, *Recueil*, p. 306, no. 132: "concedo . . . terram que dicitur Sancta Columba sicut eam dedit Niellus clericus quam eam de me tenebat in alodum, quem etiam ob hoc monachi secum receperunt sub habitu monachili. Consuetudines quoque et servicia omnia quo de terra exeunt, secundum morem Normannie, ipsi sancto et monachis in ipsa terra perpetualiter possidenda trado." Yver, "Une boutade," p. 787, n. 1, reluctantly concludes that the phrase *secundum morem Normannie* modifies *exeunt* rather than *trado*. "Allod" in Normandy normally meant a tenement by this time (Carabie, *Propriété foncière*, 1:232–36; Lucien Musset, "Réflexions sur alodium et sa signification dans les textes normands," *Revue historique de droit français et étranger*, 4th ser. 47 [1969]: 606; Tabuteau, "Ownership and Tenure," pp. 112–13).

87. Eadmer, *Vita Sancti Anselmi archiepiscopi Cantuariensis*, ed. Richard W. Southern (London, 1962), p. 94v; translation by Southern, ibid., p. 94r. The enfeoffed knights are equated with angels; mercenary knights are equated with the majority of Christians, and dispossessed but hopeful knights with monks. The same analogy is used by Anselm in *De humanis moribus per similitudines*, cc. 39, 80, in Richard W. Southern and Franciscus Salesius Schmitt, eds., *Memorials of St. Anselm* (London, 1969), pp. 52, 70; it is also reported by the monk Alexander, *Liber ex dictis Anselmi*, c. 10, in ibid., pp. 150–51.

88. For knights holding fiefs for service, where the type of service is not specified, see Fauroux, *Recueil*, p. 110, no. 24 (Saint-Ouen, between 1017 and 1023); Guérard, *Saint-Père de Chartres*, 1:108 (between 1023 and 1027), with commentary at pp. 108–9; Archives départementales de la Seine-Maritime, 14 H 255 (Saint-Ouen, between 1006 and 1033, probably about the same time as Fauroux, *Recueil*, no. 24, as it concerns the same transaction); and Arch. Eure, H 711, fols. 108r–108v, no. 320 (Saint-Pierre de Préaux, between about 1040 and 1072).

For knights holding for service land that is not called *feodum* or *beneficium*, see Fauroux, *Recueil*, p. 220, no. 80 (Saint-Wandrille, between 1029 and 1035); ibid., p. 341, no. 156C (Saint-Julien de Tours, 1063); and B.N., MS lat. 17137, fols. 39v–40r (Saint-Sauveur-le-Vicomte, about 1100).

For knights holding fiefs but not explicitly for service, see above, at n. 81 and accom-

without elaboration, to the service of knights, and two mention "free service," one of them explicitly connecting this to service by knights.[89] A charter of 1109 from La Trinité de Caen, which grants a fief "for such

panying text and at n. 85, twice; Fauroux, *Recueil*, p. 270, no. 110 (Mont-Saint-Michel, between 1037 and 1046; the fief was created between 1027 and 1035); ibid., p. 358, no. 166 (Montivilliers, between 1035 and 1066); Deville, *La Trinité du Mont*, p. 437, no. 30 (about 1060); ibid., p. 451, no. 57 (1066); Bréard, *Saint-Ymer-en-Auge*, p. 1, no. 1 (1066 or 1067); René Norbert Sauvage, *L'Abbaye de Saint-Martin de Troarn*, Mémoires de la Société des antiquaires de Normandie, vol. 34 (Paris, 1911), p. 349, no. 2 (1068); Guérard, *Saint-Père de Chartres*, 1:206 (between 1033 and 1079); Musset, *Abbayes caennaises*, p. 69, no. 6, where the tenant is called a *mariscalcus* (Saint-Etienne de Caen, between 1080 and 1082); B.N., MS fr. n. a. 21813, fols. 750r–51r (Saint-Désir de Lisieux, 1068); and Arch. Eure, H 711, fol. 100r, no. 288, where the tenant is called a *balista* (Saint-Pierre de Préaux, before about 1092). In Le Prévost, *Eure*, 2:506, a vavassor holds a fief (Marmoutier, between 1087 and 1106).

For knights holding land not called *feodum* or *beneficium* where there is no explicit mention of the services owed, see Fauroux, *Recueil*, p. 118, no. 30 (Saint-Wandrille, between 1017 and about 1025); ibid., p. 225, no. 85 (Fécamp, between 1031 and 1035); ibid., p. 227, no. 86 (Saint-Bénigne de Dijon, between 1032 and 1035, concerning a knight of Duke Richard II, who died in 1026 or 1027); ibid., p. 246, no. 94 (Fécamp, between 1035 and about 1040); ibid., p. 248, no. 95 (Saint-Wandrille, between 1037 and about 1040); ibid., p. 269, no. 109 (Saint-Ouen, 1047 or 1048); ibid., p. 291, no. 122 (Saint-Evroul, 1050); ibid., p. 297, no. 126 (Saint-Wandrille, 1051); ibid., pp. 328–30, no. 147 (Saint-Père de Chartres, 1060); ibid., p. 413, no. 218B (Saint-Martin-du-Bosc, priory of Fécamp, between 1059 and 1066); ibid., pp. 433 and 434, no. 225 (Saint-Père de Chartres, between 1063 and 1066); ibid., pp. 451 and 453, no. 234 (Saint-Wandrille, between 1082 and 1087); Marie-Josephe Le Cacheux, *Histoire de l'abbaye de Saint-Amand de Rouen des origines à la fin du XVIe siècle* (Caen, 1937), pp. 250–51, no. 11 (1067); Musset, *Abbayes caennaises*, pp. 75–76, no. 7 (Saint-Etienne de Caen, between 1080 and 1082); Le Prévost, *Eure*, 1:536 (Saint-Pierre de Préaux, between 1078 and 1096, concerning events a generation earlier); ibid., 3:136 (Saint-Taurin d'Evreux, between 1071 and 1112); Orderic, *Historia Ecclesiastica*, ed. Chibnall, 5:266 (Saint-Evroul, 1099); Orderic, *Historia Ecclesiastica*, ed. Auguste Le Prévost, 5 vols. (Paris, 1838–55), 5:194, no. 48, where the tenant is not called a knight but one of the witnesses is his *armiger* (Saint-Evroul, late eleventh century); and probably Musset, *Abbayes caennaises*, p. 76, no. 7 (Saint-Etienne de Caen, between 1080 and 1082).

For fiefs held for service, where the tenants are not called knights and the type of service is not specified, see below, at n. 120 and accompanying text; Wiffen, *Russell*, 1:522, where the service is described as *conveniens* (Saint-Etienne de Caen, between 1079 and 1096); Arch. Eure, H 711, fols. 108r–108v, no. 320 (Saint-Pierre de Préaux, between about 1040 and 1072); Arch. Orne, *Livre blanc* of Saint-Martin de Sées, fol. 46r (1088); Arch. Eure, H 262, fol. 220r, a passage that is not in the version of this charter published in the *Gallia Christiana* (Conches, late eleventh century); and B.N., MS lat. 10086, fol. 102v (Troarn, early twelfth century).

For knights doing unspecified service who are not explicitly said to hold land, see Fauroux, *Recueil*, p. 318, no. 140 (Saint-Désir de Lisieux, between 1049 and 1058); ibid., p. 390, no. 202 (La Trinité du Mont, between 1051 and 1066); and B.N., MS lat. 13816, fol. 457/462v, a passage that is not in the version of this charter published in the *Gallia Christiana* (Conches, late eleventh century).

89. Guérard, *Saint-Père de Chartres*, 1:108 (between 1023 and 1027); see also ibid., 1:108–9. For the service of knights, see the references in the preceding note. The second charter that mentions "free service" is Fauroux, *Recueil*, p. 447, no. 232 (Mont-Saint-Michel, 1066). See K. J. Hollyman, *Le développement du vocabulaire féodal en France pendant le haut moyen âge* (Geneva and Paris, 1957), pp. 60–63, for the significance of the term *liberum servitium*; he cites the charter from Saint-Père de Chartres.

service as a knight ought to do," implies that by that date there was a standard definition of knight service,[90] but no more than any other does it define the services included in that definition.[91]

The charters that enumerate particular services done for fiefs are exceedingly rare. Three of these indicate that even late in the eleventh century a fief could be held entirely for nonmilitary types of service. In 1085, Gulbert d'Auffay held a fief from the abbey of Fécamp for suit of court alone.[92] At about the same time or even later, the abbess of La Trinité de Caen enfeoffed the abbot of Saint-Etienne de Caen with part of a church for an annual payment of twenty shillings and for suit of court but for no other services.[93] At about the turn of the century, in a charter for Troarn, a man named Rabel and his son Hubert refer to "our other fief which we hold from the saint quit, without any service unless [it is done] voluntarily, except for the three services only per year within Normandy."[94] Another charter indicates that the "three services" were messenger service owed thrice annually.[95] Other charters mention only one nonmilitary service as due from a fief; but in each instance it is possible that only that service was mentioned, although others were due, because circumstances rendered its discussion advisable. In these three instances, however, there can be no doubt that only suit of court, alone or in addition to rent, or messenger service was due.

Of all the services mentioned by various sources, military service is, in fact, one of those about which the least is said. The earliest charter that links military service and feudal tenure comes from the mid-eleventh century: Gilbert Crispin gave the abbey of Jumièges "the fief of Hauville which I, *militans*, obtain from my . . . lord," that is, from Duke William.[96] *Militans* hardly need imply any definite amount of service; it may

90. Musset, *Abbayes caennaises*, p. 139, no. 27: "per tale servitium quale miles facere debet. . . ." In the abstract, the vagueness of the phrase might be taken to imply the opposite, that there was as yet no standard definition of a knight's service; but the correct interpretation is shown by analogy with a twelfth-century survey of the agricultural tenants of this abbey, in B.N., MS lat. 5650, fols. 20r–23v, where references to services that do not deviate from the norm are often made in similar terms.

91. That it is explicitly stated that this knight also escorts the abbess on her journeys within and outside Normandy suggests that such service, or perhaps such service outside Normandy, was not considered part of a knight's ordinary service.

92. Paul Chevreux and Jules-Joseph Vernier, *Les archives de Normandie et de la Seine-Inférieure: . . . recueil de facsimilés . . .* (Rouen, 1911), pl. VII.

93. Musset, *Abbayes caennaises*, p. 135, no. 25 (between 1079 and 1101, but closer to 1101). Suit of court also seems to have been the only service required of a man to whom the abbot of Saint-Pierre de Préaux committed the wardship of the sons of one of his vavassors (Le Prévost, *Eure*, 3:209 [between 1078 and 1096]). This is one of very few allusions to wardship in the eleventh-century charters.

94. B.N., MS lat. 10086, fol. 64v: "cum alio feodo nostro quod tenemus de sancto quiete sine ullo servitio nisi voluntarie, absque tribus servitiis tantum per annum intra normanniam. . . ."

95. Jean Mabillon, *Annales ordinis sancti Benedicti*, vol. 5 (Paris, 1713) (hereafter cited as Mabillon, *AA.O.S.B.*), pp. 627–28 (Rouen cathedral, between 1067 and 1079). See also B.N., MS lat. 5650, fol. 22r (La Trinité de Caen, twelfth century).

96. Fauroux, *Recueil*, p. 371, no. 188: "benefitium Alovillam scilicet, quam a predicto meo domino militans obtineo" (between 1046 and 1066).

mean no more than "fighting." Historical writings contain a few apparent references to tenure in return for military service at an earlier date than this, but their value is dubious.[97] Only in the last three decades of the eleventh century do we begin to hear any details about military service, and even then we know mostly about service owed to lords other than the duke.

The two most informative sources are the only two extant charters whose subject is the nature of the obligations of vassals to their lords. During the reign of Duke Robert Curthose, an agreement was drawn up between the bishop of Bayeux and his vassal Rannulf viscount of Bayeux "after a long disagreement between them."[98] Mostly concerned with the rectification of their dispute over various pieces of land and with arrangements for ensuring that the agreement will be kept, it says relatively little about service; but it includes among the promises that Rannulf made to the bishop that "he should aid [the bishop] also, saving the fealty of

97. F. M. Powicke, *The Loss of Normandy (1189–1204): Studies in the History of the Angevin Empire*, 2d ed. (Manchester, 1961), p. 40, cites a passage from Dudo of Saint-Quentin as concerning "lands [which] are evidently stocked, or to be stocked, with warriors (*milites*) and [which] were to be granted in return for service." The passage at issue, in Dudo's *De moribus*, p. 187, says, however, only that a rebel leader during the reign of Duke William Longsword (933–42) suggested to his co-conspirators, "Mittamus ad eum [i.e., the duke] quemdam internuntium, ut, si voluerit, nos promptos habere sibi ad serviendum, largiatur nobis terram usque ad flumen Rislam. Nos frequentia militum, si dederit, ditabimur. Ille frustratus milite annullabitur. . . ." This sounds to me more like a refusal to serve unless bribed than like a contractual relationship of lands held for service. A relationship between the possession of large amounts of land and the control of large numbers of *milites* is implied; but these *milites* need not, as Powicke recognizes, be "knights," and their relationship to either the duke or the rebels is obscure. The passage cannot, given Dudo's proven unreliability, be taken as evidence of conditions in the mid-tenth century. Even as a reflection of the ideas of the second and third decades of the eleventh century, when Dudo was writing, it hardly requires us to think that at that time feudal obligations between lords and men had been defined.

The late eleventh-century non-Norman *Inventio et miracula Sancti Wulfranni*, ed. Jean Laporte, in *Mélanges de la Société de l'histoire de Normandie*, 14th ser., *Documents* (Rouen, 1938), p. 30, says that in the middle of the tenth century the magnates of Normandy refused to allow Duke Richard I to return lands that the abbey of Ghent had held in Normandy before the Viking conquest, on the grounds that "se . . . nequaquam posse carere propriis honoribus quos sibi armis et sanguine predecessorum suorum pepererat bellicosa virtus, sive quos sibi ipsi diuturno adquisierant servitio multisque sudoribus." This may well be anachronistic; but even if it is an accurate report of the protest, the magnates may as easily have been referring to the conquest of Normandy by force of arms in the first half of the tenth century as to lands held from the duke in return for military service owed to the duke.

Brown, *Normans*, p. 42, cites the description in William of Poitiers, *Gesta Guillelmi ducis Normannorum et regis Anglorum*, ed. Raymonde Foreville (Paris, 1952), p. 52, of William count of Arques's withdrawal from the siege of Domfront in about 1052, "satelliti debitum . . . detrectans," as an allusion to the duty of a vassal to fight for his lord. It does not imply that the duty was defined by type or amount; cf. below, at n. 119.

98. Bourrienne, *Antiquus cartularius*, 1:95, no. 76: "cum diu prius discordiam habuissent." Navel, "Recherches," p. 17, gives an explanation of the circumstances surrounding this agreement that would date it to 1087 or shortly thereafter; the explanation is only plausible, however.

Count Robert [i.e., the duke], against all who wish to make war."[99] Rannulf's three sons made the same pledge of service, which is explicitly linked to their father's tenure of land from the bishop. In return, the bishop made exactly the same promise to Rannulf of aid in war, with the same reservation of fealty to the duke.[100] The document says nothing further about this service. Presumably the help would involve actual fighting, but we cannot tell how the lord and his vassal worked out the details of the obligation of military service.

A somewhat earlier agreement is much more instructive. Between 1070 and 1081, the abbot of Mont-Saint-Michel and his tenant William Paynel made an agreement about the obligations owed to William by the tenants on the land that he held from the abbey. It begins:

> If William Paynel has war in the land that the king of the English gave him with his wife, the agreement is that Hugh de Bricqueville should do him forty days of watch and ward [with seven horsemen], he himself [being] the seventh of the horsemen, at his own cost. And Hugh's nephew will also do so if he should hold his land in parage, according to what he will hold. Again, if William Paynel should summon Hugh, he will have him in his following with two knights at his own cost or his son if he is free of the abbot's summons. Nor will the lord abbot always have him so that William Paynel does not have it. And so indeed he will have in his following Hugh's nephew and Robert de Chanteloup and William Becheth and the one who will have the honor of Scollant.[101]

This list of what was owed to William, meager as it is, is the longest passage describing military service that is extant from eleventh-century Normandy. The reason for the existence of the agreement is not far to

99. Bourrienne, *Antiquus cartularius*, 1:95, no. 76: "juvaret autem, salva fidelitate comitis Roberti, contra omnes impugnare volentes."

100. Ibid., 1:96: "quod ipse episcopus Rannulfum fideliter adjuvaret contra omnes impugnare volentes, salva fidelitate comitis Roberti."

101. Haskins, *Norman Institutions*, p. 21: "Si Willelmus Paginellus habet guerram de illa terra quam rex Anglorum dedit sibi cum femina sua, conventio est quoniam Hugo de Bricavilla quadraginta diebus illi faciet de guarda vel custodia sese septimum de caballaribus ad suum cibum. Et nepos illius Hugonis similiter faciet si in parage terram suam tenuerit secundum hoc quod tenebit. Rursus si Guillelmus Paginellus illum Hugonem submonuerit, cum duobus equitibus eum in sua familia ad suum cibum habuerit vel filium suum, si liber erit de submonitione abbatis. Nec si[c] eum donnus abbas semper habebit quin Guillelmus Paginellus hoc habeat. Et ita equidem habebit in sua familia nepotem Hugonis et Robertum de Cantelupo et Guillelmum Becheth et illum qui honorem Scollant habebit." The emendation is Haskins's. My translation is heavily indebted to the translation by Thomas Stapleton, "Letter . . . Accompanying Two Transcripts of Ancient Charters Relating to Property in Normandy," *Archaeologia* 27 (1838): 21–28, at 24, and the translation by Round, *Calendar*, p. 255, no. 714. Haskins, *Norman Institutions*, p. 20, suggests the translation "watch and ward." Paul Chesnel has made two partial translations and paraphrases of the agreement, but they are less trustworthy than the translations of Stapleton and Round (Chesnel, "De quelques usages féodaux en Normandie sous Guillaume le Conquérant d'après un acte du cartulaire de Mont-Saint-Michel," *Congrès du millénaire de la Normandie* [*911–1911*], *Compte rendu des travaux*, 2 vols. [Rouen, 1912], 1:544–48; and Chesnel, *Le Cotentin et l'Avranchin sous les ducs de Normandie* [*911–1204*] [Caen, 1912], pp. 215–18).

seek. William held the fief as a result of his marriage, arranged by the duke. Nothing is known of his wife except that she was the heiress to the fief,[102] but perhaps she was also the heiress to a fief held directly of the duke and this is why he was able to control her marriage. Whether the duke arranged the marriage as direct lord or not, William Paynel would not have had previous knowledge of the tenurial conditions pertaining to the fief: it would be natural for him to have desired a precise statement of his rights in it and for the abbot to have desired a precise statement of the limits to his new vassal's rights. It is unlikely that William's agreement with the abbot and Viscount Rannulf's agreement with the bishop of Bayeux are the sole survivors of a large group of documents that have otherwise disappeared: both were drawn up in special circumstances, and in each case the lord was a prelate. Only one apparently comprehensive list of the obligations of a vassal to his lord is found in the contemporary historians, namely, the oath that Harold Godwinsson took to Duke William during his visit to Normandy in or about 1064. The provisions of the oath, as it occurs in the most detailed account, concern support for William's claim to the throne of England and the garrisoning in William's interest of castles at Dover and elsewhere in England at Harold's cost.[103] Harold's circumstances were even more exceptional than Viscount Rannulf's or William Paynel's. Feudal obligations among lay persons seem normally not to have been reduced to writing in this period.

The first part of William Paynel's arrangement with his men refers to castle-guard rather than to host service; moreover, it seems somewhat unlikely that the second part concerns service involving actual fighting rather than mere attendance in the retinue of the lord, as the term *familia* scarcely suggests an army.[104] The agreement goes on to treat other subjects—suit of court, aids, summonses, and various perquisites—on all of which it is by far the most informative extant source.[105] Our concern,

102. Later in the charter the land is called her *hereditas*. Chesnel, "Usages," pp. 544–45, and *Cotentin*, p. 211, identifies her as Alice de Romilly, a widow with one son. Alice was in fact the wife of this William's grandson, also named William (William Farrer and Charles T. Clay, *Early Yorkshire Charters*, vol. 6, *The Paynel Fee*, Yorkshire Archaeological Society Record Series, Extra Ser., vol. 3 [1939], pp. 6, 31). Ibid., pp. 1–2, discuss what is known of the earlier William Paynel. Their conjecture that the heiress of this agreement was named Lesceline, based on a later charter from Saint-Etienne de Caen, contains problems for the following reasons: the Saint-Etienne charter refers to Lesceline's *maritagium*, but this word meant "dowry," not "inheritance," in eleventh-century Norman usage; although *hereditas* could be used to refer to a dowry, the possessions transferred before the Mont-Saint-Michel agreement seem too extensive to be merely a dowry. Because a woman would not receive both an inheritance and a dowry, and because the Saint-Etienne charter post-dates William Paynel's death, but in it Lesceline is still alive, I think the most likely conjecture is that Lesceline was William Paynel's second wife.

103. William of Poitiers, *Gesta*, pp. 102–4.

104. Stapleton, "Letter," p. 24, translates the phrase as "having entertainment at the family board of the lord." Round, *Calendar*, p. 255, translates *familia* as "company." Chesnel, *Cotentin*, p. 216, thinks that this passage "prouve clairement que . . . les seigneurs normands avaient le droit de guerre"; see also Chesnel, "Usages," p. 545.

105. See Tabuteau, "Transfers of Property," pp. 417–21, 456–58, for discussions on some of these points.

however, is with military service. On this subject the agreement raises several points of interest, information on some of which is also forthcoming from other sources.

Hugh de Bricqueville owes William his own service and that of six others—if I have correctly interpreted an obscure phrase in the charter[106] —in doing castle-guard, and he or his son owes his own service and that of two others when serving in William's following; the ambiguous phrasing of the charter means that the latter may also be true of Hugh's nephew, Robert de Chanteloup, William Becheth, and the holder of the honor of Scollant.[107] Here is evidence for the existence of two different quotas of service in the late eleventh century. They are not, however, quotas owed to the duke by one of his vassals but quotas owed to a man who is, formally at least, two steps lower in the feudal hierarchy. Only one other charter refers to regular service by several knights in a way that probably indicates that this was a quota of service. The charter is of such interest that it deserves to be quoted in full:

> I, Baudry, with the consent of [my] lord William king of the English and duke of the Normans, quitclaim to the nuns of Saint-Amand de Rouen the service of two knights that they owe for forty days per year from the fee of Bacqueville until I or my heir pays the thirty pounds of [money of] Rouen that I owe to St. Amand and the nuns for my sister Elizabeth who was made a nun there. The witnesses were. . . . Before this gage the aforesaid knights were thus equipped when they did service: one of them with full arms; the other, however, with plain arms.[108]

Apparently the abbey had owed Baudry a quota of two knights for forty days per year, and the duke's consent may imply that Baudry owed the service of the same two knights to him.[109] The charter is indubitably

106. Stapleton, Round, and Chesnel are all in accord with this interpretation.

107. Chesnel, *Cotentin*, p. 216, thinks that these men are to serve only if Hugh or his son cannot; Chesnel, "Usages," p. 545, appears to think that one or another of these men—not all—is to serve if Hugh or his son cannot. Stapleton ignores the matter; Round, *Calendar*, p. 255, appears to agree with my interpretation.

108. Haskins, *Norman Institutions*, p. 20: "Ego Baldricus annuente domino Willelmo Anglorum rege et Normannorum duce clamo quetum [*sic*] sanctimonialibus de Sancto Amando Rothomagi servicium duorum militum quod quadraginta diebus debent per annum de feodo Bascheville donec ego vel heres meus reddamus .xxx. libras Rodmeisinorum quas Sancto Amando et sanctimonialibus debeo pro sorore mea Elisabeth que ibi effecta est monacha. Testes sunt. . . . Ante hoc vademonium predicti milites sic erant in servicio parati: unus horum totis armis, alter vero ad plainas armas" (between 1066 and 1087). The witness list comprises five names plus, apparently, the signatures of Baudry and of the king. For the significance of the last sentence, see below, at text accompanying nn. 135–38.

109. Le Cacheux, *Saint-Amand*, pp. 185–86, appears to think that the service of these two knights was normally owed to the abbey rather than to Baudry. Farrer and Clay, *Early Yorkshire Charters*, vol. 9, *The Stuteville Fee*, Yorkshire Archaeological Society Record Series, Extra Ser., vol. 7 (1952), p. 70, are in agreement with my interpretation of the charter. Haskins expresses no opinion on the matter. It seems to me indubitable that, whether the subject of *debent* is the nuns or the knights, if Baudry quitclaimed the service to the nuns in lieu of a payment that he owed them, then the service must normally have been

important; but it is possible that its Baudry was related to the de Bocquencé family of the Saint-Evroul charter allegedly of 1128 and, if so, his defined obligations might, again, be characteristic only of this one family, not of eleventh-century Norman feudal obligations in general.[110] In any

---

owed to him from them. It is true that his action is called a *vademonium* and that this word usually meant a mortgage; but a mortgage was a temporary surrender of something normally one's own (see Tabuteau, "Transfers of Property," pp. 155–81, esp. 155–60), and the word could be used simply for a pledge of performance (ibid., pp. 998–99, n. 76). It might be argued that the service was normally owed to Baudry by someone other than the nuns, but the use of the term "quitclaim" implies that an obligation or a claim already existing between the parties was being renounced rather than that an entirely new concession was being made. Saint-Amand is not listed as owing service in the Inquest of 1172 or in any of the thirteenth-century lists printed in *HF*, vol. 23.

Baudry's charter survives only in a *vidimus* of 1313 (Haskins, *Norman Institutions*, p. 20, n. 66). It is not found in any other pancart or cartulary of the abbey, including the other extant version of the pancart which is the subject of the *vidimus* of 1313 (Le Cacheux, *Saint-Amand*, pp. 25–26). This is puzzling but not sufficient to cast doubt on the authenticity of the charter: see also ibid., pp. 26–27.

110. See above, at n. 79 and accompanying text. The earliest evidence of a connection between Bacqueville and Saint-Amand is the presence as a witness of Nicholas de *Bascavilla* at a gift to the abbey datable to between about 1042 and 1066 (Fauroux, *Recueil*, p. 370, no. 187). His appearance suggests that the abbey already had a connection with *Baschevilla*, although it is not possible to tell whether it yet had knights there. This place is identified by both Fauroux, *Recueil*, p. 480, and Jean Adigard des Gautries, "Les noms des lieux de la Seine-Inférieure attestés entre 911 et 1066," *Annales de Normandie* 6 (1956): 119–34, at 131, as Bacqueville-en-Caux. Orderic names Nicholas de Bacqueville (*Baschevilla*) as one of the sons of Baudry the German and brothers of Baudry de Bocquencé (*Historia Ecclesiastica*, ed. Chibnall, 2:82). If the order in which Orderic lists the sons of Baudry the German corresponds to the order of their birth, as is likely, Nicholas was older than Baudry de Bocquencé. Le Prévost, in his edition of Orderic, *Historia Ecclesiastica*, 2:76, n. 1, identifies Nicholas as from Bacqueville-en-Caux, although most of his family's holdings were near Saint-Evroul, a considerable distance from the Caux district. Farrer and Clay, *Early Yorkshire Charters*, 9:70, n. 9, and 71–72, suggest certain familial and geographical relationships between the de Bocquencé family and various donors to Saint-Amand. Nicholas de Bacqueville and Baudry de Bocquencé had a sister named Elizabeth, as does the Baudry of the Saint-Amand charter. Elizabeth de Boquencé married Fulk de Bonneval and had a son who had become a monk at Saint-Evroul by 1061, probably by 1057 (Orderic, *Historia Ecclesiastica*, ed. Chibnall, 2:84 and n. 3). Orderic does not say what happened to her or to her husband thereafter; but, chronologically at least, it is certainly possible that she had become a nun at Saint-Amand by the time when Baudry's sister was described by the Saint-Amand charter as a nun and, therefore, that the Baudry to whom the abbey owed two knights was Baudry de Bocquencé. Baudry de Bocquencé and his brother Nicholas had an uncle Wiger and a brother Wiger "of Apulia." If the sons of Baudry the German are listed in order of birth in Orderic, *Historia Ecclesiastica*, ed. Chibnall, 2:82, then Wiger "of Apulia" was younger than either Nicholas or Baudry de Bocquencé. In the Saint-Amand charter witnessed by Nicholas de Bacqueville, another of the witnesses is Wiger *homo Nicolai*. It is hard to see how either *frater* or *avunculus/patruus* could be transmogrified by even the most inept of scribes into *homo*, but two things should be noticed. First, in the 1050s, Baudry de Bocquencé and his brother Wiger were joint tenants of Bocquencé and it would appear that Baudry was in some way superior to Wiger (ibid., 2:80–82). Wiger may therefore have been considered his brother Baudry's man; perhaps earlier he had been his brother Nicholas's man. For one brother to do homage to another was not impossible at this date; King Henry I of England had done homage to his elder brother Robert Curthose at some time before 1101 (ibid., 5:318). Second, the name Wiger, which is rare in eleventh-century Normandy, was in the Bocquencé family because the father and uncle of Nicholas,

case, two charters—William Paynel's and Baudry's—are slight evidence on the basis of which to argue that quotas of service were widespread in

Baudry, Wiger, Elizabeth, and their siblings had migrated to Normandy from Germany before 1026. Possibly they came with German supporters, among them one named Wiger.

Alternately, the Baudry connected with Saint-Amand may have been the son, not the brother, of Nicholas de Bacqueville. If so, he may be identifiable with the Baudry son of Nicholas, probably also called Baudry de Guitry, whom Orderic mentions as flourishing in the second half of the eleventh century (ibid., 3:250, 4:50, 100). He also appears as a witness in the charter cited above, at n. 92. Farrer and Clay, *Early Yorkshire Charters*, 9:70–71, conclude that Baudry son of Nicholas was the son of Nicholas de Bacqueville and the grandson of Baudry Teutonicus and conjecture that their dates of birth may have been approximately 1025, 1000, and 975, respectively. Baudry son of Nicholas gave possessions at Dieppe to Saint-Evroul (Orderic, *Historia Ecclesiastica*, ed. Chibnall, 3:250), and Dieppe is near Bacqueville-en-Caux; this donation therefore slightly strengthens the identification of these persons as members of one family, whether the Baudry of the Saint-Amand charter be Baudry de Bocquencé or Baudry son of Nicholas. The mistake in the Saint-Evroul confirmation charter allegedly of 1128, which speaks of Baudry son of Nicholas where it ought to name Baudry de Bocquencé (see above, at n. 78 and accompanying text), may also be evidence that the two were related. It is also noteworthy that Orderic never discusses the progeny of Nicholas de Bacqueville, although he had a penchant for tracing the genealogies of the families of benefactors of his abbey. Perhaps he expected that everyone knew that Baudry "son of Nicholas" was the son of Nicholas de Bacqueville and therefore the nephew of Baudry de Bocquencé. Baudry son of Nicholas is not known, however, to have had a sister named Elizabeth.

There are a few other tenuous connections among the various persons at issue here. Between 1032 and 1048, Nicholas son of Baudry gave the church of Guitry to Saint-Wandrille, and among the witnesses are two men named Wiger, one a cleric, the other a layman (Ferdinand Lot, *Etudes critiques sur l'abbaye de Saint-Wandrille* [Paris, 1913], p. 58, no. 16). In Fauroux, *Recueil*, p. 337, no. 153, this Nicholas is said to have a wife named Geretrudis and several sons who are not named (Saint-Wandrille, between 1047 and 1063). When Hadvis daughter of Nicholas de *Baschelvilla* or *Bachetvilla* gave land to Montivilliers between 1066 and 1087, one of the witnesses was Robert de *Novilla*, who might conceivably be related to Richard de Neuville, another brother of Nicholas de Bacqueville and Baudry de Bocquencé (*Gallia Christiana*, vol. 11, *Instrumenta*, col. 329; B.N., MS fr. n. a. 23056, fol. 63r). Nicholas son of Baudry also appears as a witness in the following charters where the details are of no help concerning his family: Fauroux, *Recueil*, p. 259, no. 102 (Saint-Wandrille, between 1037 and about 1045); B.N., fonds Moreau, vol. 341, fol. 17v (Fécamp, 1047). The same is true of the appearance of Nicholas de Guitry as a witness in a charter on behalf of Marmoutier dated 1070 (Mabillon, *AA.O.S.B.*, 5:627). There is, at least, no chronological impossibility or improbability as a result of these charters. The one directly contradictory piece of evidence comes from Robert of Torigny, who, in his interpolations to William of Jumièges, *Gesta Normannum ducum*, ed. Jean Marx (Rouen and Paris, 1914), p. 328, says that Nicholas de *Bascheritvilla* (whom ibid., n. 4, identifies as Nicholas de Bacqueville, son of Baudry the German) married a niece of Duke Richard II's wife Gunnor and that his sons were William Martel and Walter de Saint-Martin. If Marx's identification of this Nicholas is correct, this evidence runs counter to the attempt to identify Baudry son of Nicholas as the son of Nicholas de Bacqueville; but it should be noted that in the same passage, Robert, who wrote in the mid-twelfth century, made several genealogical errors; see ibid., p. 329, nn. 1 and 3. I find no evidence in the charters or the historians to confirm or deny the genealogy given by Robert of Torigny; but, as Marx notes, ibid., p. 328, n. 5, Robert elsewhere makes a mistake about the sons of Walter de Saint-Martin, and Robert of Torigny's genealogies of eleventh-century families are, in general, untrustworthy. His mistake here, if it was one, may have been a deduction from the fact that in his day Bacqueville was held by a family named Martel; see Farrer and Clay, *Early Yorkshire Charters*, 9:70, n. 9, who suggest that William Martel's mother may have been of the "Baudry" family.

eleventh-century Normandy, much less that if they existed on the lower levels of the feudal hierarchy they must, a fortiori, have existed between the duke and his immediate vassals.

The only additional evidence of the existence in the eleventh century of quotas—owed in these cases to the duke—comes from twelfth-century sources. Orderic Vitalis, in the speech that he attributes to William the Conqueror on his deathbed, makes him say of Guy count of Ponthieu, captured in William's victory at Mortemer in 1054, "I kept him in prison at Bayeux at my good pleasure, and two years later received homage from him on these terms: that in future he would always be faithful to me and would perform military service [*militare seruicium*] for me each year wherever I commanded with a hundred knights."[111] Although the accuracy of this deathbed speech is debated,[112] there is other evidence, insufficient to be conclusive, that Guy remained William's vassal and that Ponthieu was considered to be held by Guy from William.[113] The story may well be veracious in its outlines, but its least easily accepted feature is the exact figure for the amount of knight service owed to the duke.[114] Even so, this piece of evidence is more trustworthy than the other, which

111. Orderic, *Historia Ecclesiastica*, ed. Chibnall, 4:88; translation by Chibnall, ibid., 4:89.

112. Johannes Steenstrup, "Normandiets Historie under de syv første hertuger: Avec un résumé en français" (1925), in *Mémoires de l'Académie des sciences et des lettres de Danemark, Sections des lettres*, 7th ser. 5 (1936): 1–319, at 293, thinks that William actually made this speech, "qu'Orderic Vital nous a conservé." At the other extreme, Gaston Le Hardy, "Le dernier des ducs normands: Etude de critique historique sur Robert Courteheuse," *Bulletin de la Société des antiquaires de Normandie* 10 (1881): 3–184, at 53, says that the speech is "d'une invraisemblance complète"; but he is so much a defender of Curthose that he cannot be trusted as an authority on Orderic. Most scholars accept the speech as Orderic's view of the events—fairly accurately presented—of William's reign; see Orderic, *Historia Ecclesiastica*, ed. Chibnall, 4:80, n. 3.

113. John Le Patourel, *The Norman Empire* (Oxford, 1976), pp. 19–20, 77. In addition to the evidence Le Patourel cites, Guy was one of the commission of judges appointed to hear an important case in William the Conqueror's court in 1080 (Deville, *La Trinité du Mont*, p. 463, no. 82). He also appears as a witness to the record of the settlement of another important case by the default of one of the parties in Duke Robert Curthose's court in 1093 or 1094 (Marchegay, "Saint-Florent," p. 695, no. 16). The men listed as witnesses would probably have constituted the commission of judges that would have decided the issue if there had been no default.

114. See Sten Körner, *The Battle of Hastings, England, and Europe, 1035–1066* (Lund, 1964), pp. 93–96, and the references there, on the possibility that Guy or his son was at Hastings. Even if this was so, there certainly do not appear to have been one hundred knights of Ponthieu in the battle; only Wace, *Maistre Wace's Roman de Rou et des ducs de Normandie*, ed. Hugo Andresen, 2 vols. (Heilbronn, 1877, 1879), 2:276, 375, mentions any at all as present, except for Eustace of Boulogne. See Körner, *Hastings*, pp. 233, 234. There is no other evidence of knights of Ponthieu fighting on behalf of the duke of Normandy in the eleventh century. Orderic's story is accepted by most historians. The figure of one hundred knights is explicitly accepted by Haskins, *Norman Institutions*, p. 18; and Frank Barlow, *William I and the Norman Conquest* (London, 1965), p. 27. That figure is questioned by Chibnall, in her edition of Orderic, *Historia Ecclesiastica*, 4:88, n. 5. The story as a whole is rejected by du Motey, *Origines*, p. 213; but du Motey is so vehement a denigrator of the value of Orderic's work that his opinions must be regarded with extreme caution.

comes from Wace's poem on the history of Normandy, the *Roman de Rou*. In narrating the discussions leading up to the campaign to conquer England, Wace has William fitz Osbern promise on behalf of the Norman barons that each will provide double the service he customarily owes.[115] The passage mentions quotas of twenty, thirty, and a hundred knights, but it may be disregarded because it obviously relates more to Wace's own lifetime than to 1066 and is highly romantic at that.[116] There is, therefore, little evidence that quotas of service existed more than occasionally in eleventh-century Normandy, and the instances that are indubitable concern not the duke but lesser lords. Hence, the question

115. Wace, *Roman de Rou*, ed. Andresen, 2:273–75.

116. As noted earlier, this passage is the sole evidence that Round could find for the existence of *servicia debita* in Normandy in the eleventh century; see John Horace Round, *Feudal England* (London, 1895), pp. 259–60. Yet at the same time it was Round who did the fundamental work in destroying Wace's credibility as a source for the eleventh century; see ibid., pp. 403–9. His conclusion has not achieved consensus, and other historians have been just as inconsistent in their use of Wace as Round was. To cite but one example, D. C. Douglas, "Companions of the Conqueror," *History*, new ser. 28 (1943): 129–47, at 131–32, rejects Wace as an authority for the presence of named individuals at the battle of Hastings and, on that basis, drastically pares down the list of those known to have participated in the conquest. Yet in his biography of William the Conqueror, Douglas uses Wace quite freely in other contexts; see Douglas, *William*, p. 72, n. 2, for one rather striking example. It seems to me impossible to rely on Wace as an independent authority, especially on a matter of basic societal organization. A particular detail, such as whether a certain person was present at a certain battle, might conceivably survive undistorted through a century of oral tradition; the fundamental structure of society would almost inescapably be interpreted as similar to that of the writer's own day.

In 1066, William probably received contributions of ships from his supporters. The surviving list of these contributions, for which see J. A. Giles, ed., *Scriptores rerum gestarum Willelmi Conquestoris* (Caxton Society, 1845), 3:21–22, records levies of round numbers of ships, some of them very large. There is, however, reason to question the accuracy of this text; see Douglas, *William*, pp. 189–90; Douglas, "Companions," pp. 144, n. 7, and 146, n. 4; and Körner, *Hastings*, pp. 251–53. Moreover, there is no indication that such contributions were a regular exaction of service rather than an ad hoc effort directly consequent upon the projected invasion of England. The Norman dukes did not normally campaign at sea; and the only possible earlier instance, an alleged expedition by Robert the Magnificent, is much disputed; see Douglas, *William*, p. 163; and Yver, "Premières institutions," p. 334, n. 81 *bis*.

The list of ships includes the numbers of knights sent by each of four magnates. There is, however, no reason to think that these numbers, even if correct, represent quotas of service due rather than ad hoc arrangements: the abbot of Saint-Ouen, who in 1172 owed 6 knights, is alleged to have contributed 100; and the *eleemosinarius* of Fécamp, whose abbot in 1172 owed 10 knights, is alleged to have contributed 20. Hugh de Montfort is supposed to have contributed 60 knights: in 1172 Robert de Montfort owed 7½ or 8½ knights from the honor of Coquainvilliers and the fief of Orbec and had the service of just over 44 (*HF*, 23:694; *Red Book*, 2:627); Geoffrey de Montfort owed 3½ and had 13½ (*HF*, 23:695; *Red Book*, 2:631); and the honor of Montfort had the service of over 21 knights, though it was not known how much was owed (see above, at n. 69). The figure for the fourth contributor in 1066 is much closer to a figure from 1172: Walter Giffard allegedly contributed 100 knights, and in 1172 the honor of Giffard had just about that much knight service (see above, at n. 69). Even here, however, the correspondence is illusory: it was not known in 1172 how much service was due to the duke from the honor, but, judging by comparable figures in the Inquest of 1172, it was probably only a fairly small fraction of the number of knights enfeoffed.

remains open. It seems most likely that the arrangement between William Paynel and one or more of his vassals, the one between Baudry and Saint-Amand, and the one that may have existed between Duke William and Guy of Ponthieu were exceptional or, at least, were not expressions of a general and systematic practice. Against this all that can be said is that, as William Paynel's charter is one of only two extant from the whole century whose subject is explicitly the conditions of feudal tenure, the fact that it includes references to quotas for two kinds of service bears considerable weight.

William Paynel's charter is the only one that mentions the cost of serving as a knight. The charter's wording is ambiguous; but it seems likely that Hugh de Bricqueville and his nephew—and perhaps the men whom they must bring with them—will do their service of castle-guard at their own cost, whereas they and the others are to be in William's following at William's cost.[117] In later days, the question of who was to support the expense of service was closely connected with the issue of limitations on the amount of service that could be exacted, limitations both of duration and of geographical area. It is possible that the forty-day limitation on the service of castle-guard in William Paynel's charter is related to the fact, if it is one, that in this case the vassals did the service at their own cost.[118] The limit is not said to be forty days per year; this is the most likely interpretation, but it is conceivable, as the service is to be done "if William Paynel has war in the land that the king of the English gave him," that it was forty days per war. The same phrase seems to limit the castle-guard service—and perhaps also the service in William's following—to certain of William's wars. Only one other charter mentions a limitation on the duration of service: the two knights whose service Baudry quitclaimed to Saint-Amand served for forty days per year. Nothing is said about the cost of their service.

Few other sources discuss limits at all. Orderic's statement that "Duke Robert [Curthose] often commanded Gilbert, son of Engenulf of Laigle, to perform military service [*militaria seruitia crebro iniunxit*] because he was conspicuously courageous" implies that there was no limit on the frequency of service even toward the end of the eleventh century.[119] A

117. Stapleton, "Letter," p. 24, thinks that both services are to be at William's cost. Round's translation, *Calendar*, p. 255, is as ambiguous as the Latin but appears to consider the cost Hugh's in both cases. Haskins, *Norman Institutions*, pp. 20–21, and Chesnel, "Usages," p. 545, and *Cotentin*, pp. 215–16, agree with my interpretation.

When the cleric of Grainville did escort or messenger service for the nuns of La Trinité de Caen, the abbey provided his sustenance (B.N., MS lat. 5650, fol. 22r [twelfth century]). The council of Lillebonne, held in 1080, ordered that any priest who accompanied his lord on a journey as chaplain should receive his sustenance from the lord (Orderic, *Historia Ecclesiastica*, ed. Chibnall, 3:28).

118. Haskins, *Norman Institutions*, pp. 20–21, asserts that it is.

119. Orderic, *Historia Ecclesiastica*, ed. Chibnall, 4:200; translation by Chibnall, ibid., 4:201. See also Barlow, *William*, pp. 27–28, who cites William's anger at the unauthorized departure of his uncle William count of Arques from the siege of Domfront (see above, at n. 97) as another indication that there was no limitation on the duration of service.

man named Adelard, having received certain land from the abbot of Saint-Martin de Sées for which he became the abbot's man, promised "that he would serve for the same land whomever the abbot or the brothers should order [him to serve] as if for his fief without any *determinatio*."[120] If the last phrase means "without any limitation" and if the service "as if for his fief" that Adelard—and later his son—was to do was military service, which the charter never says it was, this might be an indication that limitations were a normal feature of military service by the eleventh century. It does not indicate what limitations might be expected, except that, apparently, there was not here even any limit as to the lord to be served, a provision that is otherwise unknown in Normandy in this period. To return to more conventional limits, according to Orderic, Guy of Ponthieu's hundred knights were to serve wherever Duke William wished. This, because it may imply that limits were normal, is the best evidence that a limit of geographical area could be applied to military service in eleventh-century Normandy.[121] The only charter that limits the geographical scope of military service—to "within the borders of Normandy"—is concerned with the rear-ban, a general *levée en masse* in the event of a foreign invasion of Normandy, and the limitation is stated as a special privilege.[122] Wace makes the barons of Normandy assert, in 1066, that they need not serve overseas; but he is no more likely to be reliable on this point than on the subject of quotas.[123] Because the contemporary Norman historians record Duke William's incursions into Maine, Brittany, and the Vexin with no reference to special arrangements, it is probable that what opposition there was to the campaign to conquer England—every historian records some—was based on the risk involved and the danger of never coming back, rather than on any customary restriction of service to Normandy alone.

William Paynel's agreement with the abbot of Mont-Saint-Michel provides that Hugh de Bricqueville or his son will come to serve in William's following only "if he is free of the abbot's summons. Nor will the lord abbot always have him so that William Paynel does not have it." The same apparently applies to the four other men who are obligated to serve in William's following; and there is a similar provision concerning the suit of court that the seven peers of William's honor are to do, although in this case there is no equivalent of the obscure statement about the

120. Arch. Orne, *Livre blanc* of Saint-Martin de Sées, fols. 45r–45v: "se pro eadem terra serviturum cuicunque abbas vel fratres preciperent sicuti pro feodo suo sine ulla determinatione pepigit . . . " (between 1073 and 1089). Adelard's son and heir was to hold the land after his father's death and also to serve "sicuti pro feodo suo."

121. There seem to have been limits on the distance or the place to which someone could be summoned to do suit of court; see Tabuteau, "Transfers of Property," pp. 417, 422–23. See above, at n. 91, for the possibility that a charter of 1109 implies that escort service outside Normandy was unusual.

122. Musset, *Abbayes caennaises*, p. 64, no. 4A *bis:* "intra fines Nortmanniae . . ." (Saint-Etienne de Caen, between 1081 and 1087).

123. Wace, *Roman de Rou*, ed. Andresen, 2:272: "Oltre mer seruir ne devon."

abbot.[124] That statement seems to mean that the abbot agrees not always to preempt the service of these men.[125] It would appear that William's men were also tenants directly of the abbot and that their duty to serve him preceded their obligation to William—that, in other words, the abbot was their liege lord.[126] Recall that in the agreement between Viscount Rannulf and the bishop of Bayeux each, in promising to aid the other in war, reserved his fealty to the duke, who would therefore seem to have been the liege lord of both. This is the only known instance of such a reservation of allegiance to the duke, and it cannot be taken to indicate that such reservations were common practice in Normandy at this time.[127] Instead, it is possible that the special position of each of the parties—the one as viscount and, therefore, the duke's chief official in the area; the other as bishop and, because the bishop concerned was probably Odo, the duke's uncle and one of his chief counselors—explains the appearance of the clause in the agreement between them.[128] Al-

124. Haskins, *Norman Institutions*, p. 22: "Conventio est de septem paribus de honore quem Willelmus Paginellus tenet de abbate . . . quoniam submonuerit illos in sua curia, qui si sponte sua ambulare voluerint ibunt si liberi erunt de servicio abbatis. . . . " This is the only use of *pares* in a technical sense in an eleventh-century Norman document. The only other time the word appears, it is used in a social sense: Arch. Eure, H 711, fol. 142v, no. 455: "ut quod alii divites paresque mei in suis elemosinis iure habebunt et ego habeam . . . " (Saint-Pierre de Préaux, between 1096 and 1101). William Paynel's charter does not identify the peers of his honor. It mentions only six individuals: Hugh de Bricqueville, his son, his nephew, Robert de Chanteloup, William Becheth, and the holder of the honor of Scollant. The only group of seven men in the charter is the seven horsemen (who include Hugh de Bricqueville and/or his nephew) who do castle-guard.

125. Stapleton, "Letter," p. 24: "and if he be always under summons from the Abbot, then the lord [i.e., William Paynel] not to have this service." Round, *Calendar*, p. 255: "Nor shall the abbot always prevent William from having this"; ibid., n. 1: "Sense of this clause obscure." Chesnel, "Usages," p. 545: "En cas d'empêchement motivé par le service de l'abbé. . . . "

126. Stapleton, Round, and Chesnel all assume that this is so. The inference that they reserved their service to the abbot without being his tenants seems even less likely. Of William's tenants who are mentioned in the agreement, only Hugh de Bricqueville can be identified elsewhere. He witnesses a transaction between Abbot Rannulf of Mont-Saint-Michel and a man named Guatszo (Arch. Calvados, série F, fonds de Beausse, année 1926, carton 1, liasse Mont-Saint-Michel [between about 1055 and 1085]). This reinforces the likelihood that he was one of the abbot's tenants.

127. Haskins, *Norman Institutions*, p. 22 and n. 70, assumes that it can. For the view that reservations of loyalty to the duke were by no means universal even under Henry I, see Lucien Valin, *Le duc de Normandie et sa cour (912–1204)* (Paris, 1909), pp. 61–64; Walther Kienast, *Untertaneneid und Treuvorbehalt in Frankreich und England* (Weimar, 1952), pp. 234–39; and Powicke, *Loss of Normandy*, p. 42. The argument of Valin and Kienast is criticized by Jean-François Lemarignier, "Autour de la royauté française du IXe au XIIIe siècle," *Bibliothèque de l'Ecole des Chartes* 113 (1955): 5–25, at 21–22, but largely on the basis of an unquestioned acceptance of Haskins's arguments.

128. On the position of viscounts in eleventh-century Normandy, see, most recently, Yver, "Premières institutions," pp. 325–32. On Bishop Odo's role during the reign of Robert Curthose, see V. Bourrienne, "Odon de Conteville, évêque de Bayeux," *Revue catholique de Normandie* 8 (1898–99): 507–32, at 514–23; ibid. 9 (1899–1900): 420–40, at 420–35, and 530–42, at 536–37; David R. Bates, "The Character and Career of Odo, Bishop of Bayeux (1049/50–1097)," *Speculum* 50 (1975): 1–20, at 15–19.

though the promises that the bishop and the viscount made to each other were virtually identical, Rannulf's fealty to the bishop is called "liege fealty," whereas the bishop's fealty to Rannulf is not.[129] The term "liege" occurs only twice elsewhere in the eleventh-century Norman documents: late in the century each of two not very important individuals "became the liege man" of Abbot Gilbert of Saint-Etienne de Caen in return for a fief.[130] Thus, of the four apparent references to the practice that are extant, only one concerns the duke as liege lord, and it may be an exceptional case.

The need for liege homage must have been apparent in Normandy long before Curthose's reign, and a reservation of loyalty to the duke has sometimes been thought to be one of the signs of the unusual strength of the dukes in this period.[131] Yet Orderic tells two stories which tend to show that liegeance was not yet in use. Roger de Mortemer was one of the leaders of Duke William's army at the battle of Mortemer in 1054 against the army of the king of France. In the deathbed speech attributed to William, Orderic makes him say that in the battle

> Count Ralph [of Crépy] would have been taken prisoner . . . , if Roger, the commander of my army, had not spared him. He did so because he had done homage to him. So, in his lord's hour of need, he performed a just and seemly service by protecting him in his own castle [of Mortemer] for three days and then escorting him back to his lands. I banished Roger from Normandy for this offense, but became reconciled with him soon afterwards and restored the rest of his honor to him. I withheld from him, however, acting—I believe—rightly, the castle of Mortemer in which he had preserved my enemy; and gave it to his kinsman, William of Warenne, a loyal knight.[132]

The tone of this is slightly inconsistent: perhaps Orderic forgot who was supposed to be speaking when he wrote "just and seemly." In any case, Roger's homage to Ralph apparently included no reservation of alle-

129. Bourrienne, *Antiquus cartularius*, 1:95, no. 76: "fecit . . . sibi fidelitatem ligiam idem Rannulfus. . . ."

130. Etienne Deville, *Notices sur quelques manuscrits normands conservés à la Bibliothèque Sainte-Geneviève*, vol. 4, *Analyse d'un ancien cartulaire de l'abbaye de Saint-Etienne de Caen* (Evreux, 1905), p. 24, fol. 31: "devenit homo ligis . . . " (between 1079 and 1101); ibid., p. 30, fol. 40: "devenit homo ligis . . . " (between 1079 and 1101).

131. Haskins, *Norman Institutions*, p. 22; Achille Luchaire, *Les premiers Capétiens*, pt. 2 (Paris, 1901; vol. 2, pt. 2, of the *Histoire de France*, ed. Ernest Lavisse), pp. 54–55; Jacques Flach, *Les origines de l'ancienne France*, vol. 3 (Paris, 1904), pp. 88–90; Michel de Boüard, "Le duché de Normandie," in Ferdinand Lot and Robert Fawtier, eds., *Histoire des institutions françaises au moyen âge*, vol. 1, *Institutions seigneuriales* (Paris, 1957), pp. 1–33, at 15, 21.

132. Orderic, *Historia Ecclesiastica*, ed. Chibnall, 4:88; translation adapted from Chibnall, ibid., 4:89. The story is universally accepted. Barlow, *William*, p. 37, interprets it as an example of Duke William's insistence "that his barons owed their loyalty to him alone"; see also Brown, *Normans*, p. 21. Jean Yver, "Les châteaux forts en Normandie jusqu'au milieu du XIIe siècle: contribution à l'étude du pouvoir ducal," *Bulletin de la Société des antiquaires de Normandie* 53 (1955–56): 28–115, at 61, interprets it as one of William's successful efforts to convert castles held in fee into castles held by mere custodians.

giance to Duke William. Thirty-five years later, Orderic tells us, "Ascelin Goel feloniously took the castle of Ivry away from his lord William of Breteuil and surrendered it to Duke Robert. William, who was unwilling to lose the castle, offered fifty thousand livres to the duke for it. After recovering the castle, he avenged himself by depriving Goel of the castellanship and confiscating all the property which he held of him. As a result there was prolonged war between them. . . ."[133] Although Orderic judges Ascelin harshly, from the duke's point of view his action was doubtless welcome. Ivry had been in the ducal demesne throughout the reign of Duke William, and Robert Curthose may well have been regretting the "foolish prodigality"[134] that had led him to grant it out. Certainly, no reservation of loyalty to the duke seems to have existed between Ascelin and William to prevent the latter from attempting to punish the former for doing a service helpful to the duke but harmful to the lord. At most, therefore, the four examples of reservations of loyalty and of liege homage indicate that liegeance was beginning to spread in Normandy by the last three decades of the century.

In addition to the other obscurities in William Paynel's agreement with the abbot of Mont-Saint-Michel, there is a problem concerning Hugh de Bricqueville's nephew, who owes the service of castle-guard only if he holds in parage and in proportion to how much he holds. This is the only use of the word "parage" in the eleventh-century Norman documents, but the practice seems to have been fairly well known. It would seem probable that Hugh's nephew might hold in parage as the son of Hugh's younger brother, who himself had once held in parage from Hugh. The reference to proportion suggests that Hugh and his nephew together would perform forty days of castle-guard service, each serving the same fraction of the service—fraction of the time? fraction of the total number of "horsemen" who had to serve with them?—as he held of the combined fee. The sentence construction, however, implies that Hugh's nephew's service was to be in addition to Hugh's own. No other source permits resolution of this difficulty, even by analogy, which is most unfortunate, because, if it were certain that the service was to be divided in proportion to the amount of land each man held, we should have evidence—such as is otherwise lacking—that by the late eleventh century in Normandy service was at least occasionally considered to be proportional to the amount of land held.

Only one source gives any detail at all of the requirements of military service other than the limits that might be placed upon it. At the end of his agreement with Saint-Amand, Baudry notes that the knights whose services he had temporarily renounced "were thus equipped when they did service: one of them with full arms; the other, however, with plain arms."[135] In later days, the distinction between full arms and plain arms

133. Orderic, *Historia Ecclesiastica*, ed. Chibnall, 4:198; translation by Chibnall, ibid., 4:199.

134. Ibid., 4:114; translation by Chibnall, ibid., 4:115.

135. See above, at n. 108 and accompanying text.

was the principal military distinction between knights and those vavassors who owed military service.[136] Here, however, both men are called knights, although the term "vavassor" was in current use.[137] The next time the two types of armament are distinguished is in the Bayeux Inquest, where plain arms are all that is required of vavassors.[138] Because Baudry's charter is the only extant reference to the eleventh-century requirements for military equipment, interpretation of the distinction it makes—beyond the obvious fact that two degrees of armament were known and that different degrees might be required of different soldiers as a standing arrangement—is impossible.

This, such as it is, is all the information contained in eleventh-century Norman sources on the subject of military service in return for fiefs. There is somewhat more information about castle-guard than about host service; indeed, we know at least as much about suit of court or about the feudal incidents as about either aspect of the duty to serve in arms.[139] The amount known about the definitions of the requirements of host service—supposedly one of the distinctive characteristics of the Norman feudal "system"—is truly paltry. There are three references to *servicia debita*; but that term itself never appears in a technical sense, and of the two references in William Paynel's charter one concerns castle-guard and the other only very dubiously refers to host service. William Paynel's charter is the only one to refer to the cost of service. There are two mentions—one concerning castle-guard, the other apparently referring to host service—of a forty-day limit on service; a few allusions to unlimited service, one of which may imply that a geographical limit on service was possible; and one reference to certain required types of arms. Liege homage appears by name three times, and there is one set of reservations of loyalty to the duke. There is only one possible indication that service might be predicated on the amount of land held. Moreover, these few references come from documents written in the last three decades of the century.

All this does not, of course, mean that military service was scarcely known in Normandy in the eleventh century. Obviously the duke could raise an army, and so could his magnates—for him, against him, and in

136. Navel, "Enquête," pp. 51–54; Navel, "Recherches," pp. 105, 107.

137. It is used as early as Fauroux, *Recueil*, p. 76, no. 5 (Saint-Taurin d'Evreux, between 962 and 996). The most recent work on the meaning of the term "vavassor" is Jean Yver, "'Vavassor,' note sur les premiers emplois du terme," *Revue historique de droit français et étranger*, 4th ser. 52 (1974): 548–49. Yver questions the contemporaneity of the language of Fauroux, *Recueil*, no. 5, but points out that the term was certainly in use from the early eleventh century on. On the meaning of the term, see also Navel, "Recherches," p. 78.

138. Navel, "Enquête," pp. 19, 21; see also Haskins, *Norman Institutions*, p. 20. There is no mention of the full arms presumably demanded of knights. On the armament of Norman vavassors in general, see P. Guilhiermoz, *Essai sur l'origine de la noblesse en France au moyen âge* (Paris, 1902), pp. 185–88 and nn.

139. See Tabuteau, "Transfers of Property," pp. 402–80, on these subjects. Both Gleason, *Ecclesiastical Barony*, pp. 74–75, and Barlow, *William*, p. 110, suggest that castle-guard—and, Barlow adds, messenger and escort service—were in fact more important than host service.

their own quarrels. Equally obviously, in the charters, service was owed for fiefs. The absence from the sources of all but the slightest indications of definitions of the terms of military service does, however, suggest that the still generally accepted picture of the development of feudal practices in Normandy and in Norman England is in need of drastic revision. The same conclusion would emerge from detailed study of the nonmilitary feudal obligations. It seems unlikely that precisely defined obligations were imported in developed form from Normandy to England in 1066. Instead, it is probable that at the time of the conquest, Norman practices were many and various, and often not precisely defined, and that after 1066 these practices were gradually regularized both in Normandy and in England, perhaps more rapidly in the latter country, where the situation of the conquerors gave them the opportunity and the incentive to define their own and their vassals' obligations.

If this was indeed the general course of development, a few remarks about its chronology are in order. The *terminus ante quem* for the development in Normandy of definitions of the obligations of service is 1133, when the jurors of the Bayeux Inquest stated the obligations of the bishop's tenants in terms of precise types and amounts due from specific pieces of land. Although, as we have seen, some definitions may have been made or altered after this time, an understanding that service can normally be defined in these ways underlies the Inquest. But there is little sign of such precision in the earlier documents, not only those of William the Conqueror's reign but also those from the reign of Robert Curthose. Therefore, it would seem likely that the process of definition in Normandy was most effective in the years after Henry I took control of the duchy in 1106. More than his father, who had been duke of Normandy for thirty-one years before becoming king of England, or his brother, whose contacts with England were comparatively few and brief, Henry I was English rather than Norman. Moreover, the Norman magnates of his reign were the second or even the third generation in their families to have held land in England, considerably more land in many cases than they held in Normandy. If definition had proceeded faster in England than in Normandy, it is not unlikely that such men would have attempted to introduce into their feudal relations in Normandy what they perceived as the advantages of their feudal relations in England or—less deliberately—that practices with which they had become familiar in England would, willy-nilly, have influenced their behavior and the arrangements that they made in Normandy. Detailed study of the nature of feudal relations in Normandy in the first third of the twelfth century may some day make it possible to document the course of development, whether it be this one or another. For the present, however, it remains merely the best hypothesis that Normandy became "one of the most fully developed feudal societies in Europe"[140] not under the predecessors of William the Conqueror but under the greatest of his sons.

140. Haskins, *Norman Institutions*, p. 5.

3 Inheritance by Women in the Twelfth and Early Thirteenth Centuries

S. F. C. Milsom

Inheritance and Family Provision: The Background

Inheritance and family provision in the twelfth and early thirteenth centuries were affected by two kinds of interest. The family interest had no doubt produced many differing customs, and at a humble level some survived to appear in the manor court rolls of the late thirteenth century.[1] At higher levels and in the king's court more pressure was exerted by what may be called the feudal interest; and questions were asked and answered in feudal terms. The feudal dimension has been explored elsewhere.[2] Its essence is that land was not owned, but allocated by lord to tenant in return for service. The customs were not about abstract rights, metaphysical name tags stuck into the earth. They were about powers and obligations, about what individual people could and should do.

Who should do what when a tenant dies? At least formally the lord could take the land into his own hand. But if the tenant had done homage and left an heir, the lord could not keep it for himself. That he must make a new arrangement with whomever his court decided to be the heir was a settled consequence of homage before rules were settled determining in every case who the heir was. Suppose the simplest case. The tenant had been married once, had two sons and one daughter, and is survived by all three children and by his wife. However clear it is that the elder son gets the land, he gets it not by operation of law but because the lord gives it to him.

But it does not follow that the elder son is entitled to enjoy for himself the whole of what the lord has now given to him. He may be under a similar obligation to honor allocations made from it by his father. When the father married, he would have made an allocation to his wife by way of dower. That was an internal arrangement, no concern of the lord's: and now that the father is dead, the obligation to honor it falls not upon the lord but upon the heir. Similarly, the father may have made an allocation to his daughter. Normally he does this when she marries, and the land is said to be given "with" the daughter to her husband. We shall return to the language, but may mention here the difficulties that arise when a father tries to provide for his daughter before her marriage. There is nobody to whom the land can physically be given, so he keeps it for her

1. George Caspar Homans, *English Villagers of the Thirteenth Century* (1941; reprint ed., New York, 1960), chaps. 8–14.

2. S. F. C. Milsom, *The Legal Framework of English Feudalism* (Cambridge, 1976).

as *custos*; and then it can be argued that the allocation was never made.[3] If the father's allocations were properly made, the son must warrant both the daughter's *maritagium* and the widow's dower; and it is in his court, not the lord's, that both must make their claims.

The claims of widow and daughter against the heir are of the same nature as the heir's own claim to be given his inheritance by the lord. But there is a difference in intensity. For the heir's claim to his inheritance, there is a kind of external sanction flowing from his father's homage. When we read that homage is not done for dower or *maritagium*, we are not being told just that homage does not feature in the list of incidents associated with two "estates" whose properties are independently fixed. Homage is a prime force, and its presence or absence determines many features of the relationship. In the case of *maritagium*, what we read is that the arrangement somehow changed its nature when the third heir from the original donee entered, and also that he was the first to do homage to the donor or his heir. But in reality homage could be taken at any time: the only magic about the third heir was that by custom he could require it to be taken.[4] Whenever it was taken, two consequences followed. The less important was that the land must now bear its share of the service due to the lord from the inheritance as a whole: if the *maritagium* had been *liberum*, there would have been no such obligation before. The more important consequence was that homage transformed a provisional family arrangement into a tenure as durable as that by which the heir himself held the inheritance of the lord.

Suppose that after the father's death the daughter and her husband die leaving an only son, who does homage to his elder uncle, the present tenant of the inheritance. If now the daughter's son himself dies childless, his land must go to his heir; and if we think in terms of abstract rules of inheritance, that would be the same elder uncle. But those are the wrong terms. The uncle is lord, debarred from having the land by the homage he has taken, obliged to give it to whoever is heir on that basis: and in our case it will be his own younger brother.[5] The land originally given to the daughter cannot reunite with the inheritance itself. It was precisely to avoid that result that homage was normally not taken so early. Provision for the daughter was at the expense of the heir, a subtraction from the resources available to sustain the services due to the lord. But until homage was done, it was not a permanent subtraction: if the daughter herself died childless, or if her issue failed before homage was done, the land simply came back to the heir of the donor. As the daughter's issue lengthened out, it was increasingly unlikely that it would fail, that this land would any way revert to the parent inheritance; and so there was no harm in stabilizing the situation by homage. It is now a purely feudal and not a family arrangement.

The special feature of the daughter's *maritagium* was therefore the

3. Ibid., pp. 145–46.
4. Ibid., p. 143.
5. Ibid., pp. 139–43.

obligation on her father's heir to maintain it, even beyond her own lifetime, although her husband had not done homage. This obligation existed in the heir's own court; but it had also an independent sanction. As against the father and his heirs, the daughter could claim in the church courts on the basis of a breach of faith.[6] But the feudal interest did not permit any such provision for the younger son. The father could make him an allocation, and the elder son could choose to maintain it. But there was no custom like that of dower or *maritagium* whereby the father could oblige the elder son to maintain his allocation, even for the life of the younger son. The only way in which the father could guarantee the younger son's enjoyment was to take his homage; and this he often did.[7] But the effect lasted beyond the life of the younger son and beyond the continuance of heirs issuing from him. So long as there was any other heir, the land could never come back to the parent inheritance. It was to avoid that result that grants came to be made to a man and the heirs of his body: the fee tail could mitigate the family hardship of primogeniture without permanently detaching land from the inheritance. But this paper looks backwards rather than forwards. The integrity of the inheritance was important because of the nature of the central transaction. When he first made his grant, the lord was not just allocating resources within his control. As the word and the act of homage remind us, he was securing for himself a man.

Women Inheriting

A lord would never have made his initial arrangement with a woman. Is he obliged to renew it with a woman? So long as the question was asked in those terms, and not in terms of the devolution of property, uniform answers would be slow to develop. But it is not only that uniform customs of inheritance seem to be later for females than for males. They are different in nature.

Let us begin with some familiar learning of the thirteenth century. If a military tenant left an infant male heir, the lord should at once take the infant's homage and so acknowledge his own absolute obligation to deliver the land to this heir.[8] But he did not make livery, and before 1176 did not necessarily take homage, until the heir came of age; and meanwhile he held both land and heir in *custodia*. At any rate at first, that *custodia* was not some special entity peculiar to this situation: we have seen that the father allocating land to his daughter before her marriage

6. *Tractatus de legibus et consuetudinibus regni Anglie qui Glanvilla vocatur*, ed. and trans. G. D. G. Hall (London, 1965) (hereafter cited as *Glanvill*), VII, 18 (p. 93).

7. *Glanvill*, VII, 1 (pp. 72–73); Milsom, *Legal Framework*, pp. 137–42.

8. *Glanvill*, IX, 1 (p. 103); Assize of Northampton, c. 4. For the latter text see William Stubbs, ed., *Select Charters and Other Illustrations of English Constitutional History . . .*, 9th ed., rev. by H. W. C. Davis (1913; reprint ed., Oxford, 1946), pp. 179–81.

would hold the land himself as *custos*.[9] Now suppose that the military tenant died leaving only an infant daughter. The lord cannot take homage, and so commit himself directly to her. His obligation is still that flowing from the homage he took from her father: he must not keep the land for himself and must hand it over to the father's heir, but he has not foreclosed discussion of who that is. Again, he holds land and daughter in *custodia*; but this *custodia* is not going to end when she attains some age, and he is never going to make livery to her. What he should do when she comes of age is to arrange a marriage for her; and then he will deliver land with daughter to the husband, and take the husband's homage for her inheritance. Whose now is the land? It is an anachronistic question to which this essay seeks terms appropriate to the time. Parts of the answer are that the husband has become the lord's man, and that his holding of his wife's land can be described, like the lord's own before the marriage, as in *custodia*.

Now let us turn to some familiar documents. The interior changes by which tenure ceased to be something like a contract of service and became something like an ownership of land left few visible traces in the way of demands for conscious adjustment. The most obvious are about the regularization of inheritance and its corollaries. Not counting initial assurances to the church, this is the concern of the first three clauses (in the conventional numbering) of the Coronation Charter of Henry I,[10] and of the first seven clauses of the Great Charter of John.[11] Both charters address themselves to the most fundamental point of all, the fixing of reliefs.[12] The earlier has to express the matter in elementary terms: the heir must not be made to buy back his land. Both address themselves also to what looks like a detail: widows should not be compelled to remarry. King John contemplates that the widow may have *hereditas* as well as dower and *maritagium*;[13] and though he was probably denying himself only an income from sales, it is worth recalling that even in the thirteenth century the husband's death left a widow in control of her inheritance for the first time. From her father it had passed directly into the *custodia* of the lord or his nominee, and thence into the *custodia* of the husband. Henry's undertaking extends in terms only to dower and *maritagium*.[14] He does not mention the widow with *hereditas*. Perhaps she was omitted by mistake, and he reckoned that she could make provision for the services due from her inheritance. That she could make such provision for the services due from her husband's inheritance is the assumption behind Henry's seeming liberality in conceding *custodia* to her or some

9. See above, pp. 60–61.
10. Cc. 2–4. For this text, see Stubbs, *Select Charters*, pp. 117–19.
11. (1215) cc. 2–8; (1225) cc. 2–7. For these two texts, see J. C. Holt, *Magna Carta* (Cambridge, 1965), pp. 316–37, 350–58.
12. Coronation Charter, c. 2; Magna Carta (both versions), c. 2.
13. (1215) cc. 7, 8; (1225) c. 7.
14. Coronation Charter, cc. 3, 4.

other relative.[15] This remained the logic of socage wardships. It was only when the value of military service visibly lost all relation to the actual revenues of the land that a lord would invite bids for a *custodia* or keep the revenues for himself; and that left consequential problems of waste for John's charter to deal with.[16]

But other explanations are possible for the silence of Henry's charter about the widow with *hereditas*. The simplest is that Henry would indeed compel her to remarry, in the sense of depriving her of the inheritance if she refused. The most fundamental is that he did not contemplate that she would hold the inheritance anyway. Dower was meant to be the widow's provision for life. So, as a minimum even if there were no children, was *maritagium*. Perhaps *hereditas* was hers to transmit rather than to enjoy for herself. In their dealings with baronies, it was an attitude still sometimes taken by Henry's grandson and great-grandson. Redbourne was the inheritance of Maud, granddaughter of the Domesday tenant. Maud was married to Reginald de Crevequer, who died between 1165 and 1172, and was herself still living in 1185. But her inheritance passed on Reginald's death to one of their sons; and before Maud died it had passed again to the issue of another.[17] Later, as we shall see, these events were to be rationalized in other terms.[18] But they happened. Again, when William de Mandeville died in 1189, the "heir" to his great barony of Pleshy was his aunt Beatrice de Say, who still had some eight years to live. But Richard I at once gave the inheritance to one of her two sons, then took it back and gave it to the issue of the other.[19] In each case the disposition actually made will be of interest in other contexts. But the disposition that was not made may be even more significant. The king's dealings with his tenants-in-chief seem to have been exceptional only in continuing what had been the understood powers of lords in general; and in passing over the widows, Henry II and Richard may have done what Henry I assumed that any lord would do. His charter is silent because the question has not arisen.

On the question of women inheriting in the first place, John's charter is silent for the converse reason: so far as concerned the dealings of lords with their tenants, the question seemed to be settled. But Henry's Coronation Charter has to deal with it; and it is worth reminding ourselves of the nature of such a document. The king is neither legislating nor

15. Coronation Charter, c. 4.

16. Magna Carta (both versions), cc. 4, 5.

17. *Curia Regis Rolls* (London, 1922–) (hereafter cited as *CRR*), 2:218, 223–24; *CRR*, 3:317; *The Earliest Lincolnshire Assize Rolls, A.D. 1202–09*, ed. Doris M. Stenton, Lincoln Record Society, vol. 22 (1926), pp. lxxx–lxxxii; I. J. Sanders, *English Baronies: A Study of their Origin and Descent, 1086–1327* (Oxford, 1960), p. 74.

18. See below, p. 68.

19. *Ancient Charters Royal and Private, prior to 1200*, ed. J. H. Round, Pipe Roll Society, vol. 10 (London, 1888), pp. 97–99 (no. 59); Sanders, *English Baronies*, p. 71. Cf. Sidney Painter, *The Reign of King John* (1949; reprint ed., Baltimore, 1964), p. 263: "But no king was likely to take seriously the claims of an elderly widow to the great Mandeville barony."

codifying. He is giving undertakings about his own use of his powers as lord of his own men, and commanding them to treat theirs in the same way. But until that command is regularly enforced, there is no law in these matters except what he and other lords actually do. He may be setting up as the model what he thinks the best of current practice. But he makes law only to the extent that his model is followed in current practice. For the parties to any individual dispute, it is not even current practice that matters: it is what the court dealing with that dispute actually decides.

The Coronation Charter first deals with the living tenant arranging a marriage for his daughter or other female relative. He should speak with the king or other lord, who, however, is not to demand payment, and not to refuse consent unless the proposed husband is an enemy.[20] Some ninety years later, Glanvill makes a more stringent statement. He confines it to the tenant having only a daughter or daughters, and says that he may be disinherited for arranging the unlicensed marriage.[21] For Glanvill, there is a rule by which the daughter automatically inherits her father's land; and only by disinheriting the father can the lord be saved from having to accept the homage of one who may be an enemy. For Henry I, his more relaxed provision suggests that there was some choice about a woman inheriting. One with an unacceptable husband could simply be passed over. But customs were becoming established, and it was better that the difficulty should not arise.

Henry's charter states one custom that he proposed to follow: "si mortuo barone vel alio homine meo filia haeres remanserit, illam dabo consilio baronum meorum cum terra sua."[22] This contemplates that a daughter can in some circumstances be *haeres*: but it does not show an automatic inheritance according to fixed rules, let alone the particular rules that came later to be fixed. In terms it is a promise about the marriage of a lone unmarried daughter; and she will be *haeres* in the sense that the land will be given with her to the man chosen as her husband. Nothing indicates that several unmarried daughters would all be *haeredes*. And it is possible that *filia haeres remanserit* confines the inheritance to the unmarried daughter who had remained with her father, to the exclusion of those already married. Suppose the father had three daughters, and had married off two in his lifetime. Those two would each have received *maritagium*; and even from the family point of view, it would make sense to leave the married daughters with what they had, and allow the remaining one to inherit what was left. This is an aspect of the matter to which we shall return in the last section of this paper.[23] Our present concern is with the lord's own interest; and though he might have consented to the earlier marriages, this solution would give him the homage of the man whom he himself had chosen. Nor is this pure

20. C. 3.
21. *Glanvill*, VII, 12 (p. 85).
22. Coronation Charter, c. 3.
23. See below, p. 81.

speculation. King John had so granted the whole inheritance of William de Buckland with the youngest of his three daughters; and when the two elder and their husbands sued in 1218 for their shares, the youngest and her husband sought to have the question postponed until Henry III was of age. It was, they said, a right that all his predecessors had enjoyed in such circumstances to give *postnatam filiam que remaneret in hereditate patris sui* to one of his knights with the whole inheritance.[24]

The contention was limited to the king and apparently to the lifetime of the favored daughter; and anyway it was unsuccessful. But that was in 1218 when regularization was far advanced and all daughters understood to be entitled to their shares; and there is no reason to think it was without basis in the earlier practice at least of kings. Henry's charter contemplates a single daughter, and we shall return to the question of sharing. But even when sharing was clearly established, we sometimes find that a claim is by an elder sister or her issue against a younger.[25] Generally, of course, we do not know what had happened when the ancestor died, how the younger came to get the whole. But we do know in a case of 1201–3 concerning a royal serjeanty, a tenure in which the actual service has continued to matter. A tenant dying under Henry II had left two sisters, and the issue of the elder are suing the son of the younger. He relies simply upon Henry's charter granting the whole to his father as husband of the younger sister.[26]

We do not know whether Henry II had arranged the marriage in that case or had chosen between already married husbands. Only if the youngest daughter was the only one unmarried would she be in a specially favorable position. The general principle, if anybody thought in those terms, was perhaps that the father's homage constrained the lord to choose one of the daughters; but which he chose would depend upon her husband, as much as her seniority. In one sense, as we shall see, he chose a single daughter until well into the thirteenth century; but regularization prescribed that he should choose the eldest. With holdings of mesne lords, we only once find it argued that the lord's disposition is in itself conclusive.[27] But for baronies the king clearly chose a single sister, and supposed that his choice was final. We have already mentioned the case of the great Mandeville barony of Pleshy, when Richard I passed over the widowed Beatrice de Say, made and revoked a grant to her younger son, and gave it to the issue of her dead elder son. That son had left two daughters, Beatrice II, who was married to Geoffrey fitz Peter, and

24. *Bracton's Note Book*, ed. Frederic W. Maitland, 3 vols. (London, 1887) (hereafter cited as *BNB*), no. 12.

25. (a) *Three Rolls of the King's Court in the Reign of King Richard the First, 1194–1195*, ed. Frederic W. Maitland, Pipe Roll Society, vol. 14 (London, 1891), pp. 6, 30–31, 49, 54; *Rotuli Curiae Regis*, ed. Francis Palgrave, 2 vols. (London, 1835) (hereafter cited as *RCR*), 1:13; (b) *CRR*, 5:46–47, 149; (c) *CRR*, 9:14, 284–85; *CRR*, 10:19, 20, 54, 177; *BNB*, no. 302; (d) *BNB*, no. 12.

26. *CRR*, 2:25, 68, 232; *CRR*, 3:40.

27. *CRR*, 6:119, 133, 190, 199–200, 295 (inheritance partitioned earlier, dispute over land formerly held by widow in dower).

Maud, who was married to William de Buckland (whose own inheritance, as we have seen, King John was to grant to the youngest of his daughters, to the exclusion of the two elder). King Richard gave the barony to Beatrice II, or rather to Geoffrey fitz Peter; and Maud got nothing. That was in 1191. It was not until 1218 that Maud felt able to claim her share, and even then the case disappears with an adjournment "eo quod consilium domini regis non audet facere judicium super cartas domini regis."[28] In the Mandeville case the sister preferred was in fact the elder. But consider what was done and what was said in the case of Aldington. William fitz Helte had died in 1180 leaving three sisters. In 1206–8 we find the son of the middle sister suing a third-party contender, who argues that he need not answer unless the heirs of the other two are joined. To this the demandant has his answer: "dominus rex reddidit ei jus quod fuit Willelmi Helte sicut recto heredi pro ccc. marcis argenti."[29]

The Mandeville case, and that of Redbourne, also already mentioned for the immediate grant of a widowed heiress's own inheritance to her issue, both exemplify another choice that a lord might have between possible heirs. In each the sisters concerned were daughters of a dead elder son, and there was a living younger son. An important study of the *casus regis* is expected soon; and little can be said with confidence until it comes. But the question probably seemed different when one of the possible heirs was a woman. Consider King John's own case. When Richard I died there was another claimant to the English crown: Arthur of Brittany was the twelve-year-old son of John's dead elder brother Geoffrey. A few years later Arthur died, and John is generally believed to have seen to that.[30] But for Arthur's sister Eleanor, John and his son after him judged it sufficient to keep her an honored and unmarried prisoner.[31]

28. For the original disposition see references in n. 19. For the 1218 case see *BNB*, no. 8; *CRR*, 8:117, 236; *CRR*, 9:247. Maud's claim is based on the seisin of her and Beatrice II's father, who had however died long before the Mandeville inheritance fell vacant. There is no mention of the agreement dividing the father's inheritance, apparently made in 1185 after the sisters were married (cf. *Rotuli de Dominabus* [1185], ed. J. H. Round, Pipe Roll Society, vol. 35 [London, 1913], pp. 49–50), confirmed in 1198 (*Ancient Charters*, pp. 108–10 [no. 66]), and entered on the pipe roll at Geoffrey fitz Peter's instance a few months later (*Pipe Roll, 10 Richard I*, ed. Doris M. Stenton, Pipe Roll Society, n.s., vol. 9 [London, 1932], p. 139). The confirmation is less emphatic than the enrollment about releasing Maud's rights, but it saves to Beatrice her *antenatio*. From the pedigree in *The Earliest Lincolnshire Assize Rolls*, pp. lxxx–lxxxii, Redbourne would appear similarly to have been granted to one of two sisters; but compare *Testa de Nevill*, Record Commission (London, 1807), p. 344, with *Book of Fees* (London, 1920–31), 1:189. Another barony giving rise to relevant disputes was Barnstaple. See *RCR*, 1:45; *RCR*, 2:179–80; *Pleas before the King or His Justices, 1198–1212*, 4 vols., ed. Doris M. Stenton, Selden Society, vols. 67 (London, 1948), 68 (1949), 83 (1966), 84 (1967) (hereafter cited as *PKJ*), 1, nos. 2093, 2473, 3198; Sanders, *English Baronies*, p. 104.

29. *CRR*, 4:140, 161; *CRR*, 5:19, 282; *PKJ*, 3 and 4, nos. 1746, 1785, 2120, 2374, 3159; Sanders, *English Baronies*, p. 1.

30. Painter, *King John*, p. 85: "John himself saw to Arthur."

31. Her English lands were held in *custodia*; cf. (a) *CRR*, 9:13, 237–38, 328; *CRR*, 10:215; (b) *CRR*, 9:142–43.

King John's future predicament cannot have been envisaged by Henry II in his dealings with Redbourne: they were all over before Geoffrey of Brittany was dead or Arthur born. And it is very unlikely to have been in Richard's mind when he disposed of the Mandeville barony in 1189 and 1191. Both kings first chose the living younger son in preference to a daughter of the dead elder son; and both changed their minds. In the Mandeville case, Richard's first choice of Geoffrey de Say may have owed a little to the wishes of the widowed Beatrice: but the inheritance was granted to him in return for a proffer and transferred to his niece for default of payment. When Geoffrey and his son revived his claim in 1212–14, they relied upon an alleged seisin of Beatrice and upon the short seisin of Geoffrey himself; but the claim fails on an irrelevant ground and the *casus regis* question is not mentioned.[32] It could not be directly relevant to the lawsuit that was brought about Redbourne; but a view is implicit in an argument that deserves notice for another reason. Henry II's dealings had been even more high-handed. The inheritance was Maud's; and it is relevant that she outlived not only her elder son and her husband, who died in that order, but also her younger son. This was Simon de Crevequer, to whom the inheritance was granted on the death of his father, Maud's husband. Simon enjoyed it all his life; and only when he died leaving an infant son was it transferred to his niece Cecily and her husband. In 1203, Simon's son seeks to recover it in mort d'ancestor, on the basis that Simon had died seised; and so he had. But Cecily claims that his enjoyment had been only in right of Maud, who had really been seised of her inheritance throughout.[33] By 1203 inheritance was seen as a matter of rules, and rules that were supposed always to have existed; and a widowed heiress was left in possession subject only to a possible condition of having to remarry at the lord's will. Cecily had herself been a widow for some five years, and seems to have controlled the barony until her death. Looking back on what happened from that framework, her interpretation was a natural one. But it would have surprised Henry II, who was dealing in facts rather than abstractions.

Except for the fact that she had got in, the niece in each of these cases was in the situation of Eleanor of Brittany; and King John's court could hardly have allowed the abstractions to be declared in her favor. Nor should we be misled by our own label of "representation" into assuming that from the beginning the niece's claim was indistinguishable from the nephew's. The lord's need of a man merged into a general preference for the male line. A less exalted case of 1220 shows that the younger son had again got in; and his niece, perhaps for the political reason, bases her claim on special facts. On the occasion of the elder son's marriage, she says, the father of the two sons resigned (*se demisit*) the inheritance in his favor; and the father held thereafter only by grace of the elder son. On

32. For other aspects of the matter see references in nn. 19 and 28. For the 1212–14 case see *CRR*, 6:270; *CRR*, 7:57, 110–11.

33. See above, n. 17.

that basis the elder son died seised, although in his father's lifetime, and his daughter makes her claim in an assize of mort d'ancestor. The assize finds that the elder son did not die seised; and the younger son is left in possession with no direct discussion of the point of principle.[34] But in the same year, in a case brought on the king's own behalf as guardian, the king's court has no hesitation in affirming that the son of a dead son is to be preferred to living and married daughters: "quia . . . ipse est de masculo, consideratum est quod . . . majus jus habeat in terra illa."[35]

Sharing the Inheritance

The early understanding seems to have been that a lord would grant the whole inheritance to the husband of one daughter, but might have some discretion in choosing which. This section will consider how these two propositions changed. The next will try to make out the properties of the husband's holding.

First, the lord's discretion became restricted to his control over the marriage of any daughter. He still had a voice in choosing husbands, but lost any power to choose between them. The eldest daughter and her husband acquired a right. This change could not be complete until the king's court would regularly override whatever other disposition the lord and his court had in fact made; and it is one aspect of the invisible change that came over all inheritance. If a past choice can be overridden, you cease to think in terms of choice or even of controlling choice: you think in terms of an abstract right, passing independently of what people have actually done. There is a formula in which pedigree and chronology are the only variables. By 1200 it is assumed that the eldest is automatically entitled.[36] But we have already mentioned cases about that time in which it is an elder sister who is having to sue a younger;[37] and the uniform assumption may not be very old. How did it grow? In lords' courts the natural preference would be not for the first-born but for the eldest who was unmarried when the father died, the first whose husband would be a man of the lord's own choosing. But there is enough talk of *esnecia* (which comes in many spellings) to suggest that the first-born was thought to have some inherent claim; and she was the obvious choice for a single formula. In early usage *esnecia* sometimes denotes the right of an elder son as against a younger,[38] and Glanvill's only use of the word also refers to males. He says that an inheritance partible between males will

34. *CRR*, 9:178–79, 322; *CRR*, 10:136–37, 267(?); *CRR*, 11, no. 658(?); *BNB*, no. 1462.

35. *CRR*, 9:268–69; *CRR*, 10:61.

36. *CRR*, 1:250–51. Cf. the obscure *CRR*, 12, no. 1839.

37. See above, nn. 25, 26.

38. (a) *CRR*, 7:338; *RCR*, 2:88–89; *CRR*, 1:179, 180, 226; *PKJ*, 1, no. 2973; (b) *RCR*, 1:363.

be divided "saluo tamen capitali mesagio filio primogenito pro dignitate ainsnecie sue."[39]

The word is most commonly used in connection with a changed reality in female inheritance. The lord loses any choice, but his choice ceases to be important. The invariable right of the eldest daughter is subject to a kind of trust in favor of the others. *Esnecia* is used to denote whatever features of that arrangement are under discussion in the case.[40] Glanvill's reference to an inheritance partible between males makes a good starting point. With military tenures the capital messuage was never just a matter of *dignitas*. It was the headquarters of a fee.[41] Here the lord paramount would distrain the lord of the fee; and here the lord of the fee would hold court for his own tenants. It was the heart of the inheritance, not to be allocated in dower (the usual context of its mention in lawsuits) or in *maritagium*. And when the inheritance came to be partitioned between sisters, this was something that the eldest must keep for herself, although reckoning its value as part of her share.

The essence of the parage arrangement is well known.[42] The lord still had a single tenant. The whole inheritance was held of him by the eldest sister and her husband; and it was the eldest sister's husband who did homage and who was responsible for the whole service. So far as the lord was concerned, that was that. Provision for the younger sisters was an internal arrangement within the inheritance like dower and *maritagium*. The younger sisters held of the eldest, and they and their husbands reimbursed the eldest and her husband for their share of the services. But the husband of a younger sister did not do homage to the husband of the eldest.[43] As in *maritagium*, homage would not be done for a younger sister's share until her third heir entered; and this must have been for the same reason as in *maritagium*. Suppose there were three sisters, and the husbands of the two younger did homage to the husband of the eldest: if the second sister died without issue, her third share could only pass intact

39. *Glanvill*, VII, 3 (p. 75).

40. (a) *Three Rolls of the King's Court*, pp. 6, 30–31, 49, 54; *RCR*, 1:13; (b) *Memoranda Roll, 10 John*, ed. R. Allen Brown, Pipe Roll Society, n.s., vol. 31 (London, 1955), p. 109; *RCR*, 1:147; *CRR*, 1:50, 80; *CRR*, 2:92; (c) *CRR*, 1:350; (d) *CRR*, 1:225, 447–48, 453; (e) *CRR*, 4:162; (f) *CRR*, 5:46–47, 149; (g) *Rolls of the Justices in Eyre for Yorkshire, 1218–19*, ed. Doris M. Stenton, Selden Society, vol. 56 (London, 1937), no. 304; (h) *CRR*, 8:145, 185, 213–15; *BNB*, no. 86; (i) *CRR*, 8:387; *CRR*, 9:214, 294; *CRR*, 10:17, 196; *CRR*, 11, no. 394; cf. *CRR*, 8:24–25; (j) *CRR* 10:17–18, 106; (k) *CRR*, 10:166–67, 196; (l) *CRR*, 11, no. 1223; *CRR*, 12, nos. 360, 866, 914, 1576, 2045; (m) *CRR*, 12, nos. 249, 1771; (n) *CRR*, 11, nos. 2019, 2682; *CRR*, 12, no. 256; *BNB*, nos. 924, 1053. For *antenatio*, see *Ancient Charters*, pp. 108–10 (no. 66); for the context of this document see above, n. 28.

41. (a) *CRR*, 7:25, 41, 48; (b) *BNB*, no. 1207.

42. *Glanvill*, VII, 3 (p. 76); Sir Frederick Pollock and Frederic W. Maitland, *The History of English Law before the Time of Edward I*, 2d ed., reissued with a new introduction and select bibliography by S. F. C. Milsom, 2 vols. (Cambridge, 1968) (hereafter cited as *P&M*), 2:274–78.

43. *Glanvill*, VII, 3 (p. 76); IX, 2 (p. 106).

to the youngest; and if issue of the youngest then failed, her two-thirds would have to go to a younger son of the eldest line. The homage would prevent the eldest sister and her heirs from increasing their original third share until there were no other heirs of the younger sisters. After three generations it was unlikely that the inheritance would reunite anyway, and so the dependent tenures might as well be stabilized by homage.

Except that shares are equal, the relationship between the eldest sister and her husband and the younger sisters is exactly that between a male heir and his sisters having *maritagium*; and both arrangements are a compromise between family provision and the lord's interest in the integrity of the inheritance. That interest depended upon his vision of a tenure as a source of service, the same vision that allowed Henry I to concede *custodia* to an infant heir's mother or other relative on the understanding that she would arrange for the service to be done.[44] It was the increasingly obvious unreality of military service compared with the actual revenues of the land that gave independent value to what became thought of as the separate "incidents of tenure." In the language of investment, *custodia* and escheat were the lord's residuary interest in the equity of the land. When they were what mattered, and when the integrity of the inheritance did not matter, the parage arrangement worked against a lord's interest. An infancy in a younger sister's holding properly brought no wardship either to the eldest sister or to the lord: the eldest just continued to take contribution to the service. An infancy in the eldest sister's holding could therefore bring little more than her share to the lord. Rather belatedly, parage vanished and the lord came to take homage in respect of all the sisters' holdings. But that is not our present concern.

There are many reflections of the living reality in the early records. The commonest is an express reservation of *esnecia* in claims or arrangements for partition,[45] or a reservation of the capital messuage,[46] or some reference to tenure between sisters.[47] But litigation might turn on the tenurial details of the arrangement. The question may be between the lord and the representative of the eldest line. In 1223 it concerns the power to sanction a marriage in the younger line.[48] In 1220 the lord has been distraining on the younger line, and the eldest sues to stop it; and a fine dating from Henry II is recited, which sets out the parage in detail.[49] Or

44. See above, n. 15.

45. (a) *Rolls of the Justices in Eyre for Yorkshire*, no. 304; (b) *CRR*, 10:166–67, 196; (c) *CRR*, 11, no. 1223; *CRR*, 12, nos. 360, 866, 914, 1576, 2045.

46. *BNB*, no. 137. Cf. (a) *CRR*, 4:162; (b) *CRR*, 10:17–18, 106.

47. (a) *RCR*, 1:147; *Memoranda Roll, 10 John*, p. 110; (b) *PKJ*, 1, nos. 2085, 2475, 3488; *CRR*, 1:157; (c) *CRR*, 10:97–99, 187, 281–82; *CRR*, 12, nos. 507, 1751; (d) *CRR*, 11, nos. 523, 1065, 2029; cf. *CRR*, 6:161, 200–201, 254, 282–83; *CRR*, 7:47, 194–95, 235, 298; (e) *CRR*, 11, no. 2090.

48. *CRR*, 11, nos. 132, 420, 742, 1331; *BNB*, no. 1596. Maitland thought the marriage concerned was that of the son of a younger sister (*P&M*, 2:277). Some mistake may have been made by the plea roll clerk; but the nature of the dispute is clear enough.

49. *CRR*, 8:387; *CRR*, 9:214, 294; *CRR*, 10:17, 196; *CRR*, 11, no. 394. Cf. *CRR*, 11, no. 869; *BNB*, no. 1639.

the question may be between the two lines. In 1225 the representative of the elder has to sue the younger for contribution to the relief he has paid to the lord for the inheritance.[50] In 1221 yet another tenurial level comes into it: the question is whether a tenant of the inheritance still holds of the eldest or has been attorned to a younger.[51] Another case in the same year shows that in this context, as in that of *maritagium*, it is not only historians who have found the three degrees confusing.[52] A quarrel about the share of a dead sister brings into question also the original sharing; and the representatives of the younger sisters offer homage to the lord, which the grandson of the eldest resists, saying, "ipse exiuit de primogenita sorore et fuit ad tercium genu et ideo debuit ipse facere homagium."[53] Degrees made a difference in the younger line, not the elder; and the difference they made was in the matter of homage to the eldest, not to the lord. But the case is interesting as well as odd, and serves to introduce a serious question. It was to the lord that all parties turned, proffering large sums for his protection. And it was the lord who in the end arranged an equitable partition, putting out the eldest whom he had himself put in. The action in the king's court is an assize of novel disseisin brought in consequence by the eldest against the lord. The assize returns a special verdict setting out the facts, and justices itinerant are sufficiently uncertain to adjourn the case to Westminster. Judgment is eventually given for the defendant lord, but it is more or less expressly based on the merits rather than on the law.

How and when did the younger sisters come to acquire their right to a share, and how was it protected and in what court? We will begin with the last of these questions. The lord's action in the case just considered, proper or not, was extrajudicial. Could the representatives of the younger sisters have brought a writ of right patent to his court? If the tenure was not military, so that each parcener would hold directly of the lord, that was clearly proper; and this seems to be the situation envisaged by most early precedents of the writ of right *de rationabili parte*.[54] But a younger sister claiming in parage could not bring her writ patent to the lord. Such a writ "must be directed to him of whom the demandant claims to hold, not to anyone else, not even to the chief lord."[55] On Glanvill's principle, the writ should go to the eldest sister. In the case of dower, also a dependent tenure within the inheritance, we know that the widow's writ of right

50. *CRR*, 11, nos. 2019, 2682; *CRR*, 12, no. 256; *BNB*, nos. 924, 1053.

51. *CRR*, 10:106–8; cf. *CRR*, 9:5; *CRR*, 10:99.

52. Cf. *CRR*, 4:2, 76, 118, 187, 219–20; *CRR*, 5:3.

53. *Rolls of the Justices in Eyre for Gloucestershire, Warwickshire, and Staffordshire, 1221–22*, ed. Doris M. Stenton, Selden Society, vol. 59 (London, 1940), nos. 1036, 1115, 1133.

54. *Early Registers of Writs*, ed. Elsa de Haas and G. D. G. Hall, Selden Society, vol. 87 (London, 1970), CA.2, CC.2–3, R.19–21. The writ in *Glanvill*, XII, 5 (p. 138), is untypical: a rent-paying messuage is held of the king, and the addressee may be a royal bailiff. Even the operative command is *facias habere*, not the usual *plenum rectum teneas*.

55. *Glanvill*, XII, 8 (p. 140).

must be directed to the heir.[56] We are not expressly told this in the case of the daughter's *maritagium*. But in an early claim by a daughter against her brother and a third party, the clerk by mistake enrolled the writ: it is directed to the brother himself.[57] Such accidents are rare, and only one early action between sisters has been found in which the legal records themselves tell us what the writ was: the actual document, dating from 1199, is one of the few early writs to survive.[58] It is not a writ patent at all, but a *precipe* bringing the dispute directly into the king's court. A parage arrangement seems to be involved, but because the land is held of the honor of Boulogne and had been the subject of an earlier fine in the king's court, no general conclusion can be drawn from that.

We have, however, information of another kind. When Miss Hurnard set out to discover how far the *precipe* was being used improperly before Magna Carta, she correlated entries in the pipe rolls of payments due for *precipe* writs with entries in the plea rolls of lawsuits between the same parties. She did not count claims for dower in which, though the plea roll often does not say so, the *precipe* of the pipe roll was probably a writ of dower *unde nichil habet* and therefore proper to the king's court.[59] But of the kinds of claim that she did count, that between sisters turned out to be the most frequent. The absolute number is not large, seven.[60] But because the pipe roll does not note all *precipe* writs, at most only those issued on credit,[61] and because actions between sisters are relatively uncommon on the plea rolls, even this small number is significant. It does not in itself tell us anything about parage, because once in the king's court the parage would not be relevant to the claim for a share, and we should not and do not see it. But it does tell us that before the Charter, claims between sisters were being started by *precipe* when strict propriety would require a writ patent to the eldest in parage and to the lord in other cases.

Magna Carta placed a general restriction on the *precipe* that restored the elementary principle in its full rigor.[62] One claiming right in land must always begin with a writ directed to the lord of whom he claimed to hold it, no matter how clear it was that the lord's court could or would do nothing, so that the claim would reach the king's court only after the

56. *Glanvill*, VI, 4 and 5 (pp. 60–1); *Early Registers of Writs*, CC.6 and note preceding it, R.16 and *Regula* preceding it.

57. *Memoranda Roll, 10 John*, pp. 105 (writ), 100–101; *CRR*, 1:41; *CRR*, 7:346. *Glanvill*, VII, 18 (p. 94), makes a procedural comparison in general terms with dower.

58. *PKJ*, 1, no. 3488 (writ; fine and confirmation also printed by the editor), 2085, 2475; *CRR*, 1:157.

59. N. D. Hurnard, "Magna Carta, Clause 34," in *Studies in Medieval History presented to Frederick Maurice Powicke*, ed. R. W. Hunt, W. A. Pantin, and R. W. Southern (Oxford, 1948), pp. 157–79, at p. 164.

60. Ibid., p. 166. Miss Hurnard suggested a different kind of explanation; but see Milsom, *Legal Framework*, pp. 69–70.

61. Ibid., p. 165.

62. Magna Carta (1215), c. 34; (1225), c. 24.

roundabout tolt and *pone*. The old undifferentiated *precipe* disappeared, and came to be replaced by special forms with clauses explaining why the particular *precipe* did not deprive a lord of jurisdiction.[63] The *precipe in capite* and *quia dominus remisit curiam* explain themselves to us as well as to contemporaries. The entry clause in a writ of entry showed that the dispute was between the demandant and one claiming to be in as the demandant's tenant, and therefore that the demandant's lord would not be concerned.[64] No such explanatory clause could have made a *precipe* obviously proper for the claim between sisters, which must be a claim to hold either of the eldest or of the lord; and one might expect that the claim would be driven back into the ambit of writs patent. But no: a new writ was developed, one not formulated with a *precipe*.

The action known as *nuper obiit* is first found in the earliest records to survive after the Charter.[65] Before the Charter a sister might possibly resort to mort d'ancestor.[66] For all the sisters against lord or stranger this was appropriate; but between sisters it was not appropriate, as a case soon after the Charter pointed out: *perquirat se alio modo si voluerit*.[67] It looks as though a new need prompted the hasty provision of a new writ, which does not, as does mort d'ancestor itself, define its own scope. It says only that the ancestor "died lately." There was doubt about the permissible remoteness of the relationship between ancestor and parties;[68] and a remarkable range of limitation periods was proposed.[69] Other restrictions came to be adopted for which there is no warrant in the words of the writ. One is taken from mort d'ancestor: the ancestor must have died seised. Another has the appearance of being taken from dower *unde nichil habet*: the demandant must have no part of the inheritance.[70]

If we think in our own terms of abstract rights and possessory remedies, it is possible to explain *nuper obiit* as extending to the parcener the rapid protection that the heir had in mort d'ancestor and the widow in

63. M. T. Clanchy, "Magna Carta, Clause Thirty-Four," *English Historical Review* 79 (1964): 542–48.

64. Milsom, *Legal Framework*, pp. 88–102.

65. *BNB*, no. 12. Bracton refers to a case now lost *in rotulo de primis placitis post guerram* (*Bracton De Legibus et Consuetudinibus Angliae*, ed. George E. Woodbine, trans. with revisions and notes by Samuel E. Thorne, 4 vols. [Cambridge, Mass., 1968–77] [hereafter cited as *Bracton De Legibus*], fol. 77 [2:224]). A possible forerunner is *CRR*, 4:290; *PKJ*, 3, no. 2219. And the phrase is used in an action started by different means in *CRR*, 10:166–67, 196.

66. (a) *PKJ*, 3, no. 860; (b) *CRR*, 4:79, 157–58 (against lord having other sister in *custodia* and alleging bastardy of demandant).

67. *Rolls of the Justices in Eyre for Yorkshire*, no. 322 (actually son of one sister against other sister). Cf. *Glanvill*, XIII, 11 (p. 155).

68. *Britton*, ed. Francis Morgan Nichols, 2 vols. (Oxford, 1865), III, ix, 3 (2:83).

69. *Novae Narrationes*, ed. Elsie Shanks, completed with a legal introduction by S. F. C. Milsom, Selden Society, vol. 80 (London, 1963), p. cxi. To the references there given, add *Early Registers of Writs*, note following CC. 186b.

70. *Novae Narrationes*, pp. cxii–cxiii.

unde nichil. But the promptness is hard to square with a hesitation about aiel and cosinage some twenty years later, to which we shall return.[71] And even Bracton, who saw remedies in terms of possessory protection, did not see *unde nichil* itself in that light. He has a different explanation which, as has been remarked elsewhere,[72] can be extended to cover *nuper obiit*. If dower is being refused because the marriage is denied, the issue must go to the church courts; and perhaps it was only the king's court that could demand an answer.[73] The same difficulty would arise if one claiming as parcener was being refused any share on the supposition that she was a bastard. But in neither case is there factual support for the explanation. In the earliest records, which do not reach back to the creation of *unde nichil*, dower actions are very common and denials of the marriage rare.[74] The records do reach back some twenty years before the appearance of *nuper obiit*; and though actions between parceners are not frequent, we can be sure that bastardy allegations were not a pressing problem.[75] The similarity between the two actions seems even odder now that *nuper obiit* turns out to be a substantially later creation.[76] Perhaps with *unde nichil* itself Bracton was only rationalizing the result of some different and forgotten logic.

The immediate occasion for *nuper obiit* was the restriction placed on *precipe* writs by Magna Carta. The logic of that was the logic of tenure itself. A claim to land is a claim to be the lord's tenant and must be addressed to the lord: hence the writ of right patent. But before the Charter, immediate action in the king's court was accepted as proper when there seemed no room for dispute, when the lord himself was keeping out one with a direct right against him in defiance of his obligations. We know from the legislation creating it that this was the original role of mort d'ancestor.[77] It was conceived for use against the lord himself; and legislation about damages nearly a century later still treats that as the principal case.[78] And when some twenty years after Magna Carta (and also after the creation of *nuper obiit*), the principle of mort

71. See below, pp. 75–76.

72. *Novae Narrationes*, pp. cxii–cxiii.

73. *Bracton De Legibus*, fols. 296–96b (3:357).

74. Examples noted in the plea rolls before Magna Carta are: (a) *RCR*, 2:56; (b) *CRR*, 1:233, 322; (c) *CRR*, 2:41; (d) *CRR*, 2:63; (e) *CRR*, 2:79; (f) *CRR*, 3:150; (g) *CRR*, 4:2–3, 38–39; (h) *CRR*, 6:153; (i) *CRR*, 7:99, 275; (j) *CRR*, 7:101. Cf. (a) *CRR*, 1:309; (b) *CRR*, 6:301, 391–92. Even if many have been missed, the proportion is minute in relation to the number of dower actions.

75. (a) *CRR*, 4:79, 157–58 (mort d'ancestor against lord having other sister in *custodia* and alleging bastardy of demandant; writ to bishop); (b) *CRR*, 12, no. 1537 (*nuper obiit*; issue to jury).

76. G. J. Turner, in *Brevia Placitata*, ed. G. J. Turner, completed by T. F. T. Plucknett, Selden Society, vol. 66 (London, 1947), pp. xciv–xcv, thought the two writs might be the creation of the same chancellor.

77. Assize of Northampton, c. 4 (Stubbs, *Select Charters*, pp. 179–80); *P&M*, 1:148 and 2:57, n. 1.

78. Stat. Marlborough (1267), c. 16, reaffirming Provisions of Westminster (1259), c. 9.

d'ancestor was extended to cases omitted because the dead ancestor was too remote, a wider "abstract" remedy was expressly resisted by the magnates. They were prepared to sanction the new *precipe* writs of aiel and cosinage only as against the lord himself or one who could vouch him.[79] The direct remedy is given, in the latter case by *precipe*, precisely because the lord himself is defaulting on his obligations.[80]

When dower is seen as a dependent tenure within the inheritance, the writ *unde nichil* falls into similar place. The widow claims not an abstract property right, but the benefit of an obligation falling upon the heir. If she has nothing, it is not just that he has not fulfilled his obligation: he must be repudiating or defying it. Instead of setting up a separate procedure like mort d'ancestor, the king exercises the discretion attributed to him by Glanvill and issues a *precipe* writ.[81] Like mort d'ancestor, the writ named the tenant of the land but did not identify his tenurial position; and this obscured the logic. Both came to be used against other tenants, no doubt for the same reason: if another tenant was in, that itself was the responsibility of the lord in mort d'ancestor, of the heir in dower *unde nichil*. The husband's grantee holds of the heir, is warranted by him, just as the widow claims to be. In both cases the extension had happened before the time of Glanvill, but in the case of dower the logic is expressly recollected. Whoever is named as tenant, the book warns immediately after giving the writ *unde nichil*, the heir himself must be present *qui mulieri petenti de dote sua respondeat*.[82] And though the logic was not known to Bracton, it was probably still remembered at the time of the Charter: the *precipe* writ with its explanatory clause seems not to have been questioned.

What about the other dependent holdings within the inheritance? There is little evidence linking the *precipe* with *maritagium*:[83] but normally there is no need for action when the father dies, because the daughter and her husband already have the land. But in parage it is the eldest sister who gets the land; and the claim she faces from a younger sister is exactly akin both to the mort d'ancestor claim of heir against lord and to the *unde nichil* claim of widow against heir. These are the two remedies from which *nuper obiit* takes its properties. And this is a situation in which the use of the *precipe* before the Charter would have had the same

79. *BNB*, no. 1215 (1236–37), with amended reading suggested in Milsom, *Legal Framework*, p. 84, n. 6. Notice the linking of aiel with mort d'ancestor, *nuper obiit*, and writs of entry in the objection of the tenants in *Select Cases in the Court of King's Bench under Edward I*, vol. 2, ed. G. O. Sayles, Selden Society, vol. 57 (London, 1938), pp. clvi–clvii (1239).

80. Cf. Milsom, *Legal Framework*, pp. 85–86.

81. *Glanvill*, I, 5 (p. 5); notice also the availability for claiming free tenement as well as fee.

82. *Glanvill*, VI, 15 and 16 (p. 66).

83. See Hurnard, "Magna Carta, Clause 34," at p. 166. Miss Hurnard explained these cases differently; they do not seem to be claims against the heirs; and anyway the number is hardly significant considering the frequency of actions involving *maritagium*.

justification as the *precipe* writ *unde nichil*: the eldest sister must be repudiating or defying any obligation to the younger.

But *nuper obiit* was not, and the earlier use of *precipe* writs may not have been, confined to this claim of a younger sister against the eldest; and the logic of parage may have had powerful reinforcement in a practical difficulty resulting from its mere existence. It is not just that subinfeudations reaching down to a humble level might leave parties uncertain whether or not there should be parage, and so whether or not there should be a writ patent to the lord. Suppose there should clearly be parage, but it is the youngest of three sisters who has the whole: what writ patent should the middle sister get, and what the eldest? Make the problem harder, and suppose that the inheritance is held of the king: should the eldest get a *precipe*, and should it claim just her beneficial third or the whole? Perhaps somebody actually tried to draft those writs, and decided that the niceties must be cut through. We have met the case before. It is that of the daughters of William de Buckland in 1218; and it seems to be the earliest surviving example of *nuper obiit*.[84]

These procedural questions about the established parage all reflect an earlier and substantial question: how did it become established in the first place? Let us assume a lord to have given the whole inheritance to the eldest sister and her husband: to whom did the younger sisters first turn? It cannot have been the lord, not just because they did not claim to hold of him, but because he needed a single tenant and an undivided tenement. In his court, the right thing had been done and there was an end of it. And in an important sense, there indeed was an end of it. The eldest was not disturbed in what the lord had given to her, and the rights of the younger sisters were strictly dependent. It is equally self-evident that those rights could become regular only when the king's court would regularly intervene. But should we think in terms of a customary right having, like the *maritagium*, some earlier existence in the court which the eldest sister would hold as lord of the inheritance? Or should we think of an almost legislative creation, with the king's court intervening from the beginning with some mechanism like the *precipe*?

In either case the motive force no doubt came from family arrangements customary before there were lords to upset them. And the willingness of the church courts to treat as breach of faith a failure by the heir to honor a gift in *maritagium* suggests that they saw an underlying moral duty to make such provision. But *maritagium* became a customary institution in lay courts because it was customarily given. The younger sisters may have had a moral claim well established in family custom, may sometimes even have been in the inheritance. But the only gift actually made was the lord's gift of the whole to the eldest; and hers was the only "legal" right.

That there was at some time something in the nature of a legislative act or declaration of right by some authority is a fact that we learn by

84. *BNB*, no. 12; above, p. 66. Cf. above, n. 65.

accident. A charter attributed to about 1145 refers, in passing and with tantalizing obscurity, to a *statutum decretum* by which if there is no son, daughters are to share "by spindles"; "nec potest maior natu iuniori medietatem hereditatis nisi vi et iniuria auferre."[85] Whether or not the words by which this ruling is described, *statutum decretum*, suggest some church participation, the words in which it is expounded do not suggest a legislative act providing in modern terms for the legal division of property rights. It must have declared that the elder sister would do wrong in depriving the younger of her share. The language is that of obligation; and two echoes in detail, though much later, are insistent. The formula *defendit vim et iniuriam* is common form in the plea rolls, but not in "proprietary" actions: it is the standard denial in all personal actions. Another echo is in the writ *nuper obiit* itself: it is not a *precipe*, and the operative words are *ostensurus quare deforciat*. The *ostensurus quare* formula is most at home in actions for wrongs. What the lost ruling seems to contemplate is the wrongful exercise of an undoubted power. The land is the eldest sister's, but she is under an obligation to allow the younger her share. Parage is the expression in tenurial terms of something like a modern trust.

The significance of this casual recital is further sharpened when it is placed in its context. The charter is one by which a considerable lord confirms a gift that his tenant has made to a religious house; and it recites that the tenant's daughter joined with her father in placing the land upon the altar by means of a symbolic knife, which daughter was heir of the tenant for that land "iuxta statutum decretum quod ubi filius non habetur terram patris filie per colos parciuntur nec potest maior natu. . . . " The father is still alive; and if he has a younger daughter, it must be the point of the recital that she will have no "legal" right, that the consent of the elder to this grant will be binding on the inheritance. But nothing suggests that there was in fact a younger daughter, and probably the recital of the part of the enactment relating to younger daughters was only for the sake of completeness. As a matter of syntax, the entire recital is to explain why the lord who is issuing the charter feels himself entitled to treat the daughter as heir at all: "que scilicet Agnes heres erat Walteri . . . iuxta statutum decretum quod ubi filius non habetur. . . . " Whatever the ruling was, it probably did more than state a duty to share. It took some step beyond Henry I's Coronation Charter in establishing female inheritance itself, perhaps in recognizing that an unmarried daughter herself had a right, and not just an expectation that the lord would give the land with her to whomever he chose as her husband.

85. F. M. Stenton, *The First Century of English Feudalism*, 2d ed. (Oxford, 1961), pp. 38–41, 260–61 (app., no. 5). Cf. *Regesta Regum Anglo-Normannorum*, vol. 3, *1135–54*, ed. H. A. Cronne and R. H. C. Davis (Oxford, 1968), p. 39 (no. 106).

The Husband's Interest

The important change was in the sense in which women inherited. The husband contemplated by Henry I in his "illam dabo . . . cum terra sua" is himself a grantee. When the land is the woman's by operation of law, the husband's right is derivative, flowing from the marriage. But the woman's automatic right was also, if she had sisters, a shared right; and the sharing itself had practical consequences which may have affected the way in which the husband's right was seen. We shall therefore start with those.

The most obtrusive consequence of sharing, from the husband's point of view, is that the acquisition of an inheritance by marriage becomes less simple. He, or his father, had better buy the marriages of all the daughters. When Richard de Lucy of Egremont died in 1213 he left a widow and two daughters. The widow married Thomas de Multon; and Thomas acquired from the king the *custodia* of both daughters and married them to his own two sons. Egremont was, in fact, granted whole to the elder couple; but Multon won something else for the younger. Richard de Lucy had inherited Egremont from his mother, the middle of three sisters who had each inherited a barony from their parents. When the youngest died childless in 1215, the whole of her barony of Papcastle was taken by the representative of the eldest line. Multon, acting in the king's name, recovered half (and arranged a partition in which *esnecia* was reserved to the eldest line); and it was this half that went with the younger Lucy, daughter to his own younger son.[86] Just a hundred years later their grandson was granted the other half of Papcastle, which had escheated to the crown, a delayed bonus over and above what Multon had striven for.[87]

Such calculations did not always work out. A tenant of the earl of Winchester died leaving two daughters and, though the facts were disputed, *custodia* of the inheritance and of both daughters seems similarly to have been acquired by the father of two sons. The elder son married the elder daughter all right; but a church on the inheritance fell vacant, "et placuit . . . postnato filio melius promoveri in ecclesiam illam quam uxorem ducere." Something had to be done, and the elder son did it: he placed the younger daughter in a nunnery. But it was not a very secure one; and she contrived to send for a man friend and, on their own account, he married her then and there in the nunnery. When some news reached the elder son, he arranged for her to be removed to a more secure house; and on the way the party passed her new husband. The husband's account is no doubt colored—or deliberately colorless—because he is facing an action in the earl's name for forcible abduction. He says she called to him for help, "et ipse vidit multitudinem gentium et respondit ei

86. *CRR*, 11, no. 1223; *CRR*, 12, nos. 360, 866, 914, 1576, 2045; Sanders, *English Baronies*, pp. 115 (Egremont), 134 (Papcastle), 142 (Skipton).
87. Sanders, *English Baronies*, p. 135.

quod noluit pro ea pugnare," whereupon she threw herself from her horse and went off with him on her own initiative, "et tali modo recuperavit ipse uxorem suam." The melodrama fades away, and later we find the two couples getting down to litigation over the division of the inheritance.[88]

But it is not just a stirring story. The sequence of events may not have been uncommon; though there were not necessarily two sons, and it might from the beginning be intended to dispose of the sister by making her a nun. Of one such case we have only fleeting glimpses; and it is by accident that we learn that in the end the plan failed and the lady was married without question.[89] Another such case gave rise to bitter litigation, ecclesiastical and lay, lasting some twenty-five years. The younger sister says that the elder and her husband placed her in the nunnery when she was five years old, and that she properly returned to the world when she reached the age of discretion. Properly or not, she was excommunicated; and the earliest proceedings were in church courts. The father had apparently died under Henry II. Her claim for her share of the inheritance is first seen in the king's court in 1201, and it is eventually compromised in 1220.[90] She might have had a better life without it.

Another aspect of sharing brings us back to the relationship between inheritance and *maritagium*. At all levels of society some provision was made for a daughter on her marriage, whether in land or in goods and money. If somebody else inherited, most obviously her brother, then no question arose on the father's death. But a question did arise if the daughters themselves inherited; and family equity allows two kinds of answer. Either the benefit received must exclude the beneficiary from sharing in the inheritance, or the inheritance must be shared on the footing that the benefit falls into hotchpot.[91] The question always arises with partible inheritance, and many variations of detail are possible. With impartible inheritance, the underlying question arises in another form: what lifetime gifts are permissible within the family? That is a major question for Glanvill; and his discussion, particularly of the gift to a younger son, shows family sense at odds with the feudal burden borne by the inheritance.[92] Unfortunately he discusses *maritagium* only in the same context of a male heir, and not in the context of daughters sharing the inheritance; and here it is possible that the feudal and the family forces had for a time pulled in the same direction.

88. *CRR*, 9:65–67; *CRR*, 10:92 (both concerning the abduction); *CRR*, 9:91; *CRR*, 11, nos. 190, 293(?), 306, 344, 346, 686 (all concerning the inheritance).

89. References in Milsom, *Legal Framework*, p. 156, n. 4.

90. *CRR*, 2:81; *CRR*, 3:41, 178, 334–35; *CRR*, 4:80, 155, 252, 318; *CRR*, 5:79, 79–80, 123, 171, 183–86; *CRR*, 7:108–9, 180, 246; *CRR*, 8:173, 184; *CRR*, 9:222, 241, 381–82, 385; *PKJ*, 3 and 4, nos. 171, 1654, 1724, 2117, 2695, 2783.

91. For a survey see Jack Goody, "Inheritance and Property and Women," in *Family and Inheritance: Rural Society in Western Europe, 1200–1800*, ed. Jack Goody, Joan Thirsk, and E. P. Thompson (Cambridge, 1976), pp. 10–36.

92. *Glanvill*, VII, 1 (pp. 69–71); Milsom, *Legal Framework*, pp. 121–22.

At humble levels it is clear that some customs excluded daughters with marriage portions from inheriting.[93] If the tenement barely supports a family, portions are likely to be given from family savings in goods and money; and this must be the first home of the "hearth-child" who will inherit the tenement itself. But even at higher levels, where marriage portions are generally in land, this is an approach acceptable to family feeling. By confining inheritance to unmarried daughters, it is also an approach that leaves the lord to choose the husband who will be his tenant. This is something we have already noticed as possibly relevant to the *filia haeres remanserit* of Henry I's Coronation Charter, and to the disposition that King John made of William de Buckland's inheritance: he acted on an alleged prerogative to give *postnatam filiam que remaneret in hereditate* with the inheritance to a man of his choosing.[94] Even the words in which the lost enactment about sharing is described would be consonant with an exclusion of elder daughters having *maritagium* and a division of the residue of the inheritance. It is not *primogenita* but *maior natu* who is to share *per colos* with her junior.[95] Suppose a tenant to die leaving three daughters, of whom only the eldest was married. The *maritagium* of the eldest would be balanced by the tenurially similar parage of the youngest; and apart from a possible inequality of share,[96] the only thing "wrong" with the result would be that it is the middle sister who has become the lord's tenant, not the eldest. Cases in the king's court in which it is an elder who is having to sue a younger for her share, in some of which there is also an express claim for *esnecia*,[97] do not necessarily reflect lords who simply ignored the family situation.

Even when all questions come to the king's court, we should not think too simply in terms of "the law." If the eldest, or her husband, is always to be the lord's tenant, then that in itself implies a different approach to *maritagium*. If *maritagium* does not exclude from the inheritance, the question must arise of its falling into hotchpot, and that is the result toward which the king's court works. But problems arise piecemeal. When was a grant by the father sufficiently independent of the marriage to be exempt?[98] Was a grant even on the marriage exempt if the land had

93. (a) *CRR*, 11, nos. 298, 1273, 1460, 2386, 2878; *BNB*, nos. 951, 988; (b) *CRR*, 11, nos. 1743, 2407, 2905; *BNB*, no. 1018. See also *Borough Customs*, vol. 2, ed. Mary Bateson, Selden Society, vol. 21 (London, 1906), p. 133; Homans, *English Villagers*, p. 141. Cf. the concord made in a seignorial court in the time of Henry II, *CRR*, 2:112–13.

94. See above, n. 24 and accompanying text.

95. See above, n. 85 and accompanying text.

96. *Glanvill*, VII, 1 (p. 69), says that one can give "quandem partem terre sue cum filia sua uel cum alia qualibet muliere in maritagium siue habeat heredem siue non." Both this, and the feudal burden on the inheritance, suggest that the permissible size of the gift would be the same whether there was a son or not. So long as a *maritagium* remained *liberum*, there would be compensation for any shortfall in the actual share.

97. (a) *Three Rolls of the King's Court*, pp. 6, 30–31, 49, 54; *RCR*, 1:13; (b) *CRR*, 1:225, 447–48, 453; (c) *CRR*, 5:46–47, 149. Cf. *Bracton De Legibus*, fol. 75 (2:218).

98. (a) *Rolls of the Justices in Eyre for Lincolnshire, 1218–19, and Worcestershire,*

been the father's own purchase rather than his inheritance?[99] Nor could rules be stated in the abstract: it depended upon who was suing whom. Unless both parties agreed to exclude their lifetime benefits,[100] a demandant clearly had to bring her *maritagium* in.[101] But the sister enjoying handsome *maritagium* will not be demandant: she will feature as tenant being sued.[102] Can she be made to give up any excess beyond her mathematical share?[103] And if what she has is the whole, can she hark back to the other approach to the problem and argue that there is no inheritance to divide?[104] In the early rolls, and indeed in Bracton, it looks as though the questions are somehow new.

Just as sharing affected the calculations of a husband seeking to acquire an inheritance which will descend to his issue, so does its relationship with *maritagium* affect our understanding of his own personal tenure of the land. His right to enjoy the land for his whole life, if issue had been born of the marriage, comes to be known as curtesy. Glanvill describes it, though not under that name or indeed any name; but his description comes in his account of *maritagium*, and nothing is said about the wife's inheritance.[105] Most scholars, though not all, have followed Maitland in supposing that at that time it did apply to inheritance,[106] as it does for Bracton.[107] Maitland indeed thought that inheritance was the prime case, that Glanvill can be understood as saying that the right applied "even" to *maritagium*.[108] To that proposition we shall return. But the ramifications of sharing suggest that the question itself may be oversimplified. On an obvious factual level, if there was ever a decision to be made about *maritagium* falling into hotchpot, whether in general or in a particular case, a possible change in the husband's entitlement would be at least

1221, ed. Doris M. Stenton, Selden Society, vol. 53 (London, 1934), no. 1040; (b) *CRR*, 11, nos. 2201, 2793; *BNB*, no. 934. Cf. *Bracton De Legibus*, fol. 77 (2:224–25); *Britton*, III, viii, 8 (2:79).

99. *Memoranda Roll, 10 John*, p. 109; *RCR*, 1:147; *CRR*, 1:50, 80; *CRR*, 2:92. Cf. *Glanvill*, VII, 1 (pp. 70–71). According to *Bracton De Legibus*, fol. 77 (2:224), it makes no difference.

100. *CRR*, 12, nos. 249, 1771.

101. *CRR*, 11, nos. 2201, 2793; *BNB*, no. 934. Cf. *Bracton De Legibus*, fols. 77 (2:223–24), 428b (4:331).

102. (a) *CRR*, 6:161, 200–201, 254, 282–83; *CRR*, 7:47, 194–95, 235, 298; *CRR*, 11, nos. 523, 1065, 2029; (b) *Rolls of the Justices in Eyre for Lincolnshire*, no. 1040; (c) *CRR*, 10:166–67, 196; *CRR*, 11, nos. 219, 1374. Cf. *Bracton De Legibus*, fol. 77 (2:223–24).

103. *Bracton De Legibus*, fols. 76b–77 (2:223–24); *Britton*, III, viii, 8 (2:78–79).

104. *Bracton De Legibus*, fols. 76b–77 (2:223); *Britton*, III, viii, 8 (2:78–79).

105. *Glanvill*, VII, 18 (pp. 92–93). But the discussion of homage and its consequences at least contemplates that a husband may continue to hold his wife's inheritance after her death: "nec primus maritus premortua uxore, terram illam iterum releuabit" (IX, 4 [p. 108]).

106. *P&M*, 2:420, n. 1. Followed by G. D. G. Hall, in *Glanvill*, p. 93, n. 1, and apparently by T. F. T. Plucknett, *A Concise History of the Common Law*, 5th ed. (Boston, 1956), pp. 548, 568. Doubted by G. L. Haskins, "Curtesy at Common Law," *Boston University Law Review* 29 (1949): 228, n. 5.

107. *Bracton De Legibus*, fols. 216 (3:151), 437b–38 (4:360).

108. *P&M*, 2:420, n. 1.

relevant. But there is a deeper complication. Any difference between inheritance and *maritagium* might be expected to flow from the husband's homage. But if there were two or more sisters, only one husband would do homage. The tenure of the younger sister in parage is like *maritagium.* Indeed, if, as seems possible, sharing was first confined to younger and unmarried daughters, leaving the elder undisturbed with their *maritagium*, the parage of the youngest may have been consciously modeled upon the *maritagium* of the eldest. If there ever was a difference between *maritagium* and inheritance over curtesy, it is unlikely to have survived a general principle of sharing the inheritance.

Curtesy was the right of the surviving husband to hold the land so long as he lived, provided only that a child capable of inheriting it had been born of the marriage. It did not matter that the wife had left sons by an earlier marriage so that the heir being kept out was not the husband's own child.[109] Nor did it matter that the heir, even by an earlier marriage, was an infant so that the wife's lord was losing a wardship; nor, indeed, that any child had already died, so that the person being kept out was either a collateral heir of the wife's or the lord awaiting his escheat.[110] When inheritance is automatic and when women are understood to inherit in the same sense as men, the right looks generous to the husband and hard on the wife's heirs. We inevitably think about it in the same terms as dower.

That it was not like dower is most obviously shown by the comparative frequency with which the two things figure in early litigation. The widow had in a ceremonial sense been given dower on her marriage, but, even if the land had then been specified, it remained within her husband's control. Her action to recover dower after the husband's death from his heir or grantee is one of the most frequent of all actions on the early plea rolls.[111] There was no action by which the husband could claim curtesy, and he never had to sue for it. He had had the land ever since the marriage. If he granted it away, after the wife's death or before,[112] or if after his own death it was taken as his own inheritance,[113] then of course there might be litigation between the persons claiming under the wife and

109. *P&M*, 2:416–17, and references there given. *Glanvill*, VII, 18 (p. 93), expressly places the second husband on the same footing as the first; *Bracton De Legibus*, fol. 438 (4:360), reports a contrary view, which is followed in *Britton*, II, xii, 3 (1:289), and in *Fleta*, ed. and trans. H. G. Richardson and G. O. Sayles, Selden Society, vols. 72 (London, 1953) and 89 (London, 1972), IV, 3 (3:54). There may of course be what will later be called "special tail" (*CRR*, 14, nos. 395, 1067; *BNB*, no. 487; *Bracton De Legibus*, fol. 168 [3:34]).

110. Maitland thought the remarkable fact about curtesy was its priority over the lord's wardship and escheat (*P&M*, 2:417). That depends upon a thirteenth-century view of the "incidents" as of prime importance to a lord, as opposed to the services. See below, p. 87.

111. Cf. the review by G. D. G. Hall of *CRR*, 12, in *English Historical Review* 74 (1959): 107–10, at 108.

112. *Glanvill*, VII, 3 (p. 76). Examples: (a) *RCR*, 2:202–3; *CRR*, 1:330–31, 466; *CRR*, 2:30–31; (b) *CRR*, 7:31, 109, 158, 290; (c) *Rolls of the Justices in Eyre for Yorkshire*, nos. 167, 1132; (d) ibid., no. 292 (customary power of husband to sell).

113. (a) *CRR*, 7:177, 180; (b) *CRR*, 8:335.

those claiming under himself. But curtesy was never as such the object of litigation. When the wife died, her heir might claim the land in mort d'ancestor; and because the points of the assize would presumably be answered in favor of the heir, one would expect that the case would always be recognizable from an exception made by the husband. But such assizes are not common.[114] What we find a little more often is an assize of novel disseisin brought by the husband against one who has simply taken the land on the wife's death.[115] This may be the wife's heir; and in the case of *maritagium*, which can be inherited only by issue, he is necessarily the issue of an earlier marriage.[116] Other possible defendants are the donor of *maritagium*,[117] the donor's heir,[118] or, if the land was the wife's inheritance, the lord of whom it was held.[119] In the examples found of the latter situation, in which the defendant is the woman's father or brother taking the reversion after *maritagium*, or is her lord taking his escheat, the facts again appear from an exception that he expressly pleads. But it is possible that this was unnecessary, and that other such cases are hidden behind general verdicts for the one party or the other. When the defendant is the woman's heir, we generally learn the facts only because the clerk has enrolled an explanation given by the recognitors for a general verdict. Any question about the husband's entitlement, for example, whether or not children had been born alive, goes to his having or not having free tenement,[120] and is therefore within the points of the assize. He was or was not disseised of his free tenement, and the explanation upon which the historian depends was for those concerned at the time gratuitous.

Taking all these kinds of action together, in the first thirty years after the earliest surviving plea roll the total number of cases visibly involving curtesy is of the order of one or two a year. Unless we can make that mere fact tell us something, it follows that the rolls themselves will not tell us much about curtesy. They are not even as clear as might be hoped about

114. (a) *RCR*, 1:432 (see below, n. 141, for another stage of this dispute); (b) *RCR*, 2:202–3; *CRR*, 1:330–31, 466; *CRR*, 2:30–31; (c) "Roll of the Justices in Eyre at Bedford, 1202," ed. G. Herbert Fowler, in *Bedfordshire Historical Record Society*, vol. 1 (Apsley Guise, 1913), pp. 144–247, at no. 65 (pp. 160–61); (d) *Rolls of the Justices in Eyre for Gloucestershire*, no. 1090. For mort d'ancestor in this situation see *Bracton De Legibus*, fols. 271 (3:293), 278 (3:311). For a special action see ibid., fol. 438b (4:362–63). Cf. (a) *CRR*, 1:182, 249–50, 294, 452, 476; (b) *CRR*, 6:11–12.

115. *Bracton De Legibus*, fols. 168 (3:34), 169b–170 (3:38), 206 (3:124–25), 216–16b (3:151–52); cf. fol. 404b (4:259).

116. (a) *CRR*, 6:333–34; (b) *Rolls of the Justices in Eyre for Yorkshire*, no. 309; (c) *Rolls of the Justices in Eyre for Gloucestershire*, no. 534. Cf. *CRR*, 7:7, in which it is not clear who the defendants are.

117. *Rolls of the Justices in Eyre for Yorkshire*, no. 22.

118. *CRR*, 3:66. Cf. *CRR*, 10:73–74.

119. (a) "Roll of the Justices in Eyre at Bedford, 1202," no. 63 (pp. 158–61); (b) *Rolls of the Justices in Eyre for Lincolnshire*, no. 357.

120. (a) *Rolls of the Justices in Eyre for Yorkshire*, no. 309; (b) *Rolls of the Justices in Eyre for Gloucestershire*, no. 534.

the application to inheritance as well as *maritagium*. Most cases in which the wife's interest is stated do involve *maritagium*, but at the higher levels many more women would have *maritagium* than would inherit. At the humblest level, where marriage portions would be in goods, woman heirs would be relatively more common; and many of the early cases, including some of those in which we can see that the land was indeed inheritance and not *maritagium*, are from humble levels.[121] The earliest clear allegation of curtesy from a military inheritance relates to some period before 1200; but the allegation itself is made as late as 1219, and then in litigation in which the curtesy is barely in issue.[122] Only one case has been found in which it may possibly have been argued that something turned on the distinction. It is an assize of mort d'ancestor in 1200. Walter and his wife Richolda had a son William and a daughter Maud. After Richolda's death, Walter gave some of her land in *maritagium* with Maud, and William, as Richolda's heir, is now claiming it from Maud's husband; but Maud's husband is warranted by Walter, so that the real dispute is between William and Walter. According to one enrollment, "Willelmus dicit quod non licuit patri suo dare hereditatem matris sue cum filia sua: e contra Walterus pater ejus dicit quod ipse duxit . . . Richoldam uxorem suam cum maritagio suo. . . ." But probably nothing turns on William's use of *hereditas* to describe Richolda's land as against Walter's use of *maritagium*, because Walter goes on to conclude that "ex consuetudine Anglie debet tenere hereditatem ejus et warantizare tota vita sua." Another enrollment shows William denying that he had consented to the gift by Walter, and his real concern clearly goes beyond Walter's lifetime.[123]

Walter's phrase *ex consuetudine Anglie* is as near as the early rolls come to a formula specifically denoting curtesy. In the previous year we find *secundum consuetudinem regni*;[124] and some twenty years later, that and *per legem terre* come into more general use.[125] "Curtesy" itself is much later. Nor is it just that there is no special name for this right of the husband. It has to share a name with other things. Among its other uses,

121. (a) *RCR*, 1:359, 427–28; *RCR*, 2:65, 196; *CRR*, 1:136 (lord recovering land of dead wife *salvo jure heredum illius terre*); (b) *Rolls of the Justices in Eyre for Lincolnshire*, no. 357.

122. *CRR*, 8:152, 333; *CRR*, 9:20, 57, 87, 370–71, 379; *CRR*, 10:253. Cf. *CRR*, 8:213–15; and Sanders, *English Baronies*, p. 22 (Bulwick). Robert de Courtenay was married to his second wife, Alice of Papcastle, by 1200 (*CRR*, 1:265). The suggestion that the heir was sufficiently seised to endow his wife during his father's lifetime may be an infection from dower (Milsom, *Legal Framework*, p. 145).

123. *RCR*, 2:202–3; *CRR*, 1:330–31, 466; *CRR*, 2:30–31. A similar confusion of language may be seen by comparing *RCR*, 1:432, with *RCR*, 2:124–25 (see below, n. 141, for this dispute). In one sense *maritagium* became *hereditas* when issue was born.

124. *RCR*, 1:359, 427–28; *RCR*, 2:65, 196; *CRR*, 1:136.

125. (a) *Rolls of the Justices in Eyre for Yorkshire*, nos. 167, 1132; (b) *CRR*, 13, no. 311; *BNB*, no. 266; (c) *CRR*, 8:152, 333; *CRR*, 9:20, 57, 87, 370–71, 379; *CRR*, 10:253; (d) *Rolls of the Justices in Eyre for Gloucestershire*, no. 534.

custodia is used of the husband in relation to his wife's land, whether she is alive[126] or dead.[127] When she is dead the *custodia* is sometimes specified as *cum pueris*,[128] when alive as *cum uxore*[129] or *per uxorem*.[130] But it might be neither: in one early case the issue was whether the husband had held after the death of both wife and child *ut de feodo an ut de warda*.[131] We shall ask later for whom in such a case he might be holding in *custodia*. Our immediate concern is with the lack of a specific name.

It is a fact to be placed beside the scarcity of litigation. A state of things which does not give much practical trouble and has not earned for itself a name cannot need much discussion. Glanvill devotes a book to dower, and five sentences to curtesy.[132] They come in his chapter on *maritagium*, at the end of his book on inheritance and alienation. That book is a remarkable achievement of substantive analysis;[133] and it is possible that this passage has misled us into overlooking the absence of a name and antedating curtesy as a legal entity of the same nature as dower. Even Bracton, who uses *per legem Angliae* as a name, makes only scattered procedural statements.[134] He considers problems, mainly of proof, that may arise if the husband brings novel disseisin or faces mort d'ancestor or an action in the right; and even in these short references space is devoted to monsters heard to roar as opposed to children heard to cry.[135]

We cannot solve the various problems of curtesy, but we may reduce them by starting from this point. There is no name and no need for substantive discussion precisely because the husband needs no action, does not have to formulate a count. He is in, protected so far as the king's court is concerned only by novel disseisin; and he is within the protection of the assize because he has free tenement. How was he protected before novel disseisin was introduced? It has been argued elsewhere that the assize was originally intended to protect tenants against action by their lords in breach of the customs governing the tenurial arrangement.[136] To

126. (a) *RCR*, 1:253, 393; (b) *PKJ*, 2, no. 455; (c) *The Earliest Northamptonshire Assize Rolls, A.D. 1202 and 1203*, ed. Doris M. Stenton, Northamptonshire Record Society, vol. 5 (1930), no. 450.

127. (a) *CRR*, 7:31, 109, 158, 290; (b) *CRR*, 8:152 (full references above, n. 125). It is not always clear whether the wife was at the relevant time alive or dead: (a) *CRR*, 2:37, 221; (b) *CRR*, 8:335.

128. (a) *CRR*, 1:182, 249–50, 294, 452, 476; (b) "Roll of the Justices in Eyre at Bedford, 1202," no. 65 (pp. 160–61).

129. *PKJ*, 2, no. 455.

130. *RCR*, 1:253, 393. Cf. *The Earliest Northamptonshire Assize Rolls*, no. 450.

131. *RCR*, 1:359, 427–28; *RCR*, 2:65, 196; *CRR*, 1:136. Cf. *CRR*, 7:31, 109, 158, 290.

132. *Glanvill*, VI, (pp. 58–69) (dower); VII, 18 (pp. 92–94) (*maritagium* including curtesy).

133. G. D. G. Hall, *Glanvill*, p. xxiv.

134. *Bracton De Legibus* (on novel disseisin) fols. 168 (3:34), 169b–170 (3:38), 206 (3:124–25), 216–16b (3:151–52), 404b (4:259); (on mort d'ancestor) fols. 271 (3:293), 278 (3:311); (on action in the right) fols. 437b–39 (4:360–63).

135. *Bracton De Legibus*, fols. 438–38b (4:361–62). Cf. fols. 216 (3:151), 271 (3:293).

136. Milsom, *Legal Framework*, pp. 8–25.

have free tenement was to be such a tenant, to be protected by these customs in the lord's court. The husband is simply the lord's tenant, and entitled to the same protection as any other tenant.

The conclusion is obvious enough: but obvious propositions are sometimes worth emphasizing. Dower and *maritagium* were special entities partly because they were "tenures" as much as "estates." Curtesy was not a tenure. Consider the wife's inheritance and assume for simplicity that she is an only daughter. The husband becomes the lord's man in the same way as a son would have: the lord makes livery to him and takes his homage. The tenure is that by which the wife's father had held. The lord is securing a man and his service. For Maitland it was a great puzzle that the husband's curtesy should keep out the lord's wardship if the wife died leaving an infant heir.[137] But that is a thirteenth-century puzzle. When it was his services that a lord desired, he would naturally continue to look to the husband. We have seen that Henry I was prepared to look to the widow or other relative of a dead male tenant:[138] like socage *custodes*, they could have *custodia* of the land provided they arranged for the service to be done.

All this applies equally to the second husband. Unless Magna Carta was making an otiose promise,[139] there had been a time when the widowed heiress might be compelled to take a new husband so that the lord might have a new man. If she herself wished to remarry, the lord must be asked to consent:[140] but the absence of consent could not affect the fact of a marriage, and the sanction must have been that the husband would not become the lord's man and would not get the land. But here novel disseisin probably wrought a real change: the lord had to put up with him. A case of 1199 shows one who was actually the donor of *maritagium* proceeding in the king's court against a second husband to whom he had not consented, but the terms of his challenge are those of a lord: *in feodum suum intraverat sine ejus assensu.*[141]

Questions about the second husband suggest a yet earlier stage. We have seen that the Coronation Charter of Henry I makes no promise about the marriage of a widow with *hereditas.*[142] Perhaps he might compel it. But dealings with baronies suggest that if, when the husband died, there was a male heir of full age, the inheritance might be given directly to him even though the woman was still alive.[143] Perhaps to begin with the husband was indeed seen as tenant of the wife's inheritance like any other tenant. The most that any tenant could have was the lord's war-

137. *P&M*, 2:417.
138. Coronation Charter, c. 4; see above, pp. 163–64.
139. Magna Carta (1215), cc. 7, 8; (1225), c. 7.
140. *Glanvill*, VII, 12 (p. 86).
141. *RCR*, 2:124–25. This case is discussed, and full references given, in Milsom, *Legal Framework*, p. 51. See also above, n. 114, for an earlier stage of the dispute. Cf. the action brought by the dead woman's lord in *RCR*, 1:359, 427–28; *RCR*, 2:65, 196; *CRR*, 1:136.
142. Coronation Charter, cc. 3, 4; see above, p. 63.
143. See above, p. 64.

ranty and protection for life, together with the obligation imposed on the lord by homage that when the tenant died the land would be given to an heir. If homage was taken in the wife's name, this last obligation would be toward her heirs. But if the husband was indeed the lord's tenant like any other tenant, it was his life that mattered, not hers; and the real puzzle is not why the husband could keep the land if issue had been born but why he lost it if not.

It is not impossible that this rule grew up as one of the customary properties of the *maritagium*, and was generalized in the uniformity of the king's court. At the higher levels of tenure, the *maritagium* was certainly of more frequent occurrence than the inheritance coming to a woman; and on the view taken in this essay, it is likely also to have been the earlier. And because it was a product of the family interest undistorted by feudal logic, and in particular did not attract the preordained consequences of homage, the customs may just reflect the implied terms of an arrangement that was desired. Although with *maritagium*, as with inheritance, the land is said to be given "with" the woman to the husband, the donor was providing for the woman: we have seen that he might try to make his gift before any marriage was in prospect, himself holding it as *custos*.[144] To him it was always the woman's life that mattered, not her husband's; and an understanding that he would no longer warrant the husband if there was no child at the woman's death would be entirely intelligible. But then suppose that a child survived its mother but quickly died? The practical desire for certainty could have produced the all-or-nothing conclusion that the mere birth was decisive. But it is hard not to suppose some deeper connection with the later idea of a "conditional fee."

Let us return to the case of inheritance and consider the husband's position in terms of an arrangement with the lord, rather than of the properties of some "estate" as a known entity. Even in 1219 it could be an arrangement on special terms. Because the wife had died childless a lord retook the land; but at the time of the marriage the lord's predecessor had conceded that the husband should hold for life *siue haberet heredem de ea siue non*, and so the husband recovered in novel disseisin.[145] We can be sure that in that case the lord was taking his own escheat: his predecessor could not have made such a concession at the expense of collateral heirs of the wife.[146]

A century and more earlier, what were the likely terms of the arrangement contemplated in "illam dabo . . . cum terra sua"?[147] The lord is under an obligation imposed by homage toward the dead tenant's heirs. Instead of giving the land to, say, the dead man's brother, he is making the daughter's husband his man. What has induced him to do so? Suppose the dead tenant had left a brother and a grandson by a dead daugh-

144. See above, pp. 60–61.
145. *Rolls of the Justices in Eyre for Lincolnshire*, no. 357.
146. For an arrangement with the heir see *CRR*, 6:11–12.
147. Coronation Charter, c. 3; see above, p. 65.

ter:[148] surely the lord would have felt obliged to the grandson; and if the grandson was an infant, would he not accept the dead daughter's husband as holding in *custodia*? So should not the living daughter have her chance to transmit the inheritance? But she cannot be heir in the same sense as a man; and the lord cannot take her homage and regard the matter as closed until her own death, when he will ascertain who is her heir. Her capacity is just to transmit the inheritance; and all the time there is another heir in the dead tenant's brother. If these were indeed the terms of the lord's problem, they necessarily become the terms of the arrangement he makes. It is a conditional arrangement. The homage he takes from the daughter's husband is itself conditional, obliging him to the heirs of the marriage if there are heirs. Until there are, perhaps the daughter has nothing and the husband only a *custodia* for whomever the heir will turn out to be. If children have not been born when the wife dies, nothing can keep out the alternative heir of her dead father. If a child is born, the husband's homage takes its full effect: he becomes the lord's man indeed, but still in *custodia* for the heirs of the inheritance and not his own heirs.

Direct evidence for any such proposition is so unlikely that one must be suspicious when it seems to turn up. In a case of 1199–1200, the suspicion is that lost facts would disclose some quite different explanation, such as a fine. But we have more facts than usual, because the central figure wrote a letter to the justiciar, who quoted it in a letter to the justices that has survived. She was a widowed heiress who had granted an advowson in frankalmoign to a religious house, and this grant is being contested by her son-in-law. What the letter says is that the grant was made from what had descended to her from her father, and was made before her daughter's marriage. But later she contradicts herself on the second point, and admits that the grant was made after her daughter had married and had children. As against the religious house, the son-in-law had argued that the lady could not warrant the grant, and this appears to be vindicated by her admission.[149] It is hard to imagine any basis other than a lingering idea that an heiress primarily transmits the inheritance.

148. *Glanvill*, VII, 3 (p. 77).

149. *PKJ*, 1, nos. 3063, 3104, 3475 (the letter); *RCR*, 1:239, 313, 397; *RCR*, 2:53–54, 226; *CRR*, 1:44, 65, 142, 143, 201 (the letter contradicted), 301.

4 Trial by Ordeal: The Key to Proof in the Early Common Law

Paul R. Hyams

In twelfth-century England no regular legal means existed to challenge a court decision, duly made in the proper form, simply on the ground that it was the wrong decision. The many disgruntled litigants could take the matter further only by self-help, or by alleging that the court holder had denied them justice (*defectus iustitie*) or had wilfully mishandled the proceedings (*falsum* or *iniustum iudicium*). Either allegation began new proceedings before a royal court,[1] where the holder or suitors of the inferior court might have to be fought, quite literally, in a judicial duel. Even after Henry II's reforms had introduced various kinds of trial by jury, the common law hardly recognized remedial appeal against error.[2] Certainly this is a severe deficiency for any system of law with pretensions to rationality, but final proof in early English law, as elsewhere, was generally left to the judgment of God. Because God was by definition impeccable, His judgments appeared erroneous to honest men only when there had been malfeasance on the part of those who purported to question God and interpret His verdict—that is, the judge and suitors. Genuine error was impossible, and there could be no appeal to higher authority.

The functioning of trial by ordeal, that most notorious form of God's judgment, is a subject of keen intrinsic interest. Its reexamination, together with that of its legacy to the early common law, is long overdue. The difficult questions involved have been unwarrantably overshadowed by the quest for the mystical origins of the English jury. Many English legal historians have cursorily dismissed the ordeal as irrelevant, because

I have been thinking around the subject of this paper on and off since about 1970, and have delivered a number of talks and lectures on both sides of the Atlantic. The friends, colleagues, and questioners who have corrected errors and enlightened me in different ways are too many to be thanked here. I shall do so when I write further on ordeals, as I hope to do shortly. I must, however, at least acknowledge the help of my wife, Elaine Marcotte Hyams, and the authors of several works cited below.

1. *Leges Henrici Primi*, 33, 1a–2, ed. L. J. Downer (Oxford, 1972) (hereafter cited as *LHP*); apart from this I follow the sigla for English laws of F. Liebermann, *Gesetze der Angelsachsen*, 3 vols. (Halle, 1903–16) (cited hereafter as *Gesetze*).

2. T. F. T. Plucknett, *The Concise History of the Common Law*, 5th ed. (London, 1956), p. 131 and n. 4; *Tractatus de legibus et consuetudinibus regni Anglie qui Glanvilla vocatur*, ed. and trans. G. D. G. Hall (London, 1965) (hereafter cited as *Glanvill*), p. 36, n. 1; Donald W. Sutherland, *The Assize of Novel Disseisin* (Oxford, 1973), pp. 74–76. T. F. T. Plucknett, *Edward I and Criminal Law* (Cambridge, 1960), pp. 73–76, notes the lack of full criminal appeals before the present century. François Louis Ganshof, *Frankish Institutions under Charlemagne*, trans. Bryce and Mary Lyon (New York, 1970), pp. 93–94, reveals exact Carolingian parallels.

its disappearance apparently coincided with the very beginning of that modern "scientific" law which was their major concern. This neglect is unfortunate. The functioning and demise of the old proofs actually shaped the classical common law in multifarious ways. Western Europe's transformation of the old ordeals into the seeds of its modern, supposedly rational systems involved choices about the direction of change whose consequences still affect us today, in both the Anglo-American and the Continental systems.[3] The changes involved loss as well as gain. For example, the failure of western European courts until quite recently to appreciate the community roles and standing of the individuals who came before them, outside the specific facts of the case, partly resulted from the exclusion of the ordeal.[4] A fuller understanding of medieval proofs promises rather more than mere exposition of the peculiar institutions of English law six hundred years ago.

Trial by ordeal is a very widespread institution, known and practiced in a wide range of premodern societies. Any attempt to explain its history in England can therefore draw on a vast body of comparative material. English hypotheses must also consider the ordeal's history in the other parts of western Christendom, where modes of proof based on the judgment of God predominated between (roughly) the end of the Western Roman Empire in, say, the fifth century, and the cultural renaissance of the West in the High Middle Ages.

I shall first offer a possible model for the working of the early medieval ordeal, based on the assumption that so ubiquitous an institution must have made sense within its time and context. From this sketch of the "world of the ordeal," I can try to explain the transformation of the old ordeals during the High Middle Ages.[5] Within the rough pattern of European change this reveals, each area and jurisdiction of course developed at its own pace and in its own way. England is an interesting case. Many historians see the Anglo-Norman state as a cultural laggard in the context of the twelfth-century renaissance.[6] Yet they generally agree that its legal advances began relatively early. Thus, because the eleventh-century starting point was a legal and political system not too far out of

3. The demise of the ordeal was in one respect the triumph of adversary process over other forms of legal inquiry. Does this not help to explain why the common law long thought essentially in terms of winners and losers, even in disputes over matrimonial causes or family rights?

4. S. F. C. Milsom, *The Legal Framework of English Feudalism* (Cambridge, 1976), pp. 2–3, insists on the importance of forms of proof for the understanding of the early common law.

5. By the "old ordeals" I refer to those unilateral forms, most notably the water and hot iron, which passed finally out of official use after 1215. This distinguishes them from "new ordeals" like the jury, and from oaths and duels. I consider forms used mainly in north-western Europe, thus excluding the Mediterranean lands, where written law persisted. I confess that as yet I do not begin to understand the functioning of law in the society of the Norse sagas; so I exclude those forms too.

6. R. W. Southern, "The Place of England in the Twelfth Century Renaissance," in his *Medieval Humanism* (Oxford, 1970), chap. 9, may exaggerate this lag.

line with the rest of post-Carolingian Europe,[7] the English experience furnishes a reasonably fair first test to the approach canvassed in the model. To my summary model of large-scale European metamorphosis I therefore append a summary narrative of the development of ideas and techniques of proof in English law between about the year 1000 and the mid-thirteenth century.

A final preliminary is necessary: to specify how "ordeal" will be used in this paper, to say what unites the group of practices studied. A dictionary definition runs: "an ancient . . . mode of trial, in which a suspected person was subjected to some physical test fraught with danger, . . . the result being regarded as the immediate judgment of the Deity."[8] This meets our purpose, providing that we note that ordeals were used in civil suits too.[9] The tests used varied considerably in nature. It is helpful to distinguish between those faced by a single proband (unilateral ordeals) and bilateral ordeals, such as the judicial duel, which pitted opponents against one another.[10] Most scholars would further distinguish judicial oaths. In early litigation the parties not only offered oaths to validate their assertions of fact; they also swore oaths before embarking upon proof by an ordeal, test, or duel. In addition, oaths themselves constituted a form of proof, and the performance of an important oath to conclude a case could be a moment so fraught with tension as almost to constitute a "physical test" within the ordeal definition quoted above. For example, one simoniac bishop discovered, when challenged by Hildebrand at a Council in the 1050s, that he was totally unable to pronounce the simple formula *Gloria filio et patri et spiritui sancto*.[11] Although proof-oaths are perhaps not full, genuine ordeals, they are far too closely related to be ignored here.

Unilateral ordeals, oaths, and duels share one important factor. All three methods of proof purport to work by revealing God's judgment. The proof-oath is no exception. By the standard theory that *jurare est testem Deum invocare*, those swearing understood that God and the saint on whose relics the oath was made would be their witnesses, who

7. J. Campbell, "Observations on English Government from the Tenth to the Twelfth Century," *Transactions of the Royal Historical Society*, 5th ser. 25 (1975): 39–54.

8. *Shorter Oxford English Dictionary*, 3d ed., corrected; but see below, at n. 34, on the phrase "fraught with danger." The excellent paper of J. M. Roberts, "Oaths, Autonomic Ordeals and Power," *American Anthropologist* 67 (1965): 186–209, starts from a definition too specific about "guilt and innocence."

9. See below, at n. 42, for the distinction between civil and criminal law.

10. There is a vast literature. H. C. Lea, *Superstition and Force*, 3d ed. (Philadelphia, 1878), remains the starting point; one relevant chapter is reissued as *The Ordeal*, ed. E. Peters (Philadelphia, 1973). H. Nottarp, *Gottesurteilstudien* (Munich, 1956), is a comprehensive and intelligent survey. A great deal of valuable material is assembled in *La preuve*, Receuils de la Société Jean Bodin, vol. 17 (Brussels, 1965).

11. A. Stacpole, "Hugh of Cluny and the Hildebrandine Miracle Tradition," *Révue Benedictine* 77 (1967): 341–63, at 356–58; and I. S. Robinson, "The Friendship Network of Gregory VII," *History* 63 (1978): 6, outline the story and show that it circulated widely from ca. 1060 into the mid-twelfth century.

could and would punish any perjury.[12] Lawsuits that came to proof almost always concluded, then, with some act that conveyed graphically the idea that the final say in the matter resided with God, whose vengeance could enforce His judgment. To explore the ramifications of the common rationale of these forms of proof, we begin with unilateral ordeals. The two best evidenced in England were the cold water, into which a proband was lowered to see if it would "receive" him, and the red-hot iron, which the proband carried, his hands then being bound up and examined later to see how they were healing.[13]

Let us first recount an actual criminal trial from southwestern England in the last decade of the tenth century.[14] A slave arrested for an unspecified crime was brought to trial before Eadric the reeve, at Calne, a royal hundred vill in Wiltshire, and sentenced to the ordeal by the hot iron. A freeman of good reputation with no criminal record would have expected to clear himself by some kind of oath, but this option was hardly open to a slave without free, law-worthy oath helpers.[15] Nevertheless, our informant, the Winchester monk Wulfstan Cantor, thought the judgment harsh. Eadric ordered that the slave be kept in custody until his master Flodoald, a well-known foreign merchant of Winchester, could be present to witness the proof. Flodoald hurried to the spot and, being particularly fond of this loyal slave, offered him to the reeve together with a pound of pure silver in return for the remission of the *iniustum iudicium*. The slave's own relatives added their pleas and proffers too, all to no avail. Here, far from Winchester, the proud reeve was all-powerful, and even Flodoald had little influence. The arrogant Eadric had his men bank up the fire unusually high[16] and ordered a heavier iron than was customary. At the appropriate moment in the ritual, the slave lifted the iron and experienced immediate, searing pain—apparently increased by a guilty conscience. Nevertheless, the prescribed procedure was followed: the hand was bound for reexamination after three days. By now Flodoald despaired, and in his distress turned to prayer as a last resort, offering the

12. Yvonne Bongert, *Recherches sur les cours laïques du Xe au XIIIe siècle* (Paris, 1949), pp. 205 ff.; Marguerite Boulet-Sautel, "Aperçus sur le système des preuves dans la France Coutumière du moyen âge," in *La preuve*, p. 281; Nicole Hermann-Mascard, *Les reliques des saints: formation coutumière d'un droit* (Paris, 1975), pp. 265–66. Lea, *Superstition and Force*, gives examples of oaths as ordeals.

13. Other forms known in England include trial by morsel (*corsnaed*) and various tests involving boiling water. These, and still other forms, may have been equally widespread in popular ordeals outside major centers.

14. *Frithegodi Monachi Breviloquium Vitae Beati Wilfredi et Wulfstani Cantoris narratio metrica de S. Swithino*, ed. Alistair Campbell (Zurich, 1950), pp. 150–54 (bk. 2, lines 299–434). D. Whitelock, "Wulfstan Cantor and Anglo-Saxon Law," in *Nordica et Anglica, Studies . . . S. Einarsson*, ed. A. H. Orrick (The Hague, 1968), pp. 87–92, offers valuable commentary.

15. Cf. below, at n. 82 and accompanying text.

16. L. Halphen, "La justice en France au XIe siècle: région angevine," in his *A travers l'histoire du moyen âge* (Paris, 1950), p. 188, n. 2, cites an ordeal when the water was boiled *ultra statutum morem*.

slave to St. Swithin if God could be persuaded to preserve him. On the third day after the ordeal, the court reassembled to determine the result. The bandages were unwrapped and a clean (*mundus*) hand revealed. The astounded reeve and his cronies had to admit: this man is not guilty (*inculpabilis*); there is no blame, no crime in him! The rest of the onlookers were even more surprised, for *they* could clearly discern the signs of guilt, the pus and decay on the hand. Judgment had, however, been declared. With the unexpected change of fortune, the atmosphere of the court shifted abruptly. Eadric and his crew slunk away, shamed by a judgment that condemned them and vindicated the accused slave. Meanwhile, St. Swithin at Winchester received an extra slave, who surely lived happily ever after.

Of course this account comes from a poem in honor of St. Swithin. Although all the story's details cannot be guaranteed, they nevertheless fit without strain into what we learn from the laws and rituals of the time. Despite the very unusual miraculous denouement, the anecdote certainly contains some general lessons. The poem vividly portrays the dynamics of an actual ordeal case.[17] No procedural formalism need be assumed here. Wulfstan Cantor focuses rightly on the interplay of personalities within the community—the slave and his supporters, the reeve and his, the audience in general. Everything centered on the reeve. As the court's president, he could bully and manipulate toward the judgment he desired. Whatever his motive on this occasion, he orchestrated proceedings to establish the accused's guilt and punish him in an awesome manner. This too was intended as a lesson for the whole community, which would know better in the future what he expected of it. But the planned drama miscarried, and the public rebuff undermined Eadric's own position. Local officials like a reeve must exercise power with continuous success if they are to retain it. Eadric's failure was dramatized by the exceptional emotional charge in the crowd on that third day. All present knew what had been expected. When it failed to materialize, the reeve consequently lost face and authority. This moment of truth was the grand culmination of the trial, when the court formally perceived the result of the ordeal and embodied it in a final judgment. These three high spots—the concluding decision, the performance of the ordeal itself, and the reeve's *iniustum iudicium*—were separated by public debate of the issues at the court hearings. Meanwhile, the less dramatic negotiations between the slave's party and the reeve, mostly conducted outside court, were equally important.[18] The story makes little sense until we realize that the affair was as much a quasi-political episode as a judicial inquiry. From a possibly trivial starting point, it eventually concerned power relationships that affected the whole community served by Calne's hundred court.

17. This insight into practice is an important addition to our knowledge, pace Whitelock, "Wulfstan Cantor," p. 88.

18. Ibid., pp. 89 ff., concludes that the offer was a "legal composition" and not "a barefaced attempt to bribe." This fine distinction is not important here; proffers were part of the game.

This anecdote no more establishes a general pattern for early medieval law than the arrival of the first swallow proves that an English summer will follow. But it does indicate a pattern of actual behavior that may recur. Thus prompted, one can now try to frame a model that answers two basic questions. Into what *kind* of world can the ordeal comfortably fit? And what kind of law would suit that world?

The ordeal, primarily a device of small communities, functions most comfortably in milieus where each man's personal character and standing are publicly known and affect the welfare of the rest. The community is not too tiny for variety of interest, daily occupations, and so on.[19] No one man can dominate it on personality alone, certainly not so completely as to settle all disputes without challenge. Yet the harsh realities of life demand cooperative effort, such as the administration of open-field agriculture or communal defense, and thus entail some method of enforcing a communal will against dissenters. If the level of acceptable violence seems high, influential members remain keenly aware of the premium on consensus and are prepared to act as necessary for its maintenance. They can be hardheaded, quite clear-sighted about individual and group interests, and accustomed, as farmers or warriors, to relying on their courage and common sense. At the same time, in their world the sacred and profane are everywhere inextricably intertwined.[20] No modern western distinction between the natural and supernatural inhibits their efforts to survive and prosper. They naturally seek assistance when appropriate from God and His saints, or demons and the like. They keep their powder dry—of course—but accept the possibility of miraculous intervention as feasible, indeed natural, and perhaps in the last resort, expected. Miraculous forces beyond human reach exist always as a reserve explanation for events otherwise inexplicable. For some, no doubt, the divine means considerably more, but all agree on the necessity of the reserve, because everything that happens must have a cause.[21] The apparently inexplicable must somehow be integrated into the common thought-world. The most spectacular occurrence must be described so as not to contravene the accepted basic rules of existence. This "secondary elaboration"[22] tames and slows down the pace of fundamental change. It sometimes seems as

19. Gavin I. Langmuir, "Community and Legal Change in Capetian France," *French Historical Studies* 6 (1970): 275–86, makes imaginative use of concentric communities at the levels of lordship, county, etc.

20. Peter Brown, "Society and the Supernatural: A Medieval Change," *Daedalus* 104 (1975): 133–51, at 135.

21. See Gregory VII's explicit statement, quoted by C. Morris, "Judicium Dei: The Social and Political Significance of the Ordeal in the Eleventh Century," *Studies in Church History* 12 (1975): 95–112, at 110. Today, when we no longer believe that everything has a meaningful cause, we often use coincidence as a pseudo-explanation.

22. The thought comes from E. E. Evans-Pritchard, *Witchcraft, Oracles and Magic among the Azande* (Oxford, 1937) pt. 3, chap. 4, esp. p. 319. Cf. Mary Douglas, ed., *Witchcraft Confessions and Accusations*, A.S.A. Monographs, vol. 9 (London, 1970), introduction, for exposition; and Lea, *Superstition and Force*, pp. 350 ff., for examples.

if fundamental change cannot happen at all until the arrival of outside observers, whose different system of beliefs enables them to criticize, to transform, or even to destroy a system alien to them.[23] In the absence of intervention from outside, the community has to find its own way to reconcile apparent anomalies with conventional wisdom.

The reconciliation of anomalous behavior with convention is the task of social control in general and the role of law in particular. In this world the distinction between law and other forms of control is far from clear. Violent self-help and private warfare compete directly with law as means of achieving a new status quo or maintaining the old one. Even where the society is technically literate, in some sense, legal process often remains largely oral.[24] Because there is no accurate memory of past decisions, each new case reviews the good old custom in the context of the current situation. Thus, the quiet modification of norms precludes the upheaval sometimes entailed by a direct challenge to ancient roots and the communal belief in a continuous tradition. Consequently, legal rules, in the modern sense of generalized prescriptive guides applied rigorously by the courts to diverse situations,[25] rarely figure in litigation. Early medieval Europe, unlike most of the recent societies with comparable legal systems, did, however, possess a legal literature. But we probably expect too much of barbarian law codes, whose resemblance to modern statutes and legislation is often merely superficial.[26] Unless laws can be shown to have been used in actual cases, we ought to be very cautious about accepting them as compelling evidence of practice.[27] To set custom down in writing highlights a formalism that is more apparent than real. In the longer term, written precedent inhibits the free development of custom,[28] and may ultimately lead toward genuine legal formalism later.

In fact, court proceedings in the world under scrutiny are far removed

23. Cf. below, at n. 55.

24. C. P. Wormald, "The Uses of Literacy in Anglo-Saxon England and Its Neighbours," *Transactions of the Royal Historical Society*, 5th ser. 27 (1977): 95–114.

25. L. Twining and D. Miers, *How to Do Things with Rules* (London, 1976), chap. 2.

26. The inspiration for these assumptions about the nature of the *Volksrechte* is J. M. Wallace-Hadrill, *Early Germanic Kingship in England and on the Continent* (Oxford, 1971), pp. 33 ff. Patrick Wormald, "*Lex Scripta* and *Verbum Regis*: Legislation and Germanic Kingship from Euric to Cnut," in *Early Medieval Kingship*, ed. P. H. Sawyer and I. N. Wood (Leeds, 1977), pp. 105–38, and Patrick Wormald, "Aethelred the Lawmaker," in *Ethelred the Unready*, ed. D. Hill, British Archeological Reports, British ser., vol. 59 (1978), pp. 47–79, carry on the torch.

27. See Wormald, "*Lex Scripta* and *Verbum Regis*," esp. pp. 119–23, 135–36. Wormald, "The Uses of Literacy," p. 113, n. 77, gives some Continental examples. Cf. below, at text accompanying note 73, for England.

28. Cf. M. T. Clanchy, "Remembering the Past and The Good Old Law," *History* 55 (1970): 165–76, a paper the sight of whose early draft inspired this line of inquiry. Robert Besnier, "'Vadiatio legis et leges': les preuves de droit commun à l'époque des coutumiers normands," *Revue historique de droit français et étranger* (hereafter cited as *RHDFE*), 4e sér. (1940): 88–135, is in the same direction. It is equally possible, however, that setting custom down in writing encourages kings to think of changing it, as Dr. C. J. Wickham pointed out to me; cf. Wormald, "*Lex Scripta* and *Verbum Regis*," pp. 124–25, 129, for ninth- and tenth-century developments in northern Europe.

from the highly formalistic model beloved of German legal scholarship, except for the set pieces of oath swearing and the making of proof. The argument pivots around these two elements. First the court must decide the nature of the proof to be made—by whom, when, and in what circumstances. Then, after proof, it proclaims success or failure and the consequences in a final judgment.[29] Modern courts seek to establish whether or not certain specific acts have been committed, then whether these constitute some crime of the accused or some actionable tort, and finally what the law should do. But in this more localized world of the ordeal, the goal is as much "to make the balance" and reestablish a workable peace within the community as to redress any specific grievance.[30] The strategies vary according to the desired ends. They may aim to effect a compromise between the disputants on honorable terms, for example, or even to eliminate a troublemaker from future calculations by deprivation of civil rights, expulsion, mutilation, or death. Ideally, the court inches cautiously toward the best practicable solution, and attempts to lower the emotional temperature in thrashing out the problem aloud. En route it exposes much material in open court (and also, less formally, outside) that today's practice and the rules of evidence would conceal. Passions are more open, audience involvement closer, than most modern judges would permit. The presiding judge here cannot force his preferred judgment down the court's throat. He can merely guide the deliberations through meanderings that strike an unprepared observer as aimless,[31] until a satisfactory conclusion gradually emerges. The court then declares the proof to be attempted, and now at last comes the moment for God's participation.

29. Besnier, "'Vadiatio legis et leges,'" p. 135; Frederic L. Cheyette, "Custom, Case Law and Medieval 'Constitutionalism': A Re-examination," *Political Science Quarterly* 78 (1963): 362–90, at 368–69, a paper that foreshadowed and influenced much in the current argument. English plea rolls generally call the mesne judgment *judicium* (= OFr. *iuise*, "ordeal") and introduce the final judgment with the words "Consideratum est . . . " Cf. Melville Madison Bigelow, *History of Procedure in England* (London, 1880).

30. Brown, "Society and the Supernatural," p. 137, talks of "an instrument of consensus . . . a theatrical device by which to contain disruptive conflict," but the ordeal could equally be used to crush some people in the interest of others. The phrase "to make a balance" derives from the anthropologist Laura Nader; Max Gluckman, *The Judicial Process among the Barotse of Northern Rhodesia* (Manchester, 1955), was my starting point. It must be admitted that the anthropologists tell much about informal legal process and a good deal about ordeals, but worryingly little about the two combined in the manner argued for here.

31. C. Lévi-Strauss, "The Sorcerer and His Magic," in his *Structural Anthropology*, trans. Claire Jacobson (1963; reprint ed., New York, 1967), chap. 9, brings out strongly the role of onlookers; read this essay for the extraordinary and suggestive story of Quesalid the skeptical sorcerer, pp. 169 ff. Late evidence of interference by committed spectators in English duels is some confirmation of the idea. See *Curia Regis Rolls* (London, 1922–) (hereafter cited as *CRR*), 1:100 (1199); and *CRR*, 10:189 (1221); as well as *Régistres de Grégoire IX*, ed. L. Auvray, 4 vols. (Paris, 1890), 2:4744 = *The Register of Walter Gray*, Surtees Society, vol. 56 (Durham, 1872), pp. 182–83; and further references cited in C. T. Clay, *Early Yorkshire Charters*, vol. 5, Yorkshire Archeological Society (Wakefield, 1936), pp. 224–25, for an incident of 1235; and *Calendar of Patent Rolls, 1266–1272*, p. 579 (before 1271).

In the rough de facto democracy of the court and its suitors, the constant urge to reopen *res judicata* is the law's greatest bane.[32] The conclusion of cases by God's judgment gives the court's verdict a better chance of lasting acceptance, for God is uniquely qualified to settle authoritatively just those cases most difficult for human tribunals. Such cases might hinge on an act committed in secret without witness[33] or concern the manner of commission, rather than the admitted fact. When the rift runs deepest, the community requires an especially harsh and spectacular method of seeking God's judgment, comprising more than an element of punishment.[34] The decision about proof is the crucial step to which all else is subordinate. Courts enjoyed an unexpectedly broad freedom of maneuver. Suitors might propose a whole range of draft judgments before the court chose one and stipulated terms for the performance of proof. Each part of the judgment was important. In a world where no man entirely evaded belief, a conscience unable to accept fully the wording of the oath could cause utter failure in a test that would otherwise be confidently handled.[35] Before the test, the proband was cloistered away from the everyday world of his community and submitted to intense psychological pressure.[36] By now it was common knowledge what result was desired. Even the parties knew. Concord, or straight confession and capitulation, remained possible and indeed frequently occurred right up to the final moment.[37] In a sense they were the most satisfactory conclusion to the case. A *iudicium* actually performed meant obstinate disputants, a quarrel that might yet revive. Men had to hope that the rare *spectaculum* of a "good ordeal" would mercifully release tensions and reinforce the community's standards of proper behavior. Otherwise, trouble might recur in the future. Hence the final moment,

32. *English Historical Documents, c. 500–1042*, vol. 1, ed. D. Whitelock (London, 1955), no. 102 (p. 502): "Then we all said it was a closed suit when the sentence had been fulfilled. And, Sire, when will any suit be ended if one can end it neither with money nor with an oath? And if one wishes to change every judgement which King Alfred gave, when shall we have finished disputing?"

33. S. Kuttner, "Ecclesia de Occultis non iudicat," in *Actus Congressus Iuridici Internationalis, Romae . . . 1934*, vol. 3 (Rome, 1936), pp. 227–46, esp. 230–33, indicates the continuing problem for canonists of facts hidden to all but God. *Peter Abelard's Ethics*, ed. D. Luscombe (Oxford, 1971), pp. 38–40, 42–44, gives one answer to the famous *questio* about whether a judge should give judgment according to the *allegationes* or his own knowledge. These theoretical difficulties only arose when God ceased to judge through the ordeals.

34. This is the justification for the phrase "fraught with danger" in the definition above, at n. 8. It is not applicable to all ordeals but may become truer as the ordeal declines; see further below.

35. The scenes in the Tristan stories are the best known literary illustrations of sensitivity to the precise wording of oaths. This literary depiction of a God who could be thus easily fooled may be a late reflection of genuine problems of conscience. For an example, see above, at text accompanying n. 11. Trial accounts show the care taken in decisions about the formulation of proof.

36. Brown, "Society and the Supernatural," p. 138.

37. Halphen, "La justice en France," pp. 189–91.

when the court perceived the result of God's judgment (occasionally, as at Calne, with surprising effect), was of paramount importance.

In a world of this type, trial by ordeal performs, I believe, several sensible functions in a useful manner. Admittedly our model is idealized. Not even in an ideal world could all cases follow the exact lines sketched. For one thing, institutions have a life of their own. A device like the ordeal, rational within the particular social and intellectual context where it originated, often finds new and seemingly less appropriate applications. For example, in 1077 a duel (and perhaps the fire ordeal) was held to choose between the Roman and Mozarabic liturgies.[38] However, the basic argument remains unaffected. In any case, close examination of individual anecdotes will deepen our generalized analysis.[39] In addition, early Europe certainly retained much local variation in ordeal forms and customary guidelines for the courts' judgments. All reservations acknowledged, much historical evidence about the judgment of God now becomes comprehensible without the need to dismiss early Europeans as savages bereft in this respect of rationality.[40] In its context the ordeal is rational and remains so until the transformation of its world demands a new rationality.[41] One major contention of this essay is that the transformation of northern European society during the eleventh and twelfth centuries was a main cause of the ordeal's transformation in England and generally. Before we consider how these changes occurred, one final point about law in the world of the ordeal demands attention.

Readers trained in modern law may have wondered at the rather casual dismissal of substantive law in the model. Are they asked to believe that in medieval courts everything was quasi-political and undivided, and thus lacked some of the essential distinctions around which most modern law is organized? The answer is that learned men were vaguely aware of such problems from Roman law, directly or through canons of the church.[42] But such sophisticated learning was scarce and not influential; it was usually inappropriate to society's needs. No distinction between

38. Morris, "Judicium Dei," p. 99, n. 10.

39. The complete anecdotes are much more illuminating than any brief citations suggest. When I return to this subject, it will be to supplement analysis with texts. One excellent example is Herman of Laon, *De Miraculis S. Mariae Laudunensis*, III, 28, in J.-P. Migne, *Patrologiae cursus completus: Patres . . . ecclesiae latinae*, 221 vols. (Paris, 1844–64) (hereafter cited as Migne, *PL*), 156:1011–12; and Guibert of Nogent, *De Vita Sua*, III, 15, ed. John F. Benton, trans. C. C. Swinton-Bland (New York, 1970), pp. 207–9, on the theft of cathedral treasures at Laon.

40. Rebecca V. Colman, "Reason and Unreason in Early Medieval Law," *Journal of Interdisciplinary History* 4 (1974): 571–91.

41. Steven Lukes, "Some Problems about Rationality," *European Journal of Sociology* 8 (1967): 247–64. The calculating *ragione* whose origins are traced by A. Murray, *Reason and Society in the Middle Ages* (Oxford, 1978), is what is at issue here.

42. Early European laws seldom drew a sharp distinction between criminal and civil law, as Roman law and modern systems do. The entry of this distinction into currency about the end of the twelfth century is another pointer to the nature of the changes at that time. I use

fact and law is necessary when formulating questions for the omniscient Deity's answer. God in an ordeal declares that the litigant is *justus* or *justificatus* or perhaps *culpabilis* or *incredibilis*[43] in an effortless mix of factual and legal/moral questions. Such a system encourages neither scientific factual investigation nor analysis of substantive law; these remain secondary considerations for the world of the ordeal that its law is not designed to treat. Not until the triumphant revival of the learned laws in the eleventh and twelfth centuries were such distinctions again current in the courts, to become entrenched swiftly as central criteria of a respectable, scientific legal system.[44] Men schooled in these avant-garde ideas sneered at the ordeal critically. But by this time, the ordeal and its world were already disappearing.

The present essay cannot hope to describe or even sketch the vast changes associated with the renaissance of the twelfth century, which are pertinent to the transformation of legal proof. Certainly the quickening of communications and the extension of political units able to wield more than local power, in particular, influenced the timing and pace of change. Here we concentrate on the general pattern. As the world of the ordeal atrophied, men became able to create new social arrangements. The old ordeals were progressively less useful as communities' horizons became less restricted. Their use indeed continued, but in circumstances where the idea of God's judgment was more a fifth wheel than a central theme.[45] Or men cynically imposed harsh ordeals as a deterrent or quasi punishment. Frederick II's famous exposition of the circumstances in which he was prepared to retain trial by battle demonstrates this point: "It is not remarkable that we subject defendants in treason, murderers by stealth and poisoners not so much to judgement as to terror by combat . . . [because] we desire that murderers of this kind should be put in the public view of men under a fearful test as an example to others."[46]

"civil" actions crudely to refer to suits between party and party before the mid-twelfth century.

43. I. Zajtay, "Le Registre de Varad: Un monument judiciaire du début du 13e siècle," *RHDFE*, 4e sér. 32 (1954): 527–62, at 547, 548 ff. At the hot iron of Varad, Hungary, a proband was either *justificatus* or burnt!

44. Marsilio of Padua, *Defensor Pacis*, II.x.4–6, ed. C. W. Previté-Orton (Cambridge, 1928), pp. 200 ff., gives an excellent account of how later law functioned around the distinction between fact and law—and he was aware that earlier conditions were different; cf. ibid., I.iii.4; and A. Gewirth, *Marsilio of Padua*, 2 vols. (New York, 1951), 1:140–41. Gratian, *Decretum*, Dist. 29, q.1; C.15, q.6, c.1 and gl. *que fiunt*; C.23, q.8, c.14 and gl. *homicidium*, broadcast the distinction in the twelfth century.

45. Written record of ordeals is always exceptional. Dr. C. J. Wickham makes the point that, though feud, oaths, and trial by battle (but no old ordeals) remained common in Italy well into the later Middle Ages, almost all recorded court cases are represented as turning on documents and evidence. This strengthens my view that ordeal survivals were more numerous than our evidence for them. Cf. below, n. 161.

46. *The Liber Augustalis*, II.xxxiii, trans. James M. Powell (Syracuse, N.Y., 1971), p. 93; cf. H. Conrad, "Das Gottesurteil in den Konstitutionen von Melfi Friedrichs II von Hohenstauffen," in *Festschrift . . . W. Schmidt-Rimpler* (Karlsrühe, 1959), pp. 9–21. This tendency for the ordeal to end up as a criminal proof of last resort is well illustrated by

The systematic collection of information as the basis of reasoned conclusions, a familiar practice in private everyday life, was now more frequently applied to public affairs. Gradually but inevitably, people realized the limitations of the old ordeals in the new social context. Once they had distanced themselves from the old system, albeit with difficulty, they could finally, from their new perspective, risk its complete rejection. This process did not occur overnight.[47] It was at least a century and a half old in 1215 when the Fourth Lateran Council proclaimed the church's official disapproval. "Civil" ordeals were probably extremely rare in the West when the Council met. Indeed, the canon did end the criminal ordeal, after anxious debate in Denmark and England on the form of its replacement,[48] but even these criminal ordeals had long functioned less as an inquiry into truth than as a sanction. The duel, though apparently condemned alongside the water and iron, was unaffected; its use actually revived in some areas later in the century.[49] In Navarre the prohibition merely replaced the officiating priests with lay bailiffs.[50] The Lateran canon symbolized the departure of the last vestiges of respectability from an already discredited institution. Deprived of a welcome in high-class circles thereafter, the old ordeals drifted ever outwards and deeper into the countryside, into backward areas where conditions could still sometimes approximate to that older "world of the ordeal." Miracle stories and vernacular literature[51] attest to their retention within the popular consciousness, to reemerge sporadically under favorable conditions.[52]

The supposed preeminence of 1215 in the history of ordeals largely arises from a widely held view about the reforming canon's "intellectual

---

England (see below, at nn. 114–27 and accompanying text). See also Jean-Marie Carbasse, "Le duel judiciaire dans les coutumes meridionales," *Annales du Midi* 87 (1975): 387–88; and, for customs similar to Frederick II's rule, ibid., pp. 392, 399, and nn. 33, 62.

47. Georges Duby, "Recherches sur l'evolution des institutions judiciaires . . . ," in his *Hommes et structures du moyen âge* (Paris, 1973), p. 40, says that ordeals were already rare in eleventh-century Burgundy, though not in other provinces.

48. R. C. van Caenegem, "La preuve dans le droit du moyen âge occidental: rapport de synthèse," in *La preuve*, pp. 715 ff., 718, 730, n. 4; see also below, at text accompanying nn. 189–90. Scotland did not formally abolish the ordeal until 1230 (Ian Douglas Willock, *The Origins and Development of the Jury in Scotland*, Stair Society, vol. 23 [Edinburgh, 1966], pp. 23–26).

49. John P. Dawson, *A History of Lay Judges* (Cambridge, Mass., 1960), pp. 49–50; Boulet-Sautel, "Aperçus," pp. 295–99, 300–301, 315–25; Carbasse, "Le duel judiciaire," pp. 391, 396, and nn. 29, 51; Q. Griffiths, "New Men among the Lay Counsellors of St. Louis' Parlement," *Medieval Studies* 32 (1970): 234–72, at 255–56, 266.

50. Van Caenegem, "La preuve," pp. 719, n. 2, 719–25.

51. For examples, cf. G. G. Coulton, *Life in the Middle Ages*, 4 vols. (1928; reprint ed., Cambridge, 1967), 1, no. 93; and Caesarius of Heisterbach, *The Dialogue of Miracles*, bk. I, cc. 16–17, bk. X, cc. 25–26, trans. H. von E. Scott and G. C. Swinton-Bland, 2 vols. (London, 1929), 1:148 ff., 2:202 ff. See also Nottarp, *Gottesurteilstudien*, pp. 116–17; Hans Fehr, "Die Gottesurteile in der deutschen Dichtung," in *Festschrift Guido Kisch* (Stuttgart, 1955), pp. 271–81; and R. J. Hexter, *Equivocal Oaths and Ordeals in Medieval Literature* (Cambridge, Mass., and London, 1975).

52. Lea, *Superstition and Force*, pp. 328 ff., gives some early examples of "popular"

preparation." Historians have rightly sought this among the writings of the previous generation critical of the institution.[53] But they have too easily accepted the writers' own assessment of themselves as reforming critics. Consequently, our own first reactions to a long-gone, very alien system are mistakenly attributed to the late twelfth century. Men still struggling then to escape the old thought-world could not consider it clearly or dispassionately. Even Peter the Chanter, for whom the ordeal was a kind of obsession, concentrated as much on its connection with sin and bloodshed as on his attempted "scientific" refutation.[54] Before him, few westerners hazarded an outright denial of the ordeal's validity in terms comparable to the repudiations by outsiders uncommitted to western intellectual premises.[55] The total refutation of an institution like the ordeal from within its own thought-world is next to impossible until intellectual eyes are opened by what is actually happening around them. The materials habitually assembled by scholars to illustrate the crumbling of the old ordeals under rational assault are better understood as late and untypically learned aspects of a long line of criticism that existed throughout the ordeal's history. But outside the intellectual revivals of the ninth and eleventh to twelfth centuries, they were seldom written down. The extreme moral concern of many writers is indisputable, but greater than their actual influence. At the most they would encourage readers to reform and revise, rather than to reject, the ordeals. Their arguments generally boil down to a secondary elaboration that left the system intact; that is, they do not assert roundly that the idea of God's judgment is a fraud which could never act as it claimed to do. They declare the ordeal's use inexpedient on the ground that the temptation of God is wicked; or they argue that it is so susceptible to trickery, it never in fact reveals

ordeals. See also K. V. Thomas, *Religion and the Decline of Magic* (London, 1971), chap. 8.1. Dr. J. D. Walsh informs me that comparable ordeals continued at a popular level in remote parts of Britain until the nineteenth century; see M. A. Courtney, *Cornish Feasts and Folk-Lore* (Penzance, 1890), pp. 68–70. Dr. P. Doob brought to my knowledge the most recent offer of which I am aware, from the *Toronto Globe and Mail*, 16 November 1973!

53. John W. Baldwin, "The Intellectual Preparation for the Canon of 1215 against Ordeals," *Speculum* 36 (1961): 613–36, is a learned survey of lawyers and theologians that reaches different conclusions from those in the text here. See further his valuable *Masters, Merchants and Princes*, 2 vols. (Princeton, N.J., 1970), 1:323–32.

54. Baldwin, *Masters, Merchants and Princes*, 1:326–29.

55. Compare Frederick II's unsentimental attitude (see above, at n. 46 and accompanying text) with that of a Jew (e.g., Jacob Katz, *Exclusiveness and Tolerance* [Oxford, 1961], pp. 52–53, 96; or Jacob R. Marcus, *The Jew in the Medieval World* [1938; reprint ed., New York and Philadelphia, 1964], p. 128), or a Moslem (e.g., *Memoirs of an Arab-Syrian Gentleman . . . Usamah ibn-Munquidh*, trans. Philip K. Hitti [1930; reprint ed., Beirut, 1964], pp. 167–69), or a Greek (e.g., Charles Diehl, "La société byzantine à l'époque des Comnènes," *Révue historique du sud-est européen* 6 (1929): 197–280, at 275. All three are credulous in other texts (e.g., Diehl, "La société byzantine," pp. 249 ff.) but perceive and reject the nonsense of a different culture. *The Table Talk of a Mesopotamian Judge*, trans. D. S. Margoliouth, Oriental Translations Fund, n.s., vol. 28 (London, 1922), pp. 187–89, is not to be missed as an illustration of tenth-century rationalism in the East.

genuine judgments of God.[56] These ecclesiastical gentlemen had nothing to teach experienced laymen about the dodges that fixed the results in court; they said little new.[57] The ordeal must always have attracted complaints. In every system of law, failed litigants blame their woes on fraud and mismanagement, or anything else except their own lack of a good case. These grumbles at injustice—for the most part unevidenced in the period[58]—are not easily distinguished in the extant texts. Criticism rarely touches upon the logic of the process. We may concede the odd exception, but still feel that the arguments found in the writings of the eleventh and twelfth centuries were insufficient in themselves to create so important an institutional change.

In any case the received opinion relies once again on another unargued assumption, that the initial stimulus toward change originated with writers of the time, men with some distant resemblance to modern academics like ourselves! On reflection, thinkers and intellectuals are rather unlikely to have given the lead. In any age they usually explain with the benefit of hindsight change already initiated elsewhere. In the eleventh and twelfth centuries, their representatives were all within the church, an improbable engine room of radical change. Churchmen felt the weight of tradition too directly. As keepers of authority they could not ignore awkward scriptural texts, which they had painfully to interpret out of contention.[59] The adultery test of bitter waters, for example, still reads in the Vulgate Latin of Numbers, chapter 5, like a medieval ordeal text. In the late twelfth century, some readers happily applied it—under the influence of apocryphal literature like the so-called Pseudo-Matthew—even to the exceptional marriage of Joseph and Mary.[60] As

56. The suggestion that Charlemagne encouraged duels as an alternative to oaths, because fighting was better than perjury (Ganshof, *Frankish Institutions*, p. 88 and n. 130), implies a view on the temptation of God different from that publicized later.

57. Many dodges are mentioned in the penitentials. See, for example, C. Vogel, *Le pécheur et la pénitence au moyen âge* (Paris, 1969), p. 107 for Burchard of Worms; and Adrian Morey, *Bartholomew of Exeter, Bishop and Canonist* (Cambridge, 1937), pp. 241–42, 258–60.

58. Medieval texts mention the skeptic who doubts a miracle only very occasionally, as when the saint puts him down; see John of Salerno, *Vita Sancti Odonis*, II.xxii (Migne, *PL*, 133:72–73), trans. by G. Sitwell as *St. Odo of Cluny* (London, 1958), pp. 65–66, for an example. The grumbler similarly escaped publicity.

59. Marie-Thérèse d'Alverny, "Astrologues et théologiens au XIIe siècle," in *Mélanges . . . M. D. Chenu* (Paris, 1957), pp. 31–50; *The Letters and Charters of Gilbert Foliot*, ed. Adrian Morey and C. N. L. Brooke (Cambridge, 1967), no. 237. In 1112 the noted theologian Master Anselm of Laon suggested the use of the cumbersome procedure from Joshua 7:14 to locate the thief of cathedral treasure. Other, more practical views prevailed (Herman of Laon, Migne, *PL*, 156:1013).

60. Compare Priester Wernher, *Maria*, ed. Karl Wesle, 2d ed. (Tübingen, 1969), pp. 165–73 (lines 3267 ff. of MS D), written in 1172 in south Germany, with Pseudo-Matthew, *Liber de Ortu B. Mariae et Infantia Salvatoris*, cc. 10–12, ed. C. de Tischendorf, in *Evangelia Apocrypha*, 2d ed. (Leipzig, 1876), pp. 71–75, a possible source. See also H. Fromm, "Quellenkritische Bemerkungen zum Marienleben des Priesters Wernher," *Annales Academiae Scientiarum Fennicae*, ser. B, 84 (1954): 326–27. I am grateful to Prof. Peter Ganz and Dr. R. Combridge for help here.

the learned canonist Gratian included Numbers 5:12–28 in his authoritative *Decretum*, it is not surprising that he and his fellow canon lawyers were slow to exclude the vulgar ordeals entirely.[61] And less intellectually advanced ecclesiastics remained conscious that they, who lacked the physical power of their lay neighbors, had sometimes to depend on the threat of the miraculous to protect their property and position. The twelfth century was almost as notable for the collection of relics[62] and wonder-tale miracles[63] as for intellectual inquiry. Relics indeed figure prominently at every level of society; from courts like those of Henry II and Frederick Barbarossa, and along pilgrimage routes to Compostella or the East, men fought for relics because they believed in their power. The same Lateran Council that outlawed in the ordeal one type of controlled miracle approved another by sanctioning the doctrine of transsubstantiation. Thus the twelfth century still produced a trickle of approving *exempla* about the ordeal, as well as a few cases where men confident of the justice of their cause spontaneously offered to submit to the judgment of God by the hot iron.[64]

The erroneous belief that change resulted from positive decisions has encouraged a late dating. Although explicit decisions to change existing custom after public debate may have been more common than they seem from records, genuine legislation remained abnormal before the thirteenth century. Consequently, the best publicized pronouncements about the ordeal arrive late in our story, after a slow, silent revolution that must be deduced from fragmentary direct evidence and by reading between the lines of well-known texts. The prime movers are men of affairs—doers, not writers—who seldom get to tell their own tale. They were in the eleventh century already seeking new and better ways to organize administration and to maintain order in their own best interests. In the field of law, the flexibility of the ordeal system assisted their efforts. Courts and their judges could select their preferred proofs according to the need of

61. Gratian does not seem to me to tackle *purgatio vulgaris* directly in *Decretum*, C.2, q.5, which is concerned with the purgation of a bishop. Cc. 20–26 form an appendix of texts that do tell against lay ordeals, though c. 21 is Numbers 5:12–28. Many of the texts in the *questio* could be used to illustrate the world of the ordeal. Gratian's views are extraordinarily hard to establish to the satisfaction of, for example, Prof. Stephan Kuttner. Because I do not yet convince him, I must return to the subject on another occasion. Cf. Jean Gaudemet, "Les ordalies au moyen âge: doctrine, législation et pratique canoniques," in *La preuve*, pp. 99–135, esp. 123 ff.

62. C. Morris, "A Critique of Popular Religion: Guibert of Nogent on the Relics of the Saints," *Studies in Church History* 8 (1971): 55–60, and K. Leyser, "Frederick Barbarossa, Henry II and the hand of St. James," *English Historical Review* 90 (1975): 481–506, at 487–88, give references. Also, Hermann-Mascard, *Les réliques des saints*, pp. 225–34, illustrates saintly property defense after human efforts proved inadequate.

63. For example, Southern, "The Place of England in the Twelfth Century Renaissance," pp. 171–74, surveys miracle collections. See P. Rousset, "La croyance en la justice immanente à l'époque féodale," *Le moyen âge* 54 (1948): 225–48; and the interesting remarks of Benedicta Ward, S.L.G., "Miracles and History: A Reconsideration of the Miracle Stories Used by Bede," in *Famulus Christi*, ed. Gerald Bonner (London, 1976), pp. 70–76.

64. Lea, *Superstition and Force*, pp. 356–57; cf. below, at nn. 137 and 147 and accompanying text.

the moment. Now and again we glimpse their criteria,[65] but the process is mostly unobservable.[66] The harsher old ordeals were unnecessary for the handhaving thief, whose guilt was manifest from the circumstances of his capture. Similarly, courts might use ordeals merely to crush the already condemned. As skill in the assessment of documents and evidence improved (perhaps, too, as court holders increased their power to sway decisions), resort to the ordeal correspondingly waned. One can guess that in communities approximating to the perfection of our model, ordeals had been common enough to rouse people's expectations, but not so commonplace that the spectacle lost its drama and tension. The now rarer ordeal spectacles progressively lost their glamor and degenerated into physical tests without rational context or justification.

In retrospect, the apparently deliberate general policy of change was merely the cumulative effect of many individual acts that arose from actual cases.[67] Because the great questions were never explicitly raised, there was little backlash; people seldom noticed the disappearance of their traditional ways. Where individuals led, whole groups followed. In the same kind of way that Flodoald and the rest had once sought to buy one slave off from the hot iron at Calne, whole communities now purchased from princes who could enforce their grants exemptions and the right to meet allegations with oaths instead of ordeals. As well as familiar municipal privileges, eleventh-century grants to the churches, Jews, and so on attest to the same point.[68]

65. See Galbert de Bruges, *Histoire du meurtre de Charles le Bon, Comte de Flandres (1127–1128)*, ed. H. Pirenne (Paris, 1891), esp. chaps. 76, 87, 105, 108, for the story of Lambert of Aardenburg, a guilty participant in the assassination, who survived the hot iron only to die later in battle. Galbert decided that God had spared Lambert in the hope that he would repent, but later let him die after he had acted arrogantly and without any sign of contrition. Galbert probably wrote the whole work to puzzle out the workings of divine Providence on his town in the disturbed period during the collapse of order after the count's death. He was worried by Lambert's acquittal, but concluded that God's ways were not those of men. "Unde fit, ut in bello alter inquus prosternatur, in judicio aquae vel ferri iniquus, penitens tamen, non cadat" (p. 156). Probably Galbert preferred to advocate battle for future use.

66. Most attempts at statistics use the thirteenth-century register from Varad, Hungary, on which see Zajtay, "Le Registre de Varad," pp. 527–62, and van Caenegem, "La preuve," pp. 699–700. The results are interesting but do not advance knowledge in the critical areas. We know very little even about the proportion of cases that went to the different proofs.

67. The final stages of the process in the English Curia Regis can be documented; see below, at n. 190 and accompanying text.

68. There seems to be no general survey of exemptions. R. C. van Caenegem, *The Birth of the Common Law* (Cambridge, 1973), p. 70, cites early examples from the Netherlands; and K. Helleiner, "Osterreichs älteste Stadtrechtsprivileg," in *Beiträge zur Stadtgeschichtsforschung* (St. Pölten, 1959), pp. 49–57, presents the earliest Austrian example. Carbasse, "Le duel judiciaire," is a model area study that goes beyond towns. *Materials . . . Thomas Becket*, vol. 4, ed. James Craigie Robertson, Rolls Series (London, 1879), p. 148, a plea that clerics might receive equal exemption with Jews and burgesses, suggests the way aspirations spread; and *The Chronicle of Jocelin of Brakelond*, ed. H. E. Butler (London, 1949), pp. 100–101, is a particularly instructive text. For English towns, see Mary Bateson, ed., *Borough Customs*, vol. 1, Selden Society, vol. 18 (London, 1904), pp. 32–36; and Bigelow, *History of Procedure*, pp. 296, 323 ff.

The demise of the old ordeals was, then, largely a straight shift from some kinds of proof to others, the consequence of commonsense choices unencumbered by much theory. New cases were found to be soluble by existing techniques without the need to consult God; few new techniques, if any, were invented. God was not needed to determine how things were at a particular time, for example in the Domesday Inquest. Boundaries or the dues previously paid were best established by the men who had experienced them. Though their oath was an added safeguard, the Domesday inquiry is rightly regarded as factual. But the mystery of seisin and right, for example, or the question of who *ought* to hold land under dispute in Domesday *invasiones*, was much less easily abstracted from the divine judgment. By the twelfth century many laymen so fully believed in the efficacy of the new methods of factual inquiry that they happily applied them to every question, perhaps even the choice of a wife! The spread of rational methods of inquiry is one of the age's most exciting aspects. Yet when schoolmen like Abelard applied these novel approaches to matters like the Trinity, they appalled and angered powerful conservatives. Similarly, the submission of property rights to human factual judgment with no appeal to God might have raised objections, though at a lower level. In order to avoid traditionalist reproaches, medieval innovation often had to disguise itself as a revival of good old custom, or pose as an adaptation of accepted forms.[69] Legal innovators may have tried to conceal their supersession of the old ordeal in some such fashion. The English jury of the late twelfth century could plausibly be represented as a new type of ordeal in answer to conservative challenge. Similar confrontations may have occurred elsewhere, too.[70]

Legal enactments that specify the use of the ordeal first become common in England about the middle of the tenth century. The explanation for their appearance at this moment is twofold. For the first time in England, a comprehensive Christianization of the ordeal was attempted,[71] along Carolingian lines and under direct Continental influence. Soon afterwards a royal drive was mounted against theft and disorder, also influenced from abroad and unparalleled before the Angevins.[72] The compilers of the relevant law codes concentrated on specific problems like cattle theft and never intended comprehensive coverage. "Though

69. B. Smalley, "Ecclesiastical Attitudes to Novelty, c. 1100–c. 1250," *Studies in Church History* 12 (1975): 113–31.

70. R. H. Bloch, *Medieval French Literature and Law* (Berkeley and Los Angeles, 1977), chaps. 1–2, which contains much that is pertinent to the foregoing, became available to me only after this paper was completed.

71. The ordeal was by no means new to tenth-century England. See *Ine*, 37, and the commentary of F. L. Attenborough, *The Laws of the Earliest English Kings* (Cambridge, 1922), pp. 187–89.

72. Here and in much that follows about Old English law, I lean heavily on the preliminary conclusions of Patrick Wormald, who has very kindly permitted me to see some early drafts of his work on English legislation. See nn. 24, 26, above, for publications to date. I hope I have not distorted his views in making them my own.

Anglo-Saxon codes, unlike those of the Continent, were issued in the vernacular, they probably remained marginal to what was always a largely oral system of pronouncement and enforcement. There were demands for the use of the *domboc*, but no recorded Anglo-Saxon case cites or refers to written law, and the manuscript tradition is dependent on very few preconquest scriptoria and twelfth-century collections."[73] These *leges* refer to the ordeal *only* in the context of theft. In all the enactments concerning "civil" actions for compensation, there is no mention of the ordeal. This is surprising, and one hesitates to argue from silence in such a matter. Yet it seems likely that the Old English legal system may have struck eleventh-century Norman observers as strange almost as much for its lack of "civil" ordeals as for its neglect of the judicial duel. The implication is that Old English "civil" procedure had centered on oaths.

Detailed study of the ordeal is consequently limited to the treatment of proof in theft accusations, which is useful enough for present purposes. Preferably, an accuser would lay his reputation against that of the suspect before God.[74] He had to make at least a prima facie case before the accused could be put to his law.[75] The court no doubt listened to oral argument before deciding on the details of the accuser's fore-oath[76] and the proof to be made by the accused himself. It would consider the gravity of the alleged offense[77] and the social rank of the parties,[78] but the crux of the argument was reputation, especially that of the accused in his own community. The laws impose different treatment on three categories of accused. He could class as a *getreowe* man if he persuaded his lord and two thegns to certify on oath that he had not recently failed an oath or ordeal.[79] The man whose lord dare not so swear thus revealed himself *ungetreowe*[80] or *tihtbysig*,[81] of so doubtful a reputation that

73. C. P. Wormald, "Angelsächsisches Recht," in *Artemis Lexicon des Mittelalters* (Munich, 1978).

74. For example, 2 *As.*, 23.2. But 3 *Atr.*, 4–6, follows 3 *Atr.*, 3, the much discussed text that still seems to provide for communal accusation. The laws say little of what happened when an accuser was lacking. See most recently R. C. van Caenegem, "Public Prosecution of Crime in Twelfth-Century England," in *Church and Government in the Middle Ages . . . Essays Presented to C. R. Cheney*, ed. C. N. L. Brooke, et al. (Cambridge, 1976), pp. 41–76.

75. The notion that the simple word of an accuser was insufficient to put a man to his law was already old in the twelfth century. Magna Carta, c. 38, insisted that royal officials conform too; note the changes in c. 31 of the 1217 reissue (Sir Frederick Pollock and Frederic W. Maitland, *The History of English Law before the Time of Edward I*, 2d ed., reissued with a new introduction and select bibliography by S. F. C. Milsom, 2 vols. [Cambridge, 1968] [hereafter cited as *P&M*], 2:605–6; van Caenegem, "Public Prosecution," p. 71; the Norman *Très ancien coutumier*, c. 40, ed. E. J. Tardif, *Coutumiers de Normandie*, vol. 1 [Rouen, 1881], p. 34). Some French customs were more willing to burden an accused (Boulet-Sautel, "Aperçus," pp. 282–83; Bongert, *Recherches*, pp. 184–85).

76. *LHP*, 14, is a full discussion of fore-oaths. See *Gesetze*, 2:546, s.v. *Klageeid*.

77. 8 *Atr.*, 27; 2 *Cn.*, 51.

78. *LHP*, 67.2; cf. below, at n. 184.

79. 1 *Atr.*, 1.1–4; 2 *Cn.*, 22, 30; *Leges Willelmi*, 14; *LHP*, 64.9, 67.1.

80. 2 *Cn.*, 22, 30, 33, etc.; *LHP*, 64.9a, 67.1.

81. Van Caenegem, "Public Prosecution," p. 48 n, reviews the concept of the *tihtbysig*

much weightier proof was required to clear his name. Worst of all, the friendless man who had no one to speak for him consequently had no reputation at all within this community.[82] He would be imprisoned until he could undergo his ordeal. In contrast, the *getreowe* man (or *credibilis*, as the Latin texts say) might face only a simple oath or ordeal, as opposed to the triple oath or ordeal imposed on the *ungetreowe*. This distinction between simple and triple proof is explained by the equation in the texts of a simple oath with one pound weight of hot iron, or a triple oath (thirty-six men) with three pounds or sixty shillings of silver.[83] The crucial choice between oath and ordeal might seal a suspect's fate. Although the texts do not illuminate the decision process, they do stipulate the mode of ordeal to be used in certain specified cases.[84] The relevant clauses of the laws probably cannot have served as a blow-by-blow guide for the reeves and others who presided over trials. Rather, they established rules of thumb for the general guidance of courts. The seriousness of the alleged theft and the parties' standing within the community certainly weighed strongly in the court's deliberations, as well they should. But of course more worldly, quasi-political considerations, of the kind apparent in Old English case records, also influenced their verdicts.[85]

Once the court had agreed on formal award of proof, the parties' sureties were expected to ensure that the principals reappeared on a later day fixed for the ceremonial attempt to make proof,[86] by the ordeal[87] or the swearing of oaths. Sundays and holy days were deemed inappropriate for such a solemn event.[88] The accuser swore his fore-oath and witnessed the accused's attempt to make his law.[89]

The anonymous but probably official version of these ceremonial steps

---

man. Julius Goebel, Jr., *Felony and Misdemeanor* (1937; reprint ed., Philadelphia, 1976), pp. 322 ff., is illuminating on the connection between the ordeal and the concept of *infamia*, for which see also below, at n. 168 and accompanying text.

82. 2 *Cn.*, 35; *LHP*, 65.5.

83. 2 *As.*, 4–6; 5 *Atr.*, 30; 2 *Cn.*, 57; *LHP*, 67.1b–c. *Gesetze*, 3:603, s.v. *Ordal*, says that the distinction is unique to England.

84. 3 *Atr.*, 6, says that the choice is the accused's, but in the special circumstances of *Blas*, 2 (ca. 930–75), the choice apparently went to the accuser.

85. Frederick Pollock, "English Law before the Norman Conquest," in *Select Essays in Anglo-American Legal History*, vol. 1 (Boston, 1907), pp. 88–107, at 92–94, asserts categorically that Old English procedure "was governed by traditional rules of the most formal and unbending kind" against an older view that saw a more natural informality in the popular courts. See also James Bradley Thayer, "The Older Modes of Trial," in *Select Essays in Anglo-American Legal History*, vol. 2 (1908), pp. 368 ff. (also in his *A Preliminary Treatise on Evidence at the Common Law* [Boston, Mass., 1898]). Cf. the influence of Declareuil (1898–99) on Besnier, " 'Vadiatio legis et leges,' " pp. 110–13.

86. *Gesetze*, 3:601, s.v. *Ordal*, cites 2 *As.*, 23.2, and *Ordal*, 4, as authority for another English peculiarity.

87. 1 *Atr.*, 1.1–7.

88. 5 *Atr.*, 18; 6 *Atr.*, 25; 1 *Cn.*, 17; *LHP*, 62.

89. 2 *Cn.*, 22, removed previous exceptions; see also *LHP*, 64.1, 9b–c. *Leges Willelmi*, 14.3, would make an accuser swear that he acts for *jus suum*, not *odio*.

toward the ordeal, given in the tenth-century tract *Ordal*,[90] accords closely with the prescriptions in the laws. If read together with the extant liturgical *ordines* for the holding of ordeal ceremonies, a convincing picture emerges of what *may* have happened. However, even more than the *leges*, liturgical manuscripts present the historian with severe problems of interpretation.[91] All our English rituals belong to one large Carolingian family, and may indeed descend from a single northern French archetype imported early in the tenth century.[92] Even the postconquest ones are associated with this same family. The greater detail found in these later rituals produces a rounder, more colorful picture. This, however, must not be read back into the Old English period, because the Norman compilers undoubtedly wrote in a more self-conscious vein, under occasional challenge from skeptical laymen and others. They therefore added fresh material to justify the procedures they laid down.[93] But even with the strictly contemporary rituals, evidence of actual use is lacking.[94] We can say only that they are generally compatible with stories like that of the trial at Calne. No charters, for example, enable one to match actual procedure with liturgical prescriptions.[95] And even when one assumes that an *ordo* was followed in a particular case, many details remain unclear. The celebrant priest retained considerable freedom of choice in the most densely written ritual. Some ordeal *ordines*, for example, offered him alternative forms of *oratio* to the proband;[96] none covers every

90. *Gesetze*, 1:386–87 (ca. 936–50 or a little later). Note that this text envisages boiling water as well as hot iron. Cf. 2 *As*., 23, 23–2.

91. Cf. J. L. Nelson, "Ritual and Reality in the Early Medieval Ordines," *Studies in Church History* 11 (1975): 41–51: "He who consults the early medieval *ordines* should be wary of imposing on the age of liturgy the preoccupations of an age of law" (p. 51).

92. This is argued by Patrick Wormald (see above, at n. 72) from Liebermann's *ordines* I–IX (*Gesetze*, 1:401–17). *The Portiforium of St. Wulstan*, ed. A. Hughes, Henry Bradshaw Society, vol. 89 (London, 1956), pp. 166–72, and *Pontificale Lanaletense*, ed. G. H. Doble, ibid., vol. 74 (London, 1937), pp. 108–9, 116–25, are modern editions of some of these in their MS context.

93. *Ordines* X–XVI (*Gesetze*, 1:417–29). Mr. Wormald also relates the Carolingian *ordines* to the issues and texts debated by such men as Agobard of Vienne and Hincmar of Rheims in the early ninth century. Sources for the Anglo-Norman *ordines* were more general and will be hard to identify.

94. Walter Dürig, "Gottesurteile in Bereich des Benediktinerklosters WeihenStephan (Freising) unter Abt. Erchanger (1082–96)," *Archiv für Liturgiewissenschaft* 15 (1973): 101–7, associates the rituals in a late eleventh-century MS with a particular religious house some of whose monks left evidence of coolness toward the old ordeals. He concluded that mere copying is insufficient to prove use. This is of course true, but his evidence does not establish the contrary either.

95. Halphen, "La justice en France," pp. 187–88, cites charters that could be compared with rituals known to have been used in Anjou. Liebermann pointed out (*Gesetze*, 3:239) that Eadmer, *Historia Novorum in Anglia*, ed. Martin Rule, Rolls Series (London, 1884), p. 102 (for which see further below, at nn. 139–42 and accompanying text), uses language quite strongly reminiscent of *ordines* I–II and suggests that Eadmer knew them or something similar. *The Chronicle of John of Worcester, 1118–1140*, ed. J. R. H. Weaver, Anecdota Oxoniana, vol. 13 (Oxford, 1908), p. 30, furnishes full detail of a hot iron ordeal in 1130; the work circulated to other monasteries, one of which (Gloucester) omitted this passage.

96. For example, *ordines* III, 1–2; X, 2.20.

possible variant. At best coverage was incomplete. Like the laws, for instance, extant rituals apparently envisage no "civil" uses; probands are always suspects of serious crimes or adultery.[97] Finally, some parts at least needed translation into English, if the proband were to understand fully and be impressed,[98] for, unlike the laws, *liturgica* are always in Latin.

In short, the rituals must be treated as a small selection from liturgical literature that, despite the number of copies known and their fairly wide geographical spread, might stand revealed as quite unrepresentative of actual practice, could we but view the whole scene. All the same, within the field of royal prosecution for serious crime, the rituals helpfully corroborate our global model in certain respects and prompt at least one reservation. In particular they well illustrate some of the techniques adopted to increase the chances of achieving the desired end. They show, first of all, the effort to abstract the proband from the normal atmosphere of his everyday life. Sequestrated from his community, he had to forego his family, friends, and clothes, and was compelled to spend the few days before his test in prayer and fasting with a priest he did not know as his only company inside a strange church.[99] Meanwhile the ritual begs God to manifest here on earth His divine justice. This may be all the compilers intended, but the priest's every act intensified the moral pressure on the proband. Each stage of the ritual on the day further charged the atmosphere. The priest's exhortatory address could easily be modified to suit the individual case and take advantage of any appropriate sculpture or paintings (the Last Judgment was particularly apt!) in the church. Like the repetitive litanies that followed, it cited biblical precedents to stress God's immanent justice.[100] The blessing of the ordeal equipment called upon God to harm the guilty but spare the innocent. The proband was ushered toward a mass but warned not to accept the Eucharist unless he was innocent; otherwise, he might choke! "May the Lord's body be with you at the proof today," a postconquest ritual adds.[101] Again and again the theme of no escape for the wicked thunders out. The keeper of truth and guardian of the weak will make evident any *maleficia*, and thwart all diabolic attempts to subvert the proof.[102] Despite the supernatural tone and context, I doubt whether compilers or readers intended any clear

97. Unlike the laws, the rituals are silent about accusers or observers from the two parties. Contrast in particular *Ordal*, 4. The laws envisage private accusers as well as perhaps public prosecution (cf. 3 *Atr.*, 3, etc.) or ex officio persecution by reeves and others.

98. *Gesetze*, 3:239, thought this likely, in part on the evidence of Old English glosses.

99. The proband's home village could be some way from the ordeal church. Note that fasting meant a restriction to food and water as defined by the rituals: so much bread, cress, salt, etc.

100. Morris, "Judicium Dei," p. 100.

101. *Ordo* XIII.4.1 and cf. *ordines* III.2.3–4, VII.12.1, and XIII.9.

102. For example, *ordines* I.1, II.3. Cf. *Novae Narrationes*, ed. Elsie Shanks, completed with a legal introduction by S. F. C. Milsom, Selden Society, vol. 80 (London, 1963), B. 13, for the champion's oath on the field in thirteenth-century duels.

distinction between magic and more commonplace tricks and dodges:[103] all equally were of the Devil and would fail if God willed them to do so. Meanwhile the proband was continually reminded of the iron heating nearby when holy water sprinkled on it provoked steam and spluttering, which perhaps exaggerated the temperature it had reached.[104] Only the most resolute of men entertained no second thoughts under this psychological bombardment.

Many no doubt surrendered. Others were now so jittery that they threw away their chance of success. All the while members of the affected community were watching attentively. Whatever the outcome, they too, equally uncomfortable in the alien surroundings, could perceive important lessons. The *spectaculum* presented a visible sign "so that the rest seeing this might be freed from their incredulity through God's mercy."[105] For example, the crucial distinction between fidelity and infidelity[106] had a much wider potential significance than for the suspect and his alleged crime only. Thus were the onlookers imbued with the standards of behavior. Yet at the same time, the resolution of doubt[107] apparently concentrates on the specific allegation more closely than our model suggested. God proclaims a man's guilt or innocence of a particular act in the course of a judgment on the whole man and his soul.[108]

After 1066 the Old English enactments about proof procedure in theft were repeated, ostensibly as living law, in various translations and revisions. The later *leges* are slightly more detailed.[109] England was now dominated by an alien French aristocracy who were not fully conversant with English procedure. The newcomers' possession of their own personal laws was a further minor complication, because French proof customs differed a little from the English ones.[110] The only notable innovation, however, was the introduction of trial by battle.[111] Postconquest

103. Morris, "Judicium Dei," p. 102, takes a slightly different line, which may be compared with evidence he cites later, pp. 106, 108.

104. *Ordo*, XVI.8 (1067–1210).

105. *Ordo*, II.4; cf. *ordines* VII.24, X.2.20.4.

106. *Ordo*, II.2.

107. Cf. n. 106.

108. The statement in Brown, "Society and the Supernatural," p. 127, that "God is revealing 'truth' not any specific fact" should be compared with the text he cites in n. 28.

109. References are mostly in the notes below. *LHP* has slightly more extended treatment: see below at nn. 114–16 and accompanying text. *Wl. Lad.*, 1.2, 2, and *Wl. Ep.*, 4, specify the kind of ordeal envisaged.

110. L. Delisle, "Cérémonial d'une épreuve judiciaire," *Bibliothèque de l'école des chartes* 18 (1857): 253–57, is an interesting early twelfth-century *ordo* from Fécamp including a "book" ordeal. Adolphe Tardif, *La procédure civile et criminelle au XIIIe et XIVe siècles* (Paris, 1885), pp. 90–101, is a fair general survey.

111. I am prepared to believe that the Scandinavian *holmgangr* (single combat) was practised in eleventh-century England, as suggested by C. E. Wright, *The Cultivation of Saga in Anglo-Saxon England* (Edinburgh, 1939), pp. 191–92, despite his reliance on late evidence. Equally, the English were very familiar with the idea of battles as judgments of

ordeal rituals, for example, followed the same sub-Carolingian lines as before.[112] Some conflicts of custom were, nevertheless, inevitable, although under the new regime the two peoples lived mostly apart, each organizing its own affairs. Even limited contacts, however, produced disputes; to avoid chaos, the king himself had to pronounce on the mode of trial. A decree of William I's ruled on the proofs used in certain actions directly concerning royal justice. Frenchmen could offer their accustomed battle against English opponents, but the English could decline it in favor of some other *dom*. But this was no soft option. The accused Frenchman could clear himself with an "unbroken" oath, that is an oath that need not be word perfect. On the other hand, an Englishman faced by a French accusation might evade battle only by offering to carry the red-hot iron.[113]

This decree regulated only those allegations of serious crime like homicide and theft that later classified as appeals of felony. Very little can be learned about "civil" use of ordeals elsewhere. In the century after 1066, the use of the old ordeals probably atrophied except for the repression of crime. Disappearances are hardest of all to document, but the process roughly coincided with the withering away of the old law of *bot* and *wer*. Certainly the twelfth-century *leges* proclaim no great changes from the Old English system. When the compiler of the *Leges Henrici Primi*, for example, appears momentarily to condemn *peregrina vero judicia*, he is mechanically following Pseudo-Isidore.[114] Elsewhere he comfortably accepts the old verities of his Anglo-Saxon sources and advocates ordeal and battle alongside proof by *testes* and oath.[115] He rehearses much of the preconquest material on the subject, adding detail on such matters as the court's discretion in the award of proof.[116]

Although the *Leges Henrici* are less than convincing evidence of practice, in all likelihood use of unilateral ordeals in local courts as the criminal proof of last resort was rapidly becoming their main surviving function. The great twelfth-century rise in the importance of private justice is no objection, for private lords must in any event have been responsible for most of those who went to the ordeal. Even in the tenth century, royal control of theft trials left to them a considerable role and share in the profits. Ethelred's Wantage code had ordered that ordeals always be held in a royal *byrig*, but made *landrica* responsible for putting to the ordeal any suspect whom no one would accuse.[117] In the twelfth

God. But M. Bloomfield, "Beowulf, Byrhtnoth and the Judgment of God: Trial by Combat in Anglo-Saxon England," *Speculum* 44 (1969): 545–59, strangely can produce no good evidence of the duel as a judicial institution.

112. See above, at n. 93.

113. *Wl. Lad.*, 1, 1.1, 2, 3.2; *Wl. Art.*, 6, 6.3; *P&M*, 1:90–91.

114. *LHP*, 31.7a; Downer, *LHP*, p. 135, however, translates as "judgments pronounced by strangers."

115. *LHP*, 45.1a, 87.6; see below, at n. 125.

116. *LHP*, 9.6, 18.1, 45.1a, 64.1 ff., 64.9, 65.3, 72.

117. 3 *Atr.*, 4.2, 6.1.

century private individuals clearly valued the right to hold ordeals.[118] The average baron still wished to order suspects to the ordeal and expected to hold duels regularly at his *caput* to determine disputes over his fees and other pleas.[119] Contemporaries felt that this ability was essential to baronial dignity. Yet the continuance of grants of ordeal rights long after 1215 suggests that they were a franchisal matter, theoretically of royal grant.[120] Furthermore, most of the churches that staged ordeals can be associated with hundreds[121] or hundred groups[122] from before the conquest, or with bishops to whom the Conqueror entrusted control after 1066.[123] Most barons would certainly have resented the idea that they held their ordeals by royal license; yet, royal officials attended non-royal ceremonies to ensure fair play and execute the king's justice on condemned men.[124] This context of royal theft jurisdiction and the whole public flavor of twelfth-century ordeals makes "civil" usage questionable. Of course the duel was the standard proof in land suits and a variety of other serious "civil" cases.[125] But the evidence most usually cited to

118. Naomi D. Hurnard, "The Anglo-Norman Franchises," *English Historical Review* 69 (1949): 433–60, at 436–37.

119. F. M. Stenton, *The First Century of English Feudalism*, 2d ed. (Oxford, 1961), pp. 103–4 n, approved this thesis of R. R. Reid, "Barony and Thanage," *English Historical Review* 35 (1920): 161–99, at 169–76 (with argument about France and Scotland on pp. 166–68, 180–81), despite his skepticism about other parts of her argument. Reid, "Barony and Thanage," p. 168 n, was probably right to read *LHP*, 55.1, as envisaging the holding of baronial duels; R. B. Patterson, ed., *Earldom of Gloucester Charters* (Oxford, 1973), no. 109 (1126), is an illustration.

120. Hurnard, "Anglo-Norman Franchises," p. 436. A former right to hold the ordeal was good evidence for present possession of *infangthief*, the right to hang handhaving thieves.

121. Calne's old minister may be one example; cf. *Britain before the Norman Conquest*, Ordnance Survey (Southampton, 1973), p. 56; *Domesday Book*, vol. 1, fol. 64b; and above, at pp. 93–95. For Sherburn, cf. Patterson, *Earldom of Gloucester Charters*, no. 171. For Shorne, Kent, cf. *CRR*, 15:835 = *Bracton's Note Book*, ed. Frederic W. Maitland, 3 vols. (London, 1887), no. 821 (1233). *E. Cf.*, 9.3, implies that there could be more than one ordeal church in a hundred.

122. James Tait, *The Medieval English Borough* (Manchester, 1936), p. 37; Helen M. Cam, *Liberties and Communities in Medieval England* (Cambridge, 1944), pp. 101–2, for Wye, Kent; *Domesday Book*, vol. 1, fol. 87b; A. J. Robertson, *Anglo-Saxon Charters* (Cambridge, 1939), pp. 236–39, for Taunton, Somerset.

123. *Wl. Ep.*, 4.2, *Ep.*, 5, and *Inst. Cn.*, iii.58, are the legislative texts; cf. Hurnard, "Anglo-Norman Franchises," pp. 459–60. Bishops already enjoyed control in Normandy (Colin Morris, "William I and the Church Courts," *English Historical Review* 82 [1967]: 452–63). Council of Lillebonne (1080), c. 40, which confirmed this position, was apparently later reissued in England, too; cf. P. Chaplais, "Henry II's Reissue of the Canons of the Council of Lillebonne of Whitsun, 1080 (?25 February 1162)," *Journal of the Society of Archivists* 4 (1973): 627 ff. Nottarp, *Gottesurteilstudien*, pp. 246–47, cites two papal letters to England on the subject of clerical extortion; the archdeacon of Coventry allegedly required thirty pence (!) to hold an ordeal.

124. *E. Cf.*, 9; *LHP*, 26.4; cf. R. F. Hunnisett, *The Medieval Coroner* (Cambridge, 1961), p. 6; and Reginald of Durham, *Vita Sancti Godrici*, ed. J. Stephenson, Surtees Society, vol. 20 (London, 1847), p. 235. Procedure was similar in Scotland, if the texts are to be believed. In general, the Scots seem to have followed England with a time lag; see Willock, *The Jury in Scotland*, chap. 4; and Reid, "Barony and Thanage," pp. 180–81.

125. *Hn. Com.*, 3.3; *LHP*, 48.12, 49.6, 59.16a. The implication of later evidence, like

establish "civil" use of the unilateral ordeals comes from the wholly exceptional circumstances of the Domesday *invasiones*, before a public, perhaps fiscally inspired, inquiry. The commissioners may not even have accepted the offers, which are all the references show.[126] How much, if at all, were unilateral ordeals still used in English law courts? I know of no firm twelfth-century evidence for the actual holding of ordeals in "civil" cases. An England with few or no "civil" ordeals at this stage apparently differs from her neighbors.[127] Significantly, if this really was so, she had reached that situation by natural attrition, without any formal decisions.

Meanwhile, popular ordeals continued deep in the English countryside where royal justice seldom reached.[128] Even as politicians and sophisticated thinkers advanced to newer ways, clerical writers voiced the old sentiments. Scribes copied and elaborated ordeal rituals well into the Angevin period.[129] Seven manuscripts of the mid-twelfth century or later preserve the form of benediction used by the Church of York to favor its approved champions in judicial duels.[130] Approving ordeal anecdotes were published in historical works[131] and in *vitae* of the holy men whose aid ordeal probands earnestly besought,[132] as well as in the largely oral

---

Glanvill (see below) and practice in felony appeals, is corroborated by a smattering of references to contemporary duels in charters, *vitae*, and cases such as *Bracton's Note Book*, no. 1436.

126. See below, at nn. 137 and 147 and accompanying text, for other twelfth-century offers of ordeals.

127. Civil use of ordeals certainly continued in Normandy; P. Le Cacheux, "Une Charte de Jumièges concernant l'épreuve par le fer chaude," in *Mélanges société de l'histoire de Normandie* (Rouen, 1927), pp. 203–17, describes a colorful example. See also Bongert, *Recherches*, pp. 203 ff.; and Nottarp, *Gottesurteilstudien*, pp. 117 ff.

128. The only English evidence for this assumption that I have noticed is R. W. Southern, *The Making of the Middle Ages* (London, 1953), p. 97, from the mid-thirteenth century Roger Bacon. William of Malmesbury, *Gesta Pontificum*, ed. N. E. S. A. Hamilton, Rolls Series (London, 1870), p. 181, and *Chronicon Monasterii Abbendoniae*, vol. 2, ed. Joseph Stevenson, Rolls Series (London, 1858), p. 259, tell the kind of story that would have encouraged men to hold popular ordeals.

129. See Liebermann's apparatus to *ordines* X–XVI, *Gesetze*, 1:417–29.

130. *Duel, Gesetze*, 1:430–31. By *Regesta Regum Anglo-Normannorum*, vol. 2, *1100–1135*, ed. Charles Johnson and H. A. Cronne (Oxford, 1956), no. 1083, Henry I granted duel privileges to St. Peter's, York. The privilege was confirmed in 1136 by Stephen, *Regesta Regum Anglo-Normannorum 1066–1154*, vol. 3, *1135–54*, ed. H. A. Cronne and R. H. C. Davis (Oxford, 1967), no. 975 = *Historians of the Church of York*, vol. 3, ed. J. Raine, Rolls Series (London, 1894), p. 36.

131. Earl Godwin's death from a stroke in 1053 was represented as a popular ordeal by morsel in later Norman tradition. Wright, *The Cultivation of Saga*, pp. 233–36, conveniently discusses the texts that may be compared with the contemporary *Anglo-Saxon Chronicle*, C, s.a. 1053. Geffrei Gaimar, *Lestorie des Engles*, ed. T. D. Hardy and C. T. Martin, Rolls Series (London, 1888), lines 4870 ff. (pp. 206–13), details Godwin's supposed trial for the Aetheling's death much more fully than Florence of Worcester, *Chronicon*, ed. Benjamin Thorpe (London, 1848), 1:195.

132. *Historians of the Church of York*, 2:542–43, is of special interest because the saint there modified an autonomic response; he caused a great swelling, which came up after touching the hot iron, to go down, and the woman was freed. See also ibid., pp. 289–90,

vernacular literature.[133] And, because God's judgment remained an approved theme in accounts of battle and warfare,[134] the civil duel, which flourished throughout the century, was still sometimes described (and rather less often experienced) as a test of the old providential kind. Men were still inclined to seek supernatural aid from the saints before entering upon a duel; Robert de Montfort, awaiting his treason appeal against Henry de Essex in 1163, apparently traveled, like so many others, to Soissons for a vigil before the remains of St. Drausius.[135] And a few years later, Roger de Clere added to his grant of a quarter church to a Gilbertine house the explanatory note that "I acquired the aforesaid fee with God's help by a duel in the lord king's court at London and therefore deemed it necessary to give part of the fee into God's service for the souls of my father *etc. etc.*"[136] That these sentiments probably belonged as much to the monastic draftsmen as to Roger himself only confirms the continuing clerical commitment to the old rationale. This is especially impressive in the case of the duel because of clerical feeling against violence and bloodshed. It is equally suggestive that the last two offers of an old ordeal that I have noted both came from clerics.[137] In about 1157 an aged retired prior to Worcester did not hesitate to proffer the hot iron, or any proof dictated in equity, in support of a Gloucester Abbey land claim against the Church of York. His archaic offer was intended to vindicate the testimony he based on respectable charters, chronicles, and *testes*. A little earlier, one of Archbishop William of York's clerks was ready to undergo hot iron, hot water, or battle to substantiate his allegation that Osbert the archdeacon was guilty of his master's death. Neither offer was accepted; Osbert understandably responded by seeking *ecclesiasticum iudicium*. The striking fact is that these offers were made at a time when

---

and *Chronicon Abbatiae De Evesham*, ed. William Dunn Macray, Rolls Series (London, 1863), pp. 323–24.

133. Hexter, *Equivocal Oaths*, and E. C. York, "Isolt's Ordeal: English Legal Customs in the Medieval Tristan Legend," *Studies in Philology* 68 (1971): 1–9, make some interesting points. The lack of a contemporary literature in English can fairly be met, up to a point, by recourse to French works such as the Tristan cycle, with its mass of commentary.

134. William of Poitiers, *Gesta Guillelmi*, ed. R. Foreville (Paris, 1952), pp. 174–78, on the battle of Hastings, is particularly "legal" in tone. Georges Duby, *Le Dimanche de Bouvines* (Paris, 1973), pp. 147–59, makes about as much as can be made of this theme.

135. John of Salisbury, *Ep.*, 145 (Migne, *PL*, 199, cols. 136–37), stresses the saint's wide appeal to those in search of invincibility. M. Germain, *Histoire de l'abbaye royale de N. D. de Soissons* (Paris, 1675), p. 427, prints the relevant passage from the *Vita* (tenth century or earlier). *The Chronicle of Jocelin of Brakelond*, pp. 70–71, is one account of the Montfort-Essex duel.

136. *Transcripts of Charters Relating to Gilbertine Houses*, ed. F. M. Stenton, Lincolnshire Record Society, vol. 18 (Lincoln, 1922), p. 43, no. 9 (before 1184). Cf. *The Letters . . . of Gilbert Foliot*, no. 119.

137. Melville Madison Bigelow, *Placita Anglo-Normannica: Law Cases from William I to Richard I* (London, 1879), p. 196; *The Letters of John of Salisbury*, ed. W. J. Millor, H. E. Butler, and C. N. L. Brooke (London, 1955), 1, no. 16; cf. M. D. Knowles, "The Case of St. William of York," *Cambridge Historical Journal* 5 (1937): 175.

learned opinion sanctioned the vulgar proofs only for possible use against laymen. English scholars, even those outside the learned vanguard, were certainly not unaware of the current of thought flowing against the ordeal.[138]

The rising tide of clerical disapproval of the ordeal is often illustrated with a famous story from Eadmer's *History of Recent Events*, written under Henry I.[139] Properly understood, however, this text jeopardizes the view of the church as the major force behind the transformation of proofs. Fifty men accused of forest offenses were adjudged to the hot iron, which they duly carried at the appointed time to reveal on the third day afterwards the unburnt hands of the innocent. Eadmer represented their trial as King William Rufus's attempt finally to break the Old English families of the accused, and described the king's outburst on their acquittal. Rufus railed at God's judgment, which, he complained, could be swayed by men's prayers. He would in the future, therefore, retain judgment in his own hands. Perhaps he suspected that the celebrant priests had arranged the acquittal—and perhaps he was right.[140] In that event, it would be quite understandable to seek modes of proof less susceptible to clerical management. That Eadmer, who clearly sympathized with the English accused, chose to interpret the king's attitude as religious skepticism, a straight denial almost of divine omniscience and providential power, reflects the monk's own belief in God and the ordeals. The story is an *exemplum* to demonstrate St. Anselm's difficulties with the impossible king and to justify the saint's attempt to abandon his duties on papal license.[141] Modern readers, if prepared to accept the anecdote's basic truth, may prefer to interpret it as a royal political stroke thwarted by the chicanery of interfering clerics. At any rate, the ordeal critic here is the lay king, intent on power over men. The studious monk Eadmer, his friends round St. Anselm, and more generally the Gregorian party in England probably remained sympathetic to the old ordeals into the second quarter of the century.[142]

How then might an interested and informed observer have summarized

138. The earliest English condemnation I have noted dates from 1142–44 and was produced at Paris (F. Courtney, *Cardinal Robert Pullen*, Analecta Gregoriana, vol. 64 [Rome, 1954], p. 242 and n.). See also *The Letters . . . of Gilbert Foliot*, no. 237 (1163–77), with the editors' comments in A. Morey and C. N. L. Brooke, *Gilbert Foliot and His Letters* (Cambridge, 1965), p. 241 and above, at n. 57 for Bartholomew of Exeter; and E. Rathbone, "Roman Law in the Anglo-Norman Realm," in *Collectanea Stephan Kuttner*, 4 vols. = *Studia Gratiana*, vols. 11–14 (Bologna, 1967), 1:265–66, 271, for Senatus of Worcester (before 1179) and Alanus Anglicus.

139. Eadmer, *Historia Novorum*, pp. 101–2; see van Caenegem, "La preuve," pp. 710–11.

140. An officiant might allow the iron to cool, for example, as in *Pipe Roll, 21 Henry II*, Pipe Roll Society, vol. 22 (London, 1897), p. 131: "de Philippo filio Wiardi et v. aliis pro ferro iuise bis portato de i calefactione."

141. Eadmer, *Historia Novorum*, pp. 99, 103.

142. Morris, "Judicium Dei," abundantly documents the reliance of the Gregorian party on the miraculous, including ordeals. The story cited above, at text accompanying n. 11, was certainly circulating among English Gregorians and followers of St. Anselm into the 1130s.

current practice about proof at the end of Henry I's reign? In theory the ordeal still flourished. Lordships claimed and valued the right to order men to it. Local courts and their associated churches understood its scope and procedure. Relatively little public comment was unfavorable. But practice was another matter. Actual use of the old ordeals in properly constituted courts was more or less confined to serious crimes that had defeated more mundane methods. The judicial duel was favored in land suits as well as appeals of felony, but some form of oath probably served as the judgment of last resort in many "civil" cases.[143] In general, moreover, a hypothetical observer might have noticed (where the historian tied to written evidence cannot) a steady growth of reliance on rational argument about evidence, with the aid of documents[144] and *testes*.[145] True, progress was uneven, largely confined to a few major centers and their hinterlands. And just as Anglo-Norman centralization of justice had helped before 1135, the ensuing relaxation of royal grip under Stephen and Matilda may have signaled some slight revival of the older proofs. All the same, Henry of Anjou, law reformer-to-be, came in 1154 to the throne of a country whose law of proof was already under reconstruction.[146]

Henry's legal reforms primarily affected the Curia Regis, where unilateral ordeals were seldom seen in the twelfth century.[147] The impact on the local and seignorial courts that handled most duels and ordeals is harder to assess. Nevertheless, Angevin adjustments to proofs set the pattern for the future. The battle of ideas, already underway in 1154, was still far from won. Its completion required considerable ingenuity and a real effort to justify innovation against conservative doubts.[148]

143. *Pipe Roll, 31 Henry I*, ed. J. Hunter, Record Commission (London, 1833); repr., ed. Charles Johnson (London, 1929), p. 35, records a proffer of twenty marcs "ut purgaret se de judicio ferri per sacramentum." The ordeal can be referred to as *lex*, e.g., *Pleas before the King or His Justices, 1198–1212*, 4 vols., ed. Doris M. Stenton, Selden Society, vols. 67 (London, 1948), 68 (1949), 83 (1966), 84 (1967) (hereafter cited as *PKJ*), 1, no. 3169 (1201); *CRR*, 2:56 (1201). For wager of law, see *P&M*, 2:634–37; R. L. Henry, *Contracts in the Local Courts of Medieval England* (London, 1929), chap. 2; and A. W. B. Simpson, *A History of the Common Law of Contract* (Oxford, 1975); pp. 137–44. See also above, at n. 68.

144. Hence the boom in forgery! Morey and Brooke, *Gilbert Foliot and His Letters*, chap. 7.

145. Eadmer, *Historia Novorum*, p. 138, is an enlightening anecdote about eleventh-century attitudes toward the advantages of witnesses as against documents: why should one prefer the word of monks plus a piece of sheepskin, marked with ink and a lump of lead (i.e., a papal bull!), against that of three bishops?!

146. An assessment of the extent of royal influence over the whole range of litigation and dispute settlement in the first half of the twelfth century is badly needed. I take no position here on, for example, the prehistory of the Angevin jury.

147. Two apparently serious offers of ordeals are, however, known from Stephen's court *coram rege*. In addition to those cited above, at n. 137 and accompanying text, one is recorded by Thomas of Monmouth, *The Life and Miracles of St. William of Norwich*, ed. Augustus Jessopp and Montague Rhodes James (Cambridge, 1896), p. 47 (1144).

148. In a forthcoming exploratory paper entitled "The Place of Henry II in English Legal History," I discuss this subject at greater length.

The central theme of the Angevin reforms is the institutionalizing of local community testimony in the jury.[149] Juries attracted royal advisers for two main reasons. First of all they appealed to common sense. Royal *familiares* made their political choices and managed their estates most of the time along lines that were quite rational in the terms of today. Why should they not develop court procedure similarly? Masters of the two learned laws might then sneer a little less at England's unwritten custom.[150] Furthermore, the king and his justices secured the kind of control over judgment and proof whose lack Rufus had already felt. The second consideration was probably less important. Some consciences were certainly disturbed by the sin inherent in the ordeal's tempting of God. Many *familiares* were, of course, at least conventionally religious, as is evident from their pious benefactions that often included a prayer for their royal master's soul. Nevertheless, concern for salvation was probably not a decisive factor. Rather, expediency dictated their innovations and also alerted them to the possibility of some traditionalist resistance to change.[151] Like colonial administrators, the reformers imposed progress "for their own good" on benighted rustics slow to see its benefits. To avoid giving unnecessary offense to the church was only sensible. Consequently, they armed themselves with a rationale that would satisfy critics from that quarter.

The most compelling evidence for this view comes from the civil jury in the real actions. Scholars quite rightly place the petty assizes in a rational context of judgments derived from the systematic collection and processing of relevant information. During the first generation of the reforms, however, contemporaries may sometimes have followed quite a different line of rationalization. An unsympathetic questioner could have been advised to regard the jury as a new method of putting issues to God, no more, no less. This conception of the jury as a new ordeal made some sense at the time.[152] The issues put to early assizes and recognitions were mixed questions similar to those formulated for ordeals.[153] Initially, there was no obvious awareness of the distinction between fact and law.

149. Ralph V. Turner, "The Origin of the Medieval English Jury: Frankish, English, or Scandinavian?" *Journal of British Studies* 7 (1967): 1–10, is a competent recent survey of the state of the question. *Glanvill*, XII, 25 (p. 148), seems to imply that recognitions are a royal monopoly.

150. *Glanvill*, Prologue, proves that one royal adviser was sensitive to slights from his colleagues of the two laws.

151. Recent studies have made little of the critical response to the legal reforms. Much of the material cited by M. T. Clanchy, "*Moderni* in Education and Government in England," *Speculum* 50 (1975): 671–88, is from this period. For Ralph Niger, see H. Kantorowicz and B. Smalley, "An English Theologian's View of Roman Law," *Medieval and Renaissance Studies* 1 (1941): 237–52.

152. Plucknett, *Concise History*, pp. 137–38, 417–18; F. Jouon des Longrais, "La preuve en Angleterre depuis 1066," in *La preuve*, pp. 193–274, at p. 206; Cheyette, "Custom, Case Law and Medieval 'Constitutionalism,'" pp. 372–73.

153. Early assizes were asked to decide, for example, if a plaintiff had had seisin *ut de libero tenemento* before he was disseised *iniuste* (novel disseisin: *Glanvill*, XIII, 33 [p. 167]), or if his ancestor had been seised *in dominico suo sicut de feudo suo* (mort

Jurors, selected for their local knowledge, could and did attempt to check the facts of the case,[154] but only God could say whether their views on the moral imperatives implied by questions about the manner of seisin were correct. Thus early jury verdicts were genuinely inscrutable; they do not merely appear so because of our sources.[155] One could accuse a court of mishandling and fraud, or challenge jurors to defend their perjury by battle, but as in the old ordeals, God would neither explain His motives nor change His mind on request.

This kind of justification, although required only briefly, had considerable effect. Juries answered questions about land seisin for about fifteen years before the establishment of the Grand Assize.[156] The right to land was of much greater moment than mere seisin. To call upon human beings to declare who had in the past held land made very good sense. Physical control was visible to human eyes, and could be symbolized in tangible, memorable acts.[157] But past events were merely persuasive evidence for the location of *dreit*, the right to hold land: only God could say who *ought* to be the tenant. Some hesitation before the jury was applied to questions of right is therefore to be expected. Ambiguous feelings about the new ordeal, and even more a consciousness that decisions in the right were permanently binding, explain this reluctance. A procedure for right had to be in many ways the equivalent of the judicial duel that it replaced. As Glanvill's account of proof shows, the Grand Assize was just such an equivalent.

For Glanvill, battle remained a fully respectable part of the *generalis probandi modus*[158] that could still be used to declare the right in a wide variety of disputes. For most of these, the Angevins never offered a procedure of the newer type. Battle might decide, for example, a question of right arising out of an assize of mort d'ancestor, or an action of debt, even when a written charter existed.[159] Perhaps current practice (*modo*

---

d'ancestor: *Glanvill*, XIII [p. 150]). In each case, the specifications of the *kind* of seisin involved legal questions that were not always argued in open court. The very concept of "seisin" probably referred to a legal/moral, as well as factual, state, until learned lawyers like Glanvill reduced it to a lesser counterpart of *ius* = "right." Early jurors might not separate these different strands in their own minds, but clearly their verdicts involved nonfactual judgments too.

154. Stenton, *First Century of English Feudalism*, pp. 82, 270 (app., no. 21), and David Walker, "A Letter from the Holy Land," *English Historical Review* 72 (1957): 662–65, print documents concerning information offered to jurors by great men. Jurors' enquiries of lesser folk are harder to document.

155. S. F. C. Milsom, "Law and Fact in Legal Development," *University of Toronto Law Journal* 17 (1967): 1 ff., explores this area in brilliant fashion; see also his *Legal Framework*, chap. 1 and passim.

156. Here I follow Round's dating of ca. 1179. However, if the view of Milsom, *Legal Framework*, on the *breve de recto* were correct, an earlier date for the origins of the grand assize, back almost to the first of Henry II's writs *de recto*, might follow.

157. Samuel E. Thorne, "Livery of Seisin," *Law Quarterly Review* 52 (1936): 345–64, still has a great deal to teach us.

158. *Glanvill*, X, 17 (p. 132).

159. *Glanvill*, V, 4, 5 (pp. 55–58), VI, 11, (p. 64), X, 12, 15, 17, (pp. 126, 131, 132), XIII, 11 (p. 154).

solet) preferred now to deal with disputes about grants *aliquibus certis et manifestis indiciis*,[160] but wager of a duel between charter witnesses was still perfectly legitimate. Before 1200 battle was not obviously superseded by the Grand Assize and other recognitions. Relatively few charters that refer to proof of right mention the Grand Assize.[161] In any case, battle and Grand Assize, near equivalents for Glanvill, remain genuine alternatives at the defendant's option.[162] The rules under which they operate are very similar.[163] Defenses to the Grand Assize are *pari ratione ac per duellum*.[164] And each should lead to a decision that binds the present parties forever.[165]

Why then was the *regale beneficium* a matter for praise? Glanvill's explanation reflects above all the contemporary consciousness of the chancy nature of duels. The miracle stories that emphasize the participants' desire for supernatural assistance demonstrate this same awareness.[166] The combatant risked both his life and his good name, for the cry of "craven" entailed perpetual infamy, the loss of a man's free law.[167] The new assize offered three advantages over battle; two amounted to good common sense.[168] By the Grand Assize, a freeman could avoid physical danger without thereby forfeiting his land. Initially the procedure was, too, swifter than battle, whose formalities necessitated adjournments while the proper arrangements were made. The trouble and money thus saved were an especial boon to the poor. Glanvill's third point is quite different. He explains that the assize was born of the highest equity because the oaths of twelve "suitable" witnesses are weightier in judgments than the single oath of one duel combatant. The archaic ring derives from a world where the numbers and standing of oath helpers were all-important and where jury process was understood as compurgation updated.[169] And if here, too, theory very soon advanced to more "modern" conceptions, one important reason was the reformulation of the issue in terms of *maius ius* to the disputed property. Where com-

160. *Glanvill*, X, 12 (p. 127).

161. That J. H. Round could adduce so few charters in his article "The Date of the Grand Assize," *English Historical Review* 31 (1916): 268–69, speaks for itself. Most charters specify trial by duel if they mention proof at all.

162. *Glanvill*, IX, 1, (p. 105); cf. *CRR*, 2:18–19 (1201).

163. *Glanvill*, II, 19 (p. 36).

164. *Glanvill*, III, 5 (p. 41).

165. *Glanvill*, II, 3, 18 (pp. 25, 35); cf. *Bracton's Note Book*, no. 1436 (1220), where the court would not rule a second time on an issue already submitted to trial by battle some time before 1166.

166. Reginald of Durham, *Vita Sancti Godrici*, pp. 189–91, reminds one that innocent men who had sought saintly aid nevertheless sometimes died in the duel.

167. *Glanvill*, II, 3 (p. 25); cf. *LHP*, 43.7. The letters patent, cited above, at n. 31, display something of the impact this sanction retained even in the 1270s.

168. *Glanvill*, II, 7 (p. 28).

169. Cf. n. 143 above. Milsom, *Legal Framework*, pp. 84–85, makes a very different suggestion about the Grand Assize, quite plausible in itself and not incompatible with the view in the text here. Note however that *Glanvill*, VII, 3 (p. 78), does not prohibit battle between a nephew and the uncle who is also his lord, providing that no homage has been performed.

batants had once perhaps called on God through the duel to declare which party had absolute right,[170] the knights of the assize were asked only to compare claims as well as human beings could. This formulation of the issue promoted factual discussion and argument, and facilitated "the rise of an abstract concept of property in land," perhaps for the first time in English law.[171]

So Glanvill's comments on battle and its replacements are less clear and rational than some scholars have thought. His treatment of unilateral ordeals is briefer and less controversial. He gives no hint that they were ever used in civil actions.[172] Even in appeals of felony, proof was always by battle unless the appellor was too old, physically incapable, or female.[173] Otherwise the ordeal was reserved for prosecutions *de fama* against people suspected of serious crime in the absence of a willing accuser. Glanvill is referring to the jury of presentment procedure, under the Assizes of Clarendon and Northampton,[174] which in the present context of proofs clearly stands toward the end of the old ordeals' long development as well as the start of the history of indictment.[175]

Henry II was not the first to link a royal drive against crime in the countryside with rules that put suspects to an exculpatory ordeal. The drive initiated in late 1165 or early 1166[176] perhaps differed less from its

170. Milsom, in *Novae Narrationes*, pp. xxv, xxxiv, argues from thirteenth-century evidence that the issue of a duel concerned the truth of the oaths the two champions had sworn; cf. *CRR*, 5:265–66 (1208). This may not have been the case earlier, before the evolution of the forms of action deprived courts of the freedom to formulate issues as they thought most fit. The evidence of *Glanvill*, II, 3 (p. 23), VIII, 9 (p. 100), is congruous with this possibility, in which case defenses *de verbo in verbum* would have been very exacting in the twelfth century. A precise record of the issues in duels waged at the shire would have been necessary before royal justices could determine how properly the inferior court had acted. The many allegations of procedural irregularity in the shire from the early plea rolls (C. T. Flower, *An Introduction to the Curia Regis Rolls, A.D. 1199–1230*, Selden Society, vol. 62 [London, 1943], p. 119) suggest that procedure had formerly been freer there than in the Curia Regis of the late twelfth century.

171. Milsom, *Legal Framework*, pp. 76–77. The 1201 case (*CRR*, 1:430; *Chronicle of Jocelin of Brakelond*, pp. 58–59, 123–24, 138–39) is an excellent illustration of the changes.

172. See, however, below, at n. 192.

173. *Glanvill*, X, 5 (p. 120), XIV, 1, 3, 6 (pp. 173, 174, 176); *PKJ*, 2, nos. 288, 619 (1201), is an example. Cf. Besnier, "'Vadiatio legis et leges,'" pp. 99–101. The ordeal was also used for accessories (Flower, *Introduction to CRR*, p. 321) and when an appellant withdrew (*PKJ*, 2, no. 729 [1201]).

174. *Glanvill*, XIV, 1 (p. 171). Suspected concealers of treasure trove were not, however, put to the ordeal on mere *infamia*; compare *Glanvill*, XIV, 2 (pp. 173–74), with the 1116 case recorded in *Liber Eliensis*, ed. E. O. Blake, Camden Society, 3d ser., vol. 92 (London, 1962), pp. 266–69; and Ordericus Vitalis, *Historia Ecclesiastica*, ed. and trans. Marjorie Chibnall, 6 vols. to date (Oxford, 1969–78), 3:347–58.

175. Naomi D. Hurnard, "The Jury of Presentment and the Assize of Clarendon," *English Historical Review* 56 (1941): 374–410, lies at the head of modern argument on the subject. See Thomas A. Green, "The Jury and the English Law of Homicide, 1200–1600," *Michigan Law Review* 74 (1976): 414 ff., for a brief survey.

176. Sutherland, *Assize of Novel Disseisin*, p. 7, n. 2; Janet Loengard, "The Assize of Nuisance: Origins of an Action at Common Law," *Cambridge Law Journal* 37 (1978): 144–66, at 154, n. 28.

tenth-century precedent (apart from its superior documentation) than we have realized. The suspect's reputation and record was the key in each case, though in different ways. The essence of the Angevin enactment was an order to each local community to report (through its representatives) to royal justices sitting in an afforced shire court[177] the names of any people the community feared as persistent offenders of serious crime. The community's perceptions were undoubtedly treated in a more sophisticated way, and were rigorously controlled to the king's interest, but the underlying principle was quite similar. Evil fame sufficed to force a suspect to his law and, because the fact of presentment already established this, no exculpatory oath was permitted.[178] All suspects either went to the water or were freed;[179] the justices might order acquittal, for example, if they believed the presentment malicious.[180] Distinctions like those of the Old English laws reappear only after the ordeal. Success did not ensure full freedom; men of very bad reputation could still be required after acquittal to find sureties or abjure the realm.[181] The proceedings, then, look highly mechanistic. But the justices retained enough discretion to be worth bribing. Glanvill explains that the court listened to argument before deciding to send a man to the ordeal, and the early plea rolls testify to careful inquiry into the grounds for suspicion.[182] The procedure comprised accusation, checking, and proof, but no real trial, even in the sense of the communal self-examination of popular ordeals. These hearings under the assizes were held at the king's expense[183] to repress crime and disorder in his realm to his greater credit. Hard evidence of high moral aims or any keen desire for justice is lacking. The presiding justices could have duly performed their duties without any

177. J. C. Holt, "The Assizes of Henry II: The Texts," in D. A. Bullough and R. L. Storey, eds., *The Study of Medieval Records* (Oxford, 1971), pp. 103–6, demonstrated the role of the sheriffs in the first visitation under the assize.

178. Charles L. Wells, "Early Opposition to the Petty Jury in Criminal Cases," *Law Quarterly Review* 30 (1914): 97–98, associates the shifting of the onus of proof onto the accused; this oversimplifies the previous position. Ralph Niger mentions in his *De re militari* (1189) *scelerati, quibus interdiceretur aqua et ignis in patria sua* (*Medieval Studies* 9 [1947]: 181), alongside criminals fleeing punishment by going on crusade. Presumably the *scelerati* were either convicted under the assize or forced to abjure the realm as *de pessimo testimonio*.

179. *Glanvill*, XIV, 1 (p. 171).

180. The writ *de odio et atia* is briefly mentioned below. See also above, at n. 89.

181. *Assize of Clarendon*, c. 14; *Northampton*, c. 1. *E. Cf.*, 9, assumes that those cleared by the ordeal went free.

182. *Glanvill*, XIV, 1 (p. 171); cf. ibid., XIV, 2 (pp. 173–74), for the more stringent requirements in the case of alleged concealment of treasure trove. Early plea roll illustrations include *PKJ*, 2, no. 255 (1201); *Somersetshire Pleas*, ed. Charles E. H. Chadwyck-Healey, Somerset Record Society, vol. 11 (London, 1897), pp. 88, 91, 95, 100 (1201); *The Earliest Northamptonshire Assize Rolls, A.D. 1202 and 1203*, ed. D. M. Stenton, Northants. Record Society, vol. 5 (1930), p. 726 (1203). See also Charles L. Wells, "The Origin of the Petty Jury," *Law Quarterly Review* 27 (1911): 347–61, at 348–49, 353.

183. *Dialogus de Scaccario*, ed. and trans. Charles Johnson (London, 1950), II.vii.A (p. 87), explains the pipe roll entries; cf. Holt, "The Assizes of Henry II," p. 104.

belief that the ordeal actually did reveal God's judgment. The fact is that the vast majority of those prosecuted under the procedure were of low social status.[184] The two assizes used the presentment jury and ordeal to make an example of those who could be caught.

In the end, then, the Henrician reforms occupy a rather paradoxical position in the transformation of proofs. Although the forward-looking civil jury represented to some extent a posthumous existence for the logic of the old ordeals, the one area where ordeals actually continued—public presentment of crime—exhibited toward its customers thoroughly unsentimental attitudes that belong to no single epoch or stage of legal development. By the end of the twelfth century, though, change moved unmistakably toward more juries, albeit still at a gentle canter. Sporadic batches of plea roll entries, recording criminal ordeals under the surveillance of eyre justices, remind one that the occasional peasant still had to carry the hot iron in the England of Magna Carta.[185] Ordeals may have remained quite common in private courts.[186] The number of county court duel cases whose records came before royal justices certainly implies that many battles were waged in the shires.[187] But royal justices were working to curtail the ordeal's scope long before 1215. They raised technical barriers under various pretenses to divert suspects from ordeals toward inquests.[188] Indeed, chapter 36 of Magna Carta, which freed the writ *de odio et atia* from impediments and thus helped to boost the criminal inquest, is almost as significant for the English law of proof as the Lateran Council's pronouncements in the same year, 1215.[189] In the absence of eyre visitations because of the civil war, the infant Henry III's council did not have to make a decision about the ordeal, at which no

184. This was Lady Stenton's impression too (*PKJ*, 1:41). M. T. Clanchy, "Highway Robbery and Trial by Battle in the Hampshire Eyre of 1249," in *Medieval Legal Records . . . C. A. F. Meekings*, ed. R. F. Hunnisett and J. B. Post (London, 1978), pp. 26–61, makes a similar guess about the social background of approvers. The assertion of *Glanvill*, XIV, 1 (p. 173), that villeins went to the water ordeal, freemen to the hot iron, may reflect not only learned legal sources (briefly indicated in my *King, Lords and Peasants in Medieval England* [Oxford, 1980], chap. 9) but also an awareness of the social distinctions involved. In fact, most suspects went to the water, among them at least one rich Londoner: see Roger of Howden, *Gesta Regis Henrici Secundi Benedicti Abbatis*, ed. William Stubbs, vol. 1, Rolls Series (London, 1867), p. 156 and *Chronicon*, ed. W. Stubbs, vol. 2, Rolls Series (London, 1869), p. 131. The hot iron seems to have been reserved for extreme cases, i.e., used as a quasi-punishment. In 1198 an alleged sorceress cleared herself by the hot iron (*PKJ*, 2, no. 103; *CRR*, 1:108). Lady Stenton suspected that the justices were less sure of her guilt than angry Norwich citizens were (*PKJ*, 1:45).

185. *CRR*, 3:144 (Oxford, 1204); *CRR*, 7:241 (Newgate delivery, 1214).

186. They leave little trace there. *CRR*, 8:41–42 (1219), is one example.

187. Flower, *Introduction to CRR*, pp. 113 ff., 119.

188. Lady Stenton, in *Rolls of the Justices in Eyre for Lincolnshire, 1218–19, and Worcestershire, 1221*, Selden Society, vol. 53 (London, 1934), p. lxviii, and in *Rolls of the Justices in Eyre in Yorkshire, 1218–19*, Selden Society, vol. 56 (London, 1937), pp. xl–xli, and Naomi D. Hurnard, in *The King's Pardon for Homicide before A.D. 1307* (Oxford, 1969), pp. 339–50, esp. 345–46, describe parts of the process.

189. See Hurnard, cited in the last note.

priest should now officiate, until 1219. Apparently his councillors understood the papal canons as an absolute prohibition of unilateral ordeals, because they presented the eyre justices with new guidelines that divided crimes into three crude grades, each to be treated differently. But they sensibly left the real decisions to be made locally, where the truth about suspects and their alleged crimes could be learned.[190] The justices then exploited this freedom in creative manipulation of the accused toward inquests;[191] furthermore, they occasionally exceeded their instructions by actively discouraging the duel.[192] By the middle of the century criminal duels were rare, except for the appeals of approvers,[193] and the appeal of felony was "virtually a jury action."[194] The protracted delay before the petty jury became the standard trial procedure in crime confirms that insistence from the bench, not enthusiasm for innovations, was responsible for the jury's spread. Once battle was waged, the case was outside the justices' hands, although they could bully or cajole jurors almost at will.[195] They exerted no similar pressure against civil duels, which remained quite common in mid-century.[196] Men well knew the juries' susceptibility to ties of affinity or coercion by impaneling sheriffs. Defendants therefore still sometimes preferred battle to decide their case. By the end of the century, indeed, the availability of battle was regarded as an essential liberty, rather like the jury much later.[197]

This essay has reminded its author of the importance of understanding the Old English basis of the legal system from which Henry II launched

190. Thomas Rymer, *Foedera*, vol. 1 (London, 1704), p. 228.

191. Wells, "The Origin of the Petty Jury," pp. 347–61; C. A. F. Meekings, *Crown Pleas at the Wiltshire Eyre, 1249*, Wiltshire Archaeological Society, Records Branch, vol. 16 (Devizes, 1960), pp. 89 ff.; J. M. Kaye, *Placita Corone*, Selden Society, supplementary ser., vol. 4 (London, 1966), pp. xvi, xxv.

192. The royal letters patent are silent on the duel and indeed appeal process in general, for they are clearly aimed at presentments under the assizes. *CRR*, 10:120 (1221), contains an attempt to understand the prohibition as extending to battle in actions of right, for the purposes of an old ordeal exemption.

193. On the other hand, battle remained the standard criminal proof for the Scots, according to Willock, *The Jury in Scotland*, pp. 21–22. *Dialogus de Scaccario*, II, vii (pp. 87–88), already sees approvers as deterrents; Thomas of Chobham singled them out for special condemnation ca. 1215 (Baldwin, *Masters, Merchants and Princes*, pp. 329–30). Cf. Frederick C. Hamil, "The King's Approvers: A Chapter in the History of English Criminal Law," *Speculum* 11 (1936): 238–58; and Clanchy, "Highway Robbery," pp. 29 ff.

194. Meekings, *Crown Pleas*, p. 70.

195. Kaye, *Placita Corone*, p. xxvii.

196. *P&M* 2:633; M. J. Russell, "Hired Champions," *American Journal of Legal History* 3 (1959): 242–59, at 257. Men argued for or against battle as it suited them. See the exchange of 1255–60 in E. Faral, "Le procès d'Enguerrand IV de Couci," *RHDFE* 4e sér. 26 (1948): 221; and for French practice generally, above, at n. 49 and accompanying text.

197. V. H. Galbraith, "Death of a Champion (1287)," in *Studies in Medieval History Presented to Frederick Maurice Powicke*, ed. R. W. Hunt, W. A. Pantin, and R. W. Southern (Oxford, 1948), pp. 283–95; Kaye, *Placita Corone*, p. xvi. Ecclesiastics continued to use the civil duel much as laymen did; cf. F. M. Powicke and C. R. Cheney, eds., *Councils and*

his reforms. The greatest surprise was to realize that the overwhelming proportion of ordeal evidence points to its use for crime alone, from the tenth century right through to its transformation in the twelfth. England apparently differed from its neighbors in preferring to close property disputes with a judicial oath rather than an ordeal. To understand why this was so demands a wider context; we must view the ordeal together with the other available proofs. A study of the judicial oath through its transition into the old common law's "wager of law" might explain England's apparent singularity in "civil" suits, and would enhance the arguments in this essay. The other pertinent background is the supernatural. The ordeal functioned and declined throughout in a world where miracles and relics ruled men's minds and actions. A declining belief in divine providence might have caused the old ordeals to vanish. But no such decline can be established. This paper has therefore not pursued the connections between ordeals and other manifestations of supernatural power. Further study of the manner and direction of men's choices among various means of access to this power could allocate to each certain types of dispute or social tension. The resulting deepened sense of the role of law will inevitably alter our perceptions of the early common law.

In conclusion, the underlying theme of the paper has perhaps been this: in the early Middle Ages, legal change seldom emerged directly from positive, public decisions motivated by a driving desire for a higher rationality. Perhaps it never does. Hosts of private individuals transformed medieval law in their struggles toward their own goals. Behind the transformation of the old ordeals lies the political need to condemn that unnamed villager who irritated his leaders, the urge to quash that unjust theft allegation or to win that desirable water meadow. Men's mundane needs, and not the belated, banal pronouncements of leaders of church and state, explain English development.

Northern Europe had entered the Middle Ages armed with the knowledge that testimony and evidence were the best methods of establishing the facts of a dispute. Then, over about six hundred years, men periodically sought to buttress proof by *testes* in a world that knew few men's words were to be trusted. The paradox is that the demise of the old ordeals never became the triumph of witness proof, which now survived in two eccentric forms. Either *testes* were managed in juries and inquisitions; or they figured as juristic fossils in an offer of suit, never intended to be taken up, a formal preparation for trial by jury, or indeed duel. Whether the so-called rational proofs, now revived or imported from the learned laws, functioned more justly and efficiently than the old ordeals is a matter for further discussion. The later medieval witness remains a symbol of the reasons why men once preferred God's judgments to those

Synods . . . Relating to the English Church, vol. 2 (Oxford, 1964), 1.283–84 (c. 29); and R. B. Flahiff, "The Writ of Prohibition in the Thirteenth Century," *Medieval Studies* 7 (1945): 267, n. 23.

of men. One tangible consequence of this loss of God's aid was, after all, the rise over most of Europe of judicial torture.[198] Not in England, however; and this is another fact certainly to be explained in terms of evolving doctrines of proof.

198. See J. H. Langbein, *Torture and the Law of Proof: Europe and England in the Ancien Régime* (Chicago, 1977), chap. 1, etc. I am grateful to the author for letting me see this in proof and heartened by the similarity between his quite independent line on the beginning and end of torture in European law and the hypothesis of this paper about ordeals.

5 Proof by Witnesses in the Church Courts of Medieval England: An Imperfect Reception of the Learned Law

Charles Donahue, Jr.

The study of receptions, or as one student would have it, transplants, has commanded considerable attention in the field of legal history recently. For some, the fact that the whole or a significant part of a foreign legal system can be received by another system indicates that the links between law and society are tenuous at best.[1] For others, the length of time that any reception or transplant takes in order fully to be implemented is indicative of the extraordinarily close relationship between law and society.[2] The reception of Romano-canonic witness procedure by the medieval English church courts provides some support for both points of view. What this reception may tell us about the broader question of the relationship between law and society is treated in the last section of this essay. We begin, however, first, by outlining the Romano-canonic law of witness proof; second, by examining how that law was received into the practice of the English church courts; and third, by looking at the ways English practice differed from what the learned law suggested it ought to be.

I

The most immediately practical result of the revival of academic law study at Bologna in the twelfth century was the joint development by both civilians and canonists, generally using sources from both laws, of

Research for this paper was supported in part by generous grants from the W. W. Cook Fund of the University of Michigan Law School. Earlier versions of this paper were given at a joint meeting of the Columbia University Seminar on the History of Legal and Political Thought and the Seminar on Medieval Studies and at the 1979 Annual Meeting of the American Society for Legal History. Archival material from the Borthwick Institute of Historical Research is used with the kind permission of the Director, Dr. D. M. Smith.

1. E.g., A. Watson, *Legal Transplants* (Edinburgh, 1974).

2. E.g., J. Carbonnier, "L'influence du Code français sur la société européenne," *Bulletin d'information de l'Association internationale d'histoire du droit et des institutions* 10 (1975): 19–27.

what has come to be known as the Romano-canonic procedural system.[3] Although little of the work of the first Bolognese jurists, either civilian or canonist, was designed to provide guidance on matters of procedure to practicing lawyers and judges, an outpouring of practical procedural writing began when Bolognese learning was coming to have a noticeable effect on the workings of the church courts, particularly the papal court under Alexander III (1159–81).[4] By the end of the twelfth century, books on the course of judgment, *ordines judiciarii*, had become a most popular form of Romano-canonical writing.[5] Probably the greatest *ordo* is Tancred's, composed around 1215;[6] the most comprehensive is Durantis's, the second edition of which probably was finished around 1291.[7] In addition to the *ordo judiciarius*, which describes the entire course of a legal proceeding from initial process through appeal, the academic lawyers also composed treatises on specific aspects of procedure. For our purposes the most important are the various short treatises on witnesses.[8]

When the Bolognese glossators began writing, the standard methods of proof in the secular courts were ordeal, battle, and compurgation, and ordeal and compurgation were used in the church courts as well.[9] Asking questions of those who knew or could find out about the case was not unknown, but it was clearly not the preferred method of proof. Now

3. The literature on the topic is vast. See K. Nörr, "Die Literatur zum gemeinen Zivilprozess," in *Handbuch der Quellen und Literatur der neueren europäischen Privatrechtsgeschichte*, vol. 1, *Mittelalter*, ed. H. Coing (Munich, 1973) (hereafter cited as Nörr, in *Handbuch*), pp. 383–400, esp. the literature cited on pp. 386–87.

4. The first piece of academic writing directed specifically to someone conducting a court is by the civilian Bulgarus, whose *ordo* or *excerpta legum*, written at the request of the chancellor of the Roman church, dates from between 1123 and 1141. It is edited by L. Wahrmund, in *Quellen zur Geschichte des römisch-kanonischen Processes im Mittelalter*, vol. 4, pt. 1 (Innsbruck, 1905); see Nörr, in *Handbuch*, p. 387, and literature cited. For the relationship between the work of the proceduralists and the papal court, see K. Nörr, "Päpstliche Dekretalen in den ordines iudiciorum der frühen Legistik," *Jus Commune* 3 (1970): 1–9; K. Nörr, "Päpstliche Dekretalen und römisch-kanonischer Zivilprozess," in *Studien zur europäischen Rechtsgeschichte* [*für Helmut Coing*], ed. W. Wilhelm (Frankfurt, 1972), pp. 53–65.

5. Listed by Nörr, in *Handbuch*, pp. 387–91.

6. Edited by F. Bergmann, in *Pilii, Tancredi, Gratiae, Libri de iudiciorum ordine* (Gottingen, 1842) (hereafter cited as Tancred, *Ordo*), pp. 88–316.

7. There is no modern edition. I have used Basel, 1574; reprint ed., Aalen, 1975.

8. Thirteen are listed in S. Kuttner, "Analecta iuridica vaticana," in *Collectanea vaticana in honorem Anselmi card. Albareda*, Studi e Testi, vol. 219 (Vatican City, 1962) (hereafter cited as Kuttner, "Analecta iuridica"), pp. 430–31. One (no. 13) is known only by reference. To this we may add that no. 3 (British Library Egerton MS 2819 [not 3819], fols. 3v–11v) bears a marked resemblance to no. 8 (Vatican Library MS Barb. lat. 1440, fols. 15vb–21ra), with a different *proemium*. Whether this means that the *Summa de testibus* which Johannes Andreae ascribed to Bagarottus (see Kuttner, "Analecta iuridica," pp. 425–27) is in fact the work of an Anglo-Norman "Master G." is a question that must await a future paper.

9. See generally *La preuve*, vol. 2, Receuils de la Société Jean Bodin, vol. 17 (Brussels, 1965), especially J.-Ph. Lévy, "L'évolution de la preuve, des origines à nos jours," pp. 9–70; F. Ganshof, "La preuve dans le droit franc," pp. 71–98; J. Gaudemet, "Les ordiales au moyen âge: doctrine, législation et pratique canoniques," pp. 99–136; and R. van Caenegem, "La preuve dans le droit du moyen âge occidental," pp. 691–754.

there is nothing about ordeal or battle or compurgation in the classical Roman law texts to which the early glossators addressed themselves, although some of the ancient canonic texts did deal with these methods of proof.[10] The Roman law texts deal exclusively and the canon law texts principally with proofs by witnesses and written instruments. The jurists' discovery that "the law" called for proof by "rational" methods—witnesses and instruments—rather than by "irrational" methods—ordeal, battle, and compurgation—was among the causes of the intellectuals' attacks in the twelfth century on the irrational methods of proof.[11]

We find some reflections of this hostility to the irrational methods of proof in the writings of the early proceduralists.[12] The attitude reflected in an anonymous *Summula de testibus* of the late twelfth century, perhaps by an Anglo-Norman canonist, is typical. The *Summula* repeats an injunction found in *Causa* 2 of Gratian's *Decreta*: a bishop is not to be judged unless he himself confesses or unless he is regularly convicted by innocent witnesses canonically examined.[13] This means, the summist notes, "not in single combat nor in [the trial] of hot iron, nor of cold or hot water, nor of lashes, but of oath alone."[14] Few proceduralists address themselves as specifically to the issue of irrational methods of proof, but many emphasize that witnesses are the best method of proof, better than written instruments, and, by implication, far better than ordeal or battle.[15]

At the Fourth Lateran Council in 1215, as is well known, the church withdrew her support for the ordeal.[16] The development of an alternative system of proof was the work of the Romano-canonic proceduralists up to and including Tancred. Relatively little innovation occurs after Tancred's time, and we can best explore the Romano-canonic system of witness proof by outlining Tancred's titles on witnesses.

10. See especially the texts collected in C.2 q.5; see also Gaudemet, "Les ordiales"; and J.-Ph. Lévy, *La hiérarchie des preuves dans le droit savant du moyen-âge*, Annales de l'université de Lyon, 3e sér., droit, fasc. 5 (Paris, 1935), pp. 131–35.

11. See Gaudemet, "Les ordiales"; and H. Nottarp, *Gottesurteile*, Kleine allgemeine Schriften, Geschichtliche Reihe, nos. 4–8 (Bamberg, 1949), pp. 222–97; see now P. Hyams, "Trial by Ordeal: The Key to Proof in the Early Common Law," in this volume, for the suggestion that the decline of the ordeal was the product of social rather than intellectual forces. Whatever the ultimate cause, it is clear that the beginnings of the attacks on the ordeal considerably antedated the revival of the academic study of law.

12. There is considerably more material of relevance to this debate in the writings of the decretists. See J. Baldwin, "The Intellectual Preparation for the Canon of 1215 against Ordeals," *Speculum* 36 (1961): 613–36, at 619–26.

13. C.2 q.1 c.2.

14. Cambridge, Trinity College MS o.40.70, fol. 182v: "Non in monomachiam necque [*leg.* examinacionem] candentis ferri necque acque frigide necque verberum sed solius iuramenti."

15. For the controversy on the witnesses vs. instrument point and its ultimate resolution in favor of witnesses, see Lévy, *La hiérarchie*, at pp. 84–105, and sources cited.

16. Lateran IV (1215) c. 18, *Conciliorum oecumenicorum decreta*, ed. J. Alberigo et al., 3d ed. (Bologna, 1972), p. 220 (= X 3.50.9); cf. X 5.35.3. See generally Baldwin, "Intellectual Preparation for the Canon of 1215."

The form Tancred gives for the admission, examination, and reprover of witnesses is part of the standard overall form for the course of judgment in Romano-canonic civil procedure. The case is introduced by a summons and a libel on behalf of the plaintiff and then a joinder of issue (*litis contestatio*). The plaintiff is then assigned a number of terms (three was standard; a fourth was given as an exceptional matter) to produce witnesses to discharge his burden of proof on his case in chief.[17]

Once produced, the witnesses are to take an oath to tell the whole truth, and to tell the truth for both parties. They are also to swear that they do not come to bear testimony for a price, or out of friendship, or for private hate, or for any benefit they might receive. After they have taken the oath, the witnesses are to be examined separately and in secret, after the model of Daniel's questioning of the elders.[18]

When all the witnesses have been examined, the parties are to renounce further production of witnesses. The witnesses' depositions will then be published by the notary who has written them down. The defendant now has an opportunity to except to the testimony of the witnesses. He may except to their persons, if he has reserved the right to do so when they were produced, or he may seek to demonstrate that their testimony is false in some respect.[19]

The proceduralists not only outlined the form by which witnesses were to be admitted, examined, and reproved; they also elaborated some basic principles of their system of proof by witnesses. At the core of that system are three propositions: (1) the character of each witness is to be examined; certain witnesses are not to be heard because of their status, and others' testimony is to be regarded as suspicious because of their status or mores or their relationship to one or the other of the parties; (2) witnesses are to be examined carefully to determine if they are telling the truth about events they saw and heard themselves; and (3) on the basis of the written depositions and what has been demonstrated about the character of the witnesses, the judge is to determine whether the standard of proof fixed by law has been met.

As a general matter, Tancred tells us, two witnesses make a full proof.[20] But not everyone may be a witness. Slaves, women (in certain circumstances), those below the age of fourteen, the insane, the infamous, paupers (although Tancred has some doubts about this), and infidels may not be witnesses. Criminals may not be witnesses. No one may be a witness in his own cause. Judges, advocates, and executors may not be witnesses in cases in which they have performed their official duties. Children may not testify on behalf of their parents or parents on behalf of their children, with certain exceptions. Familiars and domestics of the producing party

17. Tancred, *Ordo*, 3.8 (pp. 230–36); see generally *Select Cases from the Ecclesiastical Courts of the Province of Canterbury*, ed. N. Adams and C. Donahue, Jr., Selden Society, vol. 95 (London, 1980) (hereafter cited as Adams and Donahue, *Select Cases*), pp. 37–56.

18. Tancred, *Ordo*, 3.9 (pp. 236–37).

19. Ibid., 3.10–11 (pp. 240–45).

20. Ibid., 3.7 (p. 228).

and those who are enemies of the party against whom they are produced may not be witnesses.[21]

Witnesses are to be questioned, Tancred continues, about all the details of what they have seen and heard, for only then can it be determined whether they are consistent. They are to be asked about the matter, the people, the place, the time, perhaps even what the weather was like, what the people were wearing, who the consul was, and so on. In only a few instances, such as in computing the degrees of relationship in incest cases, is hearsay testimony to be accepted.[22]

If a witness contradicts himself, Tancred concludes, then his testimony should be rejected. If the witnesses agree, and their *dicta* seem to conform to the nature of the case, then their *dicta* are to be followed. If the witnesses on one side disagree among themselves, then the judge must believe those statements which best fit the nature of the matter at hand and which are least suspicious. If the witnesses on one side conflict with those on the other, then the judge ought to attempt to reconcile their statements if he can. If he cannot, then he ought to follow those who are most trustworthy—the freeborn rather than the freedman, the older rather than the younger, the man of more honorable estate rather than the inferior, the noble rather than the ignoble, the man rather than the woman. Further, the truth-teller is to be believed rather than the liar, the man of pure life rather than the man who lives in vice, the rich man rather than the poor, anyone rather than he who is a great friend of the person for whom he testifies or an enemy of him against whom he testifies. If the witnesses are all of the same dignity and status, then the judge should stand with the side that has the greater number of witnesses. If they are of the same number and dignity, then absolve the defendant.[23]

The doctrinal development from the first treatise on witnesses, written by Albericus de Porta Ravennate sometime in the 1170s,[24] to Tancred is substantial. Albericus's treatise, derived solely from Roman law, has a much shorter and anachronistic list of possible exceptions against the persons of witnesses, mentions the two-witnesses rule but does not go into the question of how the witnesses are to be examined, and contains no advice at all on how the judge is to resolve conflicts among the witnesses.

In the development of practical advice on questioning and on balancing discordant testimony, papal decretal law played a considerable role, as the numerous citations in Tancred to the *Compilationes antiquae* indicate.[25]

21. Ibid., 3.6 (pp. 223–28).
22. Ibid., 3.9.2 (pp. 238–40).
23. Ibid., 3.12 (pp. 245–48).
24. Edited by E. Genzmer, in "Summula de testibus ab Alberico de Porta Ravennate composita," in *Studi di storia e diritto in onore di Enrico Besta*, vol. 1 (Milan, 1937), pp. 491–510. For Gratian on witnesses see F. Liotta, "Il testimone nel decreto di Graziano," in *Proceedings of the Fourth International Congress of Medieval Canon Law*, ed. S. Kuttner, Monumenta iuris canonici, ser. C, vol. 5 (Vatican City, 1976), pp. 81–93, and sources and literature cited therein.
25. On the role of the decretals see Nörr's two articles, cited above in n. 4.

Perhaps of equal importance, however, was the work of the proceduralists of the generation preceding Tancred. The first extended discussion I have found of how to question a witness is in an anonymous *Summula de testibus*, dating from around 1200.[26] On the other hand, there are hints of what is to be the later approach as early as 1171 in the French canonist *ordo* "In principio."[27] By far the most elaborate treatment of how to evaluate conflicting testimony is to be found in Pillius's *Summula* on witnesses, which probably dates from shortly before 1195.[28] Pillius's rule-laden treatment of the issue stands in marked contrast to that of the earlier anonymous *ordo* "Si quis de quacumque re," which states: "In sum respect should never be paid to the multitude of witness but to the sincere faith of the testimony and to the testimony that the light of truth rather aids, because the judge, once he has examined what is said in the constitutions and responses of the jurists on these matters, can know more than the discipline of law can teach or permanently define."[29] Similar statements, derived from a long dictum in Gratian's *Causa* 4, may be found in the French *ordo* "Tractaturi de judiciis" of about 1170[30] and the Anglo-Norman *ordo* "Quia judiciorum" of about 1185.[31]

In sum, then, by 1215, Romano-canonical procedure had developed a means for examining witnesses in such a way as to elicit the truth. It had also developed a series of rules for rejecting the testimony of those who were unlikely to tell the truth and another series for resolving conflicts in the testimony presented. The procedure necessarily left some discretion to the judge, but the fundamental tendency of this procedural writing is to limit the judge's discretion, to prescribe rules by which he must decide, rather than to provide guidance as to how he was to exercise his discretion. This same concern with limiting the discretion of the judge is reflected in the maxim that the academic proceduralists were exploring in a number of different contexts: the judge is to judge according to things

26. Edited by E. Genzmer, in "Eine anonyme Kleinschrift de testibus aus der Zeit um 1200," in *Festschrift Paul Koschaker*, 3 vols. (Weimar, 1939), 3:399.

27. Edited by F. Kunstmann, in "Über den ältesten Ordo judiciarius," *Kritische Überschau der deutschen Gesetzgebung und Rechtswissenschaft* 2 (1855): 19.

28. Pillius, "Quoniam in iudiciis frequentissime," Vatican Library MS Chigi E.VII.218, fol. 84rb; Rome, National Library MS Sessor. 43, fol. 74r; Cambridge, Trinity College MS B.1.29, fol. 217r; for the date see Kuttner, "Analecta iuridica," at p. 430.

29. Edited by N. Rhodius, as Bk. 4 of *Placentini iurisconsulti vetustissimi de varietate actionum libri sex* (Mainz, 1530), 4.17 (p. 105): "In summa nequamque ad testium multitudinem respici opportet, sed ad synceram testimoniorum fidem et testimonia, quibus potius lux veritatis adsistit [citations] Quod iudex, discussis omnibus quae in responsis et constitutionibus de his caventur magis scire poterit, quam ulla iuris possit disciplina doceri vel in perpetuum definiet." For the work see Nörr, in *Handbuch*, p. 387.

30. "Tractaturi de judiciis," ed. C. Gross, *Incerti auctoris ordo judiciarius* (Innsbruck, 1870), 13.3 (pp. 120–21). "Si vero alter litigantium multos habeat testes, alter paucos, non pluralitati credendum est, immo conversatio et vita et fides illorum et istorum consideranda est et secundum hoc judicandum est." For the work see Nörr, in *Handbuch*, p. 388. The *dictum* is C.4 q.3 *dictum post* c.2 and c.3.

31. Ed. J. von Schulte, "Der Ordo judiciarius des Codex Bambergensis P.I.11," *Sb. Akad. Vienna* 70 (1872): 310. For the work see Nörr, in *Handbuch*, p. 387.

alleged and not according to his conscience (*judex secundum allegata non secundum conscientiam judicat*).[32]

It is not surprising that the academic writers on procedure should have been urging rules that would eliminate, or at least substantially reduce, the judge's discretion. The overall thrust, after all, of the revival of academic law was the development of coherent bodies of doctrine, the harmonization of the diverse sources that commanded academic attention.[33] Further, and perhaps more important, the academic proceduralists were urging the adoption of a system in which judgment was given not by God, invoked by battle, ordeal, or the inscrutable oath of the parties and their compurgators, but rather by all-too fallible men, judges, on the basis of the testimony of equally fallible witnesses. For such a fundamental change to have been acceptable, it was necessary for people to believe—and perhaps even for it to be true—that the ultimate decision of the case not be within human discretion but be dictated by the rules of law. People might accept a judgment of the law rather than a judgment of God; it was less likely that they would accept a judgment of man rather than one of God.[34]

Although there were relatively few advances in doctrine after Tancred, there were a number of advances in the forms by which these doctrines were implemented. For example, Tancred does not make it completely clear that the plaintiff is to submit a list of articles, statements of fact concerning which his witnesses are to be examined. Shortly after Tancred this was to become standard practice.[35] It also became standard practice for the defendant to submit a list of proposed interrogatories for the witnesses, and the examiner was bound to ask these, unless they were unduly repetitious.[36]

32. For a detailed and sophisticated treatment of the development of this maxim, see K. Nörr, *Zur Stellung des Richters im gelehrten Prozess der Frühzeit*, Münchener Universitätsschriften, Reihe der juristischen Fakultät, vol. 2 (Munich, 1967). Of course, the maxim and the rules about witnesses are directed to slightly different ends. The former limits the judge's discretion by ensuring that the parties control the process; the latter limits the judge's discretion by ensuring that what the parties produce is evaluated according to rules of law. See further below, next paragraph.

33. See especially S. Kuttner, *Harmony from Dissonance* (Latrobe, Pa., 1960).

34. For this point see J. Langbein, *Torture and the Law of Proof* (Chicago, 1977), pp. 5–8. For this point to be valid it is not necessary that the elaboration of Romano-canonical procedure have been the cause of the decline of the "irrational" methods of proof—a proposition about the truth of which there is considerable doubt. See, e.g., van Caenegem, "La preuve," esp. pp. 752–53; and Hyams, "Trial by Ordeal." Rather, it is simply necessary that the academic proceduralists have been aware that their method of proof had not been adopted by all courts and that one of the possible objections to it, whether articulated or not, might be the amount of discretion it gave to the judge. In parts II and III below, we shall see that the real alternative to the Romano-canonic system in England was the jury, judgment not by God but by the community, rather than the judge.

35. See, e.g., Gratia Aretinus, *Summa de judiciario ordine* 2.5, Tancred, *Ordo*, at p. 369; and Adams and Donahue, *Select Cases*, at p. 47.

36. Durantis, *Speculum*, 1.4.[2]*de teste*.6.21 (pp. 322–23); see generally, ibid., 1.4.[2]*de teste*.6 (pp. 319–23); and Adams and Donahue, *Select Cases*, at pp. 47–48.

One might expect that the rigidity of the doctrines announced by Tancred would have softened after judgment by human judges on the basis of witness testimony had become the accepted norm. In fact, quite the opposite is the case. One of the notable differences between Tancred's and Durantis's treatment of witnesses is the larger number of classes of people whom Durantis excludes from testifying.[37] The thirteenth- and fourteenth-century writers also refine the rules on what makes a full proof, carefully dividing and defining *indica*, *probationes semiplenae*, and *probationes plenae*.[38] It is not until the fifteenth century that we begin to find authors willing to relax the strict standards of Romano-canonical proof,[39] and the beginning of the fifteenth century will be the ending point of our exploration of the reception of the Romano-canonical law of witness proof in the English church courts.

II

The doctrines announced by the academic proceduralists had, at least in their broad outlines, an early reception in the English ecclesiastical courts.

Of the English church courts prior to 1200 we know tantalizingly little. No court archives (as opposed to litigation documents kept by one of the parties normally as a muniment of title) survive from the period before the pontificate of Hubert Walter as archbishop of Canterbury (1193–1205), so the history of the English ecclesiastical courts from the Conqueror to the reign of Richard I must be pieced together from chance survivals. There is, however, a handful of scattered documents that shed some light on how claims were proved before the English ecclesiastical courts. They indicate that the English church courts, like the secular, made considerable use of compurgation, although there seems to be no evidence that they used the ordeal.[40] These documents also indicate that

37. Compare Tancred, *Ordo*, 3.6 (pp. 223–28), with Durantis, *Speculum*, 1.4.[2]*de teste*.1 (pp. 289–304). F. Sinatti D'Amico, "Il concetto di prova testimoniale: spunti di una problematica nel pensiero dei glossatori," *Rivista di storia del diritto italiano* 39 (1966): 155–85, notes the same hardening of the doctrine in the period after Tancred, a hardening that she attributes to the influence of canonic practice. The rest of this essay will suggest that canonic practice, at least in England, was more like the arbitral justice of the Italian communes than Sinatti D'Amico would have us believe.

38. See Lévy, *La hiérarchie*.

39. See B. Schnapper, "Testes inhabiles: les témoins reprochables dans l'ancien droit penal," *Tijdschrift voor Rechtsgeschiendenis* 33 (1965): 576–616. For developments since that time, see U. Mosiek, "Der Grundsatz 'Unus testis nullus testis' und seine Geltung im kanonischen Recht," *Revue de droit canonique* 25 (1976): 371–77.

40. For compurgation see, e.g., the celebrated case of Archdeacon Osbert accused of murdering Archbishop William of York, in John of Salisbury, *Letters*, ed. W. Millor, H. Butler, and C. Brooke, 1 vol. to date (London, 1955), 1:27. For other cases involving criminous clerks *temp*. Becket, see H. Richardson and G. Sayles, *The Governance of Mediaeval England*, Edinburgh University Publications, vol. 16 (Edinburgh, 1963), pp. 303–4. Cf. P. Fournier, *Les officialités au moyen-âge* (Paris, 1880), pp. 262–70. For the use of ordeals in ecclesias-

the English church courts, like the secular, were experimenting with ways of making use of sworn members of the community to aid in the resolution of disputes. As is the case with the secular courts, the origins of the use of these jurylike bodies in the church courts may lie in Continental practices of inquest by secular or ecclesiastical officials for administrative, disciplinary, or peace-keeping purposes.[41] By the twelfth century, however, we find such bodies being used in what today we would call civil cases.

For example, between 1123 and 1148, Alexander, bishop of Lincoln, having taken counsel with the chapter of St. Mary's Lincoln, ordered one W. B. "to make a recognizance by the oath of lawful men" to determine whether the land of Banbury belonged to the demesne of the bishop of Lincoln when Alexander's predecessor, Bishop Robert, gave Eynsham abbey the tithe of Banbury. The tithe was currently the subject of litigation between the abbey and one Willelmus Gramatica. If the land did belong to Bishop Robert, the tithe was to be awarded to the abbey.[42]

Between 1160/1 and 1162, Gilbert Foliot, bishop of Hereford, and Godfrey, archdeacon of Worcester, sitting as papal judges delegate, rendered a sentence in a case between the canons of St. Mary's Warwick and the canons of the Holy Sepulchre, Warwick:

> We therefore, afforced by apostolic authority to the decision of the case, keeping in mind that proof ought by law to rest on the plaintiff and that he ought to have reasons by which he might show that what he contends is true, adjudged the proof of those things which they were claiming to the canons of St. Mary. By the oath, therefore, of six priests and six laymen it was proven that that part of the parish which the already-said canons were claiming belonged to their church, and by the oath of four priests and three laymen again it was proven that the mentioned 30d. were owed to their church by an old agreement and were paid to their church by the hand of the prior[s] of St. Sepulchre, Emery, Anthony and Ralph, on the feast of All Saints.[43]

tical courts outside England, see Gaudemet, "Les ordiales," at p. 117; and C. Morris, "Judicium Dei," *Studies in Church History* 12 (1975): 103–9.

41. For the possible connection between the ecclesiastical and secular institutions, see J. Goebel, Jr., *Felony and Misdemeanor* (New York, 1937), pp. 322–26.

42. *The Cartulary of Eynsham*, vol. 1, ed. H. Salter, Oxford Historical Society, vol. 49 (Oxford, 1907), pp. 41–42 [no. 15A].

43. ". . . Nos itaque quos ad ipsius cause decisionem apostolica vigebat auctoritate [*leg.* auctoritas], attendentes actori probacionem de iure incumbere opportere eumque raciones habere quibus quod intendit verum esse insinuet, canonicis sancte Marie probacionem eorum quod intendebant adiudicavimus. Sex itaque sacerdotum et sex laicorum iuramento probatum est partem illam parochie quam vendicabant iam dicti canonici ad ecclesiam suam pertinere et quatuor sacerdotum triumque laicorum iuramento item probatum est memoratos triginta denarios ecclesie sue ex antiqua paccione fuisse debitos et per manum prioris sancti Sepulcri Almeri, Antonii, Radulphi in solempnitate omnium sanctorum fuisse solutos. . . ." (Warwick College Cartulary, London, Public Record Office MS E.164/22, fols. 18r–19r [no. 27]).

A separate charter of the archdeacon of Worcester in the same cartulary simply states that the judges patiently heard the allegations of the parties and had adjudged that right and truth lay on the side of St. Mary's by the abundant proof of the witnesses and the faithful inspection of instruments.[44]

In 1173, Pain, the abbot of Sawtry, and Herbert, the prior of St. Neot's, made a concord concerning the amount of water that could be taken from the abbot's mills without harming the prior's. The parties chose twelve lawful men, six millers and six others knowledgeable and wise enough to settle the dispute. These men decided the case after having "sworn on the gospels that they would say the truth, all interference having been removed."[45] There are at least two other examples of arbitration under ecclesiastical auspices making use of a sworn verdict in this way, one in 1188, another from the late date of 1246.[46]

The pattern established by these cases and others like them[47] makes it reasonably clear that proof of fact by a jurylike body was not unknown to the English ecclesiastical courts in the twelfth century. Indeed, as R. C. van Caenegem has shown, such documents illustrate a typical institution, one that on the secular side was to become the assize and inquest juries in the reign of Henry II, the jury in writs of entry and trespass in the reign of John, and the criminal trial jury in the reign of Henry III.[48]

We can, however, exaggerate the jurylike characteristics of these early uses of the sworn testimony of neighbors in the ecclesiastical courts. The institution that we are looking at in the early and mid-twelfth-century documents is as much the ancestor of the canonical witness as it is the ancestor of the secular jury, as the archdeacon of Worcester's description of the Warwick case suggests. Not until the late twelfth century does a distinction appear between the two institutions, the academic law shaping the canonic institution into what today we would call witnesses and the assizes of Henry II shaping the English secular institution into the familiar jury.[49]

44. Ibid., fol. 19v [no. 30].

45. St. Neot's Cartulary, British Library MS Faustina A.IV, fols. 38r–38v, reported in R. van Caenegem, *Royal Writs in England from the Conquest to Glanvill*, Selden Society, vol. 77 (London, 1959), p. 75.

46. *Newington Longeville Charters*, ed. H. Salter, Oxford, Historical Society, vol. 3 (Oxford, 1921), p. 89 [no. 116] (1166 X 1188); Oxford New College MS 13,885 (*ex* Writtle 401) (1246).

47. E.g., *Cartulaire de Loders*, ed. L. Guilloreau, Chartes anglo-normandes, vol. 1 (Evreux, 1908), p. 59 [no. 50] (1169).

48. See van Caenegem, *Royal Writs*, pp. 40, n. 2, 65, 73, 75–76, for a discussion of all of these examples except the Writtle charter, for which see J. Sayers, *Papal Judges Delegate in the Province of Canterbury, 1198–1254* (Oxford, 1971), p. 87, n. 3.

49. That Glanvill should state that the exceptions which can be made to the jurors of the grand assize are the same as those which can be made to witnesses in the canon law suggests that contemporaries saw the connection between the two institutions (*Tractatus de legibus et consuetudinibus regni Anglie qui Glanvilla vocatur*, ed. and trans. G. Hall [London, 1965], II, 12 [p. 32]).

If we have to focus on one characteristic distinguishing the canonic witness of academic writing from the juror of English practice, it would be that the English jury's verdict is essentially inscrutable. True, an English justice will occasionally ask specific questions of the jury, occasionally will plainly disbelieve their story, but this is as far as it ever goes. The only way the jury's verdict can be upset is by the separate process of attaint.[50] In the developed canonic system, on the other hand, cross-examination is not only encouraged but required, and introducing further witnesses to disprove what the previous witnesses have said is standard practice.

Those who see the essential difference between witnesses and juries in party- rather than court-production, and those who see that essential difference as lying in the fact that witnesses are notionally eyewitnesses whereas jurors are not, have reversed at least the logic if not the chronology. It is because the testimony of witnesses can be upset by cross-examination and by introducing the testimony of other witnesses that the parties rather than the court can be relied on to produce them. It is because the testimony of witnesses must be subject to cross-examination that they must be, at least notionally, eyewitnesses of the event. Put another way, once the English secular jury has found for the plaintiff, there is nothing left for the court to do but to render judgment for the plaintiff. Once the canonic plaintiff and defendant have produced their witnesses, the court's job really begins. If this is right, then what we are looking at is an essential difference in the method of adjudication of much greater significance than simply a difference in the method of proof.

This distinction, however, operates on a somewhat theoretical level: it distinguishes the theory of witnesses in academic Romano-canon law from the theory that can be discerned as underlying fully evolved English jury practice. But however fully evolved the academic theory of witnesses was in the time of Tancred, it remains to be seen whether that theory was applied in practice, and, of course, English jury practice was anything but fully evolved by 1215. Though we cannot, unfortunately, trace the development of the inscrutable quality of the English jury, we can suggest how, if not why, the eminently scrutable quality of the canonic witness developed.

A major collection of ecclesiastical court documents survives from the pontificate of Hubert Walter.[51] Of the ninety-odd documents in this collection, some twenty-two are depositions. These give us a clear insight

50. See Sir F. Pollock and F. Maitland, *The History of English Law before the Time of Edward I*, 2d ed., reissued with a new introduction and select bibliography by S. Milsom, 2 vols. (Cambridge, 1968) (hereafter cited as *P&M*), 2:622–32.

51. Described in Adams and Donahue, *Select Cases*, at pp. *3–4, 8–12*; calendared in ibid., pp. *104–14*. A *familiaris* of Hubert Walter, Ricardus Anglicus, wrote an *ordo judiciarius*, probably some time before his return to England in 1198. The *ordo* is strictly academic and provides no help for the student of English canonic procedure. See generally W. Bryson, "Witnesses: A Canonist's View," *American Journal of Legal History* 13 (1969): 57–67.

into the extent to which Hubert Walter's court had conformed its practice to that of the academic canonists. For example, one of these depositions states:

> William de la Waie, sworn, said that he was present when it was agreed between Gilbert Martel and Hugh de Kimble at Bucklebury that the land of the said Hugh de Kimble be handed over to Gilbert in farm, and they took an oath. He was also present afterwards when Hugh handed over a signed document to Gilbert in the house of the same Gilbert, and he heard the agreement, inserted in the chirograph which Gilbert had, read; he does not know about the price of the land. Asked about the time, he said that the first agreement was entered into on a Monday, three years ago, around Hockday.[52]

Clearly this witness is being asked about what he knows. The price was a key issue in the case, but the witness was not expected to inform himself about it. Despite the fact that this type of questioning had not yet made much of an appearance in the academic writing, we already see the witness being asked about the time of the events. In another deposition in the same case the witness will be asked about the place where the agreement took place and whether the parties were standing or sitting.

"Odo de Burghfield, sworn, said that he knows nothing except by report of his son, who at that time was with Gilbert, and of others."[53] This witness's testimony is worth no more than a line. He was not an eyewitness; there were other such witnesses, and their testimony is to be preferred.

The next witness has a slightly different version of the story and knows nothing about the oath. His testimony is basically consistent, but he adds some details and omits others, and so it is reported in full.[54]

The next witness, on the other hand, is reported briefly: "John Bonell, sworn, says the same in every respect as William de la Waie."[55] Here we see what was to continue to be a usual characteristic of depositions in the southern (but not the northern) province. Witnesses who repeat previous testimony do not have their depositions given in full; the clerk simply indicates that they repeat. This is clearly the result of the press of business, but it is a practice that is criticized in academic writing, for obvious reasons.[56]

Depositions of fifteen more witnesses are given. Most of them simply repeat what has been said before; others add some detail.[57]

This production of witnesses is not numbered. Another document from the same case is labeled "first production of Gilbert Martel against Hugh

52. Adams and Donahue, *Select Cases*, A.5, p. 16.
53. Ibid.
54. Ibid., pp. 16–17.
55. Ibid., p. 17.
56. See ibid., pp. 49–50; Durantis, *Speculum* 1.4.[2]*de teste*.7.8 (p. 325).
57. Adams and Donahue, *Select Cases*, p. 17.

de Kimble," and other documents from the same period indicate that the standard practice of three productions was being followed.[58]

In these early depositions, in contrast to later depositions, there are only occasional indications that the examiner was following a set scheme of questions. For example, in another set of depositions from the Kimble case, after a witness has testified about what he does know, we find the entry: "Asked about the time of year, the payment of the money, how many years ago, if anything was put in writing between them, about any other agreement, he says he does not know."[59] Some of these questions would suggest themselves simply from what had been said before, but others, particularly those about a writing and another agreement, suggest that the examiner may have had some predetermined scheme of questions. One of the few commissions to take testimony that has survived from this period outlines the general issue at stake in the case and instructs the examiners to take testimony "on all the annexed articles" (which unfortunately have not survived).[60] We do not know, however, whether the court developed these articles or whether the producing party developed them, as he did in later practice, nor do we know whether articles were only used in cases like this one where the examination of the witnesses was committed to someone distant from the court. There is no evidence, moreover, of the use of interrogatories proposed by the adverse party, a practice that was to become usual by the end of the century.[61]

Three of the cases from this period contain depositions on behalf of both parties.[62] Although much about the defense of cases in this period remains unclear, none of the defendants' depositions refers either to the persons or the statements of the witnesses of the plaintiff, from which we may surmise that what were later called "exceptions to witnesses and what they said" were unknown in this period. One set of defendants' depositions suggests that his witnesses were produced at the same time as the plaintiff's,[63] a second probably concerns an affirmative defense,[64] the third reveals a jurylike procedure with which we shall deal shortly.[65]

The practice outlined for the *Kimble* case is common to all but two of the depositions I have found from this period. One of the unusual documents is headed simply: "the names of those sworn[66] to inquire about the marriage between Stephen de Bello and Agnes his wife."[67] Thirteen names are given, including those of Stephen and Agnes, suggesting the possibility that each of them may have been swearing twelve-handed, the

58. Ibid., p. 15; cf. ibid., p. 15 (a fourth production).
59. Ibid., p. 16.
60. Ibid., A.1, p. 1.
61. See ibid., pp. 47–48.
62. Ibid., A.2, A.3, A.6.
63. Ibid., A.2. Some of the depositions on both sides are contained in the same document (at pp. 5–6).
64. Ibid., A.6, p. 24.
65. See below, at n. 68.
66. Or is the correct translation "the names of the jurors"? The word is *juratorum*.
67. Adams and Donahue, *Select Cases*, A.8, p. 29.

standard practice in compurgation. "All of these," the document continues, "say the same thing about the affinity, to wit, that Agnes, the wife of Stephen was the wife of Elias, a cook, and Isabella, once the concubine of Stephen, was Elias's mother's sister. The whole neighborhood testifies to this, and it is well known to all." The document then considers another possibly incestuous relationship between Agnes and Stephen, arising out of the spiritual relationship of godparenthood. On this issue only five of the jurors swear, and each tells a specific story.

This document is not, at least in form, a document from a case between Agnes and Stephen, but rather the product of an inquest concerning their marriage. The suggestion is that the matter was being pursued ex officio by the court. Perhaps because of the difference between this type of proceeding and the instance procedure of the Kimble and similar cases, the report of the testimony in block and the presence of parties among those sworn in Stephen and Agnes's case stand in marked contrast to the other depositions of the period and indeed to the rest of this particular document. We are closer here to the inscrutable testimony of neighbors than we are to specific witnesses of particular transactions, which we saw in the Kimble case.

One other case suggests a jurylike procedure.[68] In an instance case between the rector of Barkway and the parishioners of the chapel of Nuthampstead concerning the respective rights of the church and chapel, the rector produces twelve witnesses—the number is chance perhaps. But what are we to say when the parishioners also produce twelve witnesses and when their depositions contain some of the elements of a joint statement that we noticed in Stephen and Agnes's case? Clearly, the transition from jury to witnesses is not yet complete.[69]

There should, of course, be nothing surprising about the ecclesiastical courts of Hubert Walter's time employing jurylike procedures. We know that the English church after Hubert Walter's time employed jurylike bodies both for the presentment of offenders against church law, for example, at synod or visitation,[70] and for administrative information gathering, for example, at inquests into the plenarty or vacancy of a church.[71] Thus the English church did not cease to use jurylike bodies after the twelfth century, bodies for which no authorization could be found in the academic proceduralists. The use of such bodies in the twelfth century suggests that it was a procedure which came naturally to the men of the time; their continued use in criminal and administrative procedure and, if our one example from the mid-thirteenth century may

68. Ibid., A.3, pp. 8–10.

69. Cf. ibid., pp. *107* [no. 22], *11*: Peter of Blois claims tithes and asks that an inquisition into the matter be made by twelve of "the more lawful parishioners of the church by their oath."

70. See C. Cheney, *English Synodalia of the Thirteenth Century* (Oxford, 1941), pp. 5–6, 8–10, 28–31.

71. See J. Gray, "The Ius Praesentandi in England from the Constitutions of Clarendon to Bracton," *English Historical Review* 67 (1952): 481–509; cf. Adams and Donahue, *Select Cases*, p. *58* and nn. 1–6, for other examples.

suffice, in arbitration procedure,[72] suggests that it continued to come naturally.

Where we do not find jurylike procedure being used after Hubert Walter's time, however, is in civil litigation. There, witnesses, occasionally supplemented by written instruments, are invariably the method of proof. Here the academic law had its greatest effect. But its effect was not to lead the English church courts to employ an institution for which they had no precedents. Rather, an institution, the sworn testimony of neighbors, that could have become the jury, as it did in the secular courts, became, under the influence of academic writing, the Romano-canonical witness. The question remains, moreover, whether the reception of the Romano-canonical witness as an institution involved the reception of all the Romano-canonical doctrine about witnesses as well.

III

Unfortunately, no depositions dating from between Hubert Walter's time and the 1270s have yet come to light. An extensive collection of ecclesiastical cause papers does survive for the vacancy of the see of Canterbury from 1270 to 1273 and another from the vacancy of 1292–94.[73] For the fourteenth and fifteenth centuries the major collection of cause papers is at York, where we find files of documents from some six hundred cases.[74]

By the time we reach the 1270s in the southern province and the early fourteenth century in the northern, the Romano-canonical system of witness proof was, in broad outlines, fully in place in the English church courts, and all the evidence suggests that it remained so throughout the Middle Ages and beyond. If we look solely to the form by which the medieval English church courts proceeded, we will conclude that the Romano-canonic system of witness proof was received by the medieval English courts. With some allowance for local variation, the form of the procedure follows the academic treatises closely, and the local variation is no greater than what one finds today in various jurisdictions purporting to follow a common body of procedural rules.

After the *litis contestatio* the party having the burden of proof gets three terms, exceptionally four, in which to make positions and produce witnesses.[75] The witnesses are produced in open court and sworn in the

72. See above, at n. 46.

73. Described in Adams and Donahue, *Select Cases*, at pp. 4, 16–17, 32–33, 35–37.

74. See D. Smith, *A Guide to the Archive Collections in the Borthwick Institute of Historical Research*, Borthwick Texts and Calendars, vol. 1 (York, 1973), p. 57; C. Donahue, Jr., "Roman Canon Law in the Medieval English Church: Stubbs vs. Maitland Re-examined after 75 Years in the Light of Some Records from the Church Courts," *Michigan Law Review* 72 (1974): 647–716, at 656–60.

75. For this and the two following paragraphs, see Adams and Donahue, *Select Cases*, pp. 45–52, and sources cited. For positions, questions posed by one party to the other, to be answered somewhat in the manner of modern written interrogatories, see ibid., pp. 44–45.

presence of the parties. Though it may have been possible for a party to take exception to the witnesses at this point, exceptions are almost invariably deferred until after the testimony is published.[76] Although this procedure somewhat reverses the logic of the order of the academic proceduralists, it is expressly authorized in academic writing as early as Tancred. Tancred requires that a litigant expressly reserve the right to except to the witnesses after their testimony has been published, but exception after publication was so common in England that the *acta* do not always mention that the reservation was made.[77]

The producing party presents a set of written articles according to which the witnesses are to be examined. The party against whom the witnesses are produced may, and frequently does, submit interrogatories to be put to the witnesses. The witnesses are then examined, normally by a court-appointed examiner, separately and in secret.[78] They are asked the questions posed in the articles and interrogatories, and their depositions are reduced to writing, occasionally with comments by the examiner. "This witness vacillates and hoots like an owl," says one waspish fourteenth-century York examiner.[79] When the producing party has renounced further production of witnesses, the depositions are published in open court.

The defendant then has an opportunity to except against the person of the witnesses and against what they said. There is normally a debate about whether these exceptions will be admitted, and if they are, the defendant is given the opportunity to produce witnesses to prove them. Sometimes there is a replication by the plaintiff, which proceeds in the same manner as the exception, and at least in the fourteenth and fifteenth centuries further pleading and production was possible.

Similarity in form can, of course, conceal considerable differences in substance and result. If the English ecclesiastical courts were not following the three basic doctrines about witnesses that we outlined above, then whatever the form that the production, examination, and reprover of witnesses took, we are dealing not with the Romano-canonical system of witness proof but with some variation of it.

But in order to determine what doctrines were being followed, we are faced with considerable evidentiary barriers. Medieval judges (and canon law judges were no exception) were not required to and generally did not render reasoned opinions.[80] Even if they had rendered reasoned

76. For one possible exception, see below, at n. 83.

77. Adams and Donahue, *Select Cases*, p. 50.

78. E.g., *Acta Stephani Langton*, ed. K. Major, Canterbury and York Society, vol. 50 (Oxford, 1950), p. 82 (no. 61): "Jurati [testes] itaque et separatim sicut moris est examinati. . . ."

79. York, Borthwick Institute CP.E. 101/13 m.1 (4 Mar. 1369): "Et videtur mihi R[icardo] de T[unstall, examinatori generali curie Ebor',] quod testis iste est vacillans et cutubans et quod modicum fides est ei adhibenda." For other examples see Adams and Donahue, *Select Cases*, p. 54, and cases cited.

80. See J. Dawson, *The Oracles of the Law* (Ann Arbor, 1968), pp. 50–54; and R. Helmholz, *Marriage Litigation in Medieval England* (Cambridge, 1974), pp. 20–22. For

opinions, they would have been unlikely to justify their decisions on the basis of anything but "the law." Further, many medieval canonic cases did not reach the sentence stage. Any reconstruction, then, of what doctrines were actually being followed must necessarily be tentative and conjectural.

One basic proposition of the Romano-canonical system that definitely was received by the English church courts is that two witnesses make a full proof. Although few documents make mention of this rule, no sentence that I know of violates it, and much that goes on in the ecclesiastical courts would make no sense if this were not a basic assumption. But it is one thing to say that there must be at least two witnesses for there to be full proof, quite another to say that those persons and only those persons whom the academic law would admit in fact served as witnesses, that they testified in a manner consistent with the principles outlined in the law, and that their testimony was evaluated in the way that the academic commentators said that it should be. Indeed, the principal deviations of English practice from the Romano-canonic law of witness proof are these: (1) people who are not qualified to testify under the Romano-canonic rules do indeed testify; (2) people who are not eyewitnesses testify, and they testify about matters of which they have no personal knowledge; and (3) the judges were considerably more flexible in evaluating testimony than at least the mainstream academic commentators suggested they should be. Let us examine these deviations in order.

1. *Unqualified witnesses testifying*: As we have seen, the academic law barred a wide variety of people from testifying.[81] Although there was some variation among the academic writers as to who was barred from testifying, it is clear that once a determination had been made that the law barred a given person from testifying, it was not within the discretion of the judge to admit him. The person barred from giving testimony should not have his deposition taken. Nonetheless, in no English case of which I am aware does the judge refuse to allow someone to testify.

This is not as surprising as it may seem at first. Obviously a witness cannot be excluded from testifying after he has done so, and equally obviously, unless some objection is raised to the witness at the time he is admitted, the fact that he should not be testifying will not normally be known to the judge at that time (particularly if he may not take into account what he knows outside of the record).[82] Because exceptions to witnesses were not raised in English canonic procedure until after the depositions had been published, no one was excluded from testifying.[83]

---

a relatively full opinion, see Adams and Donahue, *Select Cases*, B.3ee, at pp. 88–89, which, among other things, indicates that the two-witness rule was being followed.

81. See above, at text accompanying nn. 20–21.

82. See above, at n. 32 and accompanying text.

83. Adams and Donahue, *Select Cases*, C.18, pp. 292–99, is a possible exception, but the events described are more like a brawl than an attempt to raise exceptions to a witness at the time he is produced. In ibid., D.1, pp. 341–42, the party against whom witnesses were produced excepts to their persons and asks that they be excluded from testifying, but this

There are a number of reasons why English proctors and advocates consistently deferred their exceptions to witnesses until after the depositions were published. First, the academic law prohibited testimony from being raised on the same article or on one directly contrary to it until after the depositions on that article had been published. This rule was designed to hinder the subornation of perjury, but if it had been followed, it would have meant that defendants would have had to raise their defenses without knowing what it was that the plaintiff's witnesses were going to say. In order to avoid the rule about contrary articles and at the same time to have the advantage of knowing to what they were replying, defendants' proctors frequently couched their defense in the form of exceptions to witnesses. For example, rather than introducing testimony to prove that he was elsewhere at the time the plaintiff alleged he had contracted with him, the defendant would introduce the same testimony to show that the plaintiff's witnesses were perjurers: they had lied when they said they had contracted with the plaintiff on that day in that place.[84]

Postponing the exceptions to witnesses was also more efficient from the point of view both of the court and of the parties. Once the witnesses were in court it was clearly more efficient to take their depositions rather than postponing the deposition taking until the exceptions and proof on them could be presented. Postponing also gave the defendant time to discover if any exceptions could be raised against witnesses whom he might not know. Postponing until after the depositions were published allowed the proofs on the exceptions against the witnesses and those against what they said to be consolidated. It also allowed the defendant to confine his exceptions and his search for proof to those witnesses and depositions that had proved to be most damning. Finally, we cannot exclude the possibility that at least in some cases postponing the exceptions to witnesses gave the defendant an opportunity for delay. After the plaintiff's case in chief was in, the defendant could raise a blanket exception to witnesses and would be given probatory terms to see if he could find any kind of support for it.

For example, in *John, son of Emma Warner, chapman of Scampston* c. *Alice Redying of Scampston*, a York defamation case of 1367, John excepts against Alice's witnesses, John, son of Roger, and Thomas, son of Roger:

takes place after their testimony has been published. The usual formula in exceptions was to ask that "no faith be put" in the excepted-to witnesses (ibid., C.18, p. 309; see below, at n. 85; cf. Adams and Donahue, *Select Cases*, D.15, p. 556 [claim that testimony is invalid]). Of course, an examiner might have been empowered to exclude witnesses who admitted that they were incapable of testifying, but that never seems to have happened, despite the large number of witnesses who, in effect, make such admissions. See, e.g., ibid., C.2, p. 104; D.15, p. 561 (both involving witnesses of servile status); and cases cited p. *51*, n. 4.

84. For both the academic law and examples from practice, see ibid., pp. *51–52*; Donahue, "Stubbs vs. Maitland," pp. 686–95.

> [N]o or little faith is to be given to the aforesaid witnesses, their *dicta* and depositions because the said John son of Roger and Thomas son of Roger during the entire time of their reception, deposition, and examination were and still are and each of them was and still is a *nativus* and serf, of servile condition and notoriously in servitude; joined to the said Alice Redying with too much familiarity and friendship, as mediators, promoters, authors, and favorers of the aforesaid case; in this case, as if in their own, unjustly affecting victory for the party of the said Alice; paupers, ignoble, vile, and abject persons, who, unmindful of their salvation, were and are accustomed to, would, and will foreswear themselves and give false testimony for little; and the aforesaid witnesses throughout their reception and deposition in the said case were and still are capital enemies of the said John Warner, keeping company with his enemies, and evilly and maliciously pursuing this John Warner by indictments, conspiracies, and other injurious and guileful prosecutions, made up and fabricated by them on purpose for the confusion and subversion of the faculties and fortune of the said John Warner, or the total destruction of a greater part of them, as a result of which the same John Warner lost all his goods or a greater part of them unjustly and to his grave and almost irrecoverable damage. For these reasons John son of Roger and Thomas son of Roger are multifariously suspect for testifying or bearing testimony against the said John Warner.[85]

No depositions survive for this exception, but John's proctor had clearly opened the way for any kind of testimony about the witnesses's status and characters or their relations with either Alice or John.

Whatever the reason for the general practice of postponing exceptions to witnesses, the practice had substantive effect. Once the witness's testimony is reduced to writing and published, the defendant cannot object

85. York, Borthwick Institute, CP.E. 92/1: "[P]refatis testibus, dictis et deposicionibus ipsorum nulla seu modica fides est adhibenda pro eo et ex eo quod dicti Johannes filius Rogerii et Thomas filius Rogerii, testes predicti, omni tempore recepcionis, deposicionis et examinacionis ipsorum et cuiuslibet [*leg.* quilibet] eorundem fuerunt et adhuc sunt nativi et servi, servilis condicionis et in servitute notorie, dicte Alicie Redyng nimia familiaritate et amicitia coniuncti ut pote mediatores, promotores, autores, fautores cause predicte, in ipsa causa ut in propria victoriam pro parte dicte Alicie indebite affectantes, pauperes, ignobiles, viles et abiecte persone, qui sue salutis immemores pro modico solebant et solent, volebant et volunt se deierare et falsum testimonium perhibere, prefatique testes quocunque tempore recepcionis et deposicionis ipsorum in dicta cause fuerunt et adhuc sunt inimici capitales dicti Johannis Warner cum suis hostibus conversantes ipsumque Johannes Warner per indictaciones, conspiraciones et alias iniuriosas et subdolas prosecuciones fictas et fabricatas ipsorum proposito quasi in confusionem seu subversionem facultatum et fortunarum dicti Johannis Warner vel maioris partis earundem totalem deperdicionem nequiter et maliciose persequentes, quorum occasione et non aliter idem Johannes Warner omnia bona sua seu maiorem partem eorundem in ipsius grave dampnum quasi irrecuperabile amisit minus iuste, ex quibus causis predicti Johannes filius Rogerii et Thomas filius Rogerii ad testificandum seu testimonium perhibendum in hac parte contra dictum Johannem Warner multipliciter sunt suspecti." Cf. York, Borthwick Institute, CP.E. 72/4 (1356).

that the testimony should be excluded. Rather he must argue that "no or little faith" should be placed in the depositions of these witnesses because they are persons who are barred by the law from testifying. The form suggests an argument addressed to the discretion of the judge, an argument concerned with how he should evaluate the testimony, rather than whether he should receive it.

There remains the question, however, of how the judges reacted to such exceptions. The type of character assassination that John's proctor was setting up in the *Scampston* case could pose problems of judicial administration, both because of the delay that proving it (or giving terms to prove it) would cause and because of the scandalous and only tangentially relevant nature of the material that might be introduced. Further, there was a broader ethical consideration: should the law, particularly a religious law, reject out of hand the testimony of those who are of low status solely because of their birth? Tancred suggests this difficulty when he asks whether the apostles would have been rejected as witnesses because of their poverty.[86] Some combination of considerations such as these probably lies behind the ruling of an archdeacon's official in a marriage case in the 1270s. The defendant charges that one of the two witnesses of the plaintiff is of ill fame, of suspect life and opinion, a thief, and a pauper. Any one of these exceptions, if proved, would have been sufficient in the academic law to have the witness's testimony struck, and hence the plaintiff's case would have failed for failure to meet the two-witness requirement. The judge, however, simply quashes the exception. The case was appealed, although no sentence on appeal is recorded.[87]

In other cases exceptions against the person of witnesses were admitted and testimony on them allowed. But how did the judges react to such exceptions if they were proven? Did they treat the testimony of the witness in question as a nullity or did they regard the proven exception to the witness as one of a number of factors to be used in evaluating his testimony? It is difficult to prove which of these two attitudes predominated. Convincing evidence would come from cases in which four conditions are met: (1) the exception is one that the academic authors generally agree is sufficient to bar the witness from testifying; (2) the exception is proven, either by depositions which convincingly demonstrate that the exception is a valid one or by an admission by the excepted-to witness on the face of the record; (3) the witness or witnesses against whom the exception is raised are necessary for proof of the producing party's case: there cannot, for example, be two unexceptionable witnesses on his side; (4) there is a sentence in favor of the party who produced the exceptionable witnesses. Not surprisingly, there are relatively few cases in which all these conditions are met. Nonetheless, the evidence suggests that in English canonic practice of the thirteenth and fourteenth centuries there was no automatic bar to the consideration of anyone's testimony.

Lacking a large number of cases in which all four conditions are met,

86. Tancred, *Ordo*, 3.6 (p. 225).
87. Adams and Donahue, *Select Cases*, C.4, pp. 122–23; cf. ibid., pp. 119–20.

the best evidence for this last proposition is negative. There is no case of which I am aware in which a party lost because some or all of the witnesses necessary to make up his case proved to be incapable of testifying under canon law. Cases that seem at first reading to involve a straight application of the rules incapacitating certain people from testifying prove upon more careful examination to have other elements that better explain the sentence. For example, in *Thomas Bakster of North Collingham* c. *John Coke of Newark*, Bakster sued Coke for breach of faith on the ground that Coke had broken his promise to release a debt (*frangere obligacionem*) which Bakster had satisfied. Bakster introduced two witnesses to Coke's promise to release, one of whom admitted that he was of servile status. In the academic law this would have been sufficient to bar the witness's testimony, and hence Bakster's case would not have been proven. The sentence does go down for Coke. But it seems reasonably clear that the academic rule barring the testimony of those of servile status was not determinative, or, at the very least, that the academic rule was not the only reason for the sentence. In excepting to Bakster's witness on the ground of servile status, Coke raises two other exceptions: that both of the witnesses had agreed to stand surety for Bakster in a suit brought against him by Coke in the king's court and thus their testimony is to be deemed unreliable because they were financially interested in the outcome of the case, and that the witnesses did not testify consistently about when the promise to discharge had occurred, because one testified about an event that had occurred twelve or thirteen years previously and the other about an event that had occurred fourteen years previously. The factual validity of both of these exceptions is apparent on the face of the depositions of Bakster's witnesses, and either exception may well have been the principal or contributing cause to the sentence in favor of Coke.[88]

By contrast to this case there are a number of cases in which the court proceeds to sentence without regard to the fact that the witnesses on the winning side are exceptionable. For example, in *Cecilia Wright* c. *John Birkys*, Cecilia successfully petitioned for a divorce of John from his current wife, Joanna, on the ground that John had previously promised to marry Cecilia and had had intercourse with her. Cecilia produced only two witnesses, one of servile condition, the other Cecilia's sister and the wife of the other witness. Probably neither witness was admissible under the academic law. Yet despite uncontradicted testimony as to the status and the witness's admission of the relationship, Cecilia prevailed in two courts.[89] In *Alice Dolling* c. *William Smith* (1271), a marriage case more

88. York, Borthwick Institute, CP.E. 226 (1396): 226/5, Bakster's articles; 226/4, Bakster's depositions; 226/2, sentence for Coke; 226/1, Coke's exceptions.

89. York, Borthwick Institute, CP.E. 103 (1367–69). This case comes as close as any to meeting the four conditions stated above in the text following n. 87. It doesn't quite, because the witnesses on the exception of servile status (103/5), although they are convinced that the man was of servile status, hesitate to say that his mother was of servile status, and at least one (2d deposition) admits that she was of free status. If the mother was of free

fully discussed below, Alice produced three witnesses to support her basic claim of a *de presenti* marriage. Two of the witnesses were her sisters. Nonetheless, sentence was rendered for her in the court of first instance and was reversed on appeal for reasons that are clearly not confined to the exceptionable nature of her initial witnesses.[90]

More common than cases in which there is a direct conflict with the academic law are cases in which there is some ambiguity about the conflict with the academic law and in which it seems reasonably clear that the case proceeded on grounds other than the academic law. *Prior and Convent of Newburgh* c. *John Pert et al.* may serve to illustrate. The prior and convent, in their capacity as rectors of Hovingham, sued Pert and others on the ground that they had cut down trees in the yard of the chapel of Ness, which the prior and convent alleged was dependent on Hovingham church. In support of their defense the defendants introduced nine witnesses, whose depositions have not survived. The prior and convent excepted to these witnesses on the ground that three of them were of servile status and that all nine were vile, humble, and ignoble people, tenants of John Pert and in bondage. In the depositions on these exceptions the status of the witnesses as serfs and poor people is confirmed, but some of the witnesses go to considerable pains to suggest that, despite their status, the witnesses are honorable people. Others of the witnesses to the exceptions, however, testify that they believe that the excepted-to witnesses would not have testified as they did, except for the fact that they were in the power of Pert.[91] The case proceeds no further and was probably compromised, but the depositions suggest that the reliability rather than the status of the excepted-to witnesses was what was really at issue.

2. *Testimony by those who were not eyewitnesses*: In marriage and breach of faith cases the witnesses tend to be few, and the issues are quite sharply defined. Here the classic form of questioning described in the treatises on procedure is most effective: who was there, what they were wearing, whether they were seated or standing, what the weather was

status, the canon law would have recognized her son as free, at least for some purposes. See X 1.18.8; and *P&M*, 1:422–24; cf. P. Hyams, "The Proof of Villein Status in the Common Law," *English Historical Review* 89 (1974): 721–49, at 730–45. Whether being a sibling (or near affine) of the producing party automatically excluded one from testifying was also a matter of some doubt. Durantis after giving authorities *pro* and *contra* seems to conclude that it did in criminal cases but not in civil (at least where the testimony is not compelled), without discussing the intermediate category of "spiritual cases" in which marriage cases fell. Durantis, *Speculum*, 1.4.[2]*de teste*.1.8–.10, 14 (pp. 286–87).

90. Adams and Donahue, *Select Cases*, C.6, at pp. 127–38; see below, at text accompanying n. 103. For other examples see, e.g., York, Borthwick Institute, CP.E. 16 (1327) (woman testifying in a testamentary case); CP.E. 92 (1365) (serf and stepfather of a party testifying in a marriage case). The latter case is not as clear as is suggested in Donahue, "Stubbs vs. Maitland," at p. 678, n. 175.

91. York, Borthwick Institute, CP.E. 75 (1357–58): exception against the witnesses, 75/2; depositions on the exception, 75/3.

like, and so on. As we move away from this type of case with this type of issue, the relationship between witness practice and the Romano-canonic procedural treatises becomes less clear.

For example, benefice cases, tithe cases, and cases concerning the finding of a chaplain[92] frequently involve a large number of witnesses on both sides, all the way up to the canonical limit of forty.[93] Their testimony, whether it is written out in full or simply entered as being in accord with that of previous witnesses, tends to be remarkably similar: the party for whom the witnesses were produced was rightfully in possession of the benefice, a given church has always received tithes from a given field, a given chapel has always had parochial rights. We have already seen one example from the early thirteenth century of this type of case.[94] In later cases of this type the form of the depositions is less like the report of a jury verdict, but the substance is the same.

A striking example of the use of multiple witnesses to support the parties' position in a case rather than to bring out the facts occurs in the highly political dispute over the prebend of Thame in 1292–94 between Edward St. John, the son of one of the king's most trusted knights, and Thomas Sutton, the nephew of Oliver Sutton, the bishop of Lincoln. During the dispute each party in turn took possession of the prebend by force and appealed to Rome and for the tuition of the Court of Canterbury. Thomas and Oliver Sutton appealed in January 1292/3. Nine witnesses were heard on Thomas's appeal, fourteen on Oliver's. In February a year later, Edward appealed against the bishop and Thomas. Fourteen witnesses were heard on his appeal against the bishop, eighteen on Oliver's plea in opposition. Eight witnesses were heard on Edward's appeal against Thomas, twenty-two on Thomas's plea in opposition. Fifteen witnesses were heard on Thomas's cross-appeal in the same month, eight on Edward's plea in opposition.[95]

Now the issues in a tuitorial appeal are not complex. The case belongs to the Court of Rome, not the Court of Canterbury, and the only issue for the Court of Canterbury is whether the appeal was properly taken and possibly whether the appellee did anything to disturb the status quo pending appeal.[96] Some of the witnesses in the *Sutton* case, however, go deeply into the merits of the case, whereas others simply repeat what others have already said about the possession and appeals. It is hard to escape the conclusion that the purpose of introducing all these witnesses

92. "Invention" of a chaplain, a case in which the parishioners of a chapel seek to have the rector of the mother church appoint a chaplain for them at his expense. E.g., *Residents of the Vill of Subholme* c. *William Rowden, rector of Warsop*, York, Borthwick Institute, CP.E. 151 (1389–91), discussed in Donahue, "Stubbs vs. Maitland," at pp. 675–76.

93. X 2.20.37.

94. Adams and Donahue, *Select Cases*, A.3, pp. 8–10; see above, at text accompanying n. 68.

95. Adams and Donahue, *Select Cases*, D.16, pp. 567–611.

96. Ibid., pp. 64–72.

was to impress the court with the support on each side, particularly when the witnesses include the registrar of Lincoln, the official of Lincoln, and other distinguished members of Oliver Sutton's *familia*.[97]

Hugh de Saxton, vicar of Pontefract c. *Roger, vicar of Darrington* is a typical fourteenth-century tithe case that combines a jurylike quality of the depositions with exceptions to the person of the witnesses. Hugh claimed that Roger had wrongfully withheld from him tithes of wool. Roger excepted that the tithes belonged to him. Both parties introduced witnesses (six for Hugh, ten for Roger) who testified to a dispute concerning tithes from 340 sheep that grazed in an area called "Hughlaches" and who supported their principal's story that he was in the right. Hugh then excepted to Roger's witnesses. "Hughlaches," he argued, was in the parish of Pontefract and the sheep in question wintered in Pontefract. Hugh also objected to the person of the witnesses on the ground that two of them were of servile status and that all of them were of the parish of Darrington and unjustly willed and affected Roger's victory in the case because their financial obligations would be lessened if he won. Roger replied that the two witnesses were of free status but did not deny that all his witnesses came from Darrington. He also proposed that "Hughlaches" had been within the parish of Darrington from time immemorial. Hugh introduced forty witnesses in support of his exception, some of whom testified about the status of the previous witnesses and all of whom testified about "Hughlaches." Roger introduced eight(?) witnesses on his replication, all of whom confirmed the free-status point and Roger's point about "Hughlaches." Then it was Roger's turn to except to Hugh's witnesses. They are not to be believed, he said, because they are all from the parish of Pontefract and stand to gain if Hugh wins.[98]

At this point the case ends,[99] and it seems likely that it was compromised,[100] but the pleadings and depositions tell us much about the reception of the Romano-canonic law of witnesses. That two of Roger's original witnesses were of servile status is clearly a secondary point; few of Hugh's forty witnesses address themselves to the point, although

97. E.g., ibid., p. 578 (merits), p. 586 (repetition), pp. 574–81 (registrar, official, members of familia). There is a suggestion in a contemporary treatise on the practice of the Court of Canterbury that the number of witnesses was particularly important in tuitorial appeals. See ibid., p. 71 and nn. 3–4. Even if this is so, it would not explain the distinction of the witnesses and their testimony on the merits in the Sutton case.

98. York, Borthwick Institute, CP.E. 67 (1354–55): Hugh's libel, 67/17; Roger's first exception, 67/17; Hugh's six witnesses, 67/12; Roger's ten witnesses, 67/13; Hugh's exception to Roger's witnesses, 67/11; Roger's replication, 67/10; Hugh's forty witnesses, 67/6, 67/8; Roger's witnesses on 67/10, 67/5 (document damaged); Roger's exception to Hugh's witnesses in 67/8, 67/3. For similar patterns of depositions and exceptions, see CP.E. 101 (1369) (mortuary); and CP.E. 151 (1389) and CP.E. 208 (1393) (both invention of chaplain cases).

99. Roger introduces positions and articles on 67/3, 67/2, and Hugh makes a replication to 67/3, 67/1. But no depositions on these pleadings survive, and there is no record of any further proceedings.

100. For compromise, see Adams and Donahue, *Select Cases*, pp. 55–56; and Donahue, "Stubbs vs. Maitland," pp. 705–8.

Roger thought that it was at least worth rebutting. The central issue is dependent on the testimony of what are concededly interested witnesses. Further, they are not testifying to a specific fact or facts like the exchange of consent or the uttering of defamatory words, but rather to the common understanding of where a parish boundary lay. Within each group their testimony on this issue is remarkably uniform. They are reporting the *communis sententia patriae*. In short, they are behaving more like a secular jury than like Romano-canonical witnesses.

We should not be surprised that local custom about what parish was entitled to the tithes from a given field should be the core issue in this case. Canon law gave a wide range to local custom, particularly in tithe cases, and the "public voice and fame" about it was clearly one of the ways of proving it.[101] What at least the mainstream academic law does not discuss is how proof by public voice and fame is to be reconciled with Romano-canonic witness procedure. The evidence of English practice suggests that the church courts did it by using witnesses in a most unwitnesslike manner.

Thus, in cases where proof by public voice and fame was called for, the witnesses function much as a jury would, testifying not of their own personal knowledge but to the common belief of the community. Hard cross-questioning is not characteristic of these cases. Both the court and the parties seem to have been aware that the type of questioning called for in the practice manuals was not suitable in this type of case. Moreover, even in cases where the courts insisted on eye-witness testimony, such as marriage cases, the parties do not always seem to have been willing to abandon the notion that the function of a sworn neighbor is not to testify to what he knows from what he has seen but to testify to what the community believes, like a juror, or to support what the party has sworn to, like an oath helper. Corruption need not necessarily be involved, although accusations of corruption are common.[102] There are, however, enough direct conflicts of testimony between witnesses on opposite sides of a case and enough similarities of testimony, down to the last detail, among witnesses on the same side of a case to suggest that a number of medieval Englishmen were either corrupted or willing to lie for what they believed to be a higher cause—there is no other possibility.

For example, in *Alice Dolling* c. *William Smith*, a marriage case first tried before the official of Salisbury in 1271, Alice alleged that William had married her by exchanging with her words of the present tense on a given day in a given place. William excepted that he was someplace else

101. On custom see Donahue, "Stubbs vs. Maitland," pp. 675–78 and sources cited; for public voice and fame, see Lévy, *La hiérarchie*, pp. 37–40, 113–17.

102. E.g., Adams and Donahue, *Select Cases*, B.3cc, pp. 87–88; York, Borthwick Institute, CP.E. 1 (1303); Cathedral Archives and Library, Canterbury, *Sede Vacante* Scrapbook III no. 35 (1293) (cited in R. Helmholz, "Ethical Standards for Advocates and Proctors in Theory and Practice," in *Proceedings of the Fourth International Congress of Medieval Canon Law*, pp. 283–99, at 298–99). For a case in which the pattern of the examiners' questioning and comments suggests that they thought the witnesses were lying, see Adams and Donahue, *Select Cases*, A.6, pp. 18–23.

at the time, and Alice made a replication of William's presence. Alice produced three witnesses to the *de presenti* contract and four on her replication of presence. William produced ten on his exception of absence. Someone was clearly lying. Either William Smith contracted with Alice Dolling or he did not; he could not have been both contracting with Alice and attending an all-day feast four miles away at the same time. Whichever group of witnesses was lying, someone knew enough about what questions were going to be asked to allow both sets of witnesses to supply with reasonable vividness an account of the clothing, the time, and the place where it all happened.[103] Whether modern cross-examination techniques in an open courtroom would have brought the truth of the matter to light or whether they simply would have provided a keener test of whether the seven women or the ten men were the more brazen, we do not know. The medieval authorities argue that cross-examination in open court would have increased the danger of intimidation of witnesses and that allowing the defendant to hear the plaintiff's story as it was developing would simply have invited even more subornation of perjury.[104]

The interesting thing about the medieval English courts' handling of this problem is not what they did about it in marriage cases. In such cases, after all, there had to be a decision, and by far the highest percentage of cases for which we have decisions are marriage cases. The interesting thing is that in those cases where there was less necessity for an immediate decision and less likelihood that any judicially imposed decision would be permanent, the courts took a much more passive attitude in their search for the truth. As we noted above, hard cross-questioning is not a characteristic of tithe cases or cases concerning the finding of a chaplain, or even cases concerning the possession of churches. All these types of cases are eminent candidates for compromise. The *Sutton* case, for example, was settled, admittedly after royal intervention, and the cartularies are full of compromises of such cases after long and bitter litigation.[105] In such cases, what the church courts seemed to have done is to let the parties have their hearing. The parties brought in their supporters and had their statements recorded; after this, more often than not, the case disappears from view. Presumably some form of settlement was reached; presumably too, the settlement was based on some estimate of how the judge would react to the testimony. But the testimony in these kinds of cases is remarkably unrefined: it is almost as if both the court

103. Adams and Donahue, *Select Cases*, C.6, pp. 127–32; see above, at text accompanying n. 90, and below, at text accompanying n. 110. Witnesses were apparently allowed to "refresh their recollection" by discussing the matter with each other before they testified, and this may account for some of the remarkable agreement. See, e.g., Adams and Donahue, *Select Cases*, C.11, p. 175.

104. See the discussion of the various arguments among the proceduralists before the rule about separate, secret examination became fixed, in Genzmer, "Eine anonyme Kleinschrift," at pp. 391–92.

105. Adams and Donahue, *Select Cases*, D.16, p. 569; see C. Cheney, *Pope Innocent III and England*, Päpste und Papstum, vol. 9 (Stuttgart, 1976), pp. 116–18, 194–225; and Sayers, *Papal Judges Delegate*, pp. 239–42, for other examples.

and the parties recognize that the decision of the case is more a political than a judicial one and that the eminently rational Romano-canonic procedure simply is not adequate for resolving this kind of dispute.[106]

3. *Evaluation of testimony*: We have already had occasion to examine the manner in which the medieval English church courts evaluated testimony in our discussion of exceptions to witnesses.[107] There we suggested that the courts had at least a tendency not to include or exclude testimony on the basis of rules but rather to use the bias or status of a witness as one of a number of factors to weigh in arriving at a judgment.

Frequently we get the impression that even if the witnesses are suspect, their testimony will be sufficient to shift the burden of persuasion to the defendant. For example, in *John Dent* c. *John Chace*, a breach of faith case heard by the York court in the winter of 1396/7, Dent sued Chace, alleging that Chace owed him twelve shillings from a sale of iron and coal. He introduced two witnesses who testified that Chace had pledged his faith to pay Dent by the octave of Pentecost. Chace filed five exceptions to the witnesses and their *dicta*: (1) they are, he alleged, authors, favorers and special promoters, affecting the victory of Dent as in their own cause; (2) one witness lied when he said he was not an affine of John Dent, because he is his brother-in-law; (3) the second lied when he said he was not a domestic or familiar of Dent, because he is his hired man or apprentice; (4) the witnesses are too friendly with Dent and hence suspect; and (5) it wasn't Chace who made the purchase and promised to pay the money—it was one Robert Marshall.[108]

Dent denies all of these charges, but one—the one concerning his brother-in-law. Here he simply says that his brother-in-law is a layman and should not be expected to know what an "affine" is. Chace's two witnesses do not fully support his charges. They do, however, confirm that one witness had married Dent's sister and suggest that this relationship may indicate that the witness was too friendly with Dent and suspect. In the academic law the relationship might have been enough to reject this witness's testimony, and hence the two-witness requirement would not have been met. But the court finds for Dent.[109] Though it does not say so, it seems to be holding that Dent had produced enough proof to shift the burden of production to Chace. Chace's story was that Marshall made the contract, not he, but he adduced no evidence on this point, and therefore he lost.

This is not to say that we do not find evaluations that accord with the

106. Cf. Donahue, "Stubbs vs. Maitland," pp. 705–8.

107. See above, at text accompanying nn. 88–91.

108. York, Borthwick Institute, CP.E. 224: Chace's exception, 224/3; articles, 224/3, 224/5. Dent's depositions do not survive, but their content is derivable from Chace's exceptions.

109. Ibid.: depositions, 224/5, 224/2; sentence, 224/4. For the academic law on affines, see above, at n. 89; cf. *Thomas Kendall et ux., ex'rs of Peter Wolffe* c. *Henry de Nincely* [?], *rector of Foston*, CP.E. 193 (1391) (judgment for plaintiffs in a debt case despite testimony that their witnesses are enemies of the defendant and affines of the plaintiff and that one is an adulterer).

principles of evaluating testimony which we find in the academic proceduralists. For example, in *Dolling* c. *Smith*, the Salisbury marriage case described above, the official of Salisbury pronounced sentence in favor of Alice; whereupon William appealed to the Court of Canterbury. The official of the Court of Canterbury gave the documents in the case to two of the examiners of the court and asked them to give him a report concerning the case. That report has survived, and it shows us the examiners going through the *processus* of the lower court carefully and evaluating the testimony. The examiners reported: (1) Alice produced three witnesses about the *de presenti* contract. The first two testified not about a *de presenti* contract but about a *de futuro* contract; the third testified that the man used words of the present tense but the woman words of the future. The first two witnesses were sisters, and the third testified that the second witness was Alice's sister. (2) William's absence at the same time was proven by ten witnesses. (3) The replication of presence was proven by four witnesses who may not have been testifying about the same year (a reference to what may be a scribal dating error in the *processus*). In any event, ten witnesses are better than four, and the four seem to depose "less sufficiently" (a phrase which may refer to the fact that they gave relatively little detail or at least that the examiner's clerk recorded less detail).[110]

All of this is quite in accord with the academic law on reconciling conflicting witnesses. The witnesses must testify to the facts that they are produced to prove; here they are supposed to prove a *de presenti* contract, and they do not. Further, whether the status of being a sibling automatically disqualifies one from being a witness or not, it is clear that one's sibling is a suspect witness when compared to unrelated witnesses.[111] So far as the replication of presence is concerned, it is not even certain that the four witnesses conflict with the ten, because they may not be testifying about the same day. Further, they do not give enough detail, and finally, William should win his case simply on the numbers. It is not surprising that the court on appeal reverses the official of Salisbury. Its action strictly conforms to the Romano-canonic rules of procedure.

The interesting question, however, is why the official of Salisbury ever decided the case the way he did in the first place. Alice never appears in the appeal, perhaps because she knew she had a losing case, perhaps because she was prevented from appearing. It is probably true that, other things being equal, ten witnesses are better than four; but it is not inconceivable that William could have purchased the testimony of his ten witnesses. The Salisbury court asked him—why we do not know—to produce them again, and he said he could not do so, offering what seem to be formulaic excuses.[112] Though the official of Salisbury may have

110. Adams and Donahue, *Select Cases*, C.6, pp. 134–36; see above, at text accompanying nn. 90, 103.

111. Compare n. 89 above with text accompanying n. 109.

112. Adams and Donahue, *Select Cases*, C.6, pp. 129, 132.

been ignorant of the rules, bishops' officials were not normally unlearned men. If he made use of something he knew that did not appear in the record, he was, of course, violating the principle that the judge is supposed to judge according to the things alleged and not according to his conscience, but if he does not decide according to his conscience, how is he to square his conscience with the Supreme Judge?

The only principle that will explain the evaluation of the testimony in *Dent* c. *Chace*, the official of Salisbury's judgment in *Dolling* c. *Smith*, and even the judgment in the Court of Canterbury's reversal in the same case is that the judges felt that they must evaluate testimony taking into account as many factors as they could find on the record, and perhaps occasionally things that did not appear of record as well. This does not mean that status, bias, or number of witnesses was irrelevant, any more than it is today. What we do not find, however, is support for the somewhat mechanical notions of the academic commentators that testimony could be evaluated by rule. There are simply too many cases that deviate from the norms for us to believe that medieval canonic judges thought that any academic decision-rule dictated how they were to evaluate testimony.

IV

Despite these deviations of the English church courts from the principles outlined in the procedural treatises, we should not lose sight of the fact that these courts did adopt a recognizable form of Romano-canonic witness procedure. The inchoate, jurylike use of the sworn testimony of neighbors that we find in the twelfth-century documents gives way at the very beginning of the thirteenth century to a procedure that is identifiably academic in its orientations and provenance. The latter half of the thirteenth century sees an elaboration and careful following of the forms of procedure laid out in the *ordines judiciarii*. We suggested, however, that for the English church courts this was not a great change. Under the proper influences the twelfth-century use of the sworn testimony of neighbors could have hardened into the jury procedure of the English secular courts of the thirteenth, but it was not a radical shift in direction for it to have become the witness procedure of the Romano-canonic law.

We had considerably greater difficulty, moreover, tracing the reception by the English church courts of three key elements in the Romano-canonic law. The reasons why these deviations occurred are complex, and no one explanation will suffice for all of them. In the case of the failure to follow the rules about exceptions to the persons of witnesses we suggested that both the way the exceptions were normally presented and broader ethical considerations may have played some role. In the case of the use of witnesses in a jurylike manner, the nature of the issue clearly played a considerable role, as may the desires of the parties to impress the court with support for their side. In the case of the rules about evaluating testimony, the dominant force seems to have been the desire of judges for more discretion in making decisions.

It is difficult to generalize from what is necessarily speculation about a complex phenomenon, but two forces seem to predominate among those that we suggested caused the reception of the Romano-canonic law of witness proof to be less than perfect: the desire of judges to have a considerable amount of discretion and the desire of parties to have litigation proceed according to forms like those with which they were familiar. To put it more bluntly, both the judges and the parties sought to manipulate court process, and the Romano-canonic procedural principles suffered as a result.

In the case of the failure to follow the academic rules about exception practice and about evaluating testimony, the desire of the judges, by this time an elite, professional body of decision makers,[113] for greater flexibility is the force responsible for the deviations from the academic law. The parties, on the other hand, seem to have expected witnesses to behave more as jurors or oath helpers, institutions with which they were familiar from the secular and, in the case of oath helpers, the lower church courts. The parties, then, seem to have been chiefly responsible for the deviations we noted from the rule that witnesses are to speak of their own knowledge.

For the most part these two forces operated independently of each other. We have no evidence that the failure of the courts strictly to observe the rules about exclusion of witnesses greatly concerned the litigants. Indeed, it broadened the base of supporters whom they could produce in court for their cause. Nor is there evidence to suggest that litigants were concerned about the failure of the courts to evaluate testimony strictly according to the academic rules. Indeed, to the extent that the church courts were called upon to perform an arbitral function in medieval England, a more discretionary form of decision making would seem to have been called for.[114]

The courts' reaction, on the other hand, to the desire of the parties to use canonic witnesses more like jurors or oath helpers varied, as we have seen, according to the type of case. Where the issue, as in a marriage case, could be resolved by testimony in the academic fashion, the courts tended to insist on such testimony, forcing the parties and their witnesses to attempt to manipulate the process, if my guesses are correct, by perjury. Where, on the other hand, the issue was not a particularly suitable one

113. On the importance of professionalization as a critical factor in the classification and development of legal systems, see R. Abel, "A Comparative Theory of Dispute Institutions in Society," *Law and Society Review* 8 (1973–74): 217–347. In the case of medieval canonic judges another element may be of some importance: the older notion of the religious judge as father confessor. This idea was firmly rejected by the academic lawyers in their development of the maxim that the judge does not judge according to his conscience (see Nörr, *Zur Stellung des Richters*, esp. p. 13); but men all of whom were in orders and at least some of whom could, and probably did, hear confessions may have found it difficult to separate the functions of judge and confessor.

114. See Donahue, "Stubbs vs. Maitland," pp. 705–8.

for the sharp resolution called for by the academic law, as in the case of tithes or even the right to a benefice, they allowed the parties to present their sides of the case in the way to which they were accustomed, and allowed, perhaps even encouraged, a settlement to emerge from the process.

Of course, we cannot exclude other possible explanations of the failure of the English church courts fully to receive the mainstream academic doctrine on witnesses. It may be that the English judges were simply following the doctrines of the early proceduralists, particularly those of the Anglo-Norman and French schools, who, as we noted, gave the judge considerably more discretion in evaluating testimony than did such mainstream writers as Pillius and Tancred.[115] But the pattern of manuscript survival suggests that at least by the fourteenth century it was the mainstream writers, particularly those whose views were incorporated in Durantis, that were generally read, and not the more obscure writers of the 1170s and 1180s.[116]

Possibly, too, we are dealing with a phenomenon unique to England, where, it was once believed, the academic canon law was never fully received. The thesis, of course, that medieval England's relation to the Roman canon law was exceptional has largely been discredited, but whether the way her church courts dealt with witnesses was exceptional cannot be known for certain until more work is done with Continental church court records. It may be that we will find less deviation on the Continent, at least in those areas where the jury and compurgation did not continue to be used in the secular courts. The occasional criticisms of actual practice that we find in the academic writing of authors who had no connection with England, however, suggests that the phenomena we noted above were not confined to England. Further, we are not, by and large, dealing here with a failure to follow the injunctions of specific papal rulings; again by and large, the holdings (in the common-law sense) of the papal decretals concerning witnesses were followed. What was not followed were the broad doctrines that the academic proceduralists assumed underlay these decretals. Thus, the issue here is somewhat remote from the broader issue of English church-state relations.[117]

Finally, we should bear in mind that, to the extent that the procedural-

115. See above, at nn. 28–31 and accompanying text.

116. The twelfth-century treatises and *ordines* are represented normally by one or two MSS. See, e.g., Kuttner, "Analecta iuridica." On the other hand, over a hundred Tancred MSS survive. See G. Dolezalek, *Verzeichnis der Handschriften zum römischen Recht bis 1600*, vol. 3 (Frankfurt, 1972), *s.n.* "Tancredus." To my knowledge no count has ever been made of Durantis MSS, but F. von Savigny, *Geschichte des römischen Rechts im Mittelalter*, 7 vols. (Heidelberg, 1834), 5:589–91, lists over thirty printed editions prior to 1600. John Lecch, the official of the Court of Canterbury in the early fourteenth century, owned two MSS of a *Speculum iudiciale* (almost certainly Durantis's), the only procedural treatises in a well-stocked personal law library of fifty-seven volumes. See A. Emden, *A Biographical Register of the University of Oxford to A.D. 1500*, 3 vols. (Oxford, 1957–59), 2:1119.

117. On the general question see Donahue, "Stubbs vs. Maitland," and sources cited.

ists deliberately limited the discretion of the judge in order to make their procedure more palatable to people who were accustomed to resolve cases by invoking God, to that extent the underlying reason for a significant part of the proceduralists' rules was considerably less powerful by the fourteenth century. Ordeal died out rapidly in England after 1215; proof by battle lingered on, but was not a usual method of secular proof. Only compurgation remained of the ancient "irrational" methods of proof.[118] The academic proceduralists, however, continued to refine their nondiscretionary rules. The change in methods of secular proof may have made it less urgent for the church courts to follow the academic rules, but it does not explain why they deviated from them in the way they did. What we have seen above suggests, if it cannot completely demonstrate, that the force operating against the academic rules was not a societal memory of a time when the judgment of God was invoked in a lawsuit, but rather a societal awareness of the fact that cases could be resolved by the judgment of the community represented by jurors or compurgators rather than by the judgment of the judge.

So the example of witness practice in the English medieval church courts shows us that receptions can and do occur, at least where the doctrine or practice to be received simply gives direction to some preexisting idea or institution. Once the reception has taken place, however, other forces come into play that may undercut the received doctrine itself or blunt its effect. Two such forces are involved in this reception, both, perhaps, of general importance: the desire of decision makers, particularly elite, professional decision makers, not to be bound too tightly to a body of rules, and the expectations of the society using the court. To the extent that it is possible to generalize from tentative conclusions about one example, it would seem that future students of receptions should take more account of such forces. What is said by the academics is certainly important, but it hardly gives us a complete picture of the complex process of reception.

118. See generally *P&M*, 2:598–604, 632–36.

6 Adding Insult to *Iniuria:* Affronts to Honor and the Origins of Trespass

John S. Beckerman

In the development of civil liability for wrongs in English law, several changes are of fundamental importance. The common law's admission of constructive trespasses in an action previously confined to deliberate violence was, in T. F. T. Plucknett's words, "a momentous departure."[1] No less significant was the gradual modification of the idea of strict liability, still stated as principle as late as 1681 in *Lambert* v. *Bessey*: "In all civil acts, the law doth not so much regard the intent of the actor, as the loss and damage of the party suffering."[2] The idea that persons should be compensated for all injuries—as Littleton said, "If a man is damaged, it is reasonable that he be recompensed"[3]—gave way over time to principles of liability that also take account of such factors as the culpability of the offender, social policy, and expediency.

Another development as momentous for the fully evolved action of trespass and later law of torts generally was an early substantive change, the gradual restriction of liability for wrongs to the loss or damage inflicted[4] and the consequent exclusion of civil remedy for affronts to honor, contumelious insults, personal humiliation, and injured feelings. Anglo-American law today is extremely chary of redressing injuries to feelings, honor, or reputation. Even in cases of defamation, civil remedies in libel or slander are based on the damage or economic loss attendant on injury to a person's reputation, rather than on the insult involved. For personal humiliation suffered, there is no redress.[5]

The purpose of this essay is to question why and how English prin-

I wish to thank Professors B. A. Black, C. M. Gray, T. A. Green, J. H. Hexter, P. D. Johnson, and S. D. White for their thoughtful criticisms of an earlier version of this essay.

1. See T. F. T. Plucknett, *Concise History of the Common Law*, 5th ed. (London, 1956), p. 465; and S. F. C. Milsom, "Trespass from Henry III to Edward III," *Law Quarterly Review* 74 (1958): 195–224, 407–36, 561–90.

2. T. Raym. 421, 83 *Eng. Rep.* 220. See John Henry Wigmore, "Responsibility for Tortious Acts: Its History," in *Select Essays in Anglo-American Legal History*, vol. 3 (Boston, 1909), pp. 474–537, as qualified by P. H. Winfield, "The Myth of Absolute Liability," reprinted in *Select Legal Essays* (London, 1952), pp. 15–29.

3. Year Book Mich. 6 Edw. 4, f. 8, pl. 17 (1466), cited by W. S. Holdsworth, *A History of English Law*, 3d ed., 9 vols. (Boston, 1927), 2:457.

4. It is a basic principle of modern tort law that "the redress due from the defendant whose liability is established should, as nearly as possible, be equivalent in value to the plaintiff's loss" (J. A. Jolowicz, T. Ellis Lewis, and D. M. Harris, *Winfield and Jolowicz on Tort*, 9th ed. [London, 1971], p. 2).

5. I am speaking here, and shall be throughout, of the theory and provisions of the law itself, and not about what juries may do in practice. Informed comments about de facto damage measurement must await further studies of jury behavior.

ciples of civil liability developed to this end, and to suggest the outlines of the process by which liability for wrongs came to be restricted in English law so as to exclude redress for affronted honor and material solace for injured feelings. Although we mostly take for granted this restriction of civil liability to economic loss alone, it appears as an anomaly to the legal historian for three reasons.

First, the elaborate scales of "emendations" in the Anglo-Saxon laws show that in preconquest England satisfaction for wrongs was largely intended to soothe the injured feelings or assuage the wounded honor of the wronged person or his kin. This fact is well known.[6] Additionally, a considerable body of evidence, to be examined shortly, exists to show that from the Norman Conquest through the thirteenth century, the satisfaction of honor was a more important part of dispute settlement than is usually appreciated. No study has been conducted to determine how or when liability for wrongful acts was restricted to the redress of the economic loss inflicted. Instead, it has too often simply been assumed that in the thirteenth century trespass was an action in which liability was founded strictly upon economic loss, for the sole purpose of recovering damages, as it was later. This assumption, which I believe to be erroneous, makes it easy to overlook other motives victims of wrongs may have had in taking legal action. Moreover, it makes some of the courses they followed, which made no clear distinction between criminal and civil procedure—such as seeking damages in conjunction with appeals, or appending words imputing felony to what are basically damage claims—appear strange or naive.[7]

Secondly, Roman law and all of the western European legal systems based upon it do *not* restrict civil liability to exclude redress for affronted honor and solace for injured feelings. The French, Spanish, Italian, and even Scottish laws of defamation are descended ultimately from the Roman *actio iniuriarum*, in which liability is clearly founded on the idea of contumelious insult, and on that alone—not, as in the English law of defamation, upon economic loss. Why should English law have developed in so notably different a way?

Thirdly, as will be demonstrated, the Roman *actio iniuriarum* supplied a significant part of the conceptual framework of thirteenth-century trespass pleas, as well as much of the common-form vocabulary for the fully evolved action of trespass. This vocabulary consisted of words originally added to accusations in order to characterize offenses as the more serious for being particularly insulting or humiliating. With the vocabulary of trespass largely derived from Roman law, emphasizing the concept of *iniuria*—contumelious insult—it is more than a little strange that liability in the classical tort of trespass was eventually founded on economic loss alone, to the exclusion of insulted feelings and affronted honor.

6. Holdsworth, *History of English Law*, 2:51–52, 101; Francis Bowes Sayre, "Mens Rea," *Harvard Law Review* 45 (1932): 974–1026, at 977.

7. H. G. Richardson and G. O. Sayles thought them stupid. See *Select Cases of Procedure without Writ under Henry III*, Selden Society, vol. 60 (London, 1941), p. cxxii.

In order to understand better the eventual restriction of English tort liability to damages—redress for the economic loss inflicted by a wrong—we must consider three subjects: the nature of liability for wrongs and the place of honor in dispute settlement in the eleventh and twelfth centuries; the place of affronts to honor in trespass pleas in the thirteenth century; and the extent and significance of Roman law influence on the jurisprudential apparatus of early trespass.

Delictual Liability, Honor, and Vengeance in the Eleventh and Twelfth Centuries

The few specific discussions of liability for wrongdoing ca. 1100 have naturally centered on the *Leges Henrici Primi* (ca. 1114–18). The *Leges Henrici*'s pronouncements on liability are disjointed and in some instances contradictory. Its inconsistencies have been attributed to the fact that the work is a compilation drawing heavily on the Anglo-Saxon laws, rather than a treatise. Its most recent editor has concluded that the *Leges Henrici* lacks a fully coherent treatment of liability for wrongful acts, irrespective of the author's possible ability to construct one, a judgment with which it would be difficult to disagree.[8]

As anthropologists have shown, honor and personal status are interdependent.[9] It is reasonable to expect that in societies with great concern for social status, personal honor will be highly valued and conventions will exist for satisfying wounded honor. England ca. 1100 is no exception to this rule. The main tension or conflict in the *Leges Henrici*'s treatment of liability pits the consideration to be given the status and positions of the persons involved against the nature of the deed itself. Several times the *Leges Henrici* states that judgments should consider the nature of the deed rather than the status of the parties, for example, *Equum iudicium est ubi non persona set opera considerantur.*[10] Numerous other provisions, however, explicitly contradict this general principle: all legal proceedings should consider differences between persons;[11] differences in the status of the parties will determine the procedures to follow, the law to apply, and indeed the compensation appropriate.[12] One could cite many illustrative examples. A person's status determines the value of his oath: he will need different numbers of oath helpers according to whether he swears against someone of equal status (no oath helpers), of higher

8. L. J. Downer, ed., *Leges Henrici Primi* (Oxford, 1972) (hereafter cited as *LHP*), p. 11.

9. J. Pitt-Rivers, "Honour and Social Status," in *Honour and Shame*, ed. Jean Georges Peristiany (London, 1965), pp. 21–77, esp. p. 23: "If honour establishes status, the converse is also true. . . ."

10. *LHP*, c. 33, 7; see also ibid., c. 9, 9, and c. 68, 5c.

11. "Personarum distinctio est in conditione, in sexu, secundum professionem et ordinem, secundum observatam legalitatem, que in agendis omnibus pensanda sunt iudicibus" (ibid., c. 9, 8).

12. "Aliud uero est si per parem accuset uel maior minorem uel minor maiorem" (ibid., c. 9, 6a; see also ibid., c. 9, 7).

status (one or two oath helpers), or against his own lord (two or four oath helpers).[13] When one kills or harms a cleric, the victim's rank and position will determine the compensation appropriate.[14] If two persons of the same rank kill each other, the matter should rest, but if they are of different status, the relatives of the greater may demand the difference between the two wergilds or appropriate revenge.[15]

The influence of penitential literature since the mid-tenth century had, if anything, increased the emphasis on rank. The penitentials taught that although legal proceedings should consider the nature of the deed, the higher the status of the culprit, the greater should be the penance or amends. St. Jerome's directions for confessors, adopted by the English church in the time of King Edgar, state, "And always, as a man is mightier, or of higher degree, so shall he the more deeply amend wrong, before God and before the world." This passage is closely echoed in the laws of Aethelred and Canute, and similar provisions in the *Leges Henrici Primi* are derived from Pseudo-Egbert's Penitential.[16] Thus, English society ca. 1100 continued to attach importance to personal position or estate, and distinctions of rank were still a significant consideration in dispute settlement.

No less important than distinctions of rank were personal loyalties, a subject on which the evidence of the *Leges Henrici* is explicit and unambiguous. A wrong was still, in a very real way, an offense against the social group (family or lordship) to which the victim belonged. Pollock thought "the public and private aspects of injuries pretty clearly distinguished by the Anglo-Saxon terms"; the "public" interest, however, was clearly secondary.[17] Loyalties to one's kin were paramount, and according to the *Leges Henrici* a person could still join with his blood relative in every case of need (*in omni necessario*).[18] Although it would be stretching the evidence to argue that kinship ties provided conscious models for the bond between lord and man and the relationship between king and subject, some of the duties of the family group in protecting its members and taking action if any of them were wronged had gradually been assumed by lords and kings.[19] Lords were supposed to protect their men not only

13. Ibid., c. 64, 2b–3; c. 67, 2.

14. Ibid., c. 11, 8; c. 11, 12; c. 66, 3; c. 68, 5–5b. Contrast these provisions with those at n. 16 below, which suggest that the culprit's status determines the amount of compensation.

15. Ibid., c. 70, 9–9a.

16. Can. Edg., *De Confessione*, 4, in Benjamin Thorpe, ed., *Ancient Laws and Institutes of England*, Record Commission (London, 1840), p. 403; VI Aethelred, 52, 1; VI Aethelred, 53; II Canute, 68, in A. J. Robertson, ed., *The Laws of the Kings of England from Edmund to Henry I* (Cambridge, 1925), pp. 107, 207–9; *LHP*, c. 73, 1–2 (p. 388), citing Pseudo-Egbert's *Penitential*, IV, 1–2, in Thorpe, *Ancient Laws and Institutes*, p. 377.

17. Sir Frederick Pollock and Frederic W. Maitland, *The History of English Law before the Time of Edward I*, 2d ed., reissued with a new introduction and select bibliography by S. F. C. Milsom, 2 vols. (Cambridge, 1968) (hereafter cited as *P&M*), 1:46, 48.

18. *LHP*, c. 82, 7.

19. See generally J. E. A. Jolliffe, *The Constitutional History of Medieval England*, 4th ed. (New York, 1961), pp. 1–139.

against economic loss (*dampnum*) but also against dishonor (*dedecus*),[20] a conjunction of which more will be said in the next section. If vengeance were appropriate in cases of persons slain, it would be taken by kinsmen and lords (*a parentibus et dominis*).[21] The king was seen not as the fount of justice, or even as "the author and lover of peace," as he appears in Glanvill's prologue.[22] According to the *Leges Henrici*, the king stood, literally, *in loco parentis*, in the place of a kinsman, to those without relatives or lords to protect them: "the king must act as kinsman and protector [*debet esse rex pro cognatione et aduocato*] to all persons in holy orders, Frenchmen [*alienigenis*], poor people, and those who have been cast out if they have no one else."[23] Royal "justice" was appropriate when a slain man had no relatives: *Si parentes non habeat, faciat inde rex iustitiam suam*.[24]

The idea of "strict liability" emanated from the emphasis on the "private" aspects of wrongs, the tendency to view wrongful acts specifically as offenses against victims and their relatives or lords, rather than as concerns of society in general. Wronged individuals more often dwell on the harm done them than on the intent or competence of those who have wronged them. Although the *Leges Henrici* reflects this emphasis on harmful effects—*Qui inscienter peccat, scienter emendet*[25]—it also makes distinctions in delictual liability based on the actor's intent.

Historians have long known that certain provisions of the Anglo-Saxon laws and the *Leges Henrici* closely resemble those in the penitential tracts, and that distinctions in culpability based on the existence or lack of harmful intention came into the secular laws from penitential and confessional literature.[26] In this respect the penitentials exercised a civilizing influence on secular law, however deplorable Charles Plummer found them in others.[27] The *Leges Henrici* clearly states the penitential principles that harmful intent aggravates an offense and that lack of intent to harm

20. *LHP*, c. 57, 8.

21. Ibid., c. 88, 9a.

22. *Tractatus de legibus et consuetudinibus regni Anglie qui Glanvilla vocatur*, ed. and trans. G. D. G. Hall (London, 1965), Prologue (p. 2).

23. *LHP*, c. 10, 3. Cf. Edward and Guthrum, c. 12, in F. L. Attenborough, *Laws of the Earliest English Kings* (Cambridge, 1922), p. 109.

24. *LHP*, c. 92, 15a. Half the wergild of such a person was to be paid to the king (ibid., c. 75, 10b).

25. Ibid., c. 88, 6a; c. 90, 11a; see also c. 70, 12b. See Downer, *LHP*, pp. 11, 312.

26. F. Liebermann, *Über das Englische Rechtsbuch Leges Henrici* (Halle, 1901), pp. 22–24, 26–28; *P&M*, 2:476; Winfield, "The Myth of Absolute Liability," p. 20. See also Thomas Pollock Oakley, *English Penitential Discipline and Anglo-Saxon Law in Their Joint Influence*, Columbia University Studies in History, vol. 107 (New York, 1923). Intentionality was a question of great interest to monastic and scholastic theologians in the first half of the twelfth century. See D. E. Luscombe, ed., *Peter Abelard's Ethics* (Oxford, 1971), pp. xxxii–xxxvi; R. Blomme, *La doctrine du péché dans les écoles théologiques de la première moitié du XIIe s.* (Louvain, 1958); and P. Anciaux, *La théologie du sacrament de penitence au XIIe s.* (Louvain, 1949).

27. Kathleen Hughes, *Early Christian Ireland* (Ithaca, N.Y., 1972), pp. 82–89.

is an ameliorating factor, deserving of the application of mercy or clemency.[28] Though lack of harmful intent may qualify the perpetrator for milder than usual treatment, nonetheless it does not absolve him from the consequences or effects of his act. He who unwittingly commits a wrong shall consciously make amends.

This theme of "strict liability" was as characteristic of penitential discipline as it was of secular law. It is perhaps significant that in stating the rule that conscious amends should be made for unwitting offenses, the author of the *Leges Henrici* always uses the verb *peccare*, which by 1100 had acquired a specialized meaning: to sin. One could sin, as well as inflict harm, unwittingly, and regardless of the sinner's intention, penance was necessary. For example, accidental homicides require penances, albeit lesser ones than intentional homicides. One who kills his father or mother accidentally (*casu*) should do penance for fifteen years, whereas the intentional parricide (*si uoluntate*) should do penance as long as he lives.[29]

It is sometimes asserted that the idea of strict liability, emphasizing the harmful effects of the deed regardless of the actor's intention, is in conflict with another idea of the *Leges Henrici*, which seems to determine culpability solely according to the existence or absence of harmful intention: *Reum non facit nisi mens rea*, which L. J. Downer translates, "A person is not to be considered guilty unless he has a guilty intention."[30] F. W. Maitland perceived that this maxim refers in the *Leges Henrici* only to perjury. Although recent opinion has questioned his view, it is undoubtedly correct. The maxim appears in the middle of a discussion of perjury, and the author's sources read *Ream linguam non facit nisi mens rea*.[31] Perjury is defined by *mens rea*. The truth or falsity of an oath was conceived not in terms of the objective truth or falsity of the proposition sworn to, but in terms of the genuineness of the swearer's belief in its truth. To paraphrase the maxim in the *Leges Henrici*, he does not swear a false oath (*reum non facit*) unless he swears contrary to his belief (*nisi mens rea*). Nowhere else either in penitential discipline or in secular law would lack of harmful intention exculpate someone completely.[32]

There is another reason for believing that *Reum non facit nisi mens rea* in the *Leges Henrici* cannot reasonably be taken to mean that deeds should be judged solely according to the actor's intention. When Peter

28. *LHP*, c. 90, 11; c. 70, 12c; c. 75, 5.

29. Ibid., c. 70, 12, a, b, c; c. 68, 9, derived from Pseudo-Theodore's *Penitential*, 21, 18 ff. (printed in Thorpe, *Ancient Laws and Institutes*, at p. 288).

30. *LHP*, c. 5, 28b. See Downer, *LHP*, pp. 11, 312; *P&M*, 2:476; and Winfield, "The Myth of Absolute Liability," p. 20.

31. Downer, *LHP*, p. 311 n.

32. The *Leges Henrici*, c. 90, is ambiguous on the subject of accidents. If the actor can prove (*certificare*) that the accident was unavoidable, he shall be held blameless (*innoxius*) (c. 90, 7). Nonetheless, appropriate amends should be paid in cases of accidents where the actor cannot swear that the injured person was not further from life and nearer to death because of him (*per eum*) (c. 90, 11b). On the whole, strict liability tempered by mercy seems to prevail.

Abelard propounded that thesis in detail in his *Ethics* (ca. 1133–39), the idea was revolutionary, implying among other things the possible innocence of Christ's crucifiers. Conflicting with prevailing theological opinion, the *Ethics* provoked a stormy reaction of criticism.[33] The author of the *Leges Henrici* was religiously orthodox, seemingly unimaginatively so. Nowhere does he question prevailing penitential doctrine; on the contrary, he cites it approvingly numerous times. Although he is able to distinguish a deed from the actor's intention, he assumes that legal proceedings will be brought concerning the former and not the latter (*ubi opus accusetur, non uoluntas*).[34] Nor does he suggest that it should be otherwise. It is doubtful, therefore, that the author of the *Leges Henrici* should be credited with anticipating Abelard's theory of intention some fifteen to twenty years before the composition of the *Ethics*. Though lack of harmful intent may lessen the seriousness of a wrong, strict liability is the prevailing theme of the *Leges Henrici*. Lack of malicious intent does not exculpate completely, and conscious amends should be made for unwitting offenses.

Englishmen ca. 1100 did not define wrongs abstractly. The enumeration of offenses in written laws demonstrates that wrongs were identified generally by two elements: first, the damage or loss inflicted, and secondly, the affront to honor (and related injured feelings) that the deed entailed.[35] Not always wholly distinguishable from each other, these elements clearly varied according to the circumstances of the wrong. In particular, deeds with similarly damaging harmful effects were viewed very differently according to the degree to which they affronted honor or injured feelings. If the victim and perpetrator stood to each other in a special relationship of trust and support—especially that of lord to man—honor was more seriously affronted and, consequently, the wrong held more grievous, than if the victim had been harmed by someone to whom he had no relation or affinity.[36] If the deed were perpetrated with manifest harmful intent (as was the case with malicious homicide) or with treachery (as was the case with murder), the outrage was much

33. Luscombe, *Peter Abelard's Ethics*, pp. xxxiv–xxxvi.

34. *LHP*, c. 90, 11d.

35. Any interpretation of twelfth-century legal change that ignores one or the other of these elements can be no more than a partial explanation—e.g., Oliver Wendell Holmes's attempt to discern the origins of civil liability solely in "the passion of revenge" (*The Common Law* [Boston, 1881], pp. 4 ff.), and Naomi D. Hurnard's use of the kin's desire for compensation to explain the momentous changes in the law of homicide at the end of Henry I's reign (*The King's Pardon for Homicide* [Oxford, 1969], chap. 1), for which, see below.

36. For example, *LHP*, c. 75, 1, concerning those who kill their lords: "If anyone kills his lord, then if in his guilt he is seized, he shall in no manner redeem himself but shall be condemned to scalping or disembowelling or to human punishment which in the end is so harsh that while enduring the dreadful agonies of his tortures and the miseries of his vile manner of death he may appear to have yielded up his wretched life before in fact he has won an end to his sufferings, and so that he may declare, if it were possible, that he had found more mercy in hell than had been shown to him on earth." For scalping as a ritual of dishonor, see Pitt-Rivers, "Honour and Social Status," p. 74, n. 9.

greater than if the death had resulted from negligence or misadventure. The actions appropriate in response varied accordingly.[37]

In earlier centuries in Anglo-Saxon England, the best way to satisfy wounded honor had been for the victim or the victim's kinsmen or lord to take vengeance on the offender, vengeance that not infrequently resulted in blood feud.[38] For the kinsmen or lord to take vengeance was not merely a right but a solemn duty. The man who failed in his responsibility to avenge a wrong was a fainthearted coward, permanently stigmatized by his shame or dishonor.[39] The man who took vengeance or prosecuted the feud was only doing what duty, honor, and justice demanded.

In the interest of maintaining public order, the circumstances in which vengeance might be taken or the feud pursued were gradually curtailed by royal decree from the tenth century through the end of the Anglo-Saxon period.[40] In many instances pecuniary compensation (*bot* and *wer*) and monetary penalties (*wite*) were substituted for vengeance. Although the acceptance of compensation was initially voluntary on the part of the victim or his relatives, soon it became obligatory in most instances, and this explains the appearance of the detailed scales of "emendations" in the later Anglo-Saxon codes and the *Leges Henrici*.

Vengeance, then, occupied a greatly restricted position in English law at the time of the Norman Conquest. In general, into the early twelfth century, one could not take vengeance for a wrong prior to seeking legal redress. Chapter 86 of the *Leges Henrici* states, *Ne quis se uindicet de suo homine sine lege*.[41] One exception to this rule existed in the case of the adulterer taken *in flagrante delicto* by the woman's husband or immediate male relative, who might lawfully kill him, no doubt because of the special outrage accruing from sexual offenses.[42] According to the *Leges Henrici*, in cases of accidental wrongs, honor could be repaired by the acceptance of money payment (*honorificentia*, contrasted with *emendatio*).[43] Although vengeance was regarded as inappropriate in cases of accidental homicide, persons perverse enough to exact vengeance could, in theory, do so, although by greatly restricted and literally talionic means. The *Leges Henrici* provides that "If a man falls from a tree or some other man-made structure on to someone else so that as a result the latter dies

37. *LHP*, c. 90, 11; c. 90, 7–7a.

38. Dorothy Whitelock, *The Beginnings of English Society* (Harmondsworth, 1952), pp. 43–44; Pitt-Rivers, "Honour and Social Status," pp. 25–30.

39. This theme is prominent in the thirteenth-century Icelandic sagas. For a good example, see *Laxdaela Saga*, trans. M. Magnusson and H. Palsson (Harmondsworth, 1969), p. 197.

40. Hurnard, *King's Pardon for Homicide*, pp. 1–2; Holdsworth, *History of English Law*, 2:43–45.

41. *LHP*, c. 86. Downer's translation of 86, 1, is erroneous. For "against," read "with."

42. *LHP*, c. 82, 8, from Alfred 42, 7 (printed in Attenborough, *Laws of the Earliest English Kings*, p. 85). See Pitt-Rivers, "Honour and Social Status," pp. 45–47, for a discussion of the dynamics of honor and dishonor in sexual transgressions.

43. *LHP*, c. 90, 11d: "In hiis et similibus ubi homo aliud intendit et aliud euenit (ubi opus accusetur, non uoluntas), uenialem potius emendationem et honorificentiam iudices statuant, sicut acciderit."

or is injured, if he can prove that he was unable to avoid this, he shall in accordance with ancient ordinances be held blameless. Or if anyone stubbornly and against the opinion of all takes it upon himself to exact vengeance or demand wergeld, he shall if he wishes climb up and in similar fashion cast himself down on the person responsible."[44] In cases where the offender was regarded as culpable, vengeance remained a viable possibility after other avenues of seeking satisfaction or justice were exhausted. In particular, if satisfaction or justice could not be obtained through the operation of the law, vengeance might still be taken. Delay in making satisfaction aggravated the offense.[45] If an offender summoned to the county court were adjudged guilty but obstructed the execution of judgment, he was to be killed.[46] If no honor or advantage would accrue to the victim or his relatives by accepting amends from the offender, it was more praiseworthy to drop the matter, or if it proceeded, to take vengeance against him (*in eum uindicetur*).[47] In Professor Pitt-Rivers's words, "The ultimate vindication of honour lies in physical violence and when other means fail the obligation exists . . . to revert to it."[48]

It is probable that a renewal of emphasis on vengeance for serious wrongs came to England with the Normans in 1066.[49] The essence of vengeance was the recourse to violence, a tendency that, to say the least, was not unknown in Norman society. By the time of the conquest of England, a system of monetary satisfactions no longer operated in Normandy.[50] Private feuds among great lords were common, intermittently reducing the duchy to a condition approaching anarchy through the end of the eleventh century. Violent conquest was an ordinary and integral part of Norman foreign relations, and already in the twelfth century was recognized by the chroniclers as the basis for Norman landrights in England and Sicily.[51] It is hardly surprising that vengeance for personal insults is a motif prominent in the chronicles of Norman culture. In one of the contemporary accounts of the conquest of England, Harold Godwinson's perjury in assuming the English throne is described as a personal outrage (*contumelia*) that the Normans urge Duke William to avenge (*se vindicare*).[52] Matthew Paris, later adapting an anecdote lifted

44. Ibid., c. 90, 7–7a, Downer's translation.
45. Ibid., c. 9, 4.
46. Ibid., c. 53, 1a–d. For a sour comment on the uncertainty of achieving satisfaction through the operation of law, see ibid., c. 6, 6.
47. Ibid., c. 36, 1c. Downer's translation, "that some punishment should be inflicted upon him" (p. 143), and his opinion that *uindicetur* here denotes something other than vengeance (p. 416) cannot be accepted.
48. "Honour and Social Status," p. 29.
49. Hurnard, *King's Pardon for Homicide*, p. 9, suggests that the Danish conquests may have been followed by a return to vengeance.
50. *P&M*, 1:74.
51. For conquest theory generally, see D. W. Sutherland, "Conquest and Law," *Studia Gratiana* 15 (1972): 33–52.
52. "Normanni autem, hoc audito, non parvum irati de tanta contumelia, quam Heraldus Domino illorum et illis fecisset, communiter ei consilium dederunt, ut de Heraldo perjuro

from William of Malmesbury, makes King William's crushing of the Exeter revolt of 1067 seem an outraged response to an insult offered him by one of the rebels.[53]

That vengeance was an integral part of Norman judicial policy is apparent from the two main changes made by William I in the criminal law. First, the Conqueror introduced the appeal of felony along with its concomitant, trial by battle.[54] Although it is commonplace to say that the procedure of appealing criminals amounted to the institutionalization of revenge, for those appeals that proceeded to trial by battle it is nonetheless true. Secondly, William substituted mutilation for hanging. Following Brunner, F. W. Maitland saw punishments short of hanging (mutilation, monetary penalties) as mitigations of the total forfeiture of life and limb, lands and goods, incurred by those who had committed serious crimes meriting outlawry, and he remarked on the ease with which punishments were changed without ceremonious legislation from the reign of William I through that of Henry II.[55] William I's introduction of mutilation, however, was not a casual change; it was an element of a coherent political policy. Mutilation was, above all, a punishment with strong retributory, vengeful, and talionic elements. A permanent sign of dishonor—*infamia*—for those who suffered it, mutilation also served to assuage the dishonor of those whom they had wronged and to enhance the honor of the king whose justice had imposed it. The author of the Peterborough version of the *Anglo-Saxon Chronicle* (E) implies strongly that fear of mutilation contributed to the "good order" William kept in England.[56]

In cases of serious physical offenses to the person, ca. 1100, affronted honor still demanded satisfaction, as the survival of vengeance and violent retributive punishments demonstrates. If the wrong were serious enough, that is, "unemendable," the victim or kin might satisfy honor through legal proceedings initiated by appeal, through judicially sanctioned vengeance (trial by battle), or through judicially ordered retributory punishments, hanging or mutilation. According to the customary law of Wessex, cited in the *Leges Henrici Primi*, culpable homicides deserving vengeance were to be handed over to the relatives and lords of those whom they had slain.[57] One could also satisfy honor by taking vengeance

suo se vindicare procuraret, coronamque illi adeptam, si aliter non potuisset, per bellum sibi saltem restitueret" (*Brevis relatio de origine Willelmi Conquestoris*, ed. J. A. Giles, in *Scriptores Rerum Gestarum Willelmi Conquestoris* [London, 1845], p. 5).

53. "Eodem tempore rex Willelmus urbem Oxoniam sibi rebellem obsidione vallavit. Ubi quidam stans super murum nudato inguine sonitu partis inferioris auras turbavit, in contemptum videlicet Normannorum. Unde Willelmus in iram conversus civitatem levi negotio subjugavit" (*Chronica Majora*, vol. 2, ed. H. R. Luard, Rolls Series [London, 1874], p. 3). *Oxoniam* is an error for *Exoniam*. See also William of Malmesbury, *De Gestis Regum Anglorum*, vol. 2, ed. W. Stubbs, Rolls Series (London, 1889), p. 307.

54. Richardson and Sayles, *Select Cases of Procedure without Writ*, pp. cviii–cix.

55. *P&M*, 2:161.

56. *Anglo-Saxon Chronicle*, E, s.a. 1086.

57. *LHP*, c. 70, 3; c. 70, 5; c. 70, 6; c. 71, 1a.

personally and extrajudicially in cases of adulterers caught in the act,[58] or of outlaws who refused to stand to right, as noted above.

Wrongs against property also involved an element of dishonor in Anglo-Norman society. Writs of protection, of reseisin, and of *ne vexes* from the late eleventh century into Henry II's time frequently specify that the beneficiaries of the writ (in many cases religious houses) should hold their property as freely, quietly, and *honorably* as ever their ancestors or predecessors did before them.[59] Interference with their free enjoyment of their tenements, we may infer, amounted to infringements of their honorable tenure, wrongs involving affronts to honor, *iniuriae*.[60]

"Emendable" wrongs, those that did not require vengeance and were not reserved to royal justice, invited satisfaction of both economic loss and affronted honor. The economic loss or damage inflicted required redress or compensation, through either amicable settlement or judgment.[61] The honor affronted or feelings injured also demanded satisfaction. Depending on the nature of the wrong,[62] this may have been easier to achieve by settlement or agreement—even if, as was likely, it involved a compromise—for the simple reason that protracted litigation or prosecution tended to advertise the wrong and exacerbate hostility between the parties.[63]

In reconciliations effected by both amicable settlements and judgments, the satisfaction of honor was frequently a matter of giving and accepting gifts with a view to saving face and repairing appearances.[64] In addition to the compensation rendered for loss or damage—and distinct

58. This was no longer permitted by the mid-fourteenth century. See T. A. Green, "Societal Concepts of Criminal Liability for Homicide in Medieval England," *Speculum* 47 (1972): 669–94, at 689–90.

59. R. C. van Caenegem, *Royal Writs in England from the Conquest to Glanvill*, Selden Society, vol. 77 (London, 1959). Writs of seisin or reseisin: nos. 72, 94, 96, 132, 149; of protection, nos. 166, 167, 172; of *ne vexes*, no. 163.

60. Interference after the issuance of the writ amounted also to contempt of the king, a more serious act of dishonor. See *LHP*, c. 13.

61. For agreement, see *LHP*, c. 7, 3a; c. 46, 4; c. 49, 5a; c. 54, 2–3; c. 70, 11. The advantages of compromise settlements are discussed by Frederic L. Cheyette, "Suum Cuique Tribuere," *French Historical Studies* 6 (1970): 287–99; and by Stephen D. White, "*Pactum . . . Legem Vincit et Amor Judicium*: The Settlement of Disputes by Compromise in Eleventh-Century Western France," *American Journal of Legal History* 22 (1978): 281–308.

62. *LHP*, c. 70, 12c: "Amicitie tamen et uenie propius uel remotius erit si meritum eius qui occisus est interfuit, et sicut acciderit."

63. As Professor Pitt-Rivers has written, there is a fundamental conflict between the satisfaction of honor and going to law or, as he puts it, "between honour and legality": "For to go to law for redress is to confess publicly that you have been wronged and the demonstration of your vulnerability places your honour in jeopardy, a jeopardy from which the 'satisfaction' of legal compensation at the hands of a secular authority hardly redeems it. Moreover, it gives your offender the chance to humiliate you further by his attitude during all the delays of court procedure, which in fact can do nothing to restore your honour but merely advertises its plight" ("Honour and Social Status," p. 30).

64. For the dynamics of honor in gift exchange, see the classic essay of M. Mauss, *The Gift* (originally *Essai sur le don*), trans. I. Cunnison (London, 1969), esp. pp. 35, 72; see also Pitt-Rivers, "Honour and Social Status," pp. 59–60.

from it, as the *Leges Henrici* makes plain—the offender might proffer a gift or sum of money specifically for the purpose of repairing honor and facilitating reconciliation.[65] In legal proceedings, the judges were to impose it as part of the settlement.[66]

Accepting the gift, however, might place the accuser in a position of obligation or inferiority to the offender. Therefore, depending on the circumstances (concerning which the *Leges Henrici* is frustratingly vague), it was enough that the accuser be shown to be a person to be feared (*metuendus*) and it was considered a creditable and commendable act for him to renounce or return the gift that he had been offered.[67]

In the twelfth century, there were two major changes in the law, by which the royal courts greatly increased their criminal jurisdiction. The first was the assumption of all homicides as pleas of the crown toward the end of Henry I's reign; the second was the great reliance on ex officio prosecution by presentment after the Assize of Clarendon. The expansion of royal criminal jurisdiction through these devices makes any statements about the relative importance of damage and affronted honor in delictual liability highly conjectural. Nonetheless, the subject cannot be ignored.

In her study of the medieval law of homicide, Naomi Hurnard stressed the desire of the kin for compensation. She suggested that the crown took jurisdiction over homicides committed in self-defense and by accident chiefly in order to keep the victims' kin from passing off culpable homicides as accidental in order to secure compensation privately, avoiding bringing appeals.[68] Commenting on the gathering of all homicides within the royal jurisdiction and the end of the wergild system in the later years of Henry I's reign, she argues that it was "highly improbable that there was some short-lived access of vindictiveness, peculiar to England, which led to the concerted and voluntary relinquishing of their ancient right [to compensation] by bereaved relatives."[69] Miss Hurnard bases her argument on the residual desire for compensation in a way that requires her to play down a concern for honor. Along with the relatives who may have hungered for compensation, however, there were others who surely thirsted for vengeance, for whom the honor offended by a serious wrong could not be satisfied by compensation and the payment of *wite*, who not only would be unwilling to regard culpable homicides as accidental in order to secure compensation, but who also would be likely to embellish their version of events in order to increase the chances of inflicting a retributive punishment on the offender. In two instances, the *Leges Henrici* refers to the receipt of compensation by one who has been outrageously wronged (*contumeliatus*, by beating and bloodshed) as shameful

65. *LHP*, c. 36, 2.
66. Ibid., c. 90, 11d.
67. Ibid., c. 36, 1e–2b.
68. *King's Pardon for Homicide*, pp. 8, 9, 23–25. For another view of the jurisdictional change, see Green, "Societal Concepts of Criminal Liability for Homicide in Medieval England," pp. 669–94, esp. pp. 687–88.
69. *King's Pardon for Homicide*, p. 9.

(*foedus*).[70] To someone of this belief, the acceptance of blood money by the relatives of a slain person could hardly have been honorable or desirable.[71]

Another passage of the *Leges Henrici* suggests that victims, not content with the punishment that would be achieved by imposing a *wite* on the offender, artificially inflate charges and overstate the case out of "an outrageous desire to inflict injury [*nocendi cupiditate prepostera*]."[72] In cases where the resulting punishment involved physical violence, this amounted to using the procedures of the law to effect one's revenge. A famous example from later in the twelfth century is the case of Ailward of Westoning. Having been refused repayment of a penny owed him by his neighbor, and foolishly emboldened by a trip to the local tavern, Ailward broke into the man's house in his absence in order to collect the debt. Discovered and captured, Ailward was charged by his neighbor not only with the theft of the penny, but with thefts of other articles as well, for the man wished to subject him to the punishment of mutilation, which obviously was not merited by the theft of one penny. Eventually convicted by the ordeal of water, Ailward was blinded and castrated.[73]

How Henry II's legal reforms affected the satisfaction of honor remains obscure, because of the absence of judicial records and Glanvill's reticence on the subject of crime. What is certain, however, is that the prosecution and punishment of serious wrongs became increasingly impersonal. Violent self-help was suppressed after the civil wars of Stephen's reign, as presentment of serious offenses by local juries at the sheriff's tourn was regularized (or instituted, depending on one's point of view)[74] to supplement appeals. Various forms of jury trial virtually eliminated trials by battle (except in cases of approvers' appeals) during the first half

70. *LHP*, c. 39, 1; c. 84, 1. See *P&M*, 2:526, n. 2.

71. It is a well-known feature of legal anthropology of "primitive" societies that when compensation and vengeance are both available in cases of serious wrongs, the former is widely held not to satisfy wounded honor as well as the latter. As A. S. Diamond has written (*Primitive Law, Past and Present* [London, 1971], p. 93), ". . . the temptation to accept an enormous sum of blood money remains and it is sometimes taken. Nevertheless there are a number of powerful factors which militate against acceptance. There is, first, the pride and solidarity of the family, and public opinion that despises those who accept, and there is the religious aspect of the same rule. . . . It is the duty of the nearest kin to obtain revenge for the slain and the presence of the slayer in the land destroys its fertility."

72. *LHP*, c. 22, 1.

73. Ultimately, Ailward was healed by the miraculous intervention of St. Thomas of Canterbury, to which we owe the story's preservation. See *Miracula Sancti Thomae*, in *Materials for the History of Thomas Becket*, ed. James Craigie Robertson, vol. 1, Rolls Series (London, 1875), p. 156; excerpted by M. M. Bigelow, *Placita Anglo Normannica* (London, 1879), pp. 260–61. The story is also preserved in a stained glass panel in Canterbury Cathedral.

74. Hurnard argued that communal presentment of offenders long antedated the Assize of Clarendon, but no regularity is apparent in the bodies that made the presentments. See Naomi D. Hurnard, "The Jury of Presentment and the Assize of Clarendon," *English Historical Review* 56 (1941): 374–410.

of the thirteenth century.[75] Whether victims of serious wrongs or their relatives and lords felt honor satisfied by punishments inflicted after ex officio criminal proceedings cannot be known for certain.

Regardless of the changes in the law, injured individuals continued to employ judicial proceedings as a means of taking private vengeance. By the end of the twelfth century, malicious prosecutions were seen as a sufficient problem for the royal government to provide, ca. 1190, a writ to enable a person imprisoned following an appeal to challenge the *bona fides* of the appeal. This was the writ *de odio et atia*. It provided an inquest to investigate expeditiously appeals alleged to be malicious or exaggerated, and it became immensely popular during John's reign.[76] Not all artificially inflated appeals were the result of malice or vindictiveness. As Hurnard has shown, one might exaggerate an appeal as the only means of obtaining a hearing in a royal court.[77] But the writ was ostensibly directed against those who brought appeals out of "hate and spite," much of which malice probably resulted from the atavistic motivation of vengeful feelings.

Even where the punishment did not involve physical violence to the offender, the amount of compensation sought by the victim might be inflated out of vindictive feelings. In cases of woundings, chapter 10 of the laws of William, an apocryphal text from Henry II's reign,[78] required the offender to pay the victim amends of the *laecefeoh*, the "leech-fee," or costs of his medical treatment. But the same chapter required the victim to swear that he could not heal the wound for less, and that he did not inflate the amount out of hatred for the offender (*nec quod in odium illius magis justo persolvit*).[79] This text, apocryphal or not, and the writ *de odio et atia* show that by the end of the twelfth century, the *jurisperiti* who were making the law of the king's courts actively believed that royal justice ought not to be used as a means of private retribution, an instrument of revenge for wounded honor. As we shall see, this assertion was a significant step in the restriction of delictual liability solely to economic loss.

Damage and Shame in Thirteenth-Century Trespass

Were one to accept Glanvill's division of pleas into civil and criminal (*Placitorum aliud criminale aliud civile*, I, 1) as a valid practical distinction, it might be assumed that the law was generally less concerned with honor as victims, relatives, and lords became further removed from

75. J. M. Kaye, *Placita Corone*, Selden Society, supplementary ser., vol. 4 (London, 1966), p. xvi.

76. *P&M*, 2:587–89; Hurnard, *King's Pardon for Homicide*, app. I.

77. *King's Pardon for Homicide*, p. 340.

78. H. G. Richardson and G. O. Sayles, *Law and Legislation from Aethelbert to Magna Carta* (Edinburgh, 1966), p. 121.

79. Robertson, *Laws of the Kings of England from Edmund to Henry I*, pp. 258–59. The Latin text is printed in John E. Matzke, ed., *Lois de Guillaume le Conquérant* (Paris, 1899), p. 9.

prosecution and punishment. As T. F. T. Plucknett wrote, however, Glanvill's distinction "bore little relation to the state of the law in his time."[80] The need to satisfy affronted honor is still apparent in plaints of trespass from the thirteenth century, a time when trespass actions were "more punitive, more criminal . . . than at the end of the middle ages."[81]

The essential part of the late medieval action of trespass was a claim that the plaintiff had suffered some harm or loss resulting from the defendant's action, for which amends ought to be tendered. In both pleading formularies and local court records from the thirteenth century, however, money is frequently demanded not only for economic loss (*damnum*, *dampnum*) but also for shame (*pudor, huntagium*), dishonor (*dedecus*), insult or outrage (*iniuria*, *injuria*), insult, or disparagement (*vituperium*). In the law French of the formularies the usual term is *huntage* (mod. Fr. *honte*).

H. G. Richardson and G. O. Sayles committed to print their suspicion that claims for damage and shame were one prominent element of formularies which was part of the academic training offered lawyers and estate administrators by the Oxford *dictatores* but which had little influence on pleadings in court.[82] The records of local courts, the tribunals where pleas of trespass were still most commonly heard in the thirteenth century, reveal otherwise. Claims for shame or dishonor suffered were admittedly rare in pleas brought before the royal courts. In local court rolls, however, they are more frequent than Richardson and Sayles suspected. Moreover, in many cases claims for dishonor may be concealed by the abbreviation of the court roll entries, for numerous records of courts end with *ad dampnum suum ij solidorum etc.*, thus concealing permanently whatever the end of the actual count may have been.

In the evidence extant from the thirteenth century, claims for damage and dishonor occur in a wide variety of contexts. It is instructive to examine some of them, to see what light they may shed on contemporary ideas of wrong and the early nature of trespass pleas.

Usually claims for dishonor appear in regard to the injury suffered by the victim of a wrong. At Steeple Ashton, Wiltshire, for example, in 1261, Richard Tilshead (*Tiddolvesid*) accused Walter Walerand of breaking an agreement in a transaction regarding the building and sale of a house, whereof he would not have suffered the damage or shame (*huntagium*) for forty shillings.[83] At Alrewas, Staffordshire, in 1259, John Plummer (*plumbator*) accused Robert Forester of disparaging and falsely accusing him, whereof he would not have suffered the damage for twenty shillings, nor the shame (*pudor*) for half a mark.[84] At Chatteris,

80. *Concise History*, p. 422.
81. Ibid., p. 423.
82. *Select Cases of Procedure without Writ*, pp. xciii–cxv.
83. Public Record Office, SC2 208/1, m. 1.
84. *Alrewas Court Rolls*, ed. W. H. Landor, William Salt Archaeological Society, new ser., vol. 10 (London, 1907), pp. 265–66: "per verba sua viliter vituperavit et apud forestarios accusavit." The association of *vitupero* and *pudor* is interesting.

Cambridgeshire, in 1274, William Andrew complained that Andrew son of Hugh had assaulted him in the king's highway to his damage and insult (*vituperium*) of two shillings.[85] At King's Ripton, Huntingdonshire, in 1299, Ives Corner (*in angulo*) complained that Bartholomew Sweyn had insulted him with foul words in the meadow of King's Ripton, calling him larcener, incendiary (*combustor domorum*), seducer, and cuckold. Moreover, he had levied the hue on him to his further insult (*vituperium*), whence he was attached and lost twenty shillings.[86] At Lewisham, Kent, in 1299, John Smith claimed that Thomas Smith had carried off an iron hammer from his house against his will and detained it to his damage and vexation (*gravamen*) of twelvepence, and to his shame (*pudor*) of a further sum that the record, in its abbreviation, omits.[87] At Highworth Hundred, Wiltshire, in 1285, a jury reported that John Herbert, a bailiff, had released a horse he had impounded as a gage from a carter driving across a meadow, but that he (it is unclear whether John or the carter is meant) had done no other damage nor outrage (*injuria*).[88] At Abbot's Langley, Hertfordshire, in 1258, William Fulcher complained that Robert Smeed (*Smethe*) had broken an agreement with him and was deforcing him of a crop, to his damage and dishonor (*dedecus*) of two shillings.[89] At Chalgrave, Bedfordshire, in 1295, Roger Andrew complained that William Algor had wrongly carried off his goose, to his damage and shame (*pudor*) of an unrecorded sum.[90] At Alrewas, Staffordshire, in 1268, Peter son of Dick (*Dike*) accused Geoffrey le Corson of disavowing an essoin after Peter had cast it for him according to an agreement, whereby Peter was amerced to his damage and shame (*pudor*) of two shillings.[91] And in the rolls of Highworth Hundred, numerous trespasses—mostly violent assaults, the taking of chattels, some detinues—are counted *ad dampnum et pudorem*.[92]

Several things may be observed from these and other examples from the records and formularies.[93] First, the phrases alleging dishonor appear in lawsuits involving a whole variety of wrongs from defamations to forcible injuries to breaking obligations to defaulting on transactions. Any of these offenses could be counted a contumely, insult, affront to personal honor. Regardless of the specific circumstances of the wrongs, it is evident that the victims felt dishonored or disparaged by them. At East and Mid-Merrington, county Durham, as late as 1379, village ordinances

85. Public Record Office, SC2 179/3, m. 2d.

86. Ibid., SC2 179/10, m. 9d.

87. Ibid., SC2 181/47, m. 7.

88. *The Rolls of Highworth Hundred, 1275–1287*, ed. Brenda Farr, Wiltshire Record Society, vol. 22 (Devizes, 1968), p. 277.

89. Abbot's Langley Court Book, Sidney Sussex College, Cambridge, MS Δ i, 1, fol. 8v.

90. *Court Roll of Chalgrave Manor, 1278–1313*, ed. M. K. Dale, Bedfordshire Historical Record Society, vol. 28 (Streatley, 1950), p. 37.

91. Public Record Office, SC2 202/56, m. 8.

92. *Rolls of Highworth Hundred*, passim.

93. *The Court Baron*, ed. Frederic W. Maitland and William Paley Baildon, Selden Society, vol. 4 (London, 1891), passim.

required of all tenants *quod nullus eorum maledicant alios in verbis vel factis* thereafter on pain of half a mark.[94] *Maledicere* here meant "to disparage." It is notable that the disparagement prohibited could be either by words, *in verbis*, or through some action, *vel factis*.

Secondly, the specimen counts from the pleading formularies usually distinguish separate amounts claimed for damage and shame. Although this seems to have been customary on certain manors, such as Alrewas and Lewisham, most of the examples in the court rolls include an undifferentiated combined sum. In such cases, it may well have been that the allegation of shame was a vestige of older forms of pleading, added to embellish the count to inflate damage claims for punitive purposes. At Highworth Hundred, for example, in September 1279, three pleas of the taking of chattels were counted *ad dampnum et pudorem*. In each, the value of the goods taken (one mare, one horse, the crop from one acre of land) was stated to have been ten shillings; yet the combined amount claimed for damage and shame was one hundred shillings![95]

When separate amounts were claimed, the amount asked for shame was almost always from one-quarter to two-thirds of the amount asked for damage. Although it might be assumed that these proportions indicate that the dishonor was less important than the economic loss suffered, the sums claimed for dishonor may have had a mainly token value. The *Leges Henrici Primi* (c. 36, 1e–2b) suggests that in reconciling adversaries, the relationship of giving and accepting gifts was more important than what was actually given, and once the relationship was established, the gift itself might be returned. Thus, a smaller sum claimed for dishonor should not be interpreted to mean that the affront was a negligible part of the complaint.

The amount claimed for dishonor exceeds the amount claimed for damage in a few cases involving defamation or public insult, in which direct attacks on reputation led to obvious disparagement or dishonor as well as economic loss. One example is the specimen plea in the *Court Baron* treatise for "disturbing a bargain." The plaintiff, who had contracted to buy wine from a merchant of Southampton, accused the defendant of maligning him to the merchant, so that the merchant refused to give him credit and raised the price of the wine. The plaintiff was forced to return home without the wine; nevertheless, he had to pay for the rental of the cart he had hired to transport it. He claimed forty shillings for his damage, one hundred shillings for his shame—two and a half times as much.[96] Another example is from the Abbot of Ramsey's court of the Fair of St. Ives, in 1275. Thomas of London complained that Maud, wife of John Woodful, had come to Thomas's bakehouse against the peace of the abbot and bailiffs, violently assaulted Thomas's wife with abusive language, calling her a whore and a sorceress, pouring yeast

94. *Halmota Prioratus Dunelmensis*, ed. W. H. Longstaffe and J. Booth, Surtees Society, vol. 82 (Durham, 1886), p. 153.
95. *Rolls of Highworth Hundred*, pp. 133, 134, 135.
96. *Court Baron*, p. 40.

on Thomas's white meal, and committed *hamsoken*, to his damage of threepence and his insult (*ad vituperium suum eo quod fecit hamsoken*) of half a mark. The amount claimed for the insult was more than twenty-six times as much as the amount claimed for damage.[97]

Both of these cases concern defamations. The plaintiff alleged a slander in one, a public, outrageous insult in the other.[98] In one respect, these examples vary strikingly from the later common law of defamation, in which remedy was not available for insult, "mere vituperation," but only for damage or loss. In both cases cited, as may be seen from the fact that the amount claimed for dishonor far exceeded the amount claimed for damage, the heart of the complaint concerned the insult, the affront to honor. This much more resembles Roman law, which based remedy for defamation solely on the *iniuria*, the insult or outrage involved.[99] We must now consider the extent of Roman-law influence on the jurisprudence of thirteenth-century trespass.

Roman Law Influence on Thirteenth-Century Trespass: The Vocabulary of *Iniuria*

The full denial of a plea of trespass contained three distinct elements: it defended *vim et iniuriam et damnum suum*.[100]

1. *Vis*: *Vis* may be dispensed with quickly. As Professor Milsom has shown, allegations of *vi et armis*, whatever their sources, had mainly jurisdictional and procedural purposes. They did not necessarily mean what they said; their function was to get the king's court to take cognizance of the plea and impose process of arrest and outlawry.[101] In local courts, therefore, allegations of *vi et armis* were made but infrequently. Where they occur, they are of little substantive importance.

2. *Iniuria*: The allegation of *iniuria*, on the contrary, was of fundamental conceptual importance to the plea of trespass. In classical Roman law,

97. *Select Pleas in Manorial and Other Seignorial Courts*, ed. Frederic W. Maitland, Selden Society, vol. 2 (London, 1889), p. 143.

98. At King's Ripton, Hunts., in 1294, Henry of Swindon, thought by Maitland to be the local vicar, complained that John Stalker had defamed him to various villagers and to his landlord, Roger of Ashridge, rector of the church of King's Ripton, saying that Henry was a seducer and manslayer, and that he had slain his own son, Nicholas; in consequence of which, according to Henry, Roger cut three years off Henry's term in the church of King's Ripton, which he held of Roger, "ad detrimentum suum triginta solidorum et ad grave dampnum suum viginti solidorum" (*Select Pleas in Manorial Courts*, p. 116). Maitland thought that this was a claim for special damages; more likely, the word *detrimentum* refers to the dishonor Henry had suffered, the damage to his reputation, as in the two examples just discussed. It will be noted that the amount claimed for *detrimentum suum* is one and a half times as much as that claimed for damage.

99. Barry Nicholas, *An Introduction to Roman Law* (Oxford, 1962), p. 217.

100. Only the initial denial was of *vim et iniuriam (tort e force)*; the complete denial also defended the damages.

101. Milsom, "Trespass from Henry III to Edward III," pp. 573–78.

iniuria in general meant simply *omne quod non iure fit.*[102] As a special delict, however, it meant *contumelia*, insult or outrage.[103] Based on outraged feelings rather than on economic loss, the *actio iniuriarum* was, as Buckland noted, *vindictam spirans.*[104] The money payment sought thus represented "solace for injured feelings or affronted dignity," not compensation for economic loss.[105] A wide variety of wrongs came to be encompassed by the *actio iniuriarum*, related by the fact that they showed contempt of the victim's personality or tended to disparage him (or were intended to do so).[106]

It was this sense of *iniuria* that Bracton had in mind when he wrote of the *actio iniuriarum* to describe the English plea of trespass.[107] In addition to the denial of the *iniuria* or affront, as well as the various terms signifying dishonor surveyed in the last section, other allegations frequently found in trespass pleas were designed to underline the insulting or injurious nature of the offense. *Contra voluntatem suam*, the allegation that the act was done against the victim's will, characterized the wrong specifically as against the victim's personality. For the act to constitute an *iniuria* or insult, it had to be done against the victim's will. No outrage is done to him who consents: in the Year Books, English serjeants occasionally quote with approval the maxim *Volenti non fit iniuria.*[108] The allegation of *maliciose* asserted that the offender had acted willfully, with harmful intention, a factor that, as we saw in the *Leges Henrici Primi*, aggravated the dishonor or outrage involved. The allegation *et alia enormia*, "and he did other *outrageous* things to me," though vague, nonetheless speaks for itself, evoking the injurious nature of the offense. *Iniuria* in trespass pleas, then, had the specific meaning of insult, outrage, affront to honor, not the general blandness of its modern cognate "injury," as it has too often been translated.

3. *Damnum*: After denying *vim et iniuriam*, the defendant in a plea of trespass had to deny the damages claimed. It has generally been thought that Bracton, in speaking of the *actio iniuriarum* (fols. 103b, 155b, 439) was merely paraphrasing the *Institutes*, 4.4.7, concerning *iniuriae.*[109] But Bracton speaks not only of *iniuria atrox uel leuis*, which must be valued, but also of *damnum maius uel minus* (fol. 439). The *actio iniuriarum* of

102. *Institutes*, 4.4.7.
103. W. W. Buckland, *A Textbook of Roman Law from Augustus to Justinian*, 3d ed., rev. by P. Stein (Cambridge, 1963), p. 589.
104. Ibid., p. 591.
105. Nicholas, *Introduction to Roman Law*, p. 217.
106. Buckland, *Textbook of Roman Law*, p. 590.
107. *Bracton De Legibus et Consuetudinibus Angliae*, ed. George E. Woodbine, trans. with revisions and notes by Samuel E. Thorne, 4 vols. (Cambridge, Mass., 1968–77) (hereafter cited as *Bracton De Legibus*), fols. 103b, 155b, 439 (2:296, 2:438–39, 4:363). See *P&M*, 2:534, n. 2.
108. See, e.g., Beds. eyre of 1330, Lincoln's Inn, Hale MS 137 (1), fol. 175r.
109. Frederic W. Maitland, *Bracton and Azo*, Selden Society, vol. 8 (London, 1894), p. 165; Richardson and Sayles, *Select Cases of Procedure without Writ*, p. cxi.

Roman law was not concerned with *damnum*,[110] and thus could not have supplied the concept of damages to Bracton's description.

George Woodbine thought that the recovery of damages first entered English law from Romano-canonical sources in 1198, when it became possible to recover damages through the assize of novel disseisin.[111] Although 1198 marks the first evidence of a legal procedure through which damages were expressly recoverable by name in the royal courts, the principle and practice of recovering damages were not new to English law in 1198, as T. F. T. Plucknett has shown conclusively. An important purpose of Anglo-Saxon legal proceedings was to secure pecuniary compensation, and it was not a large step from *bot* to the damages of later law.[112] As early as 1114–18, the *Leges Henrici Primi* distinguished the economic loss inflicted by wrongful acts from the dishonor involved, *damnum* from *dedecus*.[113] Furthermore, it suggested that this loss could be redressed by pecuniary amends awarded by judges in litigation (*emendatio*, contrasted with *honorificentia*).[114] It would seem that these provisions incorporated both the principle and the practice of recovering damages for economic losses resulting from wrongful acts long before 1198. Although English trespass derived its vocabulary of *iniuria* from Roman law, then, there is no compelling reason to think that damages, the redress of economic loss, was anything but a native element.

The Disappearance of *Iniuria* from the Foundations of English Tort Liability

As we have seen, wrongs were widely identified in England by the early twelfth century by reference to two discrete elements: economic loss (*damnum*) and affront to personal honor (*dedecus*). Though the idea of the wrong as a personal affront was an ancient one in English law, lawyers including Bracton turned to the civil law of Rome for the vocabulary of *iniuria* with which to express accusations of affronted honor. Whereas the recovery of damages served a compensatory function, pecuniary awards for dishonor could alternatively serve soothing, face-saving, or punitive ends. Thus, the pecuniary claims for damage and dishonor encountered so frequently in thirteenth-century local court records were one way in which victims might attempt to deal with both aspects of wrongful acts, and were related to other accusations that mixed civil and

110. Wrongful damage to property (*damnum iniuria datum*) was a separate delict in Roman law, based mainly on the *lex Aquilia*. The corresponding action was the *actio legis Aquiliae*, or *actio damni iniuriae* (Buckland, *Textbook of Roman Law*, pp. 585 ff.).

111. George E. Woodbine, "Origins of the Action of Trespass," *Yale Law Journal* 33 (1924): 799–816, at 807–15.

112. *Concise History*, p. 370.

113. *LHP*, c. 57, 8.

114. Ibid., c. 90, 11d.

criminal elements, such as the appeal that sought damages and the trespass count that alleged felony.[115]

As the action of trespass flourished in the royal courts, the *iniuria* or affront to honor disappeared as an operative element in English tort liability, eclipsed totally by the element of economic loss. To return to the question with which this essay began, why did this happen? There was nothing inevitable about the disappearance of the concept of *iniuria* from tort liability. At the end of the thirteenth century, trespass pleas could still serve both compensatory and penal ends, as statutory trespasses provided not only compensation, but punitive damages, and on occasion, imprisonment for the offender.[116] Indeed, punitive damages are an occasional feature of the law of torts even today. An anomaly that blurs slightly the civil-criminal distinction we so take for granted, the award of punitive damages may remind us that there was nothing necessary or inevitable about the eventual prevalent separation of "criminal" and "civil" in English law.

As it turns out, there is nothing particularly mysterious about the disappearance of *iniuria* from the foundations of tort liability in English law. Let us consider three explanations of different types.

1. *A behavioral explanation*: This explanation depends on the conflict between honor and legality referred to above.[117] As the business of litigation in the royal courts became increasingly professionalized through the thirteenth century, victims of wrongs became further removed from the actual conduct of litigation, depending on attorneys to activate the strictures of mesne process against their opponents and on pleaders to argue their cases, often in ancient formulaic statements, in an obscure and technical language that they could understand but poorly. Even a favorable judgment could offer little more than economic redress. The satisfaction that accrued from a victory in court would have been a vicarious satisfaction at best—pleasure in a victory where confrontation between the parties took place through representatives and, although loss was recompensed, justification or vindication of the victim was minimal. As these changes occurred, victims ceased trying to satisfy wounded honor through civil remedies in the royal courts.

Three problems are immediately apparent in this explanation. The first is that persons moved to litigation by a desire for retribution or self-vindication are not likely to be deterred from their chosen end by a rational consideration of the limited satisfaction they may achieve through the law. Secondly, to laymen in any age, the impenetrable technicalities of the law create a mystique that may inflate expectations of the satisfaction attendant upon a legal victory. Thirdly, because persons kept trying to

115. George E. Woodbine, "Origins of the Action of Trespass," pp. 801–2, n. 10; Richardson and Sayles, *Select Cases of Procedure without Writ*, pp. cxxxi–cxxxvi; *Court Baron*, pp. 28, 33.

116. Plucknett, *Concise History*, p. 457.

117. See above, at n. 63.

satisfy wounded honor through trespass pleas in local courts, as was demonstrated in the section on damage and shame above, it is probably fair to assume that they would have done so in the royal courts if they could have. A behavioral explanation, then, does not suffice to explain the disappearance of *iniuria* as a foundation of tort liability in English law.

2. *A procedural explanation*: This explanation would argue that the jury, which came to be the ordinary manner of trying respass pleas in the royal courts, was not appropriate to defining and valuing affronts to honor. Although juries were well suited to valuing economic loss—taxing damages—they were ill suited to valuing damage to reputation or affronts to honor,[118] particularly when the affront or disparagement was implicit in wrongful acts that varied from assaults to wrongs against property to breaches of contract.

There is, however, no inherent reason why a jury of twelve would have been especially ill suited to valuing affronts to honor, for who could have known better what an action meant or implied than twelve men from the neighborhood in which the wrong was alleged to have been done? In many local courts, juries were trying trespass pleas that demanded sums for dishonor by the end of the thirteenth century. Perhaps, then, the procedural explanation may be reduced to the a priori assertion that affronts to honor cannot be valued. But the civil law of Scotland, based on that of Rome, successfully awarded pecuniary sums in the name of *solatium* for mere insults;[119] so it is not impossible that English trespass, with its demonstrated Roman vocabulary derived from the *actio iniuriarum*, could have done the same.

3. *The jurisdictional-conceptual explanation*: The king's courts began to employ *ostensurus quare* writs to entertain pleas of trespass only ca. 1200. As T. F. T. Plucknett showed, local courts were the usual *fora* for trespass pleas. When they first started coming into the royal courts, trespasses were counted as pleas of the crown—violations of the king's peace, acts of contempt to the royal majesty.[120] During the early thirteenth century, royal justice was being extended to provide subjects with remedies against an increasing variety of economic losses. To losses attendant upon wrongs to freehold land were added other losses occasioned by wrongs to persons or to personal property.

Though royal justice would protect subjects against losses occasioned by violent and forcible wrongs on the theory that they were acts of dishonor to the king, the royal courts had no interest at all in the personal

118. "The common law remedy of monetary payments for damages assessed by local juries, did not lend itself to a simple application in the measurement of damages to such an intangible as a man's reputation" (Colin Rhys Lovell, "The 'Reception' of Defamation by the Common Law," *Vanderbilt Law Review* 15 (1962): 1051–71, at 1056.

119. F. T. Cooper, *The Law of Defamation and Verbal Injury*, 2d ed., rev. by D. O. Dykes (Edinburgh, 1906), p. 4.

120. Plucknett, *Concise History*, p. 457; S. F. C. Milsom, *Historical Foundations of the Common Law* (London, 1969), pp. 245–46.

honor of the king's subjects. On the criminal side, as the writ *de odio et atia* taught so clearly, royal justice was not supposed to be used for purposes of private retribution. On the civil side, the king's courts provided no remedy by which subjects could vindicate personal honor. Through the fourteenth century the common law developed with no interest at all in defamation, a subject that was left to lesser tribunals, the local secular and the ecclesiastical courts.

The idea of defamation, of disparagement founded upon insult, was the central normative concept of the *actio iniuriarum*. Without it, the common law could develop no jurisprudence of affronted honor, of *iniuria atrox uel leuis*. It is ironic that the royal courts should have adopted the Roman vocabulary of *iniuria* without any interest in the honor of the subject. If the king's courts had had an earlier interest in defamation, in the first half of the thirteenth century or thereabouts, the common law of defamation might well have developed along Roman lines, and insult might have joined economic loss as a foundation of tort liability at common law, as was the case in the local courts.

As it happened, however, the seeds of Roman influence apparent in Bracton's treatise, in claims for dishonor in local courts, and in the vocabulary of *iniuria* bore no fruit in the royal courts. The future of tort liability lay in the royal courts, and throughout the Middle Ages the common law ignored dishonor to anyone but the king. By the time defamation was "received" by the common law,[121] tort liability in trespass and case had long excluded *solatium* for injured feelings or pecuniary retribution for affronted honor. Thus, the common-law remedies for libel and slander developed with a much different jurisprudential framework from the Roman *actio iniuriarum*, whose legacy to English tort law, the denial of *iniuria* in trespass, was ultimately of form rather than substance.

121. See Van Vechten Veeder, "The History of the Law of Defamation," in *Select Essays in Anglo-American Legal History*, 3 vols. (Boston, 1907–9), 3:446–73; F. Carr, "The English Law of Defamation," *Law Quarterly Review* 18 (1902): 255–73, 388–99; and Lovell, "The 'Reception' of Defamation by the Common Law," pp. 1051–71.

7 Legal Reasoning in the Fourteenth Century: The Invention of "Color" in Pleading

Donald W. Sutherland

The fourteenth century is the first age for which we can have an intimate knowledge of what went on in the English courts. For a direct and immediate introduction to the courtroom scene we need reports, and reports begin only in the 1270s. But soon after their invention they came to be produced voluminously and steadily, so that from the 1290s and through the whole following fourteenth century we have a wealth of material expressly designed to render us present in the king's court.

The early reports are meant mostly to display patterns of pleading and argument. They are less concerned to teach rules of process or substantive law, and they tell almost nothing about how trials were conducted. But arguments, and pleadings, and especially arguments about pleadings, are shown so directly and in so many cases that the system of pleading and the patterns of reasoning used in the courts ought to be plain to students of the history of law. However, this is not so. The logic of argument in the fourteenth century was not essentially different from ours, and the rules of pleading had to be simple enough that barristers could use them extemporaneously, as the procedure of oral altercation required. But I fancy that there is no one now alive who in any but the most elementary cases can anticipate the moves of fourteenth-century barristers, or the critiques of the justices, as these are time and again reported. The logical vocabulary is different. It speaks, confusingly to us, of acknowledging and traversing, of facts that are "supposed," of "the cause that supports the action," of *a*'s being "tantamount" to *b*, of *a* and *b* "standing together." The rules of pleading are cast in unfamiliar language about bars and privity and what-not else. "I'll dissolve your argument," begins a barrister in one case.[1] In another case counsel opens an argument with, "A warranty once extinguished without hope of return cannot be revived by wrongful occupation." "But," says the opponent in reply, "the fact that time has passed means that a different rule applies." An intricate argument ensued, whose most discouraging aspect for a modern reader is that the participants seem somehow to know what they are about.[2] All this sort of thing, in thousands of cases, is reported in nearly pure dramatic form, almost without commentary, a painfully honest approach and one which rewards us with its vividness but which, if we wish to understand as well as to hear, leaves us to figure everything out for ourselves. This we have not yet done.

1. *Ieo vous assoudrai ceste reson* (Lincoln's Inn Hale MS 137 [1] [hereafter cited as La], fol. 31v; the reports cited from it are of the eyre of Northamptonshire of 1329–30).
2. La, fols. 8v–9r.

Let us try in this article to take a narrow sounding into the thought of the men of the law of the fourteenth century, and let us try it at a point where their thinking seems most alien to us: let us address the matter of "color" in pleading. It is well known that in the fifteenth century and after, one of the standard moves in the game of pleading at common law was to "give color" to the opponent. Defendants gave color, originally in assizes of novel disseisin, derivatively in actions of trespass and some other forms of action. Plaintiffs often brought these actions to sue for real property, but the forms of action required the plaintiffs to say nothing specific at the outset about the basis of their claims. A plaintiff merely said that it was "his free tenement" or "his land," and instead of detailing his claim would tell of some quite incidental clash that had occurred between him and the defendant because of their rival claims to the property: "He disseised me of my free tenement," or "He broke into my land." This method of raising a case was allowed because it expedited justice, inasmuch as the law traditionally moved faster to judge of clashes between parties than to determine cases where title alone was in question. These cases in which the plaintiff was allowed at the outset to be so vague about his title were normally tried by jury, and in talking to the jurors the plaintiff would no doubt get down to the specifics of his claim to the property.

But often the defendant would want to have the plaintiff's claim explained in detail to the court, before the case ever went to a jury, so that he could then set forth his own counterclaim and draw the comparison between them—to the court. The defendant would want it this way if he believed that his claim was superior but that its superiority turned on points of law which the justices would be more likely than jurors to appreciate and respect: fine points of law, perhaps, or outright technicalities. If a fifteenth-century defendant wanted it this way, he could have it so, by himself explaining the details of the plaintiff's claim to the court as soon as the case opened, and setting forth in equal detail his own counterclaim, which he believed to be better, and concluding that, yes, of course, there had resulted from these rival claims that clash which the plaintiff described one-sidedly as a disseisin or a breaking in. The defendant might tell, for example, that the property had belonged to his own father, who gave the plaintiff a deed for it—and that was the plaintiff's claim; but that the father had in fact held onto the property so that it eventually passed by inheritance to him, the defendant—and that was *his* claim, and a far better one, for the plaintiff's deed was no good in law if the father had never parted with the property; and then there was that clash: relying on his deed even though it was legally void, the plaintiff had entered the property and the defendant had put him out of it, true enough. If the defendant pleaded in this way, the plaintiff would have to reply to what he said about the relative worth of their rival claims. The discussion would continue from there, and the plaintiff could not win unless he could show the court that his title was the better.

Now up to a point this makes plain good sense. The justices listened to the defendant's explanation of his title and took it as a basis of discussion because they thought that they could do better justice if they knew more of the facts, not an unreasonable thought. The defendant had to agree that the clash between the parties of which the plaintiff had spoken had indeed occurred, because it had to be clear that he was talking about the same case that the plaintiff had put up against him. But it is odd that the defendant should have to describe not only his own claim but also the plaintiff's. The plaintiff was going to reply. Why not leave it to him to say everything that was to be said on his side? But this description of the plaintiff's claim by the defendant was the specific element of "color," and the law insisted that the defendant include it if he wanted any discussion of the parties' rights in court before the case went to a jury.[3] And if this seems strange, it is surely much stranger that what the defendant said about the plaintiff's claim was not true and not expected to be true, but pure sham, pure fiction. Increasingly in the fifteenth century, defendants attributed the same claim to all plaintiffs, a claim that appears then, thoroughly standardized, in hundreds and in thousands of cases. When the plaintiff replied he would tell the real basis of his claim and there would be no more discussion of the sham claim that the defendant attributed to him.

It is incongruous that statements that were wholly false and known to be so should operate to turn the course of proceedings whose intent was to find facts and do justice. If the use of fictions in giving color was paralleled by counting on fictions in trover, and joined later by the fictions of common recoveries and by the imaginary roles of John Doe and William Styles in Ejectment, these and others only compound the incongruity. "We honor truth," said Justinian in one of his enactments, "and we wish our laws to tell only of things that really are."[4] Surely that is the right approach. But the use of fictions in giving color takes us far from it. Christopher St. German was troubled about this in the 1520s, for in his dialogue *Doctor and Student* he had the doctor of divinity, one of the interlocutors, object that when a party gives color he "wittingly saith against the truth." The doctor refused to be comforted by the consideration that legal fictions were not meant to deceive, for "every lie is an offense, more or less," even if it be "to the hurt of no man."[5] Three centuries later the same concern about lying moved Charles Dickens, in *The Pickwick Papers*, to excoriate the trade of the common bailsman:

> "Bail you to any amount, and only charge half-a-crown. . . ."
>
> "What! Am I to understand that these men earn a livelihood by waiting about here, to perjure themselves before the judges of the

3. There were some other ways for the defendant to obtain the same object under certain circumstances. But giving color was always the principal means, and the others need not concern us here.

4. Codex 7.5: "Nos enim qui veritatem colimus ea tantummodo volumus in nostris esse legibus quae re ipsa obtinent."

5. *Doctor and Student*, ed. T. F. T. Plucknett and J. L. Barton, Selden Society, vol. 91 (London, 1974), p. 295.

> land, at the rate of half-a-crown a crime!" . . .
> "Why, I don't exactly know about perjury, my dear sir. . . . It's a legal fiction. . . ."[6]

Our own age has rid itself of any overwrought scruples about lying but seems to find legal fictions more loathsome than ever. We feel, I believe, that it is simply undignified for serious men to mouth words that say nothing, and we have reacquired the sense of the futility of such things that afflicted Augustine in the fourth century when the young rhetorician had been chosen to deliver a panegyric upon the emperor. It would be no more veracious than other panegyrics. "I was to tell many lies, and people who knew that they were lies would applaud" the "wasting thoughts" that would teach no one any truth.[7]

Now in the fifteenth and sixteenth centuries, giving color and using fictions to do it were received, traditional devices, and it is possible therefore that they may have been accepted quite uncritically. But there must have been some time when the cast of thought of the leaders of English law was such that the devices did not at all seem pointless, incongruous, dishonest, or undignified, when on the contrary they seemed appropriate, honorable, and workmanlike. Otherwise they would never have been invented in the first place, or never received into general use when they were new. The time in question, when they were new, was the early fourteenth century.

In an assize of novel disseisin of 1330 we seem to catch the device of color being born. The plaintiff brought his assize, charging that the defendant had disseised him of his free tenement. The defendant replied that his father had held the property in fee and that when his father died he himself took it as his inheritance. The plaintiff, he said, was the lord of whom the property was held, and he claimed it as his escheat, as though there had been no heir; on the basis of that claim the plaintiff moved into the property, but the defendant put him out again. In telling here of the plaintiff's claim by escheat, the defendant was giving him color, in the way that was to become classic. But in 1330 it was not yet quite familiar, for the plaintiff in this case protested, "It is not for you to plead whether we [claimed] by escheat or in some other way." The court, however, liked the defendant's plea and took it as the starting point for further discussion.[8]

T. F. T. Plucknett recognized that color was "a product of the early fourteenth century" but believed that until much later, sometime around 1400, the color given to the plaintiff, the claim attributed to him, had to be genuine and not fictitious: "It really did represent the facts."[9] So it did in many, seemingly in most, fourteenth-century cases. In the case that we have just reviewed, although the plaintiff did not like his opponent to be

6. *Pickwick Papers*, chap. 40.
7. *Confessiones*, 6.6.
8. La, fols. 26r–v.
9. T. F. T. Plucknett, *A Concise History of the Common Law*, 5th ed. (Boston, 1956), p. 412.

telling that his own claim to the property was by escheat, it was in fact just so.[10] But it needn't have been. Fourteenth-century barristers could give fictitious color if they wanted to, and sometimes they did. In 1331 a defendant said that the plaintiff claimed to hold land in curtesy after the death of Maud, his late wife. The plaintiff actually claimed that the land was his because Maud had given it to him before they married.[11] A report of 1328 stated directly that color could be fictitious. The defendant in the case pleaded that he inherited property from a relative of his, that the plaintiff was the lord of whom the property was held, that the plaintiff tried to take possession, but that he, the defendant, put him out. It was ruled that the plea was bad because it gave the plaintiff no color. To say only that the plaintiff was lord, was not to describe any claim at all on his part to the property, not even a defective claim. "But it was said," the report continues, "that the defendant could have fabricated [*forgé*] a good bar if he had said that the lord had taken possession claiming by escheat for failure of heirs and that he himself, the defendant, was overseas in foreign parts at the time."[12] Already by 1328 some barristers were deliberately using fictions in giving color.

T. F. T. Plucknett thought that fictions could not be used in giving color in the fourteenth century because of what he saw in a case of 1388. Here a defendant, in giving color, said that the plaintiff claimed the property as the heir of her brother William Rokesey. The plaintiff replied that she never had a brother named William Rokesey, and forced an issue that left the case to turn on that point.[13] Evidently it was not safe to tell stories about a William Rokesey if "haplye there was never no such man,"[14] not safe to tell of blood-relationship between the plaintiff and another if those two were not blood relatives. So lordships had better not be invented, or husbands, or wives. But our earlier cases show that events, and ideas in the plaintiff's mind, could be conjured up out of nothing with impunity. The defendant can safely say that he was overseas and that the plaintiff, who was the lord, therefore developed the idea that he was entitled to have property as his escheat, wherever the defendant was in fact and whatever conception of his claim the plaintiff had actually entertained. This restraint on inventing persons and relationships prevented fourteenth-century barristers from using the same tired old story over and over to give color to every plaintiff in case after case, as they did from the fifteenth century. It made them work their fictions up out of the circumstances of each case. But the right to contrive imaginary events gave generous room for fiction, and still more did the right to attribute

10. Compare La, fols. 6v, 13v, and 26r–v.

11. Year Book (hereafter cited as Y. B.) Trin. 5 Edw. 3, f. 20, pl. 1 (1331) = Y. B. 5 Edw. 3 (*Liber Assisarum*), f. 8, pl. 4 (1331).

12. Y. B. 2 Edw. 3 (*Liber Assisarum*), f. 3, pl. 7 (1328–29).

13. Y. B. 11 Ric. 2 (Ames Foundation), no. 28, p. 268 (1388), cited in the Introduction at p. l and in Plucknett, *Concise History*, at p. 412. I do not see the relevance of the other case cited in the Introduction, p. l.

14. The words of St. German, *Doctor and Student*, p. 297.

any and all ideas to the plaintiff. Color, then, was invented in the years around 1330, and so, with only light restraints, was the use of fictions in giving color. The devices were adopted from that time.

So it was the men of the law of that age who invented these things, and they who first adopted them. Their thinking was such, then, that they considered them good. Fourteenth-century reports will let us work our way into their point of view.

Consider first the basic rule that color must be given, that the defendant in novel disseisin who wanted to force the plaintiff to reveal to the court the details of his claim to the property must include in his own plea a description of the plaintiff's claim too. Judges and lawyers of the fourteenth century held to the fore of their minds a rule that whenever one litigant made against another a statement that had to be answered, then the other, whatever else he might also say, must answer it directly, yes or no. He must either traverse, which was to say no—"No, I am not guilty of beating you"; "No, I do not owe you the money"—or confess, which was to say, "Yes, I admit it." If he confessed he might go on to offer further facts which would show that, even so, there was no good case against him, making his plea a confession-and-avoidance—"Yes, I beat you, but in self-defense"; "Yes, you lent me money, but I have repaid you." Or he might go on to demur—"Yes, I struck the dust from your cap, but this is not an offense."[15]

Now in an assize of novel disseisin the plaintiff's basic assertion was that the defendant disseised him of his free tenement. If the defendant answered no, if he denied disseising the plaintiff of his free tenement, or if he said anything that fairly implied a denial, then the case would go straight to the jury. So it would be if he answered flatly, "I did not wrong or disseise you." So it would be, equally well, if he replied, "I inherited the land," or "John enfeoffed me of it," or "You the plaintiff enfeoffed me of it yourself," for these replies and others of this kind implied a denial of disseisin.[16] In the assize of novel disseisin the jurors were there from the outset, instructed and prepared beforehand to pronounce a verdict whether the defendant disseised the plaintiff of his free tenement. If that *was* the question between the parties, then it should be put to the jurors without more delay to them or to the plaintiff. No doubt the defendant had material to protest and adduce, but that went without

15. Maitland cites from Bracton the hypothetical case of an appeal of felony in the terms, "wickedly and in felony you struck the dust from my cap." Sir Frederick Pollock and Frederic W. Maitland, *The History of English Law before the Time of Edward I*, 2d ed., reissued with a new introduction and select bibliography by S. F. C. Milsom, 2 vols. (Cambridge, 1968), 2:467.

16. In the later technical terminology the rule would be that in novel disseisin the plaintiff need not reply to the inducement of a special traverse. Novel disseisin may have been peculiar in this respect in the fourteenth century. It was certainly peculiar in that the defendant could make what amounted to a special traverse without stating as his conclusion an explicit denial of the plaintiff's charge of disseisin; it was enough for him to imply a denial. For example, he need not say, *Vous me enfeffastes, saunz ceo qe ieo vous disseisi*, but could plead, *Vous me enfeffastes*, and leave it at that.

saying for every defendant. He could lay it before the jury—perhaps already had done so—to help them reach their verdict.

In an assize of novel disseisin, then, if the defendant wanted to force the plaintiff to explain to the court, before the case went to the jury, the details of his claim, it would not do for him to deny the charge of disseisin even if he accompanied the denial with a statement of his own claim. If he wanted to force the plaintiff to explain himself to the court he would have therefore to confess the charge of disseisin. Then he could state further facts about his own right to the property that would turn the plea into a confession-and-avoidance. The jurors had not been prepared beforehand to speak to that. The court would as well look into it itself, requiring the plaintiff to reply and letting a discussion develop.

In all fourteenth-century pleading, however, it was a corollary of the basic rule that one must say either yes or no that, if one was going to say yes, if one was going to admit it, then this confession must be perfectly genuine, a real confession in fact of the whole gist of what the opponent charged. One could strip away the plaintiff's pejorative adjectives, where he said that what one did was wrongful, wicked, in breach of the peace, and so forth, but that was all. In particular, if you charge me with beating your servant and I am to confess, I must confess that I beat the man and that he was your servant. If you charge me with taking your horse and I am to confess, I must admit that I took the animal and that it was yours. If I admitted beating someone else's servant or taking someone else's horse it would be no genuine confession at all.

In novel disseisin the plaintiff charged the defendant with disseising him of his free tenement. If the defendant was to confess, then, he must confess that he disseised the plaintiff of the property, and that it was the plaintiff's free tenement. But of course he dared not admit that it was the plaintiff's free tenement and simply his free tenement, for that would leave no room for the "avoidance" that must follow, the defendant's explanation that justice was really on his side. The defendant must somehow acknowledge that it was the plaintiff's free tenement but that it was his in a defective sense, in a sense that was open to "defeat," open to cancellation by the defendant's action. Fortunately, the common law had always been able to feel the distinction between existence and quality, and had no scruples about recognizing that a thing might be even though it was not all that it ought to be. It could be that the plaintiff had a free tenement truly enough, but that it was wrongful, that it was legally unsound. This was what the defendant had to say. But the law always required concreteness in pleading: another fundamental rule, and a sound one. It was no good for the defendant to say that the plaintiff had a "wrongful" or "defective" or "defeasible" free tenement. He must detail facts to show the man's claim and what was wrong with it. So he might say that the plaintiff was the lord, who took the land after his tenant's death by way of escheat—but there was an heir. Or, the plaintiff's brother had owned the land and the plaintiff took it claiming as sister and heir—but the brother had been outlawed and so could have no heir. But to plead in this fashion was to give color to the plaintiff. So color had to be given.

But if part of the explanation why color had to be given was, therefore, that the court required concreteness, that the court required facts, it is on that account only the more extraordinary that the court cared not at all, even in the beginning of this business around 1330, whether there was truth in the facts, but allowed the defendant to compound them of fictions if he liked. The explanation of the license thus given seems to be in two parts. To begin with, by the early fourteenth century the courts were already used to hearing occasional fictitious statements in other connections. They had been habituated to it through the following circumstances. In general, the law required a litigant who was stating a charge or claim to state it with considerable specificity. In an action for land in 1331, for example, the defendant failed to appear and the case would have gone by default, but a third party came forward and asked to be allowed to defend the suit. The defendant was only a life tenant, he said, and he himself had the right of reversion. The plaintiff challenged him, "Describe how the right of reversion came to belong to you," and he had to tell the story in detail.[17] In 1330 an appeal of felony was thrown out of court because it was simply for " 'robbery and breach of the king's peace,' without saying what robbery."[18] If indictments of felony were sometimes allowed to charge a man as "a common thief" without more, it was noted in 1313 that in such cases the trial justice should tell the jury not to convict the accused unless of some definite act.[19] Whether the case was civil or criminal, the underlying thought seems to have been that only precise statements could be either true or false. In 1330 a claimant of franchises in Wellingborough said that he and his ancestors and all previous holders of the manor had had the franchises from time out of mind. The justice instructed him, "Say who were the other holders of the manor"; and the claimant replied, "I cannot be expected to know their names." The justice retorted, "Since you are basing your title . . . on their exercise of the franchises, you must know who they were. . . . If you name certain persons, . . . the king's attorney can take issue with you, . . . *but he cannot deny what you do not plead.*"[20]

In another case in the same court in 1330, a party asserted that com-

17. Y. B. Mich. 5 Edw. 3, f. 61, pl. 101 (1331).

18. La, fol. 37r: "un home suist vn appelle 'de roberie et de pace domini regis fracta,' saunz dire quele roberie. La cause feust adiugge nule."

19. *The Eyre of Kent 6 and 7 Edward II*, eds. Frederic W. Maitland, Leveson William Vernon Harcourt, and William Craddock Bolland, Selden Society, vol. 24 (London, 1909), p. 141: "ne les soilent pas sil ne soit pas certain fait." Developments of these rules later in the fourteenth century are shown by John Bellamy, *Crime and Public Order in England in the Later Middle Ages* (London, 1973), p. 134.

20. John Rylands Library Latin MS 180, fol. 9v: "Scrop . . . Ditez queux furunt les tenantz des maners. Bacoun. Ieo ne puisse conustre lour nons. Scrop. Quant vous affermetz title de droit par lour vsages vous le deuetz conustre." La, fols. 42v–43r: "si vous nomez certein persone . . . le seriaunt le roi purra prendre issue sur le negatif . . . mes [il] ne put pas prendre trauers sur ceo qe nest pas plede."

mon of pasture had been appendant to a certain property from time out of mind and until one Ralph of Hannington acquired the property. The opponent objected, "You are not stating who were [those earlier] holders of the property . . . *so that we might take issue with you*."[21] What is not concrete and specific cannot be quarreled with, cannot be denied, cannot be called false. Neither, presumably, could it be called true. Perhaps we need not wonder where William of Ockham acquired some of his habits of thought.

But when an opponent came to reply to charges and claims that were stated in concrete detail, the courts were usually clear that they must not allow him to rebut them by picking at their detail alone. To do so would defeat substantial justice over and over. Nominalism has its limitations, after all. What if the homicide was not committed on the day stated in the indictment? The charge was still a charge of a specific homicide and if the accused was to be judged not guilty it must be because, truly and fairly, he did not do it. In the early sixteenth century, Christopher St. German said that when a bill for theft was presented to an indicting jury they "be onelye charged with the effect of the bill, that is to say, whether he be guilty of the felony or not, and not whether he be guilty in such manner and form as the bill specifieth. . . ."[22] Back in the fourteenth century, in a civil case of 1355, a plaintiff sued Alice Halliday for some chattels, saying that he had bailed them to G. Halliday and that after G. died they came into Alice's keeping. The judge told the plaintiff that "it would be better for you if you describe" how the goods passed into Alice's keeping, and the plaintiff did so, saying that she got them as G.'s executrix. But in the discussion that followed, the court wholly refused to let Alice rebut the claim on any ground that grew solely out of her supposed status as executrix.[23]

The law knew, then, these two rules, that allegations must be specific, but that they could not ordinarily be rebutted merely by attacking their details. The implication did not escape barristers that under these circumstances the details that were alleged need not all be accurate, need not all be true. We know that from the early fourteenth century a count in trespass could allege that the defendant had opened a barrel of wine that he had in his keeping "with swords, bows, and arrows."[24] In 1330 a reporter tells us expressly that fictions can as well be used, and in some cases had better be used, to fill in between what has to be specified to round out a statement and what can be denied to rebut it. A plaintiff brought an action of *Quare impedit* for the advowson of a church. The advowson had been in his family for some time, he told. His father had presented Stephen Brown as parson. Now Stephen Brown had died, the

21. La, fol. 10r–v: "ne moustrez point quex [terre tenantz] auant cel temps auoient commune, a quei nous purrioms prendre issue . . ."

22. *Doctor and Student*, pp. 298–99.

23. Y. B. Trin. 29 Edw. 3, f. 38, the second unnumbered plea (1355).

24. Cited in S. F. C. Milsom, "Trespass from Henry III to Edward III," *Law Quarterly Review* 74 (1958): 561–90, at 567, from a case of 1317.

church was thereby left vacant, it belonged to the plaintiff to present a new parson, but the defendant was wrongfully obstructing him. The defendant answered that the plaintiff had no right to present a parson, at any rate not now, because the church was not vacant, as the plaintiff said, but "full"—it had a parson in office. With its characteristic taste for specifics the court made the defendant tell who was the parson in office and who had presented him as parson. So the defendant specified: the parson was that same Stephen Brown of whom the plaintiff had spoken, and he had been presented by the plaintiff's father just as the plaintiff said, only he was not dead but alive. The revelation of these specifics from his mouth told heavily against the defendant, in ways that we need not trouble to follow, but no wonder, for they amounted to an admission of a large share of the facts on which the plaintiff's case was founded. And, sorrowed the reporter, it was all so unnecessary, simply a technical error on the defendant's part. He wanted to allege that the church had a parson in office. To do this he had to name the parson and his patron. But "he could safely have alleged some total stranger as parson, and have said that he had the office at the presentment of someone else who never in fact had any interest in the advowson, for issue cannot be taken on this material."[25] One could fill in with fictions.

Such a dodge did not strike fourteenth-century lawyers as immoral, because the barrister's professional attitude toward the law was, and was expected to be, purely positive. A prohibition consisted in the penalty that fell upon those who violated it. If an order issues to outlaw you, you must appear at the fourth county court, for otherwise you will be outlawed; never mind the three previous court meetings where they summon you to come forth, for no penalty is laid on those days. If you default in a civil case and the grand distress is awarded against you, the sheriff must let you know the sum of "issues" with which you will be charged upon his report if you do not appear at the next day in court, so that you can decide whether you prefer to appear or to forfeit that sum. The court itself will not allow the sheriff to raise the figure after he has fixed it and informed you, for that would be to deprive you of your basis for decision.[26] So then with the pleading of fictions. As long as one was careful to use them in matter upon which the opponent could not take issue and win, there was no danger, no disadvantage, no penalty; so they were not wrong.

As for the sense of making oneself ridiculous that sticks to the use of fictions in the modern mind, it afflicts us because we understand that the law is a series of man-made arrangements continually subject to rearrangement. That such arrangements should be more elaborate than necessary is simply inefficient, and blatant examples of inefficiency smack of stupidity. But fourteenth-century lawyers did not think of the law as a human artifact, or at any rate not as one for which any one generation of

25. La, fol. 16r: "il put saluement allegger plenerte destrange persone et par presentement destrange qe vnqes nauoit riens, qar ceo nest pas traversable."

26. La, fol. 20v.

men should take comprehensive responsibility. In most respects the law was "given": given by God perhaps, given perhaps by the nation's own past. This humble view of their role saved the fourteenth-century lawyers from feeling humiliated when they sought ways within the law to change the effects of the law, however tortuous some of the ways might be. It was up to the good and honest lawyer not to design or redesign the law but to find all the ways that might be found within the law for doing justice.

Fictions could be used, then, with honesty and honor, as the fourteenth-century judges and barristers saw their work. But this is only the beginning of an explanation of why they could be used specifically in giving color. Wherever and however they were used, fictions must be alleged only in matter that was not traversable. If they were used anywhere else, where the opponent could take issue, no doubt he would in fact take issue, and would win when it appeared that the fictitious matter was false. When a fourteenth-century lawyer gave color to his opponent in an assize of novel disseisin, by saying that the opponent was in seisin of the property through events that never really occurred and on the basis of some claim that he never really made at all, why was this not traversable? The decisive reason seems to have lain in a doctrine that the courts held about the pleading of what we may call adjectival matters. If a party pleaded that John had a right, or did a deed, or whatever, and in such-and-such a way, and under such-and-such circumstances, the other party could of course flatly deny the whole statement. But if the other party wished not flatly to deny it but rather to dispute the description of it, conceding that John had the right, or did the deed, but not in that way, not under those circumstances, then in taking issue with the description alone it seems that he was required to accompany his denial with an alternative description of his own. So if a man brings a real action against me, all by myself, he is saying in effect that I am the tenant and the sole tenant of the property that he is suing for. In defense I may utterly deny that I hold any of the property. But if I wish to object that I hold it, but only in part, or that I hold it, but only jointly with someone else, then I must tell what parts I have and who has the rest, or I must name my joint tenant. So again, in 1329 a woman brought suit for some land which, she said, "was her right and free-marriage," claiming thus that she had once been seised of the land in the estate of free-marriage. The defendant pleaded that she had been seised truly enough, but not in free-marriage. The justice told the defendant that, because he had acknowledged that the woman was seised, "the court will assume that her seisin was such as she says unless you describe it as being in some other estate."[27] In the same year a defendant tried to rebut an action for recovery of entailed lands that had been alienated by saying that when the entailed lands were

27. Lincoln's Inn Hale MS 72, fol. 13r: "vous lauez conu vne seisine, quele seisine la court entent tiele com ele a counte si vous ne moustrez coment ele fust dautre estat seisi."

alienated, other lands were received in exchange for them, and that the plaintiff still held these. The plaintiff replied, "I do not hold those other lands in exchange." "How do you hold them, then?" asked the judge, and the plaintiff had to tell.[28]

In giving his opponent color in an assize of novel disseisin, the defendant said that the opponent had been seised of the property on such-and-such a basis, which was defective. The opponent could never flatly deny this, for unless he was seised he could not have been disseised, and if he was not disseised then his whole basis for bringing an assize of novel disseisin was flown from him. He had to agree that he was seised, but not in the way the defendant said. In what way, then? He must tell, because it was adjectival matter that he was disputing. He must state his own claim in detail. But of course the defendant could reply to what he said, and as having the right to reply, the defendant had the power to make the plaintiff's statement the whole basis of the rest of the discussion. What the defendant had alleged earlier need not be spoken of any more.[29] It might as well be fiction.

These were the habits of thought that made giving color a fresh and happy discovery to the judges and barristers of the 1320s and 1330s. They viewed the law and their duty to it in purely practical terms. What you must not do was what was prohibited, and a prohibition consisted in the penalty that fell on violators. If there was no penalty there was no prohibition, and if there was no prohibition there was no duty to avoid. And the law they used was, as they felt it, given them out of the past, so that they bore no general responsibility to reshape it but were doing their best as good and true men when they found ways within it to make justice prevail. Given these two features of their thought, in which they cast off from us moderns, the use of color and the employment of fictions in giving color followed for the rest from the lawyers' conscious loyalty to several rules of pleading that we of the twentieth century can admire as well as they: lean, hard rules, well designed to expedite business, exclude cant, and induce precision. Every reply to an opponent's statement must comprise a plain yes or no, a confession or a traverse. In novel disseisin, with a jury already in court prepared to pronounce on the charge of disseisin, if the defendant traverses and says that he did no disseisin, the case will go straight to the jury. A confession, if one is to be made, must be full and genuine, not at all specious and hypocritical. Adverbs and adjectives may be cast about aplenty in pleading, but they accomplish nothing substantial; any characterization of an act or state that is to be of substance must be made with nouns and verbs, must tell of beings and events, for only so can it be precise. Charges and claims made in court

28. La, fol. 19v: "il . . . dit . . . qil ne tient pas ceux tenementz en eschange, prest etc. Scrope. Comment le[s] tenetz vous donqes?" The principle is illustrated further in the case next following in La, fol. 19v, and in Y. B. Pasch. 1 Edw. 3, f. 13, pl. 49 (1327).

29. Y. B. 15 Edw. 3 (Rolls Series), no. 11, p. 27 (1341): "Il ne couient pas, quant [le pleintif] fait title, mes a destruir son title."

must be stated in concrete detail to attest their reality, but replies to them must be to their gist and not to their details alone. If in replying to an opponent's statement one wishes to leave alone the main facts that he alleged and challenge only his characterization of them, one must accompany the challenge with one's own alternative description. These principles, used together, yielded the pleading of color and the use of fictions therein. Such devices were therefore to be applauded. In these very consequences the principles stood, strong and true as they were.

8 Plucknett's "Lancastrian Constitution"

Charles M. Gray

Few phenomena oppress me with a greater sense of historic distance than Bishop Stubbs; few oppress me less with that sense than the Year Books. (Puzzlement at Stubbs's large ways of taking hold of the movement and meaning of history detracts nothing from his concrete contributions to knowledge.) Reading the Year Books seems to carry one into a perspicuous past. That presupposes some knowledge and an acceptance of the rules and values of late medieval lawyers, for it is necessary to suspend disbelief in the fine art of pleading and the subtleties of real property. One must also acknowledge that the Year Books are succinct documents for professional use, which require interpretation. But once these adjustments are made, the Year Books convey a remarkable sense of being present at discussions that, given their givens, can be followed and can be accepted as more or less the inevitable approach to the matter at hand. What the issue is, what the lawyers are trying to accomplish by their arguments—weaker and stronger ones, in the nature of legal arguments—can usually be perceived (and so, more frequently than is sometimes reputed, can the drift of the judges' opinions).

In 1924, Professor Plucknett wrote an influential article intended to exorcize the Stubbsian vision and present the authentic fifteenth century through the medium of the Year Books.[1] The contention of the present essay is that Plucknett misread his cases and attributed the wrong anachronism to the tradition descending from Stubbs. That tradition furnished Plucknett with a picture of the "Lancastrian Constitution" as an anticipation of the modern one. Four Year Book cases furnished him with evidence that the categories through which fifteenth-century lawyers approached their problems were foreign to those of later ages and the very conception of a "constitution" beyond their conceptual range. At a suffi-

1. T. F. T. Plucknett, "The Lancastrian Constitution," in *Tudor Studies Presented . . . to Albert Frederick Pollard*, ed. R. W. Seton-Watson (London, 1924), pp. 161–81. Stubbs is not mentioned by name in Plucknett's article, but he may safely be considered the father of the view of the Lancastrian constitution that Plucknett offsets. See William Stubbs, *The Constitutional History of England in its Origin and Development*, 3 vols. (Oxford, 1874–78), esp. vol. 2, chap. 17. Cf. S. B. Chrimes, *English Constitutional Ideas in the Fifteenth Century* (Cambridge, 1936), Introduction. It should be said at the start that Plucknett's article is modest in tone, written rather to evoke interest in the cases than to invite polemics by taking a polemical stance. "For the sake of argument," as Newton, C. J., has it in the first case discussed below, I shall no doubt be more polemical than Plucknett's article deserves. There is nevertheless, I think, a real difference of opinion on how the cases should be read, a difference that my perhaps closer and surely more argumentative reading will not dispel.

cient pitch of generality, I have no quarrel with that point. Under the acknowledged inspiration of Plucknett's article, Professor Chrimes wrote a useful book on the constitutional thought of the fifteenth century, with due regard for its fragmentary sources, its loose ends, and its distance from the vocabulary and substance of later thought.[2] The trouble with Plucknett's heuristic contribution is that it develops a mistaken antithesis by way of making a case against Stubbs's "Lancastrian Constitution." That, I believe, is a result of seeing the wrong things in the Year Books and of underestimating their perspicuity.

Plucknett's argument is that fifteenth-century lawyers talked about public questions in the vocabulary of private law, that they could not (with some forward-looking exceptions) see what would later be thought of as the real issues—the scope of the king's prerogative, the powers of Parliament, the resolution of conflict between those two. They could discuss such questions (talk about them almost in the sense of "talk around") only on a level appropriate to disputes between private parties. I think that thesis is misleading, the antithesis of public and private false. The fifteenth-century lawyers did not misperceive or oddly perceive the issues, in no way missed the point that they were about public policy and the competences of public authorities. Legal ideas that we may not expect to see in constitutional discussion were present, but that is because the issues were as they were, and because the lawyers' strategic needs drove them to use what ammunition they had. Plucknett attended too much to the surface language of the Year Books and too little to why it was employed—to the litigative drama in the reports, to the setting and policy thrust of the cases, to the difference between a good argument and a desperate one. Paradoxically, as his purpose was to restore the fifteenth century to itself, Plucknett saw the Year Books as strange and distant because they look that way. Is it not an error of historicism to overplay conceptual distance and underplay mere differences in what there is to think about?

Part of my contention is that the cases discussed by Plucknett, although mutually clarifying in certain ways, are fundamentally different in their issues, and that the difference is ignored in Plucknett's treatment. The earliest case, *Rector of Edington*, is not about what the other three are about.[3] (The latter three are so similar that I shall conflate them for the sake of economy after treating *Rector of Edington* by itself.) The critical distinction is that *Rector of Edington* asks in part whether there is any way to make out that *Parliament*, by voting a tax in general terms, has abrogated a tax exemption granted to an individual by royal patent, whereas the other cases go to the effect an act of *Convocation* can have on patent-based privileges held by clergymen. (I shall argue the importance of the difference in due course.) All the cases share an issue about the validity of the royal grants in question and, behind that, about the general criteria of validity.

2. Chrimes, *English Constitutional Ideas*, p. xv.
3. For citation of the cases and a skeletal account of them, see below, Appendix.

I shall discuss the problems in the cases synthetically and directly. That is, instead of debating with Plucknett along the way, I shall for the most part just present the cases as I think they should be seen; instead of following the contours of the Year Books, I shall state the substance as I interpret it, pointing in the notes to particular passages on which I rely for the interpretation. Rather than pretend to verisimilitude in language, I shall unabashedly dress the Romans in doublets and codpieces—the Year Book lawyers in ordinary modern discourse. That this technique exposes the meaning, rather than distorts it, is my claim, but whether it does is a question about method in legal history I should like to suggest in the process.

The situation in *Rector of Edington* was that the king was trying to break his own grant to the rector. The dominating reality is that he had a bad case on the main contested fronts—(1) whether the grant was valid, (2) whether, if the grant was valid, the grantee's privilege would survive Parliament's voting a tax without expressly saving the privilege. Let us start with the constitutional givens: the king had granted the rector a general tax exemption. His power to confer *that* privilege could be and was questioned. His power to confer *privileges* could not be. It was a fact of the constitution that exempting particular people and institutions from the normal run of public burdens was not a monopoly of the legislature. Observing proper form, the king could do it on his own—sometimes; when was up to the courts. Control over the king's power to grant (one can only say) rested with the judicial branch. The courts' control was not limited to enforcing due form, but extended to the substance of what was granted. They had no standard spelled out in a constitutional document purporting to describe the difference between valid and invalid royal grants. (How much such nominal guidance matters for the business of unsnarling complexly mixed systems of government is surely open to doubt.) By practice and the accumulation of cases, however, the courts had the use of ample lore on the scope of the king's granting power. Formulation of standards was not, and is not, easy. A cynical formulation, if cynicism it be, is perhaps the best one can do—"The king may make grants so long as they are not in the judges' opinion seriously harmful to the public interest." But one expects courts, save where realism flaunts its nakedness, to shade those areas where there is little else to do than fall back on common sense and intuition (and cling to the decided case when there is one, without much reasoning why). One expects—lawyers expect of themselves—a struggle to make law at the constitutional margins sound like law in its safer purlieus, to find principles in the cases, to shape distinctions whose appeal is rather to reason than to a vague feel for tolerable policy. The struggle was going on in *Rector of Edington*.

Although an extensive granting power in the king was beyond attack, his power to grant general tax exemptions was not beyond a sporting shot. The king's lawyers tried to invalidate the grant to the rector. Three things should be observed about that attempt: (1) It was against the odds. (2) It proceeded from a cavalier willingness to throw away royal power for the sake of royal revenue. One can commend that readiness in the spirit of Fortescue (who was addicted to the argument that limitations on the king conduce to his true power, as unfallen angels are not diminished by their impotence to do evil and the body is no less strong because it is incapable of disease; "true power" is legitimately assimilable to "sufficient income").[4] One can also take it as graceless for the king to try to deprive the rector of what he had given him by disputing his own power to give. In private life, people are sometimes estopped from that sort of thing.[5] (3) The proposition that the king may not confer general tax exemptions is appealing in itself. Modern sensibility should have no trouble with that. Having rid ourselves of kings, we have failed to rid tax law of inequity and political influence. Fifteenth-century judges looked out on a scene pocked with privilege, with special cases of diverse origin tending to the inevitable upshot—Jones pays more in order that Smith, for some more or less plausible reason, may go free, and the needs of government are the harder to meet when persuading or coercing Jones to do more is the cost of sparing Smith. To liberate at least parliamentary taxation from the snarls of privilege would be an understandable aspiration, even for the fifteenth century—if only a way could be found.[6]

The second and third points at least cut in favor of taking seriously anything that could be said legalistically pro and con the king's power to exempt from taxes. What can be said con is strained, whereas the pro side is easy. The strongest consideration in favor of the patent's validity is too obvious to reach the surface of the report: it is simply hard to dif-

4. See, for example, Sir John Fortescue, *De Laudibus Legum Angliae*, ed. S. B. Chrimes (Cambridge, 1942), chap. 14.

5. (Particular points are cited by the name of the speaker. The form, e.g., Fortescue-2, means Fortescue's second speech in the case. See Appendix for the names and alignments of the lawyers and judges.) Markham-1 argues that the king *was* estopped to claim the tax from the rector. Markham's context was created by the (fundamentally unsuccessful) argument that the rector was estopped to claim his privilege contrary to an act of Parliament in which he was complicit. Therefore, Markham's point is in the form of a theory that one estoppel cancels out another. The idea that the king was estopped should not be taken too seriously. It occurs only by way of parrying an argument that did not get very far, and the rector had too much going for him to require development of the notion. Taken seriously and in isolation, it is nonsense: if the king were estopped to dispute his *ultra vires* grants, the whole law of a limited granting prerogative controlled by the courts would be undermined. That he can be estopped in some special circumstances, including when he is claiming an estoppel against his grantee, is perhaps possible. It remains *graceless* for the king to try to evade his grants in the absence of a strong public interest.

6. It is worth noting that "leakage" through the king's prerogative to grant property and privileges is the heart of Fortescue's diagnosis of the practical problems of government in the later fifteenth century (Sir John Fortescue, *Governance of England*, ed. Charles Plummer [Oxford, 1885], passim). Fortescue's proposals for a significant conciliar check on the monarch—radical proposals meant to be in the royal interest—are directed more at patronage than at policy making in the areas left to the king's prerogative. Patronage and privilege are taken for granted as a feature of government; the flow is not to be cut off, but controlled—by requiring "committee approval" and keeping the committee from representing the noble factions hungriest for largesse.

ferentiate an *individual* tax exemption from the category of privileges that the king was least disputably entitled to confer. The rector had in effect been given a small piece of royal revenue; the king had diverted from himself an item of income that by itself could not exceed a tiny fraction of his expectable income. That was surely much of what the granting prerogative was for—to enable the king to meet his debts and reward the deserving by diverting revenue or canceling claims, so that he was not forced to defray his moral and quasi-legal obligations by cash payments or conveyances of property in hand. At the same time, there was no disposition among the speakers in the case to deny that the king's power to exempt from taxes must stop somewhere. Although this point is not articulated, it would probably have been agreed that a class, or at least large-class, tax exemption (to all men of a given locality or of a certain social rank) would be invalid on its face. It was a clearer point of agreement that an individual exemption would be unclaimable if the king were to grant exemptions to so many individuals as to constitute a major drain on the return from parliamentary taxes.[7]

The last consideration exposes a difficulty in the rector's otherwise convincing case. Suppose the truth is that exemptions have been given to 50 percent of the eligible taxpayers. How is this truth to be shown, so that the Exchequer may disallow the claim of a single one of the 50 percent? Newton, C.J.C.P., called attention to this problem.[8] His solution is ambiguous between two possibilities: (1) There is no satisfactory way to establish the fact of excess, and this is of course compounded by the difficulty of laying down a legal standard for what is excessive. Because tax exemptions admit of proliferation to excess and there is no adequate judicial way to find that they have so proliferated, the best solution is to hold that individual exemptions are simply invalid. (2) Because there is no adequate *judicial* way, the best solution is to leave the judgment to Parliament—that is, to hold that when Parliament has voted a tax without expressly saving exemptions, it has made a determination that privileges should not be claimed for purposes of the present tax. Newton thought, on grounds independent of the problem of judging excess, that taxes voted in general terms had a good claim to override exemptions; the problem of judging excess presumably reinforced his inclination so to

7. Most group exemptions from jury duty, as opposed to individual ones, would appear to be invalid. Cf. Convocation cases, below. This analogue is not brought up in Rector of Edington, but it seems relevant. Newton-1 and Hody-1 do not make it completely clear whether they are talking about group exemptions or an excess of individual ones—more likely the latter. How flat a distinction between individual exemptions and *any* group exemption can be attributed to the fifteenth-century judges is open to question. The jury duty parallel supports the proposition that individual exemptions cannot be claimed when there are too many; it is easier to say how many is too many in the jury case than in the tax case. (There must be enough jurors to permit cases to be tried.)

8. Newton-1. I admittedly speculate on Newton's full meaning. He is *clearly* apprehensive lest upholding one tax exemption imply that the king may exempt indefinite numbers, *and* he is sympathetic to the view that a tax without a saving for exemptions destroys them. It is my suggestion that the problem of judging excess is what justifies the apprehension.

believe. On the other hand, Hody, C.J.K.B., conceded that an individual patent would be of no force if too many such patents were granted, while holding that the rector's patent was perfectly valid.[9] Hody was expressly opposed to giving any exemption-destroying force to general taxation acts, and hence opposed to Newton's possible theory that Parliament is the only eligible judge of excess. He must have thought that the fact of a large number of exemptions could be brought before the Exchequer, or cognized by it, in an individual case, and that disallowing a patent on grounds of excess would be an appropriate exercise of judicial discretion. There is no sign of disagreement with Hody on this point except for Newton's; Hody's general view of the case lay in the majority direction, whereas Newton went out of his way to argue the king's side, though without committing himself to it.

Against the presumptive case in favor of the rector's patent, three arguments were urged. All involve claiming that parliamentary taxation is a special case, that exempting from it is not the same as forgoing or diverting other royal revenues. All are uphill arguments. The first[10] struck Plucknett as particularly private and inadequate to the constitutional issues, but it seems to me only to involve legal concepts of such generality that they necessarily overlap the public and private spheres. The basic idea is that a "grant" of something that does not exist and may never exist is an odd notion. The paradigm for this was the alleged nullity of a private grant in the form "I grant that if in the future you shall make me an obligation, said obligation shall be void." (In the terms of modern contract law, the closest analogue would be a contract on valuable consideration whereby A promises B that if A and B shall make any contracts in the future, A will not sue B for breach thereof.) If the king's counsel could win acceptance for the paradigm, their further task was to show that a parliamentary tax is like an obligation or contract that has never been made and may never be. The general proposition to be established was that the king is as helpless as anyone else to do what is in a sense *logically* unsustainable—namely, to give away what one not only does not have, but has no expectation of, save as a purely voluntary act or transaction in the future may entitle one to it. That proposition does not seem to me expressive of a private-law mentality; it is on a level with such propositions as "A sovereign legislature can no doubt do many things which private persons would not be allowed to on policy grounds, but even a sovereign legislature cannot do what is logically contradictory, and the courts have no business straining to make out an intention behind language that makes no sense."[11] However, the proposition was not easy to establish.

9. Hody-1.

10. Argument broached by Fortescue-1, developed by Vampage-1, accepted and developed by Ayscoghe.

11. This sort of statement about the legislature is arguably what is meant by saying that a statute may be void for repugnance. (See Samuel E. Thorne, "The Constitution and the Courts: A Re-examination of the Famous Case of Dr. Bonham," *Law Quarterly Review* 54 [1938]: 543–52; and Charles M. Gray, "Bonham's Case Reviewed," *Proceedings of the*

I discuss below the important counterargument that parliamentary taxes do not have the voluntary character of uncontracted obligations *et similia*. But even if that point is waived, the *king's* incapacity to convey "nonexistent" futurities is not clearly entailed by what has to be conceded as to the private incapacity. The paradigm case of the obligation was not contested. It was, however, stated from the bench and not denied that a private grant is valid if it takes the form "A grants to B that if in the future B and C (or B and unspecified other coobligors) make a joint obligation to A, said obligation shall be void as to B."[12] If that case is conceded, the generality that future things dependent on contingent acts of will are ungrantable is damaged, for B's sole obligation and the joint obligation of B and C are equally such futurities. It remains a question whether the king's grant of a tax exemption is more like a private grant purporting to void in advance B's sole obligation or one purporting to void B's and C's joint obligation *quoad* B, if it is like either. But shaking the generality about voluntary-contingent futurities opens the way to argue that the royal granting prerogative extends to such interest. No overwhelming proof to that effect was offered, but fairly good arguments were made.

It was obvious, and came out early in the debate, that there is no bar to the king's granting *futurities*—that is, things he does not have now and may never have, save as something happens that need not in the inevitable

---

American Philosophical Society 116 [1972]: 35–58.) I think the last phrase, "no business straining . . . ," is crucial to the point. It is all too easy to say that statutes spoken of as "repugnant" do not *really* contain self-contradictory language. Similarly, statements of the form "I give you what I do not have" are not really nonsense. On the other hand, the old legal idea of repugnance expresses a nice sensibility about language. As it were, the line between "unintelligible" and "eccentric" is thinner than one might assume. "Meaning" refers both to linguistic forms in the abstract and to human purposes. An expression that in the abstract *could* be followed/obeyed/given legal force verges on meaninglessness if the only intention it can be supposed to express is one no sane person can be imagined having—such as giving up something one has no reason to expect ever having. Is a sensible hearer—say, a court—supposed to think of the unintelligibility of the human act or the unintelligibility of the language? As a judicial policy, it makes sense to take some expressions as what I have called ("Bonham's Case Reviewed") "constructively repugnant," for at stake is saving people from incoherent purposes for which they have found passable words.

12. Fray-3. I change the order to bring out a logical connection that is worth noting, though not indispensable. Fray says that a joint obligation is releasable as to particular obligors in advance of its existence (clearly believing that a parliamentary tax is more like a joint obligation than a single one) *after* the arguments noted below have been made, in order to show that the king may sometimes grant what he does not "have." My point in mentioning Fray's assertion first is that other arguments are the more persuasive in the light of the proposition that not *even* all "nonexistent" obligations are ungrantable. One speech—Fortescue-3, the most cryptic one in the report—can be taken as throwing away the otherwise uncontested point that a "nonexistent" single obligation is ungrantable. Fortescue there is strongly opposed to the position later taken by Fray that a parliamentary tax resembles a joint obligation. He may at that stage of the argument want to say, "Let us forget all about obligations and concentrate on the 'estopping' power of general acts of Parliament."

course of nature.[13] It would have been convenient for the king's side to be able to maintain that all grantable futurities fall in the class of accruals from something the king already has: that is, he has a signory and therefore may grant away the relief that will accrue when the present tenant dies and his heir succeeds him, if the tenant dies seised and has an ascertainable heir; he has a court and may therefore grant away fines assessed for future offenses within the court's jurisdiction.[14] A couple of judges were impressed, however, by the untenability of the "accruals from" formula. Two types of example were urged, of which the following is the stronger: the king may grant A the right to hold a fair on A's land and take toll from it.[15] The king does not *have something* beforehand; *he* does not have a right to hold a fair on A's land and take toll in the event that anyone wants to trade there. It therefore appears that the granting prerogative can serve to *confer* rights and privileges, *ex nihilo* as it were, because the king is king—not only to *transfer* the future benefit of things already held. Why should he not be able to confer immunity from taxation?

This debate, on both sides, is entirely public. It is about the unique powers of the king, unshaped by private analogies. There is, however, nothing clinching about the points on the rector's side. This was perceived by Newton, who, again "for the sake of argument," did most to uphold the king's case.[16] Newton thought it worth insisting that a parlia-

13. Yelverton, Markham-1, Paston-2 by implication, Hody-2.

14. Vampage-1 for the generalized point that all valid examples of grantable futurities fit the "accruals from" pattern. Several concrete examples that arguably do fit that type are given in the speeches; mine are schematic.

15. Hunt. The more complicated type of example is brought up by Paston-1, with two specific illustrations. What Paston is trying to show is that some unusual grantable futurities (as contrasted to the commonplace fair) are hard to analyze as accruals from what is "in" the king, in the straightforward way in which feudal property interests yielding fairly predictable incomes are "in" him, or courts and procedures from which the king takes regular profits. Some things that he may grant he "has" only in a very tenuous sense, analogous to a "mere possibility"—as opposed to a "future interest," even a contingent one—in property law. One can of course quarrel with Paston and say that remote or odd "possibilities" are still "in" the king, compared to the benefit of undreamt-of obligations and the like. Paston's cases: (a) "I grant you the goods of A if A shall commit suicide." This grant is allegedly good. (Suicides' goods go to the king, not through the church to relatives and charities. Arguably the king has no interest or reasonable expectation in A's goods. Subject to philosophical problems about the voluntariness of self-slaughter, his "possibility" depends on someone else's voluntary act.) (b) "I grant you a rent charge out of A's land if A should subject his land to a rent charge in favor of an ecclesiastical corporation." (Were A to create such a rent charge, he would violate the Statute of Mortmain. An ordinary conveyance of land in mortmain is not void, and so the rent charge here would not be void. Rather, the lord may enter on the alienee and hold the land; the king is entitled to enter only when mesne lords have passed up the opportunity. But the rent charge created by A would not be held of A's lord; because there is no one to take advantage of the right given by the statute, and in order that the policy of the statute may be fulfilled, the king is by construction held directly entitled to the rent charge. The point is only that something that might come to the king by such a special path is hardly "in" him. Yet, *per* Paston, it is grantable.)

16. Newton-2. The context of Newton's remarks is rejection of the court profit theory (see below), but I think the insistence that a tax is a gift deserves to be separated from the

mentary tax is a *gift*, and that the power to grant away or forgo a gift one has not yet received (even in binding promissory form) remains questionable even when concessions are made to the king's special power to grant what is not "in him" and qualifications are admitted on the proposition that obligations are not releasable in advance of their existence. The argument comes back to the private analogy, or the high-level generality: *one* thing it makes no sense to speak of as givable away, by the king or anyone else—a merely free gift that has not been given or promised, may never be, and need not be on any ground of duty. Yet to insist on the similarity of gifts and taxes hardly lacks constitutional significance. "The king shall live of his own and may sometimes, but should not count on it, enjoy his subjects' generosity and desire to help" can be a fateful maxim, as can its opposite.

If it is conceded that a future gift (or future obligation of appropriate type) is not grantable, the assimilability of parliamentary taxes to such models remains a question. Plucknett found the argument against such assimilation intellectually distant, but it seems to me the straightest way. This argument says that Parliament is a court and that taxes are quasi the profits of that court, wherefore they are grantable, because the profits accruing from courts *in futuro* (e.g., fines assessed by some court with jurisdiction to fine) are surely grantable.[17] I do not think this is quaint or strained, so much as a slightly disingenous way of making a serious point. (Of course it requires the premise that Parliament *was* a court at least nominally, but so it was, long since and long after, and the sense was far from nominal.)[18] The serious point is that although parliamentary taxes were in theory voluntary—and in a sense really so, needless to say—it was factually and morally misleading to conceive them as dependent on will, the way a future gift, contract, or obligation has no expectation of existence save as one or more people will it. As a matter of fact, reasonably recurring parliamentary taxes were a reality, not predictable as to timing or amount, but as predictable an item of income as many others. They were a necessity for the realm's minimum security and

mere statement that it is not a court profit. A gift is not an obligation either (though under the common law of sealed obligations it is hard to tell whether an unconditional obligation reciting no consideration is a promissory gift or has a contractual basis—i.e., amounts to a promise to pay at a future date in consideration of a benefit received). One can still in principle concede the validity of "I grant that if B and C shall make me an obligation, it will be void as to B," and contest the validity of "If B and C shall bind themselves in terms to make me a free gift, said bond shall be void as to B." One can conceivably concede that the king, at any rate, can give away strange things—remotely possible acquisitions, the right to take toll on A's land, even nonexistent contractual rights (perhaps with an obligee's rights on a bare bond interpreted as contract rights unless the contrary appears)—and still stick at a gift.

17. Court profit analogy developed by Fray-2, Hody-2 and 3; opposed by Newton-2.

18. Fray-2 goes to the trouble of making out that Parliament is indeed a court in the ordinary sense: it has *judicial* profits from attainders and forfeitures adjudged there. Though it need not in logic (as Newton observed in effect), the fact that Parliament was a court with judicial profits appears to make it easier for Fray to think of taxes as part of an undifferentiated flow of revenue to the king via just another court.

welfare. Given this fact, it was unbecoming to assert what was at best an abstract half-truth—that taxes are merely voluntary. Of course they are "voluntary" in that the king cannot compel Parliament to vote them; they can be withheld for a time, bargained for, and used to make points about the government's policy according as they are niggardly or generous. But it is absurd to say that Parliament has no duty whatsoever to tax, that it may refrain from doing so forever and ever, while the realm crumbles around it or the king is forced into puppetry. If the unimaginable extreme of a drastically undutiful Parliament were to come to pass, one would have no recourse except to hold that royal taxation without Parliament is legal, pending the emergency.[19] These things can be said directly. I think they are as good as said in *Rector of Edington*. They do not become sayable only via the queer conceit that taxes are court profits. It is a little slick so to designate them, a little *like* lawyers and pedagogues. ("You grant me, my dear sir, that Parliament is a court and courts have profits, and you can think of nothing that would count as the profits of that court so clearly as taxes? Ergo, you see, QED.") But there is a bit more in it than that. Taxes are what accrues from Parliament, not automatically, but insofar as that "court" does its duty—voluntarily of course, as duties are mostly done, save for the special class of legal duties, whose nonperformance is supposed to bring specifiable sanctions upon the just and the unjust alike. The same can be said, in a way, of the profits of more obvious courts. They depend, not only on natural happenings or such predictable ones as the continuation of criminality, but on office-holding human beings doing their duties, "voluntarily" in the sense that failure to do them does not typically generate straightforward legal liabilities. They depend on the jury's willingness to convict the defendant when it thinks him guilty, on the judge's observance of the law, on his willingness, for example, to impose discretionary fines with some rhyme and reason and respect for practice in comparable cases.[20]

Though a major argument, the assimilation of taxes to court profits was not made to carry the whole weight of overcoming the king's argument from their giftlike quality. It was also contended that taxes are not reducible to gifts from the people to the king in that taxes require the

19. I think this proposition is implicit in the "duty to tax" theory. It was hard to deny flatly even in the seventeenth century. For royalists, it was an obvious truth (subject to the embarrassment of claiming that the last ditch of emergency had actually been reached). For the other side, it was sometimes more not-to-be-uttered (especially not as a maxim of law) than not-to-be-quietly-admitted.

20. The dependence of court profits on uncoerced willingness of course requires some qualification. A jury that neglects its duty is subject to attaint; however, the attaint jury, which goes over the same question and is confined to the same evidence, is not controllable. The punishment of jurors for untrue verdicts has a history (mostly in the Star Chamber), but the legality of that is less than clear. Legal errors by judges rectifiable by writ of error are *ex hypothesi* innocent. The means of disciplining judges whose errors are not innocent—dismissal or impeachment—rather confirm than contradict the proposition that there is no *legal* standard of when such malfeasance has occurred and what sanctions shall be visited upon it.

assent of the Lords and the king's acceptance.[21] Because of those elements in the taxing transaction, "We vote you this tax" is not so similar to "I am going to give you one hundred pounds" as it may seem offhand. What can one say taxing is except a sui generis public act, as different from the nearest private analogues as, for example, royal conveyances by sealed instrument from other men's feoffments?

Despite its vulnerability, the king's argument from the "nonexistent," voluntary-contingent, or giftlike quality of taxes was probably his strongest card. That argument cannot be so conclusively punctured as the other two made against the patent's validity: (1) One speaker, Ayscoghe, J., proposed in effect that exemptions from taxes could be held invalid without further ado than noting their public disutility.[22] This requires no premise beyond the indispensable, though vague, principle that grants of clear antisocial tendency cannot stand. Ayscoghe's example is a blank check to commit crimes—a grant of the form "If you commit felony, you will not be punished," or a futuristic exercise of the pardoning prerogative. Although one is free to intuit that a single tax exemption is as harmful as a single invitation to felony, the comparison is not convincing, and it is hard to say why such an exemption is any more objectionable than other relinquishments of royal revenue. (2) A more persuasive point was made by Fortescue, as counsel for the king: the monarch could clearly not make prejudicial grants, in the sense of giving away someone else's interest or disadvantaging A by a grant to B.[23] A single tax exemption is prejudicial in that it increases the odds that the nonexempt will ultimately have to pay more. If the tax is in the usual form of a percentage of the value of the taxpayer's property, no one will be hurt in a given case by the existence of exemptions, but in the long run public needs can only be met by a somewhat increased rate or incidence of taxation. However, this argument was not pressed, and it met with no apparent favor. It is open to the objection that minimal and uncertain prejudice does not count as legal prejudice, and, again, the same point can be made about any relinquishment of revenue.

21. Hody-3. I suppose the requirement of approval by the Lords is a better basis for differentiating taxes from gifts than the requirement of acceptance. Can there be a gift without acceptance?

22. Ayscoghe was *also* persuaded that the voluntary-contingent character of taxes makes them ungrantable. He may have been more confident in his "pure social disutility" suggestion (which I project from his felony parallel) in company with another argument than if it had stood alone.

23. Fortescue-2. Fortescue may not have had in mind the kind of prejudice described in the text, but let us give him the benefit of supposing he did, in addition to the kind he is explicit about. He wanted to make out prejudice in a much stronger sense by arguing that if the exemption were upheld, other taxpayers from the exemptee's locality would have to pay more *this time* to make up the local assessment. The judges unanimously repudiated him on this: sums due from localities would be reduced by the amount exemptees would have paid. Prejudice in a looser sense remains a plausible claim. Ayscoghe and Fortescue-2 together go to show how close "prejudice" and "social disutility" are: Fortescue explains the invalidity of such patents as "blank checks for murder" by prejudice—they are prejudicial to the murderee, as he says, but also to third parties (potential appellors).

If the rector's exemption is conceded to be valid, can anything be said for the king? Could a man be "validly" exempt from parliamentary taxes and still have to pay? The obvious answer is, "Yes, if Parliament, when it voted the tax, provided that exemptions in being should be abrogated for purposes of the present tax." I see no sign of doubt in *Rector of Edington* but that such an abrogation—amounting to a statutory one—would be effective. Conversely, I see no sign of doubt but that a proviso saving exemptions would save them. There was simply no issue about whether Parliament had power to override exemptions based on patent. The power was taken for granted, notwithstanding the moral scruples one might have about retrospective abolition of privileges people thought they had and the lack of comity in overriding the king's valid patent. In the instant case, Parliament purported *per verba* neither to preserve nor to abrogate the rector's exemption or exemptions generally.

The next question is whether Parliament meant to do either. There is no discussion of construction by intent in *Rector of Edington.* The reason, surely, is that no plausible argument can be made for the king on grounds of construction in that sense. Compare the case of statute against statute: the legislature enacts, say, an exemption from real estate taxes for churches. Subsequently, it imposes a 10 percent tax on the value of all real estate. It is hard construction to read the second statute as repealing the former. It may not be impossible, if the tax act says "all" very distinctly, or adds such reinforcing language as "all without exception," or if the legislative history suggests that such language was used with the intent of canceling prior statutory exemptions. But even in a strong case, the absence of an express repeal would be suspect, and when the case is weakened it becomes so much the harder to believe in an intent to repeal. I see no reason, in the fifteenth-century constitutional context, why intent to override exemptions by royal grant should be perceptible where intent to repeal a prior statute would not be.

If we concede that Parliament did not mean to take away the rector's exemption, is there any possible ground for holding that it nevertheless destroyed it? The king's lawyers had a go at a theory.[24] It is strained, and it was no more successful than counsel's attempt to invalidate the patent. In a way, this theory gives Plucknett's interpretation its best color, for it employs the idea of estoppel, whose normal home is private law. However, the specific use of that idea *avoids* its private sense; estoppel functions only as a highly general legal category to furnish the rationale for what can be stated as a positive public-law doctrine. Plucknett's error was to confuse the role of estoppel in *Rector of Edington* with the role of the properly private doctrine in the quite different cases discussed below.

In *Rector of Edington*, the argument comes to this: as a matter of policy—not construction by intent—tax acts that do not expressly save

24. The theory is broached by Fortescue-1; developed by Newton-1 and 2; opposed as, so to speak, "counterintuitive" by Hody-1 (more concrete arguments against it are treated below). The exposition of the theory in the text projects a good deal from the words in the report, but I think the intellectual elements are there.

prior exemptions destroy them for purposes of the present tax. This rule is a specification of a more general one: if an act of Parliament is to preserve particular privileges that militate against the objective of the act, it must do so in terms. The reason for this rule is the undisputed maxim that an act of Parliament is the act of every Englishman (with specific exceptions for the unrepresented), that everyone—being present in Parliament in person or by agent—is complicit in acts of Parliament as if they were his own. What does the maxim mean unless it means that one should strive to imagine the act of Parliament as if it were the individual act of any given person who is represented? Imagine the rector granting so much to the king by his deed under seal, nothing said about a prior grant by the king to the rector freeing the latter from all duty to pay any sum that the rector shall so grant to the king. Can one avoid holding that the rector's grant would operate as a surrender of his privilege, and that without argument as to whether he *meant* to surrender it?

This point can be made efficiently in the language of estoppel: the rector would surely be estopped from pleading the king's grant against his own grant. But that language is not essential. Instead of "estopped to plead," one can just say that the rector has granted away his privilege in the process of making a grant inconsistent with it. One does not ask whether he meant to grant the privilege away, or look at evidence going to his intention, for the grant simply fails to make sense on any alternative assumption. (Cf. statements where "What do you mean?" is a meaningless response.) If we knew that the grantor said loud and clear before sealing his grant, "Now I want it to be understood that this grant is without prejudice to my privilege," it would make no difference. Whatever account one gives of the weird state of mind in which he could say such a thing yet make such a grant, it is not a state of "intending." You cannot say what means *only x* and then say you meant something else; though there are many contexts in which it is appropriate to say that you meant something that is not apparent from your words, this is not one of them. Note the legal upshot: it makes no difference what the rector said in Parliament, if he was there, or what his representative or Parliament as a group said outside the body of the grant itself. For private estoppel, conduct sometimes matters, a protestation may save you from being estopped. Not so for estoppel by acts of Parliament.[25]

It may seem that this representation of the theory awards Plucknett his point even if the language of estoppel is avoided. The rule to be established is "Acts of Parliament override privileges in the absence of an express saving." The route is by way of the putative presence of every man in Parliament and the argument that that doctrine requires imagining the act of Parliament as if it were the private deed of any man who tries to resist the duties imposed by the act. Is Plucknett's point not that public law was only reachable in the fifteenth century by such strange bypaths?

25. Explicit in Hody-1: one objection to the (in itself unconvincing) doctrine of estoppel by act of Parliament is that it would be *unfair* to exemptees. Why? Because there would be no way for them to ward off the estopping effect.

Would the modern way not be to put the rule on grounds of policy and have done? ("It would be better for the country if special privileges created by the king were kept down. Therefore we hold that such privileges will not survive any statute of inconsistent tendency that does not go out of its way to acknowledge and preserve them.") Yes, that would be a *very* modern way, very naked about policy and judicial suzerainty. I do not believe it represents Plucknett's conception of constitutional law making in an appropriately public accent. That process appears to mean to him debate about the *powers* of public agencies conducted in its own set of legal categories—not the courts' settling political matters to suit themselves, as they no doubt often do, in the fifteenth century or at any other time. In any event, who would turn down the argument from everyone's complicity in acts of Parliament when it was there crying to be used? Perhaps an intellectual saint, someone so honest that he does not want the inevitable role of dogma and politics in life to be decently concealed, who would disdain to invent a rule of law curtailing the practical effect of royal grants without acknowledging his disapproval of the king's judgment and of a constitution generous to monarchy. Ordinary sinners seek legalisms (and contribute to the useful work of keeping up appearances in this world). The formula of universal complicity continued to be accepted long after Plucknett's constitutional prehistory yielded to his era of public-law debate. It cannot be denied as a premise to the lawyers in *Rector of Edington*. It was valuable ammunition precisely because its applied meaning was unclear: acts of Parliament are every man's act. So what? Is this maxim a piece of decoration, a truth for the theoretician, perhaps, but with no legal meaning whatever? Surely not, surely it is part of the law. But how does it make any concrete difference? The king's lawyers in *Rector of Edington* proposed an answer to this embarrassing question, and they held a good rhetorical card in the argument that the maxim would seem to be in vain unless given their meaning. What can the maxim mean unless it means that people can be worse off because of their complicity in acts of Parliament? What can that come down to but that private laws and special privileges do not hold up, or cannot be claimed, against apparently general acts of Parliament?

The questions are valid, but the conclusion to which they point was not convincing to most of the judges in *Rector of Edington*. One response may be so fundamental that it does not reach the surface of the report: perhaps universal complicity in acts of Parliament *is* a legally inert piece of theory.[26] Better to call it so than to suffer disutility (subversion of the

26. Unduly gloomy perhaps. "Every man is present in Parliament" at least has the use of expressing, and in a way justifying, such commonplaces as that no one can claim ignorance of an act of Parliament. Perhaps, indeed, the doctrine is extendable in the direction counsel pointed, but not to the inconvenient degree to which they wanted to stretch it in this case. It might not be entirely unattractive or unconvincing to say that it is a *principle* to give preference to statutes over privileges on the basis of universal complicity. But principles are not rules; they must contend with other principles—here the principle of utility embodied in the king's very power to release future revenue and the principle of fairness that must discountenance the king's turning tables on his grantees when it suits him. I suggest the

king's useful power to divert parliamentary revenue) and indecorum (permitting the king to escape his intended and socially harmless grant). Those who seem in the report only to be left cold by the "estoppel" theory were perhaps thinking such thoughts. Those who addressed themselves more particularly to the theory showed excellent reasons why it is the opposite of true: it was standard practice in statutory construction to hold that special privileges not unmistakably taken away by general legislation are preserved.[27] The bias of the law was on the side of the privilege holder, not against him (and which way the bias lay, notwithstanding the metaphysics of universal complicity, was the basic issue). It was argued in addition that no analogue to the applied doctrine of universal complicity could be found where one would most expect to find it—in the law of corporations.[28] That is, the release in general terms of a corporation, such as the City of London, does not operate to release claims of individual members of the corporation, or estop them from asserting their private claims. There is to be sure no necessary reason why the acts of corporations and acts of Parliament should be subject to the same rules. The argument from canons of construction, being specific to acts of Parliament, is the strong antidote to "estoppel." Yet it is hardly a regression to the private sphere to suggest that it would be odd for a single legal system to distinguish the natural individual and the individual

following case: The law was that all freeholders are liable for jury duty. The king grants an exemption to freeholder A. Parliament makes a statute imposing jury duty on persons with five pounds' worth of freehold property and making poorer freeholders ineligible. A, whose freehold is worth more than five pounds, now claims his exemption. It seems to me that it is relatively plausible to argue here that the statute defeats the privilege by reason of A's complicity. In a sense, of course, the "real" point is that the privilege was granted in legal circumstances that have been changed. But I am not sure the result—not letting A out of his duty on the basis of a grant made when the ball game was different—can be achieved directly. (The grant was not invalid initially and it is not disallowable now—let us assume—because there are too few freeholders in the five-pound class to raise a jury without A. It may not be convincing to say that Parliament *meant* to abolish existing privileges.) The general strength of the complicity doctrine is that it permits making no pretense that the court understands the legislative intent, as it often must not. Imagine a modern judge speaking as follows: "Privileges are a plague of political life—as they were when we had serious kings, so now when we don't, but pressure groups and democratic politics instead. I refuse to speculate, when the evidence is no better than it is, as to whether the legislature *meant* this tax bill to repeal previous privilege-creating legislation. Rather, I shall take it that a thrust of apparently general legislation is to level the existing structure of privilege. I shall take that as a 'policy of the law' in a democratic society, where everyone affected by legislation has the opportunity in numerous forms to affect legislation. I do not mean that every piece of general legislation of uncertain intent must be given such effect, but I make no apology for asserting an antiprivilege bias when I can think of no deep policies that weigh against it, when I can only suppose that the privilege in question represents a lobbyist's good luck."

27. Fortescue-4, challenged by Vampage-2, and insisted on by Fortescue-5. Fortescue's example is *De Donis* (1285), which did not give formedon in London (i.e., did not take away London's preexisting custom-based practice of accomplishing the effect of formedon by writs of right). One can of course quarrel with projecting a bias in favor of *all* sorts of privileges from that type of example.

28. Markham-2.

qua member of a collective body in one context while confounding the two capacities in another.

The other three cases discussed by Plucknett resemble *Rector of Edington* only superficially. The vocabulary of private law is more genuinely active in those other cases because in a sense they are private-law cases. The sense is special: the cases are about the effect of royal acts on the interests of the English church and the effect of acts by the church on the concerns of the government. The Reformation in England can be said to have promoted issues of that sort to constitutional status, for the church in its temporal dimension became one agency of the king among others, a component in the mixed system of government needing public-law definition and adjustment to other components. Before the Reformation, acts of the church must be thought of as in principle the acts of a "private organization"—of course a unique one, one that demanded special legal treatment many times more urgently than those "private organizations" in the modern world whose scale and social importance also demand it (AT&T or Harvard University, for example). Literally, *Rector of Edington* was a church-state case too; that it was can be ignored because the case was argued as if a layman's exemption from parliamentary taxes had been involved; nothing was made of the ecclesiastical character of the tax, presumably because *quoad* the mere act of tax granting, Convocation was considered indistinguishable from Parliament. *Quoad* anything else, it was certainly not equivalent. Missing this point vitiates Plucknett's analysis.

The other cases come to this schema: the king grants a churchman, A, an exemption from the office of collecting any future tax voted by Convocation. Convocation votes a tax, adding an express proviso that patent-based exemptions from collectorship not be taken advantage of. A is appointed collector in accord with the church's ordinary internal procedure. The king sues A for monies that ought to have been collected from the clergy in the name of the tax. This is normal procedure. That is, the law is that the collector in such case is suable as an individual ("the church" and Convocation are not suable corporations). A pleads his patent of exemption. Should his plea be allowed?

In contrast to *Rector of Edington*, this case will not translate into the lay world. A man could well hold a patent exempting him from serving as collector of lay parliamentary taxes. Imagining such, then clearly Parliament could make a statute, or accompany its tax bill with a provision, abrogating the privilege. This applies the public law that is assumed in *Rector of Edington.* It is equally clear that Convocation had no such power—no power as an agency of government to nullify royal patents or exclude their holders from pleading them in the temporal courts. If Convocation can so act as to prevent A from taking advantage of his exemption, it is not because acts of Convocation are *suprema lex*, or superior to the king's patents, or because of any constitutional principle whatever. It must be because of some "private-law" principle, properly speaking, though possibly one with no application except to the sui generis church.

On the other hand, Parliament's merely voting a tax could not plausibly be thought to destroy an exemption from the office of collector, whereas it makes at least prima facie sense to argue that merely voting a tax destroys tax exemptions. Were Parliament to name an exemption holder collector (instead of leaving the appointment to the king), it would be more than convincing to hold his exemption destroyed in the absence of a clause expressly revoking his privilege. Convocation is different. Although its merely voting a tax would be an unlikely basis for holding exemptions from collectorship destroyed, there may be reasons for holding that it cannot defeat exemptions even if it purports to do so with complete explicitness, a fortiori if it expresses an intent to do so less directly, as by itself naming an exempt person collector. The Convocation cases can only be understood by seeing that Convocation acts in the private sphere—or, in fifteenth-century language, the spiritual—and that its impingement on the king is problematic for just that reason.[29]

The public issue "What privileges are grantable by the king?" is, however, common to the Convocation cases and *Rector of Edington*. The purported exemption from collectorship was attackable on more grounds than the slender ones on which the tax exemption in the earlier case could be questioned. It is arguable, and was argued, that the king may not exempt from anything so "nonexistent" or voluntary-contingent as a future clerical subsidy (or other tax) and so may not exempt from the equally tenuous office of collecting such a contribution.[30] When a clerical subsidy rather than a parliamentary tax is in question, that argument is not answerable by assimilating taxes to court profits. For (whether or not

29. Ignoring anything that may be peculiar to the church, the following private case seems to me essentially like the Convocation cases (once the validity of the king's grant is conceded): Mallard Wildfowl Sanctuary v. Songthrush. Section 16 of the North Blackfoot Charitable Corporations Act reads as follows: "If any individual or unincorporated organization shall pledge, appropriate, or agree to donate any sum of money to any charitable corporation duly incorporated and registered under the provisions of this act, such charitable corporation may sue for such money in the courts of this State. In the event that such a pledge, appropriation, or agreement to donate is made by an unincorporated organization, the charitable corporation may bring suit against such person as the said organization designates collector of such money pledged, etc." In 1957, the Mallard Wildfowl Sanctuary, a charitable corporation duly constituted under the provisions of the act quoted above, made a contract with one Herbert Songthrush, which included the following words: ". . . in consideration of the premises, the said Mallard Wildfowl Sanctuary agrees that it will never bring suit against the said Herbert Songthrush in the capacity of collector of any sum of money pledged, appropriated, or donated to the said Mallard Wildfowl Sanctuary by any unincorporated organization." In 1969, the Polly Parrot Birdlovers' Society, an unincorporated organization, voted to charge each member one dollar, the sum collected to go as a donation to the Mallard Wildfowl Sanctuary, subjoining a proviso: "This donation is given on the understanding that no member appointed to collect the same shall have the advantage of any contract purporting to excuse him from liability for the same." The president, in keeping with his powers under the by-laws of the society, then appointed Herbert Songthrush collector, Songthrush being a member. The record shows that Songthrush was present at the meeting and offered no vocal opposition to the vote with proviso. The money being unpaid, the Mallard Wildfowl Sanctuary brought suit against Herbert Songthrush as collector. He pleaded the contract quoted above.

30. Keeble in Waltham.

the assimilation is correct in itself) Parliament *is* the king's court; on pre-Reformation assumptions, Convocation is not; if it is a "court" at all, it is an ecclesiastical court; the king clearly had no power to release or assign revenues or other duties accruing from ecclesiastical courts. In the context of the Convocation cases, therefore, the argument from the ungrantability of "nonexistent" things has to be met head on: it is merely wrong, or the conceit of court profits is superfluous for the real point that subsidies—lay or clerical—are not genuinely "voluntary," or the ungrantability of such futurities is a truth in the purely private sphere that should not be allowed to obstruct the king's useful prerogative. In the event, the argument that echoes *Rector of Edington* seems to have received no serious attention in the Convocation cases.

A second argument in the latter is that collecting a clerical subsidy amounts to an ecclesiastical office, and the king manifestly has no power to exempt from such offices.[31] The major premise of this contention is indisputable, but the minor premise failed: the collectorship was held to be a temporal office. That conclusion, which is involved with an intricate aspect of the case discussed below, has a strong intuitive appeal. Although the king obviously cannot exempt people, especially clerics, from offices of service to the church that they are compellable to perform, collecting a donation made to the king by the clergy seems an office of service to him and as exemptable as any other.

The significant excursion by the king's lawyers was into the implications of the intrinsically safe proposition that the king may not make grants which prejudice other people or defeat serious public interests.[32]

31. In Leeds: Portington, contradicted directly by Fray, indirectly by Hody-1 and 2, Newton. In Waltham: Baker (with a curious supporting citation: the king may grant cognizance of pleas even when the grantee is party, so long as the pleas are held before his bailiff. Possibly meant to say, "In the temporal sphere the king can do things that one might regard as questionable. His granting power is very broad, but that is only in the temporal sphere, and reason to keep him there"); contradicted by Jenney, Choke.

32. Objection to the grant as prejudicial comes from Fortescue in Leeds; from Nottingham and Redmayne in Waltham—contradicted there by Philpot, Fairfax, Choke, Huse. Direct argument about the jury exemption parallel is between Redmayne and Philpot. In the paragraphs that follow, I construct beyond the words of the report on these grounds: Redmayne, the lawyer on the king's side who develops the prejudice theory, seems not to say that individual jury exemptions are unlawful, only that group ones are, and that individual ones may be disallowed if there are too many. I can make sense of his contention only by supposing that he is pointing to a dilemma: either individual jury exemptions are unlawful (which is surely unlikely) or they are not true legal exemptions, but subject to that free discretion by which the present patent ought to be disallowed as prejudicial. Philpot, directly answering Redmayne, does not deny that individual jury exemptions may be disallowed if there are too many. All he seems to deny is that such exemptions are illegal (using the curious parallel that a condition against alienating generally is invalid, whereas one against alienating to a particular person is good—a general or group jury exemption is bad, but an individual one is good). But does he really understand Redmayne as contesting the bare legality of individual jury exemptions? Assuming he does not, his speech is intelligible as a response to the "uncontrolled discretion" theory: individual jury exemptions are not tenuous "recommendations," but straight rights, like any others conferred by valid royal patent. To be sure, they fail when so excessive as to obstruct the operations of the law, or to have the same effect as a general exemption. (Perhaps a condition against alienating to a

They tried and failed to sell an extreme version of the doctrine that although the king may give away his own, he is restrained from affecting anyone else's interest adversely by his grant. Carried as far in one direction as counsel tried to suggest it might be, the doctrine would rule out all exemptions from compulsory offices. For to exempt a single person from such an office is prejudicial to all others eligible to be conscripted, in that the chance of each nonexempt coeligible's being required to serve is increased, however slightly. The prejudice is more certain than that created by a tax exemption. But although it makes sense to see this consequence in the rule against prejudicial grants, insisting on it runs afoul of the commonplace example, jury exemptions, which were widespread and generally regarded as legal. Interpreting and evading that obstacle were central to a convincing case against the patent's validity.

Although exempting an individual from jury service was admittedly lawful, it was also admitted that trial courts had authority to override such exemptions on grounds of necessity. That is, if on a given occasion a jury could not be assembled from nonexempt eligibles, exemptees could be required to serve. The obvious explanation is the *public* interest: coeligibles, one may say, have no protectable private interest in keeping to a minimum the likelihood of having to serve; exemptions are disregarded only when, under the existing rules on venue and personal qualification for jury service, a case cannot be tried without using exemptees, or cannot be tried except by delaying the parties unduly and putting on the sheriff an excessive burden of hunting up nonexempt eligibles; the dispensability of individual exemptions can only be understood in the light of the admitted rule that a group exemption—as for all freemen resident in a county or hundred—would be invalid on its face; individual exemptions are dispensable only when they add up to the same effect.

However, there may be another way of seeing that dispensability. One can put the emphasis on the fact that the king cannot *absolutely* exempt from jury duty, rather than on the rationale for the power to override exemptions: the king has strict power to "give away his own." That is, he grants that his debtor A is forgiven the debt; upon being sued for the debt, A may plead his patent, and his right to be forgiven is a legal right, just as if he held the sealed acquittance of a private creditor. The exemptee from jury duty cannot be said to have a comparable "legal right," for what he has is hopelessly subject to the trial court's discretion. He holds what amounts to the king's recommendation or request to the judge to let the holder off. The judge ought to respect the king's wishes when there is no inconvenience, and the typical reason for not respecting them is public need. But public need cannot be reduced to a rule of law.

very long list of particular people, approaching the limit of all the people in the country, would fail too.) Only public grounds will cause them to fail, never prejudice to coeligibles. The grant in the present case might fail for egregious prejudice to a specific person (the bishop, if in fact he were in any danger), but it is not subject to discretionary disallowance when the courts only think there is *some* prejudice or public disutility.

One cannot say exactly when the exemptee may be forced to serve, what evidence there must be that a jury cannot be had without him, how difficult it must be to collect sufficient nonexempt eligibles. Disallowing a patent of jury exemption could never be pinpointed as legal error. Being, in sum, subject to uncontrolled discretion, such patents may be scrutinized with other values than public necessity in mind, including the values expressed in the rule against prejudicial grants. The king is not—we now concede—utterly debarred from prejudicing members of the pool of jurors, for his "recommendations" are properly respected when there is nothing against it but some slight prejudice of that sort. Neither is he *utterly* debarred from hurting the public interest, as by exempting the most capable people while leaving plenty of eligible jurors. But there is as good reason to cut off going too far in the one direction as in the other—for the sake of the public interest when, say, most of the more capable people have been exempted though abundant technical eligibles remain; for the sake of avoiding prejudice when, say, 50 percent of the pool instead of 1 percent have been exempted. (When extreme cases are imagined, it becomes nearly meaningless to say which interest is being harmed—whether the weaker half of the pool is being oppressed with excessive service, or whether justice is being impaired and the sheriff distracted from his other duties by the trouble of rounding up jurors who ought to be minding their cows for the commonwealth.)

So for jurors, and so for other compulsory offices, with appropriate attention to the nature of the office. For example, it may be proper, though not obligatory, to respect jury exemptions even when they are fairly numerous within a given venue, as jury duty is occasional and not very time-consuming, and as there is a certain piety in supposing that one eligible man will make as good a juror as the next. When an office involves real trouble and demands special competence, it lies in discretion to disallow a single exemption. It is also relevant, as in the instant cases, whether the king himself has indicated how he wants his "recommendatory" grant to be handled. When he proceeds against the exemptee, he disrecommends the carrying out of his prior recommendation. If the courts have any choice in that situation, they ought at least to weigh the king's judgment that the public interest or private fairness would be disserved by allowing the exemption this time. With the last factor taken into consideration, one might say that some grants (including all or most exemptions from compulsory offices), although not merely void like some other purported grants, amount to a mixture of nonobligatory recommendations and moral undertakings on the king's part. In the latter respect, the king says, "I intend that you should have this privilege, but I may on occasion feel obliged to urge the courts—even if I have forgone the power to compel them—to disallow your taking advantage of it. I no doubt have a moral duty to avoid so urging if there are feasible alternatives, and when I cannot avoid it, it is no doubt incumbent on me to compensate you by some other favor. You may petition me as of grace in that event." There is some virtue, under the system of government as it was, in letting the king say that, as opposed to dichotomizing his grants into those that raise clear legal rights and those that, as *ultra vires* and void, have no claim even on his conscience.

This argument (or the cruder one that exemptions from compulsory offices are merely void, whence it follows that jury exemptions are either flatly invalid or an unexplained special case) was not successful. In the end, the judges thought that the exemption from collectorship was perfectly good. It is presumably implicit in that opinion (to save the accepted rules on jury exemption) that on a showing of extreme public hardship the privilege might be disallowed. It is uncertain whether similar overriding force would have been conceded to private hardship, in the sense of greatly increasing the odds that other eligibles will have to serve. One judge had the courage to deny the generalization that prejudicial grants are invalid (courage because some probably unchallengeable grants *besides* those from compulsory offices cannot be analyzed as unprejudicial to third parties).[33] He did not speculate on whether some kinds of prejudice invalidate grants, nor on whether some degrees of private prejudice permit grants that are valid *ab initio* to be disallowed. Nor was there any attempt to say just when the degree of public prejudice becomes such that jury exemptions may be overridden, nor whether other compulsory offices are distinguishable from jury duty. The case at hand was sufficient unto the day, and the judges' basic disposition was to uphold the granting prerogative in the absence of crying hardship. One expects courts to avoid constitutional hot water when they can and usually commends them for doing so.

The judges of course reached their conclusion in a concrete situation. Owing to the crisscrossing of spiritual and temporal spheres, it is not entirely easy to move from the general arguments above to the case before us. In the abstract, the exemption in question hardly seems defeasible except by calling it merely void by reason of prejudice. I have stated a theory to justify ad hoc disallowance of a "valid" single exemption from an office, but that comes to strained extension of an already strained approach. Surely if only one person in the whole country is exempt from collecting taxes, even though the job is onerous and responsible, the public and private prejudice is infinitesimal. If a judge were satisfied that he could disallow, he still ought to hesitate. But the actual situation was more complicated than the abstract one. If Smith and Smith alone were exempt from conscription as a lay tax collector, it should be easy for the king to get the tax collected without Smith. But how is the clerical subsidy in our cases to be collected if the exemptee's patent is respected?

33. Fairfax-1. His example is a royal protection granted to a tenant in a *praecipe*, and that concession to the possibility of prejudicial grants is moderate, because the only prejudice worked by the protection is to delay the demandant. However, very modest concessions may be enough—as Fairfax thought they were—to make out that merely increasing the exposure of coeligibles is not legal prejudice.

This question involves us in the most technical side of the cases. I believe the winning position can be stated as follows:[34] When the king is told that the clergy has voted him a subsidy, a right to the contribution vests in him. He is entitled to 10 percent or whatever of the property within the scope of the tax belonging to clergyman A. That is a temporal right, no different in principle from an analogous title to raise so much from the property of layman B in the name of a parliamentary tax. From this follows the proposition that the office of collecting a clerical subsidy is inherently temporal and the further proposition that the king could appoint any collector he chose. He could appoint any layman specially or send the sheriff to assess clergyman A's property and enforce payment of the assessment. He could do this even though the church authorities designated a collector; that is, he could ignore their appointment and send someone else. This is all we need to make the essential point: a single exemption can be respected because the tax is perfectly collectable without significant prejudice to other people; at the least, the whole population of competent laymen is available for the job. (Of course the king could, instead of appointing a lay collector, request the archbishop to reconsider and choose a nonexempt cleric. But if the archbishop feels bound not to do that by the terms of Convocation's act—or at least feels that he is not bound to go to the trouble in the light of the act—and if we assume that he cannot be coerced,[35] the king still has plenty of options.)

However, a hitch occurs when one is driven back to the point that the king would be able to collect the tax by laymen. A lay collector could raise the money out of the lay property of clerics, but he could not touch their "spiritual property." Because "spiritual property" was normally within the scope of a clerical subsidy, it is not really true that the king could collect without the church's assistance. Can he have that assistance other than by disallowing the exemptee's patent—given that the archbishop is not free or not compellable to appoint a different collector, and considering that if the archbishop were answerable for the money himself the exemptee's patent would have a manifestly prejudicial effect? The winning position replies that the church's assistance could be had indirectly: if the king were to collect the money by lay hands, and there were to be a clergyman incapable of satisfying his share out of temporal property, procedures exist for invoking the ad hoc aid of the church so as to make spiritual property reachable for temporal purposes; the normal

34. Argument about the matters following by Fray, Hody-1 and 2. in Leeds; by Vavasour, Jenney, Fairfax-1, in Waltham.

35. There is some discussion scattered through the Waltham report about the bishop's position, bearing chiefly on whether the patent is prejudicial to him. Some of that is cast in terms of the conditionality of the tax donation. As I say in the text below, I do not think it was proposed to interpret the tax as conditional in the sense "We give you this money on condition that exemptees, if appointed, do the collecting," but it was suggested in effect that the king accepted the tax with the agreement that the bishop would not be liable for it himself or obligated to find a nonexempt clerical collector. Suffice it to note that at the end of the report—in response to a question by Nottingham, who remained confused as to whether the bishop was off the hook—the judges all said unmistakably that he was safe.

context for such procedures was when a clergyman had no lay property by which he could be coerced to appear as defendant in common-law litigation or on which execution of a common-law judgment could be had.[36]

The validity of the patent (with the connected questions whether valid patents may be disallowed in particular cases and, if so, whether the power to disallow is a discretionary power with respect to which only vague parameters can be described) was probably seen as the most important issue in the Convocation cases. The problem, discussed below, whether the exemptee had waived his privilege appears to have engaged the judges' interest relatively little in proportion to the lawyers' attention to it. In the end, the contention that he had waived it seemed pretty clearly unmeritorious, which throws the weight of the case back on whether his unwaived privilege was good. The competence of the king to legislate interstitially by patent is an unmistakable public issue, probably the main problematic area of constitutional law before the great cases on the absolute prerogative in the seventeenth century. It was the medium for such later issues as the monarch's power to confer legal monopolies and the extent of the dispensing power. There is no way in which fifteenth-century discussion of the granting prerogative was obfuscated by a private-law mentality.

Another equally public question was given serious attention by the judges. It was argued for the king that the patent relieved the exemptee from collecting subsidies given by "the clergy of England," whereas he had pleaded it to get off collecting a subsidy voted by the clergy of the Province of Canterbury. In other words, though concededly valid, the patent did not cover what it was applied to. Assessment of this contention involves the question how royal patents are to be construed—strictly, in the sense that the least verbal flaw that ingenuity can discover should be taken against the patentee? by probable realistic intent, in the light of how language is ordinarily used and of customary practices in the area the patent is concerned with? sometimes the one and sometimes the other? Any question about construction is apt to evoke comparisons between private and public instruments, but in the end general canons for construing royal patents (just as much as for construing statutes) are expressive of public policies, and standards for deeds and wills may well be deemed irrelevant. In the upshot, the king's best chance of winning the Convocation cases lay in the "strict constructionist" approach to patents (which of course gives voice to the bias against privilege embod-

36. The winning position stated in the text is not necessarily clinching. One could concede the technical points and still make something of the complex spiritual-temporal border: granting that the king may collect the tax by lay hands and that there are procedures for ultimately extracting what the clerics owe, it would at least be awkward to resort to any system except the usual one—collection of clerical subsidies by the church itself. If an awkward and unusual method of collecting the tax is the possible cost of allowing the exemption, that is inconvenience enough to justify disallowing it. And perhaps it is unnecessary to concede so much in this murky area of the law.

ied in the fanciful "estoppel by act of Parliament" doctrine encountered in *Rector of Edington*); on that horse, he came very close.[37]

Now, had the exemptee waived his privilege? The arguments on this question seemed to Plucknett to be especially permeated with private-law thinking. I have already stated generally why I believe that is a mistaken emphasis: private-law thinking was appropriate because the question in a sense was about a "private organization." For the rest, it seems to me that the fifteenth-century lawyers on the whole avoided drowning in private-law conceptions, so as to lose sight of the church's uniqueness and the danger of drawing too sharp a line between the public sphere and that of the supercorporation.

There is one disarming way to argue that the privilege was not waived: namely, there is no way to waive a patent-based privilege except by not pleading it in the appropriate judicial forum.[38] Whatever the exemptee did or Convocation did, the privilege was alive when the Exchequer asked the holder, "Where is the money you are supposed to be collecting?" At the first opportunity afforded him by an appropriate judicial forum, he claimed his privilege. Therefore it was not waived. For this analysis, help came again from the one familiar parallel field of practice, jury exemptions. An exemptee from jury duty does not waive his privilege by failing to show or mention his patent to the sheriff, but only by not claiming it in the face of the court. The parallel is fruitful because the sheriff is an official, and it would be a sensible enough rule, in the interest of saving time and trouble, to provide that when given an opportunity to claim his privilege by the sheriff the exemptee should do so if he intends to insist on it (whereas it would not be sensible to count his idle words outside any official context as a waiver). Leaving aside particular considerations about the status of Convocation, it is at least loosely an "official body," or at any rate an occasion on which to expect deliberate behavior. If one could waive a jury exemption by neglecting to show it to a "merely ministerial" officer, possibly a clergyman could waive his privilege by silence or complicity in so solemn a body as Convocation. But the law was the other way. It is possible that some of the judges thought this line of argument sufficient for showing that the patent was not waived. There is nothing unpublic about the doctrine that rights derived from so high a source as the king's grant cannot be waived by out-of-court acts.

37. The points in this paragraph are argued (Waltham) by Danvers, Ludworth, Browne, Catesby-4, Pigot-2, Huse, Fairfax-1 and 2, Choke. Whereas the king almost won on this point in Waltham (see Appendix for details), Shrewsbury goes decisively the other (liberal construction) way.

38. In Waltham, Ludworth, Rede, Fairfax-1. Nottingham may have had some doubt about the jury exemption parallel, but I think probably not. (He probably means only a qualification: showing one's jury exemption to the sheriff cannot be called insignificant, because if one does show it, the sheriff may properly leave one off the panel; but failure to show it to him is not in itself a waiver. In the context, Nottingham was concerned to attach significance to conduct in Convocation, not to grapple directly with the "no out-of-court waiver" theory. There is no binding reason why neglect of one's interests in Convocation should have the *same* significance as not showing a jury exemption to the sheriff.)

Let us assume, however, that the privilege might conceivably be waived by acts other than failure to plead it in the king's court. Two acts could be plausibly said to work a waiver (no further ones, such as utterances or signs of acquiescence on the exemptee's part outside Convocation, or purely *in pais*, were in the record). First would be the acts of Convocation, containing provisos purporting to override exemptions, merely as such—that is, without reference to the exemptee's behavior in Convocation, or in the light of what Convocation as a body did or was about to do.[39] Here the argument is that all clergymen are complicit in acts of Convocation just as all laymen are complicit in acts of Parliament. When Convocation grants the king so much tax provided exemptions from collectorship are not taken advantage of, it is as if the clergyman-exemptee had made such a grant, with such proviso, as an individual; his private act would obviously work a waiver or estoppel. Nothing the exemptee could have done—opposing the proviso as a member of Convocation, making a solemn protestation that he held a patent and neither wished to be taken as consenting to its loss nor admitted Convocation's power to defeat it—would alter the case. The second such act would be the conduct of the exemptee as a member of Convocation and person with interests at odds with what Convocation as a body wanted to effect.[40] This argument concedes that the acts of Convocation are not quasi the acts of every individual represented. (If you like, complicity in the acts of a representative body is a doctrine for the public sphere, whatever exactly it comes to there. There are no "representative bodies" in so full and deep a sense in the private sphere, not even in the church, notwithstanding the analogue between Convocation and Parliament.)[41] The contention is only that the exemptee—considering his opportunity, his relation to Convocation, and the obvious threat to his interest in Convocation's activity—would appear to have accepted what Convocation wanted. The appearance was created by his inactivity, for anything the record showed. The present argument requires the premise that the courts should be disposed to see privilege-waiving conduct and intent when they can, to demand that privilege holders exert themselves to preserve their privileges in contexts where sitting silent at least raises doubt about a man's state of mind and the moral excusability of doing nothing. Exactly what exertions by the exemptee would have sufficed to save his privilege makes a question; a "protestation" was regarded as his obvious move, whatever precise character it must have and whether or not any self-protective actions that would not count technically as a "protestation" could avail him.

39. The first form of estoppel is urged only in Waltham, and there as an alternative to the second form below. Catesby-1 and 3, Danvers.

40. In Leeds, urged by Portington; generally opposed by the judges, but gets support from Ayscoghe and the chancellor. In Waltham, argued by Pigot-1, Catesby-2.

41. This projected statement is of course strictly from the common-law or temporal point of view. For internal purposes, the church may have any theory or practice of representation it likes and draw whatever legal conclusions from them it sees fit.

Both of these alternative arguments are subject to one line of attack: nothing that happens in the spiritual sphere (here specifically the spiritual, not the private) can have any impact on, or be taken notice of in, the temporal.[42] Both acts of Convocation and the acts of individual churchmen in Convocation, or in relation to its proceedings, are events in the spiritual sphere. Issues about complicity and the privilege holder's duty of self-exertion need never be reached. Anything that could count as a waiver or ground for estoppel on either theory is simply beyond the cognizance of the temporal courts. That is what "separation of church and state" means.

If it is conceded that such rigid separationism is misconceived or impractical, the arguments above can be attacked otherwise. The first is open to strong objection. It is possible, though hardly worth bothering, to deny the premise that the clergy are as complicit in acts of Convocation as laymen in acts of Parliament. (No one would have thought it plausible to push the complicity theory to the lengths that were at least imagined for Parliament in *Rector of Edington*—to maintain that acts of Convocation override privileges, in the absence of an express saving, even if there are no words purporting to override them and no intent to do so is construed.) It is unnecessary to reach the metaphysics, because a complicity doctrine applied to Convocation would have manifestly dangerous results. If Convocation can defeat an exemption from collectorship just by attaching a proviso to its act of donation, why should it not defeat any other privilege held by a clergyman by the same technique? Suppose, for example, that the king grants fines accruing from the hundred of A to the abbot of X. Convocation votes the king a subsidy "provided that the abbot of X's patent be of no effect." Plainly this cannot be used to prevent the abbot from receiving the fines on the ground that the act of Convocation is as good as his own deed, and, still more plainly, Convocation may not simply pass an act, unconnected with any subsidy, nullifying the abbot's patent. If one is not worried about the abbot, one must at least be worried about the king: there is obviously no jurisdiction in Convocation, a body of which the king is not a member, to defeat his patents wholesale, and no formula for discriminating cases when complicity in the acts of Convocation should and should not have that effect. Convocation is not Parliament; it is an agency of a "private organization."

This all but insuperable argument was made from the bar by Starkey.[43]

42. This line is taken by Hody-1 and Paston in Leeds. In Waltham, urged by Vavasour, Ludworth, Rede.

43. In Waltham. Starkey is backed up by Vavasour and Browne, and by all the judicial opinion in the negative sense that it shows no sign of having been enough impressed by the "complicity" theory to need to refute it in terms. Plucknett correctly observed that Starkey's speech has a ring of general principle which many other speeches lack. In addition to counterposing Convocation to the king's prerogative, he is eloquent against the general policy of leaning in the king's favor in doubtful situations. (It is not clear what provoked his eloquence—perhaps an unreported suggestion that a king-favoring bias was appropriate to the present case, with its several doubtful points.) Chrimes, *English Constitutional Ideas*, pp. 41 ff., has shown that Plucknett was unduly impressed by the occurrence of the word

Plucknett was impressed by the more modern character of Starkey's speech, in that it uses the word "prerogative" and seems to represent the issue as between the king's prerogative and Convocation's powers. There is a verbal sense in which that was the issue, but it is misleading so to state it without regarding the context. The issue was not between one public authority and another, and there was no fifteenth-century contest between the king's prerogative and Parliament analogous to prerogative versus Convocation in Starkey's frame of reference. The point is that Convocation is *not* like Parliament, *not* a public authority; that the complicity doctrine, which possibly has serious implications in the public sphere, must not be allowed, in virtue of a tempting parallelism, to spill over to Convocation; that the effect of letting it spill over would be to give Convocation an utterly inappropriate power to curtail powers of the king—for "prerogative" means nothing more in this context—which he undoubtedly had, subject only to parliamentary control.

If Convocation cannot kill the exemption merely by pronouncing it dead, we are thrown back on the private-law doctrine of waiver or estoppel by conduct. There is nothing unreasonable about inferring a waiver from the exemptee's conduct, once the fairly strong arguments against waiver by out-of-court acts and against the possibility of waiving a temporal right by a spiritual act are conceded away. The questions become the extent to which inactivity can be held against a man and whether the kind of self-protective behavior to be expected from one in the exemptee's position can be specified well enough to erect a workable doctrine for the relevant range of cases. The part of good sense and fairness is probably to go for the exemptee, as the judges did.[44] There is a wider equity in that result—a result supportive of the homely truth that in complex and over-argued cases courts quite often end up doing the sane thing. The church was not cheated out of its power to do what it was presumably really interested in—to say to the king, "We give you this gift, not, properly speaking, on condition, not on the harsh condition that you screw any exemptees appointed to collectorship out of their privileges or you get nothing. But we give it on the understanding that collection is your problem. Whether you collect the subsidy by lay hands, or persuade any exemptees who may be appointed to abandon their

"prerogative" in Starkey's speech, though otherwise Chrimes has no apparent quarrel with Plucknett's treatment of these cases.

44. In Leeds, Fray rejects the "conduct" estoppel theory on the ground that does not require worrying about what the exemptee actually did or did not do in Convocation: individual conduct in a collective body simply does not count against the individual; his capacities as part of the body and as a natural person are simply different (a point related to the argument in Rector of Edington that corporate acts do not destroy individual members' rights—a somewhat different use of the same distinction of capacities). The same line is taken in Waltham by Brigges and Rede and probably accepted by the judges (except for Nottingham) by acquiescence. The only exchange specifically over what acts (admitting the possibility of estoppel by conduct) could be held against the exemptee is between the chancellor and the reporter in Leeds: the reporter queries the chancellor's confident reliance on "Silence is consent."

exemptions or accept a substitute reward, or choose to litigate with your exemptees in the temporal courts, is indifferent to us. Just do not pester us if you run into collection difficulties owing to your own liberality in granting exemptions." The exemptee was not cheated out of his privilege on any of several plausible, but graceless, grounds. The king escaped reduction of his granting prerogative on a couple of dangerously high grounds, as well as lower ones.

Sanity is sanity for an age. The Convocation cases, as well as *Rector of Edington*, come to about the right result for the old and truly mixed constitution, when the courts had to and *could* modulate the interaction of royal and parliamentary authority and the interplay with those of a unique institution beyond the ordinary scope of government, the church. A straight confrontation between king and Parliament, which was not present in the fifteenth-century cases to be missed by private-minded lawyers, would have signalized what it meant in the seventeenth century: constitutional problems that had outgrown judicial solution. The fifteenth-century courts went about constitutional law making, not innocent of the category, but in terms appropriate to their present. They had to all intents arrived at the cornerstone of later constitutional truth—the essential omnicompetence of Parliament. Their problem, in one dimension, was to contain that truth, lest it eat away at the existing mixture of authorities and the safety for the subject that reposed in mixture. "Keep the king's granting power broad; prevent his clever lawyers from finding ways to get him out of his grants; do not let Parliament's powers—vast if it chooses to use them unmistakably—lead to overplaying acts of Parliament as 'the law of the land,' as if there were no other; do not let the neat parallelism of temporal and spiritual turn Convocation into a 'Spiritual Parliament' to the detriment of lay authority"—that is not a bad formula for the constitutional ends most reasonably imputable to the fifteenth-century courts, and it is pretty much the formula they came to in our cases.

Appendix

In this Appendix, an anatomy of the four reports discussed by Plucknett and in the text above is given. Some details not registered in the text appear here, but the most important matter noted is the judicial lineup and other evidence bearing on the cases' outcome, to which reference in the text is general. Contrary to the impression given by Plucknett, I think there is no question about the substantive result of the cases: they all go against the king, which is to say, in favor of the holders of royal patents whose privileges the king was trying to defeat. All the cases originated in the Exchequer, but were referred to all the judges in the Exchequer Chamber, to whose deliberations the reports relate.

I. *Rector of Edington.*
Pasch. 19 Hen. 6, pl. 1. The case begins in the spring of 1441, but the last reported occasion of debate is not until Hil. 20 Hen. 6 (Jan.–Feb. 1442). This is known from the report telling that Fortescue's speeches on that last occasion were made as C.J.K.B. in the term when he was appointed to the office. The second occasion of debate could have been in any term through Mich. 20 (autumn 1441), which was Hody's last as C.J.K.B.

Facts: Henry IV granted the rector, his confreres, and his successors exemption from taxes granted to the king by Parliament or tenths granted to him by the clergy. (The patent was fairly old, which may have made it harder to break. It was to a corporation, which means a perpetual diversion of revenue.) A clerical tenth was granted to Henry VI. The collectors, accounting in the Exchequer, admitted not having taken anything from the rector by reason of his patent and asked to be discharged. The rector was called in to justify his privilege and pleaded his patent, to which the king demurred.

The rector was seeking to avoid a clerical tax, though his patent was broader. As observed in the text, the discussion of the case—in contrast to those below—makes nothing of the clerical character of the tax; all that is argued could as well be said of a lay parliamentary tax and an exemption held by a layman. I do not find this completely unsurprising. For purposes of the particular tax in question, if not in general *quoad* the act of voting a tax, the clergy was in effect taken as a "house" of Parliament. What account should be given of that? What is manifest is that the Convocation of Canterbury in the cases below was *not* treated as quasi Parliament.

Structure of the report: There are twenty-six speeches from bar and bench. Twelve individual lawyers and judges speak. Twenty-four speeches are on the substance. The other two are transitional remarks from the bench—an invitation to discuss an issue other than the main ones and a remark by the chief baron that the case required careful consideration, especially because there were several abbeys with tax exemptions similar to the rector's (in other words, "This is an important tax case"). Eight speeches are on the king's side, one is ambiguous in that it favors the rector on the merits but the king on a point of procedure, one is ambiguous in that it favors the rector in the instant case on narrow grounds while favoring one of the general doctrines urged on the king's side. Two speeches on the king's side (Newton) are noted as made "for the sake of argument." Fourteen are on the rector's side, except that one of those, by the king's principal lawyer (Fortescue), comes only to conceding the procedural point to the rector (which may have been thought in the king's interest, because all that was sacrificed was potential delay; i.e., yielding the point would expedite settlement of the case in its present form; objection to doing that came from the bench on two judges' initiative).

Most of the speeches are on one or both of the two major points discussed in the text: (1) validity of the king's patent; (2) conceding the patent's validity, whether Parliament's voting the tax in general terms destroys the exemption. Two further questions were raised. Issue (3) was whether the rector's patent exempted him from paying tax calculated on the value of property acquired after he received the patent. (This point was raised by Fray and answered by one speech from the bar, in favor of the rector—i.e., subsequent acquisitions were covered. Because the matter does not recur, it must be assumed that the answer seemed satisfactory and that the king's counsel saw no advantage in pressing the point. The issue does not transcend construction of the patent, but the answer could have an effect on the perception of [1]. Taking the king to have exempted the rector from taxes on all property he might acquire, as well as what he already had, the patent's validity becomes more portentous, for the king had purported to alienate an indefinitely large piece of potential revenue.) Issue (4) was whether, conceding the substance to the rector, it was procedurally correct to let him plead his patent *defensively*. (Two judges thought not—i.e., thought the rector should lose in the present proceeding, but that his right not to be taxed should be protected by other means, either a special writ to the Exchequer directing that he not be charged or by petition to the king. They took this position on a private-law analogy: in various situations, private parties' grants could not be pleaded in defense when the grantee was sued for that which the grant was meant to protect him from being sued for; instead, he was driven to action of covenant for breach of the grant. Fortescue, representing the king, argued *contra* and disputed some of the private law on which the analogy was based. He was backed up by one judge. Because a definitive outcome is not reported, which side prevailed on this procedural question is uncertain.)

On the principal issues: The king's side on (1) is argued for five times pretty much in isolation, though two remarks are perhaps to be taken as saying that (1) and (2) cannot be separated. The rector's side on (1) is defended in seven speeches, and one additional remark implies agreement with it. On (2), the king's position is stated or defended independently four times, but two such remarks (Newton) are noted "for the sake of argument" and one is only a defense of the general principle, accompanied by a concession that the exemption is not destroyed on the facts of the instant case. The rector's position is defended six times. Looking at the matter in this mechanical way helps to enforce the point that whereas (1) is pressed hard on both sides, (2) is broached and then argued for rather slenderly, and opposition to it is voiced by several speakers. In fact, the king's position was an extreme or too-clever one. It was not fought for by his counsel. It intrigued Newton, but he was not willing to come out for it. In an important sense, the case was seriously about the limits of the king's granting prerogative.

Lawyers and judges, result: The report gives the arguments on three separate days and then ends with an adjournment, beyond which there is no further information about the case. Therefore no outcome is known with certainty. The judicial opinion communicated by the report is summarized here. There is of course no guarantee that judges did not change their minds. However, the judicial wind was blowing strongly, though not unanimously, in the rector's favor; see the observations on the final debate below.

1. Fortescue. On the first two days of debate king's attorney; on the last C.J.K.B. As judge, strongly for the rector on (2). He does not in terms repudiate his earlier position as lawyer that the patent was invalid, but there is not much point in taking a decided view on (2) unless one has conceded its validity. He probably at least acknowledged that the votes were on the rector's side on (1).

2. Fray, C.B. Strongly on the rector's side on (1). Does not speak to (2) expressly, but one speech puts him on the rector's side by clear implication. Against the rector on (4) if he was not persuaded the other way.

3. Ayscoghe, J.C.P. In one speech on the first day of debate favors the king on (1). No position on (2).

4. Hunt, B. For rector on (1), no position on (2).

5. Paston, J.C.P. For rector on (1) and (4), no position on (2).

6. Newton, C.J.C.P. In two speeches "for the sake of argument" defends the king's position on both (1) and (2).

7. Hody, C.J.K.B. Speaks on first two days of debate, died before third day. For rector on both (1) and (2).

8. Fulthorpe, J.C.P. Speaks only on (4), against the rector. To be worried about the rector's power to plead his patent may imply agreement with his substantive case (Fray's position), but it does not have to.

Lawyers in the case besides Fortescue are Yelverton and Markham for the rector and Vampage for the king. Haydock speaks from the bar only in response to Fray's invitation to address (3)—in the rector's favor, whether speaking for himself or as one of the rector's counsel.

The report of the third day's discussion is significant for the case's probable outcome. On that day, the rector's counsel, Markham, appears with a fresh argument on (2) only. Nothing is said on the king's side on (1), implying that the validity of the patent was regarded as established, at least as the majority opinion. After Fortescue, now chief justice, has expressed himself strongly for the rector on (2), the king's remaining lawyer, Vampage, in effect throws in the towel for the purposes of the present case. He concedes that the exemption was not destroyed, but argues that the survival of the privilege need not be grounded on the doctrine that acts of Parliament leave special privileges intact unless they abolish them expressly. Vampage's concession and argument are based on the idea (which of course the king's lawyers had not thought of before) that the act of Parliament in *this* case saved the privilege by its words—not directly, but by effect of language appearing to tax what was "usually" taxed, whereas the rector had not usually been taxed. Vampage's maneuver would seem to proceed from his realization that the king was not going to win on the general doctrine that acts that do not save privileges destroy them without express language. The government was running for narrow grounds—"Let the rector go. Do not make unnecessary high-level law. Leave it open to us to reargue our general doctrine in a stronger case." Fortescue (not the only government lawyer to change his tune on the bench) wants none of that: he tells Vampage rather sharply that the rector's basis for winning was *not* the narrow one proposed; he would win if the implied saving of his privilege did not exist, so long as the exemption was not expressly abolished by Parliament; the basis for the rector's winning was the opposite of the general doctrine the government had been urging.

II. *Prior of Leeds.*

Mich. 20 Hen. 6, pl. 25 (autumn 1441). The case is contemporary with *Rector of Edington.* The report appears to deal with a single debate held before the final discussion in *Rector of Edington.* (Hody speaks and Fortescue appears as the king's counsel.) In the text, as there stated, the three reports grouped as Convocation cases are treated as one case. My discussion is mostly about the elaborately argued *Abbot of Waltham*—III below—but because the major issues in *Leeds* are essentially the same, I cite speeches from the earlier case as well as from *Waltham* as instances of the arguments reviewed in the text.

Unlike the other cases, *Leeds* is reprinted with the help of manuscripts and accompanied with the record (*Select Cases in the Exchequer Chamber*, ed. Mary Hemmant, Selden Society, vol. 51 [London, 1933], pp. 84 ff.). Though the record contributes many interesting details about Exchequer practice and the exact complexion of the case, I do not believe it affects any use I make of the black-letter version, which Plucknett was going on. The record indicates that the case was mooted without final decision on the merits; the actual result is more than consistent with the Year Book's testimony that the king was unlikely to win.

Facts: The exemption from collectorship was granted to the prior as a natural person for his life. The Canterbury Convocation voted a tenth with the proviso "that no privileged person be discharged from the collectorship thereof." Following normal procedure, the archbishop certified to the king what the clergy had voted and the king instructed the archbishop to levy the money. The prior was appointed collector and, being requested for payment, showed his patent and asked to be discharged.

Report and judicial inclinations: Only the two main issues common to the Convocation cases were raised and only some of the arguments bearing on them taken up. Issue (1) was the validity of the patent; issue (2) was, conceding validity, whether the privilege was waived.

A majority of the judges heard from favor the exemptee, with one dissent by a common-law judge, the chancellor, who also participated, siding with the dissenter.

1. Fray, C.B. On (1), the patent is not invalid for the reason originally urged by the king's counsel—viz., that the patent is a temporal thing purporting to exempt from a spiritual office. No sign that other arguments occur to him. On (2), no waiver because the conduct of a member of Convocation will not affect his rights as an individual.

2. Hody, C.J.K.B. Amounts to the same as Fray, with an additional reason on (2)—the spiritual Convocation cannot destroy a temporal right based on patent.

3. Newton, C.J.C.P. (2) only. Agrees with Hody that temporal rights cannot be hurt by spiritual events.

4. Ayscoghe, J.C.P. Does not speak to (1), but clear from his position on (2) that he regards the patent as valid at least as against the argument that it is null as a temporal attempt to grant away a spiritual thing. On (2), disagrees with the view that acts in the spiritual sphere cannot destroy interests in the temporal and supports his position with an example from the law of presentation to ecclesiastical livings. It seems clear that Ayscoghe thinks the exemptee's conduct in Convocation *did* amount to waiving the privilege.

5. Chancellor. Agrees with Ayscoghe and asserts more clearly that the privilege was indeed waived—viz., by the exemptee's silence in Convocation. Queried by the reporter for attaching too much or too certain significance to silence.

6. Paston, J.C.P. Disagrees with Ayscoghe and with the presentation-law example as interpreted by Ayscoghe. Therefore, Paston seems to be aligned with Fray et al. on (2), with the same implication that the patent was valid.

The lawyers in the report are both for the king. Portington argues that the patent was invalid as a temporal act purporting to grant a spiritual thing and that the exemptee had waived his privilege by failing to protest in Convocation. At the end of the report, Fortescue makes a different argument on (1) (confirming that a fresh argument on [1] was necessary)—viz., the patent is prejudicial (to the bishop). No response to Fortescue reported.

III. *Abbot of Waltham.*
Mich. 21 Edw. 4, pl. 6 (autumn 1481). Three days of debate are reported, with no indication that they are not all in the same term. The reporter says there was a fourth day (*in medias res*) on which he was absent.

Facts: By virtue of a long quotation from the pleadings in the report, several factual refinements are available, but it is unnecessary to take account of those here. There is no critical difference from *Prior of Leeds*. Here the patent was old (Richard II) and corporate. Convocation formulated its proviso purporting to cut off exemptions somewhat differently, presumably in the hope of making it more surefire (providing that after appointment of a collector was reported to the Exchequer, said appointment should not be "repealed," and that the Exchequer should not take any steps to secure the appointment of someone else, notwithstanding any patents of exemption that might exist). The appointment of the patent-holding abbot in this case was the work of the bishop of Winchester—that is, he was appointed diocesan collector (thus drawn from the pool of eligibles from a single diocese).

Structure and outcome: There are twenty speeches by thirteen lawyers. King's side: Catesby, Pigot, Danvers, Keeble, Redmayne, Baker. Abbot's: Vavasour, Starkey, Browne, Brigges, Ludworth, Rede, Philpot.

Issues: (1) validity of the patent; (2) whether, even if valid, the privilege is waived; (3) whether the patent, referring to subsidies granted by the clergy of England, applies to a subsidy granted by the clergy of a single province; (4) two pure pleading questions—(*a*) whether, because the patent recited a consideration for granting the privilege, the abbot's plea need allege that the consideration (the monastery's maintaining a free chapel) was fulfilled, and (*b*) whether matter of record mentioned in the abbot's plea was properly alleged (fully enough, or with sufficient recitation beyond a mere reference).

Toward the end of the report, Huse, C.J.K.B., gives what is represented as the unanimous opinion of the judges:

On (1), the patent is not invalid as prejudicial. Nothing said about other arguments against its validity, but it is clear enough that the judges agreed that there was no basis for invalidating it.

On (2), without explanation, the privilege is not waived. Alternate waiver theories and alternative arguments against them not distinguished.

On (3), the patent is held to apply to the present provincial tax. In Huse's own opinion, at least, the patent should not be construed liberally, and, taken strictly, it does not apply. However, Huse does not propose to push this point because the patent is ancient and has been allowed before. (It may be that on this issue Huse in effect declined to dissent. There was some judicial opinion against him unless he had persuaded his brethren.)

Shortly after this opinion on the substance, Huse rejects for himself the view that (4*a*) cut against the abbot, and we are told that the others agree, probably with the exception of Brian, who originally expressed the view. The discussion then turns to (4*b*), on which the judges eventually reach unanimous agreement against the abbot. That is, his pleading on that highly technical point was fatally defective, wherefore judgment is given that he be charged with the collection this time, without prejudice to his substantive right to be discharged in the future.

Individual judicial expressions:

> 1. Nottingham, C.B. On (1), patent invalid as prejudicial (both to the bishop and to coeligibles). On (2), abbot's conduct would have waived the privilege if it were valid.
>
> 2. Jenney, J.K.B. On (1), patent not invalid as a temporal

act purporting to grant a spiritual thing. No opinion on (2). On (3), patent should be construed liberally and applies.

3. Fairfax, J.K.B. On (1), not invalid as prejudicial, and clearly Fairfax does not think it invalid on any other ground. On (2), arguments designed to make out that the privilege was waived are generally incorrect; nothing would count as waiver except failure to plead the patent. On (3), patent applies, liberal construction. On (*4a*), the pleading point is not against the abbot.

4. Choke, J.C.P. On (1), patent not invalid either for prejudice or for violating the temporal-spiritual line. No opinion expressed on (2). On (3), patent applies, liberal construction.

5. Brian, C.J.C.P. On (1), patent is valid. No opinion expressed on (2). On (3), patent applies, not necessarily because it should be construed liberally, but because, as Brian reads it, it applies even if taken strictly. On (4a), the pleading point goes against the abbot.

IV. *Abbot of Shrewsbury.*

Mich. 2 Ric. 3, pl. 9 (autumn 1484). To this fourth report, Plucknett attached considerable significance. It seemed to him to reflect a more modern and more public approach to the issues than its predecessors. I think that is entirely mistaken. Plucknett was deceived by the brevity of this memorandum-report. It lacks the intricate arguments and private analogies only because it is little more than a summary of conclusions. The conclusions basically agree with *Leeds* and *Waltham*, from which it is in no material way different. Plucknett came upon this case with a misleading interpretation of the others and for that reason was impressed by superficial differences. Herewith my view of as much as need be said about *Shrewsbury* (of which I make virtually no use in the text, for it contributes only a couple of detailed twists).

The report summarizes the apparently unanimous opinion of the judges on four questions:

1. The space is mostly taken up by whether a patent covering subsidies given by the clergy of England covers a provincial subsidy. The apparent importance of this question is quite consistent with *Waltham*; liberal or reasonable construction in the light of usage was endorsed.

2. The king's grant of exemption from collectorship was apparently attacked only as an invasion of the spiritual sphere, as if to suggest that this reason seemed the best bet in the light of recent experience with other reasons. The patent was upheld, with a different emphasis as to why the office was temporal and therefore exemptable. (The bishop's appointment of a collector was pursuant to the king's instructions.)

3. A proviso by Convocation similar to those in the other cases was, as before, held ineffectual to destroy the exemption. So far as can

be gathered from a brief report, the king's attempt was to sell the "complicity" theory; there is no mention of the abbot's behavior in Convocation.

4. The one original question—presumably factually unique to this case—was whether the abbot, who as collector for a different diocese had chosen not to plead his privilege, had waived the right to plead it *quoad* the diocese here in question. Held: no waiver—that is, he was not estopped by an act that one might suppose to be more meaningful than failure to protest in Convocation.

9 The Tudor Revival of Quo Warranto and Local Contributions to State Building

Harold Garrett-Goodyear

Two centuries separated the quo warranto proceedings ordered by Edward I[1] and the lectures by Robert Constable at Lincoln's Inn in 1494 on the law of quo warranto.[2] Between 1278 and 1294, Edward had used the action of quo warranto systematically to identify and recover fiscal, jurisdictional, and other regalian rights improperly held by his subjects. Whatever Edward's achievement—and the franchises recovered for the crown may have been few—the broad scope of his undertaking is evident both in his ordinances and in the bulky rolls of claims, titles, and pleadings that resulted from the quo warranto sessions before justices itinerant throughout most of England.[3] Prior to Constable's reading, however, little surviving evidence indicates that Edward's successors wished to repeat his efforts to investigate and challenge.[4] But following the reading at Lincoln's Inn, renewed interest in quo warranto is unmistakable. Other readings soon followed Constable's: the lectures of Edmund Dudley a few years later,[5] of William Marshall in 1516,[6] and of John Spelman in 1519[7] testify to sustained interest in the summons of quo warranto within the Inns of Court. More importantly, Henry VIII's attorneys—or people who acted in the king's name and ostensibly on his behalf—used quo warranto to challenge the titles by which some English-

1. Donald W. Sutherland, *Quo Warranto Proceedings in the Reign of Edward I, 1278–1294* (Oxford, 1963), esp. pp. 33–70.

2. British Library Lansdowne MS (hereafter cited as B.L. Lansd. MS) 1119, fols. 68v–72v; Samuel E. Thorne, Introduction to Robert Constable, *Prerogativa Regis* (New Haven, 1949), p. xlvi, n. 193.

3. *Placita de Quo Warranto*, ed. W. Illingsworth (London, 1818); Sutherland, *Quo Warranto*, pp. 176–89.

4. For evidence of occasional revivals and threats of eyres in the fourteenth and fifteenth centuries, see Bertha Putnam, *Proceedings before the Justices of the Peace in the Fourteenth and Fifteenth Centuries: Edward III to Richard III* (London, 1938), pp. xlvi–xlvii. Additional evidence for infrequent use of quo warranto before Henry VII includes Year Book 15 Edw. 4, ff. 6–8 (1475); *Calendar of Patent Rolls* (hereafter cited as *CPR*), *1467–1477* (London, 1900), p. 605; Public Record Office, Duchy of Lancaster (hereafter cited as DL) 42/19, fol. 97v; and Robert Somerville, *History of the Duchy of Lancaster*, vol. 1, *1265–1603* (London, 1953), pp. 252–53.

5. Cambridge University Library, MS Hh. 3. 10, fols. 1–18v (between Lent 1496 and Nov. 1503); Bertha Putnam, *Early Treatises on the Practice of the Justices of the Peace in the Fifteenth and Sixteenth Centuries* (Oxford, 1924), p. 183, n. 7.

6. Lincoln's Inn Library, Maynard MS 70, fols. 90–end; St. John's College (Cambridge), MS S. 28, fols. 162–84v; B.L. Lansd. MS 1122, fols. 35–81.

7. University of Nottingham MS MiL 18b; Gray's Inn Library, Chaloner MS (hereafter cited as G.I. Chal. MS), fols. 277–88; St. John's College (Cambridge) MS S. 28, fols. 147–60v.

men enjoyed hunting privileges, or held courts, or collected fines imposed by royal judges, or exercised any one of the various rights that were lumped under the label "franchises and liberties."

The records resulting from Tudor interest in quo warranto do not compare in bulk to the massive collection of cases recorded in Edward I's eyre rolls, but the evidence for renewed use of the royal action by which subjects had to answer for their franchises is substantial after the first decade of the sixteenth century. Twice, Henry VIII's government experimented with general summons of quo warranto, and the experiments produced proceedings on claims to franchises in the county of Middlesex and in the borough of King's Lynn between 1519 and 1524. After the latter date the government turned away from further trials of the proceedings before justices in eyre that had originally inspired lectures on quo warranto in the Inns of Court. But efforts devoted to explicating the law of quo warranto were not wasted, because individual actions against franchise holders, initiated by informations instead of the more traditional chancery writs, had become part of the routine responsibilities of the attorney general and the justices of King's Bench by the early 1520s. Last used extensively in the early fourteenth century, quo warranto had been revived and modified in the early sixteenth century, to survive as part of modern English judicial practice.

What prompted the interest of Tudor lawyers in quo warranto after almost two centuries of neglect? Why did they and royal justices experiment with the ancient general summons and adopt new forms for individual actions? What made quo warranto attractive enough that it became a permanent part of the crown's legal repertory? Answers to these questions are suggested by the nature of the franchises and liberties claimed in response to general summons or listed in informations: they were "royal rights in private hands," alike, and alike only, in that the king should have them unless a subject, if challenged, could produce title by grant or prescription and could demonstrate that he had used them properly.[8] Such rights might be deer parks and rabbit warrens; they also included rights that gave subjects potential royal revenues or fiscal advantages which the king ordinarily enjoyed by virtue of his feudal lordship. It was probably not a coincidence that the lawyers who explicated quo warranto also engaged frequently in analysis or implementation of *prerogativa regis*, and the links between the revival of quo warranto and the Tudors' discovery and transformation of *prerogativa regis*, described and analyzed by Professor Thorne and others, appear strong ones.[9] Quo warranto probably appealed to Tudor governments because,

8. This definition is Sutherland's (*Quo Warranto*, p. 6); in addition to his discussion of the rights and privileges classified as franchises and liberties, see W. H. Holdsworth, *A History of English Law*, 7th ed., vol. 1, ed. A. L. Goodhart and H. C. Hanbury with introduction and additions by S. B. Chrimes (1956; reprint ed., London, 1969), pp. 15*–25*, 87–176; and J. H. Baker, *An Introduction to English Legal History* (London, 1971), pp. 15–18.

9. Thorne, Introduction to *Prerogativa Regis*, p. v, n. 1. John Spelman as well as Robert

like *prerogativa regis*, it promised additional success in the campaign to recover and increase fiscal resources and political advantages lost or neglected during the fourteenth and fifteenth centuries.

But franchises and liberties included more than sources of profits and fiscal privileges; among them were jurisdictional rights and responsibilities that constituted the very stuff of governance in premodern Europe. In "private" hands were rights to regalian authority and jurisdiction that ranged from courts leet to commissions of the peace, from appointment of constables to nomination of coroners, from return and execution of royal writs to jurisdiction over suits begun by those writs. John Spelman recognized that quo warranto had a dimension different from investigations of the king's feudal rights when he reminded his listeners in 1519 that the king had a duty to prevent either usurpations or abuses of his authority and jurisdiction. Precisely because the king could use quo warranto to insist upon his exclusive responsibility for justice, Spelman explained, his procedures needed to be understood by lawyers.[10] Spelman's notion of the king's responsibility for justice and the oversight of franchisal jurisdiction was not new; his remarks could have been paraphrased from Bracton or from arguments of some of the lawyers who acted for Edward I in the course of thirteenth-century quo warranto proceedings.[11] In the context of modern scholarship on Tudor government, however, it is tempting to find in Spelman's justification for his reading the key both to the motives behind revival of quo warranto and to the significance of that revival in early Tudor history. In the judgment of Professor Elton, the late medieval problems of fragmented authority, competing jurisdictions, and areas exempt from royal control could have "no solution except for the crown to assert the exclusive and general competence of the state"; and Tudor sovereigns and their ministers, Elton and others argue, adopted the only available solution.[12] Quo warranto

Constable read on both quo warranto and *prerogativa regis* (ibid., p. li). On Dudley's association with implementation of *prerogativa regis*, see D. M. Brodie, "Edmund Dudley: Minister of Henry VII," *Transactions of the Royal Historical Society*, 4th ser. 15 (1932): 131–61, at 156. On the revival of the king's right to feudal incidents, see, in addition to Thorne's introduction to *Prerogativa Regis*, W. C. Richardson, *Tudor Chamber Administration, 1485–1547* (Baton Rouge, La., 1952), esp. pp. 120–21, 198–99; and Joel Hurstfield, *The Queen's Wards* (London, 1958).

10. University of Nottingham MS MiL 18b, fol. 1.

11. *Bracton De Legibus et Consuetudinibus Angliae*, ed. George E. Woodbine, trans. with revisions and notes by Samuel E. Thorne, 4 vols. (Cambridge, Mass., 1968–77), fols. 55b–56 (2:166–67); Sutherland, *Quo Warranto*, pp. 182–84.

12. G. R. Elton, *England under the Tudors*, 2d ed. (London, 1974), pp. 14–15. Arthur J. Slavin, *The Precarious Balance: English Government and Society, 1450–1640* (New York, 1973), pp. 79–80, 85, 146, and elsewhere, makes a similar argument, as does, less emphatically, D. M. Loades, *Politics and the Nation, 1450–1660: Obedience, Resistance and Public Order* (London, 1974), pp. 129, 175. In addition to such opinions expressed in recent textbook surveys, see the similar judgments found in the following specialized studies: Helen Cam, "The Decline and Fall of English Feudalism," in her *Liberties and Communities in Medieval England* (1944; reprint ed., with corrections, London, 1963), pp. 205–22; Helen Cam, "The Evolution of the Medieval English Franchise," *Speculum* 32 (1957):

proceedings, in which monarchs challenged subjects who claimed authority and jurisdiction like that of the king himself, appear an obvious tactic for governments determined to establish a monopoly on public jurisdiction and law enforcement and to destroy all obstacles to that monopoly. Almost forty years ago, Professor Cam, who had little more than Edmund Dudley's reading on which to assess interest in quo warranto, pointed to this explanation for its revival when she suggested that readers on the ancient statute were outlining a "programme for the attack upon the franchises by the Tudor judges." The law of quo warranto, she speculated, threatened the existence of franchises well before Henry VIII and Thomas Cromwell launched a direct attack on them in the Reformation Parliament.[13]

I began systematic investigation of quo warranto fully expecting to find that legal encounters between early Tudor monarchs and their subjects over franchises would help clarify the steps by which the Tudors launched the English state upon "its career of exclusive and all-embracing power."[14] But the longer I examined results and royal conduct of experiments with general quo warranto sessions and the more durable innovations that characterized revival of quo warranto prosecutions in King's Bench, the less confident I became that Henry VIII's government was using quo warranto to suppress rival jurisdictions or immunities. And in time, I began to wonder whether early Tudor governments were indeed committed firmly and consistently to a policy that would destroy franchises in order to solve the problems created by franchises and liberties. Franchises were losing much of their former importance in local governance, and some early Tudor ministers recognized the liabilities incurred by tolerating immunities; but the evidence of the quo warranto revival did not confirm that the declining role of private jurisdictions owed very much to royal decisions or actions. Although royal lawyers and justices revived and refashioned a procedure by which they could force subjects to defend private interests in public authority, and although those procedures were used on a scale unmatched for the previous two centuries, the results from the proceedings proved strikingly small if measured by rights recovered or the number of jurisdictions eliminated or curtailed.

Negligible results from quo warranto proceedings by themselves do not mean that Henry VIII or his ministers were ready to tolerate private exercise of royal authority or immunities from the king's own adminis-

427–42; I. D. Thornley, "The Destruction of Sanctuary," in *Tudor Studies Presented . . . to Albert Frederick Pollard*, ed. R. W. Seton-Watson (London, 1924), pp. 182–207; and R. R. Reid, *The King's Council in the North* (London, 1921), pp. 1–21, 116–17.

13. "The Decline and Fall of English Feudalism," pp. 216–17. For a similar argument regarding quo warranto in Cheshire, see Geoffrey Barraclough, "The Earldom and County Palatine of Chester," *Transactions of the Historical Society of Lancashire and Cheshire* 103 (1952 for 1951): 23–57, at 44–45.

14. Elton, *England under the Tudors*, p. 14. Although my differences with Professor Elton will be evident, I depended heavily on his scholarship and I am grateful for the thoughtful reading that he gave an earlier version of this essay.

tration of justice and law enforcement. They do, however, challenge the convenient assumption that quo warranto was part of a Tudor process of "integration that was to knit together the regions and the center and finally sweep away the great lay and ecclesiastical franchise,"[15] and they even justify doubts that the Tudors pursued a consistent policy of "integration" at the expense of private interests in jurisdiction. To explain the revival of quo warranto without glossing over the limited impact that those proceedings had on franchises and their claimants, one cannot simply point to rivalry between monarchs bent upon centralizing and rationalizing government and lords of liberties equally determined to resist encroachment by the central government. The search for a more satisfying interpretation takes one behind the unity and coherence of purpose proclaimed on the face of the king's general summons and informations, to competing and sometimes contradictory objectives within the government that put a consistent policy of destruction beyond reach. And it leads beyond the contest between monarch and franchise holder described in the plea rolls, to local rivalries in which the crown could play only a limited role, and seldom the role that initiated or controlled events. By looking for different goals among the king's ministers and agents responsible for quo warranto, it is possible to see not only the royalist objectives that threatened the existence of franchises, but also the interests within the central government that helped to preserve franchises. And by looking at the rivalries within local communities, it is possible to see not only subjects whose private interests in jurisdiction prompted their resistance to royal expansion but also subjects who, probably with little thought for the king's advantage, saw in quo warranto a tactic useful for their own local and private ends. And in the context of competing goals within the government and of rivalries over franchises in local communities, both the revival and the limited consequences of quo warranto are understandable.

The analysis of the revival of quo warranto under Henry VIII that follows begins with a survey of the conduct and results of the general sessions for Middlesex and Bishop's Lynn (now King's Lynn) and a similar survey of the procedural innovations that accompanied renewed prosecutions in King's Bench, along with the outcome of those prosecutions. Such a survey is needed because the Tudor revival of quo warranto has had no chronicler;[16] but it is primarily designed to illustrate reasons for doubting that the revived proceedings were part of an aggressive campaign against private jurisdiction. Once the limited gains made by the government against franchise holders have been established, we shall look more closely at the circumstances of the general summons and at the opinions expressed at the time by royal justices, ministers, and lawyers. Thanks to reports of discussions over quo warranto and franchises gen-

15. Slavin, *The Precarious Balance*, p. 85.

16. Scholars have, of course, discussed some features of early Tudor quo warranto proceedings, and their works are cited below at appropriate places. No one has yet attempted a general survey.

erated by the initiative of 1519, we are permitted a glimpse of differences among those acting ostensibly for the king's advantage and against claimants of liberties. And in the case of Bishop's Lynn, we can reconstruct much of the local context that shaped the government's decisions and helped to determine the eventual results of the general summons. In the third part of this analysis, the several categories into which informations can be grouped are used to suggest that, although fiscal motives lay behind some of the government's prosecutions, other cases had their origins in local struggles to which the government was only one, and perhaps the least important, party. The conclusion attempts an assessment of the implications of the quo warranto revival not only for our understanding of Tudor policy toward franchises and liberties, but also for our understanding of the Tudor contribution to state building.

I

Interest in quo warranto before Henry VIII's reign was not entirely restricted to lawyers reading on Edward I's ordinances. A general summons for the county palatine of Chester brought sixty-six claims to franchises and liberties in 1499.[17] The summons of that year, however, issued not in Henry VII's name but in that of Arthur, Henry's son and the titular earl of Chester, and it may have been less a signal of new intentions toward franchises than a survival within the county palatine of a practice abandoned elsewhere long before.[18] Possibly more significant for the history of quo warranto were the three writs that issued during the spring of 1505 against Henry Lord Clifford for his hereditary sheriffwick of Westmoreland,[19] against William Lord Tailboys for his extensive

17. Public Record Office, Chester 38/26/9, 34/3, and 34/4; and for an account of the proceedings, see R. Stewart-Brown, "The Cheshire Writs of Quo Warranto in 1499," *English Historical Review* 49 (1934): 676–84.

18. Stewart-Brown, "The Cheshire Writs," p. 677, suggests that although the eyre for pleas of quo warranto had been introduced in Chester only after it had been abandoned elsewhere, it had not been used for almost a century and a half. On the other hand, a general summons of quo warranto had ordinarily accompanied the great sessions during the fifteenth century in marcher lordships, where the practice was used almost exclusively to raise money for the marcher lords: see *The Marcher Lordships of South Wales, 1415–1536: Select Documents*, ed. T. B. Pugh (Cardiff, 1963), pp. 6–7, 40–43, and also 21, 27–28, 31, 84–86, 101, and 113–14, for records of quo warranto summons, claims, and pardons in return for a collective fine. Not long before the quo warranto for the county palatine of Chester, the bishop of Durham used quo warranto to strengthen his revenues and power in his county palatine (G. T. Lapsley, *The County Palatine of Durham* [Cambridge, Mass., 1900], pp. 34–35). There is also some evidence that the county palatine of Lancaster may have been the scene of quo warranto proceedings similar in scale to those found in Chester (*CPR, 1485–1494* [London, 1914], p. 439; Ramsey Muir and Edith Platt, *A History of Municipal Government in Liverpool* [London, 1906], p. 401).

19. Public Record Office, King's Bench (hereafter cited as KB) 27/977, Rex m. 14; KB 29/135, m. 14; Public Record Office, Chancery (hereafter cited as C) 43/1, nos. 1, 4.

jurisdictional and fiscal rights in the border liberty of Redesdale,[20] and against Thomas Lord Dacre for similar franchises in the lordship of Gillesland in Cumberland.[21] Neither the summons issued in the name of Earl Arthur nor the royal writs that summoned the three northern lords to King's Bench, however, reduced the number or extent of existing liberties. The bulky rolls produced by the Chester proceedings record little more than claims. Blank spaces on the rolls remain where challenges by the earl's attorney—other than the apparently perfunctory demands for definitions of ancient terms in claims—were to be entered, and no judgments have been found.[22] Proceedings, it seems likely, were terminated in return for fines from franchise holders in the county, and the sessions may have been designed from the outset to raise money, not to reform jurisdictional anomalies or to eliminate immunities within Chester.[23] Money also appears the most obvious result for Henry of the writs against Clifford, Dacre, and Tailboys, although there was at stake in one case a hereditary sheriffwick and in the other two cases, liberties that included appointment of justices of the peace and of gaol delivery and that excluded virtually all royal officers and justices.[24]

The isolated examples of quo warranto proceedings under Henry VII contrast with the firmer evidence of experimentation and systematic use of quo warranto in his son's reign. When John Spelman read on quo warranto in 1519, John Fineux, the chief justice of King's Bench, attended and took part in some of the arguments that accompanied the lectures.[25]

20. KB 27/976, Rex m. 16; KB 29/136, mm. 24, 27d; KB 29/137, m. 12; KB 145/9/23, mm. 215–16.

21. KB 27/975, Rex m. 11; KB 29/135, m. 32.

22. For the principal roll of pleas, see Public Record Office, Chester 34/4.

23. Stewart-Brown, "The Cheshire Writs," pp. 678–79; cf. Barraclough, "The Earldom and County Palatine of Chester," pp. 44–45.

24. Two days before Henry agreed to forgive Clifford's failure to defend himself and to recognize his title to the sheriffwick, Clifford bound himself in an obligation of four hundred marks, "for the general pardon . . . as touching the quo warranto for the sheriffwick of Westmoreland and intrusion of the coronage of the same" (B.L. Lansd. MS 160, fol. 311, printed in John Bruce, "A Second Letter on the Court of Star Chamber," *Archaeologia* 25 [1834]: 331–93, at 391; M. E. James, "The First Earl of Cumberland [1493–1542] and the Decline of Northern Feudalism," *Northern History* 1 [1966]: 43–69, at 44, n. 7). Tailboys received a pardon in Dec. 1508, and letters patent shortly afterwards conceded him anew the contested franchises, although no record of a payment has been found (KB 29/136, m. 27d; KB 27/998, Rex m. 13; Public Record Office, Exchequer [hereafter cited as E] 368/287, Easter *Recorda*, m. 15; *CPR, 1494–1509* [London, 1916], p. 611; *Letters and Papers, Foreign and Domestic, of the Reign of Henry VIII*, ed. John S. Brewer et al., 21 vols. and Addenda [London, 1862–1932] [hereafter cited as *LP*], 12 [pt. 1]: 273 [no. 595], for evidence of later possession of the liberty of Redesdale by the Tailboys family, contrary to M. E. James, "Obedience and Dissent in Henrician England: The Lincolnshire Rebellion, 1536," *Past and Present*, no. 48 [1970], pp. 3–78, at 46). Dacre's case disappears from the rolls without indication of the outcome.

25. Bodleian Library Rawlinson MS (hereafter cited as Bodl. Rawl. MS) C. 795, fols. 128–39; British Library Harleian MS (hereafter cited as B.L. Harl. MS) 5265, fols. 112–28v.

The chief justice's presence may be as significant as the lectures themselves, for a few months later he again debated points of quo warranto law when the cases were no longer hypothetical. As a result of a general summons that Fineux attested in June,[26] all of Henry VIII's subjects in Middlesex who claimed franchises or proprietary rights to royal offices had to submit and defend their titles before the justices of King's Bench, who sat in a special session convened to hear and adjudge the validity of such titles. Almost certainly the first general quo warranto sessions held in the king's own name since the fourteenth century, the Middlesex proceedings that began in August were impressive both in number and status of claimants. Over fifty claims were received, and among the claimants were prominent ecclesiastical lords and laymen like the abbot of Westminster, the mayor and citizens of London, and the archbishop of Canterbury. The survival of only fragmentary records unfortunately makes it difficult to determine whether the results of the proceedings were similarly impressive.[27] Chief Justice Fineux forced franchise holders in the county to acknowledge the king's stake in their franchises and his right to review their holdings in jurisdiction and other regalian benefits; the conduct of the proceedings included suspension of franchisal jurisdiction until claimants proved their right to have them, or at least until they had provided pledges that they would recompense the king for usurpation or abuse should the court eventually reject their claims.[28] A handful of reports show the judges weighing arguments over the validity of titles and the ways in which franchise holders had exercised their jurisdictional responsibilities, and in at least three cases the justices imposed fines for neglect and abuse before allowing claimants their franchises.[29] Such fines may have been common, but it is noteworthy that the justices imposed the fines in these cases after rejecting arguments that the claimants should

26. KB 27/1032, Rex m. 14; KB 29/151, m. 17d.

27. G.I. Chal. MS, fols. 288v–89, includes reports of cases; British Library Additional MS (hereafter cited as B.L. Add. MS) 25168, fols. 559–63, has transcripts of entries from what may have been rolls and writ files similar to those that survive from the Chester proceedings of 1499. John Spelman reported discussions of one case arising from claims before the King's Bench justices in their special session. His report can be read to mean that the proclamation of quo warranto for Middlesex was made after the general quo warranto for Bishop's Lynn (almost certainly in Aug. 1521, but no later than 31 Mar.–1 Apr. 1522); but he must have intended to say only that the discussion of the particular case occurred after he had returned from the quo warranto sessions in Bishop's Lynn (*The Reports of Sir John Spelman*, ed. J. H. Baker, 2 vols., Selden Society, vols. 93 [London, 1977] and 94 [1978], 1:199–200).

28. For Fineux's arguments on this point, see Keil. 196, 72 *English Reports* (hereafter cited as *Eng. Rep.*) 375; Bodl. Rawl. MS C. 705, fol. 129v; and G.I. Chal. MS, fol. 288v. For evidence of pledges by claimants, see B.L. Add. MS 25168, fols. 561v–62. London aldermen appointed persons to be bound in King's Bench for obtaining replevin of the liberties they had claimed (London Records Office, Repertory of the Court of Aldermen [hereafter cited as London Rep.], vol. 4, fol. 60). A plaintiff in a case of error later argued that the court of St. Katherine's Hospital had sat without jurisdiction because it had been in the king's hands by virtue of quo warranto proceedings (KB 27/1042, m. 70).

29. G.I. Chal. MS, fols. 288v–89v (John Newdegate); B.L. Add. MS 25168, fol. 562 (the archbishop of Canterbury); Westminster Abbey Muniments 12739 (the abbot of Westminster).

forfeit their franchises. The three fines are the only gains that can be firmly credited to the government's side, and the only other record of a final judgment from the proceedings shows a ruling in favor of the claimant.[30] At least seventeen of the claimants who appeared in 1519 were subsequently prosecuted by informations in King's Bench,[31] and those informations argue that the proceedings on the general summons, however profitable in monetary or political terms to the crown, had not given the king possession of the franchises claimed during the special quo warranto session. The Middlesex proceedings gave royal justices and lawyers practical acquaintance with the procedures and issues explained by readers on Edward I's ordinance on quo warranto; they put many Englishmen on notice that they were answerable for the titles by which they held royal jurisdiction, fiscal rights, and other privileges, and also for the use they made of them; and they may have added to the king's extraordinary revenues. But unless the scanty evidence is largely misleading, the justices left franchisal jurisdiction and immunities intact.

The general summons of quo warranto soon had another trial, although the second experiment covered a much smaller territory. Two years after Middlesex franchise holders submitted their claims, and indeed while the justices of King's Bench were still considering those claims,[32] Henry VIII, using the formula that originated with Edward I, authorized Robert Brudenell, Sir Richard Broke, and eight East Anglian gentlemen to hear and judge pleas of liberties and also grievances against franchisal and royal officers in Bishop's Lynn. The sessions, which began on 19 August 1521, were conducted by Brudenell and Broke along the lines laid out by Spelman in his readings and by Chief Justice Fineux during the proceedings two years earlier. Offices and franchises were suspended and all insignia of authority within the borough were surrendered into the hands of the justices at the outset of the sessions, and franchise holders appeared to claim the rights they had been using and to defend their titles.[33] Only six claimants appeared, and four of the claims,

30. E 368/300, *Recorda*, m. 6.

31. See the Appendix of King's Bench cases at the end of this essay (hereafter cited as App.), nos. 54, 56, 60–63, 71–72 (Hil. 1532); 73–77 (Trin. 1532); 103–4, 114 (1537); and 162 (1543). All of the defendants in these cases are included in the list of claimants recorded in B.L. Add. MS 25168, fols. 559v–60, and some of them are mentioned in the reports in G.I. Chal. MS, fols. 288v–89.

32. See above, at n. 27.

33. John Spelman, one of the bishop of Norwich's lawyers during the proceedings, reported briefly on the sessions in British Library Hargrave MS (hereafter cited as B.L. Harg. MS) 388, fols. 18–18v, printed in *Reports of Sir John Spelman*, 1:199–200. For the royal commission and the record of the bishop's claim and plea, see KB 27/1054, Rex m. 11; and for other claims, see DL 41/7/16. Although Baker places the eyre on 31 Mar.–1 Apr. 1522, claims were received and titles offered on 19–20 Aug. 1521. The later dates were the occasion of presentments on usurpations and abuses by jurors, again in sessions held by Brudenell, Broke, and others, possibly sitting by virtue of the same commission issued in the summer of 1521. Presentments by the jurors refer to the claim made on 19 Aug. by the bishop, against which the jurors contrast his practice in using his liberties (KB 27/1045, Rex m. 19).

for trading privileges or the right to constitute a social guild, left little mark on the records.[34] The liberties and franchises claimed by the burgesses of Lynn and by the bishop of Norwich, however, brought before the justices virtually the entire range of governmental authority and jurisdiction exercised within the borough; and Thomas Fitzhugh, the king's attorney, responded to the two claims with challenges that, if accepted by the special court, would have transferred direct responsibility for the governance of Lynn to the king's own hands. The justices sitting in Lynn did not, however, decide the merits of the claims or Fitzhugh's objections. When the bishop's lawyers asked for a delay to answer the king's attorney, Broke and Brudenell adjourned the sessions, although not before they had stipulated that local officials could exercise their duties only by special royal license until final judgments were given. In the following summer, justices of King's Bench formally took custody of the records by a writ of certiorari. The general pardon of 1523 ended further action on the claim by the townsmen of Lynn, as well as the perfunctory challenge to four other claimants; but the pointed exclusion of Bishop Nix's claim from the benefits of the pardon meant that Henry VIII might still acquire possession of the bishop's franchises and, as a result, take direct responsibility for a wide range of jurisdictional and administrative responsibilities in Lynn.[35] Yet when the proceedings were finally ended by a judgment on the bishop's claim in 1524, Nix remained lord of the town and retained title to the jurisdiction and authority that accompanied his lordship. The attorney general acquiesced in a judgment that the bishop should go *sine die*, his franchises still intact.[36]

Once more, in the summer of 1524, the king authorized commissioners to hear and weigh claims for franchises, this time in Norwich.[37] But no sessions were held, and the government thereafter abandoned attempts to imitate the general summons and the use of itinerant justices characteristic of Edward I's quo warranto campaign. The story of quo warranto during the first decades of Henry VIII's reign, however, included more than unsuccessful or temporary experiments with ancient procedures. Even before Fineux and his colleagues sat as special justices to hear claims from Middlesex franchise holders, less dramatic experiments with the form of individual actions were bringing franchise holders before the justices in their ordinary capacity. By the time the justices dismissed Bishop Nix and thereby ended experimentation with the general summons before justices assigned specifically to receive claims, proceedings against individuals or corporations based on informations were no longer exceptional items on the rolls of King's Bench.

34. The bishop of Ely and the burgesses of Cambridge claimed exemption from tolls, and St. George's Guild and the Guild of the Holy Trinity claimed corporate status (DL 41/7/16).

35. Stat. 15 Hen. 8, c. 17 (ix).

36. KB 27/1054, Rex m. 11.

37. "Doomsday Book," *The Records of the City of Norwich*, vol. 1, ed. W. Hudson and J. C. Tingey (Norwich and London, 1906), fol. 91v (p. 311); see also E 159/302, Mich. *Recorda*, m. 12; and *LP*, 4 (pt. 3):2556 (no. 5750 [ii]).

An assessment of the vigor with which Henry VIII's government pursued the advantages offered by quo warranto must finally rest on the outcome of the prosecutions initiated by the new procedure, which soon replaced the old writ of quo warranto. Henry VIII's attorney general, in the only three quo warranto prosecutions of that reign before royal justices, had relied on writs issued by Chancery. But in 1512 the new attorney general, John Ernley, bypassed Chancery to submit an information in King's Bench, charging that the abbot of Glastonbury had usurped a view of frankpledge and other liberties in the manor of Newton Castle, Gloucester.[38] Ernley and the court seem briefly to have remained undecided about the advantages of informations over Chancery writs, for Walter Trelawney was summoned to answer for franchises in Trinity 1516 by a writ of quo warranto in the ancient form. In the following term, however, Trelawney was again the defendant in quo warranto, this time as a result of an information alleging usurpation of franchises virtually identical to those named in the writ.[39] When seven actions of quo warranto were initiated the following year, all were begun by informations in King's Bench.[40] Individual prosecutions thereafter ordinarily began with an information in which the attorney general listed franchises allegedly used to the detriment of the king's authority and dignity, gave the duration for which they were illegally used, and requested the court to summon the defendant to show by what authority he had used them.[41] Ernley may have also been momentarily uncertain about the most appropriate court in which to bring his informations. In 1517 he informed the barons of the Exchequer that residents of Wenlok, Shropshire, had usurped the titles and functions of bailiffs and burgesses along with other

38. KB 9/964, m. 134.

39. The writ, dated 29 Apr., 8 Hen. 8, is recorded on both KB 9/148, m. 27d, and KB 27/1020, Rex m. 8; the information, KB 9/471, m. 4, was delivered in person by the attorney general in the Michaelmas term. The information is slightly more detailed than the writ; view of frankpledge was added to jurisdiction over pleas of "chattels and debts"; Trelawney was charged with refusing execution of royal writs and of prohibiting inhabitants from suing process outside the town.

40. App., nos. 3–9.

41. Show. 115–18, 89 *Eng. Rep.* 485–87, points to an increase in informations ex officio for prosecutions in King's Bench during Henry VIII's reign, and the adoption of quo warranto informations was probably part of larger changes in common-law procedures, changes that deserve further study. Holdsworth, *History of English Law*, 1:230, n. 4, points out the difference between judgments in proceedings by writ, which were binding on the king, and by information, which were not. Such a distinction between procedures, however, is ignored by Sir Edward Coke; see, for example, 9 Co. Rep. 24a, 77 *Eng. Rep.* 765, and Edward Coke, *Book of Entries* (London, 1614), fols. 540–43v, for the case of the abbot of Strata Marcella (1591). I am grateful to C. A. F. Meekings for his suggestion that the attorney general may have been moved by motives similar to those that led litigants in civil proceedings to use bills instead of writs: informations were cheaper and more convenient to use. Replacement of the writ of quo warranto, the king's "writ of right" for franchises, by an information alleging "trespass" against the king's prerogatives and dignity may also be comparable to the replacement of writs of right for subjects by other actions, including those of trespass (Holdsworth, *History of English Law*, 3d ed. [1944; reprint ed., London, 1966] 9:236; S. F. C. Milsom, *Historical Foundations of the Common Law* [London, 1969], pp. 54–57).

jurisdictional rights in the town; but a year later, Ernley submitted another information against the Wenlok residents, which differed little from that of 1517.[42] Instead of the Exchequer, however, King's Bench was the court chosen by Ernley on the latter occasion, and thereafter quo warranto informations, with only a few exceptions, were the responsibility of justices in King's Bench.[43]

During the period between the first use of an information and the end of Henry VIII's reign, numbers in each year varied widely, but few years passed without one or more prosecutions.[44] The total number of cases for the period—at least 188—does not compete for the label "campaign" given to Edward I's proceedings, and it falls far short of the number possible had the government continued the use of general summons. The number is even less impressive when we take into account actions that represent proceedings recommenced after the king's legal officers had neglected to pursue an earlier information against the same party. But contrasted to the use of quo warranto during the fifteenth century, the proceedings on informations testify that quo warranto had something to offer the king's ministers, or his subjects, or both. A review of the disposition of cases recorded on the court's rolls, however, reveals that informations did not offer the government many opportunities to reverse usurpations of illegal uses of franchises, the ostensible purpose of the prosecutions. Of forty-seven actions begun in King's Bench by the end of Hilary term 1529, only three brought victories for the king, and they resulted from disclaimers. At least two of the defendants had in fact assigned the coroners whom they disclaimed, but the government lost even fines for usurpations as a result of the general pardon of 1523, pleaded by all three of the defendants.[45] Quo warranto defendants before

42. E 159/206, Trin. *Recorda*, m. 9d (Exchequer information); KB 9/473, m. 103 (King's Bench information). E 159/270, Mich. *Recorda*, mm. 19, 23, contains similar informations against the abbot of St. Augustine's in 1493, the only such informations in Exchequer that I could find for Henry VII's reign.

43. An exceptional information of Nov. 1523, before the barons of the Exchequer, alleges that the men and inhabitants of the city of Norwich had usurped the king's authority by electing mayors and sheriffs: E 159/302, Mich. *Recorda*, m. 12. Occasional proceedings in the nature of quo warranto resulted from inquests before escheators or special commissioners later in Henry VIII's reign: E 368/298, East. *Recorda*, m. 1 (cf. E 150/475, m. 1); E 368/300, East. *Recorda*, mm. 5, 6, 15 (cf. E 150/480); and E 368/304, Mich. *Recorda*, m. 53, before escheators; and the following four actions initiated on the basis of presentments before commissioners who were assigned by Exchequer seal and sat during the autumn of 1521, in Westmoreland and Northamptonshire: E 368/296, Mich. *Recorda*, mm. 20, 21; E 368/296, East. *Recorda*, m. 31; and E 368/304, Trin. *Recorda*, m. 28. Fifteen actions were generated by Stat. 34 & 35 Hen. 8, c. 16, which was designed to eliminate confusion over monastic franchises by transferring them from the jurisdiction of Exchequer officers to the supervision of the Court of Augmentations: E 368/319, *Recorda*, mm. 28, 44, 48, 50, 61–62, 71–72, 77–78, 129; E 368/321, *Recorda*, mm. 16, 36, 50; and E 368/324, *Recorda*, m. 3.

44. All of the cases I have identified are arranged chronologically in the Appendix, with a brief summary of the franchises challenged and process on each information. Cross-references show the frequency of informations brought more than once.

45. App., nos. 5, 7, 13.

1529 pleaded more successfully than the king's attorney. Six of them between 1512 and Wolsey's fall in 1529 offered royal charters and confirmations that, despite demurrers in two cases, enabled all to go *sine die* with their right to appoint coroners unimpaired.[46] Two other defendants, the bailiffs of Kingston-upon-Thames and the burgesses of Wenlok, also went *sine die* after pleading Edward IV's letters patent for view of frankpledge and other liberties.[47] Of the actions begun before Hilary 1529, three were continued into the next decade, and in two cases the defendants finally submitted pleas in 1534 after discontinuances for eight and twelve years; both received favorable judgments. Eight informations were resubmitted in 1532, along with informations based on the Middlesex claims of 1519.

The government's conduct of quo warranto prosecutions produced similarly meager results during Cromwell's ascendancy. Thirty-four actions that challenged franchisal coroners between 1529 and the summer of 1540 produced only one victory for the king, and that victory rested on the lord's disclaimer.[48] Coroners of five boroughs were dismissed *sine die* and their rights to the offices affirmed on the basis of royal grants.[49] Four prelates also retained their rights to appoint coroners after submitting royal letters patent.[50] Northampton and the dean of St. Peter's, York, also left the court with their rights to have coroners still intact; according to the controlment rolls, no one bothered to prosecute.[51] Cryptic notations on the controlment rolls of *cess proc'* or *pard'* terminate other proceedings against coroners or those who appointed them, and other cases disappear from the rolls without any explanation.[52] In proceedings that did not originate on coroners' inquests, the government fared little better. Only twice did the attorney general even contest a plea offered by a defendant.[53] And on the one occasion on which franchises were ordered seized into the king's hands, the court gave the order only after the burgesses of Cambridge had defaulted following an initial appearance.[54] The attorney general and the government may have regarded the outcome of other cases as victories, even if no judgment for the crown was awarded. The earl of Essex, for example, won allowance of a con-

46. App., nos. 6 and 26, 8, 18, 19 and 44, 22 and 27, 37. Two more defendants went *sine die* in 1534: nos. 15, 29.

47. App., nos. 9, 10.

48. App., no. 127.

49. App., nos. 92, 100, 133, 138, 146.

50. App., nos. 83, 88 and 89, 95 and 97, 52.

51. App., nos. 79, 89, 131 and 132.

52. In only one case is a parliamentary pardon explicitly cited as the reason for dismissal: App., no. 87. In some cases, *pard'* or *cess proc'* indicates an end only to controlment roll entries, not to the prosecution; for example, such notations appear in entries for a defendant against whom a new information was submitted: nos. 67 and 119. In other cases, *pard'* marks the last appearance of a case, e.g., no. 106.

53. App., nos. 82 (in which the attorney general traversed a title based on prescription) and 102 (in which the attorney general pleaded a parliamentary resumption of the franchise under Edward IV).

54. App., no. 136.

tested fair only after he had purchased a new charter,[55] and full and partial disclaimers in at least six cases may have accomplished the government's objectives, if the alleged usurpations had in fact occurred.[56] Even if disclaimers are counted as royal successes, however, defendants appear both more aggressive in pleading and more successful with judgments, as eight of them summoned to answer for liberties other than appointment of coroners won allowance of their liberties.

Results of both the general summons and prosecutions in King's Bench, therefore, demonstrate indifference or ineptitude more than they reveal a determination to curtail private interests in royal authority and jurisdiction. Indirect benefits of the revived quo warranto proceedings, of course, may have been more significant than the handful of clear victories for the crown; the number of franchise holders who quietly abandoned use of franchises that could not be defended if subjected to critical scrutiny, or the number who conformed their use to royal requirements out of fear of prosecution, may be much larger than is apparent from the dispositions of cases on the rolls. The small number of defendants who lost their franchises as a direct result of quo warranto, however, cannot be completely overlooked in favor of intangible results, and the few judgments favorable to the crown do not appear highly effective deterrents to other subjects who might be tempted to retain franchises of doubtful origin or questionable use. The informations that were submitted more than once testify to persistence in pursuit of franchise holders, but the same informations also suggest that the king's law officers had been less than determined or aggressive prosecutors in the first instance.

Inherent limitations of judicial methods and legal process can in part account for the limited results produced by quo warranto, whether in the form of a general summons or in that of individual actions by information. Although skillful royalist lawyers could find and expand grounds on which the Tudor monarchs might challenge subjects' titles to fiscal privileges and jurisdictions, even as they had found grounds to increase the king's benefits from *prerogativa regis*, the readings that identified invalid claims and unlawful usages also spelled out conditions under which private rights to jurisdiction could be defended. Chief Justice Fineux may have learned something about the king's advantages from John Spelman's 1519 reading on quo warranto; but Bishop Nix also benefited from the lawyer's expert knowledge when he paid Spelman for his legal counsel during the proceedings on claims in Bishop's Lynn.[57] Although quo warranto offered the government legal principles and procedures to force franchise holders to account for the use of royal authority and jurisdiction, the very use of legal tactics set boundaries for the king's agents. Reliance on quo warranto informations in King's Bench meant that the government accepted not only the restraints imposed by the court's limited resources and time but also those created by legal

55. App., nos. 88 and 94.
56. App., nos. 78, 118, 119, 124, 130, 135.
57. *Reports of Sir John Spelman*, 1:199.

process and principles. At best quo warranto could contribute only to the "piecemeal tinkering" that, according to Professor Elton, the government replaced in the 1530s with more comprehensive and effective parliamentary measures for reforming franchises and immunities.[58]

Yet the crown's poor showing in quo warranto prosecutions is so striking that we must ask whether the government's infrequent victories reflected only the limits of legal process and the Tudors' respect for those limits. The campaign to restore and expand the king's revenues from his feudal lordship was also based on construction and application of legal principles and techniques, but the results there were scarcely negligible. Instead of trying to explain away the government's unimpressive performance with quo warranto, should we not ask whether franchises survived quo warranto challenges so often because the government of Henry VIII undertook no campaign, and had no plans, for the recovery and suppression of private interests in jurisdiction? And should we not go further and ask whether others had more to gain from attacks on franchises than Henry VIII's ministers, who would lend the king's name and procedures for such assaults, but not the time or energy necessary to make quo warranto an effective weapon in suppressing or curtailing franchises?

To suggest that Henry VIII's government did not pursue a consistent policy regarding quo warranto proceedings is not to argue that he lacked ministers who saw the wisdom of destroying franchises, nor is it to deny that some of them envisioned use of quo warranto for a campaign of recovery and curtailment. And to suggest that behind royalist language and forms were propertied subjects, able and eager to use the king's authority to advance their private and local interests, is not to argue that quo warranto added nothing to the king's power in local politics and administration. And even should analysis of quo warranto under Henry VIII demonstrate that his law officers did not use it to destroy or curtail franchises, conclusions based on quo warranto would have to be reconciled with Parliament's enactments, especially those of the 1530s, to reach a balanced assessment of Tudor "policy" toward private interests in authority or jurisdiction. But if we are to make sense out of the revival of quo warranto, we must forgo the clarity and neatness that come from an explanation that contrasts the king in pursuit of centralized authority and unified allegiance to individuals and communities jealous of local liberties but capable only of reaction to royal initiatives.

The following analysis of quo warranto initiatives under Henry VIII—first of experiments with general sessions in Middlesex and Bishop's Lynn, and then of proceedings on informations in King's Bench—does throw light on the steps by which Englishmen built a state with "exclusive and general competence." In the light shed by quo warranto, however, the Englishmen who built that state were not, as we have supposed,

58. *The Tudor Constitution: Documents and Commentary*, ed. G. R. Elton (Cambridge, 1960), p. 32.

usually agents of kings determined to unify administration of justice and to improve law-abiding orderliness through greater control from Westminster. They were often propertied subjects who used the forms and substance of royal authority for their personal and local ends, and who used them no less successfully than the king's ministers exploited local rivalries to their own and the king's political advantage.

II

For one seeking evidence that the Tudors revived quo warranto in order to reform abuses in local government and to eliminate obstacles between the king and his subjects, the reported arguments made by Chief Justice John Fineux are extremely welcome. During the year before he attested the writ of July 1519, which set in motion claims and trials of franchises within Middlesex, he had more than one occasion to talk about franchises and quo warranto. What he said on those occasions suggests strongly that he lent more than his name and presence to the undertaking of 1519. A few months before the general summons, when Fineux had joined arguments over quo warranto at Gray's Inn, his remarks left little doubt that he expected the king's justices to supervise rigorously inferior jurisdictions, including those held privately, and that general summons of quo warranto impressed him as a means to monitor and correct the use of franchisal rights. Fineux asserted that whether or not justices in eyre issued instructions that franchises should be seized into the king's hand, a franchise holder's failure to claim suspended his right to use franchises until he had sued for their return from the king. And, he added, should the franchise holder ignore several general summons, he would lose forever the opportunity to use the suspended franchises. Because "the king must see that justice is executed, since he is the head of justice," a franchise holder who refused to accept the scrutiny of royal justices must forfeit his estate, regardless of the origin of his title.[59]

Close to the time that Fineux debated academic points of quo warranto with Spelman and others, he presided over two cases that illustrated the problems created by proprietary rights in royal authority or jurisdiction and the need for an aggressive response to those problems. His comments during the cases argue that his interest in quo warranto was more than academic. One of the cases began with a Worcestershire indictment of 1516, in which Sir John Savage, the sheriff, was charged with wilful complicity in the escape of two prisoners. When the attorney general submitted the substance of the indictment to King's Bench in an information, the justices ordered the office seized, although Savage held it for life by letters patent. Savage, in Easter term of 1519, protested that he should not lose possession of his office until convicted of the charges against him.[60] King's Bench justices, led by Fineux, firmly rejected the protest

59. Bodl. Rawl. MS C. 705, fol. 129v.
60. KB 9/471, mm. 26–28; KB 9/472, m. 3; KB 29/148, m. 43; KB 27/1021, m. 21.

and pointed out that regardless of the estate created by the letter patent, he held the office on condition that he justify the king's confidence; on the presentment of wrongdoing alone, the king had cause to withdraw his confidence and deprive him of use of the office.[61] The chief justice made clear not only the principle on which Savage's argument failed, but also his conviction that the principle applied no less to franchises than to the life interest in the shrievalty: "All liberties and all such offices at their origins come from the king; and for this reason, by the intent of the law, all such liberties and offices shall be understood to be in the king's hands. Therefore, the king can at any time put them to their claim, that is, to show quo warranto or quo jure they claim such liberties and offices."[62] At least one of Fineux's fellow justices thought that the chief justice had gone further than necessary or acceptable to justify the seizure of Savage's office. Although Justice Conyngsby and other members of the bench agreed that they had succeeded to the responsibilities and powers of justices *ad omnia placita*, who had heard claims to franchises for Edward I, Conyngsby emphasized that neither the king nor his justices could seize an office or franchise and force the occupant to prove his right to its return unless the court had specific or particular cause on which to order seizure. Only after a general summons before justices in eyre were franchise holders obliged to seek return of their franchises from the king's hands, whether or not they were individually summoned. The justices' exchange over the respective powers of justices in eyre and King's Bench may explain why, when soon afterward a general summons required franchise holders to appear before justices of King's Bench to claim their rights, the writ was directed to the sheriff of the one county in which King's Bench was a permanent court *ad omnia placita*.

But more than the ease with which Fineux could convoke a general session of quo warranto in Middlesex may account for the decision to proceed there. In the second case that gave Fineux an opportunity to discuss quo warranto shortly before the summer of 1519, he had good cause to conclude that the problems generated by proprietary rights in jurisdiction existed not only in Worcestershire but also close to Westminster. Appropriately, it was Sir John Savage's son who revealed obstacles to royal authority in Middlesex at the same time that his father's case provoked Fineux's speculations about the advantages of a general summons. On an appeal of murder, the younger Savage was removed from the sanctuary he claimed in one of the Middlesex holdings of the prior of St. John of Jerusalem.[63] To his plea for return to the prior's privileged lands, Fineux responded with a blistering attack on all sanctuaries in which felons or traitors resided, save for those which could show that justices in eyre had previously allowed their titles to such immunities. Although, as the reporter of the case noted, others present for debate on

61. Keil. 194–96, 72 *Eng. Rep.* 372–75; Dyer 151, 73 *Eng. Rep.* 329–30.
62. Keil. 196, 72 *Eng. Rep.* 375.
63. KB 27/1020, m. 60; George Francis Savage-Armstrong, *The Ancient and Noble Family of the Savages of the Ards* (London, 1888), pp. 32–33.

the plea were less confident that claims for sanctuary had been required by eyre justices in the past,[64] Fineux had hit upon an effective basis for destroying sanctuaries. If a general summons did not exempt ecclesiastical claimants to sanctuary, moreover, not only the sanctuary rights of St. John of Jerusalem but also the privileged precincts of Westminster Abbey and St. Martin's-le-Grand were vulnerable to attack by the king's justices. The younger Savage's flight to sanctuary had demonstrated the obstacles to law enforcement that lay virtually at the court's doorstep, and Fineux had seized upon quo warranto both as grounds to invalidate titles to sanctuary and as a method for proceeding against them.

In the cases involving the two Savages, Fineux made clear his interest in quo warranto and his conviction that it should be used to review and correct, even to destroy, franchises and jurisdictional immunities. Not surprisingly, the same conviction characterized the chief justice's arguments in the handful of reports that survive for the general quo warranto sessions over which he presided in 1519,[65] and the opportunity he found then to implement his earlier opinions may have been an opportunity that he had created for himself. Most of the cases that can be traced directly to the general summons involved neither major jurisdictional franchises nor prominent immunities,[66] but Fineux did not relax his rigorous expectations simply because the franchises in question were relatively minor or common. He held claimants to a standard of performance that, if accepted by his colleagues, would have radically reduced the number of franchisal jurisdictions in Middlesex and deprived a large number of propertied residents of rights widely exercised by lords of manors. In arguments on John Newdegate's prescriptive claim to view of frankpledge, infangthief and outfangthief, and assize of bread and ale, for example, Fineux drew out clearly and emphatically the implications of the king's obligation to see justice done, regardless of his subjects' proprietary interests. The attorney general pleaded that because Newdegate lacked the tumbril and gallows needed to exercise his franchises, he had obviously failed to use them. Compounding the nonuse, he argued, Newdegate had, contrary to common law, substituted monetary fines for corporal punishment of second offenders against the assize of bread. If indeed the franchise had been given in order that justice should be administered to the king's subjects, Fineux argued, then failure to carry out the duty fully should be punished, not simply by the fine for nonuse proposed by readers on quo warranto, but by forfeiture. To emphasize the point, Fineux noted that the franchise "is granted as well for the commonwealth as for the advantage of the party; and it should be used, or else a

64. Keil. 188–90, 72 *Eng. Rep.* 365–69.

65. See G.I. Chal. MS, fols. 288v–89, for reports that appear at the end of a copy of Spelman's reading on quo warranto; and for Spelman's own brief report of issues raised by pleadings in the Middlesex proceedings, see B.L. Harg. MS 388, fols. 18–18v.

66. See the Middlesex informations summarized in the Appendix cited above, at n. 31.

forfeiture results." Misuse or nonuse of even one part of franchisal jurisdiction, moreover, justified forfeiture of the whole.[67]

Newdegate by no means lacked defenders, who responded that "nonuser is not grounds for forfeiture, because the liberty is granted to him to use if he wishes; and it is for his advantage." If he failed to use it, no harm occurred, because the offenses could be punished in the sheriff's tourn. For abusing the assize of bread, Newdegate's advocates agreed, a fine was appropriate, but forfeiture of his leet jurisdiction was an excessive penalty to pay for misuse of the assize. His defenders did not carry the day, but neither did Fineux impose his view on the court. In this case and in decisions on similar liberties claimed by the archbishop of Canterbury and the abbot of Westminster, a majority of the court took a middle position between Fineux and those lawyers who argued that nonuse should not prejudice an estate in jurisdiction. Newdegate, the archbishop, and the abbot were allowed to make fines.[68]

Had the court followed Fineux's lead, the proceedings of 1519 not only would have curtailed sharply franchisal jurisdictions in Middlesex but also would have established a precedent for similar assaults throughout England. But colleagues with a more conservative interpretation of quo warranto than Fineux's helped insure that the Middlesex proceedings would offer little precedent for using general summons for a broad campaign destructive of franchises. In the absence of complete records from the proceedings, no balance sheet can be drawn, but the existing reports and cases argue strongly that Fineux's fellow justices, in their reluctance to accept arguments destructive of proprietary interests in jurisdiction, produced more fines for the king than fundamental reforms or changes in the status of franchises.[69]

Whether Henry VIII shared Fineux's probable disappointment in the results of the general summons is unclear, but there are hints that Wolsey, Henry's principal counselor and minister, had less cause than the chief justice to regret the course followed by the court's majority. Wolsey had few legalistic scruples about overriding franchisal rights, and in his continuing struggle with the mayor and citizens of London, he may have welcomed proceedings that brought their liberties under review along

67. G.I. Chal. MS, fol. 288v. Other evidence also suggests that on procedural points and substantive issues, Fineux followed an emphatically "royalist" interpretation of quo warranto during the Middlesex proceedings. By convening the special session of the court for hearing claims, Fineux had suspended all franchises and offices held by letters patent: see above, at n. 28. In arguments on a prescriptive claim by the prioress of Clerkenwell, Fineux expressed willingness to treat all franchises held by prescription as invalid unless allowances in eyre could be shown, a position that would have ended many courts leet as well as sanctuary rights (G.I. Chal. MS, fol. 289).

68. G. I. Chal. MS, fol. 288v; B.L. Add. MS 25168, fol. 562; and Westminster Abbey Muniments 12739. For Spelman's and Richard Broke's opinions on the consequences of nonuse, see Bodl. Rawl. MS C. 705, fols. 132v–33v.

69. See the discussion of Middlesex proceedings, above, at nn. 25–31 and accompanying text.

with those of major ecclesiastical lords.[70] That he intended sweeping reform or curtailment of franchises and liberties is not, however, very likely. The proceedings could advance Wolsey's purpose, not by enforcing the superiority of the common-law courts over private jurisdictions or by eliminating immunities that excluded agents of royal justice and law enforcement, but by improving the minister's ability to get what he wanted from civic authorities. To Wolsey, redressing London's liberties meant the suppression of resistance to his demands for fiscal aid and for the nomination of officers within the city. This at least is how Wolsey's goals appeared to the Mercers, who later complained of his encroachments on the city's liberties,[71] and to the Grocers, who were forced to surrender their charter of liberties because Wolsey wanted the nomination of their officers.[72] Despite the general summons and its implied threat to the city's privileges, Wolsey's demands on Londoners faced continuing opposition; but the city's claim before royal justices may have given Wolsey a needed bargaining chip when the government had to overcome the city's resistance to a subsidy in 1523. Wolsey won the subsidy, but only in return for a general pardon that, among other benefits, ended proceedings on claims by London's authorities and other Middlesex franchise holders.[73] The subsidy should perhaps be counted among the principal returns from the quo warranto proceedings for Wolsey and, indeed, for the king.

A contrast between Wolsey's probable expectations from quo warranto and the goals pursued by Fineux was obvious before 1523. Although his reasons differed from those of Fineux's colleagues on the court, Wolsey showed himself as hesitant as they had been about Fineux's solution for sanctuary abuses. Conferences in Star Chamber during November 1519, when the privileges of the prior of St. John's and the abbot of Westminster were vigorously debated, cannot be traced directly to the general summons of the preceding July, but the timing of the debates points to a close connection between the two events. Consistently with his earlier positions, the chief justice insisted, with Wolsey present, that, whether for debtors or for felons, sanctuary could not be tolerated by the law of the land. Even the king, Fineux believed, was barred from making privileges so clearly contrary to law and good order. Wolsey did not deny that felonies committed by sanctuarymen who then escaped punishment by returning to the sanctuary must be stopped, but his remedy fell far

70. A. F. Pollard, *Wolsey, Church and State in Sixteenth-Century England*, 2d ed. (New York, 1953), p. 319; Helen Miller, "London and Parliament under Henry VIII," *Bulletin of the Institute of Historical Research* 35 (1962): 140–43.

71. Quoted by Miller, "London and Parliament," p. 142.

72. Public Record Office, Star Chamber (hereafter cited as STAC) 2/24/50. I am grateful to Dr. J. A. Guy for discussing this incident with me. Other evidence that civic governors in London faced threats to their independent authority as a result of Wolsey's conduct include London Rep., vol. 4, fols. 33–34; *LP*, 4 (pt. 1):97 (no. 245); and *LP*, 4 (pt. 2):1227 (no. 2749).

73. Stat. 15 Hen. 8, cc. 16 and 17, which pardons, inter alia, "all and every usurpacions of any liberties or fraunchesies non claymyng non usyng mysusyng and abusyng of liberties or fraunchesies."

short of the consequences implicit in Fineux's arguments. The cardinal proposed to establish more precisely and more narrowly the boundaries of privileged places, and he advocated an oath to be administered to each sanctuaryman, by virtue of which immunity from arrest would be stripped from felons who left sanctuary to commit another crime. Wolsey, as legate *a latere*, would administer the oath, according to his plan for correction of abuses.[74]

Wolsey's response to obstacles created both by London's liberties and by abuses of sanctuary rights was to circumscribe liberties more closely without destroying them. His remedy for the disorder generated by sanctuaries would have increased the legate's power among ecclesiastics like the abbot of Westminster, but it left unsolved the fundamental issues raised by the chief justice.[75] We can piece together from Fineux's comments on quo warranto a program for its use either to eliminate franchises or to integrate them firmly into royal law enforcement and administration of justice. From Wolsey's conduct, however, we can find little confirmation that Fineux's opinions were shared and implemented by Henry VIII's principal minister. Wolsey and his master stood to gain from implementing quo warranto against Middlesex franchise holders, and he may share responsibility with Fineux for the decision to issue a general summons; but the goals that Wolsey sought do not fit the rationale for quo warranto put forward by the chief justice. The more limited but better-documented proceedings of 1521 in Bishop's Lynn show even more clearly Cardinal Wolsey's readiness to take advantage of quo warranto, but they also point to differences between his expectations of quo warranto and those implicit in Fineux's arguments.

The forms observed by Broke and Brudenell in the 1521 sessions suggested only another attempt to enforce the king's responsibility to protect his prerogatives and oversee the use of his authority for doing justice.[76] The variations in the royal attorney's responses to the six claims submitted in Lynn, however, betray a purpose obscured by the language of the records. Thomas Fitzhugh gave only perfunctory attention to the exemption from tolls claimed by the bishop of Ely and the burgesses of Cambridge, and he similarly ignored the claim to corporate status made by St. George's Guild and the Guild of the Holy Trinity.[77] But in response to the claims and titles submitted by the burgesses of Lynn and by the town's lord, the bishop of Norwich, Fitzhugh took a much more aggressive posture. Against the burgesses, who claimed corporate status and the

74. Keil. 190–92, 72 *Eng. Rep.* 367–71, contains a report of the conferences, which continues without a break the report on the younger Savage's plea for restitution to the sanctuary of St. John's. Although Savage's plea and the prior of St. John's liberties probably helped to bring about the conferences, the participants made clear that more than Savage's plea was at stake.

75. Cf. the respective contributions of Fineux and Wolsey to the debate over ecclesiastical privileges during the Hunne affair in 1515, where a similar pattern is evident (Keil. 184–85, 72 *Eng. Rep.* 361–63).

76. See above, at nn. 33–36 and accompanying text.

77. DL 41/7/16.

right to elect a mayor and other officers, the royal attorney alleged failure to cite allowances in earlier eyres and argued that, despite their royal charters and confirmations, the nonclaim required forfeiture of the franchises. Even more striking was the scope of Fitzhugh's challenge to the extensive franchises of the bishop. He repeated his arguments against the burgesses' privileges, but he added further reasons why the justices should strip the bishop of his privileges and authority in Lynn. Because the bishop had failed to use his rights to appoint justices of the peace, to hold view of frankpledge and a hustings court, or to exercise return of writs, Fitzhugh argued that he ought to lose those rights regardless of recent charters for them from Edward IV and Henry VII. Although the royal attorney acknowledged that the bishop had indeed held the civil pleas which he claimed, the prelate's reliance on a deputy to the substeward, instead of the steward who by royal charter was authorized to hear pleas, was cause in the attorney's eyes for seizure of the jurisdiction. Bishop Nix was also charged with failure to maintain the equipment necessary for fully exercising leet jurisdiction, and with providing inadequate custody of prisoners in his gaol; if the justices accepted Fitzhugh's plea on these issues, the bishop should lose both his gaol and his leet jurisdiction to the king.[78]

Fitzhugh had exalted the king's responsibility for justice and law enforcement high above the proprietary interests of subjects, even of those who could cite recent royal charters to defend their interests. Significantly, he had insisted so emphatically on the superior responsibility of the king only against Lynn's lord. The four franchises ignored by Fitzhugh were minor compared to the privileges claimed by the town and the jurisdictional rights asserted by the bishop, but subsequent events suggest that the four minor claims were ignored by the government not because they were unimportant but as a result of Wolsey's preoccupation with controversy between Bishop Nix and the burgesses of the bishop's town. Two years after Broke and Brudenell adjourned the sessions without judgment on the pleas, and one year after the justices of King's Bench formally took custody of the records, the general pardon traded by Henry and Wolsey for a parliamentary subsidy removed the threat of further prosecution from the burgesses and the four claimants of relatively minor franchises. Bishop Nix and his claims, on the other hand, were excluded,[79] and shortly afterwards the government resumed active prosecution of Fitzhugh's pleas against the prelate's extensive secular authority in Lynn. Results of further proceedings were, at first glance, disappointing to the government. Citing a royal warrant, the attorney general accepted Nix's titles and agreed to a judgment dismissing the bishop with his franchises *sine die*.[80] The proceedings in Lynn had achieved little obvious change in the franchises of the bishop or the governance of the borough, and no obvious gain for the king.

78. DL 41/7/16; KB 27/1054, m. 11.
79. Stat. 15 Hen. 8, c. 17, (ix).
80. KB 27/1054, Rex m. 11.

Changes there were, however, and changes probably intended by Wolsey when the proceedings were conceived. Faced by a vigorous and often violent conflict between townsmen of Lynn and their episcopal lords, which stretched back to the fourteenth century, Wolsey intervened in the community's affairs soon after he reached power. Initially, his efforts as mediator met little success, and further violence and increased bitterness between municipal officials and the bishop's officers forced him to a more drastic remedy.[81] Against a bishop who had resisted compromise, quo warranto could intensify pressure for concessions. In a later assessment of Wolsey's achievements and failures, John Palsgrave noted that it was the cardinal who "put in execution the writ of quo warranto sued against my lord of Norwich";[82] whether the "writ" was the general summons of 1521 or the *scire facias* that reopened active prosecution in 1523, the result fitted Wolsey's dealings with the rival parties in Lynn. While Nix's lawyers conducted his defense against Fitzhugh's challenges in the quo warranto, they also negotiated with Wolsey on terms for a settlement with the Lynn burgesses. It was no coincidence that the attorney general abandoned prosecution of Nix shortly after the bishop and townsmen began arrangements for transferring the exercise of the bishop's jurisdiction and privileges by indenture.[83] The bishop's "victory" in the quo warranto pleadings was largely empty, because the judgment depended on an agreement that the townsmen should lease his jurisdictional and fiscal privileges on terms dictated by Wolsey. The government, however, also had no victory to show for its efforts, because the franchises remained intact. Only the people exercising them had changed.

At the time the government was concluding quo warranto process against Bishop Nix, Wolsey was probably responsible for the threat of a general summons against franchise holders in Norwich,[84] a threat intended for ends similar to those of the proceedings in Lynn. A summons for Norwich franchise holders in 1524 produced no claims or pleadings, perhaps because the undertaking lost its point when the city and the cathedral priory accepted a settlement, again dictated by Wolsey, in their long-standing controversy over the jurisdictional immunities and com-

81. Evidence of fifteenth-century conflicts, and of the role played by justices and other royal ministers in mediating the disputes, includes KB 27/644, Rex m. 14; Historical Manuscripts Commission (hereafter cited as Hist. MSS Comm.), *Eleventh Report*, app. 3 (London, 1887), pp. 245–46; and Lynn Borough Records, Assembly Book (hereafter cited as Lynn Ass. Bk.) 3:322, 323, 326, 341, 355, 357, 382, 431, 446. Growing bitterness early in Henry VIII's reign appears in the bishop's petition against a commission of the peace issued to the mayor and burgesses in 1512 (C 1/342/48) and in violence between townsmen and the bishop's bailiff in 1515 and 1520 (KB 27/1017, Rex m. 17; KB 27/1040, Rex m. 10). For the townsmen's complaints in 1521 about abuses by the bishop's officers, some of which may have aided Fitzhugh in his plea to Nix's claim, see KB 27/1045, Rex m. 19. For Wolsey's participation in negotiations, see Lynn Ass. Bk. 4, fols. 219v, 225v.

82. *LP*, 4 (pt. 3):2556 (no. 5750 [ii]).

83. STAC 2/34/20; Lynn Ass. Bk. 4, fols. 241, 249, 263v; Hist. MSS Comm., *Eleventh Report*, app. 3, p. 246.

84. *LP*, 4 (pt. 3):2556 (no. 5750 [ii]).

mercial rights of the monks.[85] In this controversy also, Wolsey had been playing an active part in negotiations, and the city's capitulation to terms favorable to the priory so soon after the summons was issued probably explains why nothing can be found to show that the government demanded or prosecuted claims there.[86]

The result of the summons threatened against Norwich franchise holders, as well as the outcome of the proceedings actually held in Middlesex and Lynn, demonstrated the ability of Wolsey and the central government to exploit general summons for aggressive and effective interference in local government. But interference was not reform. So long as Henry VIII's principal minister followed a course of personal intervention in local controversies and pursued immediate political and fiscal advantages against individual franchise holders, the general summons would not become an instrument for either systematic curtailment or supervision of franchisal jurisdictions. Although Wolsey's goals help to account for the revival of quo warranto, they also help to explain why the revival of the general sessions did not prove permanent. As a tactic for bending local authorities to his will, general sessions were expensive and cumbersome. If he wished to use quo warranto, individual actions could serve much the same purpose more efficiently; and Wolsey could rely on Star Chamber and Chancery, which he controlled directly, should he prefer judicial weapons that did not depend on cooperation from the common-law courts.[87] Whatever advantages Wolsey could secure from the experiments, his objectives gave him little stake in continuing them. More significantly, the advantages he sought were incompatible with the more systematic and fundamental challenge to franchisal jurisdiction implicit in Fineux's interpretation of quo warranto. Rivalries among franchise holders enabled Wolsey to impose his will upon local authorities and to increase their dependence on his judgment, and he took full advantage of competition for local jurisdiction to dictate terms to rivals. The result increased the personal role of the king's principal minister in local affairs, but the role he played—it must be emphasized—depended upon the *survival* of franchises.

The significance of the Tudors' brief experimentation with general

85. See above, n. 37; Norwich Record Office, Liber Albus, fols. 14v–20; and for evidence of Wolsey's active part in the negotiations, STAC 2/23/268 and 2/34/21.

86. A few informations similar to quo warranto actions were submitted to Henry VIII's Exchequer before 1543. Among them is one against the mayor and citizens of Norwich for abuse of their franchises, brought in 1523; it too may have induced concessions from the citizens: E 159/302, Mich. *Recorda*, m. 12.

87. Palsgrave pointed to Wolsey's readiness to intervene personally in local controversies as a weakness, and mentioned Bury St. Edmunds as well as Norwich as occasions on which Wolsey, although active, had solved little (*LP*, 4 [pt. 3]: 2556 [no. 5750 (ii)]). For Wolsey's reliance on conciliar jurisdiction in the case of conflict between the abbot and townsmen of Bury, see STAC 2/36/220 and 7/159–63; and for examples of similar activity in disputes in the two university towns, see Charles H. Cooper, *Annals of Cambridge*, 5 vols. (Cambridge, 1842–53), 1:323–24; *Medieval Archives of the University of Oxford*, ed. H. E. Salter, vol. 1, Oxford Historical Society, vol. 70 (Devizes, 1920), pp. 255–72; and W. H. Turner, ed., *Selections from the Records of the City of Oxford* (Oxford, 1880), pp. 33–35, 62–63.

summons of quo warranto does not, however, lie only in the contrast between Wolsey's tactics of personal intervention and the goal of fundamental reform articulated by Fineux and attributed to Thomas Cromwell and the legislative program of the 1530s. The contrast between Wolsey and Fineux, or between Wolsey and Cromwell, should not obscure the initiatives of subjects whose struggles to acquire franchises from rivals or to defend them against local competition gave Wolsey his opportunity to intervene and, indeed, forced the problem of franchisal rights onto men like Fineux. The role of local contestants in provoking the government's intervention is especially clear in Lynn and Norwich, where Wolsey as well as the common-law justices were only the latest of a long line of royal agents called upon to mediate between lay authorities and ecclesiastical lords over jurisdictional and fiscal rights. But even the incentive for the Middlesex undertaking can be discovered not only in the reforming aims of Fineux or the fiscal and political requirements of Wolsey, but also in the interests and aspirations of London's lay governors. London's civic authorities had fought throughout the fifteenth century to destroy the privileges that enabled debtors to escape the jurisdiction of civic authorities and the immunities that encouraged criminals to persist in their felonious careers. And even if royal ministers preferred to overlook problems arising from privileged lands in Middlesex, London's long campaign against the liberties of Westminster Abbey, St. Martin's-le-Grand, and St. John of Jerusalem would not permit the government the luxury of indifference or inaction.[88] That the younger Savage had been taken from sanctuary in Finsbury may well be related to London's claim during the sessions of 1519 to jurisdiction there.[89]

The vigor and persistence of laymen's challenges to franchises asserted by ecclesiastical lords in Middlesex, Lynn, and Norwich gave a willing government occasion to expand the royal presence in local communities, but the occasion for intervention also implied limits to its scope. Parties who invited—even demanded—royal interference made themselves dependent on royal authority, whether they did so as challengers or defenders of long-established franchises. The government had not been invited, however, to substitute itself for local authorities, and the very terms on which royal authority was invoked excluded systematic destruction of franchisal rights. The role of mediator gave the king's ministers a chance to shape local politics; and when aggressively exploited by someone like Wolsey, that chance could produce gains for the central government. The crown was not, however, the only party to gain, and the settlements in Lynn and Norwich illustrate the advantages that civic authorities or their ecclesiastical rivals could draw from ostensible assertions of royal prerogatives. Whether Lynn burgesses or other competitors for local jurisdiction would have encouraged or even acquiesced

88. Thornley, "Destruction of Sanctuary," pp. 182–207, surveys the conflicts of the late fourteenth and fifteenth centuries.

89. App., no. 162. The city claimed view of frankpledge in the manor of Finsbury as well as the chattels of felons and other forfeitures arising there.

in the government's intervention, had they stood to lose by it, may be doubted.

Wolsey may bear responsibility for sacrificing the opportunity that general quo warranto summons gave for reforming local jurisdictions, but it is more likely that the circumstances in which the government undertook general summons ruled out reforms that would curtail jurisdictional franchises indiscriminately or widely. The conduct and outcome of general summons reflect competing motives among the king's justices and ministers; they also reflect the initiative of subjects who saw in the king's prerogative a weapon against their own opponents, not an instrument for destruction of private interests in authority or jurisdiction.

III

Despite the possibilities opened by Fineux's views on both quo warranto and the role of King's Bench, general summons did not have a lasting impact on franchises in local government or on the relationship of the court to inferior jurisdictions. The outcome of proceedings in Middlesex and Lynn, however, did not signal an end to quo warranto; nor did these proceedings terminate the activity of King's Bench in weighing titles to the exercise of the king's administrative and jurisdictional responsibilities. Informations of quo warranto against individual franchise holders had been established as a usual, if not extremely frequent, practice in King's Bench by the time the parliamentary pardon of 1523 ended proceedings on most of the claims submitted in Middlesex and Lynn. Individual actions of quo warranto offered little hope for broad and systematic curtailment of franchises, but actions aimed at selected major franchises or franchise holders, or proceedings against serious obstacles to royal officers in local communities, were not an unrealistic or inefficient method for pursuing reforms of the sort anticipated from quo warranto by Fineux. The actions brought under Henry VIII, however, suggest a government that, although ready to use quo warranto, possessed little enthusiasm for a judicial campaign to rationalize local government or to centralize royal authority. And behind some of the cases on the court's plea rolls are motives and initiatives only remotely inspired by concern for more effective or pervasive royal authority.

The franchises challenged in the first large batch of informations submitted to King's Bench point to the kind of benefits the central government did seek from individual actions of quo warranto, and to the reasons why quo warranto proved a convenient device for reaping such benefits. In 1517 six of the seven informations alleged usurpation of the right to appoint coroners, and all six informations can be traced to coroners' inquests turned over to the court two terms earlier.[90] Although

90. App., nos. 3–8, can be traced, respectively, to KB 9/471, mm. 103, 97, 66, 94, 93, and 52.

the conduct of some franchisal coroners had provoked injured parties to complain,[91] the most likely source of the government's concern with coroners in 1517 was their responsibility for appraising and seizing chattels of felons and suicides for the king. Two centuries earlier, Edward III, noting the long interval since eyre justices had surveyed goods and chattels forfeited to the crown, instructed justices of King's Bench to examine coroner's rolls in each county where the court sat and to determine what property the king should have from suicides, fugitives from justice, or convicted felons.[92] His initiative had no lasting effect. The permanent decline of the eyres and the increasingly sedentary habits of King's Bench meant that for most of the late Middle Ages both coroners and also the property they seized in the king's right would go unsupervised. Henry VII's concern for the profits of justice resulted in commissions on concealed rights and in the office of the surveyor of the prerogative. He also made it possible for King's Bench to do the job assigned by Edward III, even if the court no longer traveled beyond Middlesex. By an enactment of 1487, coroners' inquests were regularly to be turned over to gaol delivery and assize justices, who in turn were to transfer them to the justices of King's Bench.[93] During the first Tudor's reign, actions were common in King's Bench for property that, according to the inquests now routinely supplied the court, was in the custody of shire or franchisal coroners or in the hands of lords of franchises.[94]

A government determined to cultivate the profits of justice not only could use King's Bench to sue for goods mentioned in inquests, but also could exploit a revived and modified action of quo warranto to check routinely on the authority by which lay and ecclesiastical lords as well as municipalities appointed the men who assessed and held such goods. By 1527 quo warranto actions against franchisal coroners or the persons who appointed them had become so ordinary a part of the court's work that formal bills submitted in person by the attorney general were abandoned in favor of notations directly on the inquests filed with the court.[95] Not all franchisal coroners who appeared in records of the court were marked for prosecution, and prosecution in some cases was at best per-

91. See, for example, charges that the coroner of Pickering Lythe protected his servants with false verdicts returned by the juries he convened in a case of murder, in *Yorkshire Star Chamber Proceedings*, ed. John Lister, vol. 4, Yorkshire Archaeological Society Record Series, vol. 70 (Leeds, 1927), p. 62; and also STAC 2/31/53.

92. *Select Cases in the Court of King's Bench*, ed. G. O. Sayles, Selden Society, vols. 74 (London, 1955) and 76 (1957), 4:lxvi, 5:101.

93. Stat. 3 Hen. 7, c. 2.

94. Examples include KB 29/126, m. 18v; KB 27/1138, Rex mm. 2, 8d; KB 27/1101, Rex m. 3; and KB 29/168, mm. 3, 24d. In only three cases did quo warranto informations name felons' chattels alone, as opposed to actions against a collection of franchises in which felons' chattels were included: App., nos. 49, 96, 140.

95. The transition is evident in informations that included a summary of the inquest (e.g., App., nos. 15–18 in 1522) and notations for quo warranto made directly on the inquests (e.g., App., nos. 28, 42).

functory. But rights to appoint or to perform the duties of coroners received broad and steady scrutiny by Henry VIII's bench.[96] Because fewer than two hundred actions have so far been identified on the rolls of the court, the sixty-seven actions against persons who appointed or acted as coroners represents a principal share of the energy devoted by royal law officers to quo warranto. The potential fiscal advantages of such actions and the ease with which they could be initiated may account for the large place they occupy in the record of quo warranto under Henry VIII.

In addition to coroners' inquests, the government had another source of data on franchises immediately to hand after 1519, a source that played a part in another group of actions that also bulk large in the list of cases for Henry's reign. Claimants of Middlesex franchises had supplied the crown's legal officers with detailed descriptions of their fiscal and jurisdictional rights; and even if the claims led to few immediate gains for the crown, the Middlesex proceedings left the attorney general a readily available source for framing informations. In 1532 the government turned once more to the records of the 1519 proceedings in order to summon fourteen of the original claimants before King's Bench, as part of an unusually extensive and vigorous use of quo warranto during that year. Altogether, twenty-six actions were begun during 1532, including eight informations that had been earlier submitted to the court without a definitive result.[97]

The decision to resume the legal challenge to Middlesex franchises and to renew inconclusive prosecutions of earlier defendants did not signal a program of systematic curtailment or elimination of franchises. Although it was probably not simple coincidence that the attorney general revived actions on the Middlesex claims in the year that saw Thomas Cromwell secure a firm place in the king's counsels, it is also unlikely that the twenty-six prosecutions were prompted by the goal, expressed in a parliamentary memorandum by Cromwell several years later, of "utter dissolution of all franchises and liberties throughout this realm, and specially the franchises of spirituality."[98] If either Cromwell or royal law officers regarded the informations as a major move toward eliminating franchises from local government, the decision to prosecute minor jurisdictional privileges in Middlesex, and to ignore the more extensive secu-

96. Some cases were dismissed with the notation *Cess proc' que nullus ven' ad informand'* (App., nos. 79, 89, 131–32); allowance of charters was frequently noted only on the controlment rolls (App., nos. 43, 92, 97, 98, 133, 138, 146); in at least one case, persons who had acted as coroners were, according to a note scrawled on the inquest, told to appear at the next assize session to "claim ther atorite for the offec of the coroner as is above wretyn" (KB 9/447, m. 97); and a statement by the attorney of the Duchy of Lancaster was sufficient to end proceedings against the coroner for a duchy estate (App., no. 139).

97. Although claims from 1519 have been lost, the fourteen Middlesex defendants' cases listed in the Appendix for 1532 are all included on the list of claimants in B.L. Add. MS 25168, fols. 559v–60. Where the informations of 1532 can be compared with data on claims to be found in reports or transcripts from the 1519 proceedings, no discrepancies can be found.

98. *LP*, 10:91 (no. 252).

lar jurisdiction and immunities of the abbot of Westminster, the bishop of Durham, the bishop of Ely, or the archbishop of York, is puzzling; and equally puzzling is the failure to attack any major franchises in the hands of powerful lay aristocrats. If the actions were part of a campaign to destroy or sharply curtail franchisal jurisdiction, results of the twenty-six actions must have been acutely disappointing, as no recoveries for the crown resulted from the informations of 1532. The only final judgments given in the actions constituted victories for three of the defendants.[99]

The government's extensive use of quo warranto in 1532 may well have been aimed against the "franchises of spirituality" of Cromwell's memorandum, but the emphasis fell much more heavily on the "spirituality" than on the secular franchises exercised by members of the spirituality. J. J. Scarisbrick has pointed out that all but six of the defendants were ecclesiastical lords of franchises, and he compared the quo warranto actions to the *praemunire* charges used only shortly before to coerce the clergy into greater compliance with the king's wish for a divorce and for acknowledgement of his supremacy over the English church. If Scarisbrick is correct in his analysis of the government's plans for a legal campaign that would subordinate the clergy to Henry VIII's will,[100] the attorney general turned to the Middlesex claims of 1519 because they included a large number of ecclesiastical franchises, described in the kind of detail that made the job of drafting informations simple. The particular franchises claimed in 1519 were less important to the government than its ability, through quo warranto prosecutions, to drive home the point that unless the clergy courted royal favor, its role in local government stood in jeopardy. In order to achieve immediate political goals, the government did not need to deprive churchmen of secular liberties; it needed only to demonstrate that those liberties were vulnerable. For that purpose, the use of quo warranto against any substantial number of clergymen would serve, and the Middlesex claims, along with other proceedings from the preceding decade, were a convenient source of targets.

Quo warranto attacks on clergymen in 1532 contributed to the politi-

99. App., nos. 58 and 108, 62 and 102, 68. In one other case, all franchises except appointment of coroners, which was disclaimed, were allowed (App., nos. 65, 124).

100. J. J. Scarisbrick, *Henry VIII* (Berkeley and Los Angeles, 1968), pp. 296–98; he has also analyzed the informations and their place in the attack on the clergy more fully in "Conservative Episcopate in England, 1529–35" (Ph.D. thesis, Cambridge University, 1956), pp. 193 ff. In *Henry VIII*, p. 297, he speculated that a memorandum of early 1533, listing bills from the previous session, indicated that the government had introduced a measure for "comprehensive clearing away of all local territorial rights enjoyed by the clergy rather than those of only the actual victims of the Quo Warranto attack." This speculation suggests that Scarisbrick regards the use of quo warranto proceedings not only as a political tactic in Henry's contest with the clergy but also as a preliminary move in a major campaign against all franchises. Yet reference in the memorandum, Public Record Office, State Papers (hereafter cited as SP) 1/74, fol. 46, to "the resumption of the liberties, &c of the prelates," is more probably related to Stat. 25 Hen. 8, c. 14, "An act that the liberty given to the church in the days of Richard II, Henry IV, and Henry V be repealed," which revised the law for heresy trials and limited episcopal control over heresy prosecutions.

cal strength of the government, and routine proceedings against franchisal coroners may have reinforced the fiscal position of the crown. In neither case, however, can we find much evidence that Henry VIII's government intended major reform of abuses in franchisal jurisdiction, nor do we see many signs that the Tudors had marked franchises as obstacles to royal authority that had to be destroyed. But the proceedings against franchisal coroners or their lords and the 1532 informations do not account for all actions begun by the attorney general against subjects who claimed the right to use and profit from justice and law enforcement. Even if such actions were prosecuted too infrequently or irregularly to constitute a systematic program of curtailment, some were brought against laymen and ecclesiastics whose possession of power and independent authority could disturb ministers anxious to strengthen the central government and rationalize the administration of justice. And in at least a few instances, the plea rolls describe encounters that we should expect from a king and ministers determined to eliminate private jurisdiction that sheltered subjects from royal law enforcement efforts or encouraged injustice and disorder. Yet when such encounters are placed in the context of local interests and rivalries, they also resist explanation as confrontations between centralizing monarchs and independent subjects defiant of royal authority.

The records of quo warranto proceedings against Sir John Hudleston, for example, show on their face a sustained contest between the central government and a northern gentleman defending his autonomous authority against expanding royal power. Neither the interests of the king nor the ends of justice, however, were central to the conflict in which the quo warranto originated and was pursued. In 1519, at a time when John Spelman and Chief Justice Fineux were weighing the potential benefits from quo warranto to royal authority, Hudleston's extensive franchises in his lordship of Millom, Cumberland, were challenged by an information in King's Bench.[101] But local rivals who wanted to cripple Hudleston's jurisdictional and fiscal powers may deserve more credit for the action than royal advisors. The franchises challenged in the information against Hudleston—sheriff's tourn, appointment of coroners, and return of writs—were described in 1511 by jurors in a "capital court" held soon after Hudleston inherited Millom. In 1518, moreover, jurors had clarified and reaffirmed the jurisdictional rights exercised "by prescription and custom of the manor of Millom." On the second occasion, jurors ordered that no freeholder should hear, try, or determine any matters or punish any offenses justiciable in Hudleston's courts for the lordship, unless they or their ancestors had used such jurisdiction during the past forty years. Bailiffs of freehold tenants were instructed to deliver to the capital court all estreats awarded in inferior courts, to be sure that

101. App., no. 11; for biographical data on the family, see H. S. Cowper, "Millom Castle and the Hudlestons," *Transactions of the Cumberland and Westmoreland Archaeological and Architectural Society*, new ser. 24 (1924): 203–27.

the lord did not lose his profits. And all residents were directed to obey precepts of mandates served in the name of the lord, under pain of forty shillings for each default, and to obey writs served in the name of the king under pain of five pounds. The jurors also confirmed the authority of the steward to use either stocks or a fine against anyone who failed to pay penalties decreed by the lord's courts for disobedience to the king's or the lord's own precepts.[102]

The records of the 1511 court and more especially the decrees of the 1518 court reveal assertions of independent authority inconsistent with a Tudor policy of centralization and increased national unity; and the quo warranto information of 1519 could be a response to jurisdictional claims based on "prescription and custom" that checked the progress of centralization and integration. But the affirmation of the lord's authority and jurisdiction and the efforts to buttress them in 1518 may mean that Hudleston had more to fear from defiant tenants than from encroaching monarchs, and resistance to his franchisal authority within Millom may account both for his need to reinforce his authority in 1518 and the challenge to his franchises in 1519. In February, before the information was submitted, Hudleston purchased an exemplification of Edward I's quo warranto proceedings regarding Millom, which he eventually pleaded when, after a third information,[103] he defended his franchises in 1538. When he purchased the exemplification, however, the king had not yet demanded a defense, and Hudleston may have needed it to defend himself against a nearer threat. Such a threat existed in the person of Charles Pennington, who sometime in the year after August 1518 petitioned the king for redress of injuries sustained at the hands of Hudleston's servants, allegedly committed soon after the lord's court made the decrees described above. Because Pennington had defended himself against ill-disposed persons who tried to rob him, the petition charged, Hudleston used his court to amerce Pennington; and to collect the amercement, Hudleston had his bailiffs distrain the petitioner.[104] The petition points to Hudleston's readiness to use his franchisal authority aggressively, but it also points to the difficulties that he faced in maintaining his authority, and to the existence of local opponents ready to carry their defiance to the king's court.

The information against Hudleston listed, with only minor variations in wording, the same franchises identified in Hudleston's own court in 1511. If the attorney general did not draw on Hudleston's defense of his franchises elsewhere in drafting the information, he may have depended on an informant with close ties to the lordship—ties close enough, indeed, to irritate the informant. Complaints to the king's Council could have prompted the attorney general to proceed against Hudleston on his own initiatives. But when Hudleston, in his eventual plea to the informa-

102. Carlisle Record Office, D/Lans/W, Millom Court Book, 1510–23, pp. 73–84, 107–19.

103. *LP*, 3 (pt. 1):31 (no. 102).

104. STAC 2/17/109.

tion, referred to the "purchase" of the bill against him, he may have been thinking of a tenant who had persuaded the attorney general, or paid him, to prosecute an action more useful to the lord's local opponents than to the king.[105] If the government initiated the action to suppress franchises threatening to royal power, Hudleston proved remarkably successful in efforts to delay an answer that, when he offered it in 1538, relinquished everything except free chase, assize of ale, infangthief, and half of felons' chattels in the lordship. And when he offered this plea that in substance demonstrated usurpation of most of the challenged franchises, the attorney general did not bother to ask for a judgment against him. In 1543, the information was submitted for the fourth time, only to disappear from the rolls at last, still without a decision on the contested franchises.[106]

Even when they were turned against franchise holders by local rivals, quo warranto informations could, of course, simultaneously benefit royal officers, ministers, and the king himself. The action brought against the earl of Arundel in 1539[107] was at once a move in a contest for local power between two aristocrats and a maneuver by Thomas Cromwell to strengthen his and the king's control in Sussex. According to the information, Arundel had usurped views of frankpledge, felons' chattels, and appointment of justices of the peace within the honor of Petworth; he had, in effect, arrogantly set about establishing a virtually independent shire for himself within the honor, if the information accurately described his conduct. Arundel may well have attempted to exercise various jurisdictional and fiscal rights in Petworth, as the attorney general alleged, but his attempt was less clearly an affront to the dignity of the crown than the charges in the quo warranto action suggest. As the lords of the Rape of Arundel, the earl and his predecessors had long tried to exercise their franchisal rights over the tenants and officers of the honor of Petworth, which lay within the boundaries of the Rape.[108] In asserting his claims against the lord and officers of the honor, the earl continued a long struggle to maintain his family's proprietary rights as fully as possible. But the struggle took a new turn after Henry Percy's surrender of the honor made Henry VIII its lord and William Fitzwilliam, the earl of Southampton, its steward. The jurisdictional conflict remained a rivalry between two aristocrats, but one of the rivals would now identify his local interests with the royal dignity. Equally important, Southampton

105. App., no. 119.

106. App., no. 157. The four informations between 1519 and 1543, all futile if assessed in terms of recoveries of franchises by the king, are especially striking in light of the affray, between the second information in 1532 and the third in 1537, when Hudleston's supporters were supposed to have said that "There shall nother Wrytt nor processe be servyd uppon oure kyng & lorde ne never was." The remark was made as they resisted attempts to levy distresses against Hudleston, to compel his appearance on the information of 1532 (KB 29/168, m. 44).

107. App., no. 135.

108. *Victoria County History: Sussex*, vol. 3, ed. L. F. Salzman (London, 1935), pp. 95–96; 1 Bulst. 194, 80 *Eng. Rep.* 882.

could count on direct support from Thomas Cromwell, who in turn relied on Southampton to use his authority over Petworth tenants for returning Cromwell's choices for parliamentary seats.[109] Arundel therefore found himself, early in 1539, summoned to answer for his encroachments; and, not surprisingly, he backed down, disclaiming any right to the franchises named in the information. The government, on the other hand, contented itself with the disclaimer, and the attorney general did not press for a fine on account of the alleged usurpation.[110]

Arundel's case suggests that the government could exploit for political advantage a well-timed quo warranto information against a powerful lay aristocrat, much as the 1532 prosecutions had been used against clergymen, and as Wolsey had exploited the general summons for political ends in 1519. But the most striking implication of the Arundel case is not the government's ability to use quo warranto as a political tactic, but its ability to use it to protect the king's interest as lord of Petworth and its liberties. The suit against the earl of Arundel was probably only one of several actions brought ostensibly on behalf of the king's prerogatives and the dignity of his crown, but in fact intended to guard or reinforce the authority of his estate officials. Among the four new informations during 1532, for example, three probably originated in conflicts between the defendants and the king's own estate or franchisal officers. Behind the information against the abbot of Eynesham were earlier complaints that the abbot had interfered with the king's steward for Eynesham when he tried to hold a court leet for the manor.[111] The king's officials for the manor of Darlington may have moved the information against John Meryng, accused of usurping not only jurisdictional privileges but also rights of common, an unusual and inappropriate subject for quo warranto suits. But if the attorney general drew up the information from complaints of manorial officers, the inclusion of rights of common, over which Meryng and tenants had been at odds, is understandable.[112] William Crowmer faced the charge, among others, that he had illegally claimed exemption from the hundred court of Middleton, a liberty then in the king's hand.[113] In all three cases, as in the Arundel case, royal officers may have initiated the legal challenge to the defendants, but the officers acted to protect jurisdictional and fiscal rights that differed little from those enjoyed by other lords of lands and liberties. Used on behalf of the king's own franchisal officers, quo warranto neither threatened the existence of proprietary interests in royal jurisdiction nor altered the traditional distribution of power between the central government and

109. E 321/10/7; *LP*, 14 (pt. 1):201 (no. 520); Stanford E. Lehmberg, *The Later Parliaments of Henry VIII, 1536–1547* (Cambridge, 1977), pp. 41–42.

110. Other prosecutions probably related to rivalries among local governors that spilled over into political struggles at the center were those against the earl of Essex in 1534 and 1535: App., nos. 88, 94; *LP*, 7:420 (no. 1084), 439 (no. 1120), 458 (no. 1180).

111. App., no. 59; KB 9/479, m. 70.

112. App., no. 57; STAC 2/27/70, 2/3/247, 2/31/57.

113. App., no. 78.

propertied subjects who ruled local communities. Quo warranto in such instances illustrates the power of the central government to intervene in local affairs, but it also illustrates the king's continuing dependence on subjects who expected a return on their loyalty and service, and who regarded the exercise of franchisal jurisdiction as an appropriate payment.

Quo warranto informations enabled the government to exploit local rivalries to the advantage of the king and his ministers, but in some prosecutions the government appears to have undertaken little more than the task of mediating between two competitors for the king's prerogatives. Much as Wolsey used the expensive, time-consuming, but at least temporarily successful, general summons to resolve the contest in Bishop's Lynn, individual actions in King's Bench gave royal ministers one more tactic to try when compromise proved elusive. Simultaneous prosecutions in 1539 of Thomas Wyatt and of the mayor and citizens of Rochester, both for usurpations of royal rights in the Medway River, accompanied attempts by royal councillors to resolve conflict between the two over rights listed in the informations. And almost certainly, these legal actions, initiated in the term in which the council had to suspend an earlier decree on the matter, were responses to a controversy that would not yield to negotiations or mediation.[114] The simultaneous prosecution of both claimants was exceptional, but the use of quo warranto against one party in a jurisdictional dispute was not uncommon. Quo warranto was the king's action, but in practice his subjects may have prompted the decision to defend "his" prerogatives.

Lay governors of boroughs were among those subjects to whom quo warranto appealed, not because it could destroy franchises, but because it might transfer them from ecclesiastical to lay hands. The prior of Tynemouth, summoned in 1519 to answer for franchisal rights that included appointment of his own justices of the peace,[115] had less to fear from the king than from the Newcastle townsmen against whom, a few years earlier, he had used his justices. The governors of Newcastle, long engaged in battle with the prior, continued the struggle in Henry VIII's Council, in his Parliaments, and, it is likely, with quo warranto in Henry VIII's bench.[116] The king's law officers, on the other hand, showed little vigor in a prosecution that they had to renew in 1532 and again in 1537, without offering any response to the prior's titles throughout the lengthy proceedings.[117] If the government's goal was an agreement be-

114. App., nos. 144, 145; B.L. Add. MS 4521, fols. 133v–35; *Victoria County History: Kent*, vol. 3, ed. William Page (London, 1932), p. 433.

115. App., no. 12.

116. KB 9/964, m. 133; KB 9/467, m. 44; *Select Cases before the King's Council in the Star Chamber*, ed. I. S. Leadam, 2 vols., Selden Society, vols. 16 (*1477–1509* [London, 1902]) and 25 (*1509–1544* [1911 for 1910]), 2:68–74; KB 27/1002, Rex m. 15; C 1/389/32; *LP*, 4 (pt. 1):189 (no. 448); Stat. 21 Hen. 8, c. 18. For earlier contests, see *A History of Northumberland Issued under the Direction of the Northumberland County History Committee*, 15 vols. (Newcastle-upon-Tyne, 1893–1940), 9:79–82; and Leadam, *Star Chamber*, 2:xciii–xcvi.

117. App., nos. 64, 112. The prior's plea to the information was not a strong one,

tween Newcastle and the priory, or if the prosecution had been initiated at the insistence of the citizens, unaggressive prosecution by the government is no longer puzzling. Similarly, resolution of a jurisdictional conflict probably inspired the information of 1533 against the prior of Hawtenprice, whose use of a view of frankpledge annoyed the citizens of Kingston-upon-Hull.[118] In the case of another long-standing conflict, the role played by civic authorities in promoting an information of quo warranto is even less problematical. Citizens of London, who had tried a variety of legal and political tactics against the immunities of St. Martin's-le-Grand, and whose agitation may indeed have encouraged the government's general summons of 1519, secured a decree from Star Chamber in the summer of 1538 which directed the attorney general to sue out a quo warranto against the abbot of Westminster, then the lord of St. Martin's franchises. A copy of an information against the abbot was recorded in the journals of the Common Council, followed by the record of a request that the attorney general enter it of record.[119] The government had reason enough to move against privileged ecclesiastical lordships, but London's role in drafting the information and urging the prosecution of quo warranto against St. Martin's suggests that assaults on immunities in London originated as much in the self-interested concerns of London's citizens as in Tudor commitment to reform of immunities.

Henry VIII's political and fiscal needs during the 1530s made the decade a favorable one for laymen hostile to secular privileges and jurisdictions held by ecclesiastical lords. At least two quo warranto actions during Cromwell's ascendancy, however, suggest that informations were used against as well as on behalf of municipal governors who contested the secular authority of prelates. Indeed, the two cases illustrate use of quo warranto under Cromwell to preserve ecclesiastical franchises against challenge from lay rivals. Cromwell rebuffed Nicholas Shaxton, bishop of Salisbury, for his inflexible stand against citizens there who struggled to reduce the extensive franchises of his church, and the minister sternly reminded Shaxton that he owed his enjoyment of secular power in the city to the king.[120] Cromwell's attitude, on the other hand, forced the mayor and citizens to retreat from proposals that the king use his "most highest emperyall power" to deprive the bishop of his franchises.[121] Instead, citizens found themselves summoned in 1538 to

---

because he offered principally a charter of Richard I, framed in general terms, to justify such franchises as appointment of justices of the peace (KB 27/1078, Rex m. 7).

118. App., no. 82; *Victoria County History: Yorkshire*, vol. 3, ed. William Page (London, 1913), pp. 213–14; James J. Sheahan, *History of the Town and Port of Kingston-upon-Hull*, 2d ed. (Beverley, 1866), pp. 77–78.

119. Corporation of London, Record Office, Journals of the Court of Common Council 14, fols. 78, 90–92. Dissolution of the abbey not long after the decree explains why no information can be found on the court's rolls.

120. Roger B. Merriman, *Life and Letters of Thomas Cromwell*, 2 vols. (Oxford, 1902), 2:128; *LP*, 13 (pt. 1):211 (no. 572).

121. Salisbury City Archives, "Tin Box 4," bundle 2, and Salisbury Diocesan Records,

answer for their own franchises.[122] Although the language of quo warranto informations asserted the unique rights and responsibilities of the king, citizens of Salisbury discovered that Cromwell's government could use it to protect, rather than to destroy, the bishop's secular privileges and jurisdiction. The quo warranto of 1538 also taught them that Cromwell, whatever his convictions about the bishop's obligations to the king whose jurisdiction Shaxton claimed, would not countenance contempt for established rights.

The burgesses of Cambridge were taught the same lessons, and again quo warranto provided the instruction. Early in 1539 they were required to defend their claim to jurisdiction over commercial activity and transactions in Sturbridge Fair.[123] The fair and other franchises were at the center of a persistent controversy between municipal authorities and the university, and Cromwell had declared his intention of seeing the disputes ended when he became the university's steward.[124] Townsmen readily invoked the language of royal authority to protest university jurisdiction that hindered municipal officers in "the execution of the king's laws" and the "accomplishment of the King's pleasure and commandment,"[125] but their royalist sentiments did not persuade Cromwell to side with them against the university. He warned them in 1537 that they could not expect to retain their own franchises, should they use violence against the franchises of others or treat with "open and apparent contempt of suche graunts as his maiestie hath made to others." The quo warranto that issued when townsmen persisted in their campaign against the university made good Cromwell's threat that, if they refused to respect the university's liberties, "I must and will . . . be a party agenst you for the obteyning of Justice."[126] The lesson administered to Cambridge burgesses proved painful. Justices of King's Bench, after the burgesses appeared and then defaulted, ordered the liberties seized and the mayor arrested to make fine for the alleged usurpation.[127]

Miscellaneous Documents 23, are articles submitted by citizens against the bishop in 1537, "to be optayned of his grace by his lauful power accordyng unto Justice and equitie of his lawes and not after his most highest emperyall power in this behalf," which contrasts with earlier articles to be obtained from the king "Any grantes by charters or compositions to the contrary notwithstandinge" (SP 1/241, fol. 200; *LP*, Addenda, 1 [pt. 1]:439 [no. 1290]). On controversy between bishop and citizens, see Fanny Street, "The Relations of the Bishops and Citizens of Salisbury between 1225 and 1612," *Wiltshire Archaeological and Natural History Magazine* 39 (1915–17): 319–28; and G. R. Elton, *Policy and Police: The Enforcement of the Reformation in the Age of Thomas Cromwell* (Cambridge, 1972), pp. 100–107.

122. App., no. 130.

123. App., no. 136.

124. Cooper, *Annals of Cambridge*, 1:332–33, 346–71; Merriman, *Thomas Cromwell*, 1:408–9, 422, 431–32, 437–38; G. R. Elton, *Star Chamber Stories* (London, 1958), pp. 52–57, 62–74.

125. Cooper, *Annals of Cambridge*, 1:349–50.

126. Ibid., 1:389–90; Merriman, *Thomas Cromwell*, 2:74–76.

127. For subsequent efforts to recover the fair, see Cooper, *Annals of Cambridge*, 1:393;

The seizure of the Cambridge liberties was the only occasion under Henry VIII on which the justices of King's Bench gave the king liberties challenged by an action of quo warranto. This is not to say, of course, that quo warranto informations contributed nothing to the tasks of royal governance in the sixteenth century. By allowing systematic review of franchisal coroners, informations supplemented other Tudor fiscal measures. By adding to the crown's judicial armory, they increased the options for coercion and persuasion available to king and ministers, and—most important of all—improved the crown's political position in confrontations with the clergy during the 1530s. And by giving the government a convenient means of challenging selectively the exercise of jurisdiction and fiscal privileges, quo warranto made easier royal intervention in local affairs, either to mediate local rivalries or to throw the weight of royal authority behind a competitor for authority who could be useful to the central government. But quo warranto informations had not armed Henry VIII's government with a weapon for destroying or crippling franchisal jurisdictions; or, at least, his ministers did not use them as instruments of destruction. We cannot ignore the fact that the government's most impressive gain from quo warranto informations was made at the expense of defendants, the burgesses of Cambridge, whose claim to franchises injured the royal dignity less than it injured the jurisdiction exercised by the university.

IV

Neither general summons nor informations of quo warranto effected significant change in franchises or in the relationship between central authority and local governors. But the revival of quo warranto was not without consequence in shaping the early modern English state. The absence in England of special administrative courts with distinctive rules for proceedings against public authorities has been traced to writs of certiorari, prohibition, and mandamus used by King's Bench in the sixteenth and seventeenth centuries.[128] To such writs quo warranto informations should be added. Although quo warranto under the early Tudors did not lead immediately to improved or significantly closer supervision of local authorities, its use by the government in local controversies preserved for King's Bench a prominent place in the affairs of local governors; it also accustomed local authorities and their critics to the court's intervention. When justices of Henry VIII's bench presided over prosecutions brought in the course of conflicts over franchises, neither they nor the attorney general appeared very determined to enforce vigor-

and *The Charters of the Borough of Cambridge*, ed. Frederic W. Maitland and Mary Bateson (Cambridge, 1901), pp. 97–117.

128. S. A. deSmith, "The Prerogative Writs," *Cambridge Law Journal* 11 (1951): 40–56, at 48.

ously Spelman's and Fineux's assertions that such proceedings should correct abuses in the exercise of royal authority. But the informations did reinforce the capacity of royal justices to perform the traditional responsibility of mediating, resolving, and containing conflicts between rival aspirants to fiscal privileges and jurisdictional power. By enabling justices to review the authority by which local governors acted, whether they did so at the instigation of local rivals or on demand of the king, the revived quo warranto helps to explain the modern role of King's Bench as a "supreme court of administration" for England.

In other more subtle but perhaps more important ways, quo warranto shaped the distinctive contours of the English state. Under Cromwell as well as under Wolsey, quo warranto was seldom a simple assault by the crown on the independence and power of a franchise holder. But by throwing the weight of royal authority behind one rival for franchisal rights against another, quo warranto not only reminded the defendant of royal claims to supremacy but also strengthened the ties between the crown and the party who benefited from the king's suit. And precisely because quo warranto allowed the government to intervene in local rivalries for franchises, it may have increased royal tolerance for proprietary interests in jurisdiction and authority and preserved an accommodation between them and royal authority into the early modern period. The victims of quo warranto prosecutions were often those whose ancestors and predecessors had enjoyed, as a result of royal charters and letters patent, the patronage of past monarchs. With quo warranto, Tudor ministers and law officers could develop a new form of patronage, a legal process available to subjects contesting and defending the franchises given or allowed by earlier monarchs. Whatever the consequences of the "Cromwellian revolution" for royal administration, it did not mean changes in the local police machinery available to the Tudors. Cromwell was, Elton has pointed out, "compelled not only to use the locality but, to a point, to defer to the locality."[129] Quo warranto prosecutions illustrate the Tudors' dependence on the locality and their deference toward it; they also illustrate how, despite such dependence and deference—indeed, because of it—early Tudor governments added to the power and authority of the monarch. The revival of quo warranto meant that men like Wolsey and Cromwell could more readily accommodate local interests to the needs of the central government. Even as it invoked the unique prerogatives and dignity of the crown, quo warranto in practice acknowledged the validity of private interests in jurisdiction. It may be no distortion to argue that the revival of quo warranto contributed to the centralization of authority not because it enabled Tudor governments to eliminate private interests in governance, but because it allowed some propertied subjects to use royal authority in pursuing or defending their claims to local authority.

129. *Policy and Police*, p. 383.

If this argument from quo warranto does not distort Tudor attitudes toward franchises, a thoroughgoing reassessment of Tudor legislation on franchises is needed. That statutes, especially statutes of the Reformation Parliament, had an impact on franchises and their lords is evident even from the records of quo warranto. King's Bench rolls record in a handful of cases that no further process was possible or necessary against a defendant, because his monastery had been dissolved.[130] Parliament's measures on sanctuaries went far toward eliminating the abuses created by privileged church lands that Chief Justice Fineux denounced.[131] And in a measure that appeared explicit in its criticism of past royal concessions of jurisdiction, Parliament in 1536 denied subjects in the future the right to keep the peace or to issue writs in their own names, and took from them rights of appointing justices of assize, gaol delivery, or the peace.[132]

Serious and extensive reconsideration of these legislative initiatives is not possible here, but the conduct of quo warranto prosecutions under Henry VIII forces us to ask whether the statutes were as broad in their consequences as they were in their ostensible ends, and also to ask whether Parliament acted primarily to implement a royal design for reforming local government by eliminating franchises. The weight of the 1536 Act for Recontinuing Liberties fell equally on all who appointed their own justices of the peace; but if most franchisal justices were appointed by ecclesiastical lords, we should probably hesitate before insisting that the government wanted the act in order to reduce generally the role of franchises in local government. And if legislation on franchises had the largest impact on secular jurisdiction held by churchmen, we should also hesitate before attributing sole responsibility for the legislative attacks to the government. The Act for Recontinuing Liberties made strong claims for the king's exclusive authority to give justice, but its language was already familiar to lay subjects who had invoked similar ideas against bishops and monastic lords exercising secular franchises. And through quo warranto, some of the king's subjects already had experience in using royal prestige and a royal procedure for their own ends. In conflicts over local jurisdiction and authority, laymen had taken advantage of the king's action against franchise holders. The Act for Recontinuing Liberties may show a similar achievement in Parliament, and it should be reexamined, not primarily as a measure for extending the reach of royal authority or improving royal administration of justice, but as another stage in the transfer of local authority and power from ecclesiastical lords to propertied laymen. Much as quo warranto prosecutions can often be understood fully only in the context of local

130. App., nos. 82, 105, 123.

131. In addition to Thornley, "Destruction of Sanctuary," see G. R. Elton, *Reform and Renewal: Thomas Cromwell and the Common Weal* (Cambridge, 1973), pp. 135–38.

132. Stat. 27 Hen. 8, c. 24, in Elton, *Tudor Constitution*, pp. 37–39; see also Stanford E. Lehmberg, *The Reformation Parliament, 1529–1536* (Cambridge, 1970), pp. 163–211.

rivalries, so the legislation of the 1530s should be reinterpreted within the framework of lay resentment against churchmen who enjoyed secular franchises and privileges.

The point here is not that laymen, determined to capture for themselves the jurisdiction and power held by ecclesiastical franchise holders, forced an unwilling government to accept the Act for Recontinuing Liberties or statutes that curtailed immunities. Lay resentment served Cromwell's and Henry's purposes; it did not create their goals. But it is reasonable to argue that laymen who were hostile to the secular role of churchmen in local government saw the opportunity created by royal needs during the 1530s to increase their advantage against ecclesiastical lords and their franchisal officers. And if legislative initiatives against franchises originated at least in part in the competition for local power among the king's subjects, we can less confidently cite them solely to demonstrate plans for centralizing power in the king or for rationalizing local government by eliminating private interests in the administration of justice. On the contrary, the central government must be treated as one party to a complicated rearrangement of power and authority in local communities.

The pressures that simultaneously encouraged and vitiated the impact of legislative attacks on franchises can be detected behind quo warranto proceedings initiated against the burgesses of Reading in 1543.[133] For the burgesses, the dissolution of the abbey of Reading meant an exceptional opportunity to seize the authority and jurisdiction that the abbot had exercised over resentful townsmen. The crown's acquisition of the monastery's properties and liberties, however, had a less favorable outcome than the townsmen expected. Into the place of the abbot's officers stepped the bailiff appointed by Henry, who obviously had not seen the dissolution of the monastery as an occasion for eliminating its franchises. The bailiff, Thomas Vachell, proved no less dedicated than the former abbot to preserving fiscal and jurisdictional rights in the liberty. When the burgesses succeeded in their campaign for a new charter covering many of the rights formerly contested with the abbot, Vachell did not acquiesce quietly in their victory. The quo warranto, which followed soon after the new charter, was not necessarily the act of a government ready to take with one hand what it had given with the other; it was the response of the king's franchisal officer, who had no desire to see the franchise or his office reduced.[134]

Whether or not ministers like Cromwell hoped to rationalize local government and improve law enforcement by eliminating or reducing franchises, the king could not ignore both the municipal authorities and the landed gentlemen who expected a share in the jurisdictional benefits, as well as in the lands, of former monastic lords. The expectations of men like Vachell and the burgesses of Reading help account for not only the Act for Recontinuing Liberties and legislation against sanctuary, but also

133. App., no. 165.

134. SP 1/56, fol. 108 (*LP*, 14 [pt. 2]:355 [no. 811]); *Reading Records: Diary of the Corporation*, ed. J. M. Guilding, 4 vols. (London, 1892–96), 1:172–75.

for the government's refusal to suppress franchises acquired during the 1530s from laymen or churchmen. And to remove any doubt about the refusal, Parliament in 1542 confirmed the validity of franchises held within three months prior to the dissolution of a monastery or of the attainder of a lay franchise holder.[135] Neither subjects who expected to enjoy liberties or offices in them nor the king who needed to satisfy the expectations of his propertied subjects was ready to destroy franchises.

The private interests in jurisdiction represented by franchises yielded in time to the state and its monopoly on authority and jurisdiction. To explain the decline of franchisal jurisdictions and immunities that took place between the fifteenth and seventeenth centuries, we cannot look solely to the goals and policies of kings and their ministers. The revival of quo warranto under Henry VIII suggests that subjects largely indifferent to the king's benefits from centralization and unification played a leading role in shaping "royal" conduct toward franchise holders. And we may well find that the eventual disappearance of private rights in public authority owed less to royal initiatives than to propertied subjects who stood to gain more by cooperating in the concentration of authority than by supporting the widespread exercise of private jurisdiction.

135. Stat. 32 Hen. 8, c. 20.

Appendix

Listed below are individual acts of quo warranto brought in Henry VIII's King's Bench. Because almost all files of *ancient indictments* (KB 9) and controlment rolls (KB 29) of the court during Henry VIII's reign were inspected, the chart should include most actions initiated between 1508 and 1547. The list is arranged in the order of law terms in which cases were begun.

In the column "Franchises," the key used to identify them unavoidably obscures the precise terms in which the attorney general described the privileges or jurisdiction used by the defendant. I have made no attempt to maintain the order in which they were listed in informations.

Key to Identification of "Franchises"

I. View of frankpledge, sheriff's tourn, or court leet (usually associated with appointment of constables, the assize of bread and ale, and supervision of weights and measures).
II. Felons' chattels (usually associated with chattels of fugitives, outlaws, suicides, and other forfeitures, fines, or amercements).
IIIa. Appointment of coroner.
IIIb. Exercising office of coroner.
IV. Return and/or execution of writs.
V. Sanctuary.
VIa. Appointment of justices of the peace.
VIb. Exercising office of justice of the peace.
VIIa. Fair(s) and/or market(s).
VIIb. Clerkship of market.
VIIIa. Waif and/or stray.
VIIIb. Treasure trove.
IX. Infangthief and (usually) outfangthief.
X. Free warren and/or chase.
XI. Jurisdiction over civil pleas, e.g., debt, trespass.
XII. Hundred court and/or exemption from hundred or shire court.
XIII. Exemption from purveyance and clerk of royal household.
XIV. Exemption from tolls.
XV. Pleas of *vetitio namio*.
XVIa. Appointment or election of municipal officers.
XVIb. Admission of burgesses.

"Outcome" gives a brief indication of final disposition or last recorded stage of proceedings. If records were insufficient to place a case in one of the following categories, the space is blank or includes the number of an identical or similar information against the defendant in a later term.

Key to "Outcome"

Title.	Defendant pleaded title, but final disposition not recorded; asterisk (*) indicates that attorney general contested defendant's plea.
Def. dead or House dissol.	Process ended on sheriff's return that defendant had died or that monastic house had been dissolved.
Seizure after default.	Contested franchises seized for the king after defendants made default following an appearance before the court.
Allowed.	Judgment for defendant, or a process terminated by court after letters patent shown; asterisk (*) indicates that attorney general challenged title.
Pardon and/or Disclaim.	Defendant dismissed *sine die* after pleading parliamentary pardon and/or disclaiming franchises.
Dismissed.	Process terminated by court for reasons other than title pleaded or letters patent shown (e.g., *supersedeas*, "certain considerations," no prosecutor appeared, etc.; the notations *pard'* or *cess proc'* without further explanation are not treated as decisions of the court).

All references are to King's Bench (Crown Side). All references to the plea rolls (KB 27) are to the "Rex" side of the rolls. For reasons of space, membrane numbers are preceded only by commas and not by *m*'s.

Term	No.	Defendant	Franchises	Counties	Outcome	References
Mich. 1512	1	Abbot of Glastonbury	I; II; VIIa; VIIIa	Newton Castle, Dors.	Pardon	9/964, 134; 29/144, 37d
Trin. 1516	2	Walter Trelawny	II; VIIIa; XI	Menheniot, Corn.	Title; Def. dead	29/148, 22d, 27d; 27/1020, 8 (writ)
Mich. 1516	2a	" "	I; II; VIIIa; XI	" "		29/148, 22d, 39d (information)
Trin. 1517	3	Bishop of Salisbury	IIIa	Sherborne, Dors.	Dismissed	9/473, 45; 23/149
" "	4	" "	IIIa	Bishop's Cannings, Wilts.	Dismissed	9/473, 46; 29/149
" "	5	Edward Croft, Chief Forester, Malvern Chase	IIIa	Hanley in Malvern Chase, Worc.	Pardon; Disclaim.	9/473, 47; 29/151, 8d; 27/1067, 11
" "	6	Abbot of Burton on Trent	IIIa	Bronston, Staffs.	Allowed	9/476, 48; 29/150, 43; 151, 23; 27/1033, 23†
" "	7	Prior of Newburgh	IIIa	Newburgh, N. R., Yorks.	Pardon; Disclaim.	9/473, 49; 29/149, 9d; 27/1060, 2d
" "	8	Abbot of Whitby	IIIa	Haknes, N. R., Yorks.	Allowed	9/473, 50; 29/154, 40; 27/1065, 4

Term	No.	Defendant	Franchises	Counties	Outcome	References
" "	9	Bailiffs, Kingston on Thames	XII	Kingston & Emelebridge, Surrey	Allowed	9/473, 51; 29/150, 43d; 156, 13; 159, 37d; 27/1052, 10
Mich. 1518	10	John Mynsterly & others	I; XI; XVIa, b	Wenlok, Salop	Allowed	9/476, 105; 29/150, 21; 27/1037, 3
East. 1519	11	John Hudleston	I; II; IIIa; IV	Millom & elsewhere, Cumb.	Below, no. 67	29/151, 5d; 155, 13d
Trin. 1519	12	Prior of Tynemouth	I; IIIa; VIa	Tynemouth, Northumb.	Title; Below, no. 64	9/478, 3; 29/151, 13d; 27/1078, 7
Mich. 1519	13	Abbot of Waltham Holy Cross	IIIa	Loughton & Waltham, Essex	Pardon; Disclaim.	9/479, 74; 29/151, 25; 27/1033, 19
Hil. 1520	14	Abbot of Beaulieu	I; II; IIIa; IV; V; VIIIa, b; IX	Beaulieu, Hants.	Below, no. 70	9/480, 53; 29/151, 35, 37d
Trin. 1522	15	Abbot of Ramsey	IIIa	Ramsey, Hunts.	Allowed	29/154, 13d, 25d; 27/1045, 18; 1090, 13
" "	16	Prior of St. John of Jerusalem	IIIa	Rokeland Tustes, Norfolk		29/154, 14d; 156, 13d; 27/1052, 13
" "	17	Abbot of Bury St. Edmund's	IIIa	Rougham, Suffolk		29/154, 14d, 26d; 27/1045, 14

Term	No.	Defendant	Franchises	Counties	Outcome	References
" "	18	Abbot of Peterborough	IIIa	Peterborough, Northants.	Allowed	9/488, 122 (inq.); 29/154, 14d, 26; 27/1045, 16
Trin. 1524	19	Prior of Norwich Cathedral	IIIa	Martham, Norfolk	Adjudged with no. 44	9/494, 60 (inq.); 29/156, 11; 159, 11; 160, 38; 27/1071, 13
" "	20	George Lord Hastings	IIIa	Veymer, Rape of Hastings, Sussex		9/495, 1; 29/156, 12; 159, 37; 27/1066, 6
" "	21	John Veer of Bradwell	I; II; IV; VIIIa; XII	Tendring Hundred, Essex		29/156, 13; 27/1054, 7
" "	22	Robert Smith & George Foryster	IIIb	Cambridge, Camb.	Adjudged with no. 27	29/156, 11
Hil. 1524	23	John Clere & others of Colchester	VIb	Colchester, Essex	Dismissed	29/156, 30d
" "	24	Thomas Flynggaunt & Robert Northern	IIIb	" "	" "	
East. 1526	25	Thomas Jekys	IIIb	Rectory of Ashridge, Bucks.	Dismissed	9/501/1, 31 (inq.); 29/158, 6

Term	No.	Defendant	Franchises	Counties	Outcome	References
" "	26	Abbot of Burton on Trent	IIIa	Stretton, Staffs.	Adjudged with no. 118	29/158, 2
" "	27	Thomas Saye & Henry Gylson; later Edward Sleyye	IIIb	Cambridge, Camb.	Allowed	29/158, 6, 42; 27/1064, 64
" "	28	Bishop of Winchester	IIIa	Southwark, Surrey		9/501/1, 96, 97
Trin. 1526	29	Abbot of Shrewsbury	IIIa	Monks' Foregate, Shrewsbury, Salop	Adjudged with no. 83	29/153, 14d; 27/1091, 8
Mich. 1526	30	Archbishop of Canterbury	IIIa	Archbishop's Manors in Sussex	Below, no. 66	29/158, 21d
Hil. 1527	31	John Wastell, Prior of Dunstaple	IIIa	Dunstaple, Beds.	Below, no. 43	29/158, 38
Trin. 1527	32	Abbot of Bruton	I; II; IV; VIIIa, b; IX	Bruton, Somerset	Dismissed	29/159, 13, 36d; 27/1067, 3d
" "	33	Prior of Ely	IIIa	Prior's Manors in Camb.	Dismissed	29/159, 21, 38; 27/1066, 9
" "	34	George Lord Hastings	IIIa	Hooe & Wartling, Rape of Hastings, Sussex		29/159, 19; 27/1066, 8

Term	No.	Defendant	Franchises	Counties	Outcome	References
" "	35	Bishop of Ely	IIIa	Impington, Camb.	Dismissed	29/159, 11, 26d
Mich. 1527	36	John Hunt	IIIb	Kingston on Thames, Surrey	Dismissed	9/504, 105 (inq.); 29/159, 19; 160, 18
" "	37	Robert Strete, Mayor	IIIb	Clifton Dartmouth Hardness, Devon	Allowed	29/159, 20d, 27; 27/1081, 10
Hil. 1528	38	John Dowell & John Lant	IIIb	Scarborough, Yorks.		29/159, 33
East. 1528	39	John Wythers, John Smith, Hugo Saunders, prebendaries of St. Paul's Cathedral	I	Willesden, Midd.	Below, no. 71	9/506/1, 120 (presentment); 29/160, 4d
Trin. 1528	40	Bishop of Ely	IIIa	Soke of Somersham, Hunts.	Dismissed	9/507, 6 (inq.); 29/160, 17
" "	41	Richard Halam & Thomas West	IIIb	Bedford, Beds.		29/160, 16d, 38; 27/1070, 11
Mich. 1528	42	Prior of Winchester	IIIa	Redbridge, Hants.		9/508, 38†
" "	43	Gervase Markham, Prior of Dunstaple	IIIa	Dunstaple, Beds.	Allowed	9/508, 148; 509, 106 (inq.); 29/160, 20d; 161, 2d

Term	No.	Defendant	Franchises	Counties	Outcome	References
" "	44	Prior of Norwich Cathedral	IIIa	Catton, Norfolk	Allowed	29/160, 20, 38; 27/1071, 13
Hil. 1529	45	Anthony Bradstone	I; II; IIIa; IV; V; VIIIa, b; IX; XI	Winterbourne, Glouc.	Title for I; Below, no. 69	29/160, 34; 161, 19d, 40; 27/1074, 2
Mich. 1529	46	John Fen, Mayor, & bailiffs of Syon Windsor	IIIb	Syon Windsor, Bucks.	Pardon	29/161, 39; 9/512, 40
" "	47	Robert Whytney, Steward of Abbot of Bruern	IIIb	Bruern, Oxford		29/161, 27d
" "	48	John Chascombe, Abbot of Bruern	IIIa	" "		
" "	49	John Wyche, Abbot of Hulton	II	Hulton, Staffs.	Below, no. 119	9/511, 40; 29/159, 1d
East. 1531	50	William Maunsell	IIIb	Painesthorpe (Liberty of St. Mary's, York), E. R. Yorks.	Dismissed	9/511, 40 (inq.); 29/164, 41; 27/1081, 4
" "	51	Richard Malibroke, Mayor of Marlborough	IIIb	Marlborough, Wilts.		29/164, 4, 41d; 27/1081, 9d

Term	No.	Defendant	Franchises	Counties	Outcome	References
Mich. 1531	52	Bishop of Norwich	IIIa	Bakston, Suffolk	Allowed	9/509, 116 (inq.); 29/164, 33, 50; 27/1085, 23
Hil. 1532	53	Abbot of Bruton	As above, no. 33	As above, no. 33		9/518, 1; 29/164, 47d
" "	54	Prioress of St. Helen's Bishopgate	I	St. Helen's Bishopgate, Midd.		9/518, 2; 29/164, 48d
" "	55	Francis Hampden	I; VIIIa; X	Theydon Garnon, Essex		9/518, 3; 29/164, 48d; 27/1065, 21
" "	56	William Babington	IV	Westminster, Midd.	Below, no. 120	9/518, 4; 29/164, 48d
" "	57	John Meryng	I; II; VIIIa	Darlton, Notts.	Dismissed	9/518, 5; 29/164, 48d; 27/1085, 17
" "	58	Warden of St. Mary's, Winchester (Sanctuary College)	I	Isleworth, Midd.	Below, no. 108	9/518, 6; 29/164, 48d; 166, 16
" "	59	Abbot of Eynesham	I	Eynesham, Oxford		9/518, 7; 29/164, 48d; 165, 43; 27/1086, 8
" "	60	Abbot of St. Albans	I	Stanmore Magna, Midd.	Title; Below, no. 107	9/518, 8; 29/164, 48d; 165, 8d; 27/1083, 12

Term	No.	Defendant	Franchises	Counties	Outcome	References
" "	61	Abbot of Walden (in Essex)	I	Enfield, Midd.	Below, no. 105	9/518, 9; 29/164, 48d; 166, 16d
" "	62	Warden of All Souls College, Oxford	I	Edgeware, Midd.	Below, no. 102	9/518, 10; 29/164, 48; 165, 43d; 27/1086, 11
" "	63	Andrew Lord Windsor	I; VIIIa; IX; X	Stanwell & South Mimms, Midd.	Below, no. 106	9/518, 11; 29/164, 48; 165, 8d
" "	64	Prior of Tynemouth	As above, no. 12	As above, no. 12	Below, no. 112	9/518, 12; 29/164, 48; 166, 41; 27/1090, 10
" "	65	Dean of St. Paul's Cathedral	I; II; IIIa; IV; VIIIa, b; IX	Chiswick & elsewhere, Midd.	Below, no. 124	9/518, 13; 29/164, 48; 165, 20
" "	66	Archbishop of Canterbury	As above, no. 30	As above, no. 30	Below, no. 112	9/518, 14; 29/164, 48
" "	67	Sir John Hudleston	As above, no. 11	As above, no. 11	Below, no. 119	9/518, 15; 29/164, 48; 165, 32; 168, 40d
" "	68	Abbot of Glastonbury	As above, no. 1	As above, no. 1	Allowed	9/518, 16; 29/164, 48; 27/1089, 5
" "	69	Anthony Bradstone	As above, no. 45	As above, no. 45	Below, no. 121	9/518, 17; 29/164, 48; 165, 31; 170, 14d; 27/1104, 13

Term	No.	Defendant	Franchises	Counties	Outcome	References
" "	70	Abbot of Beaulieu	As above, no. 14	As above, no. 14	Below, no. 123	9/518, 18; 29/164, 48; 166, 7
" "	71	John Wythers, John Smith, & Hugo Saunders, prebendaries of Willesden	As above, no. 39	As above, no. 39		9/518, 19; 29/164, 48; 165, 20; 27/1085, 14
" "	72	Provost of King's College, Cambridge	I; II; IIIa; VIIIa, b; Xa; XIII; XIV	Ruislip, Midd.	Below, no. 122	9/518, 20; 29/164, 48
Trin. 1532	73	Edward, Earl of Derby	I; VII; VIIIa; IX	Colham, Midd.	Below, no. 110	9/520, 1; 29/165, 17d
" "	74	Prioress of St. Leonard's, Stratford	I; II; VIIIa	Bromley, Midd.	Title	9/520, 2; 29/165, 17d, 32d; 27/1085, 20
" "	75	Abbot of Abingdon	I; VIIIa, b	Kensington, Midd.	Below, no. 111	9/520, 3; 29/165, 17d; 166, 16
" "	76	Abbot of St. Mary Graces	I	East Smithfield, Midd.	Below, no. 113	9/520, 4; 29/165, 17d, 43d; 27/1086, 10
" "	77	Archbishop of Canterbury	I; II; IV; VII; VIIIa, b; XV	Harrow & Hayes, Midd.	Below, no. 125	9/520, 5; 29/165, 17d

Term	No.	Defendant	Franchises	Counties	Outcome	References
" "	78	William Crowmer	I; II; VIIIa, b; Xa; XII; XV	Tunstal & Munston, Hundred of Middleton, Kent	Title for I, XII in Tunstal	9/520, 73; 29/165, 13d, 19d, 35; 27/1084, 6
East. 1533	79	Richard Dyxson & others of Northampton	IIIb	Northampton, Northants.	Dismissed	29/166, 5
" "	80	Abbot of Battle	IIIa	Wye, Kent		29/166, 3; 167, 33; 168, 27; 27/1093, 12
Mich. 1533	81	Ralph Harriots	IIIb	Leominster, Heref.		29/166, 30d; 27/1089, 15
" "	82	Prior of Hawtenprice	I	Hawtenprice, in Kingston on Hull, Yorks.	Title*	9/525, 55; 29/166, 25, 40; 167, 17; 27/1092, 4
" "	83	Abbot of Shrewsbury	IIIa	Astley Abbotts, Salop	Allowed	29/166, 25d; 27/1091, 8
Hil. 1534	84	Thomas Lymyll	IIIb	Bridgenorth, Salop		29/166, 40
East. 1534	85	William Waryner, Coroner of Archbishop of York	IIIb	Scroby, Notts.		29/167, 7d
" "	86	Peter Parfaye	IIIb	Thetford, Norfolk		29/167, 1, 33d; 27/1093, 15

Term	No.	Defendant	Franchises	Counties	Outcome	References
" "	87	John Oxborowe	IIIb	Sudbury, Suffolk	Pardon	29/167, 1
Trin. 1534	88	Henry, Earl of Essex	II; VII	Hoddesdon, Herts.	Below, no. 94	9/528, 57; 29/167, 14
Mich. 1534	89	Dean & Chapter, St. Peter's, York	IIIa	Dringhouse, Yorks.	Adjudged with nos. 131 & 132	9/529, 182 (inq.); 29/167, 23; 27/1110, 9
" "	90	Abbot of Bury St. Edmund's	IIIa	Bury St. Edmunds, Suffolk		29/167, 30; 27/1101, 3d
" "	91	Thomas, Earl of Wiltshire	IIIa	Rape of Hastings, Sussex		29/167, 24d
East. 1535	92	Richard Dylson	IIIb	Stafford, Staffs.	Allowed	29/168, 5
" "	93	James Abbis & others of Neylond	IIIb	Weyston, Suffolk	Dismissed	9/531, 91 (presentment); 29/168, 3
" "	94	Henry, Earl of Essex	As above, no. 88	As above, no. 88	VII Allowed	9/531, 74; 29/168, 10; 27/1100, 8
" "	95	Bishop of Ely	IIIa	Rettendon & elsewhere, Essex	Allowed	29/168, 3d
Trin. 1535	96	Henry, Earl of Essex	II	Stapleford, Herts.		9/532, 55; 29/168, 10, 40d; 27/1098, 13

Term	No.	Defendant	Franchises	Counties	Outcome	References
Mich. 1535	97	Bishop of Ely	IIIa	Soke of Somersham, Hunts.	Allowed	29/168, 24
" "	98	Archbishop of York	IIIa	Beverley, Yorks.	Allowed	29/168, 25
" "	99	Archbishop of York	IIIa	Westow, Yorks.	Allowed	29/168, 25
East. 1536	100	Christopher Vespye	IIIb	Sutton Regis, Warw.	Allowed	29/169, 2d; 172, 10d; 27/1112, 10
East. 1537	101	Bishop of Salisbury	IIIa	Sherborne & Hundred of Bempster, Dors.		29/170, 4d, 14
Trin. 1537	102	Warden of All Souls, Oxford	As above, no. 62	As above, no. 62	Allowed	9/536, 39; 27/1104, 11
Mich. 1537	103	Master of St. Katherine's Hospital, next the Tower	I; II; VII; VIIIa, b; IXa	St. Katherine's, Midd.	Below, no. 160	9/537, 1; 29/170, 24d
" "	104	Dean of St. Stephen's Chapel, Westminster	I; II; VIIIa, b; IXa	St. Stephen's, Westminster, Midd.	Below, no. 159	9/537, 2; 29/170, 24d
" "	105	Abbot of Walden	As above, no. 61	As above, no. 61		9/537, 3; 29/170, 24d
" "	106	Andrew Lord Windsor	As above, no. 63	As above, no. 63		9/537, 4; 29/170, 24d; 171, 41; 27/1110, 14

Term	No.	Defendant	Franchises	Counties	Outcome	References
" "	107	Abbot of St. Albans	As above, no. 60	As above, no. 60		9/537, 5; 29/170, 24d
" "	108	Warden of St. Mary's, Winchester	As above, no. 58	As above, no. 58	Allowed	9/537, 6; 29/170, 24d; 171, 41d; 172, 9; 27/1111, 15
" "	109	Abbot of Hammond	I; II; VIIIa	Hammond, Salop	Allowed	9/537, 7; 29/170, 24d; 171, 10; 27/1107, 14
" "	110	Edward, Earl of Derby	As above, no. 73	As above, no. 73	Below, no. 161	9/537, 8; 29/170, 24d, 35d; 27/1106, 8
" "	111	Abbot of Abingdon	As above, no. 75	As above, no. 75		9/537, 9; 27/170, 24d
" "	112	Prior of Tynemouth	As above, nos. 12 & 64	As above, nos. 12 & 64		9/537, 10; 29/170, 24d, 35d
" "	113	Abbot of St. Mary Graces	As above, no. 76	As above, no. 76		9/537, 11; 29/170, 24d
" "	114	Master of St. Lazarus of Jerusalem	I; VIIIa; IX	St. Giles & Fletham, Midd.		9/537, 12; 29/170, 24d
" "	115	Abbot of Hulton	I; II (see above, no. 49)	Hulton & Milton, Staffs.		9/537, 13; 29/170, 24d
" "	116	Prior of Wenlok	I; II; VIIIa	Wenlok, Salop		9/537, 14; 29/170, 24

Term	No.	Defendant	Franchises	Counties	Outcome	References
" "	117	Archbishop of Canterbury	As above, nos. 31 & 66	As above, nos. 31 & 66		9/537, 15; 29/170, 24
" "	118	Abbot of Burton on Trent	I; II; IIIa; IV; VIIIa, b; IX	Burton on Trent, Staffs.	Allowed, except VIIIb	9/537, 16; 29/170, 24, 35; 27/1108, 3
" "	119	John Hudleston	As above, nos. 11 & 67	As above, nos. 11 & 67	Title for II, IX, X	9/537, 17; 29/170, 24; 171, 9; 27/1107, 8
" "	120	Thomas Babington	As above, no. 56	As above, no. 56		9/537, 18; 29/170, 24, 35; 27/1106, 7
" "	121	Anthony Bradstone	As above, nos. 45 & 69	As above, nos. 45 & 69		9/537, 19; 29/170, 25
" "	122	Provost of King's College, Cambridge	As above, no. 72	As above, no. 72		9/537, 20; 29/170, 24
" "	123	Abbot of Beaulieu	As above, nos. 14 & 70	As above, nos. 14 & 70	House dissol.	9/537, 21; 29/170, 24
" "	124	Dean of St. Paul's Cathedral, London	As above, no. 65	As above, no. 65	Allowed, except IIIa	9/537, 22; 29/170, 24, 36; 172, 33d; 27/1116, 18
" "	125	Archbishop of Canterbury	As above, no. 77	As above, no. 77	Title; Below, no. 163	9/537, 23; 29/170, 24, 35d; 173, 18d; 27/1116, 9

Term	No.	Defendant	Franchises	Counties	Outcome	References
" "	126	Bishop of Salisbury	I; II; IIIa; IV; VIIIa, b; IX	Sunning, Berks.		9/537, 29
" "	127	Richard Sampson, Dean of St. Paul's & prebendary of Lambourn	IIIa	Lambourn, Berks.	Disclaim. (see below, no. 143)	9/536, 129 (inq.); 29/170, 20; 27/1111, 3d
" "	128	James Worsley	IIIb	Isle of Wight, Hants.		29/170, 23
Hil. 1538	129	Abbot of Pershore	I; II; VII; VIIIa; XI	Pershore & other manors, Worc.		29/170, 31; 171, 18; 27/1108, 4
" "	130	Henry Goliston, Mayor, & residents of Salisbury	I; VIIb	Salisbury, Wilts.	Allowed, except I	29/170, 33; 171, 40; 27/1131, 1
East. 1538	131	Dean of St. Peter's Cathedral, York	IIIa	Riccall, Yorks.	Dismissed	29/172, 2; 27/1110, 9
" "	132	" "	IIIa	Beverley, Yorks.	Dismissed	" "
Mich. 1538	133	Hugo Walsh, Mayor of Hereford	IIIb	Hereford, Heref.	Allowed	29/171, 24; 172, 9d
" "	134	Bishop of Ely	IIIa	Fen Ditton, Camb.	Allowed	29/171, 25

Term	No.	Defendant	Franchises	Counties	Outcome	References
Hil. 1539	135	William, Earl of Arundel	I; II; IIIa; IV; VIIb; VIIIa, b; IX; X; XII; XV	Honor of Petworth, Sussex	Disclaim.	9/542, 1; 29/171, 38; 27/1112, 11
" "	136	Mayor & burgesses of Cambridge	VIIa	Barnwell & Stourbridge, Camb.	Seizure after default	9/542, 2; 29/171, 38; 172, 9d
East. 1539	137	Moream Orrell & Thomas Dockar	IIIb	Nottingham, Notts.		29/172, 2
" "	138	Hugo Aston & Thomas Cross	IIIb	Leicester, Leics.	Allowed	29/172, 2d, 30d
" "	139	William Herdman & Robert Stowton (later Richard Robyns & John Bulleyn)	IIIb	Godman-chester, Hunts.	Dismissed	29/172, 3, 10
" "	140	Robert Smyth & others, Mayor & bailiffs of Cambridge	II	Cambridge, Camb.		29/172, 2d
" "	141	George Charneley	IIIb	Derby, Derb.		29/172, 2d
" "	142	Robert Grene	IIIb	Coventry, Warw.		29/172, 2d

Term	No.	Defendant	Franchises	Counties	Outcome	References
Trin. 1539	143	William Pleydell, Coroner of King & Dean of St. Paul's	IIIb (see above, no. 127)	Lambourn, Berks. (see above, no. 127)		29/172, 16d
" "	144	Mayor & citizens of Rochester	Fishing rights	Medway River (at Rochester), Kent		9/543, 1; 29/172, 15d
" "	145	Thomas Wyatt	Fishing rights	" "		9/543, 1; 29/172, 15d
East. 1540	146	William Stokeman	IIIb	Newbury, Berks.	Allowed	29/173, 7
Trin. 1540	147	Mayor, Sheriff, & citizens of York	I; II; IIIa: IV; VIIb; VIIIa, b; IX	York, Yorks.	Allowed	9/547, 27, 28; 29/173, 15d; 174, 9
Hil. 1541	148	Aldermen & burgesses of Grantham	"Divers liberties"	Grantham, Lincs.		29/173, 38d
" "	149	Bailiffs of Shrewsbury	"Divers liberties" (Probably II)	Shrewsbury, Salop	Allowed	29/173, 38d; 174, 17d
East. 1541	150	George Hadley	IIIb	Havering-atte-Bower, Essex		29/174, 6
Mich. 1541	151	Thomas Tydely & William Ayes	IIIb	Worcester, Worc.		29/174, 26d; 27/1126, 4
" "	152	Thomas Wanten	I	Great Stoughton, Hunts.	Allowed	29/174, 24, 34d; 27/1125, 9

Term	No.	Defendant	Franchises	Counties	Outcome	References
" "	153	Bishop of Salisbury	IIIa	Sherborne & Yetminster, Dors.		29/174, 32; 27/1104, 6
East. 1542	154	Mayor & community of Plymouth	II; IIIa	Plymouth, Devon	Allowed	29/175, 5, 31d; 27/1127, 13
East. 1543	155	John Rogers	I; II; IV; VIIIa, b; IX; X	Bryanston & Langton, Dors.		9/554, 1; 29/176, 7d, 40d; 27/1130, 11
" "	156	Bishop of Salisbury	I; II; IIIa; IV; X	Sunning, Berks.		9/554, 2; 29/176, 7d
" "	157	John Hudleston	As above, nos. 11, 67, & 119	As above, nos. 11, 67, & 119		9/554, 3; 29/176, 7; 178, 37; 27/1137, 1
" "	158	Richard Cromwell	I; II; IIIa; IV; VIIIa, b; IX	Warboys, Hunts.		9/554, 4; 29/176, 7d
" "	159	Dean of St. Stephen's Chapel, Westminster	As above, no. 104	As above, no. 104		9/554, 5; 29/176, 7d, 40d; 27/1130, 13
" "	160	Master of St. Katherine's Hospital, next the Tower	As above, no. 103	As above, no. 103		9/554, 6; 29/176, 7d, 40d; 27/1130, 15
" "	161	Edward, Earl of Derby	As above, nos. 73 & 110	As above, nos. 73 & 110	I Allowed	9/554, 7; 29/176, 7d, 40d; 27/1138, 1

Term	No.	Defendant	Franchises	Counties	Outcome	References
" "	162	Mayor, sheriff, & citizens of London	I; II; VIIIa, b	London, Midd.		9/554, 8; 29/176, 7d, 40d
" "	163	Archbishop of Canterbury	I; II; IV; VIIa, b; VIIIa; X; XIV; XV	Harrow & Hayes, Midd.		9/554, 9–10; 29/176, 7d, 40d; 27/1130, 9
Mich. 1543	164	Richard Warecombe	I; II; IV; VIIIa, b; IX; X	Lugwardon, Heref.	I, VIIIa Allowed	9/556, 1; 29/176, 29d; 27/1135, 2
" "	165	Mayor & burgesses of Reading	I; II; IIIa; IV; VIa; VIIIa, b; IX; X; XI; XVI	Reading, Berks.		9/556, 2; 29/176, 29d
Hil. 1544	166	Mayor & commonality of Winchester	I; II; VII; VIIIa, b; XI	Winchester, Hants.		9/557, 2; 29/176, 38
East. 1544	167	Bishop of Ely	IIIa	Mitford, Norfolk		29/177, 1
Mich. 1544	168	Bailiffs of Ipswich	I; II; IV; VIIIa, b; IX; XI	Westerfield Parish, Suffolk	Dismissed	9/560, 41; 29/177, 20d, 35; 27/1139, 4
East. 1545	169	Robert Payton	I; II; IV; VIIIa, b	Springwell & Little Chesterford, Essex		9/562, 2; 29/178, 1d
" "	170	Richard Oswald	IIIb	Wenlok Magna, Salop		9/562, 72;†† 29/178, 37; 27/1137, 2

Term	No.	Defendant	Franchises	Counties	Outcome	References
" "	171	Henry Moybes	IIIb	Portsmouth, Hants.		9/562, 186;†† 29/178, 1, 35
" "	172	Edward Restwold	II; IV; VIIIa, b; IX; X	Monk Risborough, Bucks.		9/562, 188; 29/178, 1d
" "	173	William Chewarton	II; IV; VIIIa, b; IX; X	Escall in Parish of Senon, Corn.		9/562, 189; 29/178, 1d
" "	174	Thomas Checheley	I; II; IV; VIIIa, b; IX	Richmond Fee (in Camb., Hert., Essex), Camb.		9/562, 190; 29/178, 1d
" "	175	Nicholas Tempest	II; IV	Wakefield, Yorks.		9/562, 191; 29/178, 1d
" "	176	Elizabeth Turwytt	II; IV	Sturton, Lincs.		9/562, 192; 29/178, 1d
" "	177	Bailiffs of Colchester	II; IV; VIIIa, b	Colchester, Essex		9/562, 193; 29/178, 1
" "	178	George Gryffyth	I; II; IV; VIIIa, b; IX	Alrewas, Staffs.		9/562, 194; 29/178, 1d
" "	179	Robert Endolfe, Bailiff of Cinque Ports	II; IIIb; IV; VIIIa, b; IX	Romney Marsh, Kent		9/562, 195; 29/178, 1
" "	180	Bailiffs & burgesses of Stafford	VIb	Stafford, Staffs.		9/562, 40; 29/178, 5; 27/1139, 4

Term	No.	Defendant	Franchises	Counties	Outcome	References
" "	181	" "	I; II; IV; VIIIa, b	Marston Manor, Staffs.		9/563, 1; 29/178, 28d; 179, 19; 27/1139, 4
" "	182	Roger Young	I; II; IV; VIIIa, b; IX; X	Bastildon, Berks.		9/563, 2; 29/178, 24d
Hil. 1546	183	Mayor & burgesses of Saltash	I; II; VIIa; VIIIa; IX; XI; XIV; XVIa, b; prison; fishing rights	Saltash, Corn.		9/564, 7; 29/178, 34d
East. 1546	184	Humphrey Lee	I; II; IV; VIIIa, b; IX	Nordley Regis, Salop		9/565, 179; 29/179, 32
Trin. 1546	185	James Leveson	I; II; VIIIa; IX; prison; goods of deceased	Wenlok, Salop		9/566, 4; 29/179, 16d
" "	186	John Harecourt	I; II; IV; VIIIa, b; IX; X	Ellenvale & Ellenhall, Staffs.		9/566, 6; 29/179, 16d
Mich. 1546	187	George Throckmorton	Park	Boughton, Warw.		29/179, 28

Term	No.	Defendant	Franchises	Counties	Outcome	References
Hil. 1547	188	Mayor & citizens of London	Measurement of Sea Coal on Thames, with profits	London, Midd.		9/568, 9; 29/180, 1

† Does not contain allowance, but it was subsequently pleaded successfully; see references for no. 118.

†† Note on inquest.

10 Crime, Sanctuary, and Royal Authority under Henry VIII: The Exemplary Sufferings of the Savage Family

E. W. Ives

The notion that sanctified ground will protect the fugitive is rooted in the primeval past. In historic times, however, it appears in England as the privilege of sanctuary, together with benefit of clergy a classic abuse in the medieval church and the target for Henry VIII's reforming legislation. Both abuses, as it happened, escaped final extinction and lingered to provide some completely haphazard mercy toward offenders and debtors, but the old importance was gone. The story of the destruction of sanctuary was told more than fifty years ago in a masterly contribution by Isobel Thornley to another volume of essays, those presented to A. F. Pollard.[1] She demonstrated the way in which sanctuary had long been under attack from Parliament, the City of London, and the royal judges, so that what Henry VIII swept away by statute was only a residuum of the privilege. Time has not destroyed the authority of her study, but she necessarily summarized the series of early Tudor sanctuary cases and, in particular, the last of these, the prosecution of Sir John Savage the younger. The purpose of this essay is to put that final judicial assault upon sanctuary into the wider context of Tudor government policies on church and state, law and order, and to explore by bringing in associated court proceedings what was a single cause célèbre in early sixteenth-century politics involving one of the great families to whom Henry VIII and his father had owed the throne.

The principals in this episode were Sir John Savage the elder (V) of Clifton in Cheshire and Hanley in Worcestershire, and his son, Sir John the younger (VI). There were two main prosecutions. The first, indexed in Keilwey's *Reports* as *Savage's (Sir John) Case*, was an appeal of murder brought in Trinity 1516 against the younger Sir John by Bridget, widow of John Pauncefote, Esq., of Hasfield in Gloucestershire.[2] Appealed with him as principals were a relative, Antony Savage, and thirteen other gentlemen and yeomen; and Sir John, Sr., was accused, with a John Brereton, Gent., of being an accessory before the fact. The second prosecution, known confusingly as *Savage's Case*, began in Michaelmas 1516; Sir John, Sr., was the defendant here, and the charge, gross abuse of the royal offices he held in Worcestershire and Gloucestershire.[3] Ancillary

1. I. D. Thornley, "The Destruction of Sanctuary," in *Tudor Studies Presented . . . to Albert Frederick Pollard*, ed R. W. Seton-Watson (London, 1924), pp. 182–207.
2. Keil. 188–92, 72 *English Reports* (hereafter cited as *Eng. Rep.*) 365–70.
3. Keil. 192–96b, 72 *Eng. Rep.* 370–75.

prosecutions in Michaelmas and Hilary 1516, 1517, charged one or other of the Savages or various groups of their clients (to the total of fifty individuals and more) with numerous counts arising from the main offenses.[4]

I

John Pauncefote was killed on Monday, 31 March 1516, and the first recorded move in *Savage's (Sir John) Case* came on 10 May when Sir John, Jr., took refuge in the Priory of St. John of Jerusalem in Clerkenwell. He was removed by force on 20 June and taken to the Tower, a few days after his father had been committed there by the king's Council.[5] Both were promptly brought up before the King's Bench, and the elder Sir John took the simple course of pleading not guilty and waiting to be dealt with until the principals had been tried. Sir John the younger, however, not only pleaded not guilty but turned the case into a question of sanctuary by also challenging the legality of his removal from St. John's and calling the prior to attest the immunity.

In 1516 the leading case on sanctuary was *Humphrey Stafford's Case*, heard in Trinity term 1486.[6] Attainted after Bosworth, Stafford had fled to the sanctuary at Colchester, but he issued out in April 1486 to attempt to raise a rebellion. When this collapsed, Stafford had taken sanctuary again, this time at Culham Abbey near Oxford, but was forcibly removed to face a commission of oyer and terminer. When asked to show cause why the sentence of attainder should not be carried out, Sir Humphrey had pleaded the privilege of the abbey and been transferred to the Tower while his claim was considered. After much debate, political and judicial, the judges had ruled that the right to protect fugitives could not be sustained except in cases where it had been specifically granted by the sovereign and where the privilege had been allowed by a court of record. Some stress was placed on the distinctive and heinous nature of treason, but the argument was, apparently, held to apply to accusations of felony as well. Culham had not qualified and Stafford was duly executed.

Sir John Savage, Jr., seems to have been aware of the 1486 ruling, for the sanctuary at Clerkenwell was not only one of the most famous but

4. The King's Bench records of both main and subsidiary cases are to be found together, principally in the Public Record Office, King's Bench (hereafter cited as KB) 9/472; KB 27/1020, m. 60; KB 27/1021, Rex mm. 17, 18, 19d, 20, 20d, 21; KB 27/1040, mm. 29, 34, Rex mm. 3, 3d, 5d, 19; KB 29/148, mm. 37d–38d, 44, 50–55.

5. Huntington Library Ellesmere MS (hereafter cited as Hunt. Ell. MS) 2652, fol. 3. (I owe this reference to the kindness of Dr. J. A. Guy.)

6. Year Book (hereafter cited as Y. B.) Pasch. 1 Hen. 7, ff. 22–24, pl. 15 (1486); Y. B. Trin. 1 Hen. 7, ff. 25–26, pl. 1 (1486); *Select Cases in the Exchequer Chamber*, ed. Mary Hemmant, 2 vols., Selden Society, vols. 51 (London, 1933) and 64 (1948), 2:115–24; *Select Cases in the Council of Henry VII*, ed. C. G. Bayne and William Huse Dunham, Selden Society, vol. 75 (London, 1958), p. 8; Thornley, "Destruction of Sanctuary," p. 199. For the most recent discussion of the law of sanctuary see *The Reports of Sir John Spelman*, ed. J. H. Baker, 2 vols., Selden Society, vols. 93 (London, 1977) and 94 (1978), 2:339–46.

one that met the requirements laid down in *Stafford's Case*. The original claim was by prescriptive right as something enjoyed time out of mind, but papal bulls of 1213 had expressly mentioned the protection of fugitives and Henry III had ratified all existing rights in 1253. What is more, he had strengthened the prescriptive title by a *non obstante* that covered lapse of the liberty by nonuse. The 1253 charters had been confirmed on nine subsequent occasions by English sovereigns, most recently by Henry VIII himself, and the right of sanctuary had been continuously allowed by the Westminster courts.[7] In 1493, under the presidency of Sir William Hussey, who had masterminded the judgment in *Stafford's Case*, King's Bench had ruled that the privilege did not extend to St. John's Fields, but had gone on to confirm that a fugitive *in le Meason de S. John ou in le circuit del' Meason* would be protected.[8] Furthermore, if he had been removed he would be restored without having to demonstrate the prescriptive title of the sanctuary. In 1515, months only before Savage's removal, a felon had so been restored. To make protection even more sure, the prior was able to produce the relevant charters in good condition with the seals intact.

The strength of Sir John's plea clearly presented great problems to Bridget Pauncefote, who asked leave to imparl, and it was not until Hilary 1517 that she replied challenging his claim. Savage stood by his right to be restored and the problem then passed to the judges, who thereupon adjourned the plea for advisement for five terms in succession before even calling the prior to demonstrate his claim. He did so in Michaelmas 1518, but the court once more adjourned the matter "for difficulty," and all the time Savage and his father remained in the Tower. The case did eventually proceed in Hilary 1520 but only by a dramatic change on the part of Sir John the younger, who, on his counsel's advice, abandoned the plea to be restored to sanctuary and confessed himself guilty of the Pauncefote murder.[9]

What explained this unexpected development was, in part, a move toward agreement with the crown on the related *Savage's Case*, but also a drastic reinterpretation of the law of sanctuary.[10] Congratulating Savage on his wise decision, the chief justice of the King's Bench, Sir John Fineux, proceeded to explain that there was no privilege at St. John's Clerkenwell beyond the forty days allowed by the common law to every parish church. To claim more, Fineux said—driving a coach and horses through Hussey's ruling in 1493—the prior must show usage time out of mind, in addition to his charters and recent usage. The notion of a permanent sanctuary, he declared, "is a thing so derogatory to Justice and contrary to the common good of the Realm that it is not sufferable

7. *Letters and Papers, Foreign and Domestic, of the Reign of Henry VIII*, ed. John S. Brewer et al., 21 vols. and Addenda (London, 1862–1932), 1 (pt. 1):294 (no. 485 [49]). (Hereafter cited as *LP*. All references to vol. 1 are to 2d ed., rev. by R. H. Brodie, 1920.)

8. Y. B. Hil. 9 Hen. 7, f. 20, pl. 15 (1494).

9. For the date of this change see below, at n. 14.

10. For the settlement of Savage's Case see below, at nn. 104–13 and accompanying text.

by the law" unless usage time out of mind, that is, before 1189, had been recognized at a general eyre.[11] Not that this exception meant much: as Fineux remarked, nobody had ever found such an allowance in the records of the eyres, and the 1253 *non obstante* shows that the prior of St. John's obviously had no such recognition. At this point the report of the case gives a systematic analysis of the precedents, in part certainly the work of the reporter but possibly following Fineux (*Wawe's Case*, 1422–23; *Humphrey Stafford's Case*, 1486; *Boswel's Case*, 1513–14) and this shows title after title as inadequate. The one possible exception which the reporter could offer (working on a recollection of *Stafford's Case* by Justice Coningsby) was a royal grant with papal confirmation and use before legal memory, supported by royal confirmation and use since; if that conceit did not justify the privilege, then "it would otherwise be difficult to maintain any ancient Sanctuary in England."[12]

This was precisely what the chief justice was setting out to achieve and he now produced his sharpest weapon. The St. John privilege derived from an initial grant by Urban III, and the 1253 charters were only in confirmation of this. But a papal initiative of this kind was clearly in breach of *praemunire* and hence invalid; subsequent royal confirmations did not mend the defect and so the privilege was void *ab initio*. Fineux also pointed out the grave technical risk in pleading sanctuary at all; a defendant who did so would be allowed no amendment to his plea should the holder of the liberty, in this case the prior, not support him exactly; it was safe only to pray for the prior's help before making the plea. For good measure, Fineux clarified Hussey's rule on *le circuit del' Meason*; this included church, cloister, dorter, and cemetery, but not barns, stables, and gardens.[13] It is at this point that it becomes apparent that Fineux was speaking with the formal approval of his colleagues because when he went further than this, to prohibit the buttery and the pantry, they intervened to query what would have made nonsense of even the forty-day rule.

The sudden switch from continual adjournments "for difficulty" to this confident enunciation of new doctrine was the result of three meetings of the king's Council, all apparently in the previous Michaelmas term.[14] Arguments of the sort Fineux was to present in Hilary 1520 must already have been in the air because at the first meeting—attended by the chancellor, Cardinal Wolsey, by Fineux and Robert Brudenell, J.K.B.,

11. Keil. 189b, 72 *Eng. Rep.* 367.

12. Keil. 190, 72 *Eng. Rep.* 368.

13. The exclusion of gardens was followed in an assize judgment at Coventry in 1520 (Keil. 189a, b, 72 *Eng. Rep.* 367).

14. Keil. 189–90b, 72 *Eng. Rep.* 366–69, would suggest that these Council meetings came after Fineux's argument, which in turn followed Savage's withdrawal of the plea for sanctuary, despite the prior's appearance on his behalf in Michaelmas 1516. KB 27/1020, m. 60, shows that the plea was made in Trinity 1516, the prior appeared in Michaelmas 1518, and Savage changed his plea in Hilary 1520. The reporter in Keilwey may have taken the initial date, Michaelmas 8 Hen. VIII, from the appearance of Savage on adjournment from Trinity term, by association with Savage's Case, which did begin in Michaelmas 1516.

and by other councillors—the canon lawyer representing the prior of St. John's, Dr. Peter Potkin, set out to counter them. Royal tolerance of a privilege time out of mind was, he suggested, the equivalent of a royal grant. Hence "usage of sanctuary with notice and sufferance of Kings time out of mind etc. and the confirmation of Pope Urban within legal memory etc. are as good Sanctuary as patents of the King and confirmation by the Pope could make."[15] On this argument the sanctuary of St. John's was warranted, and his submission silenced the councillors.

The story was different at the second meeting, held on 10 November 1519, when Henry VIII was present in person with Wolsey, a swarm of bishops, canonists and other ecclesiastics, and all the judges. The purpose of the meeting was quite explicit: "Many mischiefs were rehearsed which had been done in time past and which increased from day to day because of the Sanctuaries of Westminster and St. John's etc., and what remedy and redress could be provided was the principal reason why the King was there in his royal person that day."[16] First, St. John of Jerusalem was called to answer. The prior was informed that his papal grant of 1213 was illegal because the pope by himself could not set up a sanctuary, and hence the subsequent royal confirmations were void. He quickly expressed a readiness to abandon any claim to sanctuary for debt, but Fineux rejected the concession: "Yet you have claimed this privilege in time past and divers other privileges which the King himself cannot grant now by order of the laws and so these cannot have had a valid origin. Therefore the privilege will not lie by prescription."[17] To continue to defend St. John's might verge upon questioning royal authority and risk the dreaded charge of *praemunire*, so the churchmen surrendered and admitted that the pope could not create a sanctuary without the king. They sought to soften the effect of this by arguing that where an ancient right had been allowed, for example a forty-day privilege to every parish church, then the pope could extend the immunity beyond that period for all offenses, including treason. The claim, and with it all hope for the Clerkenwell sanctuary, was ignored.

When John Fineux set out the law of sanctuary in Hilary 1520, he was, therefore, enunciating a new interpretation on the authority of the Council and the personal approval of Henry VIII himself. But what makes the episode more significant is its obvious affinity with the Hunne affair of 1514–15.[18] In one as the other, the king and the judges had lined up against clerical privilege, as they were to do again in the 1530s. In each the threat of *praemunire* had been made, a threat that was carried out against Wolsey in 1529. There may even be a closer connection. Who gave the order to remove John Savage from sanctuary? The crown was

15. Keil. 190b, 72 *Eng. Rep.* 368.
16. Ibid.
17. Keil. 190b, 72 *Eng. Rep.* 368–69.
18. Keil. 180b–185b, 72 *Eng. Rep.* 357–63; a substantially complete translation is to be found in the fullest account of Hunne's Case, A. Ogle, *The Tragedy of the Lollards' Tower* (Oxford, 1949), pp. 144–54.

clearly not ready to cope with the legal problems his removal posed. And yet his removal does not look like an act of impulse; it was held back until a clear forty days had elapsed, the common-law right of the St. John's sanctuary that Fineux was to recognize in 1520. It is easy to conjecture that in the aftermath of *Hunne's Case* there may have been lawyers in government service willing to probe church privilege further.[19]

In the agitation of 1514–15, one man had been in a position to mediate between the crown and the church, Thomas Wolsey, and in 1519 he had again to intervene to save something of clerical privilege. St. John's was a lost cause, but the abbot of Westminster had still to be dealt with. He could offer a title very much in line with the conceit of the reporter of *Savage's (Sir John) Case* and was a much tougher obstacle than the prior of St. John's. The initial and specific grant of sanctuary by the Anglo-Saxon kings (actually a forgery) had been confirmed by later popes and kings and allowed by the courts.[20] The strength of Westminster's claim was met by the king attempting to bluster his way through: "I argue that St. Edward, King Edgar and the other Kings and Holy Popes who made the Sanctuary never intended that the sanctuary should serve for wilful murder and larceny outside the sanctuary, done in the hope of re-entering, and such like cases, and I believe that the sanctuary was never used at the beginning [sic]. Therefore I will have reformed the abuses which have encroached and have the matter reduced to the true intent of the original makers."[21] Fineux followed with a sweeping declaration that sanctuaries violated the principle of both divine and English law that public good must come first; thus they had to fail.

Yet royal charters were not so easily to be dismissed by the huffing and puffing even of Henry and his chief justice. Fineux had reiterated also that any privilege could extend only to the actual church and its environs,

19. The problem of sanctuary had been raised at a Council meeting on 4 Feb. 1516 after "certain thieves and murderers" had taken refuge in "Strond Church," presumably St. Mary-le-Strand (British Library Lansdowne MS 639, fols. 44v–45). This meeting (attended by the prior of St. John's and one named lawyer, C. J. Fineux) took place only eight weeks before the Pauncefote murder, but the issue appears to have been not the special sanctuaries but the forty-day rule, which was allowing a notorious gang of highwaymen to stave off arrest. Conciliar interest in the abuses of general sanctuary could, however, have encouraged a challenge to the special privileges at St. John's. That judicial rejection of certain earlier claims to sanctuary was not part of an assault on the principle (as distinct from the practice) of sanctuary is indicated by the allowance of the privilege of St. John's as late as Apr. 1515 (KB 27/1020, m. 60) as well as crown unpreparedness in Feb. 1516 and later in *Savage's (Sir John) Case*. Wolsey's attitude in Feb. 1516 had been congruent with the position he was to take up on the claim of Sir John VI; the decision of the Council was to "speak with the bishop of London in the premises" at a further meeting on Thursday 7 [*recte* 6] Feb. to which were called "certain doctors of the law spiritual and other justices and learned men in the law temporal . . . to the debating of the said cause." Nothing is known of this later meeting. For opposition to Wolsey and the church in 1515–16 by a lawyer in the king's Council see the episode of Sir Robert Sheffield in J. A. Guy, *The Cardinal's Court: The Impact of Thomas Wolsey in Star Chamber* (Hassocks, Sussex, 1977), pp. 76–78.

20. Thornley, "Destruction of Sanctuary," p. 199.

21. Keil. 191, 72 *Eng. Rep.* 369.

at Westminster just as much as elsewhere. This was Wolsey's cue. If the problem was one of boundaries, so vaguely described in the charters as "surroundings and precincts," then a commission could settle them "according to the due order of the law." But as in *Hunne's Case* and the later Reformation, churchmen were divided and the cardinal's neat bureaucratic diversion was spoiled by disputes between clerical "doves" and "hawks." John Veysey, the newly appointed bishop of Exeter, had argued against clerical privilege in 1515, and he now claimed that by common law, crimes committed outside a sanctuary disqualified a sanctuaryman from further protection.[22] Cuthbert Tunstall, M.R., showed his characteristic support for clerical status in leading the canon lawyers to rebut this claim; it was crimes done within a sanctuary that forfeited immunity.[23]

Wolsey now brought all his tact and learning to a second attempt. Princes of the ancient world, he told the Council, were accustomed to set up places of refuge. Five hundred and twenty years before Christ, Donevaunt, the first crowned king of all England, had set up the Temple as such a refuge; the pagan king, Romulus, had set up a similar sanctuary. This proved that the creation of a sanctuary belonged to temporal princes and not to the pope. Papal creation usurped the regality of the prince and any such bulls were void; ecclesiastical sanctions against those who interfered with the immunity were without force, and anyone attempting to put the papal anathemas into effect was guilty of *praemunire*. We can imagine the king's approval; the sanctuary at Clerkenwell had been most comprehensively dealt with and his own dignity vindicated. But when the Council reassembled the next day for the third meeting on sanctuary, Wolsey's practical proposals for Westminster fell far short of his theory. Some time before, the Council was told, the cardinal and the abbot had tried to control sanctuarymen by requiring an oath not to commit treason or felony outside the limits.[24] This had proved ineffective because disobedience risked only the penalties of perjury, "which they regard as nothing." The cardinal, therefore, proposed that his legatine powers should be used to require the abbot to expel those who offended after swearing the oath; the logic of the day before, that the king should resume into his own hand what his predecessors had granted away, was quietly ignored. The abbot demurred on the ground that his privilege was absolute, but he seems to have promised to take action himself. Sanctuarymen who committed crimes were, in theory, kept in prison by the abbot; this would now be done in fact, although the liberty of those who did not break the law further would not be curtailed.

22. Keil. 183, 184, 191b, 72 *Eng. Rep.* 360, 361, 369.

23. J. J. Scarisbrick, *Henry VIII* (Berkeley and Los Angeles, 1968), p. 276. Tunstall's letter from Cologne purporting to be dated 6 Nov. 1519 (*LP*, 3 [pt. 1]:173 [no. 498]) should be dated 1520 and be paired with *LP*, 3 (pt. 1):383 (no. 1043), which should be addressed to Henry VIII. It is thus no obstacle to Keilwey's dating of the Council of 10 Nov. 1519.

24. This may refer to action taken by Wolsey to forestall criticism of sanctuary following Council meetings in Feb. 1516. See above, at n. 19 and accompanying text.

This was a somewhat banal ending to an episode that had absorbed the attentions of the highest in the land and drawn from the king such proud words. True, the sanctuary of St. John's had been discredited. True, Fineux could lay down a new version of the law that made it impossible for sanctuaries to continue which did not have an initial royal charter and an explicit grant of immunity for fugitives.[25] Yet even if it had been made the exception and an exception justified on royal authority alone, the sanctuary nearest the center of government at Westminster had escaped with promises of good behavior and no more; fifty years later the dean of Westminster would still be arguing his privilege before the Council.[26] But a compromise was the frequent end to disputes of this kind when Henry VIII was king. If ever his authority seemed to be impugned, the king would insist on abject and complete acknowledgement of his regality, but on the practical outcome he was prepared to be lenient. In *Hunne's Case* he had asserted his rights in a public humiliation of the leaders of the church but had allowed the actual participant in the affair to escape quietly.[27] His behavior over the Pardon of the Clergy in 1531 is of a piece with this, and so too his fury a year later when he found that in recognizing his status as head of the church, the clergy had not understood what he had.[28]

The prosecution of Sir John Savage the younger certainly belongs to the story of the destruction of sanctuary, but its real importance was the assertion of Henry VIII's authority over the church. As in the crisis following the death of Richard Hunne, the church had appeared to derogate from the king's title and Thomas Wolsey had had to intercede with his master; perhaps we should revise accepted opinion and see the cardinal as the last great defender of the medieval church. *Savage's (Sir John) Case*, like *Hunne's Case*, saw the king demonstrating his fixed conviction that in church-state relations, royal authority took precedence as of right. Together they were early essays in the concept of the royal supremacy.

II

A changed law of sanctuary was thus not the most significant consequence of the trial of Sir John Savage the younger, but neither had it been the original issue. The crown had not seized a chance to attack sanctuary; it had had that attack forced on it, perhaps by some of its own officers. But what was it about Savage, unlike the felons regularly restored to St. John's, which set in motion events that led to a constitu-

25. Cases cited in *Reports of Sir John Spelman*, 2:344–45 show the new doctrine being applied.
26. Thornley, "Destruction of Sanctuary," pp. 205–6.
27. Ogle, *Tragedy of the Lollards' Tower*, pp. 156–59.
28. J. J. Scarisbrick, "The Pardon of the Clergy, 1531," *Cambridge Historical Journal* 12 (1956): 22–39; M. J. Kelly, "The Submission of the Clergy," *Transactions of the Royal Historical Society*, 5th ser. 15 (1965): 97–119.

tional battle over ecclesiastical privilege? To understand what it was, we need to look at the Savage family itself.

The task of investigating the Cheshire Savages invites confusion because for nearly two centuries the heir was always named "John," so that there could be as many as four John Savages alive at a time. John Savage I (d. 1450), of Clifton in Cheshire, served Henry V in his French wars, where he was knighted, and went on to establish a prominent place in the affairs of the county palatine of Chester, notably in the area of Macclesfield.[29] His son, John Savage II (d. 1463), added a considerable interest in Middlewich and its salt industry—for twelve years from 1446 a half share of the salt revenues there and also from 1446 to his death an interest in the chamberlainship.[30] It was this John, or more probably his son, John Savage III (d. 1495), who entered the service of Richard duke of York, so that the family was well placed when York's son came to the throne in 1461.[31] John II received an office in Cheshire and North Wales; John III was given further appointments in Macclesfield, and he also became steward of the Duchy of Lancaster's honor of Halton as deputy to his father-in-law, Thomas Lord Stanley.[32] A Stanley connection, indeed, runs all through the Savage story—the Stanleys too had fought for Henry V and later supported the Yorkists—and it was probably in the 1450s that this had been cemented by the marriage of John III to Catherine Stanley.[33] This John Savage was knighted at the coronation of Elizabeth Woodville in 1464.[34] He became knight of the body and later knight banneret, following the Scottish campaign of 1482.[35] The son of the Savage-Stanley match, John IV (d. 1492), made rapid progress at the court of Edward IV. Probably knighted at the battle of Tewkesbury, he rose from royal carver to knight of the body, and when the king died in 1483, Savage was second in precedence in the cortege that conveyed the body to Windsor.[36] Rewards naturally accompanied this service to the crown. Apart from posts in Cheshire, John IV had substantial annuities

29. J. T. Driver, *Cheshire in the Later Middle Ages* (Chester, 1971), p. 13; *Reports of the Deputy Keeper of the Public Records*, 64 vols. (London, 1840–1903) (hereafter cited as *DKR*), 31:238, 243–46; ibid., 37:642, 643; R. Somerville, *History of the Duchy of Lancaster*, vol. 1, *1265–1603* (London, 1953), p. 510.

30. *DKR*, 31:238; 37:542, 643; *Middlewich Chartulary*, vol. 1, ed. J. Varley, Chetham Society, new ser., vol. 105 (Manchester, 1941), pp. 55, 168, 208; ibid., vol. 2, ed. J. Varley and J. Tait, Chetham Society, new ser., vol. 108 (1944), p. 220.

31. *Yorkshire Star Chamber Proceedings*, ed. W. Brown, vol. 3, Yorkshire Archaeological Society Record Series, vol. 51 (Leeds, 1914), p. 73.

32. *DKR*, 31:238; 37:644, 645; Somerville, *Duchy of Lancaster*, 1:511.

33. See below, at n. 39 and accompanying text; his son John IV was born before 1461 (*DKR*, 37:645).

34. *Letters and Papers Illustrative of the Wars of the English in France . . .*, ed. Joseph Stevenson, 2 vols., Rolls Series (London, 1861–64), 2:784.

35. W. A. Shaw, *The Knights of England*, 2 vols. (London, 1906), 1:17; *DKR*, 37:646, assuming this to be an appointment continued by Richard III.

36. Shaw, *Knights of England*, 2:15; *Calendar of Patent Rolls*, 70 vols. (London, 1891–in progress) (hereafter cited as *CPR*), *1476–85*, p. 94; *Letters and Papers Illustrative of the Reigns of Richard III and Henry VII*, ed. J. Gairdner, 2 vols., Rolls Series (London, 1861–63), 1:5, 8.

and, significantly for the later *Savage's Case*, was granted in 1478 the constableship of Hanley Castle in Worcestershire.[37]

Side by side with this rise to national importance was the exercise of local authority arising from landed wealth and crown office. Sometimes this followed a royal commission, but in the fashion of the time, much more was simply the assertion of an autonomy that the state had to tolerate, especially if exercised by a family that supported the dynasty. The Savages certainly had a history of self-help. The best-documented example of this concerns the Derbyshire manor of Mellor, a few miles from the center of their authority in Macclesfield and Macclesfield Forest.[38] Owned initially by the Ainsworths, the property passed through a female heir to Alexander Pilkington of Rivington in Lancashire, but a rival claimant emerged in the person of William Ainsworth, the bastard son of the last male heir of the line. He was supported by John Savage II, "father unto Sir John Savage that married the Earl of Derby's sister," who "came to Mellor and brought with him two hundred men & more in harness, and drove the said Alexander out of Mellor and with strength held him out so as he was never able to dwell in Derbyshire nor at his own land in Mellor, the Savages were so great and mighty, and ever the longer the greater."[39] Pilkington was succeeded by his grandson, Robert, and John Savage II by his son, John III, but the struggle went on. In 1478, Savage raided Rivington by night and took Robert prisoner to Macclesfield in an endeavor to force him to surrender. This failed, according to Robert's version, when Sir John drew back from murder:

> In the inning days of harvest then next ensuing, William Ainsworth brought a mess of green pottage on a Friday at noon to the dinner of the said Robert, and or he was [a]ware, he had eaten a great part of that mess which had poison put in; and or midnight, the said Robert was swollen so great that he was girt about his body in three places with towels and girdles for bursting. Then the said Sir John Savage repented and said he knew no deceit done to the said Robert and said that the said Robert should have all manner of things that might do him good or pleasure; and then put a cunning physician to the said Robert and he did great cures to him and cost [*sic*] the said Robert much good, and else he had not escaped.[40]

More probably, Sir John was frightened at the prospect of a prisoner of his own dying in the gaol he kept at Macclesfield for the king.[41] At any rate, a peaceful few years followed, with Robert Pilkington in possession,

37. *CPR, 1476–85*, p. 94.

38. North Yorkshire Record Office, ZDV XI, unpaginated. References are given below to the substantial summary and transcription of this manuscript in Historical Manuscripts Commission (hereafter cited as Hist. MSS Comm.), *Various Collections*, vol. 2 (London, 1903), pp. 28–56.

39. Hist. MSS Comm., *Various Collections*, 2:28.

40. Ibid., 2:30.

41. *Letters and Accounts of William Brereton of Malpas*, ed. E. W. Ives, Lancashire and Cheshire Record Society, vol. 116 (Chester, 1977), p. 130.

but the parallels between the behavior of the Savages and the great men we find in the Paston correspondence need no emphasis.

Richard III naturally regarded the Savage family with some caution. Apart from the loyalty to Edward IV and the connection with the Stanleys and through them with Henry of Richmond, the sheer size of the clan made for danger. Sir John IV had nine brothers, and in an impressive display of family confidence early in 1485, eight were admitted freemen of Chester at a single ceremony; their father was already mayor there, and Sir John IV was made a freeman himself three months later.[42] As for the remaining brother, Thomas, he was a cleric studying abroad and almost certainly in touch with Henry Tudor.[43] Richard tried to buy their loyalty, but John IV was, according to Polydore Vergil, one of the group that invited Henry Tudor to invade, and in this he may have been also a "front man" for his uncle, Lord Stanley.[44] Sir John was certainly involved in the alarums of the early days of the invasion and may either have been trying to mislead the king into thinking him loyal or simply hedging his bets. In the second week of August the situation cleared, with Richard proclaiming Savage a traitor, and by Thursday the eighteenth John had actually joined Henry.[45] He was, it was hoped, a token of Lord Stanley's continuing sympathy with his stepson, and Henry Tudor placed Savage in command of the left wing in an endeavor to secure action rather than promises from that "shifty trimmer."[46]

We know nothing of Sir John Savage's conduct at the battle of Bosworth, but victory justified all and brought its rewards. Within the month, he and three of his brothers received royal grants of office, and Sir John's were important enough to warrant a clause of exemption in the 1485 Act of Resumption.[47] The next year, "in consideration of his services with a great multitude of his brothers, kinsmen, servants and friends at great costs and risks to his person in the conflict and battle against [the king's] great adversary, Richard III, eminent in arms, in character and counsel," Sir John IV was granted lands worth (by a later valuation) £158 per annum and more, and in 1488, a year in which he

42. *Rolls of the Freemen of Chester*, vol. 1, ed. J. H. E. Bennett, Lancashire and Cheshire Record Society, vol. 51 (Chester, 1906), pp. 8, 9; MSS of Chester Corporation, Hist. MSS Comm., *Eighth Report*, vol. 1 (London, 1907–9), p. 368.

43. Thomas Savage studied at Bologna and Padua (*Historians of the Church of York*, ed. J. Raine, 3 vols., Rolls Series [London, 1879–94], 3:375) and left the latter not before 1482 (R. J. Knecht, "The Political and Intellectual Activities of Cardinal John Morton and his Episcopal Colleagues" [M.A. thesis, University of London, 1953], p. 67). Given his immediate promotion after Bosworth (see below, at nn. 50–51), it is highly likely that he had some contact with the exiled Henry during the return journey.

44. *CPR, 1476–85*, pp. 413, 534; *DKR*, 37:645, 646; *Polydore Vergil's English History*, ed. H. Ellis, Camden Society Publications, no. 29 (London, 1844), p. 215.

45. *Polydore Vergil's English History*, pp. 216, 221; S. B. Chrimes, *Henry VII* (London, 1972), pp. 44, 45.

46. Edward Hall, *Chronicle . . .*, ed. H. Ellis (London, 1809), p. 414; Charles D. Ross, *Edward IV* (London, 1974), p. 143.

47. *CPR, 1485–94*, pp. 9, 10; Somerville, *Duchy of Lancaster*, 1:550–54; *Rotuli Parliamentorum* (London, 1783), 6:361.

was elected Knight of the Garter, he secured further royal appointments.[48] The land he obtained was in the Midlands, but many of the offices were in Worcestershire and Gloucestershire, where he already held Hanley Castle. The result was a veritable corner in royal office in that area. He was sheriff of Worcestershire for life, steward of the town of Tewkesbury, and steward and bailiff of Hanley, as well as constable, steward, and bailiff of eight other royal manors, master of the game at Malvern Chase and Corse Lawn Chase, and parker of six royal parks.[49] Coupled with this was a position of influence with the new king. Sir John was, it seems, the one former military supporter who belonged to the inner ring of Henry VII's counselors, and his brother Thomas, who had become a royal chaplain immediately after Bosworth, was also intimate with the king.[50] Thus, of eleven known meetings of the king's Council in the months June-July 1486, one or both brothers were present at eight.[51] "Ever the longer the greater" would have been a highly appropriate motto for the family.

Thus far the story of the Savage family has exemplified the realities of politics in fifteenth-century England, the ultimate dependence of the monarch on the social and economic power of his supporters and a consequent toleration by the crown of local autonomy. No doubt men like John Savage and his multitude of relations expected this to continue unchanged, but under the new king the situation began to alter. This was not a change in kind; there was no "new monarchy," no "Tudor despotism," no assault on the social realities of retaining. The change was a change of balance. If Henry VII was to avoid the fate of his predecessor he had to be dominant in his kingdom. Certainly he would need to rely on the "power" of the great man, but he had to assert a veto on its use. At the same time he had to tighten control over his own "power," that proportion of local influence and authority which men like Savage exercised by virtue of holding royal offices and estates. From the start these intentions are clear, and the longer Henry Tudor survived the more vigorous did the policies become. A statute of 1487 (3 Hen. 7, c. 15) decreed loss of office or lands by any royal officer or farmer who retained others or was himself retained or who failed to report retaining by those under him; by the end of the reign there was a relentless pursuit of every significant disregard of royal authority and every hint of independence. Even close supporters would have their knuckles rapped—and worse—if the king scented a challenge. In 1492, Richard Savage, brother of the Bosworth veteran, failed to appear to answer an accusation of murder;

48. *CPR, 1485–94*, pp. 101, 102, 204 (for the full text see G. Ormerod, *History of the County Palatine and City of Chester*, ed. T. Helsby, 3 vols. [London, 1875–82], 1:713); *Letters and Accounts of William Brereton*, pp. 126–47; Shaw, *Knights of England*, 1:18.

49. Although sheriff, he apparently sat for Worcestershire in the 1491–92 Parliament; see J. C. Wedgwood and A. Holt, *History of Parliament: Biographies* (London, 1936), p. 742.

50. *Select Cases in the Council of Henry VII*, pp. xxx, xxxi.

51. Ibid., pp. 8–12.

his father was imprisoned and only released when Sir John IV himself guaranteed to produce his brother.[52]

Henry VII, of course, could only risk pursuing these policies against individuals; hence the idea that he set out to attack the nobility is absurd, and certain supporters in whom he had special trust were clearly given more latitude than others and, indeed, might be in a position to exploit their influence with such a stern disciplinarian. This was true of Richard Empson in his well-attested endeavor to strip the assets of the Plumpton family, and it was also true of the Savages.[53] As it happened, the key person here was Thomas Savage, not his elder brother Sir John IV. In 1492, the latter died at the height of his favor with Henry VII and with much still in prospect as the Tudor dynasty settled ever more firmly on the throne he had helped to win.

The circumstances surrounding the death of Sir John Savage IV at the siege of Boulogne verged on the ludicrous: "There was few or none killed, saving only Sir John Savage, knight, which going privily out of his pavilion with Sir John Riseley [another Bosworth veteran], rode about the walls to view and see their strength, was suddenly intercepted and taken of his enemies. And he being inflamed with ire, although he were captive, of his high courage disdained to be taken of such villains, defended his life to the uttermost and was manfully, I will not say wilfully, slain and oppressed, albeit Sir John Riseley fled from them and escaped their danger."[54] Thomas Savage, on the other hand, rose steadily in Henry VII's service, eventually becoming president of the king's Council, and his rewards rose from the see of Rochester to the see of London and finally to the archbishopric of York.[55] We may presume his influence in the regrant of the offices lost by the Boulogne fiasco to his brother's son and heir, John V, the future defendant in *Savage's Case*.[56] We may also suspect the hand of Thomas in the introduction of the nephew to court, where he followed his father and grandfather in the rank of knight of the body.[57] John V himself was already married to a Cheshire heiress, Anne Bostock, but court connections—and almost certainly Uncle Thomas—enabled him to secure an outstanding match for his young son, John VI, later to be the refugee in Clerkenwell sanctuary.[58] The bride was Elizabeth, the eldest daughter of Charles Somerset, Henry VII's illegitimate cousin, soon to be earl of Worcester and from 1508–26 lord chamberlain of the royal household, and the match brought the Savages four hundred pounds.[59]

Behind the favor Archbishop Savage enjoyed, and provided it gave no

52. *DKR*, 26:28.

53. *Plumpton Correspondence*, ed. T. Stapleton, Camden Society Publications, no. 4 (London, 1839), pp. cii–cxxiii.

54. Hall, *Chronicle*, p. 459.

55. *Select Cases in the Council of Henry VII*, pp. xxxviii, xxxix.

56. *CPR*, *1485–94*, p. 454; ibid., *1494–1509*, p. 62.

57. *Select Cases in the Council of Henry VII*, p. 134. He was in office by 1501.

58. *DKR*, 26:28; 37:646.

59. Cheshire County Record Office DCH/E293.

hint of insubordination, the family was able to enjoy a considerable autonomy. Anne Bostock claimed the manor of Kinderton as coheiress to the Venables family, against the heir-male, Thomas Venables. Sir John V renewed this claim in Star Chamber in right of his wife, but Venables, surprisingly, succeeded in having the case remitted to common law.[60] Thomas Savage thereupon pulled strings with the earl of Shrewsbury over the composition of the jury, and when the Savages won, part of the winnings were granted to Sir Thomas Lovell and Edmund Dudley, two of the king's confidants, and the Venables family was forced to renounce any remaining rights to the crown.[61] When John IV had been alive, he and his father had joined in a renewed assault on Robert Pilkington's title to Mellor. In 1492 they "sent out many divers letters to divers gentlemen in Lancashire, Cheshire and Derbyshire and also to Mellor, Chapel [en le Frith] and other places, read and shewed on festival days in the pulpit, desiring and charging all manner of men that would do for them, to rise against the said Robert with John Ainsworth their near kinsman and household servant as they would think to have them to do for them in time coming or in any wise to be their good masters or friends."[62] After Boulogne, when the dispute was taken before the king's Council, there was the bishop of Rochester to maintain Ainsworth "by awe or law," and when in 1496 the parties began litigation we find John V assisting his uncle in laboring the jury so that it gave a verdict against Pilkington in defiance of directions from the bench. "These were known and proved to be for the most partial quest that ever passed at Derby that any man could think or heard tell. They were as bondmen to the Savages, divers ways related or allied, old household servants, free tenants retained by fee or livery (and some were both), gain-dwellers to the Savages and their children, and divers of them related to Ainsworth or his wife so that they were all partial and non-equal, with much subtle craft amongst some of the quest that some wist not of."[63]

The only threat to the position of the Savage family came from Sir John Savage V himself. Although he had passed his apprenticeship at court and in local affairs under the guidance of his highly experienced uncle, he seems not to have recognized that autonomy and influence had to be exercised with discretion and a wary eye on the king. Among his father's offices, he had succeeded to the Duchy of Lancaster stewardship of the High Peak in Derbyshire.[64] In November 1494 (as Pilkington recorded), "Young John Savage, esquire, set a session at Tideswell in the High Peak, and there he caused many men to be judged of felony, riot

60. *Select Cases in the Council of Henry VII*, pp. 130–34.

61. Hist. MSS Comm., *Calendar of the Shrewsbury and Talbot Papers*, ed. C. Jamieson and G. Batho (1966–71), 1:18; *Lancashire and Cheshire Cases in the Court of Star Chamber*, ed. R. Stewart-Brown, Lancashire and Cheshire Record Society, vol. 71 (Manchester, 1916), pp. 111–12; *DKR*, 37:480.

62. Hist. MSS Comm., *Various Collections*, 2:32.

63. Ibid., 2:31, 38–42.

64. Somerville, *Duchy of Lancaster*, 1:551.

and trespass that belonged unto Master Vernon, for ill will."[65] The royal Council canceled the indictments after enquiry, but the intent to use crown office to strike at a rival family was evident. Four years later, Sir John Savage V lost the High Peak office on the grounds of inefficiency, and in 1507 it was in the hands of "Master," that is, Sir Henry Vernon.[66] What we know of Sir John's private affairs certainly suggests extravagance and assertion. He burdened his estates with family annuities and kept a high style, even maintaining his own standard bearer.[67] When the archbishop died in 1507, the nephew was in debt to him to the tune of £414 13s. 10d., and even more heavily to the king.[68] One of Henry VII's devices was "to have many persons in his danger at his pleasure" by extorting from them acknowledgements of debts to the crown and in many cases actual payments.[69] Among the debts when Thomas Savage died were three such bonds by John V to the king, totaling 300 marks, which the archbishop had paid on his behalf.[70] Over and above this, John V was further obliged to the crown to pay £550 over five and a half years, and there were probably other sums as well.[71] Certainly John V appears persistently as a debtor to the king in the early years of Henry VIII's reign, and by 1515 some of his estates were being taken over to secure payment.[72] The menace of Henry VII is well seen in a note attached to the bonds paid by the archbishop, to the effect that they had been left uncanceled to encourage Sir John to repay the money to his uncle under threat that otherwise they would be returned to the king!

If the record of John Savage V invited royal displeasure that even his uncle could not divert entirely, the death of Thomas Savage exposed the family in a way it had not experienced for twenty years. For the first time since Bosworth, the Savages had nobody with a close contact with the king. True, the place of John V as knight of the body kept him in touch with court (in 1509 he would take his place in the funeral procession for Henry VII as a prominent member of the household).[73] True, his son had married the lord chamberlain's daughter. But the family was clearly vulnerable in a new way. There was also another omen; eighteen months after the death of Archbishop Savage, Henry VII died. What would be the policies of the new reign?

At first sight the wave of reaction against Henry VII's methods that

65. Hist. MSS Comm., *Various Collections*, 2:34, 35.

66. Somerville, *Duchy of Lancaster*, 1:551, 552.

67. *Letters and Accounts of William Brereton*, pp. 82–83, 147, 218–19, 229–30, 256–57, 261; Ormerod, *Chester*, 1:714, 715 and nn.

68. *Testamenta Eboracensia*, ed. J. Raine et al., 6 vols., Surtees Society (Durham, 1836–1902), 4:309; see below, at n. 71.

69. C. J. Harrison, "The Petition of Edmund Dudley," *English Historical Review* 87 (1972): 86, 87.

70. *Testamenta Eboracensia*, 4:309.

71. *Calendar of Close Rolls*, 60 vols. (London, 1892–1963) (hereafter cited as *CCR*), *1500–09*, p. 306 (no. 811).

72. *LP*, 1 (pt. 1):680 (no. 1493); *LP*, 1 (pt. 2):1452 (no. 3483); *LP*, 2 (pt. 1):370 (no. 1364); *LP*, 3 (pt. 2):1527 (no. 3694).

73. *LP*, 1 (pt. 1):14 (no. 20).

began on his death might seem to favor the Savages and those like them.[74] The apparatus and much of the will for the late king's policy of rigor was abandoned. Some ministers were disgraced, others lost status, many of those "in danger" had their debts and obligations canceled. Influence with the king passed from the hardheaded bureaucrats to the more gallant courtly tradition represented by Charles Brandon, Edward Neville, and the younger Howard brothers. But the Savages were outside this group; their recognizances were not canceled; and although John V provided a contingent for the 1512 campaign and his son, John VI, led a company in 1513 and was knighted at Tournai, they belonged to the past.[75] It is a truism, fully accepted only by the Ottoman state, that the loyal and therefore favored servants of one ruler all too easily become in themselves or their children a political liability to his successor. In any case, the Tournai campaign was the final step in the rise to power of Thomas Wolsey and marks the end of the period of reaction after 1509. Wolsey would take the strong rule of Henry VII, which had been a reflection partly of the first Tudor's instinct for survival and partly of his calculating temperament, and make it a permanent feature of English government. After Wolsey there would still be local autonomy and high-handed behavior, but politics would no longer turn on the ability of this or that great man to "make" in harness so many men. At the crisis of his reign, Henry VIII would find that a majority of his critics were not willing to call out their powers to support the Pilgrimage of Grace. In the later sixteenth century the Savages would still be prominent, but prominent as leaders of the Cheshire elite, providing more sheriffs than any other family, not as counters worth so many men in the political game.[76] Between the days when the Savages had been important because of "a multitude of brothers, kinsmen, servants and friends" and the days when the Savages would be important as county magistrates lies the rule of the cardinal and the discipline of *Savage's (Sir John) Case* and *Savage's Case.*

III

Wolsey announced his "law and order" campaign at an assembly of the Council in the presence of the king on 2 May 1516, a deliberately large and ceremonious gathering that saw the first demonstration of the new policy in the public humiliation of the earl of Northumberland "for divers contempts."[77] This was only a month after the Pauncefote killing,

74. J. A. Guy, "Wolsey, the Council and the Council Courts," *English Historical Review* 91 (1976): 481–505; B. P. Wolffe, *The Crown Lands, 1461–1536* (London and New York, 1970), pp. 76–78; Chrimes, *Henry VII*, pp. 314–17.

75. *LP*, 1 (pt. 1):552 (no. 1176 [ii]), *LP*, 1 (pt. 2):927 (no. 2053 [6ii]), 963 (no. 2130 [5]), 1027 (no. 2301), 1070 (no. 2414).

76. B. Coward, "The Lieutenancy of Lancashire and Cheshire in the Sixteenth and early Seventeenth Centuries," *Transactions of the Historic Society of Lancashire and Cheshire* 119 (1967): 42–45.

77. Guy, "Wolsey," p. 485; Guy, *The Cardinal's Court*, pp. 30–33, 72–78.

and there can have been few fresher examples of the "enormities usually exercised in his realm" that Henry, under Wolsey's promptings, vowed to root out. What lay behind the murder can only be inferred. There was no long history of friction, for in 1507 Pauncefote had acted as guarantor for one of Sir John's obligations to the crown; perhaps the link had come from their mutual Worcestershire-Gloucestershire connections or via the court where Pauncefote was a gentleman usher.[78] What could have disturbed the relationship was the rise in Pauncefote's importance. In 1504 he had become justice of the peace for Gloucestershire; in 1510 he joined the commission for Herefordshire and in 1515 that for Savage's principal territory, Worcestershire.[79] To see elevated the gentleman usher he had so outranked could well have galled a more equable knight of the body than Sir John Savage, especially at Corse Lawn, where Pauncefote had some property; having ruled there since 1492 as master of the chase, and his father before him, Sir John now found himself with a rival.[80] There was also trouble over property at Bentley Pauncefoot, across the county, for twelve days after the murder, a group of almost certainly Savage supporters occupied John Pauncefote's messuage there.[81] Nor would Pauncefote's second marriage have helped relations; his wife, Bridget Tate, was the daughter of a former lord mayor of London and member of a family that was buying into Worcestershire.[82]

This much is circumstantial, but it is easier to explain government reaction. Unprotected by association with the king, backward-looking and lacking in caution, Sir John Savage and his son were likely to figure on Wolsey's agenda in due course. But two factors account for the immediate and crushing assault that was launched against Sir John the elder and could be made to justify even a violation of church privilege. The first was pressure from the widow, whose determination is shown by her persisting in her appeal until 1520.[83] In all probability family connections helped here; her cousin, Bartholomew Tate, was a prominent member of the Calais Council and in frequent touch with Wolsey—indeed, he visited the cardinal only three weeks after the murder.[84] The second factor was that John Pauncefote had been killed in performance of his duties as justice of the peace. The records repeatedly mention his office, and the appeal of Bridget Pauncefote makes the allegation in detail.[85] Her husband was traveling to the quarter sessions at Cirencester when at nine

78. *CCR, 1500–09*, p. 306 (no. 811); *LP*, 1 (pt. 1):15 (no. 20).

79. *CPR, 1494–1509*, p. 641; *LP*, 1 (app., pt. 2):1537, 1538, 1546.

80. J. N. Langston, "Old Catholic Families of Gloucestershire," *Transactions of the Bristol and Gloucestershire Archaeological Society* 71 (1952): 13.

81. KB 9/472/11.

82. Langston, "Old Catholic Families," p. 13; Wedgwood and Holt, *Parliament: Biographies*, pp. 841, 842.

83. See below, at n. 114 and accompanying text.

84. *LP*, 1 (pt. 1):651 (no. 1424); *LP*, 1 (pt. 2):1043 (no. 2337), 1243 (no. 2861 [15]), 1405 (no. 3338); *LP*, 2 (pt. 1):129 (no. 452), 507 (no. 1790); *LP*, 2 (pt. 2):1346 (no. 4363); Public Record Office, Prerogative Court of Canterbury: Probate Registers PROB 11/24, 185.

85. KB 27/1020, m. 60.

o'clock in the morning he was set upon and killed at Haw, in the parish of Tirley, apparently when he was about to cross the Severn. Details elsewhere in the case suggest that he may have been intending to lay information against the Savages.[86] A group of their supporters had met on 24 March, allegedly to plot his murder but more probably in connection with a raid that took place two days later against the fishponds of a certain William Leyceter at Crofton Hackett, a few miles from Bentley Pauncefoot. Why is not clear, perhaps a poaching affray, but Pauncefote's connections with the area would have brought him information. He was, moreover, at Hasfield or Corse Lawn at the time, in the middle of the district from which the raiders had come, and might well have known a good deal about the episode.[87]

Whether or not there was any connection with the Crofton Hackett offense, what is clear is the crown's response to the justice's death. It was not the killing itself that was significant, but the contempt displayed to royal authority. The charge of murder was left to the widow's appeal and, as we have seen, it raised severe political and constitutional difficulties. The focus of government attention was the rule Sir John Savage V and his son kept in the territory committed to them. There had been other contempts besides the death of Pauncefote. A year before, John Grimesdiche, a Savage client from Cheshire who lived at Great Malvern, had assaulted Elizabeth, the wife of Clement ap Howell, in Malvern Church and so terrified her and her husband that they could not go about their normal business.[88] Summoned a few days later to appear before the justices of the peace and give security for the good behavior of himself and his wife toward the Howells, John refused to go, "to the contempt of the king."[89] Robbery was common. As far back as 1511, Savage followers had been helping themselves to other people's grain.[90] In 1515 another group had robbed a man of six shillings and eightpence.[91] Three weeks after the Pauncefote killing the younger Sir John had led a dozen or so of his men to seize a sum of the victim's money variously stated as between ten and eighty pounds.[92] Under the indulgent eye of Sir John the elder, sheriff of Worcestershire and royal representative in manor after manor, his own family was running a local Mafia. The Savages were particularly strong in the southwest of the county but had supporters as well in the northeast, above Pershore, and in Gloucestershire about Tewkes-

86. KB 9/472/6, m. 18.

87. Haw is the natural river crossing to use from either place to Cirencester. Difficulties with the Crofton Hackett connection are that the offense was not indictable at Cirencester because committed in Worcestershire and that, although one of the murderers was, none of the plotters was at the Crofton Hackett offense. But Pauncefote could have presented the conspiracy and identified others among the sixty "unnamed" offenders who were involved.

88. KB 9/472/23; cf. *Letters and Accounts of William Brereton*, pp. 29, 188–89, 219, 230, 256, 260–61.

89. KB 9/472/22. The Howells were possibly clients of Pauncefote (KB 27/1020, m. 60).

90. KB 27/1040, Rex m. 19.

91. KB 9/472/19.

92. KB 9/472/24–30, 54–59; KB 27/1040, m. 19.

bury.[93] In typical style, the local constables were blind and refused to make arrests or behaved in a strong-armed way themselves.[94] If any of his men were taken, Sir John V was in a position to arrange their release. Of particular interest in the lists of Savage supporters are several names from their estates further north, in Cheshire, Shropshire, and the Midlands. In addition to Grimesdiche, outsiders brought in included the bailiff of the family property in Shropshire, William Slade, a number of men with Derbyshire connections, and others who figure as recipients of annuities from Sir John, such as Towcher Breket [Birkenhead] from Cheshire, John Brurton [Brereton] from Staffordshire, and Arthur Gathagur [Gataker] from Shropshire.[95]

Sir John Savage the elder was called before the Council on 5 June. His offense at this stage was "negligence (being Sheriff of [Worcestershire]) in apprehending the murderers of Pauncefote and for cherishing some of them," and after a second day's hearing he was committed to the Tower.[96] There followed the appearance to answer the appeal of murder and the remand to the Tower following his son's plea to be returned to sanctuary, but no action on any other count. Not until 5 November was a commission set up to inquire into riots, ill deeds, and other offenses in Herefordshire, Gloucestershire, Worcestershire, and the Marches of Wales.[97] The reason for the delay was probably a struggle at court between friends of the Savages and those who, for whatever reason, wished to see them harshly dealt with. John VI's father-in-law, the lord chamberlain, had returned to England from Tournai just before the Pauncefote murder, and the prosecution did not begin until he was on the point of departing again.[98] Mary, the king's sister, was possibly already involved also; she was certainly pressing Wolsey later on behalf of Antony Savage, the brother to one of her women servants.[99] For Wolsey, the attack on the lawlessness and consequence of the Savages was part of a general policy, but he too was reinforced by court intrigue.[100] Sir William Compton, a rapacious courtier with considerable influence on Henry, was at this time "marvellous great" with the cardinal, and it was ominous when the commission was at last issued that Compton was one of the quorum of three.[101] A month later he actually replaced Sir John, Sr., as sheriff of Worcester and in the following July acquired all his other offices in the

93. From the styles of those indicted.

94. KB 9/472/31; KB 27/1040, Rex 19.

95. *Letters and Accounts of William Brereton*, pp. 105, 141–44, 219, 222, 230, 256–57, 261, 273, 275; Public Record Office, Star Chamber (hereafter cited as STAC) 2/21/242; *DKR*, 39:234; *LP*, 3 (pt. 2):972, at 973 (no. 2297 [12]); *LP*, 4 (pt. 2):1270 (no. 2839 [28]).

96. Hunt. Ell. MS 2652, fol. 3.

97. KB 9/472/1.

98. *LP*, 2 (pt. 1):420 (no. 1509), 856 (no. 2706).

99. See below, at n. 121 and accompanying text.

100. The Council debates on sanctuary in early Nov. 1519 were preceded on 27 and 28 Oct. by renewed meetings on the "law and order" theme (Guy, "Wolsey," p. 486).

101. Edmund Lodge, *Illustrations of British History . . . in the Reigns of Henry VIII, Edward VI, Mary, Elizabeth and James I*, 3 vols. (London, 1838), 1:22; KB 9/472/1.

area.[102] The topographer John Leland echoed the affair twenty years later: "[Hanley] Castle stands in a park at the west part of the town. Sir John Savage and his father and grandfather lay much about Hanley and Tewkesbury as keepers of Hanley. The Earls of Gloucester were owners of this castle and lay much there. Mr. Compton clean defaced it in his time, being keeper of it after Savage."[103] This element of court intrigue would also explain why Sir John V resisted with such intransigence; there was no point in appealing for royal favor when the king had already been persuaded to prejudge him.

The delay after June, however explained, is in marked contrast to the haste that takes over on the issue of the commission of 5 November. On the fourteenth the first indictments were taken at Worcester, and on the twenty-fifth both the Savages and one of their men who was also in the Tower, William Phippes, were produced in King's Bench.[104] Sir John the younger and Phippes were charged with theft from Pauncefote and Sir John the elder with aiding and abetting. Sir John, Sr., was also charged with allowing prisoners to escape from custody and with abusing his tourn or sheriff's court. Having pleaded "not guilty" the accused were returned to the Tower, but next day the king's attorney returned to the question of the escapes and the tourn. He laid an information before the King's Bench and asked for the office of sheriff to be seized into royal hands.[105] The justices agreed.

In the meantime the commission was still at work, and the full case against the Savages, father and son, and their supporters reached King's Bench on 12 February 1517.[106] Twenty-three indictments had been received in November and now there were at least forty-four more.[107] Two refer to the Pauncefote murder, twenty-seven to the theft of money from Pauncefote, four to the release of prisoners by Sir John, Sr., and twelve to various offenses of murder, assault, riot, forcible entry, and the like by his men. Twelve counts alleged retaining, two against Sir John V for offending himself, nine against him for failing to report his son's retaining of royal tenants in breach of 3 Hen. 7, c. 15, and one against those retained. Also presented were six abuses of office as keeper of various parks by unlicensed hunting. The recital owes something of its impact to the repetition of offenses for each of the manors and offices John Savage V held, and to recapitulation with differing lists of accessories, but it shows nevertheless a massive royal determination to humble the Savage family and to destroy its hereditary influence in Worcestershire and Gloucestershire, once and for all. The care is evident in many of the indictments,

102. *LP*, 2 (pt. 1):846 (no. 2684); *LP*, 1 (pt. 2):1106 (no. 3483).

103. John Leland, *The Itinerary of John Leland* . . . , ed. L. T. Smith, 8 vols. in 5 (London, 1906–10), 8:135.

104. KB 27/1021, mm. 17, 18, 19d, 20, 20d.

105. KB 27/1021, m. 21; KB 29/148, m. 44.

106. KB 9/472/1.

107. Eight other indictments are in the file but not demonstrably associated with the Savages: KB 9/472/15, 16, 17, 20, 50, 51, 52, 53.

which carry annotations made in preparation for or in the conduct of the case. The indictment of John VI for the death of Pauncefote is headed *Murdro* and glossed with a note against two others accused, "Memorandum to enter this by her self for Bryked & Heritage—Gloucestershire"; other documents are annotated as appropriate—*de ingressu, de deliberatione signorum, de contemptu, de felonia, negligencio escapio.*[108]

Despite this formidable weight of accusation, everything would ultimately turn on a jury selected from the very region where Savage influence had reigned supreme and where Sir John, as sheriff, had had responsibility for the selection of jury panels. It was, perhaps, to lessen this influence as well as to benefit Compton that the king's attorney, John Erneley, had laid the information and secured seizure of the office. Keilwey's *Reports*, however, show that this also enabled the crown to avoid action on the indictments and initiate *Savage's Case* proper on a *scire facias*, calling on Sir John to show cause why his office should not be forfeit.

With Savage in the Tower and the offices already granted or earmarked for Compton, the crown could take its time, and it was not until Michaelmas 1518 that Sir John the elder was able to begin his answer. His object throughout seems to have been to get before a jury, and he opened with a formidable plea. The indictments on which the information had been grounded had referred to his holding office by virtue of a patent of 1512, granted jointly to himself and his son in survivorship.[109] Sir John now claimed that this patent had been obtained without his knowledge or consent, that he had never exercised office by reason of it, and that there was no record of his accepting it. He held by an earlier grant of 1495 to himself alone and disclaimed entirely any benefit from the later patent; he offered to prove this and asked to be restored to his offices.[110] The case was adjourned and argued at length in the following Easter term. Savage kept up his pressure. He argued that procedure by *scire facias* was improper because the commission had been asked to investigate felonies, not titles to office, and on a felony the accused could go to trial. Moreover, the court had acted *ultra vires* in suspending his posts because his letters patent had not been revoked; the crown was claiming on a simple unproven allegation which he had the right to traverse—after all, the court had called him to answer the presentment! The court, however, would not go so far. It pointed out that although loss of land only followed a jury verdict, with an office the position was different; an office was granted on an implied condition of trust, and if that trust was violated, this was ground for forfeiture. As for the propriety of *scire facias*,

108. The murder indictment memorandum (KB 9/472/6) is clearly addressed to the clerk entering the roll. It is, however, erroneous in giving the date of the murder as 21, not 31 Mar.

109. *LP*, 1 (pt. 1):708 (no. 1524 [47]); the grant is annotated that it differs from previous grants only by being granted jointly to father and son.

110. *CPR, 1494–1509*, p. 62; this replaced earlier grants, one to his father, John IV, and himself in survivorship, and one to John V alone (*CPR, 1485–94*, pp. 204, 454).

Fineux accepted the contention of the royal lawyers that this was equivalent to a quo warranto: "All liberties and all such offices came initially from the King, and for this reason the law concludes that all such liberties and offices will be understood to be in the King's hands and therefore the King can at all times require holders to prove their claim."[111] The king's serjeants then attempted to counter the demurrer on the indictments. The office was at risk following the indictment for allowing prisoners to escape, irrespective of which patent was alleged; because Savage had not taken issue on the escapes, he had "confessed by implication," his office was plainly forfeit, and they asked for the cancellation of both patents. This the court refused to do, but it did cancel the 1512 patent.[112]

The crown could hardly have been pleased with its progress, and a year later, Hilary 1520, Savage appeared again to answer a *scire facias* against his original grant. The escape of prisoners was once more alleged and this time the abuse of the tourn was taken up. The particulars were that his undersheriff in 1513–14 had held the court at Pershore and Piddle; this, it was claimed, violated Magna Carta, which required the tourn to be held in the "proper and accustomed place," which was Worcester. This time there was no defense in law to fall back on and Savage pleaded not guilty to the escapes and traversed the finding on the tourn; Pershore and Piddle were the time-honored locations, not Worcester. Once more he was taking a position to force jury trial on favorable terms. For the crown, Serjeant Thomas Pigot could only press the royal privilege to pursue multiple pleas by joining issue on both indictments for escape and by challenging the location of the tourn as well.[113] But by this time it began to look less and less likely that any jury would ever sit on Sir John Savage's misdeeds. It was in this same term that his son had dropped the plea for sanctuary and confessed to the murder of Pauncefote. An additional sign was the unexplained failure of the widow to appear as usual to press her appeal, and she was accordingly nonsuited. A deal was being done behind the scenes; the king's sister Mary was pressing Wolsey, and it was hard to deny an earl of Worcester on whose endeavors the success of the Field of Cloth of Gold depended.[114] The royal case against Sir John, Sr., went through the mo-

111. Keil. 196, 72 *Eng. Rep.* 375.

112. Keil. 196b, 72 *Eng. Rep.* 375, notes the gossip that if Savage had risked a plea of "not guilty" and been unsuccessful he could not have been condemned for felony because he was answering a *scire facias* and not arraignment, but it might have estopped a plea of "not guilty" on a subsequent indictment. No discussion is reported on the voiding of the grant by 6 Hen. 8, c. 25 (*LP*, 2 [pt. 1]:846 [no. 2684]). This act attempted to suppress regrant of offices to an existing holder and a newcomer, jointly in survivorship, but presumably it was construed that in vesting the offices in the 1512 patent in the original grantee alone, John V, the act nevertheless preserved his rights under that patent and did not produce a reversion to the patent of 1495.

113. Keil. 192a, b, 72 *Eng. Rep.* 370–71; the crown chose to join issue on the tourn in general terms.

114. *LP*, 3 (pt. 1):160 (no. 455) (28 Sept. 1519), 203 (no. 602) (22 Jan. 1520). Worcester was deeply involved in the arrangements for the diplomatic meeting in June (*LP*, 3 [pt. 1]:205 [no. 609], 259 [no. 738]).

tions for two more terms, but in Michaelmas 1520 he abandoned his defense and produced a royal pardon dated 27 November.[115] On the same day his son was pardoned and after four and a half years in the Tower, both were freed.[116]

In return for the pardon and release of all royal claims against him, Sir John the elder had to suffer. Following the guilty plea, all his patents for office in Worcestershire and Gloucestershire were brought in to be canceled.[117] There were financial penalties too, a fine to the king of 4,600 marks and 1,000 marks to Bridget Pauncefote and her children.[118] To secure this, almost all the Savage estates outside Cheshire were taken over by royal feoffees and leased back to the family at a rent of £160 per annum, which would clear the debt in some twenty-four years. The net income from those lands was probably about £200, leaving the family significantly impoverished.[119] What is more, their Cheshire property, worth £250–£300 net, was also recovered by the crown, apparently as extra security.[120] As for the rest of those involved, many charged as accessories had surrendered to the court and been released on bail, but the pardon of Sir John and his son was the signal for those who had been outlawed as principals in the murder to make their peace with the crown. The experience of outlawry had been more than an inconvenience. William Horton of Staunton had seen his property granted away to the queen's attorney, and, according to the king's sister, Antony Savage was so impoverished that he had nothing to live on.[121] With their leaders in the Tower, perhaps the retainers had suffered more than most outlaws. Horton and Savage were pardoned in the spring of 1521.[122] In Trinity term a large group of Savage supporters appeared in King's Bench and were discharged on the report of the king's attorney that they had been indicted "by sinister means of their adversaries!" Individuals continued to appear until Michaelmas 1529 at least; Wolsey would not allow men to take even a pardon as a formality.

Did the Savages learn their lesson? Probably not. Within a year of the pardon they were feuding with Ralph Leche, who had bought the lease of their manor of Ilkeston while they were in the Tower.[123] Once again the

115. KB 29/148, m. 51; *LP*, 3 (pt. 1):397 (no. 1081 [27]).

116. KB 29/148, m. 51d; *LP*, 3 (pt. 1):397 (no. 1081 [27]).

117. *CPR, 1485–94*, pp. 9, 204, 454; *CPR, 1494–1509*, p. 62.

118. Public Record Office, Chancery (hereafter cited as C) 66/671, m. 20 (*LP*, 12 [pt. 1]:352 [no. 795 (38)]).

119. *Letters and Accounts of William Brereton*, p. 19.

120. The rent was not increased by this (ibid., p. 19). The Cheshire lands may have been held against good behavior, because Peter Leycester records as part of the financial settlement deed, dated 24 Nov. 1520, a requirement that the Savages keep out of Worcester and Cheshire unless given a royal license, which John, Jr., received in 1524 (Ormerod, *Chester*, 1:714, 715 and nn.).

121. *LP*, 2 (pt. 2):1230 (no. 3960); *LP*, 3 (pt. 1):203 (no. 602).

122. *LP*, 3 (pt. 1):479 (no. 1262 [18]), 529 (no. 1324 [6]). KB 27/1040, Rex m. 3d, shows that the pardon to Savage on 6 May 1520 (*LP*, 3 [pt. 1]:297 [no. 854 (6)]) was premature or is an error.

123. STAC 2/21/242.

Council had to investigate tales of riot and violence by their followers, some still outlawed on the Pauncefote charge, and allegations that Sir John and his son did "not regard and dread the punishment of the laws."[124] Leche was a difficult man, but when Wolsey attempted a solution by arbitration in 1525, it was Sir John, Sr., who would have none of it.[125] The long-standing feud with Sir Piers Dutton of Halton had gone on even while the two Savages were in the Tower.[126] Again the Council had to step in, as it had in 1523 over a theft committed by a servant of Sir John, Sr.[127] In 1528 the quarrel with Dutton flared up with new intensity over the succession to some property in Cheshire.[128] But shorn of public office and heavily in debt to the crown, the Savages were not what they had been. Sir John, Sr., died in 1527.[129] Already, in 1515, Sir John the younger had sold part of his maternal inheritance; in 1523 he was further in debt and within months of succeeding his father he had defaulted on the payments to the crown for the Pauncefote fine.[130] On Lady Day 1528, the crown foreclosed.[131] John did not live much longer; within months he also was dead, and his property and the wardship of his infant son, John VII (d. 1597), were granted to the Cheshire courtier William Brereton, groom of Henry VIII's privy chamber, who proceeded to marry the widow.[132] Sir John the elder and Sir John the younger lay in monumental effigy in the church of Macclesfield, dressed in the traditional armor of the medieval magnate, but the power base along the Severn that John IV had built up was gone for good; indeed, so too was much of the winnings from his successful gamble at Bosworth.[133] John Savage VII would grow to be a worshipful Elizabethan gentleman, separated by more than years from the world of his father, grandfather, and great-grandfather.

Isobel Thornley concluded her seminal study of the destruction of sanctuary with the words of Hallam: "In the rapine and tumult of the Middle Ages, the right of sanctuary might as often be a shield to innocence as an impunity to crime. We can hardly regret, in reflecting on the desolating violence which prevailed, that there should have been some green spots in the wilderness where the feeble and the persecuted could

124. Leche complains that the Savages are harboring Henry Whetely, who is outlawed for the Pauncefote murder; cf. KB 29/148, m. 36d.

125. *Letters and Accounts of William Brereton*, pp. 54, 278; STAC 2/21/242/1.

126. *Letters and Accounts of William Brereton*, pp. 32–33; *Lancashire and Cheshire Cases in Star Chamber*, pp. 48–50.

127. Hunt. Ell. MS 2652, fol. 10.

128. *Lancashire and Cheshire Cases in Star Chamber*, pp. 87–92, 115; *LP*, 4 (app., pt. 3):3170 (no. 207).

129. *DKR*, 39:233; Ormerod, *Chester*, 1:714, 715.

130. *DKR*, 39:231; *Letters and Accounts of William Brereton*, pp. 19, 59.

131. *Letters and Accounts of William Brereton*, p. 113.

132. Ibid., pp. 1–2.

133. F. H. Crossley, "Medieval Monumental Effigies Remaining in Cheshire," *Transactions of the Historic Society of Lancashire and Cheshire* 76 (1924): 1–51, at pp. 25, 27, 47, 48.

find refuge."[134] It is not just the passage of time that makes this humane Victorian sentiment seem unwarranted. To explore the disgrace of the Savage family is to become aware of much wider implications. What in legal terms might be seen as a timely vindication of national interest over a now outmoded privilege will appear to the constitutional historian as a rehearsal for the royal supremacy. The student of administration finds the assertion of central authority under the control of the cardinal and the Council against the tradition of delegated local authority and high-handed provincial autonomy. The historian of society sees in the experience of one great family an example of a nationwide divide in values and attitudes. The historian of politics sees the end of a chapter opened in 1485 at Bosworth or even at St. Albans, thirty years earlier, or equally a demonstration of the identity in Tudor times of law with politics, what may appear to the legal historian as an instance of the legislative function assumed by the judicial bench. The saga of Sir John Savage V and Sir John Savage VI warns of the impossibility of historical apartheid; it has much to tell us of each of these topics, but above all it calls us to see them all together, as one untidy, complicated, multifaceted piece of human experience. Hallam's plea of sanctuary must fail because there was more to it than that.

134. Thornley, "Destruction of Sanctuary," p. 207.

11 Future Interests and Royal Revenues in the Sixteenth Century

J. L. Barton

If an estate may be well limited in contingency, it is possible to confer an interest by purchase upon a person not yet born. For the crown, this was not an indifferent matter. If the tenant by knight's service settled his land upon his wife or children, the Statute of Wills and the Act of Explanation[1] secured the king the wardship of the body of the heir and of one-third of the land, if the heir were an infant, or relief and primer seisin for one-third, if the heir were of full age. If the settlement limited interests to the settlor's grandchildren in remainder after the interests to his children, the king would be entitled to nothing when the children died. The grandchildren did not take by descent, and they did not take under a settlement made by their father. In practice, land would be settled on the marriage of the settlor's children rather than upon the settlor's death, for the relations of a prospective bride of suitable rank would be unwilling to part with her portion except in exchange for a satisfactory provision for her. The children of an intended marriage are, in the nature of the case, not yet born. Thus, the question how far the prudent settlor could protect his family against feudal incidents by the limitation of successive interests depended on the further question how far it was possible to limit such interests to persons not in being.

There was still considerable force in the argument that a remainder must pass out of the settlor by the original livery, and that it cannot pass unless there be then some person in whom it may vest. In the sixteenth century, it was too late to contend that a remainder might not be well limited to the heir of J. S., though J. S. were living at the date of the conveyance. St. German appears even to have thought that if the tenant for life predeceased J. S., the remainderman might be relieved in Chancery if the settlement were made for value.[2] It was still arguable that the remainder to the heirs of J. S. was a special and anomalous case,[3] and it was long before the point was finally settled. As late as 1595 it could be observed *obiter* that a remainder may arise well enough by way of use to one who is born after the date of the limitation, but it is otherwise by way of possession.[4] According to the report of Anderson, C.J., on *Archer's*

1. Stat. 32 Hen. 8, c. 1; Stat. 34 Hen. 8, c. 5.
2. Christopher St. German, *Doctor and Student*, ed. T. F. T. Plucknett and J. L. Barton, Selden Society, vol. 91 (London, 1974), Dialogue I (Latin version), c. 18 (p. 128).
3. Colthirst v. Bejushin (1551), Plowd. 21, at 28, *per* Morgan, Sjt., *arguendo*, 75 *English Reports* (hereafter cited as *Eng. Rep.*) 33, at 45.
4. Blodwell v. Edwards, Mo. 430, 72 *Eng. Rep.* 675.

Case,[5] to which he was a party, the principal ground of the decision was that the remainder to the right heir of tenant for life was void in its limitation, because it could not vest during the particular estate. In *Arden* v. *Darcy*[6] in the same series of reports, land was limited to the use of A for life or until her remarriage, and after her death or remarriage to the use of B. It was held that nothing vested in B, because the remainder was to begin upon a disjunctive, and it was uncertain which event would first happen. The remainder would have been in abeyance if limited in these terms at common law, assuming that it might have been validly limited, which was doubtful. It had been held in 16 Eliz. that a remainder to the heir of A will be void if limited after an estate for the life of A, because it cannot vest until A dies. Thus, if this remainder were to commence at all, it must commence upon condition, and it was at least debatable whether an interest granted to a third party might validly be limited to take effect upon a condition precedent.

The point at which the line between a vested and a contingent interest should be drawn was clearly still in doubt. The argument that a remainder limited upon a condition can be supported only if we hold that a third person may take advantage of a condition had been urged and rejected in *Colthirst* v. *Bejushin*,[7] but was accepted in 1594 in *Cogan* v. *Cogan*.[8] An estate cannot be well limited to commence upon a condition precedent, and in so far as *Colthirst* v. *Bejushin* may be taken as authority to the contrary, it is bad law. The sixteenth-century controversies over the common-law rules of limitation have been largely concealed from posterity by the systemizing endeavors of Sir Edward Coke. Whatever criticisms may be made of his reports, his success in itself is proof that the age was much in need of a reporter with the courage of his convictions, who would take it as his mission to provide the student with an anthology of authorities for the correct opinions. He settled the law for the next generation, however, rather than for his own, and even in the *Reports* there are some traces of the prevailing uncertainty. Posterity was to have some difficulty in determining the effect of the principle that a remainder must vest upon a necessary and common, rather than a remote, possibility,[9] or that contingencies must be single, and may not be double.[10]

Before the Statute of Uses, there had been no serious question that much might be done by use which could not be done by limitation of the common-law estate. In the last years of the sixteenth century, when the

5. 2 And. 37, 123 *Eng. Rep.* 533 (1597).

6. 2 And. 93, at 103, 123 *Eng. Rep.* 563, at 568 (1596).

7. Plowd. 21, 75 *Eng. Rep.* 33 (1551); see also John Perkins, *A Profitable Book* (London, 1657), §56.

8. Cro. Eliz. 360, 78 *Eng. Rep.* 608.

9. Cholmley's Case (1597), 2 Rep. 50a at 51a, 76 *Eng. Rep.* 527, at 530. This seems to be a reminiscence of the argument of Serjeant Morgan, cited above, at n. 3.

10. The Rector of Chedington's Case (1598), 1 Rep. 153a, at 156b, 76 *Eng. Rep.* 343, at 351.

implications of the decision in *Chudleigh's Case*[11] were being worked out, there were some suggestions that no interest could be limited by way of use if it could not validly be limited as a remainder, or even that all contingent uses were void, because the statute did not execute them.[12] Neither view was directly supported by decision, and in the earlier years of the century either would have led to practical difficulties that the judges understandably preferred to avoid, for the effect upon existing settlements executed by the statute would have been at once drastic and capricious. It was therefore natural that settlors should prefer upon the whole to limit uses rather than common-law estates, especially because the conveyance to uses had the additional practical advantage that the settlor himself might take an interest under the settlement without a reconveyance. Contingent uses, therefore, were a problem of more immediate concern than contingent remainders.

By definition, a contingent use is vested in no one. There were thus two possible views that might be held: that the statute converted the contingent use into a legal possibility, or that the statute did not execute the contingent use until it vested. On the latter view, until the use vested, something must remain in the feoffees out of which it could be executed. If this were the case, it was at least possible that the feoffees might prevent the use from arising by extinguishing or parting with that something, just as they might have destroyed the use at the common law by parting with their estate to a purchaser for value without notice. A possibility, on the other hand, is a singularly indestructible form of interest, if it be correct to call it an interest at all. Because it is no estate, it cannot be divested or discontinued. So far as the reported decisions go, the first of these two views seems to be slightly the earlier. Three years after the Statute of Uses, we have a very remarkable case. A covenants with B that when B shall enfeoff A of three acres of land in Dale, A and his heirs and all those who shall be seised of the lands of A in Sale shall stand seised thereof to the use of B and his heirs. A makes a feoffment of his lands in Sale. B enfeoffs A of three acres in Dale. A's feoffee is seised to the use of B and his heirs, and it is not material whether he have notice of the covenant. The land is bound by the use into whosesoever hands it may come. This is not like the case of a feoffee to uses who sells to one who has no notice of the first use, for here there is no use until B has enfeoffed

11. 1 Rep. 120a, 76 *Eng. Rep.* 270; Pop. 70, 79 *Eng. Rep.* 1184; 1 And. 309, 123 *Eng. Rep.* 489 (1595).

12. Wells v. Fenton (1601), Cro. Eliz. 826, 78 *Eng. Rep.* 1053, *per* Anderson. The other members of the court disagreed, and it is not easy to be certain just how seriously this observation was intended, but compare Bacon in his reading on the statute: "... as to what Glanvile, justice, said, he could never find by any book, or evidence of antiquity, a contingent use limited over to a stranger; I answer, first, it is no marvel that you find no case before E. IV his time, of contingent uses, where there be not six uses in all &c." (Francis Bacon, *The Works of Francis Bacon, Baron of Verulam, Viscount St. Alban, and Lord High Chancellor of England*, 5 vols. [London, 1778], 2:423).

A of three acres, and then the use arises.[13] In 1552, however, land had been mortgaged by feoffment to the use of A and his heirs until payment, and upon payment to the use of B and his heirs. In the view of the majority, B would be seised in fee if he paid the money and reentered, but there were some who thought that the feoffees would have to enter in order to raise the use, and Brooke therefore thought it the safest course for the mortgagor to enter claiming in his own name and in the names of the feoffees.[14] In other words, the opinion that the feoffees retain something to serve the future use is held, and cannot be dismissed out of hand.

Whether they retained enough to enable them to destroy a future use was a question discussed at length in *Brent's Case*[15] in 1575. A feoffment had been made to the use of the feoffor's wife for her life, remainder to the use of the feoffor and such wife as he might subsequently marry for their lives, remainder to the use of A in fee. With the consent of the feoffor, A and the original feoffees joined in a new feoffment to X, to the use of the original feoffor and his wife for their lives, remainder to the use of B in tail, remainder to the use of the feoffor in fee. The feoffor subsequently levied a fine to yet other uses. The feoffor's wife died. The feoffor took another wife and died. The widow entered by command of the first feoffees. The question was whether her entry were lawful. Mounson and Harper, who held for the wife, argued that the statute had left nothing in the feoffees. The contingent use in favor of the feoffor's second wife was therefore in the custody of the law, and no act of the feoffees could affect it. Dyer adds that they also held that if anything did remain in the feoffees, it could be nothing more than a bare possibility, which could not be divested. Dyer and Manwood argued that by the express words of the statute the use must be executed in some certain person. It follows that if there be no person to take at the date of the feoffment, an interest out of which the future use can be executed must remain in the feoffees. This interest must necessarily be something more than a bare possibility, and there was nothing in the statute to prevent the feoffees from destroying an unexecuted use by parting with their interest, in the same manner as they might have destroyed a use at the common law. According to Leonard, Dyer held that the feoffees retained a determinable fee simple. In his own report of the case, which may have been revised, he terms the interest of the feoffees a *scintilla juris*: an expression that had a long and controversial future before it. He also held that the remainder to the second wife of the feoffor had failed in any event, because it was not vested when the previous estate determined. In this opinion he was alone, for his colleagues held that uses differed from remainders. Because the Common Pleas was equally divided upon the principal question, the

13. Sir Robert Brooke, *La Graunde Abridgement* (London, 1573), Feoffements al uses, pl. 50 (30 Hen. 8).

14. Brooke, *Abridgement*, Feoffements al uses, pl. 30 (6 Edw. 6).

15. Dyer 339b, 73 *Eng. Rep.* 766–67, 2 Leo. 14, 74 *Eng. Rep.* 319. Dalison 111, 123 *Eng. Rep.* 316, appears to be a report of an earlier argument in the same case.

case was adjourned into the Exchequer Chamber, but was settled by agreement after the first argument.

So the controversy continued, and formed the subject of an elaborate written disputation, some ten years later, between the aged Edmund Plowden, who had been counsel in the cause,[16] and Popham, then attorney general. Plowden argued that future uses were executed *instanter*, and that a contingent use was until it vested no more than a bare possibility of estate, which could not be touched by any alteration of the freehold. It might be compared to a right of entry for condition broken, or to the right of the wife endowed *ex assensu patris* to enter after the death of her husband, or to the right of the party to whose use a disseisin had been committed to agree to the disseisin and enter, whether or not the estate of the original disseisor continued. Popham contended that a use which was not vested could not be executed. So long as it remained in contingency, it might be defeated by any act that would have destroyed a use before the statute. If Plowden's view were to be accepted, not only would the mischiefs set out in the preamble to the Statute of Uses continue, they would be increased. The multitude of perpetuities would render the position of heirs insecure, and would lead to dissension in families. Lords would be deprived of their incidents by shifting uses. No purchaser would ever be sure of his title. No demandant could know against whom to bring his action. Titles by the curtesy and in dower would be defeated. It would be a perverse course to construe the statute to increase the mischiefs that it was intended to remedy. The consequences would be even worse than those of the old entail, and they had been grave enough to induce the sages of the law to search out a means by which entails might be barred. Over the Christmas of 1584, Plowden, who died in the following February, was asked by his nephew whether Popham's answer had satisfied him, and he put his reply into writing. The inconveniences that Popham had mentioned were a matter for Parliament rather than for the common lawyer. It might indeed be well if Parliament were to take steps to remedy some of the inconveniences of future uses, and more especially of those perpetuities that were becoming so fashionable, but the inconveniences of overthrowing contingent uses by judicial decision would be at least as great as the inconveniences of supporting them. "We should argue by affirming the law as it is, and not argue like burgesses of Parliament, who may make new laws."[17]

16. Dalison 111, 123 *Eng. Rep.* 316.

17. "Case de toller le future use per act del tenant del terre escry per Plowden et Popham attorney le royne," Bodleian Library Rawlinson MS C. 85, fol. 165 ff. The case appears to be a hypothetical one. A covenants to stand seised to certain uses when B marries his daughter, and makes a feoffment for value without notice before the celebration of the marriage. We are told, however, that "Le matters del case vst devant ceo ester argue in le common banke per la terre de vn Brent in le County de Somersett," and the disputants seem to assume that uses limited by covenant and uses limited upon a feoffment, like executory uses and remainders in use, are upon the same foot.

It is interesting that Plowden should at least represent himself to be defending the literal and accepted construction of the statute against an overenthusiastic application of the "mischief rule" of statutory interpretation. Plowden was a skilled debater, and we must assume that the approach he adopted would have appeared reasonably plausible to contemporaries, whether or not it would have been universally accepted. So in the first argument in *Brent's Case*, Bromley, S.G., asked rhetorically, "And if a man make a feoffment to the use of himself for life, and after to the use of his first issue male thereafter to be born, here no use vests in the son: do you mean that in this case the tenant for life can make a feoffment and disappoint the other uses? If so, you would overthrow many great conveyances."[18]

Bacon tells us in his reading that as a result of the decision in *Chudleigh's Case*,[19] " . . . the false and perverted exposition, which had continued for so many years, though never countenanced by any rule or authority of weight, but only entertained in a popular conceit, and put in practice at adventure, began to be controled."[20]

Whether or not it be strictly true that the false and perverted exposition was never judicially adopted,[21] it was apparently thought to be quite possible that it might be, for the litigation over Sir Richard Chudleigh's settlement caused considerable alarm in exalted quarters. Sir Richard had enfeoffed eleven persons, to the use of himself and of the heirs of his body by a series of ladies at that time married to others. The reason, according to Popham,[22] was that his eldest son, Christopher, was at that time in some danger of being convicted of felony, and he therefore wished to be seised of an estate of inheritance that could not descend to the possible felon, but that might be converted after his conviction into a new fee simple which could descend without impediment to his unattainted younger sons. In remainder after these estates in special tail the use was limited to the feoffees for the life of Christopher, remainder to the first, second, third, fourth, fifth, sixth, seventh, eighth, ninth, and tenth sons of Christopher successively in tail, with remainders over in tail to Sir Richard's younger sons, and a final remainder to the right heirs of Sir Richard. Sir Richard died. The feoffees enfeoffed Christopher in fee, without consideration, and with notice. Christopher had issue Stracheley, his elder son, and John, his younger son. Christopher died. Stracheley died without issue. In Hilary term of 27 Eliz. an ejectment was brought in the King's Bench for the manor of "Laurets" by George Chudleigh, on the demise of John Chudleigh, against George Dyer, who claimed under an alienation by Christopher. In Trinity term of 28 Eliz., after the case had been twice argued,

18. Dalison 111, at 113, 123 *Eng. Rep.* 316, at 316–17 (translated).
19. See above, at n. 11.
20. *Works*, 2:416.
21. There is an anonymous decision of 1574 in 2 Leo. 224, 74 *Eng. Rep.* 497, in which the Common Pleas appears to hold that a recovery does not bar a contingent use.
22. Pop. 70, at 76, 79 *Eng. Rep.* 1184, at 1190.

> Her Majesty being informed by divers of her Privy Council that she should lose many privileges and prerogatives, and that many titles of purchasers depended in the same difficulty, she thought it well to let sleeping dogs lie, and deputed Sir Christopher Hatton, Chancellor, and Lord Walsingham, Secretary, to bring the parties to agreement, who awarded that Chudley, forasmuch as he had title to claim divers other lands in possession of other men to a great value by the same title, that he should have an estate in all the manor of which the land in question was parcel by Trevannion lord thereof and maintainer of Dyer on condition that if he paid £2500 at five several days that then it should be to him and to his [heirs] and that if not that then Trevannion should reenter, and upon this such assurance to be made as the counsel of Chudley should devise &c. And to this the parties agreed.[23]

Because the negotiations that led to this settlement were apparently thought too delicate to be mentioned in the Privy Council minutes, we do not know how the settlement came to break down. Possibly, the queen intervened too late. The feoffment to John Dillon, upon which the second action was brought, bore date the previous March. It could be that John Chudleigh had been attempting to turn a part of his prospects into ready money, and that his feoffee was not prepared to abandon his chance of making a large profit from his speculation. By the same token, we know nothing of the comings and goings behind the scenes while *Chudleigh's Case* was depending. It was argued and reargued for nearly five years, first in the King's Bench and then before all the judges assembled in the Exchequer Chamber, and final judgment was delivered only in 1595.

Eight of the ten judges held that the feoffment to Christopher had destroyed the contingent interests limited to his unborn sons. Only two, Periam, C.B., and Walmesley, J., held the contrary. In their view, all the uses limited upon the feoffment, whether vested or contingent, were executed *instanter*. The contingent uses were therefore in the custody of the law, and no act of the feoffees could affect them. Gawdy, J.—with whom, according to Popham, Clench, J., concurred[24]—agreed with the minority in holding that the statute left nothing in the feoffees, though he held that contingent uses were executed by the equity rather than by the letter of the statute. Once executed, however, they acquired the charac-

23. "Et puis *in Trin. an° 28°* Eliz. Sa maieste estant acertise per diuers de son privy counseil que el devroit perdre plusiours priviledges et prerogatiues, et que plusiours titles de purchasors dependoient en mesme le difficulty, el pensa bien de ne muer le chien dormant, et manda a *Sr. Chr. Hatton, Chancelor, et Sieur de Walsingham Secretary* pur faire agreement entre les parties, lesquelx agarderont que *Chudley*, en respecte que il avoit title de claimer diuers autres terres en le possession dautres homes a grand valew per mesme le title, que il devoit aver estate de tout le manor dont le ter en question fut parcel de par *Trevannion* seignior de ceo et maintayner de Dier sur condicion que sil paioit 2500 *l* a 5 seuerall iours, que donque serra a luy et a ses et si nemy que donque *Trevannion* reentra. et sur ceo tiel assurance destre fait come le counsel de Chudley devisera. &c. Et a ceo les partyes agreont." The report is in Bodleian Library Rawlinson MS C. 85, fols. 173–80.

24. Pop. 70, at 74, 79 *Eng. Rep.* 1184, at 1188.

teristics of legal estates. The feoffment in the case at bar would have destroyed a contingent remainder depending on the estate of the feoffees. It followed that it would also destroy a contingent use. The remaining judges of the majority all held with varying degrees of emphasis that no contingent use could be executed while it remained in contingency. If it were to be executed when it vested, there must at that moment be a seisin out of which it could arise. Therefore, some interest must remain in the feoffees. Whatever this interest was (and in view of the difference between the reports it is well to be cautious about the judicial opinion on the point), it was more than a bare possibility. Not only might it be bound by the act of the feoffees, but any act which divested the estates that had been executed out of the seisin which had passed by the original feoffment would divest the interest of the feoffees as well. If these estates were subsequently revested by the reentry of *cestuy que use* entitled in possession, the interest of the feoffees would also be revested, and the contingent uses would be executed in due time. If *cestuy que use* did not reenter and the contingency happened while he was out of possession, when his estate determined, the feoffees might enter and revive the contingent use. If *cestuy que use* had lost his right of entry the contingent use could never arise, any more than it might if the feoffees had lost their right to enter. Because Sir Richard Chudleigh's feoffees could not enter against their own feoffment, the contingent uses were gone, and it was not material that the feoffment to Christopher Chudleigh had been voluntary, nor that he had had notice of the uses. At common law the use had depended upon privity of estate. It could not be enforced against a disseisor. By the feoffment of the tenants *pur auter vie*, Christopher Chudleigh was in of a new fee simple, not subject to the uses, and there was nothing in the statute to make the use binding upon anyone whom it would not have bound at common law.[25]

The effects of this decision took some time to work out. They were particularly important for the popular settlement by covenant to stand seised. Anderson, C.J., had observed in *Chudleigh's Case*[26] that there were some who took a distinction between estates executed and covenants upon good consideration. The distinction was only logical, for where future uses were raised by covenant, the covenantor retained the estate out of which they were to arise. Hence, he could bar the future uses even by a conveyance that had no tortious operation, at least if it were made to a purchaser for value without notice. The only question was how far this principle extended. In 1601, a settlor had covenanted that he would stand seised to certain uses upon his marriage.[27] After the covenant, and before the marriage, he demised the land for years. It was argued that this was a sufficient alteration of the estate to destroy the

25. 1 Rep. 120a, 76 *Eng. Rep.* 270, Pop. 70, 79 *Eng. Rep.* 1184, 1 And. 309, 123 *Eng. Rep.* 489.

26. 1 And. 309, at 334–35, 123 *Eng. Rep.* 489, at 502–3.

27. Wood v. Reignold (1601), Cro. Eliz. 764, 78 *Eng. Rep.* 996.

future uses. The majority of the court held that the uses might still arise, because the demise had not touched the freehold, but that the beneficiaries under the settlement would take subject to the lease, because the lease of the tenant of the legal estate would have bound *cestuy que use* at the common law. Popham, C.J., said that he had consulted the other judges at Serjeants' Inn, and they had agreed that this was the correct view. Fenner, J., dissented, on the ground that if the uses were executed at all, they related back to the original covenant.[28] Again, Sir Edward Coke, in a very memorable case, had covenanted to stand seised to the use of himself for life, remainder to the use of his wife for life, remainder to the use of his daughter for life, remainder to the use of his daughter's sons successively in tail, with an ultimate reversion to himself in fee. He later made a lease for years, granted over his reversion to A, and made a feoffment to other uses. He died. His wife entered. His daughter bore a son and died. His wife died. It was held that the grant of the reversion to A would have destroyed the uses to the daughter's unborn sons, had the settlement not been recited in the deed of grant. A was thus a purchaser with notice, he had given no consideration, and his estate was therefore subject to the uses limited by the covenant. This estate had indeed been divested by the feoffment, but the entry of Sir Edward's widow had revested it, and the daughter's son might enter.[29] From another case on the same title,[30] it would seem that the real difficulty was felt to be that a decision in favor of Sir Edward's grandson appeared to imply that Sir Edward himself had been guilty of an error in conveyancing.[31]

If the use upon a feoffment were limited upon a contingency to B in fee simple, after a previous use in fee simple to A, the position would be rather more difficult. If the use were limited back to the feoffor, it might be deemed a common-law condition, and indestructible as such.[32] There were practical as well as theoretical arguments in favor of this opinion. Wray, C.J., who took a more benevolent view of contingent interests than was later to become fashionable, had pointed out in *Manning and Andrews' Case*[33] that a feoffment to the use of A and his heirs until payment, and then to the use of B and his heirs, had become "the common manner of mortgage," and to hold that a shifting limitation of this kind might be destroyed would be to enable mortgagees to defraud their borrowers. If the fee were limited over to a third party, there was in

28. See also Bould v. Wynston (1608), Cro. Jac. 168, 79 *Eng. Rep.* 147.

29. Wegg v. Villiers (1651), Sir Henry Rolle, *Un Abridgement des Plusiers Cases et Resolutions del Common Ley* (London, 1668), Uses, p. 796, pl. 10.

30. Hayns v. Villars (1658), 2 Sid. 64, 82 *Eng. Rep.* 1259 (1659), 2 Sid. 157, at 158, 82 *Eng. Rep.* 1309, at 1310, *per* Newdigate, J.

31. Cf. his own observations, in Edward Coke, *The First Part of the Institutes of the Laws of England; or, A Commentary upon Littleton*, 19th ed., 2 vols. (London, 1832), 2:337b, on the dangers of acting as one's own conveyancer.

32. 1 And. 309, at 335, 123 *Eng. Rep.* 489, at 503; Smith v. Warren (1601), Cro. Eliz. 688, 78 *Eng. Rep.* 924.

33. 1 Leo. 256, at 259–60, 74 *Eng. Rep.* 234, at 236–37 (1576).

principle much to be said for the argument that the feoffor who had once limited a fee simple had left nothing in the feoffees. A second limitation of the fee, therefore, was an attempt to limit a use out of a use. This was the argument of Coke in *Woodliff* v. *Drury*,[34] in the Michaelmas term after the delivery of judgment in *Chudleigh's Case*. He failed to convince the court, but the judges were left with an awkward problem. A fee simple is the greatest estate known to the law. It necessarily follows that no disposition by tenant in fee can have any tortious operation, for there is no means by which he can pass a greater estate than he has. Thus, if a feoffment be made to the use of A and his heirs until B marries, and after the marriage of B to the use of B and his heirs, it is not immediately obvious what A can do that will disturb the future use to B. This problem appears to have been first solved by holding that any conveyance whatever by A will be a bar to B's interest. In *Strangways* v. *Newton*[35] in the Court of Wards, A had levied a fine to the use of himself and his heirs until the celebration of a marriage between his son, B, and C, and thereafter to the use of himself for life, remainder to B and C in tail, with a power to A to limit a term of years in remainder after his life estate by his will, in order to raise portions for his other children. A died before the celebration of the marriage, having by his will charged the land with portions in terms that it would have been difficult to treat as an exercise of the power, even on the assumption that it was already exercisable. The two chief justices, who were consulted, refused to decide whether this were a bar to the future uses, because they found the question too difficult. They were quite positive that had A devised the land itself, the further uses limited upon the fine could never have arisen.

The feoffment in *Barton's Case*[36] was to the use of the feoffor for life, remainder to the use of his wife for life, remainder to the use of the right heirs of the feoffor, proviso, that if the heirs of the feoffor or any person claiming under them should disturb the possession of the wife, the use limited to the right heirs of the feoffor should cease, and the feoffees should be seised to the use of the wife and her heirs. The feoffor subsequently made a lease for years, to commence after his wife's death. The two chief justices agreed that the lease would prevent the future use from arising, though, as Moore points out, it was no more than an *interesse termini* during the life of the wife. It is significant that in this case (and probably in the former case also)[37] the two chief justices were those doughty foes of contingent interests of every description, Popham and Anderson, and that they seem to have held that there was no difference, at least in such a case as this, between a feoffment and a covenant. It might perhaps have been argued that this last decision must be taken to

34. Cro. Eliz. 439, 78 *Eng. Rep.* 679 (1595).

35. Mo. 731, 72 *Eng. Rep.* 870. The decision is earlier than Wood v. Reignold (1601), Cro. Eliz. 764, 78 *Eng. Rep.* 996, because it is cited in the latter case.

36. Mo. 742, 72 *Eng. Rep.* 876 (1601).

37. This on the assumption that it can hardly be earlier than Chudleigh's Case.

proceed on the ground that the use limited to the heirs of the feoffor was his old use, and that he, like a covenantor, was therefore seised of the estate out of which the uses were to be raised. Contemporaries, however, do not seem to have been tempted to distinguish it upon this ground. Indeed, after the decision in *Pells* v. *Brown*,[38] Hedley could still observe in argument in *Beck's Case*[39] that where one fee simple was limited after another there was a difference between a devise, where the second fee could not be destroyed, and a limitation of the use, where it might be docked by the tenant of the freehold. The point seems by this time to have been more controversial than he suggested. In 1633[40] the Common Pleas was equally divided, although, on the view that the court took of the construction of the instrument, the question did not have to be decided. The earliest explicit decision that a fine will not destroy a shifting use appears to be *Lloyd* v. *Carew*,[41] in the reign of William III. By this time attitudes had changed. The only question seriously argued was whether the limitation infringed the rule against perpetuities.

According to six of the eight judges who formed the majority in *Chudleigh's Case*,[42] a contingent use limited after a particular estate could not vest so long as the estates that had passed under the original limitation were divested. The effect of the divesting of the prior estate upon a contingent remainder was more controversial. At the common law, a recovery suffered by tenant for life would bar even a vested remainder. According to 32 Hen. 8, c. 31, and 14 Eliz., c. 8 (which repealed and replaced it),[43] such recoveries were void only against those to whom the reversion or remainder should *then* appertain, and not against those to whom it would appertain when a contingency should happen. On one view, however, this meant only that they would be entitled to falsify at common law, because the "intended recompense" would not go to those who had no estate in the land at the time of the judgment.[44] In 1574 the King's Bench expressly decided that a contingent remainder was not destroyed by a fine with proclamations levied by tenant for life.[45] However, opinion was changing, and *Archer's Case*[46] is generally taken to

38. Cro. Jac. 590, 79 *Eng. Rep.* 504, Bridg., J., 1, 123 *Eng. Rep.* 1157, 2 Rolle 196, 216, 81 *Eng. Rep.* 746, 760, Palm. 131, 81 *Eng. Rep.* 1012 (1621).

39. Lit. 253, at 254, 124 *Eng. Rep.* 233 (1629).

40. Earl of Kent v. Steward, Rolle, *Abridgement*, p. 795; Cro. Car. 358, 79 *Eng. Rep.* 914.

41. Prec. Ch. 72, 106, 24 *Eng. Rep.* 35, 51 (1697).

42. See above, at n. 11.

43. The second act was rendered necessary by the decision in Anon. (1563), Benl. 131, 123 *Eng. Rep.* 100, that Stat. 32 Hen. 8, c. 31, did not apply where the tenant for life suffered a recovery as vouchee rather than as tenant.

44. Anon. (1574), 2 Leo. 224, 74 *Eng. Rep.* 497.

45. Humfreston's Case, Dyer 337a, 73 *Eng. Rep.* 760, 2 Leo. 216, 74 *Eng. Rep.* 490, Benl. 195, 123 *Eng. Rep.* 136, 1 And. 40, 123 *Eng. Rep.* 342, sub nom. Lane v. Cowper, Mo. 103, 72 *Eng. Rep.* 469.

46. 1 Rep. 66b, 76 *Eng. Rep.* 146 (1597).

have established that if the particular estate were prematurely destroyed any contingent remainders dependent upon it would be destroyed with it. Though, as we have seen, there is some variety in the reports of that decision, the common opinion is probably correct, for the point does not seem to have been called in question thereafter. Nonetheless, one very significant difference between remainders and uses remained. A remainder might vest, and the remainderman would be entitled to enter in due time, though the estate that supported the remainder had been turned to a right of entry. If a contingent use could be executed only out of a *scintilla juris*, which must be deemed to remain in the feoffees, it necessarily followed that if the estates were once divested, nothing short of an actual entry, whether by the particular tenant or by the feoffees, could serve to vest a contingent use. A use could be executed only out of a seisin, not out of a right. There was thus still room for more than one view on the extent to which contingent uses were to be assimilated to contingent remainders. In *The Earl of Bedford's Case*,[47] counsel argued that a contingent use would not fail if the particular estate determined naturally before it vested, for the feoffees were tenants to the *praecipe*, and there was no hazard of an abeyance of the seisin. This still appears to be the view of Bacon: ". . . I make a feoffment in fee to the use of my wife for life, the remainder to my first-begotten son; I having no son at that time, the remainder to my brother and his heirs: if my wife die before I have any son, the use shall not be in me, but in my brother. And yet if I marry again, and have a son, it shall divest from my brother, and be in my son, which is the skipping they talk so much of."[48]

It could be supported by the opinions of three out of the four justices of the Common Pleas in *Brent's Case*.[49] *The Earl of Bedford's Case* itself might be deemed an authority to the contrary,[50] but it was held in that case that the remainder limited to the right heirs of the settlor was his old use, which vested in him as a reversion, and that the heir took nothing by purchase, so that the question did not in strictness arise.

The continuing uncertainties about the precise scope of the remainder rules also left the earlier authorities open to more than one interpretation. It had been assumed in *Humfreston's Case*[51] that there was no objection to a limitation to the settlor and his wife for their lives, remainder to the eldest child of the settlor in tail, remainder to the settlor in tail, remainder over in fee, though the question whether the settlor's remainder in tail were vested or contingent seems to have provoked some inconclusive discussion. *Mildmay* v. *Mildmay*[52] was a case upon a "clause of per-

47. Mo. 718, 72 *Eng. Rep.* 861, Pop. 3, 79 *Eng. Rep.* 1126, 2 And. 197, 123 *Eng. Rep.* 618 (1593).

48. *Works*, 2:443.

49. Dyer 339b, 73 *Eng. Rep.* 766, 2 Leo. 14, 74 *Eng. Rep.* 319 (1574).

50. See e.g., 1 Rep. 130a, *per* Coke, *arguendo* in Chudleigh's Case, 76 *Eng. Rep.* 296–97.

51. See above, at n. 45.

52. Mo. 632, 72 *Eng. Rep.* 805 (1602).

petuity," by which, if tenant in tail resolved or went about to bar his entail, his estate was to cease as though he were naturally dead and to go over for his life to the person next entitled under the settlement. In the Common Pleas two of the judges, Warburton and Walmesley, JJ., were prepared to hold this clause valid, and they cited *Humfreston's Case* as an authority to show that it was not repugnant to the estate granted, because a contingent use might well be interposed between two estates. They apparently held *Humfreston's Case* to be a decision upon uses,[53] for they distinguished *Germin* v. *Ascott*[54] on the ground that it was a case of possession, not of use. Though the language of the report is obscure, it would seem that in their view a contingent remainder could not be interposed at common law between two vested estates, for when it vested it would replace the vested remainder that followed it. If a use limited in these terms were good, it would follow that such a limitation could not be objectionable merely upon the ground that it suspended an existing estate for a time. They refused to follow *Corbet's Case*[55] on the ground that it was a decision in a feigned action, and therefore not binding. The two other justices took the opposite view, and the case was eventually taken to the King's Bench, which did follow *Corbet's Case* and *Germin* v. *Ascott*, and held the proviso void.[56] It may serve to show, however, that if Hedley's observation that there is no difference between a remainder limited at common law, by devise, or by use[57] was a seventeenth-century axiom, it had not yet attained this status in the previous century.

In an age when the best means of securing the future welfare and preserving the standing of a family was felt to be ensuring that its landed wealth remained so far as possible intact, to render contingent limitations useless for this purpose was to reduce their attractions for the owners of great estates. However, even in the sixteenth century, the strength of dynastic sentiment varied. If it were possible to limit an infinite series of contingent estates, this would not prevent the land from being disposed of out of the family. It would, on the other hand, ensure that so long as the land was not disposed of in fact, it would never descend from an-

53. The original conveyance in that case was to A and his wife for their lives, remainder *seniori puero* of A in tail, remainder to A in tail, remainder over. A and his wife then levied a fine to the use of themselves for their lives, remainder to the *eldest child* of A in tail, remainder over as before. A subsequently had issue: first a daughter and then a son. Because the court held that the fine had not destroyed the original remainder, the principal question in the cause was whether the Latin *puer* should be taken to include the female sex as well as the male, and it became known as the case of *seniori puero*. By 1602 it could hardly be contended that a fine would not destroy a contingent remainder, and to treat the case as a decision on the deed to lead the uses of the fine is a piece of reinterpretation of the kind that often proves necessary in any system based upon precedent.

54. Mo. 364, 72 *Eng. Rep.* 631, 1 And. 186, 123 *Eng. Rep.* 422, 2 And. 7, 123 *Eng. Rep.* 517, 4 Leo. 83, 74 *Eng. Rep.* 745 (1591).

55. 1 Rep. 83b, 76 *Eng. Rep.* 187 (1600).

56. Sir Anthony Mildmay's Case (1606), 6 Rep. 40a, 77 *Eng. Rep.* 311.

57. Beck's Case (1629), Lit. 253, at 254, 124 *Eng. Rep.* 233.

cestor to heir, and thus that no feudal incidents would be due after the first generation. Indeed, if a perpetual freehold were so limited that each estate in remainder vested only *eo instanti* with the determination of the previous estate in possession, the tenant in possession would have substantially the same powers of disposition as a tenant in fee simple, but his issue would be spared the financial inconveniences of having a parent seised of an estate of inheritance.

There were, it was accepted, some restrictions upon the contingencies on which a remainder might be limited to vest at common law, though it was not easy to state them precisely. Coke, in his argument in *Perrot's Case*,[58] asserts that perpetual freeholds are mischievous to the commonwealth and a great inconvenience to the crown, for should they be valid this would defeat the crown of all escheats, wards, liveries, and primer seisins. He also asserts that such interests are against law, save for those that are settled in remainder in any person during the continuance of the frank tenement in possession. It was held in *Haddon's Case* that a perpetual series of life estates limited to every person who should be right heir of the settlor successively was good to the first taker, and to his heir, but that all the further limitations were void. This somewhat resembles Popham's rule against double possibilities,[59] but is not altogether the same. According to Popham, if a contingent remainder be limited after a particular estate, a further remainder upon another distinct contingency will be void. Coke appears to argue that all contingencies must happen during the *first* particular estate. A remainder originally contingent cannot support another contingent remainder even after it has vested. *Haddon's Case* is unhappily not reported elsewhere, so we have only Coke's word for the ground of the decision. Serjeant Moore, on the other side, contended that uses differed from remainders. A limitation to a person unborn would be bad at common law, but good by way of use, like a limitation to such wife as A might marry. The court contrived to decide for the crown upon the form of the pleadings, without ruling on any of the substantive questions that had been raised in the argument. In *Mildmay* v. *Mildmay*,[60] however, Warburton, J., observed that the Statute of Uses did not execute fraudulent or troublesome uses, and he placed perpetual freeholds in the "troublesome" class. He tactfully refrained from stating whom they would trouble most. The rule that a remainder to the issue of a person unborn cannot be limited after a remainder to his parent acquired in a later age the name of "the old rule against perpetuities." Its original purpose was not to protect the public from perpetuities, which

58. Mo. 368, 72 *Eng. Rep.* 634. The discussion cannot be earlier than 1595, because counsel find it necessary to consider the effect of Chudleigh's Case. Moore's date of Mich. 36 & 37 Eliz. is two terms before the judgment in Chudleigh's Case was given, and probably refers to the commencement rather than to the decision of the proceedings.

59. The Rector of Chedington's Case (1598), 1 Rep. 153a, at 156b, 76 *Eng. Rep.* 343, at 351.

60. See above, at n. 52.

could not be effectively created by settlements in this form, but to guarantee the queen her feudal incidents at least in every alternate generation.

The final compromise between the interests of landowners and those of the crown was long to outlast not only the reasons for its existence, but even the memory of them, for there can be few subjects of less interest to posterity than the protection or avoidance of a revenue that has ceased to be exacted.

12 Origins of the "Doctrine" of Consideration, 1535–1585

J. H. Baker

No other doctrine in English law can compete with "consideration" for the greatest diversity and complexity of historical explanations.[1] Most of these explanations can be seen as attempts to answer two groups of questions. Was "consideration" an unbroken development of a single idea from medieval times; or was there a break with medieval thought, and perhaps a combination of different ideas? Second, was it a wholly indigenous development; and, if so, was it an incidental consequence of the exigencies of the forms of action or a direct result of juristic speculation about contractual liability? Alternatively, was it something reflected or borrowed from the canon law or the civil law? And, if so, was the influence brought to bear on the common law directly through Renaissance humanism, or indirectly by way of the canonist chancellors or ecclesiastical judges? It has been customary to seek some single answer to all these questions; but that approach in itself begs another question, for there is no reason to suppose that sixteenth-century lawyers were unanimous as to the nature, let alone the intellectual sources, of the doctrine of consideration. Indeed, the one safe assumption to begin with is that if the matter had been plain then, it would be more readily clarifiable now.

Anyone who attempts to augment, even by a few pages, all that has already been written on this vexed subject must at the outset acknowledge his own foolhardiness; for, in the apt language of our old books, *serra rette son foly demesne.* Nevertheless, there is one large evidential stone

1. The principal theories are to be found in the following works: Frederick Pollock, *Principles of Contract: A Treatise on the General Principles concerning the Validity of Agreements in the Law of England* (London, 1876), pp. 149–52; C. C. Langdell, *A Summary of the Law of Contracts*, 2d ed. (Boston, 1880), pp. 58–62; O. W. Holmes, *The Common Law* (1881; reprint ed. by Mark DeWolfe Howe, London and Melbourne, 1968), pp. 200–213, 222–25; J. I. Clark Hare, *The Law of Contracts* (Boston, 1887), pp. 132–36, 141; John W. Salmond, "The History of Contract," *Law Quarterly Review* 3 (1887): 171–78; John W. Salmond, *Essays in Jurisprudence and Legal History* (London, 1891), pp. 187–94, 207–24; James Barr Ames, *Lectures on Legal History and Miscellaneous Legal Essays* (Cambridge, Mass., and London, 1913), pp. 129–30, 142–48; W. T. Barbour, *History of Contract in Early English Equity* (Oxford, 1914), pp. 59–65, 160–68; C. H. S. Fifoot, *History and Sources of the Common Law* (London, 1949), pp. 395–415; A. K. Kiralfy, *The Action on the Case* (London, 1951), pp. 170–85; S. F. C. Milsom, *Historical Foundations of the Common Law* (London, 1969), pp. 309–15; W. M. McGovern, "Contract in Medieval England: The Necessity for Quid pro Quo and a Sum Certain," *American Journal of Legal History* 13 (1969): 173–201, esp. 190–97; J. L. Barton, "The Early History of Consideration," *Law Quarterly Review* 85 (1969): 372–91; A. W. B. Simpson, *A History of the Common Law of Contract* (Oxford, 1975), pp. 316–488; and S. J. Stoljar, *A History of Contract at Common Law* (Canberra, 1975), pp. 38–39.

still unturned. We have never known quite when or how "consideration" appeared in the *assumpsit* declaration, nor what legal discussion (if any) accompanied the process of its becoming a material allegation. It would be idle to expect the discovery of this missing information to end all doubt and speculation concerning the origins of the idea of consideration, if only for the very good reason that the idea seems to have been present in English law long before it acquired the name. But whether we are endeavoring to trace the idea backward or forward from its first appearance in modern guise, our most convenient focus must be the point at which the innominate idea lurking in older jurisprudence became a nominate "doctrine" capable of shaping arguments and controlling decisions. Of course, the focus will not be very sharp. The common law was not in the habit of changing overnight, and its exponents were adept at concealing any overt evidence that it had changed at all. With reasonable confidence, however, we can reduce our concentration to the half century from 1535 to 1585. By the 1580s the reports are full of discussions about consideration; usually the matter arose on a motion in arrest of judgment, but it could also be raised by a demurrer,[2] or writ of error,[3] or special verdict,[4] or argument upon the evidence.[5] Objecting to the declaration "for want of sufficient consideration" had become the lawyer's first resort in attacking any *assumpsit* action that seemed to raise some arguable point, and the procedure was already raising a wide range of questions both substantive and technical. Consideration had achieved the status of a doctrine, and could be defined as a profit to the defendant or a labor or charge to the plaintiff.[6] A mere fifty years earlier there was no trace of "consideration" in *assumpsit* declarations or in the few reported discussions relating to such actions. This fifty years, then, is the period on which attention must be fixed; and it is no accident that it is precisely the period that most previous speculation as to the history of consideration has studiously or unwittingly avoided.

2. Lucy v. Walwyn (1561), for which see below, at n. 43 and accompanying text, p. 348 (demurrer to bar); Richards v. Bartlet (1584), 1 Leo. 19, 74 *English Reports* (hereafter cited as *Eng. Rep.*) 17 (demurrer to bar); Fooly v. Preston (1586), 1 Leo. 297, 74 *Eng. Rep.* 270 (demurrer to declaration; judgment later affirmed on a writ of error: see next note).

3. Isack v. Barbour (1563), Public Record Office, King's Bench (hereafter cited as KB) 27/1207, m. 55 (quoted in n. 61, below); Page's Case (1585), Cambridge University Library (hereafter cited as C.U.L.) MS Ii. 5. 38, fols. 4v–5; Preston v. Tooley (1587), Cro. Eliz. 74, 78 *Eng. Rep.* 334; Howell v. Trevanion (1588), 1 Leo. 93, 74 *Eng. Rep.* 87, Cro. Eliz. 91, 78 *Eng. Rep.* 349.

4. Gramson v. Bower (1584), C.U.L. MS Ii. 5. 38, fols. 126–27; Fuller's Case (1586), Harvard Law School (hereafter cited as H.L.S.) MS 16, fol. 229.

5. Snowe v. Jourdan (1572), H.L.S. MS 1192, fol. 22v; Anon. (1577), Lincoln's Inn (hereafter cited as L.I.) MS Misc. 361, fol. 81; Anon. (1588), H.L.S. MS 16, fol. 423.

6. Webb's Case (1577), 4 Leo. 110, 74 *Eng. Rep.* 763; Richards v. Bartlet (1584), 1 Leo. 19, 74 *Eng. Rep.* 17. See also Coke's formulations in Stone v. Withypoll (1588), 1 Leo. 114, 74 *Eng. Rep.* 106 ("no consideration can be good, if not, that it touch either the charge of the plaintiff, or the benefit of the defendant"), Owen 94, 74 *Eng. Rep.* 924 ("consideration is the ground of every action on the case, and it ought to be either a charge to the plaintiff or a benefit to the defendant").

Origin of the "Consideration" Clause

The first appearance of the *in consideratione* clause in the *assumpsit* declaration may be dated with reasonable precision to 1539.[7] No contemporary, we may be sure, regarded it as a significant event; actions on the case were still in the fluid, experimental stage, and it would be another thirty years or more before the new phrase ousted its predecessors. The most we can hope to discover from the circumstances of its introduction is some sense of what "consideration" originally meant and of the extent to which it represented new thinking about contractual liability. In order to draw the contrast, we must first step back a little before our chosen period.

In the fifteenth century, *assumpsit* actions rarely proceeded beyond the *optulit se* stage, and therefore the precedents in the rolls are mostly of uncontested writs. Hundreds of these precedents recur in the most elementary form: "whereas, in return for [*pro*] a sum agreed or paid beforehand by Y, X had undertaken to build a house for Y, X failed to build the house." The *pro* clause here bears more than a superficial resemblance to the later consideration clause, and a discussion in 1425 suggests that it did indeed reflect a notion of reciprocity: it was because the carpenter had been paid, or could bring debt for the agreed sum, that he himself should be liable in return.[8] By the end of the century, however, the usual formula had become more sophisticated, with the *pro* clause demoted to a recital: "whereas, for a sum agreed or paid, A had agreed to build a house for B, and A had undertaken to build the house within a certain time, A had failed to build within the time as undertaken." The undertaking had been gently separated from the principal bargain, to become in effect a promise to carry out the bargain on time or (in negligence cases) in a careful manner. This verbal divorce was no doubt designed to avert technical objections to overlapping remedies, yet in so doing it introduced a new problem. The undertaking now seemed imperfectly explained; it was no longer expressed to have been made in return for the sum of money, and it was linked to the bargain only by the implication inherent in the word "and." Now, it may seem an absurd subtlety to hold that "and" did not adequately fuse the bargain and the undertaking into one single transaction, but the dilemma arose inevitably from the object of the expanded formula: either the action was founded on the bargain or covenant itself, in which case it would probably fail on formal or

7. The following account of the records is based on a study of the King's Bench rolls (KB 27) down to 1550, the results of which are related in more detail in *The Reports of Sir John Spelman*, ed. J. H. Baker, 2 vols., Selden Society, vols. 93 (London, 1977) and 94 (1978), 2:286–97. Forays into the Public Record Office, Common Pleas (hereafter cited as CP) 40, suggest strongly that the King's Bench led the way. It is possible that a full search will shake the details given here, and that in searching about five miles of King's Bench parchment between 1535 and 1550 the writer may have missed something significant.

8. Year Book (hereafter cited as Y. B.) Hil. 3 Hen. 6, f. 36, pl. 33 (1425), *per* Rolf, Sjt. There is no reported reply to this aspect of Rolf's argument.

evidential grounds, or it was founded on the collateral undertaking, in which case it had to be shown why that undertaking should be independently actionable. By the time of Henry VIII at the latest, pleaders seem to have been aware of this problem and increasingly they took care to avoid all mention of a precedent bargain or contract—by reciting a delivery rather than a sale of goods, or a discussion (*colloquium*) instead of a bargain—or else to give the undertaking an explanation of its own. The formulas they devised for the latter purpose are so varied as to defy classification, and include some phrases in which consideration is clearly foreshadowed;[9] but the commonest device was to say that the undertaking had been given in return for (*pro*) a small sum of money, usually twelvepence. This last device was probably in many cases a fiction and is therefore hardly a true precursor of consideration;[10] but the need for such a fiction shows the reality of the pleader's dilemma, and his uneasiness about leaving the undertaking unexplained on the face of the record.

The need for a connecting link between the recited bargain and the undertaking to perform it was the subject of an unreported King's Bench decision in *Marler* v. *Wilmer* (1539).[11] The plaintiff complained in the mayor's court at Coventry that he had sold goods to the defendant's testator for a sum to be paid on request, and that after the testator's death the defendant executor *super se assumpsit et fideliter promisit* to pay the sum but had not done so. The local court gave judgment for the plaintiff, upon demurrer, and the defendant brought a writ of error in the King's Bench. One of the points assigned for error was "that it does not appear in the declaration for what cause [*quam ob causam*] he made the aforesaid undertaking, either for money paid beforehand, or receipt of part of the aforesaid goods, and so *ex nudo pacto non oritur actio*." He also objected that the action should have been debt, not "deceit on the case," and that the plaintiff should have produced a deed. Unfortunately, the King's Bench proceedings end with the *scire facias* to summon the defendant in error; but it is significant that already by 1539 it could be argued that no action would lie on an undertaking without "*causa*" because it is *nudum pactum*. The declaration had to explain the under-

9. E.g., Browne v. Cornely (1533), KB 27/1086, m. 28 (*ob gratitudinem credenciam et benevolenciam* toward his sureties, he undertook to save them harmless; judgment for the plaintiff).

10. In at least four cases the payment was denied by protestation: Tayllor v. Kyme (1533), KB 27/1088, m. 24; Wyvell v. Frenche (1534), KB 27/1092, m. 72; Pynnok v. Fyndern (1539), KB 27/1112, m. 32; Annesley v. Kytley (1539), KB 27/1113, m. 62. In 1567 it was said to be a common-form fiction and untraversable (Lord Grey's Case, as printed in Simpson, *History of Contract*, p. 633, *per* Dyer, C.J.).

11. KB 27/1111, m. 64. This case was discovered and brought to the writer's notice by Mr. David Ibbetson of Corpus Christi College, Cambridge. Mr. Ibbetson has also persuaded the writer that he read too much into the earlier error case of Quasshe v. Skete (1538), KB 27/1109, m. 74: as to which see *Reports of Sir John Spelman*, 2:289. The objection in that case, that the plaintiff below had not set out the *causa actionis*, evidently related not to the declaration but to the curt entry of the plaint as being simply "in an action on the case."

taking, and it was not enough merely to recite a precedent bargain. The consideration required for an executor's promise would continue to give difficulty throughout the century, but the relatively simple objection in 1539 would have applied with equal force to the common declaration in *assumpsit* for the price of goods. Some linking phrase was needed between the recital and the *assumpsit* clause to explain the undertaking, and it can hardly be a mere coincidence that within a year or two of *Marler* v. *Wilmer* several new formulas had been invented for the purpose. The most common of the new devices can best be described as a *quid pro quo* clause. It was used mainly in actions to recover the price of goods, which had become the principal function of *assumpsit* by 1540. The plaintiff alleged a sale of goods for a certain sum, or a delivery of goods worth a certain sum, "for which goods [*pro quibusquidem bonis*]" the defendant undertook to pay. Thus the goods were treated as the *quid "pro quo"* the undertaking was given. The buyer could use the same formula, alleging that the promise to deliver was made *pro* the money paid.[12] For over twenty years the *quid pro quo* clause dominated *assumpsit* declarations, and bid fair to jostle consideration out of use.

The consideration clause that appeared in 1539 performed exactly the same linking function as the *quid pro quo* clause. At first it was simply an alternative, chosen whenever it seemed more apt or elegant than *pro*. The first recorded case illustrates this very well. The plaintiff complained that, whereas the defendant's wife had before marriage been indebted to the plaintiff for board, lodging, and a loan, the defendant in full knowledge afterwards, in consideration of his impending marriage and for twelvepence paid to him, undertook to pay off the debt, but had not done so.[13] The plaintiff's counsel had seen fit to make use of the fictional shilling in addition to the true cause, and so the *in consideratione* clause was used to avoid the repetition of *pro*, a word much more appropriate to introduce a payment than a marriage.[14] In the next instance on the King's Bench rolls, the undertaking to pay was in consideration of wrongs done and *pro* twelvepence paid; again *in consideratione* is a companion to *pro*, and it is more apt to describe a motive founded on something past.[15] In a third early case, the two phrases occur together as past and present moving causes, where a woman had asked a man to ride on a

12. E.g., Grey v. Botte (1544), KB 27/1133, m. 105 (judgment for the plaintiff).

13. Harvy v. Stone (1539), KB 27/1112, m. 65.

14. Marriage had often been treated as a "consideration" to raise a use, and it was more accurate to describe it so than as *quid pro quo* because there were doubtless other reasons for the marriage than the payment of the debt. See below, at n. 46 and accompanying text.

15. Phyllyp v. Heeth (1540), KB 27/1116, m. 23d. For the association of consideration with causes past or "precedent," see Dyer 49, 73 *Eng. Rep.* 108–9; and Christopher St. German, *Doctor and Student*, ed. T. F. T. Plucknett and J. L. Barton, Selden Society, vol. 91 (London, 1975), p. 229. St. German distinguishes between an "accord" (for past wrongs) and a contract. The first mention of consideration in an *assumpsit* action occurs not in a declaration, but in a plea of accord: Hewton v. Forster (1536), KB 27/1099, m. 76.

journey with her, and for (*pro*) his company and in consideration that he had lent her money, she promised to give him a ring.[16]

In the decade after 1540 there are at least thirty-two instances of consideration clauses in the King's Bench rolls, but there is little uniformity in their form or function. In one back-to-front case the *assumpsit* was the consideration for the plaintiff's promise to perform.[17] In nearly all the cases, however, the consideration was used to explain a promise to pay money. It might be a past act (often the delivery of goods), or a present bargain, or a future act. Sometimes it was combined with the word *pro*, as in the phrase *pro et in consideratione*[18] or the general, meaningless *pro diversis considerationibus.*[19] As a mere alternative to *pro* it could mean "in return for," and this sense of reciprocity is underlined in such phrases as *in consideratione et recompensatione.*[20] But it had more subtle connotations of its own: there was the sense of *causa*, itself ambiguously hovering between the two shades of meaning "because of" and (more subjectively) "having taken into consideration" or "being moved by." The latter sense is clearly manifest in the general form *pro diversis aliis causis et considerationibus ipsum E. adtunc et ibidem moventibus.*[21] It is therefore impossible to assert that the nascent phrase represented precisely the notion of *quid pro quo* or *causa*. There is a very strong case, on the other hand, for saying that it actually combined both notions, and that its triumph over the various *pro* clauses was eventually secured by its convenient ambivalence.

Attempts to Delimit Consideration

On turning to the reports, we meet with an apparent lack of concern with general principles of liability. Not only are there no discussions of the nature of "consideration" before 1560, but when the discussions do begin the profession seems already to be engulfed in a torrent of complex learning gushing out in every direction from no apparent source. Ironically, the commonest types of *assumpsit*—actions for the price of goods or services—received the least attention. Although consideration had begun in such actions, it was by now thought unnecessary for them and if alleged could not be traversed; under such liberal conditions even a conditional gift of money could be enforced.[22] We have seen that consid-

16. Turfote v. Pytcher (1543), KB 27/1130, m. 104.
17. Owtrede v. Whyte (1546), KB 27/1138, m. 24d (judgment for the plaintiff).
18. E.g., Rent v. Danyell (1549), KB 27/1150, m. 104.
19. Usually added to a money payment: e.g., Cawenfeld v. Elder (1546), KB 27/1137, m. 113d (*pro* 4d. *et pro aliis subsequentibus consideracionibus*); Pynnok v. Clopton (1547), KB 27/1141, m. 79 (*pro* 5s. *et pro aliis consideracionibus inter ipsos concordatis*); Holmes v. Harryson (1549), KB 27/1149, m. 32 (*pro* 2s. *et pro diversis aliis causis et consideracionibus*); Norman v. Moore (1549), KB 27/1149, m. 117 (similar).
20. Pyrry v. Appowell (1545), KB 27/1134, m. 67d.
21. Newman v. Gybbe (1549), KB 27/1152, m. 135; Kiralfy, *Action on the Case*, p. 176.
22. Not traversable: Lord Grey's Case (1567), printed in Simpson, *History of Contract*,

eration in these common cases served to link circumstances that had always given rise to liability with the undertaking that enabled *assumpsit* to be brought instead; whatever problems that caused with respect to overlapping remedies, they were not problems relating to the nature of consideration. The doubts were not as to the existence of liability, but as to the form of the remedy and the mode of proof; in the seventeenth-century common counts consideration was to become virtually meaningless, certainly unimportant. It was outside the context of sale that consideration came to be of fundamental importance, because there was no preexisting substantive law of contractual liability and so consideration not only explained the undertaking, but thereby determined whether an action would lie for its breach. This was the context in which discussion began as to what constituted a "good" consideration. Would a merely subjective motive (such as affection), or a "continuing" motive (such as kinship), give binding force to an undertaking; or must the plaintiff have done or promised something in return? If the plaintiff had done something in return, must it have been done in return for the promise; or would it be sufficient if it had been done at the defendant's request, or simply for the defendant's benefit? If the plaintiff had not done, but *promised*, something in return, was it necessary that he should subsequently have performed his promise; or would it be enough that the promise would have been performed if the defendant had not broken his promise?

Adequacy and Contemporaneity

The courts do not seem ever to have been troubled about economic disparity between consideration and promise; it was a common maxim that for a penny consideration a man could bind himself for a hundred pounds.[23] In the earlier cases past consideration is not unusual,[24] and there are also several examples of the vague general clause *pro aliis*

---

p. 633; Anon. (1572), British Library Lansdowne MS 1067, fol. 28, *per* Lovelace, Sjt.; Anon. (1577), L.I. MS Misc. 361, fol. 81, *per* Wray, J. (no need to prove any consideration beyond the debt); Smith v. Hitchcocke (1587), H.L.S. MS 16, fol. 445. Not necessary: Anon. (1581), Godb. 13, 78 *Eng. Rep.* 8; Anon. (1582), L.I. MS Misc. 488, p. 100, *per* Wray and Gawdy, JJ.; also reported, C.U.L. MS Ii. 5. 38, fol. 60; Whorwood v. Gybbons (1587), Gould. 48, 75 *Eng. Rep.* 986, sub nom. Gill v. Harewood, 1 Leo. 61, 74 *Eng. Rep.* 57. Conditional gift: Bedford v. Eyre (1559), KB 27/1192, m. 178 (upon a marriage treaty, the father undertook that *if* the plaintiff married his daughter he would pay twenty pounds; judgment for the plaintiff).

23. J. Rastell, *Exposiciones terminorum* [ca. 1525], sig. B4v ("*ex nudo pacto non oritur accio* but yf any thyng were gevyn for the xx s. though it were not but to the valew of a peny, then it was a good contract"); Howell v. Trevanion (1588), H.L.S. MS 16, fols. 423v–24, *per* Drew; Knight v. Rushworth (1596), Duck's reports, British Library Hargrave MS (hereafter cited as B.L. Harg. MS) 51, fol. 134, *per* Anderson, C.J.

24. E.g., Phyllyp v. Heeth (1540), KB 27/1116, m. 23d (injuries done); Busshewell v. Rye (1546), KB 27/1138, m. 67d (money previously received); Tyll v. Brockhouse (1548), KB 27/1147, m. 103d (goods previously taken).

considerationibus tacked on to a small prepayment.[25] By the 1580s, however, it was common learning that consideration had to be something of value; and it was a standard objection to the consideration that it was "insufficient" or "past." That position may well have been reached in a haphazard way, as defense lawyers persuaded courts to reject particularly dubious kinds of moving cause; but its attainment is significant as marking the emergence of a "doctrine" of consideration. The choice of direction open to the courts was provided by the ambiguity of the word "consideration." In the *causa* sense it might more easily encompass motives, and things past or continuing, whereas in the *quid pro quo* sense it called for some reciprocal act done or promised. Common lawyers were not wont to distinguish these senses, and in the law of uses it was already the practice to speak of "insufficient cause" to denote the absence of *quid pro quo.*

The first area of difficulty seems to have been the consideration of friendship or kinship. That "natural love and affection" should have been rejected as consideration was by no means a foregone conclusion. At the beginning, the word "consideration" was closely associated with the context of marriage;[26] and in 1549 a surety launched an action on an undertaking given "in consideration of friendship and good will."[27] The reaction is first encountered in a case of 1565 concerning uses, which Plowden argued and made into a leading case by reporting verbatim the arguments of counsel. The attack by Serjeants Fletewoode and Wray was based very much on the *quid pro quo* school of thought. Affection or kinship were of no monetary value, and they were continuing states of affairs that would continue even if no promise had been made; as recompense, therefore, they were quite illusory:

> For if a man makes a grant to John Style in consideration of his long acquaintance, or of great familiarity between them, or that they were schoolboys together in their youth, or upon such like considerations, that he will stand seised of his land to the use of him: this will not change the use, for such are not taken as considerations worthy in law to make a use, for they are not of value or recompense. For if I promise you, in consideration that you are of my great familiarity or acquaintance, or are my brother, to pay you £20 at such a day, you shall not have an action on the case or action of debt for it, for it is but a naked and barren pact and *ex*

25. See above, at n. 21 and accompanying text. In 1584 it was held that such general consideration could not raise a use, because it did not appear whether it was sufficient (which Coke interpreted as requiring *quid pro quo*) (Mildmay v. Standysh [1584], 1 Rep. 175, 76 *Eng. Rep.* 379; C.U.L. MS Ff. 5. 4, fol. 111).

26. See Yorke's reports, B.L. Harg. MS 388, fol. 180 (1530); Pollard's reports, ibid., fol. 76v (1532); Dyer 17, §100, 73 *Eng. Rep.* 37 (1536); Harvy v. Stone (1539), KB 27/1112, m. 65; Dyer 49, §11, 73 *Eng. Rep.* 109 (1541); and Holt v. Oxenden (1542), KB 27/1125, m. 38 (judgment for the plaintiff in *assumpsit*).

27. Rent v. Danyell (1549), KB 27/1150, m. 104 (imparlance).

> *nudo pacto non oritur actio*, for the cause is not sufficient. And nothing is done or given from the one side, for you were my brother before and will be so afterwards, and you were of my acquaintance before and will be so afterwards.[28]

There was also an evidential reason: "the common law requires fresh cause, whereof the country may have intelligence or knowledge for the trial if need be." Plowden maintained that natural causes were sufficient consideration, and in an ingenious argument based on the law of nature and philosophy demonstrated that the continuance of male heirs was good consideration because men are more reasonable than women and have more discretion in managing affairs. His eloquence won the day, but he had not met the objections squarely and the doubts had been sown. Two years later, Dyer, C.J., seems to have been wavering; according to one report, he ruled that a father's indebtedness was no consideration for a son's promise to pay off the debt, whereas another has him declaring that "whatever goes in ease and benefit of my friend is my ease and benefit also."[29] By 1588, at any rate, the courts had ruled out "love and affection" as consideration for an *assumpsit*, apparently for the reasons advanced on the losing side in 1565.[30]

The later cases on adequacy were mostly about such trivia as forbearances to sue "for a little while,"[31] showing the party a document,[32] permitting a party to do what he was already entitled to do,[33] or releasing a nonexistent right.[34] These transparently artificial considerations were introduced for ulterior reasons: to convert debt into *assumpsit*, to extend liability to personal representatives, or to enable *assumpsit* to be brought to enforce quasi-contractual or noncontractual obligations. The parent principle, however, had more significant offspring in the doctrine that past consideration was insufficient. The objection to past consideration was close, both in spirit and in chronology, to the objection to love and affection. There had been dissent in Mary's reign as to whether a past consideration could support a use, and the context seems to have been the continuing relationship.[35] The doubt spread to *assumpsit* by 1568,

28. Sharington v. Strotton (1564–66), Plowd. 298, at 302, 75 *Eng. Rep.* 454, at 460 (translated).

29. Watton's Case (1567), C.U.L. MS Ii. 3. 14, fol. 145; Lord Grey's Case (1567), H.L.S. MS 2071, fol. 18v. (Cf. Simpson, *History of Contract*, p. 633.) These may be reports of the same case.

30. Harford v. Gardiner (1588), 2 Leo. 30, 74 *Eng. Rep.* 332. For a full discussion of the cases, see Simpson, *History of Contract*, pp. 434–37.

31. Lutwich v. Hussey (1583), Cro. Eliz. 19, 78 *Eng. Rep.* 286.

32. Sturlyn v. Albany (1587), Cro. Eliz. 67, 78 *Eng. Rep.* 327.

33. Lile v. Frencham (1587), H.L.S. MS 16, fol. 418v (permitting finder of goods to retain them until asked for them). This seems to be an attempt to use *assumpsit* instead of trover.

34. Anon. (1584), L.I. MS Misc. 487, fol. 192v (held good, because *est quiett a son mynde*). Cf. Stone v. Wythipoll (1589), Cro. Eliz. 126, 78 *Eng. Rep.* 383; and Tooley v. Windham (1590), Cro. Eliz. 206, 78 *Eng. Rep.* 463.

35. Sir Robert Brooke, *La Graunde Abridgement* (London, 1573), Feoffments al Uses, pl. 54; Simpson, *History of Contract*, pp. 453–54.

and again the context was friendship; a consideration of gratitude for a past favor was rejected, on a motion in arrest of judgment, on the ground that it had been spent when the promise was made.[36] The teaching of Fletewoode and Wray had again prevailed: something past will remain done and cannot be undone, and so it is not a fresh cause moving the promise. The decision would have threatened the growing practice of laying the consideration in the pluperfect tense and the *assumpsit* in the perfect tense, were it not for the common allegation of a "special instance and request." The precedent request linked the past event, in a reciprocal sense, with the undertaking, and thereby avoided the objection.[37] In practice, therefore, the objection to past consideration usually arose only when the pleader had for some reason omitted to lay a request.[38] In many cases the request was no doubt either fictional or (in modern language) "implied in fact"; but in theory a present consideration had to be proved. In a case of 1584, where a friend had undertaken to pay the arrears of account incurred by a beer-clerk if his master would release him, it appeared in evidence and was found specially that the release had occurred before the undertaking was made. Fuller argued that, as the issue was *non assumpsit*, the jurors ought not to enquire into the consideration. The court of Queen's Bench, however, ordered judgment to be entered for the defendant; if the consideration was not proved in evidence, said Wray, C.J., the whole action failed.[39]

Mutual Promises

It has been generally assumed that the question whether a promise could be consideration for a promise was the last important question to be asked, and that its answer in the affirmative finally transformed consideration into a doctrine based on a consensual view of contract. The hurdle, as historians have seen it, was a logical one: a promise was only of value if binding, and to say that it was binding because it was given in consideration of another promise would trap one in a vicious circle from which the only escape would be to suppose that the reciprocal promises somehow breathed life into each other at the same instant, so that they could support each other. Unfortunately for this view, no contemporary discussion has been found in which the problem is treated in those terms. One recent writer has concluded from this that the problem never entered anyone's head, and that "all talk about the recognition of 'wholly execu-

36. Hunt v. Bate (1568), Dyer 272, 73 *Eng. Rep.* 605–9. See also Hurleston v. Lord Dacre (1568), entry in British Library Harley MS 7648, fol. 114, citing Hil. 10 Eliz. 1, m. 850 (D. undertook to pay fourteen pounds *tam in consideracione laboris et industrie* of H. about his affairs *quam in recompensacione onerum et custagiorum* laid out by H. in the same; demurrer to declaration; court takes advisement until Easter term).

37. For a full discussion, see S. J. Stoljar, "The Consideration of Request," *Melbourne University Law Review* 5 (1966): 314–28.

38. E.g., Cooke's Case (1581), L.I. MS Misc. 488, p. 91; Crewe v. Curson (1582), C.U.L. MS Ii. 5. 38, fol. 56v. For the later cases see Simpson, *History of Contract*, pp. 455–58.

39. Gramson v. Bower (1584), C.U.L. MS Ii. 5. 38, fols. 126–27.

tory,' 'bilateral,' or 'consensual' contracts in [the sixteenth] century is wholly misconceived."[40] The only contemporary problem, on this view, was whether the plaintiff had to aver the performance of his own promise; and the answer lay in the "sharp distinction" between a promise and a future act. If A promised B ten pounds if B would build a house, then B had to show that he had built the house before he could sue for the ten pounds; but if A promised B ten pounds in consideration that B then and there promised to build a house, then B's promise was a sufficient consideration to bind A. This was not so much a consideration problem as that of determining whether promises were dependent or independent: a problem eventually to be solved by a mass of abstruse learning centered upon Serjeant Williams's notes to *Pordage* v. *Cole* and then lost (in England) in the confused law about conditions, warranties, and discharge by breach.[41]

Neither approach seems entirely satisfactory. It is true that mutual promises are found at an early date,[42] and that the discussions are not in terms that anyone affected toward the traditional story would wish. But it is equally true that the reported cases do reveal a consideration problem; indeed, the three most extensive early discussions of consideration arose from mutual promises.

The first reported discussion is also the very first case so far discovered in which an objection was taken to the consideration by that name. Such are the vagaries of sixteenth-century law reporting that the report is only to be found in a manuscript notebook, in private possession and hitherto unnoticed, containing reports by Anthony Gell of the Inner Temple. It concerned a mutual friend (Simon Walwyn) who had been asked by one friend (Thomas Lucy) to obtain an assignment of a lease for him from the other friend (John Swyfte). Walwyn in the event bought the lease for himself, and was sued in *assumpsit*. The declaration recited a lease of the manors of Hampton Bishop and Hatton by Queen Mary in 1554 to John Swyfte for sixteen years, and continued:

> and the aforesaid Thomas Lucy, coveting and desiring to acquire and purchase the aforesaid interest and entire estate of the aforesaid John Swyfte for some reasonable sum, to the same Thomas's own use, and having great faith in the same Simon and being fully

40. Simpson, *History of Contract*, pp. 461, 467. Much of the material that follows was not available in print when Simpson wrote.

41. There is a valuable account in Stoljar, *History of Contract*, pp. 147–63, which is "an abridged and much revised" version of a longer article in the *Sydney Law Review*, 2:217–52.

42. Perhaps the earliest is Fyneux v. Clyfford (1517), KB 27/1026, m. 76, in which the ingenious and elaborate bill was drawn for (perhaps by) Fineux, C.J. It was an action against a vendor of land who had sold to another; but Fineux, C.J., had not, like William Shipton in Doige's Case, been tricked into paying anything. Fineux had to lay mutual undertakings on each side, a tender of payment by himself, and then a direct assertion that the defendants schemed (*machinaverunt*) to deprive him of the bargain and sold to another. The case has not been traced beyond imparlance. Its uniqueness bears testimony to the peculiar problem raised by a wholly executory contract.

> confident in him on account of the long fellowship and acquaintance which existed between the said Simon and John Swyfte, warmly requested and desired the same Simon [at such a time and place] to do whatever he could to obtain and purchase the aforesaid interest [etc.] from the said John for a reasonable sum of money for the said Thomas Lucy, to the use of him the said Thomas Lucy and his assigns.
>
> And the said Thomas then and there promised [*pollicitus fuit*] the same Simon for his labour to be bestowed in that behalf, and for purchasing and procuring the said interest [etc.], to give and deliver to the said Simon immediately upon the purchase of the said estate and interest as aforesaid all the charges, expenses and sums of money paid and spent by him the said Simon in that behalf, and also a gelding to the value of 100s. or 100s. in cash. . . .
>
> Whereupon the same Simon, afterwards on the same [day], in consideration that the same Thomas Lucy would pay the said Simon all his charges, expenses and sums of money paid and spent by him the said Simon in that behalf, and also in consideration of the aforesaid gelding to be delivered to him as aforesaid (or of the aforesaid sum of 100s. to be paid to the same Simon as aforesaid) . . . took upon himself and faithfully promised the said Thomas Lucy that he the same Simon would do as much as he could, with as much speed as possible, to obtain, purchase and procure the said estate and interest [etc.] for the said Thomas Lucy, to the use of him the said Thomas Lucy and his assigns.

The long declaration went on to allege a breach of the undertaking, in that Simon had not obtained the lease for Thomas but had acquired it himself. The defendant pleaded that for three weeks following the undertaking he had done all he could to obtain the lease from John Swyfte, who had utterly refused to sell it to Thomas but had (at the end of the three weeks) granted it to Simon himself, so that Simon could no longer procure it from John for Thomas. To this plea the plaintiff demurred, and the matter was argued in the King's Bench. The original ground of the demurrer was that the defendant, having undertaken to do his best, should have gone on trying for the rest of his life; his confession that he had abandoned his efforts was therefore a confession of breach. This point was not hotly pursued, because it was arguable that the words "with as much speed as possible" would make a mere demand and refusal sufficient; so the argument shifted to the declaration, and to the consideration.

Thomas Nicholls argued that the consideration was nugatory, because the defendant "was to have nothing before the obtaining and so no *quid pro quo*, but *nudum pactum*." Onslow countered with the argument that the gelding was partly "for his labor to be bestowed," and labor had been bestowed in the three weeks of negotiation; but this argument was opposed by Plowden, in a speech that our reporter has irritatingly omitted. The record shows that, after five continuances, the court gave judgment on the demurrer for the plaintiff; and upon the writ of inquiry the inquest returned damages of one hundred pounds and twenty shillings' costs, whereupon the court took advisement again for two terms. The meaning of this last adjournment is obscure, but because judgment had already been given "that the aforesaid Thomas do recover his damages" the court must have decided that the consideration was good as alleged.[43] This is not a clear case; the plaintiff's promise (or "pollicitation") is mentioned in the recital, not directly in the consideration clause, and so it could be argued that the consideration was not the promise but a future act that never fell to be performed, and that the problem was therefore one of dependency. According to Gell's report, the unsuccessful argument was apparently that something conditional on the defendant's performance was not *quid pro quo*. If A promises B that he will do *x* if B does *y*, and B in consideration of A's promise to do *x* undertakes to do *y*, but fails to do it, the consideration for B's promise logically fails because it is subject to a condition that is not fulfilled. This is a more subtle point than the historians' conundrum about a promise for a promise; but without a text of Plowden's argument we cannot be certain that the more general problem of mutual promises was not also raised. What we do know is that while *Lucy* v. *Walwyn* was depending, and during the readership of Richard Onslow (Lucy's counsel), the general point was argued in the Inner Temple. Again Anthony Gell is the source, and it is worth reproducing his report in full:

> Note that Kelway said that if I give another 20s. or a penny in consideration that he to whom the gift is made should make an assurance to me of his manor of Dale for the sum of £20 to be paid later, and if he who takes the penny does not make assurance, the other may have an action on the case and recover damages to the value of the land; because it was a contract and there was *quid pro quo*.
>
> And Thomas Gawdy said that, even if no money had been paid, but one promised the other to enfeoff him of his manor of Dale before such a day, and the other promised to pay him £20 for it, if the feoffor did not make the feoffment the other could have an action on the case notwithstanding that no money was paid. But Kelway denied this, and said that it is but *nudum pactum* upon which *non oritur actio*, without *quid pro quo*. And see *Lucy's Case*, above, well argued in a similar action on the case.[44]

43. Lucy v. Walwyn (1561–63), KB 27/1198, m. 183 (extracts translated in the text); Anthony Gell's manuscript reports (hereafter cited as Gell MS), fols. 154v–63v (quoted below, at text accompanying n. 60). The report ends, "Plowden argue al contrary et le grand reason que il fist fuit ceo que ouste le respondre sur *quid pro quo*." The writer is most grateful to Mrs. A. E. Gell for permission to copy the manuscript in her possession.

44. Gell MS, fol. 198 (translated). It is reported under Michaelmas term 1562, and there

Again we must lament the absence of detailed reasons, but it is clear that no less a lawyer than Robert Kelway (Keilwey) regarded mutual promises as *nudum pactum*, because the counter-promise was not *quid pro quo*, and that Anthony Gell thought this to have been the main point in *Lucy* v. *Walwyn*.

A similar division of opinion occurred in the next reported discussion, which arose from Lord Effingham's victory in an archery contest. The agreement was a ten-pound wager on the result, between the loser and a noncompetitor. As yet there was no objection of public policy to wagering contracts, and so the defendant's argument turned on the consideration. The only consideration for the defendant's promise to pay ten pounds was the plaintiff's counter-promise to pay ten pounds if the defendant won the competition. It is proper for us to note that again the counter-promise was conditioned upon an event that never happened; but that point is not expressly taken in the printed report. Mounson, J., thought a counter-promise was a good consideration because it was "reciprocal." Manwood, J., however, took the more conservative view that it was not; between the competitors, he said, there was good consideration in preparing equipment, attending the match, and "the labour in shooting and the travell in going up and down between the marks"; but between the "bettors by" there was no such consideration.[45]

The third of our discussions was occasioned by a somewhat mercenary love affair. A suitor for the hand of the defendant's sister had entered into negotiations with the defendant, and the crucial bargaining point was whether the girl was worth fifteen hundred pounds (that is, in property). She was not, and the plaintiff did not marry her; instead he brought *assumpsit* against the brother for breach of an undertaking that she was worth the sum mentioned. The consideration for the defendant's undertaking was the plaintiff's counter-promise that, if the girl was worth fifteen hundred pounds, he would pay the defendant two hundred pounds. The transaction smacks of wagering, but that point was not taken. Yelverton moved in arrest of judgment that there was no consideration because, at the time when the promise was broken (the same instant as it was made), the plaintiff had sustained no prejudice. Gawdy, J.—the same Thomas Gawdy who had advocated the recognition of mutual promises in 1562—thought there was consideration, because of the suitor's financial interest in the girl's wealth: "It seems his intent was to marry as much for the riches as for love." But Wray, C.J., and Ayloffe, J.,

---

is no express reference to the Inner Temple, but Gell often noted discussions in the inn. Keilwey (d. 1580) read in 1547, Gawdy (d. 1588) read in 1553 and 1560, and Gell (d. 1583) was reader-elect in 1563–64.

45. West v. Stowell (1577), 2 Leo. 154, 74 *Eng. Rep.* 437. The record in CP 40/1346, m. 719 (Trin., 1577), ends with an imparlance; the declaration corresponds closely to the report, the consideration being laid as a conditional past promise ("in consideracione quod [the plaintiff] assumpsisset super se et fideliter . . . promisisset quod si . . . [the defendant] assumpsit et . . . promisit quod si. . . .").

decided there was no consideration, because the defendant had no reciprocal remedy for the two hundred pounds; if the counter-promise was not binding, it was no consideration for the defendant's promise.[46]

In so far as there is a discernible theme in these discussions, it is not the need for the plaintiff to aver performance of his counter-promise[47] but an uneasiness about the want of reciprocity or *quid pro quo*. How could a promise be consideration for another promise, when it was itself conditioned on the performance of the other promise? Could even an unconditional promise be regarded as *quid pro quo*? However readily these questions may have been answered at the end of the century, the opinions of such distinguished lawyers as Plowden, Keilwey, and Wray, in the third quarter of the century, are enough to show that the difficulties then were serious. When general statements about the effectiveness of mutual promises began to appear in the books, the explanation of their efficacy was that there were reciprocal remedies.[48] The constant repetition of that proposition in the reports indicates in itself that it was not altogether digestible. On the other hand, there was never any difficulty over "future acts" as consideration; it only became necessary to explore the distinction between promise-consideration and act-consideration, in the context of the need to aver performance by the plaintiff, once the difficulties about promise-consideration had been overcome. The value of the early discussions is not only the unsureness they reveal, but the testimony they bear to the widespread belief that good consideration was synonymous with *quid pro quo*.

Was Consideration Old Law or New?

By 1600 there were so many decisions touching the doctrine of consideration that recourse to earlier ideas was seldom necessary. To that extent the doctrine of consideration was plainly novel, so novel in fact that none of the cases after 1568 was in print until the seventeenth century. In the earliest discussions, however, lawyers saw no incongruity in citing Year Book cases for propositions about consideration: in the

46. Butterye v. Goodman (1583), C.U.L. MS Ii. 5. 38, fols. 85v–87. Gawdy, J., dissented from Wray, C.J., and Ayloffe, J., on a similar point in Smith v. Smith (1584), 3 Leo. 88, 74 *Eng. Rep.* 559.

47. Simpson, *History of Contract*, pp. 461 ff., in arguing that this was the question, relies on cases beginning in 1596. In the cases of 1561, 1577, and 1583 any such averment was out of the question because the plaintiff's promise never became due for performance.

48. E.g., Anon. (1579), L.I. MS Misc. 488, p. 61 ("si jeo promise al J. S. leas de mon parsonadge pur 10 li. annual rent et J. S. agrea a ceo, que en cest case si jeo ne performe ceo accordant il avera accion sur le case sur cest assumpcion, et le consideracion fuit assetts sufficient car la ad equall remedie envers lauter si le contract ne soit performe"); Anon. (1584), C.U.L. MS Ii. 5. 38, fol. 120v; Anon. (1584), ibid., fol. 159v; Fuller's Case (1586), H.L.S. MS 16, fol. 229 (either performance of act or "cross-assumption" required); Lile v. Frencham (1587), ibid., fol. 418v; Strangborough v. Warner (1589), 4 Leo. 3, 74 *Eng. Rep.* 686.

middle of the sixteenth century, Brooke and Plowden explained the nonfeasance cases of 1409 and 1425 as showing that *assumpsit* would not lie without consideration;[49] Wyndham, J., in 1581 adapted a definition of consideration from a remark of Serjeant Jenney in 1476;[50] and, in 1588, Coke professed to have based his "charge or benefit" definition on the marriage-money case of 1477.[51] Should we conclude that consideration was but an amalgam of old ideas in a new guise, or were lawyers trying to disguise, or at least authenticate, completely new ideas?

Of one thing we may be sure: the law of consideration was English. Of course, we know that St. German had some slight acquaintance with the canonist learning about *causa*, and that Plowden was able to quote a brief civilian definition of *nudum pactum*.[52] But these superficial flirtations with Romanism had no noticeable effect on the history of consideration, except perhaps on Plowden's notion of "deliberation" or intention to be bound; but that notion bore little fruit until Lord Mansfield tried unsuccessfully to revive it two centuries later, and it is now treated by English lawyers as a requirement distinct from consideration. The sixteenth-century cases contain no discussion of error or of vested pacts. Both before and after the introduction of "consideration," English lawyers admittedly made free use of the phrase *nudum pactum*;[53] but they were borrowing language, not legal doctrine. It can also be admitted that the notion of consideration to raise a use, a generation older than consideration in *assumpsit*, played an influential role;[54] indeed, it was probably not until late in Elizabeth I's reign that it occurred to anyone that there might be two "doctrines." This, however, is far from acknowledging canonist influence; the law of uses was the creation of the common-law courts, not (as so many have assumed) of canonist chancellors.[55] The most we can say of Roman influence is that St. German and Plowden

49. Brooke, *Abridgement*, Action sur le Case, pll. 7, 40; Plowd. 309, 75 *Eng. Rep.* 470.

50. Lord Gerard's Case (1581), L.I. MS Misc. 361, fol. 21v: "al primes il monstre que fuit un consideracion, le quel il define solonque le definition de Genney in 16 E. 4. en tiel manner: un consideracion nest que un reasonable cause pur de mover ou pur de passer chose etc." This is a reference to Y. B. Mich. 16 Edw. 4, f. 9, pl. 5 (1476), where Jenney, Sjt., explained that an accord must be pleaded with satisfaction, "car per nostre ley parols sans reason ne liera nulluy, car si jeo die a vous que jeo dona ou paya a vous xx li. a certain jour *nihil operatur* per ceux parols."

51. Stone v. Withepoole (1588), Owen 94, 74 *Eng. Rep.* 924. The case referred to is Y. B. Mich. 17 Edw. 4, f. 5, pl. 4 (1477).

52. *Doctor and Student*, pp. 228–29; Plowd. 309, 75 *Eng. Rep.* 470–71.

53. E.g., Y. B. Mich. 9 Hen. 5, f. 14, pl. 23 (1421), *per* Cokaine, J.; Y. B. Pasch. 11 Hen. 6, f. 43, pl. 30 (1433); Y. B. Trin. 17 Edw. 4, f. 4, pl. 4 (1477), *per* Townshend, Sjt.; Yorke's reports, B.L. Harg. MS 388, fol. 215 (before 1537); Gray's Inn reading, probably that of James Hales in 1537, B.L. Harg. MS 253, fol. 12; Gell MS, fol. 198 (quoted in the text accompanying n. 44); Sharington v. Strotton (1565), Plowd. 298 at 302, 305, 306, 308v; 75 *Eng. Rep.* 454, at 460, 464, 465, 470; West v. Stowell (1577), 2 Leo. 154, 74 *Eng. Rep.* 437; Cook v. Pyne (*temp.* Eliz. 1), L.I. MS Misc. 487, fol. 275v.

54. See Simpson, *History of Contract*, pp. 327–74.

55. Ibid., pp. 327–28, 372–74.

were curious to see whether foreign solutions were capable of adaptation to fill the jurisprudential void; but they did not delve very deep, and if their knowledge of other laws was so limited, it is inconceivable that the profession as a whole paid the least attention to canon or civil law.

Causa

Both in the plea rolls and in the reports, consideration was not infrequently associated with or defined in terms of "cause."[56] Some have jumped to the conclusion that this betokens some reliance on Roman conceptions of *causa*; but it seems rather that, as with *nudum pactum*, all that was borrowed was the vocabulary. And, like other borrowed words such as *injuria*, it was virtually devoid of precise technical meaning: indeed, it was probably borrowed as a nontechnical word. There is an ambiguity in the word "cause"—and also in "consideration" when used in that sense—quite distinct from the other ambiguity in "consideration" to which attention was drawn above. For, in addition to the sense of *causa promissionis*, the reason why the promise was made, it could also denote the "cause of action," the reason why the law made the promise actionable. No doubt in some minds the two coalesced, so that what made the promise actionable was the sufficiency of the reason why it was made; but no assertion in such clear terms appears in the books. If we compare three early sixteenth-century statements about the liability of carpenters for nonfeasance, we find the requirement of advance payment consistently treated as *causa* in the sense of *causa actionis* rather than *causa promissionis*:

> If I covenant with a carpenter to build a house, and pay him £20 to build the house by a certain day, and he does not build the house by the day, now I shall have a good action upon my case because of [*per cause de*] the payment of my money; and yet it sounds only in covenant, and without payment of money in this case there is no remedy. . . . And so it seems to me in the case at bar the payment of the money is the *cause of the action* on the case.[57]
>
> If I promise you to build you a house by a day, which I do not do, this is but *nudum pactum* upon which [you] shall not have an action. . . . [But] if I give certain money to someone to build me a house by a day, and he does not build it by the day, there this is a

56. For the association in the words of pleadings, see above, at nn. 11, 19, 21. For definitions, see, e.g., Calthorpe's Case (1574), Dyer 336b, §34, 73 *Eng. Rep.* 759 ("un consideration est un cause ou occasion meritorious . . ."); Lord Gerard's Case (1581), L.I. MS Misc. 361, fol. 22, *per* Dyer, C.J. ("un consideracion est *causa meritoria* pur que il granteroit, et poet estre appell per bien *causa reciproca*, s. un mutuall cause"); and Sydenham v. Worlington (1585), Godb. 31, 78 *Eng. Rep.* 20, *per* Peryam, J. ("it is sufficient if there be any moving cause or consideration precedent, for which cause or consideration precedent the promise was made").

57. Orwell v. Mortoft (1505), Keil. 78, pl. 25, 72 *Eng. Rep.* 239, *per* Frowyk, C.J. (translated).

> *consideration why I should have an action* on my case for the nonfeasance.[58]
>
> If a man comes to me and says, "Give me £10 and I will build you a barn of so much in length," now if he does not build I shall have an action on my case. It is the contrary where no money was given, for then it is but *nudum pactum*. And this is nonfeasance; but, because I have no remedy for my money, this is the *cause why* I shall have this action.[59]

When we come to *Lucy* v. *Walwyn* in 1561, we find "consideration" still being used in this sense, and may even allow ourselves a little surprise on finding talk of consideration for an action in tort:

> Always in an action on the case there must be a consideration in fact or in law. Thus, if a man menaces my villeins of my manor of Dale so that they run away from it, I shall have an action on the case because it is wrong, and against law and reason, which makes a consideration in law. And so it is for slandering me: it is a consideration in law. But if there is no consideration in fact or in law, no action on the case lies. And this is why the book is agreed in 11 Hen. 4, where one erected a school which was to the nuisance of another, and yet no action against him who erected it. . . . And so in our case there is no consideration in fact or in law, for he who undertook to obtain the lease was to have nothing before the obtaining; so that there is no *quid pro quo*, but only *nudum pactum*, upon which an *assumpsit* cannot be.[60]

If "consideration" were here used in its later sense, we might argue that "consideration in fact" was *quid pro quo* and that "consideration in law" was our modern duty of care. But it is obviously not used as a term of art in this passage; it means "the reason why I can sue." If the passage reflects current thought in 1561, there was evidently still no doctrine of consideration; the word was the name of the problem, not of its answer.

Again it is the plea rolls that provide the best evidence of a refinement of meaning. In 1563 an administratrix, who had been sued in London on a promise to pay the debt of the deceased, had the judgment against her reversed in the King's Bench for error because "no consideration is alleged by reason of which [she] promised and undertook to pay."[61] Considera-

58. Anon. (between 1526 and 1537), Yorke's reports, B.L. Harg. MS 388, fol. 215 (translated). This is the first use of the word "consideration" in a reported contract case; but it is obviously not used in the later sense.

59. Gray's Inn reading, probably that of James Hales in 1537, B.L. Harg. MS 253, fol. 12 (translated).

60. Lucy v. Walwyn (1561), Gell MS, at fol. 161, *per* Nicholls (translated). The case referred to is The Case of Gloucester School, Y. B. Hil. 11 Hen. 4, f. 47, pl. 21 (1410).

61. Isack v. Barbour (1563), KB 27/1207, m. 55: "nulla allegatur consideracio ob quam predicta Elizabetha promisit et super se assumpsit." The writer is indebted to Dr. R. H. Helmholz for bringing this case to his attention.

tion here is not only *causa promissionis*, but it seems to have acquired a technical sense, at least for the pleader. The *causa promissionis* sense had always underlain the consideration clause of the declaration, which was introduced with the object of showing cause for the undertaking. It was in this sense that past and insufficient considerations were at first recited without demur; they were sound reasons for promising. It also explains such seemingly unreciprocal considerations as natural love and affection, being found in arrears upon an account,[62] having goods in the capacity of an administrator,[63] or having goods by finding.[64] These were all held good in their time, until they were struck down by the countervailing notion of reciprocity. But the only ultimate legacy of this looser view of consideration was the *indebitatus* formula; it was to be by far the most important species of *assumpsit*, yet it was a species in which consideration in the established sense played no real part and which in the seventeenth and eighteenth centuries spread itself well beyond the bounds of "contract." Once consideration was not merely a cause, but a "reciprocal" or "mutual" cause, then the older sense of *causa* was defunct. Consideration had come to mean the price of the promise, not the motive behind it.

Quid pro Quo

The *causa reciproca* mentioned by Dyer, C.J., was better known to common lawyers as *quid pro quo*. Much controversy has raged over the suggestion, promoted by Langdell and Holmes, that consideration was somehow "derived" from *quid pro quo*. The arguments put forward by those pioneers of the law of contract now seem incredibly odd. Yet the reaction against the *quid pro quo* school has at worst been equally misconceived. In its bluntest form, the traditional learning was that *quid pro quo* was a precise and technical doctrine in the law of debt; this doctrine was then either transferred to or absorbed into the law of *assumpsit* because of the close analogy between *indebitatus assumpsit* and debt; or, according to the opposing school, it was not precisely followed in *indebitatus assumpsit* because that action was tortious in origin and there was no need to prove an indebtedness in any technical sense. This traditional learning—which has been on the wane in recent years—rests on two false assumptions. In the first place, *quid pro quo* was not a

62. Snowe v. Jurden (1572), KB 27/1242, m. 481; KB 27/1244, m. 228; H.L.S. MS 1192, fol. 22v; C.U.L. MS Hh. 2. 9, fol. 59. In the first action the consideration was an accounting together and being found in arrears; in the second it was altered to a being found in arrears (reciting the account in the *cum* clause) *and* twelvepence paid (probably a fiction).

63. Hudson's Case (1558), cited in Howell v. Trevanion (1588), H.L.S. MS 16, fol. 423v; Becher v. Mountjoye (1573), in E. Coke, *Booke of Entries* (London, 1614), fols. 2–3 (citing Mich. 15 & 16 Eliz. 1, m. 1959).

64. Lile v. Frencham (1587), H.L.S. MS 16, fol. 418v; C.U.L. MS Ii. 5. 38, fol. 259 (executor; case of finder put in argument); Ireland v. Higgins (1589), Cro. Eliz. 125, 78 *Eng. Rep.* 383, Owen 93, 74 *Eng. Rep.* 924, 3 Leo. 219, 74 *Eng. Rep.* 644, Het. 50, 124 *Eng. Rep.* 334 (finder of animal).

precise doctrine carefully worked out in medieval times in the context of debt. The prevalence of the general issue prevented any discussion of the basis of liability in debt, except in those rare cases where there was a tentative demurrer to a novel kind of declaration: and when that happened, as in the marriage-money cases of the fifteenth century, everyone who spoke seems to have had a different conception of *quid pro quo*. The second error lay in supposing that the notion belonged exclusively to the action of debt, and could therefore have influenced only *indebitatus assumpsit*. This was doubly wrong. First, the consideration in *indebitatus assumpsit* never was the *quid pro quo* of the debt-creating contract, but was either the indebtedness itself or something collateral (such as the fictional shilling, or a forbearance). Second, and more important, *quid pro quo* was a constituent element of a "bargain," only one side of which was remedied by debt. It had therefore been as relevant in *assumpsit* for not performing a bargain as in debt, and it continued to play a more prominent role in "special" *assumpsit* than it ever did in *indebitatus assumpsit*.

Thus, in *Doige's Case* (1442), Newton, C.J., and Fortescue, C.J., both gave as the reason for allowing *assumpsit* against a defaulting vendor of land that it achieved reciprocity of remedies: "it would be wonderful law if a bargain could be made by which one party was bound by an action of debt but was without remedy against the other."[65] One of the clerks of the King's Bench actually described the payment for the promise as *quid pro quo*.[66] In some of the early Tudor discussions of *assumpsit* to perform acts, the prepayment that was regarded as the cause of action is described as *quid pro quo*.[67] The first reported nonfeasance case where there was no prepayment, *Sukley* v. *Wyte* (1543), occasioned a discussion in terms of reciprocity; the word "consideration" does not appear, but Shelley, J., in reserving judgment, remarked that nothing was given in return for the undertaking "except a thing which by law he could do anyway."[68] For Keilwey, in 1562, it was only *quid pro quo* that could save a promise from being *nudum pactum*.[69] Likewise, Beaumont, also of the Inner Temple, said in a case about uses a few years later: "In every bargain there must be *quid pro quo* or else it is *nudum pactum* and no perfect bargain. If I bargain with a carpenter that he will build me a house, and he agrees to do it, but it is not agreed what he will have for his labor, this

65. [Shipton v. Dogge] (1442), Y. B. Trin. 20 Hen. 6, f. 34, pl. 4 (1442) (translated).

66. Simpson, *History of Contract*, p. 626, citing H.L.S. MS 156. William Broune or Brome was filazer for Yorkshire and Lincolnshire from 1434 to 1458 and chief clerk from 1458 to 1461.

67. Yorke's reports, B.L. Harg. MS. 388, fol. 215; Sir Anthony Fitzherbert, *La Nouvelle Natura Brevium* (London, 1534), fol. 145 G.

68. Library of Congress, Gell MS, Pasch. 34 Hen. 8, fol. 12v (translated); Simpson, *History of Contract*, pp. 631–32. These reports were written by the same Anthony Gell who is mentioned above.

69. See above, at n. 44 and accompanying text. See also Nicholls's argument, above, at text accompanying n. 60.

is a void bargain unless the money be paid immediately, or a day of payment appointed, or earnest given."[70] And Coke, who showed little interest in *assumpsit*, was sure that the consideration required to raise a use was nothing more nor less than *quid pro quo*.[71]

"Labor or Charge"

Although the notion of a bargain, or *quid pro quo*, seems to have been responsible for ousting vaguer notions of *causa* from English law, it does not explain the whole story; for, by the 1580s, it was repeatedly being stated that a promise could be supported by considerations which did not amount to *quid pro quo*.[72] The tradition of legal history was that these further considerations, usually summarized in the misleading phrase "detriment to the promisee," were a legacy of the delictual origins of *assumpsit* for nonfeasance. The cases which established that *assumpsit* lay for nonfeasance had all stressed the need for the plaintiff to show that he had been deceived out of his money, or had suffered consequential loss in reliance on the promise.[73] Ironically, the very prepayment that had been treated as *quid pro quo* was in the same cases treated as "tortious" damage: the confusion of ideas was present from the start. There is no doubt that the delictual approach held considerable sway in the reigns of Henry VII and Henry VIII. Frowyk, C.J., repeatedly stressed the deceit or "misdemeanour" as the cause of action,[74] and an illuminating moot of 1516 shows a general supposition in Gray's Inn that *assumpsit* lay only for a tort (*injuria*) that caused damage.[75] For Spelman, J., in 1532, a breach of promise was actionable in *assumpsit* because it was a "tort."[76] And declarations in *assumpsit* from this time onward nearly always alleged some form of consequential damage. In assessing this evidence, we should not deceive ourselves into confusing form and substance: the main reason for the delictual approach was to find a justification for using actions on the case instead of "general" writs of debt or covenant,

70. Bracebridge's Case (1583?), B.L. Harg. MS 9, fol. 136, *per* Beaumont "le puisne" (translated). The speaker is probably Henry Beaumont (d. 1585), who became a bencher in 1584; his elder brother Francis (d. 1598) became a bencher in 1578.

71. Mildmaye's Case (1584), 1 Rep. 175a, 76 *Eng. Rep.* 379; Wiseman v. Barnard (1585), 2 Rep. 15, 76 *Eng. Rep.* 418.

72. Webb's Case (1577), 4 Leo. 110, 74 *Eng. Rep.* 763; Baxter v. Read (1584), Treby's notes to Dyer 272 (73 *Eng. Rep.* 606) in marg.; Sydenham v. Worlington (1585), Godb. 31, 78 *Eng. Rep.* 20; Foster v. Scarlet (1587), Cro. Eliz. 70, 78 *Eng. Rep.* 330; Preston v. Tooley (1587), Cro. Eliz. 74, 78 *Eng. Rep.* 334.

73. E.g., Shipton v. Dogge (see above, at n. 65); Orwell v. Mortoft (see next note); Pykeryng v. Thurgoode (see below, at n. 76). In the last case, consequential loss alone is relied on, and deceit is no longer discussed.

74. Y. B. Mich. 20 Hen. 7, f. 8, pl. 18 (1504); Keil. 69, 77, 72 *Eng. Rep.* 229, 239. The case is Orwell v. Mortoft (1505), CP 40/972, m. 123.

75. Moot at Peter Dillon's reading, L.I. MS Misc. 486(2), fol. 7v; printed in *Reports of Sir John Spelman*, 2:272. The question was whether an action on the case lay against a carpenter for nonfeasance. Harlakenden and Hales thought not; Tingleden said that consequential physical damage was necessary; Dillon and Martin said that it was sufficient if there was *injuria*. None of the speakers took the point about prepayment and *quid pro quo*.

76. Pykeryng v. Thurgoode (1532), printed in *Reports of Sir John Spelman*, 1:5, *per* Spelman, J.

and we need not suppose that the notion of deceit denoted much more than a disappointed expectation. There does, nevertheless, seem to have been a substantive principle as well: the principle that a promisor should be liable for breaking his promise if the promisee has relied on the promise in such a way as to incur loss. The defaulting carpenter could be seen, on this view, as being liable because of the "wrong" he had done the client both by taking his money and by keeping him without a home.[77]

Having granted all this, we must face the near impossibility of linking either the delictual history or the substantive principle with the "doctrine" of consideration in the way suggested by Hare and Ames. The elements of deceit and consequential loss were never incorporated in the consideration clause, but were destined to wither away as fictions. And in the cases that established "detriment to the promisee" as good consideration, the consideration in question had nothing in common with the earlier deceit cases: it was a reciprocal future act, or a promise to act, by the plaintiff. Even the line between "detriment" consideration and *quid pro quo* was unhistorical, probably the result of a Tudor restriction of the latter, which later generations would receive as medieval.[78] Salmond was correct, therefore, in supposing a "breach of continuity" between the rationale of the nonfeasance cases and the doctrine of consideration. On the other hand, there was no breach of continuity in the development of *quid pro quo*; and so the conclusion drawn from Salmond's theory, that consideration must have been imported into English law *ab extra*, was as unnecessary as it is improbable.

Conclusion

We began with a warning against an undue desire for historical neatness. When the legal historian sees confusion or inconsistency, unless it is of his own making, he is probably looking at law being made. If a legal historian of the twenty-fourth century purported to reveal the perfect clarity of, say, the English doctrine of fundamental breach in the 1960s and 1970s, he would be a bad historian; we of the 1960s and 1970s know how many plausible ways there are of looking at the same problem, but we cannot know (as our successor will) which view will ultimately prevail, and so the state of uncertainty is itself the historical truth. It rather looks as though "consideration" was in the same plight in

77. Ibid.; Anon. (before 1537), Yorke's reports, B.L. Harg. MS 388, fol. 215.

78. For the uncertainty of the judges in 1458, see Y. B. Mich. 37 Hen. 6, f. 8, pl. 18 (1458). Prisot, C.J., apparently thought *quid pro quo* unnecessary to maintain debt; Danvers, J., thought a future act was *quid pro quo*; and Moyle, J., thought a future act done for a third party was "tantamount" to *quid pro quo*. The medieval uncertainty is fully discussed by McGovern, "Contract in Medieval England," pp. 173–201. The later definitions of *quid pro quo* may, ironically, have been more influenced by Roman law than consideration was: not by way of canon law or St. German, but through the revival of interest in Glanvill and Bracton.

the period we have examined. Most lawyers could identify the questions without difficulty, but the search for a clear answer was complicated and delayed in practice by divergent views about the forms of action, by the infinite variety of special declarations, and by the tireless ingenuity of opposing counsel. The survival of older ways of settling disputes had rendered a detailed law of contractual liability unnecessary, or at least unattainable, before the establishment of *assumpsit* for nonfeasance. The comfortable certainty of that old world ended when the special declarations in case, with their myriad permutations of facts, began to throw up endless questions of law that had never been posed before. These new questions required new, more precise formulations of shadowy medieval notions, and the nascent learning suddenly converged in the 1560s upon a simple phrase which was calculated merely to avoid or deflect a number of disparate problems raised by the development of *assumpsit* declarations. Contemporary sources suggest that the only novelty lay in the refinement of earlier ideas; for the spiritual sources of the law of consideration were the two simple, timeless, and ubiquitous moral principles that bargains should bind both parties and that men should be held to promises on which others have actively relied. The technical "doctrine of consideration" in which these principles came to be enshrined in the time of Elizabeth I was occasioned by nothing more arcane than the fertile ambiguity resulting from a little shift of wording by the pleader. It is true enough that the life of the law has not been scholastic logic: it has been the conversion of loose words into jargon.

13 A Cheshire Seductress, Precedent, and a "Sore Blow" to Star Chamber

Thomas G. Barnes

When Professor Thorne was invited to give the first Selden Society Lecture in March 1952, he was enticed away from Henricus de Bratton long enough to cast new light on Bracton's worthiest successor (though possibly not Bracton's intellectual peer), Sir Edward Coke. In suggesting some canons for discovering in Coke's corpus what was his confection and what was truly old law, Professor Thorne gave us good direction and timely warning:

> As a rule of thumb it is well to remember that sentences beginning "For it is an ancient maxim of the common law", followed by one of Coke's spurious Latin maxims, which he could manufacture to fit any occasion and provide with an air of authentic antiquity, are apt to introduce a new departure. Sentences such as "And by these differences and reasons you will better understand your books", or "And so the doubts and diversities in the books well resolved", likewise indicate new law. If I may formulate a theorem of my own, I advance this—the longer the list of authorities reconciled, the greater the divergence from the cases cited.[1]

The Thorne Theorem might not be provable, but it is a sound approach to analyzing the use of precedents by Coke's contemporaries as well as by Coke himself. His luminous rival and intellectual adversary, Francis Bacon, is not to be excepted. In Star Chamber in Trinity term 1614 special day was given to hear "presidentes" touching the power of the court; never before or after were precedents so extensively used in Star Chamber. The dispute at the hearing was less between the adversary parties than between Attorney General Bacon for the relators and the common-law judges on the bench, led by Chief Justice Coke. Though Bacon carried the day with the court, the victory was so narrow as to be parlous. Neither Bacon nor Coke distinguished himself in arguing precedent. *Brereton's Case* is a classic set-problem in the use of precedents in that age—and Sam Thorne is our Euclid!

Even as Star Chamber cases went, *Attorney General ex rel. Sir Richard Egerton* v. *Richard Brereton et al.* was unusually lurid. Sir Randall Brereton was a Cheshire magnate with extensive properties in that and neighboring counties. A passionate and choleric man, a famous litigant, and a

1. Samuel E. Thorne, *Sir Edward Coke, 1552–1952* (London, 1957), p. 7.

notable libertine, he found old age cruel, blindness, increasing feebleness, and senility clouding his last years. Three or four years before his death in 1611, Randall fell under the flattering wiles of the wife of a neighboring magnate and second justice of Chester, Sir Henry Townsend. Lady Dorothy Townsend was a courtesan of no mean talent, and with her husband's tacit allowance if not connivance she set out to seduce old Randall and induced him to move to the Townsend mansion with most of his valuables. Dorothy (and perhaps Henry) conspired with Randall's younger brothers, Richard Brereton, Esq., and Sir Thomas Brereton, and their sons to make a prey of his estate to the disherison of Randall's only surviving child and heir presumptive, Mary, wife of Sir Richard Egerton. Randall had made a will in about 1605 leaving virtually his entire personal estate to Mary and the seven children of her marriage to Egerton; the Egertons were named executors. The old man had further secured the will by a deed of the property, which, because he feared seduction, he kept in his own custody. About four months before he died, Dorothy Townsend, Henry Townsend, and Richard Brereton's wife burned the will—Randall was then resident in the Townsend mansion. In late April 1611, Randall became comatose. He had one last lucid moment on Sunday, 4 May, said "Jesus" and "God bless her" (apparently referring to Dorothy), and signed a will that had been concocted that morning by which much of his realty was bequeathed to his younger brothers (who were named executors) and most of his personalty to Dorothy. One John Davies, D.Med., falsely subscribed as a witness though he did not see the will signed. When Randall finally gave up the ghost about four P.M. on Thursday, 8 May, Davies disemboweled the cadaver before it was cold. The new will was entered in the Prerogative Court of Canterbury for probate by a vagrant, hired by the conspirators to act as their proctor and to put in scandalous allegations against the Egertons as well, in order to color the matter. It took two trials in PCC and reference to Delegates to prove the will. By it, the Egertons stood to lose over three thousand pounds of the seven- to ten-thousand-pounds estate of Randall Brereton. In April 1612, Attorney General Hobart filed an information in Star Chamber on the Egertons' relation, charging the principal conspirators and a host of small fry with fraudulently suppressing the old will, fraudulently moving the new will, suborning libel, and perpetrating the misdemeanor of "bowelling" Randall before he was cold.[2]

Considering that the proceedings in the case were one of the most massive on file, the case was prosecuted with unusual celerity. Dozens of witnesses were examined on many interrogatories (587 interrogatories for the plaintiff), the last of them in June 1613. The trial, on 26 November 1613, took only one sitting-day. Hobart having been promoted to the chief justiceship of the Common Pleas on the same day, his successor as attorney general opened: Sir Francis Bacon. Bacon was doubtless sec-

2. Public Record Office, Star Chamber (hereafter cited as STAC) 8/14/7, proceedings in the case.

onded by the relators' counsel, Francis Moore.[3] Eleven defendants were convicted. Richard and Thomas Brereton and Dorothy Townsend were each fined £800; the Townsends' servant, Edward Davies, who had taken a particularly unsavory role in the conspiracy, was fined £1,000; Dr. Davies was fined £200 for his overzealous dissection; and other defendants were fined £100 each. All of the charges were found against some of the defendants. The notable acquittal was that of Sir Henry Townsend. He was not cleared outright, but the case against him was found *non liquet*. Richard and Thomas Brereton and Dorothy Townsend were ordered to pay £3,000 damages to the Egertons, and afterwards they were taxed £150 costs.[4]

The fines were moderate in light of the heinousness of the offenses and the qualities of the defendants, the costs were heavy but not incommensurate with the massiveness of the proofs, and the damages awarded were just on the basis of the proven loss to the Egertons occasioned by the fraudulent will. As a general rule every conviction in Star Chamber resulted in a fine to the king. Costs, on the losing party, were a matter of course, whether awarded by the whole court in the decree of judgment or taxed afterwards by the lord chancellor; "very good costs," that is, penal costs, were not unusual. Damages, however, were another matter. Under the early Tudors the awarding of damages grew steadily, though they never became a matter of course, and were prayed by successful plaintiffs much more often than they were granted. Such relief was in line with the early Tudor perception of Star Chamber as a great tribunal not tied to ordinary powers and procedures.[5] Then the court also "meddled" with title, summarily restored parties to possession, readily provided restitution of goods, and generally wielded its injunctive power freely. Early in Elizabeth's reign, Star Chamber rather suddenly became what in theory it had always been, a court of general (and largely uncircumscribed) criminal jurisdiction for the repression of serious misdemeanors. Within five years of the queen's accession it resolutely refused to "meddle" with title, only reluctantly granted possession and restitution, and reduced its prodigal employment of injunctions. The circumstances surrounding and the reasons for this abrupt change are not clear. It also became very niggardly in the matter of damages. Though the loss of the court's order and decree books makes a categorical statement impossible, for the first thirty years of Elizabeth's reign the surviving instances of damages awarded can be

3. Moore, Middle Temple, shortly to be created serjeant, signed the information (in STAC 8/14/7) with Hobart, Att. Gen.

4. Huntington Library Ellesmere MS (hereafter cited as Hunt. Ell. MS) 2790, cause-list, 26 Nov. 1613, with notes by Ellesmere of trial; Public Record Office, Exchequer (hereafter cited as E) 159/448, Trin. 13 James 1, rot. 145, estreat of fines in Star Chamber, tested 28 June 1615; Public Record Office, State Papers (hereafter cited as SP) 14/77/51B, copy of decree on precedent hearing, Star Chamber, 29 June 1614.

5. See J. A. Guy, *The Cardinal's Court: The Impact of Thomas Wolsey in Star Chamber* (Hassocks, Sussex, 1977). I am grateful to Dr. Guy for helping me run down Henrician cases relevant to this essay.

counted on one hand, and most involved unusual cases.[6] Beginning in 1588, and continuing without noticeable interruption until *Brereton's Case*, Star Chamber became more ready to award damages. It added a subpoena *ad solvendum dampna* (similar to the subpoena *ad solvendum costagium*) to its process; failure to pay constituted contempt, attachment would issue, and the contemnor would be committed until he purged his contempt by paying. Damages assessed by the court in the decree (as in *Brereton's Case*) were rare; usually a commission to local gentlemen to assess damages was issued and the court ordered the amount found, by order postdecree.[7] However, damages were still not common—no more than two or three cases per year resulted in an award.

In due course, subpoenas for both the damages and the costs were served on the two Breretons and Dorothy—in the Fleet prison, because pursuant to the court's practice they were committed at pleasure until they had paid their fines to the king or arranged for payment. Having nothing to lose by their contempt, the three sat out the subpoenas. Similar subpoenas were then served on Sir Henry Townsend, doubtless on the analogy of the well-established practice of Star Chamber by which a principal defendant convicted was responsible for his servants', son's, or wife's fine to the king.[8] Townsend also chose to stand in contempt. The relators were stalemated. On the post-term day of Hilary 1614, the Egertons' counsel moved Sir Henry's commitment for contempt, and moved, further, that the damages and costs be levied on the lands and goods of the contemnors "accordinge to former presidentes of this honorable court in like cases."[9] He also prayed injunction to stay suits brought by the defendants against the Egertons and their tenants for the lands descended to Mary Egerton as heir of Sir Randall. The court favored the motion but could only grant day the next term for the defendants to show cause to the contrary.

In Easter term counsel on both sides were heard. The relief requested was so unusual that the court called for precedents to be shown a week later. When the relators produced what precedents they could, the defendants took strong exception, denying that the court had power to grant the relief sought. The court took this as an affront and responded with alarm "for that the power and authoritie of this highe and honourable Court . . . is hereby drawne in question."[10] The court set the first day of Trinity term, 29 June 1614, for a full hearing of the matter and precedents, and directed a thorough search of Star Chamber's precedents,

6. Based upon British Library Harleian MS (hereafter cited as B.L. Harl. MS) 2143 (extracts from Star Chamber order and decree books, Edw. 6–James 1) and British Library Lansdowne MS (hereafter cited as B.L. Lansd. MS) 639 (William Hudson's extracts from same, Hen. 8–Chas. 1).

7. E.g., STAC 10/11/1; B.L. Harl. MS 2143, fol. 61, Baldwin v. Smyth (Trin., 1594), indicating this is usual course.

8. E 159/413–35, estreats of Star Chamber fines, on King's Remembrancer Memoranda Rolls.

9. SP 14/77/51B.

10. Ibid.

which were to be circulated to the lords of the Privy Council and judges prior to the hearing. Thus was set the great debate.

Precedent

The three questions to be settled at law were stated by the court to be:

> [First] whether this court hath used to graunt anie such proces [extent] for the levyeinge and payement of damages and costes uppon the landes and goodes of the parties that ought to paie the same;
>
> Secondly, whether Sir Henry Towneshend standinge not convicted by the saide decree ought to be chargeable with the paiement of the fyne [to the king], damages, and costes imposed uppon his wife;
>
> And lastlie, whether this court hath used to staie all suites in other courtes brought by such as shall not performe the decrees of this court for other matters not concerninge the matters heere dependinge althoughe they were betweene the same parties.[11]

In so stating the case, the court defined the first and third questions as resting wholly upon determination by precedent, and implied that the second was to be governed by precedent. Moreover, the court's reluctance to determine the issue as a matter of policy at the second hearing in Easter term—upon cause shown—raised the issue of the power of Star Chamber to enforce its decrees. This was unusual. For a century, the king's Council in the Star Chamber had demonstrated little tenderness about extending its jurisdiction, seldom questioned its own procedures or entertained fundamental questions about them, and had created a body of substantive misdemeanors that went far beyond what its mediaeval predecessor, the Consilio Regis, or the tribunal established by the so-called Act Pro Camera Stellata (1487) and absorbed by the Council, had been prepared to repress.[12] The citation of procedural precedents in trials in Star Chamber was relatively rare, and counsel showed, understandably, considerable reluctance to question the court's procedural powers. But in Easter term 1614, Star Chamber itself posed the question counsel usually feared to ask, and in such terms that if precedent did not appear to support the court's powers it stood in danger of having to limit them.

It is difficult to see what else Star Chamber might have done. Two circumstances surrounding the case in hand militated against following

11. Ibid.

12. See Guy, *Cardinal's Court*, chap. 1. See also the introduction to *Select Cases in the Council of Henry VII*, ed. C. G. Bayne and William Huse Dunham, Selden Society, vol. 75 (London, 1958); and reviews of ibid. by G. R. Elton, in *English Historical Review* 74 (1959): 686, and Thomas G. Barnes, in *Speculum* 34 (1959): 649–51.

the time-honored course of ruling peremptorily, as had been the court's wont. The first was the unfortunate timing of the relators' motion. The post-term day of Hilary (15 February 1614) was the least auspicious sitting-day to try to make new law surreptitiously. Star Chamber sat that day not only to tidy up term business by hearing motions and to entertain pleas in mitigation of fines and corporal punishment imposed by decrees in the previous two terms; it was also the day when all of the common-law court judges attended to hear the lord chancellor's charge before they rode the Lent assizes. Whereas usually only the two chief justices sat (or in the absence of one of them, the chief baron or a puisne of any of the three courts), on that day all of them were present. We don't know what response from the *jurisperiti* the Egertons' motion evoked, but the allegation that what was prayed was according to former precedents of the court was likely to have been challenged from the bench. That day was given to show cause might well have resulted as much from Lord Chancellor Ellesmere's desire to stifle discussion then as from the course of the court. The second circumstance that made it nearly impossible to rule peremptorily at the show cause hearing was the quality of Sir Henry Townsend. Not only was he a magnate, he was also learned and a judge in the Palatinate of Chester.[13] Given a less august and less qualified party, the court would have been at least in a stronger position to accept the allegations as to its past practices without determining how well the allegations were founded. If hard cases make bad law, big men make hard cases.

Star Chamber was probably in no position to do otherwise than to call for a search of precedents in *Brereton's Case*—even had the two particular circumstances not been present. Star Chamber had been for a decade in the same throes of precedent hunting that had revolutionized the common law in the late years of Elizabeth's reign and during the first decade of James's. As Dr. J. H. Baker has pointed out, the "principal authority advanced for the King's Bench view [of using action on the case as alternative to writ action] was the continuous practice of the court itself."[14] For the same ends (neither more nor less) and by the same means, Star Chamber had assumed and fashioned an increasingly coherent civil jurisdiction based upon fraudulent acts prosecuted in Star Chamber as misdemeanor: fraud, forgery, perjury, subornation, embracery, maintenance, extortion, deceit in trade, lawyer's malfeasance, and conspiracy. Although these offenses (conspiracy, i.e., combination, excepted, as a substantive offense) were staples of Star Chamber activity for decades, even a century, the motivation behind the prosecution of them and the ends sought in prosecution of them were civil.[15] The awarding of dam-

13. Townsend was admitted to Lincoln's Inn in 1558, called 1568, bencher 1579, and read Autumn 1581; he was second justice of Chester, 1603–25.

14. J. H. Baker, "New Light on *Slade's Case*," *Cambridge Law Journal* 29 (1971): 51–67, 213–36, at 221.

15. Thomas G. Barnes, "Star Chamber Litigants and Their Counsel, 1596–1641," in *Legal Records and the Historian*, ed. J. H. Baker (London, 1978), pp. 7–28; Thomas G.

ages was the clearest indication of what the Jacobean litigant sought and the court was prepared to provide. Star Chamber from the mid-1590s was in the process of making "precedent" almost every Wednesday and Friday in term. From that time dates the large corpus of reported cases in the court, most of them destined by the court's abolition in 1641 to remain in manuscript, but all of them reflecting the new science of reporting.[16] Star Chamber had as far to go as King's Bench to make instant "precedent"; further, in fact, because it was throughout the sixteenth century a court theoretically less formal procedurally and less structured in its substantive law than the King's Bench. Yet increasingly in these latter years it operated implicitly on the contentious, though not easily refutable, dictum of Popham, C.J.K.B., in *Barkley* v. *Foster* (1597) that "Although it be error, yet the long use and multitude of precedents must draw it into a law, for *communis error facit jus.* . . ."[17] Indeed, Star Chamber proved an apt disciple of King's Bench; just possibly, the roles of master and student were reversed, but that can't be delved into here.

To the new, instant, "precedent" was added genuine old precedent. The curious compilations, extracts from the Council registers of Henry VII and Henry VIII, called *Libri Intrationum*, date from the last decade of the sixteenth century, and were done by clerks in the office of the clerk of the Council in the Star Chamber, William Mill, probably at the behest of Lord Keeper Egerton (afterward, Lord Chancellor Ellesmere).[18] Shorter extracts from the order and decree books proper of the Star Chamber from Henry VIII's reign onward were amassed under the same quasi-official auspices.[19] And the clerk himself kept an "alphabet kallender to give light of divers especiall presidentes" from Henry VII to Elizabeth.[20] Counsel practicing in the well-defined sub-bar of Star Chamber made their own extracts—that of William Hudson, the most eminent practicer at that bar, survives and was the basis for his widely circulated and highly esteemed manuscript treatise on the court.[21] Mill, in the last years of the

---

Barnes, "Star Chamber and the Sophistication of the Criminal Law," *Criminal Law Review*, 1977, pp. 316–26.

16. I am preparing some one thousand such reported cases from manuscript sources for publication by the Ames Foundation. See L. W. Abbott, *Law Reporting in England, 1485–1585* (London, 1973), chap. 7, "Edward Coke and the New Era."

17. Baker, "New Light on *Slade's Case*," p. 222.

18. See text of *Select Cases in the Council of Henry VII*; for Ellesmere's copies of the *Libri Intrationum*, see Hunt. Ell. MSS 2654, 2655, 2768.

19. B.L. Harl. MS 2143, fols. 1–71v. contains 1,033 extracts of orders and decrees, almost 800 of them from Elizabeth's reign. There are a few *temp*. Hen. 7 and Hen. 8, most of them the precedents cited by Bacon, Att. Gen., in Brereton's Case, added to it on fols. 69v–70.

20. Hunt. Ell. MS 2725, inventory of clerk's books received by Sir Francis Bacon as clerk of the Council in Star Chamber in succession to William Mill, Aug. 1608.

21. B.L. Lansd. MS 639, fols. 22–112, are extracts of orders and decrees arranged under various headings of convenience to a practicer, mostly compiled by Hudson, the remainder by his protégé and successor as barrister in practice there, John Lightfoot, also of Gray's Inn. Hudson's treatise exists in about a score of known manuscript copies; it is most

1580s, helped that assiduous antiquary, William Lambarde, in his search for the origins of English judicature, and was rewarded by being supplied with precedents back to Edward I for the king in his Council (in and out of Star Chamber) and a treatise over half of which was devoted to that jurisdiction.[22] With such a literature available, Star Chamber could not escape increasing emphasis on precedent as the basis of authority for substantive and procedural developments.

What had long dampened the bar's enthusiasm for citing precedent in Star Chamber was not only the court's self-esteemed grandeur but the existence of a living oracle of the court's precedents in the person of William Mill, the clerk. Time and again, Mill would have the last word on precedent when a question arose, insofar as it was Star Chamber's course. By the narrow view of precedent as expressed by Popham, that was the only precedent that weighed heavily with the court—a predilection reinforced by Star Chamber's own sense of its greatness and uniqueness. With Mill's death in July 1608, the court lost its oracle. He was succeeded as clerk by the reversioner to the office: Sir Francis Bacon, solicitor general. Henceforth, the office was executed by deputy (three of them between 1608 and *Brereton's Case* alone), and none ever enjoyed the confidence reposed in Mill. Not until William Hudson, by virtue of his command of the court in practice and in theory, became an equally unimpeachable oracle, about 1620, could court and counsel rely on anyone to have the last (or very nearly the last) word on Star Chamber's precedents.

From Mill's death to *Brereton's Case* a number of cases arose that compelled the court to a search of precedents; citation, or at least allusion, to precedent became more prominent in advocacy at trial. The last such instance before *Brereton's Case*, coeval with it and involving substantially the same bench in Star Chamber, is instructive. In Hilary 1614 in *Proctor's Case* the court split evenly, four to four, as to the guilt of Sir Stephen Proctor and other defendants on the charges of conspiracy against and libel of the earl of Northampton and Lord Wooton. Upon reference, Coke, C.J.K.B., and Hobart, C.J.C.P. (who at the trial had been for conviction), after consultation with the king's counsel learned, certified in Easter term that "this question must be determined by the precedents of the Court of Star-Chamber. . . ."[23] Counsel for Proctor—none other than William Hudson—made the search, producing only two cases. Both were recent; neither was entirely on all fours with the case in hand. Hudson's brief concluded: "Theis two presidentes doe shewe, that uppon equall voyces the sentences hath benn entred with the Lord Chauncelors

familiar to scholars as printed in Francis Hargrave's *Collectanea Juridica*, vol. 2 (London, 1792).

22. William Lambarde, *Archeion*, ed. C. H. McIlwain and Paul L. Ward (Cambridge, Mass., 1957).

23. 12 Co. Rep. 118, 77 *English Reports* (hereafter cited as *Eng. Rep.*) 1393, at 1394. For conviction of Proctor, Coke and Hobart, C.JJ., Tanfield, C.B., and the earl of Northampton; for acquittal, Ellesmere, L.C., two prelates, and Caesar, Chancellor of the Exchequer.

voyce wheather it hath beenn for the conviccion or for dissmission. And it cannot bee fownde uppon all the searche that hath benn made for both partes, that any sentence of conviccion hath benn entred against the Lorde Chauncelors voyce when the court hath stoode uppon equall vouces. Much paines hath benn taken therein, but such a president cannott be fownde."[24] Hudson's conclusions (and his despair at finding anything more) speak for themselves. Because in *Proctor's Case*, Ellesmere, L.C., was for acquittal, no decree was made.

If *Proctor's Case* is instructive of how faithfully Star Chamber could adhere to Popham's dictum, how its use of precedent would result in a conclusion based simply on which side the chancellor favored and no more, it is also indicative of the circumstances that impelled the court increasingly to the search of precedents, the search for more or less old, established authority for determination in unusual situations rather than a conclusion dictated by policy and reason. What is striking about the decisions of Star Chamber to about 1608 is how unanimous they were. There was nothing remotely *per curiam* about its procedure for factual conclusions or legal judgments: each privy councillor, each common-law judge, and the bishop sitting rendered a separate judgment in ascending order of precedence, beginning with mere knightly councillors, followed by the judges, and then the councillors-peers by dignity, concluded by the lord chancellor. Although individual differences as to amount of fine, and so on, were common enough, there was seldom a division as to conviction or acquittal. In 1608 this began to change, with *Piggott* v. *Newdigate*. Coke, C.J.C.P., was adamant for acquittal, carrying Bishop Ravis of London and Archbishop Bancroft of Canterbury with him, against his brother Fleming, C.J.K.B., and seven others including the lord chancellor.[25] Increasingly, Coke took an independent line and one that more often than not saw him at odds with Ellesmere. This is not to say that Coke played an obstructionist role. But he asserted himself whether he had a company or merely marched off alone. The bench divided time and again on factual issues. When the question was one of law, the division inevitably led to a search of precedents. There was no other way to satisfy Sir Edward Coke. This might have been a good thing, but it was a significant departure from past practice. Inevitably it brought tension and animosity, particularly between Coke and Ellesmere.

The significance of that animosity when it rose to high matters of state and judicature has been well treated by recent scholars.[26] The only foot-

24. Hunt. Ell. MS 2764. The only manuscript report of Proctor's Case is in Harvard Law School, L. MS 1128, no. 17—the report is by Hudson, contained in the reports (of later date) of his protégé, John Lightfoot.

25. Hunt. Ell. MS 2730, Oct. 1608.

26. See J. H. Baker, "The Common Lawyers and the Chancery, 1616," *Irish Jurist*, new ser. 4 (1969): 368–92; William J. Jones, "Conflict or Collaboration? Chancery Attitudes in the Reign of Elizabeth I," *American Journal of Legal History* 5 (1961): 12–54; William J. Jones, *The Elizabethan Court of Chancery* (Oxford, 1967), chap. 13; William J. Jones, *Politics and the Bench* (London, 1971), pp. 32–52.

note to be added is that it went back to the late 1590s in Star Chamber when Coke as attorney general clashed repeatedly with Ellesmere (then Sir Thomas Egerton, lord keeper). The point is that Coke's assertiveness in Star Chamber was the same affront to Ellesmere and his notions of high prerogative as it was in Chancery. Whether Ellesmere's, or for that matter James's, ideas of the prerogative really were a threat to the dominance of the common law is debatable and will probably become more so the deeper we delve into the legal history of the early Stuart period. That the judges between 1608 and 1616 became increasingly concerned that the prerogative was a threat is not in question. Star Chamber was not openly involved in the conflict, which touched principally Chancery, Requests, and the ecclesiastical jurisdiction, and which ultimately unseated Coke from the King's Bench in 1616. The High Court of Star Chamber was not a "prerogative court" (in the Whig sense of the term) in the eyes of anyone, though king and judges lauded it as a bulwark of the king's prerogatives as it was of law and good order. Yet Coke and some of his fellow judges were not prepared to see the bulwark raised higher, and in 1614, Coke apparently was prepared to open a second front in Star Chamber. It would not be fought with prohibitions and *praemunire*: I have not been able to find a single common-law court process issued in denigration of or hindrance to Star Chamber's powers and jurisdiction. Coke undertook to challenge the court not from his place in Westminster Hall but while sitting in Star Chamber. So long as Coke fought alone in Star Chamber as the defender of the common law, as he defined it, he was a nuisance. After death removed Fleming, C.J.K.B., in August 1613, Coke was translated from Common Pleas to King's Bench in October. Attorney General Sir Henry Hobart was made C.J.C.P. in the following month. Coke was joined in Star Chamber by a judge who hardly shared his apprehension of the danger to the common law but who was easily flattered and stood in some awe of Coke. Coke and Hobart joined in common cause in *Proctor's Case*. In *Brereton's Case*, on the three questions of law, they were as one. The alliance lasted, though Hobart was the weaker partner, throughout the next three troubled years in the great conflict between the judges on the one side and Ellesmere and Bacon on the other. No less was the working agreement of the latter forged in the same two cases.

Star Chamber's alarm in Easter term over the exception to the court's power taken by the Breretons and the Townsends afforded Attorney General Bacon an opportunity hitherto denied him. At the time he opened at the precedent hearing on 29 June 1614, Bacon had been attorney general for eight months. He had trounced duelers, seditioners, and slanderers of the great, but had not yet found an issue where he could vaunt the greatness of Star Chamber and establish the magnitude of its power—and that by a display of erudition and oratorical splendor. This was his object in *Brereton's Case*, and there could be no doubt that his target was Coke, C.J.K.B.

Bacon could not have cast the matter higher. He began with the dignity of the court: "the King himself has his seat prepared here always and many of his progenitors have sat in person, and the King is supreme judge and the Council are as assistants, as the King really judges in this court where in others he is judge but by fiction."[27] For the "assistants," they were the "great magistrates of the realm," councillors of state, judges, prelates. The causes heard were "those that are new or irregular and exorbitant." The delinquents were not shielded by privilege or honor "from the power of this court." It was a court of mercy, because capital offenses could be tried there and reduced to "offences finable." Star Chamber "*est sicut civitas super montem*, the great court of state of the realm." (The Evangelist could not have predicted that Star Chamber would be a floor above Westminster Hall in the Palace.) Star Chamber "is not confined to ordinary principles as other courts are to which the common law or statute laws have assigned limits."

Having thus concluded on the dignity of the court—note the claim for its extraordinary nature—Bacon went on to deal with the importance of the three questions at issue. If it could not levy damages and costs on lands and goods, its decrees would be "scarecrows," and none would bring actions in it (hyperbole), and it would in this be inferior to all other courts that had power to award elegit for costs and damages. "Moreover, this court was more ancient than the statute [of Elegit, Westm. II, c. 18 (1285)] and has a transcendant jurisdiction by royal prerogative, for necessity of state, to hear and end the great and very high offences of the people that tend to the subversion of the public state," and if other courts have power to levy "*a fortiori*, by the rule of the most supreme law, which is *salus populi*, [it] should have such power." He pointed to the significance of the second issue, the husband's responsibility for his wife's misdemeanors, by again stressing that Star Chamber would be in a more base condition than the common-law courts, where the husband was responsible for the wife's damages in mere battery or action for words. As for the third issue, injunctive power to stay suits, this he likened to outlawry in Common Pleas (a well-aimed jibe) and excommunication in courts Christian, which were for "disobediences and contempts to the said courts for not obeying the judgments and sentences there."

The thrust of Bacon's introduction was patently to demonstrate Star Chamber's empyrean distinction and to warn that if the court could not grant the relief sought it would be in worse state than the lowliest common-law courts. This really was the issue—though whether all of the dreadful consequences so solemnly rung would in fact have resulted is questionable. One can reasonably ask how Star Chamber had managed

27. All of Bacon's opening, except where otherwise indicated, is taken from the manuscript reports of Francis Moore of cases in Star Chamber, the best copy of which is Folger Library, MS (hereafter cited as Folg. MS) V. a. 133, fols. 32v–39v (at fol. 33v). It is a full and sound report by the relators' counsel in the case. There is no other manuscript report of the precedent hearing, which is reported in Noy 103, 74 *Eng. Rep.* 1069 (brief, but accurate), and 4 Leo. 249, 74 *Eng. Rep.* 852 (atrocious and completely botched, virtually nothing correct in it).

to survive so long without (or only fitfully possessing) such power. Yet it was a tocsin that Bacon rang, directed to the privy councillors present. If Star Chamber did not emphatically confirm that it had the powers the relators moved that it use, it was in danger of losing its preeminence. By leading with the best—the king—Bacon implied that if the court was reduced, the king by virtue of his prerogative was also reduced. It was a clever submission, and one that almost made the rest of his speech, devoted to the precedents, irrelevant.

Bacon divided his treatment of precedents into two parts: "the force of precedents in law" and "the difference among precedents and which will be more binding." In the first he stole a march on his prime antagonist on the other side of the bar at the Board. The three cases that he cited to prove that the judges in "ancient times" had accepted precedents and had taken them to have the force of "law and reason" were

1. formedon against the *Prior of St. Swithins*, Mich. 11 Edw. 3 (1337);
2. *John Paston's Case* upon an outlawry, Hil. 4 Edw. 4 (1465);
3. *Case of Mines*, Mich. 1567.

These three cases Attorney General Coke had relied upon in *Slade's Case* in 1602![28] Never one for faint pleading, Bacon drove the point home in his first citation with respect to the nature of precedents and which will be more binding: "First, precedents among clerks, which pass in silence without debate, and those will not bind so strongly as those that have attained allowance of the justices by long continuance. Secondly, judicial precedents, established by the knowledge and rules of the judges, and they will be binding, as *Morley and Slades Case* in Lord Coke's Fifth Report."[29] If Coke flushed he could not have argued with Bacon's conclusion: "And all the law of England in effect is precedent law, that is to say, when the judges upon deliberation have resolved and adjudged the controversy, this judgment and resolution is precedent to all posterity afterwards." To illustrate, Bacon cited two cases from Star Chamber, one from 1601 where, though Glanvil, J.C.P., on reference and after consultation with other judges, rejected a bill of revivor, the whole court allowed it upon the "presidentes of the court being understood";[30] and the other, *Proctor's Case*, where the rule of follow-the-chancellor was a "particular usage allowed by so many precedents of this court." From Coke's own pen, Bacon had established the general; and leaving aside *Proctor's Case*, which would hardly satisfy even contemporary criteria for relevance, he had defined Star Chamber's authority in precedent by a case of relatively

28. 4 Co. Rep. 92b, at 93b, 76 *Eng. Rep.* 1074, at 1075–76; Prior of St. Swithins, Year Book (hereafter cited as Y. B.) 11 Edw. 3 (Rolls Series), p. 267 (1337); John Paston's Case, Y. B. Hil. 4 Edw. 4, f. 41, pl. 3 (1465); Case of Mines (1567), Plowd. 310, at 320, 75 *Eng. Rep.* 472, at 486–87.

29. Folg. MS V. a. 133, fol. 35.

30. Alnwick Castle MS (hereafter cited as Aln. MS) 10, fol. 476, notes by Sir Julius Caesar of precedent hearing in Brereton's Case.

recent vintage that demonstrated the court triumphant over the judges in fixing its own course.

So far, so good, but Bacon was not home yet. The particular precedents requisite to establish that Star Chamber had levied upon lands and goods, had required nonconvict husbands to bear financial responsibility for their wives' offenses, and had stayed actions brought by defendants in contempt in Star Chamber were harder to come by. Bacon rightly did not rely on the precedents retrieved by the clerk and circulated to the councillors and judges between Easter and Trinity terms. The sixteen cases extracted, from 1485 to 1600, were all directed to the sole question of levying on lands and goods. Of these, only five cases were relevant to the issue; the rest dealt with various other means for Star Chamber to enforce its decrees (including injunction and commitment for contempt of it, which was not in question) and some of the precedents touched fines, not damages and costs.[31] At the hearing, Bacon chose to cite only four of the five relevant cases, for reasons that will be made clear. Rather, Bacon cast a wider net. He had the order and decree books searched—not folio by folio, since for the period 1552–95 alone there were eleven volumes of between 250 and 500 folios each—but by the clerk's "alphabet kallender," which had been compiled by old Mill's underclerk, Thomas Mynatt, latterly Bacon's deputy clerk in Star Chamber.[32] The seventeen cases that Bacon cited at the hearing were the results of this search. Because the order and decree books have long since disappeared, the historian cannot play Monday-morning quarterback, though a search of the *Libri Intrationum*, quasi-official extracts from the records, and counsels' compilations, as well as precedents extracted from the books by Ellesmere, does not turn up anything relevant missed by Bacon.[33] Yet even with seventeen precedents, Bacon found himself in the uncomfortable position of an advocate having to make a summer with very few swallows, or few swallows very far between.

Bacon showed his precedents chronologically under each of the three issues, seriatim. Albeit sound practice, it helped to paper over the cracks in his edifice. Of the seven cases demonstrating the court's exercise of the power to levy on lands and goods, one of them was not to the point: *Hore* v. *Slauter* (1545) was an injunction to a defendant to make a grant of an annuity out of his lands for damages to the plaintiff.[34] The latest case cited, *Stretley* v. *Dorne* (1600), was silent on levying but could

31. Hunt. Ell. MS 2757. These precedents are referenced to the "alphabet kallender."

32. Thomas G. Barnes, "The Archives and Archival Problems of the Elizabethan and Early Stuart Star Chamber," in *Prisca Munimenta: Studies in Archival and Administrative History Presented to Dr. A. E. J. Hollaender*, ed. Felicity Ranger (London, 1973), p. 137.

33. Only two of these seventeen cases have I been unable to find in any of these extant sources, both of them relating to a husband's responsibility to pay his wife's fine, etc.: Jane wife of Robert Arundell (1549) and Tunstall v. Brakenbury (Pasch., 1605). I can discover nothing further on Jane; Tunstall's Case is well reported by John Hawarde, *Les Reportes del Cases in Camera Stellata*, ed. William Paley Baildon (1894), p. 195.

34. B.L. Harl. MS 2143, fol. 69v.

count obliquely in support of the responsibility of a husband to pay his wife's damages and directly in support of the court's power to stay suits, because a purchaser of the defendant's lands who still had the purchase money in hand was ordered to pay the damages awarded against the defendant, and injunction was granted to stay all suits on the bonds.[35] *Stretley* at least indicates action against a third party with funds in his hands liable to the damages, but it would require considerable stretching to bring husband and wife within its scope. If, in using *Hore* and *Stretley*, Bacon meant to show lands as being liable to damages, he was in danger of tripping; no other sanction than injunction was involved in these cases, and that was a well-accepted remedy because it touched person, not property. *Stretley* didn't even involve lands, but merely chattels, the purchase money and bonds for the payment of the same. On the face of it, *Stubbes* v. *Sidley* (1573) was one of Bacon's strongest precedents. The defendant, if he did not pay damages awarded, was to be a close prisoner and writ issue to the sheriff to levy the damages on his lands.[36] What enfeebled *Stubbes* was the fact that the writ used had been created two terms previously in *Cromwell* v. *Taverner*, for levying damages occasioned by forgery prosecuted under 5 Eliz. 1, c. 14. Bacon did not cite this case (which was in the clerk's brief of precedents) because the damages were granted according to the statute, which also provided for payment of them from profits of lands: as the clerk's brief noted, "the case nowe in hande doth not sort with it."[37] Although *Stubbes* was not a case upon the statute, obviously the use of process from *Cromwell*, appropriate to *Cromwell* on the basis of the statute, was irregular—an inference given force by the fact that the process was not used again. *Stubbes* was worthless in light of *Cromwell*, and if *Cromwell* was raised *Stubbes* would fall—as it did. Therefore, the strength of Bacon's case for the court's power to levy on lands and goods depended on the first four cases he cited, all from between 1507 and 1519. *Hales* v. *Sherley* (1507), in which the defendants retook possession of land they had been enjoined to restore to the plaintiff and writ was directed to the sheriff to levy on the lands and goods of the defendant to recompense the plaintiff for the profits lost during the repossession; *Brookesbanks* v. *Merchants of the Steelyard* (1518), wherein the sheriffs of London were, if damages were not paid, to raise the posse and batter down the doors of the Steelyard and levy on the goods of the merchants; *Broadgate* v. *Sewall* (1519), where the plaintiff was to pay costs to the defendants or else the mayor of Carlisle was to attach Broadgate until he paid, and if he did not, then to levy on his goods and lands—all were sound and to the point, though the

35. Ibid., fol. 70; Hunt. Ell. MS 2757 (precedents prepared for Brereton's Case); reported, Inner Temple, Petyt MS 511, v. 13, fol. 136.

36. B.L. Harl. MS 2143, fols. 6v, 70; B.L. Lansd. MS 639, fol. 22v; Hunt. Ell. MS 2757.

37. Hunt. Ell. MS 2757. Cromwell v. Taverner is reported in 3 Dyer 322b, 73 *Eng. Rep.* 729; see also B.L. Lansd. MS 639, fol. 22v, and Hunt. Ell. MS 479. There is a manuscript copy, verbatim, of Dyer's report of the case in Bacon's papers, Hertfordshire Record Office, Verulam MS XII. A. 4.

last one involved only costs.[38] Bacon's best case was *Slane* v. *Bellewe* (1518). Bellewe, ordered to restore mesne profits to the plaintiff, refused to do so in court and was committed. The attorney general was directed "to make proces to the Shireff of Devon aforesayed to see this decree put in due and parfaitt execucion"; the sheriff, in default of restitution, was to levy first on Bellewe's goods, then on his lands by extending them.[39] Extent was what the Egertons prayed—and extent was what the court had given in *Slane*. Yet starting with seven, Bacon had been reduced to four swallows, one of them on perfect point, but all of them a century old.

For the responsibility of a husband not convicted to pay damages for his wife, Bacon cited three cases, none of them entirely to the point. All of them were relatively recent, and since the time when, under the Tudor Henries, damages had been more common than in the late sixteenth century. One was for the fine on a single woman since married, whose new husband was enjoined to pay her fine; in the second the husband, though not convicted, was ordered to pay the fines of his wife and his servants for the riot; in the third, Combes of the Middle Temple, though not convicted of the forgery, was ordered to pay part of the damages.[40] The first two involved fines, not damages, and although fine was at issue as the court had stated the case, it was only part of the second question. As to Combes, Bacon was only half correct when he said Combes was not convicted but "suspect" of forging the will. Combes had pleaded his pardon and so was not convicted, but the court found the will forged and Combes was "Condemned for a Cunninge & suttle practise."[41] It is hard to see how this case would help against a husband and wife, because it was so sui generis as to be worthless. There was no case directly to the point with respect to damages ordered against a husband not convicted.

The seven cases Bacon cited in support of the proposition that Star Chamber could stay suits in other courts were weighty insofar as they proved that the court had freely used the injunction (or Henrician analogue) to prevent individuals from suing or continuing suits in other courts, including common-law courts.[42] There were, though, two prob-

38. Hales, B.L. Harl. MS 2143, fol. 69v; Brookesbanks, B.L. Harl. MS 2143, fol. 69v, and Hunt. Ell. MS 2652, fol. 12; Broadgate, B.L. Harl. MS 2143, fol. 69v, and Hunt. Ell. MS 2757.

39. Public Record Office, Chancery (hereafter cited as C) 66/634, enrolled Star Chamber decree; STAC 2/15/114–116; Hunt. Ell. MSS 2655, fol. 13, and 2757; B.L. Harl. MS 2143, fol. 69v; B.L. Lansd. MS 639, fol. 22. See Guy, *Cardinal's Court*, pp. 128–30.

40. Jane wife of Robert Arundell (1549); Paston v. Seamor (Mich., 1560), B.L. Harl. MS 2143, fol. 70, and B.L. Lansd. MS 639, fol. 70; Tunstall v. Brakenbury (1605), Hawarde, *Reportes*, p. 195.

41. Hawarde, *Reportes*, p. 197.

42. Doggett v. Lord Fitzwater (1493), B.L. Harl. MS 2143, fol. 70, Hunt. Ell. MSS 2652, fol. 2v, 2654, fol. 14v, and 479, and Guy, *Cardinal's Court*, pp. 16–17; Rogers v. Lady Kelbelley (Mich. 1506), B.L. Harl. MS 2143, fol. 70; Dean & Chapter Lincoln v. Mayor & Burgesses Lincoln (Pasch. 1510), B.L. Harl. MS 2143, fol. 70, and B.L. Lansd. MS 639, fols. 30, 30v, 31, 34, 34v; Inhabitants Kings Norton v. Midlemore (1517), B.L. Harl. MS 2143, fol. 70; and Hunt. Ell. MS 2652, fol. 6v; Kitchman v. Dawney (1535), B.L. Harl. MS

lems with them. Only one was post-1530, and all of them—as opposing counsel would point out—were to stay suits elsewhere while the cause depended in Star Chamber. Thus, none of them was on all fours with *Brereton's Case*, where the defendants had already received judgment and were in contempt of it. One case certainly did Bacon's cause no disservice. The king in Council in 1493 in *Doggett* v. *Lord Fitzwater* sent an "injunction" (a privy seal letter) to the Common Pleas judges directing them to surcease all causes between the parties—apt to cite, but a precedent, not a guide for 1614.

Henry Finch of Gray's Inn represented the Breretons and the Townsends. Unfortunately we have only scrappy notes of a councillor at the hearing from which to try to retrieve his presentation. Finch was as learned as any counsel of the time, a legal positivist and a thoroughgoing Ramist logician, of great intellect and a wayward eccentricity, highly successful as an advocate and a man whose skills would have carried him to the bench if he had not been so heterodox in religion.[43] At the outset of his argument, he admitted that the "presidentes of every court are the common lawe of England for the government of that court and particularly in the court of Starchamber."[44] Consequently, as he said, he could except only against the impertinency of the precedents on the other side. As a general argument this was sound, and Finch fell to particulars with great skill and without the fanfare and tediousness of Bacon's argument. He distinguished only one case in detail, *Edgcombe's Case* (1587), arguing that the injunction there was only to stay multiplicity of suits at common law—a contention that can no longer be tested but that if correct would hardly have damaged Bacon's case. More to the point, he characterized all of Bacon's precedents for power to stay suits as being for causes depending in Star Chamber, unlike *Brereton's Case*, which had been concluded by the decree in Michaelmas 1613. This was telling, but only if he could demonstrate that the defendants' contempts in the present case did not constitute a continuation of the case beyond decree. Finch did damn all of Bacon's precedents as to levying by pointing out that none was for "damages adjudged to bee extended uppon landes when the party is in execution." And he cited two recent Star Chamber cases, *Hayward* v. *Whitbrooke* (1609) and *Wharton* v. *Langdale* (1609), in both of which the judges on reference held that, the defendant being in prison, no sequestration could be granted of his lands.[45] We cannot check this contention, but if correct it was well taken. These cases went to the

2143, fol. 70; Higgins v. Abbot of Haughwood (Trin. 1530), Hunt. Ell. MS 2659, and B.L. Harl. MS 2143, fol. 70; Edgecombe v. Long (Trin. 1587), B.L. Harl. MS 2143, fol. 70.

43. See W. R. Prest, "The Art of Law and the Law of God, Sir Henry Finch (1558–1625)," in *Puritans and Revolutionaries: Essays in Seventeenth-Century History Presented to Christopher Hill*, ed. D. Pennington and K. Thomas (Oxford, 1978), pp. 94–117.

44. Aln. MS 10, fol. 476v. These notes of Caesar's are the only indication of Finch's appearance and of counsel's submission *ex parte* the Breretons and the Townsends.

45. Hayward, B.L. Harl. MS 2143, fol. 68; Wharton, B.L. Harl. MS 2143, fol. 38v, and Cambridge University Library, MS Ll. 3. 2, fol. 10.

issue of levying as did none of Bacon's, and the factual situations in them all were indistinguishable from that of the Breretons and Lady Townsend. Their sole weakness was that only the judges, not the whole Star Chamber, had so ruled—in *Brereton's Case* the whole court would decide. Finch went on to argue by analogy and extension of the law that the court could not levy or make a husband unconvicted pay for his wife. The statutes against forgery give Star Chamber power to levy damages; without such explicit authority it has no such power. A husband will not suffer bodily punishment for his wife;[46] therefore, Sir Henry cannot be imprisoned to compel him to pay his wife's debt. At law a master answers for his servants when he himself is condemned, but not when he is discharged. Yet Finch's best point was saved for the end. There was no "concurrency of presidentes from time to time" in his adversary's argument. He had counted the swallows and noted their age. Bacon was led to reply, rather weakly, that in "rare cases some presidentes without concurrency are sufficient." *Rara avis.*

Whether Bacon replied at length to Finch is not clear. What is clear is that as the court began to render its opinions, Bacon's case was in trouble. The first two to speak would have found no fault with it. Sir Julius Caesar, chancellor of the Exchequer, a civilian and former master of Requests, shortly to become master of the Rolls and an active participant in the great controversy over Chancery, had composed a treatise in the 1590s extolling the antiquity and greatness of the conciliar jurisdiction, particularly Requests.[47] Sir Ralph Winwood, civilian and diplomat, had been appointed secretary of state three months before, and this was his first day in Star Chamber;[48] he was known as a strong prerogative man. But Sir John Croke, J.K.B., close friend of Coke since their student days together at the Inner Temple and of like mind with him on most questions juridical and political, opened fire on Bacon's case. The judges "in their judgment ought *ponere ante oculos Deum, regem, legem, et gregem.*"[49] For the King's fine, body, goods, and land are all to be taken by common law; but not on process from Star Chamber but from Exchequer upon estreat of the fine. Damages to the party are governed either by common law, whereby only land in the hands of the heir by descent is liable, or by statute, where by the Statute of Elegit, only one-half the lands and goods are liable, to be levied upon reasonable price or extent and the extent to be by inquisition. Elegit is not awardable by Star Chamber, and even if it were it would not extend to all the land. Therefore, Star Chamber cannot award a writ to the sheriff to levy upon lands. None of the precedents matches the present case, anyway, because in the precedents the order to levy on lands was parcel of the body of the decree and in the present case the decree did not appoint levying of damages; and because the damages

46. Citing Y. B. Pasch. 9 Hen. 6, f. 8, pl. 20 (1431).
47. *The Ancient State, Authoritie, and Proceedings of the Court of Requests by Sir Julius Caesar*, ed. L. M. Hill (Cambridge, 1975).
48. SP 14/77/58.
49. Folg. MS V. a. 133, fol. 37v.

in the precedents were awarded to parties but in the present case to a relator, the attorney general being the party. With these distinctions, Croke was in danger of becoming over-fine. The strength of his argument turned on the inapplicability of elegit to Star Chamber. It appears he was prepared to admit that because common law, not statute, gave execution upon goods, Star Chamber might levy upon goods.

Whether Croke or Hobart, C.J.C.P., or Coke, C.J.K.B., raised *Cromwell* v. *Taverner* is not clear, but it was used to demolish Bacon's emphasis on *Stubbes*.[50] It also served to unleash Coke. With considerable disingenuousness, Coke began by arguing that if Star Chamber could levy for damages it would put the party damaged in better state than the king for his fine, the estreat into Exchequer taking longer than issuance of Star Chamber process. This would be against 25 Edw. 3, St. 5, c. 19 (1350–51), and 33 Hen. 8, c. 39 (1541–42), whereby the king was to be preferred in executions. Then Coke launched into a long disquisition to establish that Star Chamber "is as ancient as any court at Westminster." Characteristically, the disquisition took the form of a long string of "precedents," fifteen references to the Council or Star Chamber in a judicial role beginning in 1217 and ending—triumphantly—with 1486.[51] He concluded from the string of instances, "By which it is proved that this court [of Star Chamber] was a court of ancient jurisdiction before the statute of 3 Hen. 7 [c. 1, Pro Camera Stellata, 1487], and was not first erected by this statute as some have held. . . ." It is not clear what this essay in history was intended to contribute to his opinion that Star Chamber could not levy on lands. Perhaps he got carried away with himself, warming to his expected performance of playing Clio's nuncio, though such pedantic expositions were seldom without purpose. More likely, he meant to argue (though there is no record that he made the point) that so ancient was the court that if it had by common law the power to levy there would be indication in old times that it had exercised the power, or otherwise it would have had that power given it by statute, which it had not. If such was Coke's intent, it was a dangerous line: who was to say that such an ancient court came not within the Statute of Elegit, enacted almost three-quarters of a century after the first indication of "Star Chamber's" existence cited by Coke? Before finishing, he cited one last precedent, from 1459, that "this court is not able to make decree to bind any

50. See above, at nn. 36–37 and accompanying text. Coke's opinion is in Folg. MS V. a. 133, fols. 37v–38v.

51. Most of these references were from the close rolls or the patent rolls. The earliest was an order for the appearance of Philip de Ulecote "coram consilio" in Mich., 2 Hen. 3, *Rotuli Literrarum Clausarum*, ed. T. D. Hardy, 2 vols., Record Commission (London, 1833), 1:336b. One was from Y. B. 28 Edw. 3 (*Liber Assisarum*), f. 155, pl. 52 (1354); three were from Y. B. Pasch. 13 Edw. 4, f. 9, pl. 5 (1473), Y. B. Mich. 2 Ric. 2, f. 2, pl. 4 (1378), and Y. B. Mich. 1 Hen. 7, f. 3, pl. 3 (1485)—this last being the latest cited by Coke. Coke also cited a bill and answer "in this court," from the "Petitions Rolls," i.e., Public Record Office, Ancient Petitions, S.C. 8. From Sir Anthony Fitzherbert's *La Nouvelle Natura Brevium* (London, 1534), fol. 233, he cited the writ *de idiota inquirendo et examinando*, "Ideota probanda coram Rege et consilio."

right any more than Chancery."[52] The case was appropriate so far as it touched Chancery, but its applicability to Star Chamber depended upon an equation of the two courts that not even Coke was prepared to make.

The three judges, having rendered their opinions that Star Chamber could not levy on lands, then turned to the second question. Coke stated that in civil causes, the husband will answer for his wife, but in criminal cases not. He illustrated the point by the resolution of all the judges in Hilary 1593, wherein they held that the Statute of Recusancy (1586–87) was insufficient to make the husband responsible for the fine for his wife's recusancy, but the Statute of Sectaries (1592–93) did. The resolution was torturous.[53] It could be distinguished as not going to the general responsibility of a husband for his wife's criminal acts; anyway it could not defeat precedents making clear that Star Chamber did otherwise. The other two judges agreed with Coke on the second question. They do not appear to have considered that damages, even if given "*ex accidenti et ex consequenti*" in Star Chamber (as they had argued earlier),[54] were a form of civil remedy and that therefore analogy to civil law rather than criminal law was warranted.

The three judges did agree that an injunction would issue against one in contempt of Star Chamber's decree to surcease all suits in all courts concerning the same matter as in the original suit in Star Chamber and, as well, any suit against the party at whose suit he was in contempt in Star Chamber—with the proviso that when the party had purged his contempt the injunction would cease.

The opinions of the three judges denying the court's power on the first two questions and conditioning (though not seriously limiting) its power on the third were perhaps not unexpected, given the increasingly hostile stance of the common-law judges toward the non-common-law courts. Doubtless, better was expected of Hobart, so recently attorney general. What caused consternation, however, was the next voice. William Lord Knollys, treasurer of the household, had been a privy councillor since 1596, longer than anyone on the bench that day save Ellesmere, also admitted to the Council in the same year. Knollys agreed with the three judges on all three questions. So far, four voices against the attorney general and two for. There were four more councillors sitting. Edward Lord Zouch, the two prelates, Bishop John King of London and Archbishop William Abbot of Canterbury, and Ellesmere found for the attor-

52. Y. B. Hil. 37 Hen. 6, f. 14v, pl. 3 (1459).

53. The Statute of Sectaries (35 Eliz. 1, c. 1) was, according to J. E. Neale, used as a vehicle for catching husbands of recusant wives in the toils of the penalties for recusancy—something that parliamentary vigilance prevented being done by Stat. 35 Eliz. 1, c. 2, the Statute of Recusants of the same Parliament. However, the resolution of all the judges referred to by Coke did not take place before the passage of the Statute of Sectaries, as he said, but afterwards.The judges resolved that *per* the statute, a husband was responsible for his wife's recusancy though he was not himself a recusant. See J. E. Neale, *Elizabeth I and Her Parliaments, 1584–1601* (London, 1958), pp. 280–97.

54. Aln. MS 10, fol. 475v.

ney general on the first two questions and accepted the judges' proviso on the third. Ellesmere went out of his way to emphasize that

> use makes law and the precedents of each court is the usage of the court and use guides law. . . . and precedents are the common law and the authority of the common law are the precedents, merely the judgment and resolutions of the judges. And in this he did much regard the precedents, and it seemed to him that the precedents will agree in substance with the present case on both [the first two] points. . . . And how reasonable it is [and] not inconvenient that this court that gives judgment of damages will have means and authority to execute the judgment; nor is it against reason that this court, consisting of so many peers, judges, and bishops, will have power for judgment of the law and for discretion among themselves to award damages to the party grieved as well as jurors or judges in other inferior courts will do.[55]

It is difficult to fault Ellesmere's argument. If Star Chamber was in the business of giving damages—and it could be argued that it ought not to have been—it could hardly be denied the capacity to provide relief enjoyed by other courts that awarded damages. *Brereton's Case* was ultimately decided not on the precedents, but on policy. Ellesmere's evocation of the rule of reason was the proper approach; it was of a higher intellectual order than either Bacon's precedents or Coke's attempts to distinguish them. It was really the only approach.

The court ordered writs of extent to issue to the sheriffs of the counties in which the Breretons and Townsends had goods and lands. The writ, in Latin, was almost indistinguishable from Exchequer's *extendi facias*, and directed the sheriff to extend the manors, lands, and tenements, goods, and chattels of the defendants and keep them in his hands until the damages and costs were satisfied.[56] The court further decreed that the resolution on the three questions was to be a "rule and order to bee observed and putt in execucion in all such like cases hereafter." Damages and costs awarded to parties grieved might be levied by writ to the sheriff upon the lands, goods, and chattels of those who refuse to pay the same, whether in prison or not; where the husband is a party to the bill though not convicted, he will pay the fine, damages, and costs imposed upon his wife; where a party stands in contempt for not satisfying damages, costs, or anything else decreed to be paid, restored, or satisfied to or on behalf of the party grieved, the party in contempt "shall and maie" at the court's discretion be stayed from prosecuting any suits in any courts by himself or by others against the party grieved or for any matter concerning him until the contemnor has purged his contempt and conforms himself to the court's orders.[57]

55. Folg. MS V. a. 133, fol. 39.
56. B.L. Lansd. MS 639, fol. 108.
57. SP 14/77/51B.

The impact of the court's general "rule and order" was not as great as one might have expected. If, as Bacon argued, the denial of the power to levy would discourage plaintiffs from suing in Star Chamber, it might be argued that the addition of the extent to its armory of process would encourage more suits. In fact, the number of bills put in in Star Chamber continued to decline steadily from about 400 per annum at the beginning of James's reign to around 250 per annum in 1624. Certainly, prayer for damages became more common, and damages were awarded with greater frequency, giving point to Hudson's observation that "For damages to the wronged party this court [Star Chamber] is the best jury; and when they have justly discerned the wrong, they make the most ample recompense, and requite the wronged person's labour and travel sometimes with all his injury."[58] There is evidence that the subpoena to pay damages or costs was still generally effectual and that extent remained more a threat than a weapon of use. For example, for seven terms and their vacations following, 1624–25, 7 subpoenas for payment of damages, 292 subpoenas for payment of costs, and only 20 extents (12 for costs, 8 for damages) were sealed.[59] Most of the extents were repeaters, and three were for damages and costs pending from a case in Elizabeth's last years. As for the husband's responsibility for his wife's fines, damages, and costs, that was finally definitively established, but inasmuch it was rare for a husband to be acquitted and his wife convicted, the effect of the rule was slight. It did have one interesting and unforeseen effect: in *Langley* v. *Symnell* (1627), a woman was dismissed from the suit because her husband was not a party to it![60] There is no evidence of any marked increase in the number of injunctions to stay suits; the situation envisioned in the rule, requiring as it did long standing-out in contempt postdecree, was not very common. All in all, if hard cases make bad law, rare hard cases don't make much bad law.

A "Sore Blow"

The impact of *Brereton's Case* at the political level was another matter. Contemporaries were immediately aware of its significance. The newsletter journalist, John Chamberlain, wrote the ambassador in Venice that "On Wenesday the last weeke was a great Star-chamber day about the jurisdiction of that court in divers cases. . . . [Winwood] went with the major part in the affirmative (which is counted a hard case) and contraried by all the judges that were present."[61] Indeed it was hard. Never before had a major question concerning the Star Chamber's power been settled by a vote as close as six to four. Never had the common-law

58. W. Hudson, in *Collectanea Juridica*, 2:226.

59. Public Record Office, Gifts and Deposits, PRO 30/38/21, Star Chamber process book.

60. B.L. Lansd. MS 639, fol. 103.

61. SP 14/77/58, Chamberlain to Sir Dudley Carleton, 7 July 1614.

judges stood so obstinately against affirming the court's power, and never before unanimously. But then, never before had the question been cast so high and been so thoroughly searched and debated.

The court could have moved more circumspectly by the well-tried procedure of referring the issues to a judge or judges-referee, carefully selected to avoid a negative response in the referee's certificate to the court for its rule. Hobart, C.J.C.P., might have proved safe if insulated from Coke's influence. Laurence Tanfield, C.B., was thoroughly reliable. Augustine Nichols, J.C.P., was little favored by James, but he was balanced and solid and no partisan of Coke. Humphrey Winch, J.C.P., eschewed judicial politics. George Snigge, B., and Peter Warburton, J.C.P., were the most senior judges and not very susceptible to Coke's blandishments or suasion. Any of these judges would have done—and it was in the lord chancellor's discretion to choose the option and the referees. At the hearing of the full court upon the certificate, Coke and Hobart could not have been denied seat, but Croke had no claim to be present. The attendance of privy councillors and prelates ought to have been twelve or thirteen, not seven. Coke and Hobart would have had their say, but if the certificate was favorable they would have found themselves breasting a wave. A vote of six to four would have been avoided, and given enough pressure on Hobart, it might have been eleven or twelve to one nay.

The suspicion remains that any quieter—and safer—course than the one actually taken was rejected by Ellesmere and Bacon because they sought confrontation. It was a dangerous game, characteristic of Bacon's hubris and the aging Ellesmere's animus toward Coke. Yet the narrowness of his victory appears to have been instructive for Bacon. He realized that overreliance on precedent as authority, especially in critical matters, was too restrictive of Star Chamber, perilous to the exercise of its extraordinary jurisdiction, innovative capacity in procedure, remedy, and substantive law. He recognized, belatedly, that to cast a matter so high in Star Chamber as to summon the king and his prerogative to his aid eroded Star Chamber's authority with those increasingly uneasy about the prerogative. Neither as attorney general nor later as lord chancellor did Bacon allow issues of such high and critical moment to be fully debated in Star Chamber, and he demonstrated reluctance to give exceptional weight to precedent as authority in Star Chamber. Francis Bacon had been chastened by *Brereton's Case*.

That Edward Coke learned something from the affair cannot be doubted. He certainly never again showed any inclination to make Star Chamber an arena for his struggle against the prerogative. He continued to take an active part in its judicature as chief justice until his dismissal in 1616, but it was as a dutiful *jurisperitus*, a veritable "assistant" to that tribunal. And when as plain Sir Edward Coke, privy councillor, he was recalled to the Council and the Star Chamber in 1617, he was grateful for the opportunity to sit again in a judicial way and showed himself more royalist than the king in the major state trials that took place in Star Chamber from 1617 to 1619. That the trials enabled him to settle some old scores with old adversaries added to the pleasure. But at a more profound level, Coke might have begun to recognize that the particular conception of precedent as authority on which he had made his career in law (and was about to unmake it in politics) was an imperfect instrument, either to structure law or to safeguard the law. *Communis error facit jus* had its corollary, that the course of the court by making precedent makes law. That is to say, the course of the individual court makes the law relevant to that court. Bacon's case might not have been strong on the precedents, but what there were of them was better than virtually no precedents against them. These feeble precedents made new law in Star Chamber. Bacon had used Coke's own tools against him, if not entirely effectually at least effectively. Because there was no higher tribunal than Star Chamber to impose a law common to all the courts upon Star Chamber, its course carried the day. When in 1621 Coke became parliamentarian extraordinary, he sought to make out of the course of the High Court of Parliament a law so powerful that it would overarch all other law and resist the encroachment of the prerogative by piecemeal conquest of part of the law court by court.

One not present at the hearing of *Brereton's Case*, but who was more interested than any other in its outcome, save only the parties themselves, was James I. The translation of Coke from Common Pleas to King's Bench to staunch the flow of prohibitions had not caused him to become any less troublesome, and to his increasingly annoying conduct on King's Bench, Coke had now added the opposition in Star Chamber. *Brereton's Case* further marked Coke in James's eyes. Moreover, the affair rendered James even more dependent on Ellesmere and Bacon. As the great conflict over Chancery developed, James saw in *Brereton's Case* evidence of a wide-scale combination of the common-law judges against all of the non-common-law courts, including Star Chamber. It served the purposes of Ellesmere and Bacon not to disabuse the king. James's apprehension was exaggerated, but paranoia was never far beneath the surface of his pedantic rationality. Consequently, just two years after *Brereton's Case*, James I came to the Star Chamber in full regal panoply to take his seat as the king in his Council in the Star Chamber, the first time that a monarch had done so since the first Tudor. His purpose in coming on 20 June 1616 was to give solemn decree in settlement of the dispute over Chancery, to charge his judges before they went circuit, and to demonstrate that "Kings are properly Iudges, and Iudgement properly belongs to them from God: for Kings sit in the Throne of God, and thence all Iudgement is deriued."[62] Having upheld the Chancery, James launched into a disquisition on Star Chamber, beginning, "The *Starre-Chamber* Court hath bene likewise shaken of late, and the last yeere it had receiued a sore blow, if it had not bene assisted and caried by a few voyces. . . ."[63] There

62. James I, "A Speach in the Starre-Chamber," in *The Political Works of James I*, ed. C. H. McIlwain (Cambridge, Mass., 1918), p. 326.
63. Ibid., p. 335.

was no mistaking that he referred to *Brereton's Case*, though two years was the correct time.

The "sore blow" had been averted, or so James believed. Had it? William Hudson, the court's staunchest supporter, writing some seven years after *Brereton's Case*, remained fearful that the close decision as to the court's powers might still be undone. Addressing himself to the new lord keeper, Bishop John Williams of Lincoln, Hudson contrasted the present with the times of Elizabeth, when "there was scarce a man found so impudent as would struggle with the sentence of this high court. It therefore behoveth the great judge of this high court [i.e., Lord Keeper Williams] to maintain this power to execute the sentence, which was so worthily regained by the industry of the *lord chancellor Egerton*, of whose care and pains in this particular I was more than *oculatus test.* for I can say without boasting, *quorum pars magna fui. . . .*"[64] In the event, the rule from *Brereton's Case* was not undone. Yet at a more profound level, the "sore blow" had at least grazed and wounded, if it had not maimed, Star Chamber. The court did escape the controversy that touched Chancery, Requests, Admiralty, and the ecclesiastical courts, and licked at the provincial conciliar courts. So far James was correct. James himself, however, in his compulsion to tidy up Westminster Hall and its neighboring chambers, to play the peacemaker among hostile judicial factions, saw fit to deliver himself on the High Court of Star Chamber. In doing so, he made it a party to a *causa* in which it had not been involved since 29 June 1614. When Star Chamber was, finally, openly attacked in 1640–41, it tumbled in a matter of months. The erosion of its reputation began, however, on 20 June 1616, the court tarred by association drawn in the king's own words. The text for James's homily in Star Chamber that day was the first verse of Psalm 72: "Give the king thy judgments, O God, and thy righteousness unto the king's son." To James was vouchsafed the judgment of God. Upon his son was visited the "righteousness" of the Saints that among other things swept away the High Court of Star Chamber.

64. Hudson, in *Collectanea Juridica*, 2:231. The reference to Hudson's part seems to indicate that he played some role, probably in the precedent search (though there is no direct proof of this); he was not, apparently, of counsel with any of the parties.

14 "Of No Mean Authority": Some Later Uses of Bracton

D. E. C. Yale

In the year 1821 the Court of King's Bench found itself engaged in a debate upon the right of the public over the marine foreshore and concerned with the question of the authority to be accorded to Bracton's *De Legibus*.[1] Bracton, avowed Best, J., was "a man of no mean authority for what the common law was at the time he wrote." And the conclusion was reached that though the Bractonian passage in question was evidently borrowed from the text of the civil law, the incorporation of that text into the treatise had incorporated the doctrine into English law. But the doubts expressed in this case as to the status of Bracton's treatise merely echo an old objection, one indeed that goes back a long time to an age in which lawyers had not begun to trouble themselves over Bracton's Roman law.

Professor Thorne's work has illuminated the scene of the thirteenth century when the treatise was composed, but we remain less well informed, in fact very poorly informed, on the fate of Bracton over the next two centuries. The number of surviving manuscripts, about fifty, indicates a felt need to preserve copies (whether or not they were much studied), but it is noteworthy that very few seem to have been made after the mid-fourteenth century.[2] The work had ceased to interest a profession that had little use for thinking in terms of substantive law. And so Bracton's "was the last English law-book for centuries to be written with such terms in mind."[3]

For upward of two centuries there is a silence until in the early Tudor age Bracton is quoted not only in Westminster Hall[4] but also and perhaps

1. Blundell v. Catherall, 5 Barn. & Ald. 268, 106 *English Reports* (hereafter cited as *Eng. Rep.*) 1190.

2. John P. Dawson, *The Oracles of the Law* (Ann Arbor, Mich., 1968), p. 54, remarks that "Bracton, whose work for a time had been avidly read, was first digested in more usable form by two other authors (Fleta and Britton) and then fell rapidly into disuse." Some of the numerous extant manuscripts were not in the hands of lawyers till the sixteenth century; Bodleian Library Rawlinson MS C. 159, for example, was in the library of St. Augustine's, Canterbury, before belonging to the Manwood family. "Itt was my father his booke and lay in hys studdy att Sergeants Inn." This was Sir Roger Manwood, whose relative John Manwood wrote the well-known treatise *Forest Laws* (London, 1665), making use of Bracton among his "old authorities."

3. S. F. C. Milsom, *Historical Foundations of the Common Law* (London, 1969), p. 32.

4. Year Book (hereafter cited as Y. B.) Mich. 10 Hen. 7, f. 6v, pl. 12 (1494), *per* Sjt. Keble; Y. B. Trin. 13 Hen. 8, f. 16, pl. 1 (1521), *per* Sjt. Shelley. The printed Y. B. Mich. 9 Hen. 4, f. 2v, pl. 8 (1407), contains a sizable quotation that does not seem to be an editorial embellishment. It occurs in the Year Book manuscript, Cambridge University Library MS Gg. 5. 8 at fol. 21v (second gathering): "antiquus liber de Breton."

more significantly in readings at the Inns of Court.[5] But this freshet of interest received a check of some consequence on the publication in the second decade of the century of Anthony Fitzherbert's *Great Abridgement*. For in abridging a case of 1457 concerning the marriage of wards the compiler added this comment: "Vide de ceo matter en 35 dauter report et Bracton dis. que lage le male et female fuit tout un et tout le court dis. que Bracton ne fuit unques tenus pur auctor en nostre ley."[6]

If we turn to the printed Year Book no such denial of Bracton's authority is to be found, and it is questionable whether such an opinion was ever delivered.[7] Maitland in adverting to this comment remarked that "it proves very little. Many things had happened in those two centuries; a new idea of 'authority' had been evolved, and it would have been strange if in the year 1457 this old text-book had not become antiquated. . . ."[8] But whatever the validity of this supposed dictum in 1457, its force was not to be denied when it appeared in the *Great Abridgement*, and there is evidence of a long-continued effect. One particularly powerful repetition occurred half a century later during the Exchequer Chamber debate in *Stowel* v. *Lord Zouch* (1565), which was amply reported by Plowden and in which Bracton was freely cited, but subject to and under express qualification.[9] Thus, Saunders, C.B., quoted Bracton "not as an author in the law; for he said that Bracton and Glanvil were not authors in our law, but, he said, he cited him as an ornament to discourse where he agrees with the law." And similarly Catline, C.J., said "that he did not cite him as an author in our law, but for consonancy and order where he agrees with better authorities."[10] These statements give no reason for the denial

5. Bracton was freely quoted by George Treherne in his Autumn reading, 1520, at Lincoln's Inn upon *Carta de Foresta* (of which there are many MSS, the best being National Library of Wales, Wynnstay 39, British Library Hargrave MS 15, and Cambridge University Library MS Dd. 3. 39). Dr. J. H. Baker has kindly supplied me with other references to Bracton in readings: Cambridge University Library MSS Ee. 3. 46, fols. 24–33 (Ticheborne, Inner Temple), Ee. 5. 19, fol. 113 (Anon., *temp.* Hen. 7), Hh. 3. 10, fol. 59 (Dudley, Gray's Inn). See generally Baker's discussion in *The Reports of Sir John Spelman*, ed. J. H. Baker, 2 vols., Selden Society, vols. 93 (London, 1977) and 94 (1978), 2:33.

6. Garde, pl. 71. As is well known, Fitzherbert used *Bracton's Note Book* as the source for his cases from the time of Henry III in his *Abridgement* (Sir Anthony Fitzherbert, *La Graunde Abridgement* [London, 1516]), but there is no evidence that he connected these reports, or extracts from the rolls, with Bracton.

7. The absence of reference to Bracton in the Year Book cited induced John Reeves, *A History of English Law*, 3d ed., 4 vols. (London, 1814), 4:571, to write: "It was a pleasure to discover that the Year Book had given him [Fitzherbert] no warrant for this monstrous opinion." The case is Y. B. Hil. 35 Hen. 6, f. 52, pl. 17 (1457), with which is associated the earlier stage, Y. B. Hil. 35 Hen. 6, f. 40, pl. 2 (1457) (perhaps the "other report"), in which Prisot, C.J., quotes Britton. If Britton was the work under discussion, the disparagement may refer to that work, the names of Bracton and Britton being commonly confused in writing and printing. For a modern edition of the case, see *Select Cases in the Exchequer Chamber*, ed. Mary Hemmant, 2 vols., Selden Society, vols. 51 (London, 1933) and 64 (1948), 1:132–43.

8. Frederic W. Maitland, *Selected Passages from the Works of Bracton and Azo*, Selden Society, vol. 8 (London, 1894), p. xxxii.

9. 1 Plowd. 353, at 357–58, 75 *Eng. Rep.* 536, at 542–44.

10. But the chief justice was not very consistent. See his remarks at the duke of Norfolk's

of authority and do not seem even to imply a contrast of Bracton's law with "our law" (an implied contrast with the civil law); they seem simply restatements and testify to the great influence of Fitzherbert's work upon the minds of lawyers of the Tudor age. This passage in the *Abridgement* was in the minds of lawyers throughout the sixteenth century and even later.[11] Thus, Coke reports that in *Paine's Case* (1587) "it was well observed that Glanvil, Bracton, Britton and Fleta, may be vouched for antiquity and ornament in cases where they concur with the later authority of law and do not impugn the common experience and allowance in judicial proceedings at this day."[12]

Against this discouraging doubt voiced by Fitzherbert and repeated in the Elizabethan courts of common law Bracton's "authority" made slow progress. That it did progress may be attributed to the services rendered to Bracton by two men, Richard Tottel and Edward Coke, the one in publishing the treatise and the other in publicizing it professionally. Unfortunately, all too little is known of the circumstances of the first printing of the treatise in 1569. Britton had been published earlier, around 1540,[13] but the priority is doubtless due to its being written in familiar French and to its utility, it being the only work to give in summary form the legislation of Edward I. In 1557, Tottel had published Sir William Staunford's *Pleas of the Crown*,[14] and Staunford had included substantial passages from Bracton. Staunford in his preface gave his reasons for so doing: "Citavi etiam non pauca, ex Bractono et Brittono, vetustis legum scriptoribus, hoc nimirum consilio: ut cum leges Corone, magna ex parte

---

trial in 1571 (see below, at n. 34), and ten years before, on 20 Apr. 1561, he wrote a report for Cecil on the law relating to the punishment of witchcraft and sorcery. On this practical question he had referred to the opinions of Bracton and included an extract from Britton. (See *Calendar of State Papers, Domestic Series . . . 1547–1580*, ed. Robert Lemon [London, 1856], p. 174.)

11. At least it was in Sir Bartholomew Shower's mind in 1690 in an argument set out in his reports, 1 Show., at 121, 89 *Eng. Rep.*, at 488. Percy H. Winfield (*Chief Sources of English Legal History* [Cambridge, Mass., 1925], p. 256) said of this citation of the *Abridgement*, "nor is the court reported to have raised any protest"; but the court had no opportunity, for the argument was never delivered.

12. 8 Co. Rep. 34a, at 35, 77 *Eng. Rep.* 524, at 526, the reporter indicating approval but without attribution to bench or bar.

13. Redman's edition is undated. Robert Brooke, who died in 1558, includes in his *Abridgement* (*La Graunde Abridgement*, [London, 1573]) a wider range of sources than Fitzherbert and has references to Britton, but not to Bracton.

14. A modern reprint in the Classical English Law Texts (London, 1971) has an introduction by Mr. P. R. Glazebrook. Staunford's work on the king's prerogative, though not published till 1567, was composed before 1548, and it contains Bractonian citations. When Staunford became a judge of the Common Bench, he soon found occasion to use Bracton. In Throckmerton v. Tracy (1555), Plowd. 145, 75 *Eng. Rep.* 222, he cited Bracton for two of his "three rules of the understanding of deeds" (Plowd., at 160, 75 *Eng. Rep.* at 247), and in the same case Saunders, J., recited from Bracton the couplet on the civil-law clothing of pacts (Plowd., at 161, 75 *Eng. Rep.*, at 250). In this case, Dyer had introduced Bracton into his argument on the interpretation of conveyances *ut res magis valeat quam pereat* (Plowd., at 159, 75 *Eng. Rep.*, at 246, Dyer 125b, pl. 44, 73 *Eng. Rep.* 274), and Plowden noted as reporter how he later verified with Dyer "the true words of Bracton."

iure statutario constant, ponatur ante legentis oculos commune ius, quod fuit ante ea statuta condita. Nam ea res maxime conducit recte interpretandis statutis." As contrasted with this cautious explanation the editor of 1569 expressed himself more freely. He asserted a long-standing demand among the profession for the publication of *De Legibus*. He then made some informative remarks concerning consultations with colleagues and collations of copies. He drew attention to Bracton's reliance upon the institutional scheme of the civil law, making comparison with the state of common-law literature, *indigesta confusio*.[15] He then launched into a lengthy diatribe by way of warning the reader that Bracton if not himself benighted had written in an age of religious darkness, and concluded with a short and sensible admonition that the reader should be ready to make allowances for changes in the law, both statutory and judge-made, since Bracton's day. Finally he signed his initials, T.N., leaving no further clue to his identity. If that identity could be revealed,[16] some new light might be shed on the publication of 1569. One is tempted to link the printing of Bracton to some general development of the age, and we might plausibly suppose a humanistic influence or inspiration, the revival of a classical text.[17] Plucknett himself believed that "the first edition of Bracton is part of the Romanising movement of the reign of Elizabeth," though he at once added that "English law was still too medieval to feel the force of such an argument."[18] It might equally well be regarded as a practical step toward introducing some system into the exposition of English law. The printing of Britton a quarter of a century earlier had been offered as an attempt to give the law a simpler shape, because the Year Books "many times, for lack of good grounds plainly expressed in the same yeares, have so amased, dulled and discouraged many noble wits learning the same." And Staunford writing a little later had pleaded for systematic exposition of the law. At a more mundane level there is

15. "Quod eius institutum, illis quibus in hoc genere indigesta confusio semper displicuit atque multum indies et molestiae et impedimenti obiicit, non potest non esse inprimis et iucundum et utile. Videmus quantum pauci illi libri quos eruditi nonnulli, non multi tamen, de Iuris nostratis argumentis vel Titulis (ut vocant) aliquot recte & ordine non malo ediderunt, quales sunt Litletonus de tenuris, Fitzherbertus de Brevium natura, Stanfordus de Placitis Coronae, & Regia Praerogativa, et eius generis reliqui, studiosis in hac facultate tyronibus adiumenti afferant."

16. A candidate who deserves close consideration is Thomas Norton, for whose career see the *Dictionary of National Biography*, s.v. Norton, Thomas. No direct proof has been found, but there are many circumstantial indications in his direction. The preface certainly expresses beliefs that Norton held, and there are features of his career in literature and the law that are suggestive. He was very close to Tottel, through the Stationers' Company and in Fleet Street and the Temple.

17. Louis A. Knafla has suggested ("The Law Studies of an Elizabethan Student," *Huntington Library Quarterly* 32 [1968–69]: 221–40, at p. 232) that the lawyers of the 1560s saw in Bracton nothing relevant to their own law. "Because Bracton used Roman Law in the thirteenth century historians of Tudor England cannot draw the conclusion that avant garde lawyers who began to read and use civil law were reviving Bracton's work and the 'Bracton tradition.' Bracton was read in the sixteenth century by historians who were interested in him and by lawyers who were interested in thirteenth-century common law."

18. T. F. T. Plucknett, *Concise History of the Common Law*, 5th ed. (Boston, 1956), p. 263.

the reason given in the opening words of the preface. The words may have a conventional tone, but they may nevertheless express the immediate truth. Tottel had become aware of a demand and as a publisher he was evidently not disposed to let gaps go unfilled. He certainly produced a very fine book; as Plucknett said, "a stately volume, perhaps the best printed law book we have ever had."[19]

The printing of Bracton naturally introduced the work to a range of readership beyond the reach of manuscripts, whether bought, borrowed, or otherwise acquired. Such a large and costly volume would not be easily acquirable by the ordinary student,[20] but during the next thirty years citations and quotations increasingly appear. Within ten years, Simon Theloall had written and published his *Digest of Original Writs* (1579), in which he made a very liberal use of Bracton's text.[21] And there were also more academic uses. Thus, Abraham Fraunce in his *Lawyers' Logic* (1588) was concerned to bring the newly cultivated Ramist logic from Cambridge to the lawyers in London, and he made considerable use of Bracton.[22] A little later a pedestrian and totally unphilosophic author, Edward Hake, can be found turning apposite Bractonian definitions and passages to his purpose.[23] But the principal promoter was certainly Coke. He made extensive use of Bracton in his *Reports* and *Institutes*.[24] The general effect was that the authority of Coke carried the acceptance of

19. Ibid., p. 263.

20. Egerton, when a student in the 1560s, may have been exceptional in possessing a copy, and he had it by gift from Thomas Owen (later a justice of the Common Bench). But he annotated only the introductory parts of the treatise, and most of the later folio pages remained uncut. (See Knafla, "Law Studies"; and, more generally, Louis A. Knafla, *Law and Politics in Jacobean England: The Law Tracts of Lord Chancellor Ellesmere* [London, 1977], chap. 1, "The Making of a Legal Mind.") A typical student of the same time, the 1560s, John Savile, read the *Old* and the *New Tenures*, the *Natura Brevium*, Perkins's *Profitable Book*, a selection of statutes and the Year Books of Ric. 3, Hen. 7, and Hen. 8 ("Autobiography of Sir John Savile of Methley, Baron of the Exchequer, 1546–1607," ed. J. W. Clay and John Lister, *Yorkshire Archeological and Topographical Journal* 15 [1900]: 420–27). Savile acquired his copy of Bracton only in 1590, but four years before being created serjeant. The book (Trinity College, Cambridge: Grylls, 1. 139) was, unlike Egerton's, read from cover to cover, for his pen runs through the whole and he concludes on the last page with a "laus deo."

21. This work was inspired by Staunford's plea in his *Exposition of the King's Prerogative* (see above, at n. 14) for a more systematic treatment of English law. Theloall's use of Bracton was to quote passages as leading texts on which to expand, e.g., lib. 3, cap. 1, s. 2: "Ore nous verrons coment nostres anciens sages *Judges* ont prise cells leys ainsi escripts per *Bracton*."

22. *The Lawiers Logike exemplifying the praecepts of Logike by the practise of the common lawe*, commenting at fol. 118v that "Bracton foloweth the order of the civill law altogether insomuch as he that hath seene the one may easily iudge of the other." The other principal work of Ramist logic, Henry Finch's *Law* (London, 1613), cites Bracton on the first page but then has no more to say of him. See generally Wilfred Prest, "The Dialectical Origins of Finch's *Law*," *Cambridge Law Journal* 36 (1977): 326–52.

23. Edward Hake, *Epieikeia, a Dialogue on Equity in Three Parts*, ed. D. E. C. Yale (New Haven, 1953), to which Professor Thorne kindly contributed a valuable preface.

24. It has been suggested (Alan Harding, *A Social History of English Law* [London, 1966], p. 202) that after publication, Bracton's work "at last exercised its due influence, for it inspired another comprehensive work, Coke's four Institutes, the first of which appeared

Bracton, so much so that after Coke the denials and doubts as to Bracton's "authority" seem to fade. Coke indeed was aware that Bracton might require buttressing with more recent authority on certain matters, but it seems evident that in Coke's writings Bracton was treated as an authority, that is, an author whose statements of law deserved acceptance unless contradicted by subsequent statute or judicial modification of the common law.

To say that Coke "carried" Bracton may be true, but there is also the larger truth that the legal climate was changing. Not that Bracton's position improved because the position of Roman law was improving, and certainly at the practical level Coke would never have employed Bracton's text if he had thought of Bracton as infiltrating a foreign legal influence. The change in climate was that English lawyers were beginning to think of their law in substantive terms. An illustration of this change may be found in the law of servitudes. This branch of the common law was beginning in the sixteenth century slowly and uncertainly to emerge out of the medieval law of nuisance, which regulated legal duties between neighbors. The text of Bracton provided one ready source of material to give some order and substance to this development. Thus, Coke drew on Bracton in classifying rights of way,[25] and even before the publication of Coke on Littleton, Whitlocke, J., is reported as expounding in the King's Bench the nature of praedial servitudes from the pages of Bracton.[26] Though many of the civil-law features of this field of common law were introduced later, from the *Corpus Juris* and as late as the nineteenth century, yet the effect of Bracton must have been considerable. The judges and lawyers at large were now beginning to consider questions of *iura in re aliena* in terms of legal principle instead of concentrating attention on the procedural problems of the assize of nuisance and other similar remedies.

In the seventeenth century, therefore, Bracton's use was more widespread and his status more secure. The first printed abridgment to include extracts from Bracton, Henry Rolle's (1668), was in fact compiled in the earlier part of the century.[27] And as long as readings continued, Bracton

in 1628." Coke doubtless saw that Bracton was framed on an institutional scheme, and he called his own commentaries Institutes, but the first is a gloss on Littleton and both in form and function is very far removed from Bracton's treatise.

25. Edward Coke, *The First Part of the Institutes of the Laws of England; or, A Commentary upon Littleton*, 19th ed., 2 vols. (London, 1832), 1:56a. Moreover, Coke frequently quoted Bracton in his judgments, as also did Doderidge, J.

26. Sury v. Albon Pigot (1626), 3 Bulst. 339, 81 *Eng. Rep.* 280, Pop. 166, 79 *Eng. Rep.* 1263 (the latter report is of course not Popham's but one of the "remarkable cases reported by other learned pens since his death"), a case on unity of possession over natural rights, in this case watercourses.

27. Though not published till 1668 under the auspices of Matthew Hale, Rolle's *Abridgement* (Henry Rolle, *Abridgement des Plusiers Cases et Resolutions del Common Ley*, 2 vols. [London]) was compiled in the earlier half of the century. It may be noticed in the preface that in his advice to law students, Hale does not include Bracton among the recommended reading.

might be freely cited.[28] But occasional extraction and citation are less significant than visible effect upon the course of legal development, and in this connection one of the more striking instances occurred in the law of bailments when at one blow, in *Coggs* v. *Bernard* (1703), Lord Chief Justice Holt attempted a revolutionary revision of the common law with the aid of Bracton.[29] The existing case law appearing chaotic, Holt was minded to reorder the law on first principles, and to this end he found Bracton admirably suited. But he cited the treatise in cautious language: "I cite this author, though I confess he is an old one, because his opinion is reasonable, and very much to my present purpose, and there is no authority in the law to the contrary." Though Holt applied Bracton with no sparing hand, the tone of this remark and others is a curious echo of the old view of Bracton; but Holt certainly regarded Bracton as an authority and his use of his "old author" certainly is consistent only with a view of Bracton as having legal authority; indeed he quotes the treatise as "a full authority, if it not be thought too old." When later in the eighteenth century William Jones wrote his remarkable essay designed to place the law of bailments on a rational basis,[30] he had to refer to Holt's handling of Bracton, and with bare respect he had this to say of it: "I am perfectly aware that he [Bracton] copied *Justinian* almost word for word, and that Lord *Holt* who makes considerable use of his treatise, observes three or four times 'that he was an *old* author'; but although he had been a civilian, yet he was also a great common-lawyer, and never, I believe, adopted the rules and expressions of the Romans except when they coincided with the laws of *England* in his time; he is certainly the *best* of our juridical classicks. . . ."[31]

Such was the belief that in the course of time came to ensure Bracton's status as an "authority." Doubtless a variety of causes contributed; some have already been indicated and there were some others of a more adventitious nature.[32] But apart from the uses of Bracton within the field of private law we have to reckon with his uses in the fields of public law and politics. This development came with the seventeenth century, though there are incidental uses earlier. Apart from the quotations from Bracton in the *Pleas of the Crown*, Staunford had used the treatise in his *Exposition of the King's Prerogative*.[33] In 1571 at the trial of the duke of

28. A notable instance is Robert Callis's Gray's Inn reading of 1622 on Sewers (Stat. 23 Hen. 8, c. 5), especially the first lecture.

29. 2 Ld. Raym. 909, 92 *Eng. Rep.* 107.

30. *Essay on the Law of Bailments* (London, 1781), a work not only of great historical and analytical power but of some prophecy, for Jones has good claim to have invented "the reasonable man."

31. Ibid., p. 75.

32. Such as the long-lived belief that Bracton had been chief justiciar. John Lord Campbell (*Lives of the Chief Justices of England* . . . , 2 vols. [London, 1849], 1:62) was disposed in the mid-nineteenth century to this view on "the authority of Lord Ellesmere and others, who have carefully studied the subject." Coke in the preface to 9 Co. Rep. was content with "Curiae de Banco Judex." This belief as to judicial status was material to the authority of *De Legibus*.

33. See above, at n. 14.

Norfolk the prisoner himself invoked Bracton on a point concerning the admissibility of certain witnesses and did so to such effect that the attorney general was moved to complain to the duke: "You alledge Books, Statutes, and Bracton. I am sure the study of such books is not your profession."[34]

With the turn of the century, Bracton's book came to assume a role in constitutional matters, and probably the most important case in which Bracton was used on an issue of constitutional law was the great case of the postnati in 1608.[35] The question whether such persons as Robert Calvin, born in Scotland after the accession of King James in 1603, were aliens and foreigners in England raised the whole legal principle of allegiance to the level of an Exchequer Chamber discussion. On this subject, Bracton was a particularly important source, for the earliest occasion the common law had had to form a doctrine concerning allegiance was during Bracton's own time, not because of the accession of a foreign king, but because of the loss of the Duchy of Normandy to France. Accordingly, Bracton was much quoted and, as Francis Bacon described him in addressing the judges, treated as an author "of great credit," not only by the bar and common-law judiciary but by Lord Chancellor Ellesmere too; he had revisited Bracton and found useful material.[36] In these discussions there is no trace of political acrimony, and even Bacon was happy to quote some of the more "feudal" passages in the treatise concerning regal authority.[37] Nevertheless, such happy harmony in the use of Bracton was not to prevail.

The first note of controversy had already sounded. In 1607, Coke had had his celebrated confrontation with King James, when the chief justice had denied the king's authority to give or direct judgment in his courts.[38] "With which the king was greatly offended," reported Coke, "and said that then he should be under the law, which was treason to affirm, as he said. To which I said that Bracton saith *quod Rex non debet esse sub*

34. *A Complete Collection of State Trials . . .*, comp. Thomas B. Howell, 34 vols. (London, 1809–26), 1:957, reported by Thomas Norton (see above, at n. 16), at pp. 1026–27, where the duke submitted that a self-confessed traitor should not be admitted as a witness. To which Catline, C.J., replied that "Bracton indeed is an old writer of our law, and by Bracton he may be a witness; a stranger, a bondman may be a witness. Ask you all the Judges here. And the Judges affirmed that he may."

35. The speeches and reports are collected in Howell's *State Trials*, 2:559. There are a few sixteenth-century instances of political use. Thus, Thomas Cromwell (who may have recalled the treatise from student days in Gray's Inn) recommended Bracton for giving the king the title of "vicarius Christi" (G. R. Elton, "The Political Creed of Thomas Cromwell," *Historical Studies of the English Parliament*, ed. E. B. Fryde and Edward Miller, 2 vols. (Cambridge, 1970) 2:193–216, at 203.

36. For a modern edition of the lord chancellor's speech see Knafla, *Law and Politics*, pp. 202–53. Ellesmere even felt able (pp. 217–18) to question Bracton's statement that *sola Anglia usa est iure non scripto* on the ground that the civil law also had been in origin an unwritten law.

37. He emphasized (Howell, *State Trials*, 2:580) that the law gave title to the king, "and in that sense Bracton saith well, lib. 1, fol. 5, and lib. 3, fol. 107, *Lex facit quod ipse sit rex*."

38. *Prohibitions del Roy*, 12 Co. Rep. 63, at 65, 77 *Eng. Rep.* 1342, at 1343.

homine sed sub deo et lege." Evidently, Coke was answering the king on the spur of the moment, and it is clear that an instinctive resort to Bracton produced the words that were over the following years to become well worn. As Maitland said, "We see these old words of Bracton doing service again and again."[39] They were to do service in more serious scenes than a Council chamber row. Bracton was brought firmly into the field of controversial politics with *Shipmoney*.[40] The references by the judges in their Exchequer Chamber speeches are not numerous, but they were much nearer slogans than previous uses of Bracton's text and they brought Bracton well within the scope of political debate. Nor were such uses or abuses forgotten. The treatise itself was given a new circulation by the second edition in 1640,[41] and the partisan employment of Bracton's text reached a climax in 1649 when Bradshaw delivered his speech upon the condemnation of King Charles. In looking back to the thirteenth century, Bradshaw saw an age "when the nobility of the land did stand out for the liberty and property of the subject, and would not suffer the kings that did invade to play the tyrant freer but called them to account for it."[42] In the calling to account, Bradshaw was able to invoke the passages of Bracton that suited his argument, not least the notorious text on coercing or "bridling" a faithless king.[43]

It was in the aftermath of regicide and when it came to justifying the king's death to the world at large that Milton found many passages of Bracton apt to enforce his arguments.[44] His quotations from "our ancient and famous lawyer, Bracton," were to mark the beginning of another use of the treatise in political argument, for in the second part of the seventeenth century the political use of Bracton was more in the direction of the controversial literature upon political theory. Though many of such users had claims to scholarship, nevertheless the use made of Bracton was essentially of an unhistorical nature. From Sir Robert Filmer upon one extreme to Algernon Sidney on the other, Bracton was shuttlecocked

39. Frederic W. Maitland, *The Constitutional History of England* (1908; reprint ed., Cambridge, 1909), p. 269.

40. Howell, *State Trials*, 3:825.

41. This edition was a mere reprint of the first edition and tells us nothing of the circumstances of the reissue. Britton was republished in the same year as a genuine reedition.

42. Howell, *State Trials*, 4:1009.

43. *Bracton De Legibus et Consuetudinibus Angliae*, ed. George E. Woodbine, trans. with revisions and notes by Samuel E. Thorne, 4 vols. (Cambridge, Mass., 1968–77) (hereafter cited as *Bracton De Legibus*), fol. 34 (2:110): the *addicio de cartis* that "Rex habet superiorem, deum scilicet: item curiam suam, videlicet comites et barones, quia comites dicuntur quasi socii regis, et qui habet socium habet magistrum." Bradshaw of course had no reason to doubt the authenticity of his text; the text (*Bracton De Legibus*, fol. 34 [2:110]) was considered in later times to be interpolated, but it now appears that "this addicio is as Bractonian as any other and was certainly in his manuscript" (*Bracton De Legibus* [3:xlvi, n. 9]).

44. These are in John Milton, *A Defence of the People of England* (London, 1651), chaps. 8 and 9. The principal passages are given in John Milton, *Prose Works*, Bohn's Library, 5 vols. (London, 1848–81), 1:174–75; and in *The Complete Prose Works of John Milton*, ed. Don M. Wolfe (New Haven, 1966), vol. 4, pt. 1, pp. 492–93.

about from one partisan position to another. The historical context was not much regarded or indeed understood. Thus it has been said of Dr. Brady in his view of the legal scene of Bracton's time that "he was inclined to regard the common law of the thirteenth century as the force hostile to monarchy which it appeared to be in its own time."[45] In this literature, which was vigorously pursued between Puritan Rebellion and Whig Revolution, Bracton seems to have been regarded as a useful ally in both camps. It was possible to use the treatise from opposed points of view, because the texts were chosen selectively and the contemporary context, that of the thirteenth century, taken with much partiality. Among the various authors it may be sufficient to adduce one by way of example, if only because of his exceptional ability in political theory. Thomas Hobbes, discussing sovereignty in a specifically legal context, drew on Bracton as "the most authentick Author of the Common Law," and proceeded to extract from Bracton a strongly monarchical interpretation. "If Bracton's Law be Reason, as you and I think it is, what temporal power is there which the King hath not?"[46]

Such uses of Bracton did not survive into the eighteenth century, during which the silence of the earlier age returns. By mid-century, Blackstone was preparing to supersede Bracton and all previous general statements of English law. In relation to public law the last occasion in which Bracton occupied a leading role occurred soon after the Hanoverian succession. It was an odd episode, starting in circumstances of triviality and farce, but nevertheless an episode that "became of dramatic importance for the course of English politics."[47] George I quarreled with his son and expelled the prince from St. James's Palace, but he kept his grandchildren and insisted that he would himself be responsible for their further education. The question whether the king as grandfather, or the grandfather as king, had the right to supersede the father was referred to the judges.[48] The relevance of Bracton to this imbroglio was that in the treatise paternal authority had been described in terms of *patriapotestas*. Those who sought to support the king's case therefore relied on Bracton and the passages on *patriapotestas*. Those who favored the prince's case were concerned to distinguish or disparage. To disparage was to deny authority to Bracton, but the attempt was unsuccessful. Fortescue-Aland, B., gave the fullest refutation:

45. This *Complete History of England* . . . by Robert Brady, the Master of Caius College, Cambridge (London, 1685), was composed to inculcate the virtues of loyalty and obedience. The comment is by Professor J. G. A. Pocock, *The Ancient Constitution and the Feudal Law* (1957; reprint ed., New York, 1967), p. 221.

46. Thomas Hobbes, *A Dialogue between a Philosopher and a Student of the Common Laws of England* (1681), pp. 38–39, ed. J. Cropsey (Chicago, 1971), pp. 74–75.

47. J. H. Plumb, *Sir Robert Walpole: The Making of a Statesman* (London, 1956), pp. 259–61.

48. *The Grand Opinion for the Prerogative concerning the Royal Family*, reported in Fort. 401, 92 *Eng. Rep.* 909, and Howell, *State Trials*, 15:1195, adding the opinions of the two dissenting judges.

> These law books [Bracton and Fleta] are so strong that there has been no way thought of to evade them but by denying the authority of them, and calling it civil law. But I own that I am not a little surprised that the books should be denied for law, when in my little experience I have known them quoted almost in every argument where pains have been taken, if anything could be found in those books to the question in hand, and I have never known them denied for law but where some statute or usage time out of mind has altered them. We have been told indeed that they were quoted in the case of ship-money,[49] but I believe that objection would not have been made if they had been aware that these very books were quoted on both sides of the question; which destroys the objection and shows they were approved of by all who argued that case, both of one side and the other.[50]

In the instant case the bias of Bracton was all one way and in favor of the paterfamilias, that is, King George. And the judges, with no more than two dissents, were able to affirm an opinion favorable to the king. But it seems almost perverse to place *patriapotestas* as a part of the private law of England, and it is difficult to see how such an opinion can be supported without resorting to circumstances of prerogative or just plain political prejudice.[51] This question did indeed interest William Lee, later to become chief justice, for he composed "a Treatise of Paternal Power" in order to test the validity of the conclusions reached by the judges.[52] He traced the passages in Bracton and Fleta to their sources in Justinian's *Institutes*. He made a meritorious attempt to account for the revival of civil-law studies in Bracton's time and particularly for the use of civil law in the treatise. He felt unable to give Bracton an independent status as authority: "It is not his opinion can make anything law which was not so before. The common law of England is founded on immemorial custom and usage and judicial decisions of courts of justice on the proper evidence of this custom, but the treatises of particular men though of great learning and character are to be considered only as private collections; they are of great use in the construction and interpretation of laws but have no authority in themselves to establish a rule not agreeable

49. Thus Price, B.: "Bracton and Fleta are old civil law books; they may fetch out of these books shipmoney and the dispensing power, they were all fetched out of these old books" (Fort. 401, at 429, 92 *Eng. Rep.* 909, at 921).

50. Ibid., Fort., at 419, *Eng. Rep.*, at 917.

51. It would be wrong to make too much of the fact that one of the two dissenting judges, Eyre, J., held a position in the prince's household, but it is worth remark that in this case, the first case of political significance after the Act of Settlement came into operation, the judges do not appear to have acted with conspicuous independence.

52. This is unprinted and exists in a manuscript in my possession. It is undated but was evidently written before the end of the reign in 1727. It is in Lee's handwriting, and a note of provenance by Dr. Lee of Hartwell in 1850 shows that the manuscript was once among the chief justice's papers at Totteridge Park.

to former precedent." This view, though it denies Bracton an independent status of authority, does so not because Bracton wrote in the very distant past or because his treatise was infected with civil law, but simply because textbooks were not to be put on the same plane as statutes and judicial decisions. Nor apparently was Lee disposed to any idea that a textbook could acquire "authority" by professional evaluation. In the event and after a long and close examination of all relevant sources he came to the conclusion that Bracton's *patriapotestas* was not warranted by the sources so consulted. But, he continued, "since we have been contesting the authority of Bracton, we may be thought to have failed in doing him right if we do not take in his whole scheme and consider *quibus modis*, he says, *Patriapotestas dissolvitur*, as well as the power itself." He was then able to reach the conclusion that full age, marriage, or forisfamiliation (according to modern civil law) worked emancipation. In the rest of his work he considered whether the king had a prerogative in this respect, but because Bracton's proposition was concerned not with prerogative but purely with a matter of general law, that part of Lee's treatise did not oblige him to do battle with Bracton or consider further propositions of law in *De Legibus*.[53]

Though this was the last occasion on which Bracton was invoked in a matter of serious political significance, it is noteworthy that it was plain to all that an important issue was the civil-law content of *De Legibus*. That the treatise had a Roman model was clear to the editor of 1569 and to others in the sixteenth century, but they were aware of it in the way that we today are aware that Blackstone in the eighteenth century used an institutional scheme for his *Commentaries*. An awareness of the presence of Roman law as a matter of substantial content was slower in coming. On the question to what extent Roman law is indeed present in the text of Bracton the final answer has not come till our own time and Professor Thorne's edition, but the question was beginning to stir in the early modern period, and we cannot leave Bracton in this period of history without considering the beginnings of the academic study of Bracton, which may be said to begin with Selden's investigations.[54]

When the text of Fleta was put into print in 1647 the publishers applied to Selden for an introduction. He complied, having as he tells us a few days at his disposal because of an indisposition. The result in ten remarkable chapters was his *Dissertatio ad Fletam*.[55] The second and

53. The conclusion reached by Lee was that "it is indifferent in regard to the question of right between the king and the prince whether Bracton be law or not, for if his authority be not allowed the Prince will have his children in his power as their father, and if it prevails, he will have them as the children of a son emancipated . . . and therefore in whatever view we consider this case we cannot but concede that the care and education of His Majesty's grandchildren belong of right to the Prince their father." For the text of Bracton, see *Bracton De Legibus*, fols. 6–6b (2:34–35).

54. Works that the reader might expect to examine the question are disappointing. William Fulbeck's *Parallel* (London, 1618) has nothing of significance, and John Cowell's *Interpreter* (Cambridge, 1607) has a fair quantity of extraction but of a superficial sort.

55. *Ioannis Seldeni Ad Fletam Dissertatio*, ed. David Ogg (Cambridge, 1925).

third chapters are particularly concerned with Bracton and the epitomes, among which of course Fleta is to be numbered. But in the first chapter, Selden had alluded briefly to the question of "authority." In his view the vulgar opinion that such writers were unauthoritative but employable only "pro ornamentis tantum orationis in disputationibus juris nostri forensibus scholasticisque" was quite wrong. Such works retained authority, he thought, subject to later alterations and abrogations in law. "Atque ita certe tam autoritatem e qua juris interpretatio pendeat eos habere manifesto in disputationibus forensibus scholasticisque est agnoscendum quam ornamento esse." As for the authority of the civil law itself, Selden concluded that in Bracton's time the civil law was used solely in a supplementary role, "ut tum ubi deesset nostri juris praescriptum expressius, ad rationem juris etiam Caesarei ratione suffultam recurreretur, tum ubi jus utrumque consonum, etiam Caesarei quasi firmaretur explicareturve res verbis."

Selden's whole treatment of his subject seems academically detached. The discussion of *lex regia* that bulks large in the third chapter had some bearing on general questions of government, but Selden made no contemporary allusion or application. With regard to Bracton's treatise it has been said that "Selden's acquaintance with the texts of Bracton was apparently not such as to give him a hint of the profound modifications and even discrepancies which crept in mainly through the incorporation of glosses. . . ."[56] It is certainly true that Selden did not give any very close attention to the textual state of *De Legibus*, at least for the purpose of writing his introduction to Fleta. Having started with a disclaimer of responsibility for the poor editing of Fleta, he later on deplored the errors in the editing and printing of 1569. But it is probable that he had seen less of the manuscripts than had Tottel's editor.[57]

Selden's contribution to Bractonian studies was not in the elucidation of the text; his main service was in setting the context by relating Bracton to his own age in legal history and particularly the history of the civil law in Europe and England. It is this aspect of Selden's essay that enables one to credit him with making a start on the true academic study of Bracton. He was not concerned with using Bracton either for legal argument or for political polemic. But while Bracton was so used the question of authority required an answer. Only when such uses ceased could the question itself cease.

As might be expected there was in fact no single answer to the question. Not only do we have to take account of changes over long periods of time in notions of authority, but we have also to listen to discordant

56. Ogg, *Dissertatio ad Fletam*, p. xxxvii.

57. "Atque in editionibus illis utriusque menda sunt perplurima eaque crassissima, partim e librariorum inscitia, partim ex operarum incuria" (Ogg, *Dissertatio ad Fletam*, pp. 20–21). This judgment on the editor of 1569, who had collated some dozen manuscripts, is not justified. Even so severe a critic as the late H. G. Richardson (*Bracton: The Problem of His Text* [London, 1965], p. 13) considered that "he had some notion of textual criticism, the principal criteria being that the text should make sense and that it should be inclusive, with nothing Bractonian left out," and concluded that he did not deserve Selden's censure.

voices. Some said that the use of Bracton was ornamental, to decorate an argument; others considered that the use was interpretative, to understand the old statutes; others saw in Bracton a source of law, at least where not superseded by change; it was long before Bracton was seen as a source of history, purely evidence of what the law and customs of England had been in the thirteenth century. As to the intermixture of thirteenth-century English law and the texts of the civil law, that inquiry could make serious progress only with modern critical methods, and the modern inquiry started with Carl Güterbock. Güterbock himself had considered tracing the influence of Bracton's book upon the later development of English law but had abandoned the plan as too ambitious.[58] It is to be hoped that now the beginnings of the book have been definitively settled, one day that plan will be fulfilled.

58. Carl Güterbock, *Bracton and His Relation to the Roman Law* (1862; trans. Brinton Coxe, Philadelphia, 1866), pp. 173–74; Plucknett gave an interesting sketch in his *Concise History*, at pp. 262–64.

Bibliography of Samuel E. Thorne

Books

A Discourse upon the Exposicion and Understandinge of Statutes. San Marino: Huntington Library, 1942.

Prerogativa Regis. Tertia Lectura Roberti Constable de Lyncolnis Inne Anno 11 Henry VII. New Haven: Yale University Press, 1949.

Readings and Moots at the Inns of Court in the Fifteenth Century, vol. 1. Selden Society, vol. 71. London, 1954.

Bracton on the Laws and Customs of England. 4 vols. Cambridge, Mass.: Harvard University Press, 1968–77.

Articles

"St. Germain's *Doctor and Student*." Transactions of the London Bibliographical Society. 4th ser. x, 421 (1930).

"The Assise *Utrum* and Canon Law in England." *Columbia Law Review*, xxxiii, 428 (1933).

"Le droit canonique en Angleterre." *Revue historique de droit français et étranger*, xiii, 499 (1934).

"Notes on Courts of Record in England." *West Virginia Law Quarterly*, xl, 347 (1934).

"*Statuti* in the Post-Glossators." *Speculum*, xi, 452 (1936).

"Livery of Seisin." *Law Quarterly Review*, lii, 345 (1936).

"The Equity of a Statute and Heydon's Case." *Illinois Law Review*, xxxi, 202 (1936).

"Fitzherbert's *Abridgement*." *Law Library Journal*, xxix, 59 (1936).

"Courts of Record and Sir Edward Coke." *University of Toronto Law Journal*, ii, 24 (1937).

"Dr. Bonham's Case." *Law Quarterly Review*, liv, 543 (1938). Reprinted in *The Constitution Reconsidered*, edited by Conyers Read. New York: Columbia University Press, 1938.

"Praemunire and Sir Edward Coke." *Huntington Library Quarterly*, ii, 85 (1938).

"Gilbert de Thornton's *Summa de Legibus*." *University of Toronto Law Journal*, vii, 1 (1947).

Preface to W. O. Hassall, *A Catalogue of the Library of Sir Edward Coke*. New Haven: Yale University Press, 1950.

"Tudor Social Transformation and Legal Change." *New York University Law Review*, xxvi, 10 (1951).
Preface to Edward Hake, *Epieikeia: A Dialogue on Equity*, edited by D. E. C. Yale. New Haven: Yale University Press, 1953.
"Sir Edward Coke, 1552–1952." Selden Society Lecture Series. London, 1957.
"English Feudalism and Estates in Land." Maitland Lecture. *Cambridge Law Journal*, 193 (1959).
"Early History of the Inns of Court." Gray's Inn Lecture. *Graya*, 179 (1959).
"History of Law." In *Bibliography of British History, 1485–1603*, edited by Conyers Read. New York: Oxford University Press, 1959.
"Sovereignty and the Conflict of Laws." In *Bartolo de Sassoferrato studi e documenti per il VI centenario*, ii, 675. Milan: Giuffrè, 1962.
"Magna Carta." In *The Great Charter*. New York: Pantheon, 1965.
"Bibliografia." In *Charles Howard McIlwain e la storiografia sulla revoluzione americana*. Bologna: Il Mulino, 1965.
"English Law and the Renaissance." In *Atti del primo congresso internazionale della società italiana di storia del diritto*. Florence: Olschki, 1966.
"Henry de Bracton." University of Exeter, 1970.
"The Text of Bracton's De Legibus Angliae." In *Atti del secondo congresso internazionale della società italiana di storia del diritto*, ii, 803. Florence: Olschki, 1971.
"Henry I's Coronation Charter, Chap. 6." *English Historical Review*, xciii, 794 (1978).

Contributors

J. H. Baker is a fellow of St. Catharine's College, Cambridge, and a lecturer in law at the University of Cambridge. He has written over forty articles, notes, and reviews on the subject of English legal history. Dr. Baker is the author of *An Introduction to English Legal History* and has edited *The Reports of Sir John Spelman* for the Selden Society.

Thomas G. Barnes is professor of history and law at the University of California at Berkeley. He is the author of numerous articles and his books include *Somerset 1625–1640: A County's Government during the Personal Rule*; *Hastings College of Law: The First Century*; and *List and Index to Star Chamber Proceedings, James I* (3 vols.).

J. L. Barton is a fellow of Merton College, Oxford, and is All Souls' Reader in Roman Law at the University of Oxford. He has published a large number of articles on Roman law, English legal history, and modern English law. He is the author of *Roman Law in England* and the editor of the Selden Society edition of St. Germain's *Doctor and Student.*

John S. Beckerman taught medieval history at Yale from 1972 to 1977 and at Haverford College from 1977 to 1980. He has published several articles on the history of medieval English law.

Charles Donahue, Jr., is professor of law at Harvard Law School. He was a member of the faculty at the University of Michigan Law School from 1968 until 1980 and has been a visiting professor at the law schools of Columbia University and the University of California at Berkeley. He has written extensively on law and legal history and is coeditor of a casebook on the law of property. Professor Donahue (with N. Adams) has edited for the Selden Society a selection of thirteenth-century cases from the ecclesiastical courts of the province of Canterbury.

Harold Garrett-Goodyear is associate professor of history at Mount Holyoke College. His main research interest is in determining and investigating the initiatives responsible for the centralization of justice in England during the fifteenth and sixteenth centuries.

Charles M. Gray is professor of history at the University of Chicago. He has published articles on English legal history and the history of legal theory in England. He is the author of *Copyhold, Equity, and the Common Law* and *Renaissance and Reformation England*.

Paul R. Hyams is official fellow and tutor in modern history at Pembroke College, Oxford, and lecturer in modern history at the University of

Oxford. His articles and reviews in various economic, legal, and historical journals reflect his concern to treat legal phenomena as part of the historical mainstream. His book *King, Lords and Peasants in Medieval England: The Common Law of Villeinage in the 12th and 13th Centuries* was published in 1980.

E. W. Ives is a senior lecturer in modern history at the University of Birmingham. He is the author of numerous articles in learned journals and has a special interest in the history of the legal profession.

S. F. C. Milsom is a fellow of St. John's College, Cambridge, and professor of law at the University of Cambridge. He was formerly a fellow of New College, Oxford, and professor of legal history at the University of London, and he has been a visiting professor at the Harvard, New York University, and Yale law schools. He is the author of *Historical Foundations of the Common Law* for which he received the Ames Prize and the Swiney Prize for Jurisprudence. His Maitland Memorial Lectures, *The Legal Framework of English Feudalism*, were published in 1976. Professor Milsom has been a literary director of the Selden Society since 1964.

A. W. B. Simpson is professor of law at the University of Kent at Canterbury. He was a fellow of Lincoln College, Oxford, from 1954 to 1973 and has been a visiting professor at the University of Chicago Law School. He is the author of *An Introduction to the History of the Land Law* and *A History of the Common Law of Contract*.

Donald W. Sutherland is professor of history at the University of Iowa. He is the author of *Quo Warranto Proceedings in the Reign of Edward I, 1278–1294* and *The Assize of Novel Disseisin*.

Emily Zack Tabuteau is assistant professor of history at Michigan State University and was an Andrew W. Mellon postdoctoral Fellow in Humanities at Duke University in 1976–77. Her main research interest is in eleventh-century Norman customary law.

D. E. C. Yale is a fellow of Christ's College, Cambridge, and Reader in English Legal History at the University of Cambridge. In addition to being the author of various articles, notes, and reviews, he has edited works by Lord Chancellor Nottingham and Sir Matthew Hale for the Selden Society, of which he is a literary director. He is also general editor of *Cambridge Studies in English Legal History*.

Index of Persons and Places

Legal titles where given refer to the highest rank attained.

See and *See also* references in boldface refer to entries in the Index of Subjects.

Index of Subjects

See and *See also* references in boldface refer to entries in the Index of Persons and Places.

MORRIS S. ARNOLD
is professor of law and history
and vice-president–director of
the Office of the President at
The University of Pennsylvania.

THOMAS A. GREEN
is professor of law and history at
The University of Michigan.

SALLY A. SCULLY
is associate professor of history at
San Francisco State University.

STEPHEN D. WHITE
is associate professor of history at
Wesleyan University.